# INDIAN WISDOM

# INDIAN WISDOM

## RELIGIOUS, PHILOSOPHICAL, AND ETHICAL DOCTRINES. OF THE HINDUS:

WITH A BRIEF HISTORY

OF THE CHIEF DEPARTMENTS OF SANSKRIT LITERATURE,

AND SOME ACCOUNT OF THE

PAST AND PRESENT CONDITION OF INDIA, MORAL AND INTELLECTUAL.

BY

**MONIER-WILLIAMS,** M.A.

SECOND EDITION

GYAN

*Published by*

GYAN

Gyan Publishing House
5, Ansari Road
Daryaganj, New Delhi-110002
Phone: 011-47034999, 9811692060
E-mail: books@gyanbooks.com

*Distribution Network*
gyanbooks.com
India, USA, Canada, UK, Australia, France



ISBN : 978-81-212-6611-6 (PB)
First Published, 1875

2nd Impression 2022

*Printed at:* Gyan Press, Delhi.



**INDIAN WISDOM**
Author: MONIER-WILLIAMS

# INDIAN WISDOM

OR

## EXAMPLES

OF THE

RELIGIOUS, PHILOSOPHICAL, AND ETHICAL DOCTRINES OF THE HINDŪS:

WITH A BRIEF HISTORY

OF THE CHIEF DEPARTMENTS OF SANSKRIT LITERATURE,

AND SOME ACCOUNT OF THE

PAST AND PRESENT CONDITION OF INDIA, MORAL AND INTELLECTUAL.

BY

MONIER-WILLIAMS, M.A.

BODEN PROFESSOR OF SANSKṚIT IN THE UNIVERSITY OF OXFORD.

*SECOND EDITION.*

1875.

# PREFACE

## TO THE SECOND EDITION.

THE increasing interest felt in India and Indian literature has led to such a demand for the present work, that it was found necessary to begin printing a second edition almost immediately after the issue of the first. I have, therefore, been unable to avail myself of the suggestions contained in the Reviews which have hitherto appeared. Nevertheless, a few unimportant alterations have been made in the present edition; and through the kindness of Professor W. D. Whitney, who lost no time in sending me some valuable notes, I have been able to improve the chapter on Astronomy at p. 180.

Being on the eve of quitting England for a visit to the principal seats of learning in India, I have for obvious reasons deferred addressing myself to the fuller treatment of those portions of Sanskṛit literature of which I have merely given a summary in Lecture XV.

India, with all its immutability, is now making such rapid strides in education, that a Professor of Sanskṛit at Oxford, if he is to keep himself up to the level of advancing knowledge and attainments, ought to communicate personally with some of those remarkable native Pandits whose intellects have been developed at our great Indian Colleges and Universities, and who owe their eminence in various branches of learning to the advantages they have enjoyed under our Government.

In undertaking so long a journey my only motives are a sense of what is due from me to the Boden Chair, a desire to extend my sphere of work, a craving for trustworthy information on many obscure portions of Indian religious literature not yet examined by European scholars, and a hope that on my return, should health and strength be spared to me, I may have increased my powers of usefulness within my own province, and be enabled to contribute more than I have yet effected towards making England and India better known to each other, or at least towards making Oxford an attractive centre of Indian studies, and its lecture-rooms, museums, and libraries sources of accurate knowledge on Indian subjects.

*Oxford*, October 1875.

---

# PREFACE

## TO THE FIRST EDITION.

THE present volume[1] attempts to supply a want, the existence of which has been impressed upon my mind by an inquiry often addressed to me as Boden Professor:—Is it possible to obtain from any one book a good general idea of the character and contents of Sanskṛit literature?

Its pages are also intended to subserve a further object. They aim at imparting to educated Englishmen, by means of translations and explanations of portions of the sacred and philosophical literature of India, an insight into the mind, habits of thought, and customs of the Hindūs, as well as a correct knowledge of a system of belief and practice which has constantly prevailed for at least three thousand years, and still continues

---

[1] The volume is founded on my official lectures.

to exist as one of the principal religions of the Non-Christian world[1].

It cannot indeed be right, nor is it even possible for educated Englishmen to remain any longer ignorant of the literary productions, laws, institutions, religious creed, and moral precepts of their Hindū fellow-creatures and fellow-subjects. The East and West are every day being drawn nearer to each other, and British India, in particular, is now brought so close to us by steam, electricity, and the Suez Canal, that the condition of the Hindū community—mental, moral, and physical—forces itself peremptorily on our attention. Nor is it any longer justifiable to plead the difficulty of obtaining accurate official information as an excuse for ignorance. Our Government has for a long period addressed itself most energetically to the investigation of every detail capable of throwing light on the past and present history of the Queen's Indian dominions.

A Literary survey of the whole of India has been recently organized for the purpose of ascertaining what Sanskṛit MSS., worthy of preservation, exist in public and

---

[1] See the caution, last line of p. xxxi, and p. 2. Although European nations have changed their religions during the past eighteen centuries, the Hindūs have not done so, except very partially. Islām converted a certain number by force of arms in the eighth and following centuries, and Christian truth is at last creeping onwards and winning its way by its own inherent energy in the nineteenth; but the religious creeds, rites, customs, and habits of thought of the Hindūs generally have altered little since the days of Manu, five hundred years B. C. Of course they have experienced accretions, but many of the same caste observances and rules of conduct (*āćāra, vyavahāra,* see p. 217) are still in force; some of the same laws of inheritance (*dāya,* p. 270) hold good; even a beggar will sometimes ask for alms in words prescribed by the ancient lawgiver (*bhikshām dehi,* Manu II. 49, Kullūka); and to this day, if a pupil absents himself from an Indian college, he sometimes excuses himself by saying that he has a *prāyaś-ćitta* to perform (see p. 278, and Trübner's Report of Professor Stenzler's Speech at the London Oriental Congress).

private libraries. Competent scholars have been appointed to the task, and the result of their labours, so far as they have hitherto extended, has been published.

Simultaneously, an Archæological survey has been ably conducted under the superintendance of Major-General A. Cunningham, and we have most interesting results published and distributed by the Indian Governments in the shape of four large volumes, filled with illustrations, the last issued being the Report for the year 1871–72.

An Ethnological survey has also been set on foot in Bengal, and a magnificent volume with portraits from photographs of numerous aboriginal tribes, called *Descriptive Ethnology of Bengal*, by Colonel Dalton, was published at Calcutta in 1872. This was preceded by a valuable guide to the *Ethnology of India*, written by Sir George Campbell.

Even an Industrial survey has been partially carried out under the able direction of Dr. Forbes Watson, who proposes that a new Museum and Indian Institute shall be built and attached to the India Office.

Moreover, Sir George Campbell caused to be prepared, printed, and published, during his recent administration in Bengal, comparative tables of specimens of all the languages of India—Āryan, Drāviḍian, and aboriginal—the practical benefit of which requires no demonstration on my part.

But there are other official publications still more accessible to every Englishman who will take the trouble of applying to the proper authorities.

Those whose horizon of Eastern knowledge has hitherto been hopelessly clouded, so as to shut out every country beyond the Holy Land, have now a clear prospect opened out towards India. They have only to study the Report of the *Moral and Material Progress and Condition of India during* 1872–73, published by the India Office, and edited by Mr. C. R. Markham. At the risk of being thought impertinent, I must crave permission to record here an opinion that this last mentioned work is worthy of a better fate than to be wrapped in a blue cover, as if it were a mere official statement of dry facts and statistics. Its pages are full of valuable information on every subject connected with our Eastern Empire—even including missionary progress—and the carefully drawn maps with which it is illustrated are a highly instructive study in themselves. The revelation the Report makes of what is being done and what remains to be done, may well humble as well as cheer every thoughtful person. But emanating as the volume does from the highest official authority, it is in itself an evidence of great advance in our knowledge of India's needs, and in our endeavours to meet them, as well as an earnest of our future efforts for the good of its inhabitants.

The same must be said of Sir George Campbell's exhaustive Report on his own administration of Bengal during 1872–73. This forms a thick 8vo volume of about nine hundred pages, and affords a mine of interesting and valuable information[1].

Most significant, too, of an increasing interchange of Oriental and Occidental ideas and knowledge is the circumstance that almost every number of the *Times* newspaper contains able articles and interesting communications from its correspondents on Indian affairs, or records some result of the intellectual stir and ferment now spreading,

[1] Another very instructive publication, though of quite a different stamp from the official documents mentioned above, is M. Garcin de Tassy's Annual Review (*Revue Annuelle*) of the literary condition of India, which is every year kindly presented to me, and to many other scholars, by that eminent Orientalist. It is delivered annually in the form of a discourse at the opening of his Hindūstānī lectures. Though it deals more particularly with the development of Urdū and other linguistic studies, it gives a complete and reliable account of the intellectual and social movements now going on, and of the progress made in all branches of education and knowledge.

as it has never done before, from Cape Comorin to the Himālaya mountains.

Another noteworthy indication of growing inter-community of thought between the East and West is the fact that every principal periodical of the day finds itself compelled to take increasing account of the sayings and doings—wise or unwise—of young Bengal, Madras, and Bombay. Our attention is continually drawn by one or another publication to the proceedings of native religious societies—such as the Brahma-samāj, Sanātana-dharma-samāj, Dharma-sabhā, &c.[1]—or to the transactions of literary and scientific clubs and institutions; while not unfrequently we are presented with extracts from vernacular journals[2], or from the speeches of high-minded Hindūs, who occasionally traverse India, not as Christian missionaries, but seeking, in a spirit worthy of Christianity itself, to purify the Hindū creed and elevate the tone of Indian thought and feeling. All this is a sure criterion of the warm interest in Oriental matters now taking possession of the public mind in Western countries.

But still more noteworthy as an evidence of increasing personal intercourse between England and India is the presence of Hindūs and Muslims amongst us here. Many of the more intelligent and enlightened natives, breaking through the prejudices of caste and tradition that have

---

[1] There appear to be two sections of the Brahma-samāj or Theistic society established in India. One clings to the Veda and seeks to restore Hindūism to the pure monotheism believed to underlie the Veda. These theists are followers of the late Rammohun Roy. The other society rejects the Veda and advocates an independent and purer theism. Its present leader is Keshab Ćandra Sen.

[2] The increase in the number of journals and newspapers in the vernacular languages, conducted with much ability and intelligence by native editors, is remarkable. An Urdū and Hindī paper called *Mangala-samāćāra-patra*, printed and published at Besvān, by Ṭhākur Guru Prasād Siṉh, is, through his kindness, regularly transmitted to me.

hitherto chained them as prisoners to their own soil, now visit our shores and frequent our Universities to study us, our institutions, laws, and literature. Some of them, too, have already received a thorough English education at Indian colleges. It is even asserted that they sometimes come amongst us knowing our language, our history, and our standard authors better than we know them ourselves. Be this as it may, thus much, at least, is clear that Englishmen and Hindūs are at length holding out the right hand of fellowship to each other, and awaking to the consciousness that the duty of studying the past and present state—intellectual, moral, and physical—of their respective countries can no longer be evaded by educated men, whether in the East or in the West.

In truth, it cannot be too forcibly impressed upon our minds that good laws may be enacted, justice administered, the rights of property secured, railroads and electric telegraphs laid down, the stupendous forces of Nature controlled and regulated for the public good, the three great scourges of war, pestilence, and famine averted or mitigated—all this may be done—and more than this, the truths of our religion may be powerfully preached, translations of the Bible lavishly distributed; but if, after all, we neglect to study the mind and character of those we are seeking to govern and influence for good, no mutual confidence will be enjoyed, no real sympathy felt or inspired. Imbued with the conciliatory spirit which such a study must impart, *all* Englishmen—whether resident in England or India, whether clergymen or laymen—may aid the cause of Christianity and good government, more than by controversial discussions or cold donations of guineas and rupees. Let us not forget that this great Eastern empire has been entrusted to our rule, not to be the *Corpus vile* of political and social experiments, nor yet for the purpose of extending our commerce, flattering our pride, or increasing our prestige, but that a vast population may be conciliated, benefited, and elevated, and the regenerating influences of Christianity spread through the length and breadth of the land. How, then, have we executed our mission? Much is now being done; but the results effected are mainly due to the growth of a more cordial feeling, and a better understanding between Christians, Hindūs, Buddhists, and Musalmāns. And these good results may be expected to increase if the true character of the three principal systems of religion opposed to Christianity, and now existing in India, British Burmah, and Ceylon, are fairly tested by an impartial examination of the written documents held sacred by each; if the points of contact between Christianity, Brāhmanism, Buddhism, and Islām become better appreciated, and Christians while loyally devoting themselves—heart and soul, body and mind—to the extension of the one true faith, are led to search more candidly for the fragments of truth, lying buried under superstition and error.

Be it remembered, then, that Sanskṛit literature,—bound up as it has ever been with all that is sacred in the religion and institutions of India,—is the source of all trustworthy knowledge of the Hindūs; and to this literature Englishmen must turn, if they wish to understand the character and mind of nearly two hundred millions (or about five-sixths) of India's population (see pp. xvi–xx of Introduction).

Some departments of Sanskṛit literature have been fully described of late years by various competent and trustworthy scholars. Good translations, too, of isolated works, and excellent metrical versions of the more choice poems have from time to time been published in Europe, or are scattered about in Magazines, Reviews, and ephemeral publications. But there has never hitherto, so far as I know, existed any one work of moderate dimensions like the present—accessible to general readers—composed by any one Sanskṛit scholar with the direct aim of giving Englishmen who are not necessarily Sanskṛitists, a continuous sketch of the chief departments of Sanskṛit literature, Vedic and Post-vedic, with accompanying translations of select passages, to serve as examples for comparison with the literary productions of other countries[1].

The plan pursued by me in my endeavour to execute a novel and difficult task in a manner likely to be useful to Oriental students, yet intelligible to general readers, and especially to those men of cultured minds who, not being Orientalists, are desirous of accurate information on subjects they can no longer ignore, will be sufficiently evident from a perusal of the lectures themselves, and their appended notes. To avoid misapprehension and exaggerated ideas of my scope and aim, as well as to understand the extent of my obligations to other scholars, let the reader turn to pp. 1–4 with notes, p. 15, note 2. I will merely add to what is there stated, that as Vedic literature has been already so ably elucidated by numerous scholars in Europe, and by Professor W. D. Whitney and others in America, I have treated this part of the subject as briefly as possible. Moreover, my survey of so vast and intricate a field of inquiry as Indian philosophy, is necessarily a mere sketch. In common with other European scholars, I am greatly indebted to Dr. Fitz-Edward Hall for his contributions to this and other departments of Sanskṛit literature, and especially for his translation of Nehemiah Nīlakaṇṭha's 'Rational Refutation of the Hindū Philosophical Systems.'

I should state that, although the present volume is intended to be complete in itself, I have been compelled to reserve some of the later portion of the literature for fuller treatment in a subsequent series of lectures.

[1] Great praise is, however, due to Mrs. Manning's valuable compilation called 'Ancient and Mediæval India,' published by W. H. Allen and Co.

It is possible that some English readers may have given so little attention to Indian subjects, that further preliminary explanations may be needed by them before commencing the perusal of the following pages. For their benefit I have written an Introduction, which I hope will clear the ground sufficiently for all.

Let me now discharge the grateful duty of tendering my respectful thanks to the Governments of India for the patronage and support they have again accorded to my labours. Let me also acknowledge the debt I owe to two eminent Sanskṛitists—Dr. John Muir of Edinburgh, and Professor E. B. Cowell of Cambridge—for their kindness in reading the proof-sheets of the present series of lectures. These scholars must not, however, be held responsible for any novel theories propounded by me. In many cases I have modified my statements in accordance with their suggestions, yet in some instances, in order to preserve the individuality of my own researches, I have preferred to take an independent line of my own. Learned Orientalists in Europe and India who are able adequately to appreciate the difficulty of the task I have attempted will look on my errors with a lenient eye. As I shall welcome their criticisms with gratitude, so I shall also hope for their encouragement; for, often as I have advanced in my investigations, and have found an apparently interminable horizon opening out before me, I have felt like a foolhardy man seeking to cross an impassable ocean in a fragile coracle, and so have applied to myself the well-known words of the great Sanskṛit poet:—

तितीर्षुर्दुस्तरं मोहादुडुपेनास्मि सागरम् ॥

*Titīrshur dustaram mohād uḍupenāsmi sāgaram.*

M. W.

*Oxford,* May 1875.

# CONTENTS.

# INTRODUCTION.

IN this Introduction[1] I shall endeavour, first, to explain how Sanskṛit literature is the only key to a correct knowledge of the opinions and practices of the Hindū people; and, secondly, to show how our possession of India involves special responsibilities and opportunities with reference to the study of the three great systems of belief now confronting Christianity in the world—Brāhmanism, Buddhism, and Islām.

To clear the ground let me review very briefly the past and present history of the great country whose teeming population has been gradually, during the past two hundred and fifty years, either drawn under our sway, or, almost against our will, forced upon our protection.

The name India is derived from the Greek and Roman adaptation of the word Hindū, which was used by the Persians for their Āryan brethren, because the latter settled in the districts surrounding the streams[2] of the Sindhu (pronounced by them *Hindhu* and now called Indus). The Greeks, who probably gained their first conceptions of India from the Persians, changed the hard aspirate into a soft, and named the Hindūs Ἰνδοί (Herodotus IV. 44, V. 3). After the Hindū Āryans had spread themselves over the plains of the Ganges, the Persians called the whole of the region between the Pañjāb and Benares Hindūstān or 'abode of the Hindūs,' and this name is used in India at the present day, especially by the Musalmān population[3]. The classical name for India, however, as commonly

---

[1] Some detached portions of the information contained in this Introduction were embodied in a lecture on 'The Study of Sanskṛit in Relation to Missionary Work in India,' delivered by me, April 19, 1861, and published by Messrs. Williams & Norgate. This lecture is still procurable.

[2] Seven rivers (*sapta sindhavaḥ*) are mentioned, counting the main river and the five rivers of the Pañjāb with the Sarasvatī. In old Persian or Zand we have the expression Hapta Hendu. It is well known that a common phonetic interchange of initial *s* and *h* takes place in names of the same objects, as pronounced by kindred races.

[3] The name Hindūstān properly belongs to the region between the Sutlej and Benares, sometimes extended to the Narbadā and Mahā-nadī rivers, but not to Bengal or the Dekhan.

employed in Sanskṛit literature and recognized by the whole Sanskṛitic race, more particularly in Bengal and the Dekhan, is *Bhārata* or *Bhārata-varsha*—that is to say—'the country of king Bharata [1],' who must have ruled over a large extent of territory in ancient times (see pp. 371, 419 of this volume).

It will not, of course, be supposed that in our Eastern Empire we have to deal with ordinary races of men. We are not there brought in contact with savage tribes who melt away before the superior force and intelligence of Europeans. Rather are we placed in the midst of great and ancient peoples, who, some of them tracing back their origin to the same stock as ourselves, attained a high degree of civilization when our forefathers were barbarians, and had a polished language, a cultivated literature, and abstruse systems of philosophy, centuries before English existed even in name.

The population of India, according to the census of 1872, amounts to at least 240 millions [2]. An assemblage of beings so immense does

---

[1] Manu's name (II. 22) for the whole central region between the Himālaya and Vindhya mountains is *Āryāvarta*, 'abode of the Āryans,' and this is still a classical appellation for that part of India. Another name for India, occurring in Sanskṛit poetry, is *Jambu-dvīpa* (see p. 419). This is restricted to India in Buddhist writings. Strictly, however, this is a poetical name for the whole earth (see p. 419), of which India was thought to be the most important part. *Bharata* in Ṛig-veda I. xcvi. 3 may mean 'a supporter,' 'sustainer,' and *Bhārata-varsha* may possibly convey the idea of 'a supporting land.'

[2] Of these about 27 millions belong to the native states. In the Bengal provinces alone the number, according to the census of 1871–72, amounts to 66,856,859, far in excess of any previous estimate. Of these, only 19,857 are Europeans, and 20,279 Eurasians. A most exhaustive and interesting account of its details is given by Sir George Campbell in his Bengal Administration Report. This is the first real census of the country yet attempted. Sir William Jones in 1787 thought the population of Bengal, Behar, Orissa (with Benares also) amounted to 24,000,000; Colebrooke in 1802 computed it at 30,000,000; in 1844 it was estimated at 31,000,000; and of late years it was assumed to be about 40 or 41 millions. Now it is found that the food-producing area of Bengal numbers 650 souls to the square mile, as compared with 422 in England, and 262 in the United Kingdom. The three Presidency towns number 644,405 inhabitants for Bombay (called by the natives *Mumbaī*); 447,600 for Calcutta (*Kalikātā*); and 397,522 for Madras (*Ćenna-pattanam*): but

not, of course, form one nation. India is almost a continent like Europe. From the earliest times its richness has attracted various and successive immigrants and invaders, Asiatic and European. Its inhabitants differ as much as the various continental races, and speak languages equally distinct.

We have first the aboriginal primitive tribes, who, migrating from Central Asia and the steppes of Tartary and Tibet, entered India by successive incursions[1].

Then we have the great Hindū race, originally members of that primeval family who called themselves Arya or noble, and spoke a language the common source of Sanskṛit, Prākṛit, Zand, Persian, and Armenian in Asia; and of the Hellenic, Italic, Keltic, Teutonic, and Slavonic languages in Europe. Starting at a later period than the primitive races, but like them from some part of the table-land of Central Asia—probably the region surrounding the sources of the Oxus, in the neighbourhood of Bokhara—they separated into distinct nationalities, and peopled Europe, Persia, and India. The Hindū Āryans, after detaching themselves from the Persian branch of the family, settled in the Pañjāb and near the sacred river Sarasvatī. Thence they overran the plains of the Ganges, and spread themselves over the region called Āryāvarta (see p. xvi, note 1), occupying the whole of Central India, coalescing

---

the suburbs have been calculated in the case of Bombay, making it come next to London as the second city in the Empire. If this had been done in Calcutta and Madras, the numbers for Calcutta (according to Sir G. Campbell's Report) would have been 892,429, placing it at the head of the three cities. Almost every one in India marries as a matter of course, and indeed as a religious duty (see p. 246 of this volume). No infants perish from cold and exposure. As soon as a child is weaned it lives on rice, goes naked for two or three years, and requires no care whatever. The consequent growth of population will soon afford matter for serious anxiety. The Hindūs are wholly averse from emigration. Formerly there were three great depopulators—war, famine, and pestilence—which some regard as evils providentially permitted to exist in order to maintain the balance between the productive powers of the soil and the numbers it has to support. Happily, our rule in India has mitigated these scourges; but where are we to look for sufficient checks to excess of population?

[1] These aboriginal tribes, according to the last census, amount to 14,238,198 of the whole population of India. For an account of them see p. 312, note 1, and p. 236, note 2, of this volume.

with and, so to speak, Āryanizing the primitive inhabitants, and driving all who resisted them to the south or towards the hills.

But India, even after its occupation by the great Aryan race, appears to have yielded itself up an easy prey to every invader. Herodotus (IV. 44) affirms that it was subjugated by Darius Hystaspes. This conquest, if it ever occurred, must have been very partial. The expedition of Alexander the Great to the banks of the Indus, about 327 B.C., is a familiar fact. To this invasion is due the first authentic information obtained by Europeans concerning the north-westerly portion of India and the region of the five rivers, down which the Grecian troops were conducted in ships by Nearchus. Megasthenes, the ambassador of Seleukos Nikator, during his long sojourn at Palibothra (see note, p. 231), collected further information, of which Strabo (see p. 281, note), Pliny, Arrian, and others availed themselves. The next immigrants who appear, after a long interval, on the scene are the Pārsīs. This small tribe of Persians (even now, according to the last census, not more than seventy thousand in number) were expelled from their native land by the conquering Muhammadans under the Khalīf Omar in the seventh century. Adhering to the ancient religion of Persia—the worship, that is, of the Supreme Being under the symbol of fire—and bringing with them the records of their faith, the Zand-Avastā of their prophet Zoroaster (see p. 6), they settled down in the neighbourhood of Surat about 1100 years ago, and became great merchants and shipbuilders[1]. For two or three centuries we

[1] The Pārsīs appear to have settled first at Yazd in Persia, where a number of them still remain. The Zand-Avastā consists of 1. the *five Gāthās*, or songs and prayers (in metres resembling Vedic), which alone are thought to be the work of Zoroaster himself, and form part of the *Yazna* (or *Yaśna*=yajña), written in two dialects (the older of the two called by Haug the Gāthā); 2. the *Vendidad*, a code of laws; 3. the *Yashts*, containing hymns to the sun and other deities. There is another portion, called the Visparad, also a collection of prayers. Peshotun Dustoor Behramjee Sunjana, in a note to his *Dinkard* (an ancient Pahlavī work just published at Bombay, containing a life of Zoroaster and a history of the Zoroastrian religion), informs us that the Avastā has three parts: 1. Gāthā, 2. Dāte, and 3. Mathre; 1. being in verse and treating of the invisible world, 2. in prose and giving rules of conduct, 3. comprising prayers and precepts and an account of the creation. The Hindū and Zoroastrian systems were evidently derived from the same source. Fire

know little of their history. Like the Indo-Armenians[1], they never multiplied to any extent or coalesced with the Hindū population, but they well deserve notice for their busy active habits, in which they emulate Europeans.

Then came the Muhammadans (Arabs, Turks, Afghāns, Moguls, and Persians), who entered India at different times[2]. Though they

---

and the Sun are venerated in both; but Zoroaster (properly *Zarathustra Spitama*) taught that the Supreme Being created two inferior beings—Ormuzd (Ahura-mazda) the good spirit, and Ariman the evil. The former will destroy the latter. This dualistic principle is foreign to the Veda.

[1] The Armenians of India hold a position like that of the Pārsīs, but their numbers are less (about five thousand), and they are more scattered, and keep up more communication with their native country. There are often fresh arrivals; but some have been in India for centuries, and are dark in complexion. They are frequently merchants and bankers, and being Christian, generally adopt the European dress. They may be called the Jews of the Eastern Church: for, though scattered, they hang together and support each other. At Calcutta they have a large church and grammar-school. Their sacred books are written in ancient Armenian. Of the two modern dialects, that spoken S.E. of Ararat by the Persi-Armenians prevails among the Indo-Armenians.

[2] Muhammad's successors, after occupying Damascus for about one hundred years, fixed their capital at Baghdad in 750, and thence their power extended into Afghānistān. The Arabs, however, never obtained more than a temporary footing in India. Under the Khalīf Walīd I, in 711, Muhammad Kāsim was sent at the head of an army into Sinde, but the Muslims were expelled in 750; and for two centuries and a half India was left unmolested by invaders from the west. About the year 950, when the power of the Arabs began to decline in Asia, hardy tribes of Tartars, known by the name of Turks (not the Ottoman tribe which afterwards gained a footing in Europe, but hordes from the Altai mountains), were employed by the Khalīfs to infuse vigour into their effeminate armies. These tribes became Muhammadans, and gradually took the power into their own hands. In the province of Afghānistān, Sabaktagīn, once a mere Turkish slave, usurped the government. His son Mahmūd founded an empire at Ghaznī in Afghānistān, and made his first of thirteen incursions into India in the year 1000. During the thirteenth century the Mongol or Mogul hordes, under the celebrated Jangīz Khān, overthrew the Turkish or Tartar tribes; and in 1398 Tīmūr, uniting Tartars and Mongols into one army, made his well-known invasion of India. After desolating the country he retired, but the sixth in descent from him, Baber (*Bābar*), conquered Afghānistān, and thence invading

now form about one-sixth (or, according to the last census, about forty-one millions) of the entire population, a large number of them are supposed to be the descendants of Hindūs converted to Islām[1].

India about 1526, founded the Mogul empire, which his grandson Akbar (son of Humāyūn) established on a firm basis in 1556; a very remarkable man, Shīr Shāh Sūr, having previously usurped the empire of Hindūstān, and raised it to great prosperity. The power of the Moguls, which rapidly increased under Akbar, Jahāngīr, and Shāhjahān, until it culminated under Aurangzīb, began to decline under Shāh 'Ālam (Bahādur Shāh), Jahāndār Shāh, and Farrukh-siyar; and under Muhammad Shāh, the fourth from Aurangzīb, took place the Persian invasion of Afghānistān and thence of India, undertaken by Nādir Shāh (A.D. 1738) to avenge on the Afghāns their inroads into Persia. Hence it appears that in all cases the Muhammadan invaders of India came through Afghānistān, and generally settled there before proceeding to conquer the Hindūs. On this account, and from the proximity of Afghānistān, it has followed that the greater number of Muhammadan immigrants have been of Afghān blood.

[1] The total number of Muhammadans in the Bengal provinces alone is 20,664,775—probably more than in any other country of the globe; so that if England had merely these provinces, she would stand at the head of all Muhammadan powers, ruling more Mussulmāns than the present representative of the Khalīfs himself (see p. xxxv, note 1). The great bulk of Indian Muhammadans are Sunnīs (see p. xlii), very few Shī'as being found in Bengal, or indeed in any part of India (except Oude, and a few districts where there are descendants of Persian families). It is noteworthy that in Behar the mass of the people is Hindū, and singularly enough it is not in the great Mogul capitals of Bengal, such as Dacca, Gaur, and Murshidabad, that the Muslims are most numerous, but among the peasants and cultivating classes. Sir George Campbell has remarked that in Bengal the Musalmān invasion found Hindūism resting on weak foundations. Its hold on the affections of the people was weak. The Āryan element was only able to hold its own by frequent importation of fresh blood from Upper India. Hence it happened that when the Muslim conquerors invaded the lower Delta with the sword and the Kurān, they were not wholly unwelcome. They proclaimed equality among a people kept down by caste. Hence in Bengal great masses became Muhammadans, being induced to embrace Islām by the social elevation it gave them. In the North-west provinces and neighbourhood of the great Mogul capital Delhi, where the Hindūs have always been more spirited and independent, there are only about four million Musalmāns. In the Panjāb, however, there are nearly nine millions and a half.

One grand distinction between Islām and Hindūism is, that the former

Politically they became supreme, but they were never able to supplant the Hindūs, as these had done their predecessors. Moreover, it was the policy of the Muhammadan conquerors to bend, in many points, to the prejudices of their Indian subjects. Hence the Muslims of India became partially Hindūized, and in language, habits, and character took from the Hindūs more than they imparted[1].

Nor has the Hindū-Āryan element lost its ascendancy in India, notwithstanding the accession and admixture of European ingredients. The Portuguese, the Dutch, the Danes, the French have one after the other gained a footing on its shores, and their influence still lingers at isolated points[2]. Last of all the English have spread themselves over the whole country, and at this moment our political supremacy is everywhere greater than that which once belonged to the Musalmāns[3]. Yet the mass of the population is

---

is ever spreading and seeking converts, whereas the latter, theoretically, can never do so. A Brāhman is *born*, not *made*. Practically, however, any number of persons may form themselves into a new caste by community of occupation, and the Brāhmans of the present day are ready to accept them as Hindūs.

[1] Hence it happens that the lower orders of Indian Muhammadans observe distinctions of caste almost as strictly as the Hindūs. Many of them will eat and drink together, but not intermarry.

[2] In later times there has been a constant immigration of Chinese into India, but only of the male sex. The Portuguese still hold three places in India, viz. Goa, Damān, and the island of Diu on the western coast. The Dutch once held Chinsura on the right bank of the Hooghly, and Negapatam on the coast of Tanjore; but about the year 1824 they made both over to us, receiving in return our possessions on the coast of Sumatra. Our cession of the coast of Sumatra was afterwards considered a blunder, to remedy which the formal transfer of Singapore to the British was effected in 1824 by Sir Stamford Raffles (a treaty being made with the neighbouring Sultan) as an intermediate port for our trade with China. The Danes once possessed Tranquebar and Serampore, both of which were purchased from them by us in 1844. In 1846 they ceded a small factory to us at Balasore, where the Portuguese also, as well as the Dutch, held possessions in the early periods of European intercourse. The French still retain Pondicherry and Karical on the Coromandel coast, Chandernagore on the right bank of the Hooghly, Mahé on the Malabar coast, and Yanaon near the mouths of the Godāvarī.

[3] Although our annexation of province after province cannot always be justified, yet it may be truly said that our dominion has been gradually

still essentially Hindū, and the moral influence of what may be called the Indo-Āryan race is still paramount.

---

forced upon us. Our first dealings with India were merely commercial. The trading corporation entitled 'Governors and Company of London Merchants trading to the East Indies' was formed in 1600. The first Court of Directors was held on the 23rd September 1600, and the first charter was dated by Queen Elizabeth on the 31st of December in that year. The first factory was built at Surat, near the mouth of the Tapty, north of Bombay, in 1613. In 1661 the island of Bombay was ceded to the British by Portugal, as the marriage portion of the Infanta Catharine, on her marriage with Charles II, but its final possession was withheld for four years. It was handed over by Charles to the East India Company in 1669. Another factory was built on the Hooghly above Calcutta in 1636; Madras came into the Company's possession in 1640, and they purchased Calcutta itself in 1698. The battle of Plassy, from which dates the real foundation of the British empire, was fought June 23, 1757.

There are still a large number of native states in India. According to the India Office Report they exceed 460. Some merely acknowledge our supremacy, like Nepāl; but even this frontier country receives our Resident. Others are under a compact to govern well; others pay us tribute, or provide for contingents. Some have power of life and death, and some are obliged to refer capital cases to English courts of justice. Nearly all are allowed to adopt successors on failure of heirs, and their continued existence is thus secured. The Official Report classes them in twelve groups, thus: 1. The Indo-Chinese, in two subdivisions, comprising—A. the settled states, *Nepāl* (whose chief minister and virtual ruler is Sir Jung Bahādur), *Sikkim* (whose king lives at two cities, Tumlung and Chumbi, and who has lately ceded some territory to us), *Bhutān* (a turbulent hill-district), and *Kūch Bahār;* B. the hill-tribes, of Chinese character and physiognomy. 2. The aboriginal *Ghoṇḍ* and *Kole* tribes in *Chota Nāgpur*, *Orissa*, the Central Provinces, and the *Jaipur* (in Orissa) Agency. 3. The states among the *Himālayas*, from the western frontier of Nepāl to Kaśmīr, ruled generally by Rājput chiefs. 4. The *Afghān* and *Belūchī* frontier tribes beyond the Indus. 5. The *Sikh* states in the *Sirhind* plain, occupying the classic ground between the Sutlej and the Jumnā, and once watered by the Sarasvatī. 6. Three Muhammadan states, geographically apart, but having much in common, viz. *Rāmpur* (a district in Rohilkhand, representing the Rohilla state of the days of Warren Hastings), *Bhāwalpur* (separated from the Pañjāb by the Sutlej), and *Khairpur* (or Khyrpur) in Sind. 7. *Mālwa* and *Bundelkhand*, the former representing part of the Marāṭhī power, and including the impor-

Nevertheless, however closely bound together this race may be by community of origin, of religion, of customs, and of speech, and however powerful the influence it may exert over the Non-Āryan population, differences distinguish the people of India as great as

---

tant states of Central India, viz. that of *Gwālior*, ruled over by Mahārāja *Sindia;* the district governed by *Holkar;* the state of *Dhār*, ruled by the third Marāṭhī family, called Puars; the Muhammadan state of *Bhopāl;* and Bundelkhand, including the district of *Rewah*. 8. The ancient sovereignties of *Rājputāna*, including fifteen Rājput states (such as Odeypur, Jaipur, &c.), two Jāt and one Muhammadan (Tonk). 9. The *Gujarātī* native states, north of Bombay, the principal being that of *Baroda*, ruled over by the *Guikwār* or *Guicowār*. [*Gui* is for *gai*, 'a cow,' and *kwār* or *cowār* (*kuwār*) is possibly a corruption of *kumār*=*kumāra*, 'a prince;' but there is a Marāṭhī word *Gāyakyā*, 'a cowherd.' He is of the herdsman caste, and descended from a Marāṭhī general.] 10. The *Marāṭhī* states south of Bombay, representing the remains of the Marāṭhī power founded by Sivājī. Of these *Satāra* was annexed in 1848, but *Kolapur* remains; nineteen others are under our management owing to the minority of the chiefs. 11. The Muhammadan state of *Haidarābād* (or Hyderabad), in the Dekhan, ruled over by the *Nizām*, at present a minor, the government being conducted by Sir Salar Jung and Shams-ul-Umra. 12. The state of *Mysore*, whose old Rāja remembered the siege of Seringapatam. He died in 1868, and was succeeded by a child for whom we are now governing the country. To this must be added the two neighbouring Malayālam states on the Malabar coast, called *Travancore* and *Cochin*, both of which are excellently governed by enlightened Rājas and good ministers. Here is a Muhammadan historian's account of the first settlement of the English in India: 'In the year 1020 (A.D. 1611) the Emperor of Delhy, Jahāngīr, the son of king Akbar, granted a spot to the English to build a factory in the city of Surat, in the province of Guzerat, which is the first settlement that people made on the shores of Hindūstān. The English have a separate king, independent of the king of Portugal, to whom they owe no allegiance; but, on the contrary, these two nations put each other to death wheresoever they meet. At present, in consequence of the interference of the Emperor Jahāngīr, they are at peace with each other, though God only knows how long they will consent to have factories in the same town, and to live in terms of amity and friendship.' (Quoted in Sir George Campbell's Modern India, p. 23.) An excellent account of the rise of the British dominions in India is given by Professor W. D. Whitney in the Second Series of his Oriental and Linguistic Studies, procurable from Messrs. Trübner & Co.

or even greater than those which once divided and still distinguish the whole continent of Europe. The spirited Hindūstānī, the martial Sikh, the ambitious Marāṭhī, the proud Rājput, the hardy Gurkha[1], the calculating Bengālī, the busy Telugu, the active Tamil, the patient Pariah differ *inter se* as much as or more than the vivacious Celt, the stubborn Saxon, the energetic Norman, the submissive Slave, the enterprising Englishman, and the haughty Spaniard.

Many causes have combined to produce these distinctions. Difference of climate has had its effect in modifying character. Contact with the aboriginal races and with Muhammadans and Europeans has operated differently in different parts of India. Even in districts where the Hindūs are called by one name and speak one dialect they are broken up into separate classes, divided from each other by barriers of castes far more difficult to pass than the social distinctions of Europe. This separation constitutes, in point of fact, an essential doctrine of their religion. The growth of the Indian caste-system is perhaps the most remarkable feature in the history of this extraordinary people. Caste as a social institution, meaning thereby conventional rules which separate the grades of society, exists of course in all countries. In England, caste, in this sense, exerts no slight authority. But with us caste is not a religious institution. On the contrary, our religion, though it permits differences of rank, teaches us that such differences are to be laid aside in the worship of God, and that in His sight all men are equal. Very different is the caste of the Hindūs. The Hindū theory, according to Manu (see p. 240), is that the Deity regards men as *unequal*, that he created distinct kinds of men, as he created varieties of birds or beasts: that Brāhmans, Kshatriyas,

[1] The word *Gurkha* for *Gorkha*—a contraction of the Sanskṛit *Go-raksha*—means 'cow-keeper.' The aborigines of Nepāl are mostly of the Bhot or Tibetan family, and are therefore Buddhists; but tribes of Hindūs immigrated into this mountainous region at different periods within memory, and obtained the sovereignty of the country. They were probably of the cowherd caste from the adjacent country of Oudh and from the district below the hills, known as *Gorakhpur*. 'The tutelary deity of Nepāl is a form of S'iva, denominated *Gorakhnāth*, whose priests are Yogīs, and the same sect and worship had formerly equal predominance at Gorakhpur.'—Asiatic Researches, vol. xvii. p. 189.

Vaiśyas, and S'ūdras are born and must remain (at least in each separate existence) distinct from each other; and that to force any Hindū to break the rules of caste is to force him to sin against God, and against nature. It is true, that the endless rules of caste in India principally hinge upon three points of mere social economy and order: 1. food and its preparation[1], 2. intermarriage[2], and 3. professional pursuits[3]; but among a religious people, who regard these rules as sacred ordinances of their religion, an offence against any one of them becomes a great crime. It is a remarkable fact, that the jails in India often contain hardened criminals, who have fallen in our estimation to the lowest depths of infamy, but who, priding themselves on the punctilious observance of caste, have not lost one iota of their own self-respect, and would resent with indignation any attempt to force them to eat food prepared by the most virtuous person, if inferior to themselves in the social scale.

A full account of the origin and development of caste—of the strictness of its rules, and of the power it still exerts as a religious rather than as a social institution—will be found at p. 218, p. 231, &c. Moreover, for a description of the rise of Buddhism and its influence in the opposite direction the reader must refer to p. 53, &c.

It remains to point out that the very nature of the Hindū religious

---

[1] The *preparation of food* is quite as vital a point as *eating together*. Food prepared by a person of inferior caste causes defilement. Some castes cook with their shoes on: but most Hindūs would abhor food thus prepared, because leather causes defilement. Food cooked on board a boat or ship is supposed to destroy caste; thus, a boat proceeding down the Ganges sometimes stops to allow native passengers to cook their food on shore; perhaps, because wood is regarded as a conductor of defilement. It cannot, of course, be said that the rules of caste are *confined* to these three points. A Hindū's ideas about unclean animals are very capricious. He dreads the approach of a fowl to his house or person, as a source of contamination; but he does not mind ducks. Happily caste can no longer hold its own against necessity and advantage—against railroads and scientific inventions. (See the quotation at bottom of p. 219.)

[2] See the note on the mixed castes, p. 218, and p. 232 with note.

[3] It is the restriction of employments caused by caste which necessitates a large establishment of servants. The man who dresses hair feels himself degraded by cleaning clothes, and one who brushes a coat will on no account consent to sweep a room; while another who waits at table will on no consideration be induced to carry an umbrella.

creed has been the source of great diversities among the people of India.

Every religion worthy of the name may be said to develope itself in three principal directions: 1. that of faith, 2. that of works and ritual, 3. that of doctrine or dogmatic knowledge; to one or other of which prominence is given according to peculiarities of mental bias or temperament. I have endeavoured to show at pp. 36 and 327–329 that the first two lines of development represent a religious exoteric or popular side, while the third exhibits its esoteric aspect, and is the only exponent of its more profound meaning.

Nothing can possibly be more simple than esoteric Hindūism. It is a creed which may be expressed by the two words—*spiritual Pantheism* (see p. 36). A pantheistic creed of this kind is the simplest of all beliefs, because it teaches that nothing really exists but the one Universal Spirit; that the soul of each individual is identical with that Spirit, and that every man's highest aim should be to get rid for ever of doing, having, and being, and devote himself to profound contemplation, with a view to such spiritual knowledge as shall deliver him from the mere illusion of separate existence, and force upon him the conviction that he is himself part of the one Being constituting the Universe.

On the other hand, nothing can be more devoid of simplicity, nothing more multiform and capable of divergence into endless ramifications than the exoteric and popular side of the same creed. This apparent gulf between esoteric and exoteric Hindūism is bridged over by the simple substitution of the word *emanation* for *identification*.

Popular Hindūism supposes that God may for his own purposes amuse himself by illusory appearances; in other words, that he may manifest himself variously, as light does in the rainbow, and that all visible and material objects, including superior gods (*īśa*, *īśvara*, *adhīśa*), secondary gods (*deva*), demons (*daitya*), demi-gods, good and evil spirits, human beings, and animals, are *emanations* from him, and for a time exist separately from him, though ultimately to be reabsorbed into their source. Both these aspects of Hindūism are fully explained at pp. 36 and 323–336 of the following Lectures. From the explanations there given, the multiform character and singular expansibility of the Hindū religious creed will be understood.

Starting from the Veda, it ends by appearing to embrace something from all religions, and to present phases suited to all minds[1]. It has its spiritual and its material aspect, its esoteric and exoteric, its subjective and objective, its pure and its impure. It is at once vaguely pantheistic, severely monotheistic, grossly polytheistic, and coldly atheistic. It has a side for the practical, another for the devotional, and another for the speculative. Those who rest in ceremonial observances find it all-satisfying; those who deny the efficacy of works, and make faith the one thing needful, need not wander from its pale; those who delight in meditating on the nature of God and man, the relation of matter to spirit, the mystery of separate existence, and the origin of evil, may here indulge their love of speculation. And this capacity for almost endless expansion and variety causes almost endless sectarian divisions even among those who worship the same favourite deity. And these differences are enhanced by the close intertwining of religion with social distinctions. The higher classes are supposed capable of a higher form of religion than the lower, the educated than the uneducated, men than women; just as the religions of Muhammadans and Christians are held (like their complexions) to be most suited to their peculiar constitutions, circumstances, and nationalities.

In unison with its variable character, the religious belief of the

and one literature, accepted and revered by all adherents of Hindūism alike, however diverse in race, dialect, rank, and creed. That language is Sanskṛit, and that literature is Sanskṛit literature—the repository of *Veda*, or 'knowledge' in its widest sense; the vehicle of Hindū theology, philosophy, law, and mythology; the one guide to the intricacies and contradictions of Hindūism; the one bond of sympathy, which, like an electric chain, connects Hindūs of opposite characters in every district of India. Happily, too, the most important and interesting parts of that literature are now accessible to all, both in the original and in good translations.

And here let me explain that the name Sanskṛit as applied to the ancient language of the Hindūs is an artificial designation for a *highly elaborated form* of the language originally brought by the Indian branch of the great Āryan race into India. This original tongue soon became modified by contact with the dialects of the aboriginal races who preceded the Āryans, and in this way converted into the peculiar language (*bhāshā*) of the Aryan immigrants who settled in the neighbourhood of the seven rivers of the Pañjāb and its outlying districts (*Sapta Sindhavas*=in Zand *Hapta Hendu*). The most suitable name for the original language thus moulded into the speech of the Hindūs is Hindū-ī (=Sindhū-ī), its principal later development being called Hindī [1], just as the Low German dialect of the Saxons when modified in England was called Anglo-Saxon. But very soon that happened in India which has come to pass in all civilized countries. The spoken language, when once its general form and character had been settled, separated into two lines, the one elaborated by the learned, the other popularized and variously provincialized by the unlearned. In India, however, from the greater exclusiveness of the educated few, the greater ignorance of the masses, and the desire of a proud priesthood to keep the key of knowledge in their own possession, this separation became more marked, more diversified, and progressively intensified. Hence, the very grammar which with other nations was regarded only as a

---

[1] It may be thought by some that this dialect was nearly identical with the language of the Vedic hymns, and the latter often gives genuine Prākṛit forms (as *kuṭa* for *kṛita*); but even Vedic Sanskṛit presents great elaboration scarcely compatible with the notion of its being a simple original dialect (for example, in the use of complicated grammatical forms like Intensives); and Pāṇini, in distinguishing between the common language and the Vedic, uses the term *Bhāshā* in contradistinction to *Ćhandas* (the Veda).

means to an end, came to be treated by Indian Pandits as the end itself, and was subtilized into an intricate science, fenced around by a bristling barrier of technicalities. The language, too, elaborated *pari passu* with the grammar, rejected the natural name of Hindū-ī, or 'the speech of the Hindūs,' and adopted an artificial designation, viz. *Saṉskṛita*, 'the perfectly constructed speech' (*sam*=*συν*, *con*, *kṛita* =*factus*, 'formed'), to denote its complete severance from vulgar purposes, and its exclusive dedication to religion and literature; while the name *Prākṛita*—which may mean 'the original' as well as 'the derived' speech—was assigned to the common dialect. This of itself is a remarkable circumstance; for, although a similar kind of separation has happened in Europe, yet we do not find that Latin and Greek ceased to be called Latin and Greek when they became the language of the learned, any more than we have at present distinct names for the common dialect and literary language of modern nations.

The Sanskṛit dramas afford a notable specimen of this linguistic elaboration on the one side, and disintegration on the other (see p. 469). The two forms of speech thus evolved may be compared to two children of the same parent—the one, called Sanskṛit, refined by every appliance of art; the other, called Prākṛit, allowed to run more or less wild.

The present spoken languages of India—Bengālī, Uṛiya or Oṛiya (of *Oḍra-deśa* Orissa), Marāṭhī, Gujarāti, Pañjābī, and Hindī[1], with its modifications—represent Prākṛit[2] in its later stages of decom-

---

[1] By Hindī I mean the speech of the Hindūs as represented by the Prem Sāgar, and the Rāmāyaṇa of Tulasī Dās. According to Dr. Fitz-Edward Hall, the Prem Sāgar does not furnish a model of the most classical Hindī. There is certainly a modern literary Hindī which borrows largely from pure Sanskṛit, and another which is so mixed with Arabic and Persian words as to receive another name, Hindūstānī (p. xxxi, note). Besides Hindī and Hindūstānī and the languages above named, there are Sindhī, Kaśmīrī, Nepālese, Assamese, Pushtū (of Afghānistān), Siṉhalese (of Ceylon), Burmese, the five Drāviḍian (xxx, 2), and the half Drāviḍian Brahū-i. See Mr. Beames' valuable Comparative Grammar.

[2] The various kinds of Prākṛit introduced into the Sanskṛit dramas (the two principal forms of which—Mahārāshṭrī and Sauraseni—are explained by *Vararuči* in his grammar, the *Prākṛita-prakāśa*, edited by Professor E. B. Cowell) represent the last stage of development in the direction of the modern vernaculars. The earlier form of the ancient spoken language, called *Pāli* or *Māgadhī*, has a grammar and extensive litera-

position, and variously modified by collision with the primitive dialects of different localities.

It must not, however, be supposed that in taking this view of the formation of Sanskṛit, I mean to imply that it does not also stand in a kind of parental relation to the spoken dialects. Sanskṛit, when too highly elaborated by the Pandits, became in one sense dead, but in another sense it still breathes, and lives in the speech of the people, infusing fresh life and vigour into all their dialects [1]. For, independent of Sanskṛit as the vernaculars probably were in their first origin, they all now draw largely from it, for the enrichment of their vocabulary [2].

---

ture of its own, the study of which will be greatly facilitated by the Dictionary of Mr. R. C. Childers. Pāli was introduced into Ceylon by Buddhist missionaries from Magadha when Buddhism began to spread, and is now the sacred language of Ceylon and Burmah, in which all their Buddhist literature is written. Singularly enough, it found a kindred dialect established in Ceylon, which had developed into the present Siṉhalese. Pāli is closely connected with, and was probably preceded by the language of the Rock Inscriptions of the second and third centuries B.C. The language of the Gāthās, as found in the Lalita-vistara (see p. 55, note 1) of the Northern Buddhists of Nepāl, is thought by some to be a still earlier form of the popular language; so that four separate stages of Prākṛit, using that term generally for the spoken languages of the people which preceded the modern vernaculars, can be traced: 1. the Gāthās; 2. the Inscriptions; 3. the Pāli; 4. the Prākṛit of the plays. (Professor E. B. Cowell's edition of Colebrooke's Essays, II. 21.)

[1] The Sanskṛit colleges founded at Benares, Calcutta, and other places, for the cultivation of the learned language and literature of the Hindūs, are doing a good work; but, after all, the bearing of Sanskṛit upon the vernaculars constitutes a point of primary importance. For we must not forget that the general diffusion of education throughout India must be chiefly effected through the medium of the vernacular dialects, and not merely through English. A knowledge of this fact has led to the establishment of Sir William Muir's new college at Allahabad (the 'Muir University College'), to which numerous vernacular schools will be affiliated. With reference to the study of the vernaculars and the spread of education by their means, let me recommend a perusal of Sir Charles Trevelyan's 'Original Papers on the Application of the Roman Alphabet to the Languages of India,' edited by me in 1859 (Longmans).

[2] This applies even to the South-Indian languages—Tamil, Telugu, Kanarese, Malayālam, and Tulu; although these are not Āryan in structure, but belong rather to the Turanian or agglutinating family.

If, then, the mere language of a people—the bare etymology of isolated words, and the history of the changes they have undergone in form and meaning—furnishes an excellent guide to its past and present condition, moral, intellectual, and physical, how much more must this be true of its literature! And here again we are met by the remarkable fact that India, notwithstanding all its diversities of race, caste, customs, creed, and climate, has to this day but one real literature, accepted by all alike—the common inheritance of all. In European countries, literature changes with language. Each modern dialect has its own literature, which is the best representative of the actual condition of the people to whom it belongs. To know the Italians, we need not study Latin, when the modern literature is at our command. But the literature of the Hindū vernacular dialects (except perhaps that of Tamil) is scarcely yet deserving of the name. In most cases it consists of mere reproductions of the Sanskṛit[1]. To understand the past and present state of Indian society—to unravel the complex texture of the Hindū mind; to explain inconsistencies otherwise inexplicable—we must trust to Sanskṛit literature alone. Sanskṛit is the only language of poetry, drama, law, philosophy—the only key to a vast and apparently confused religious system, and a sure medium of approach to the hearts of the Hindūs, however unlearned, or however disunited. It is, in truth, even more to India than classical and patristic literature was to Europe at the time of the Reformation. It gives a deeper impress to the Hindū mind, so that every Hindū, however unlettered, is unconsciously affected by it, and every Englishman, however strange to the East, if only he be at home in Sanskṛit literature, will rapidly become at home in every corner of our Indian territories.

These considerations will, I trust, justify my attempt to give some idea of the history and character of India's literature.

Let it be clearly understood, however, that the examples of Indian wisdom given in this volume generally present *the bright side of the*

---

[1] With regard to Hindūstānī (otherwise called Urdū), the proper language of the North-western districts and passing current, like French in Europe, over all India, it cannot be said to rank as a distinct language till the time of Tīmūr, about A.D. 1400, when it was finally formed in his Urdū or camp by blending Hindī with the Arabic and Persian of the Muhammadan invaders. Its prose literature, such as it is, certainly owes more to Arabic than to Sanskṛit, and is quite modern. The productions of its greatest poet, Sauda, are not much more than a hundred years old.

*picture only*. To make the sketch a faithful portrait of the reality, many dark lines and shadows must be introduced.

My reasons for giving prominence to all that is good and true in the Hindū system are stated in the note to p. 3 of Lecture I. Let me now add a few remarks to what is there asserted.

It appears to me high time that all thoughtful Christians should reconsider their position, and—to use the phraseology of our modern physicists—readjust themselves to their altered environments. The ground is now being rapidly cleared for a fair and impartial study of the writings of Eastern nations. The sacred books of the three great systems opposed to Christianity—Brāhmanism, Buddhism, and Islām—are now at length becoming accessible to all; and Christians can no longer neglect the duty of studying their contents[1]. All the inhabitants of the world are being rapidly drawn

---

[1] With regard to the books on which the three great false religions of the world rest, not only have we access to those of Brāhmanism and Islām—viz. the Veda and the Kurān—both in printed editions of the originals and in various translations (see pp. 6–9), but even the Buddhist sacred Canon—written in the ancient language called Pāli (see p. xxix, note 2)—is now becoming accessible. Its name *Tri-piṭaka*, 'three baskets or caskets,' denotes its distribution under three divisions, viz. A. *Sūtra* (Pāli *Sutta*), works containing the doctrinal and practical discourses of the great Buddha. B. *Vinaya*, ecclesiastical discipline, or works prescribing rules and penalties for the regulation of the lives of the monks (Bhikshukas, see p. 58). C. *Abhidharma* (Pāli *Abhidhamma*), metaphysics and philosophy. These three classes of works were rehearsed at the first council by the Buddha's three pupils, *Ānanda*, *Upāli*, and *Kāśyapa* respectively.

*A*. has five subdivisions, viz. 1. *Dīgha-nikāya* (*dīrgha-n°*), collections of long Sūtras. 2. *Majjhima-nikāya* (*madhyama-n°*), collections of Sūtras of a middling length. 3. *Saṃyutta-nikāya* (*saṃyukta-n°*), groups of Sūtras. 4. *Anguttara-nikāya*, collections of other Sūtras. 5. *Khuddaka-nikāya* (*kshudraka-n°*), collections of short Sūtras in fifteen different works, viz. 1. *Khuddaka-pāṭha*, lesser readings, edited and translated in the 'Journal of the Royal Asiatic Society' by Mr. R. C. Childers; 2. *Dhamma-pada*, religious precepts (lit. verses or words, on Dharma); 3. *Udāna*, hymns of praise; 4. *Itivuttakam*, precepts in which Itivuttam, 'it has been so said,' occurs; 5. *Sutta-nipāta*, occasional Sūtras; 6. *Vimānavatthu*, stories of celestial mansions; 7. *Petavatthu*, stories of Pretas; 8. *Thera-gāthā*; 9. *Therī-gāthā*, relating to elders among priests and priestesses; 10. *Jātaka*, the Buddha's previous births; 11. *Mahā-niddesa*, great commentary; 12. *Pati-sambhīdā*, exposition of the Patis; 13. *Apadāna*, heroic actions;

together by increased facilities of communication, and St. Paul's grand saying—that God has made all nations of men of one blood (Acts xvii. 26)—is being brought home to us more forcibly every day. Steam presses, as well as railroads and telegraphs, are doing a great work, and bringing about rapid changes. They are every day imposing upon us new duties and responsibilities in the opening out of hitherto unexplored regions. Surely, then, we are bound to follow the example of the great Apostle of the Gentiles, who, speaking to Gentiles, instead of denouncing them as 'heathen,' appealed to them as 'very God-fearing' (δεισιδαιμονεστέρους), and even quoted a passage from one of their own poets in support of a

---

14. *Buddha-vanśa*, history of Buddhas who preceded Gotama; 15. *Ćariyā-piṭaka*, casket of rites and deeds.

*B.* has five subdivisions: 1. *Pārājika;* 2. *Pāćittiya;* 3. *Ćūlavagga;* 4. *Mahāvagga;* 5. *Parivāra.*

*C.* has seven subdivisions: 1. *Dhamma-saṅgaṇī;* 2. *Vibhanga;* 3. *Kathāvatthu;* 4. *Puggala;* 5. *Dhātu;* 6. *Yamaka;* 7. *Paṭṭhāna.*

Of the fifteen works under the fifth subdivision or *Khuddaka-nikāya* of A, the *Dhamma-pada*, *Sutta-nipāta*, and *Jātaka* are the most important.

The *Dhamma-pada*, or precepts of law—entirely in verse—has been edited by Dr. Fausböll, of Copenhagen, with parts of the commentary (*Artha-kathā* or *Aṭṭha-kathā*), and translated by Professor Weber (Indische Streifen, I. 118) and by Professor Max Müller.

The *Sutta-nipāta* has lately been translated by Sir M. Coomāra Swāmy (Trübner, 1874). It consists of maxims on doctrine and practice, in prose and verse—sometimes in the form of dialogues—possibly as old as the third Buddhist council, in Aśoka's reign, 246 B.C. (see p. 60). They are compared to the discourses of Vasishṭha, addressed to Rāma, in the Vāsishṭha-rāmāyaṇa (see p. 370).

The tenth work of the fifteen, viz. the *Jātaka*, has also been partially edited and translated by Fausböll (ten of the Jātakas very recently, Trübner, 1872; five others in 1861).

The above long list of works under A. B. C. constitutes the sacred Canon of the Southern Buddhists of Ceylon. The Tri-piṭaka of the Northern Buddhists of Nepāl has probably become corrupted and amplified in some of its details, though the names of the works—as far as has yet been ascertained—are in all likelihood the same. The *Sad-dharma-puṇḍarīka* and the *Lalita-vistara* (see p. 55, note) were once thought to belong to this Canon, but this is now held to be a mistake. In Burnouf's translation of the former (called by him *Lotus de la bonne loi*), a note was commenced on the difference between the Northern and Southern Tri-piṭakas, but left unfinished in consequence of his untimely death.

Christian truth (Acts xvii. 28); and who, writing to Christians, directed them not to shut their eyes to anything true, honest, just, pure, lovely, or of good report, wherever it might be found, and exhorted them, that if there be *any virtue*, and if there be *any praise,* they were to think on these things (Phil. iv. 8). Surely it is time we ceased to speak and act as if truth among Gentiles and truth among Christians were two wholly different things. Surely we ought to acknowledge and accept with gratitude whatever is true and noble in the Hindū character, or in Hindū writings, while we reflect with shame on our own shortcomings under far greater advantages.

Nor ought we to forget the words of St. Peter, when—looking down from our undoubted pre-eminence on the adherents of false systems, such as Brāhmans, Buddhists, Pārsīs, Fetish-worshippers, and Muslims, wholly distinct from one another and separated by vast chasms though they be—we are accustomed to bracket them all together as if they were equally far from the kingdom of God. To continue to label them all, or even the first four, with the common label *Heathen*[1], as if they were all to be placed in the same category as

[1] I lately read an able article, written by a Christian and a man of high culture, in which the term 'heathen' was applied to murderers and villains—I presume from the fact that the inhabitants of heaths and outlying districts are often lawless and benighted. Another author, speaking of certain ignorant vagabonds, says, 'These heathen,' &c. In point of fact, I believe that this is not an unusual application of the term, and such phrases as 'heathenish conduct,' 'heathenish ideas,' are commonly current amongst us as opprobrious epithets. Are we, then, justified in still using this single term as a common label for *all* unbelievers in Christianity, however God-fearing and righteous (like Cornelius of old) they may be. We make an exception in favour of Muhammadans, forgetting that *corruptio optimi pessima*. True, the translators of the Bible generally use 'heathen' as an equivalent for τὰ ἔθνη, 'Gentile nations;' but this rests on a false notion of some etymological affinity between the two words. The Greeks and Romans who called the rest of the world 'Barbarians,' the Hindūs who call all other persons 'Mlećchas,' and the Muslims who call all unbelievers in Muhammad 'Kāfirs and Gabrs,' never have, so far as I know, applied these expressions to villains and criminals. It becomes a question whether, if we are to follow the example of the Founder of Christianity, we ought not to substitute some such term as 'Gentiles' or 'Unbelievers' or 'Non-Christian nations' for an epithet now become somewhat too opprobrious.

equally idolaters, seems, under the present altered circumstances of our increasing acquaintance with these systems, a proceeding wholly opposed to the spirit of that great Apostle, who, when addressing Gentiles, assured them that God had taught him not to call any man *common or unclean;* and declared that *God was no respecter of persons, but that in every nation he that feared Him and worked righteousness was accepted by Him* (Acts x. 34, 35; see also Rom. ii. 10, 11, 14, 15, iii. 29).

If, then, it is becoming more and more a duty for all the nations of the world to study each other; to inquire into and compare each other's systems of belief; to avoid expressions of contempt in speaking of the sincere and earnest adherents of any creed; and to search diligently whether the principles and doctrines which guide their own faith and conduct rest on the one true foundation or not—surely we Englishmen, to whose rule India has been intrusted, have special opportunities and responsibilities in this respect. For in India the three great systems which now confront Christianity—viz. Brāhmanism, Buddhism, and Islām—are all represented. Brāhmanism is, of course, numerically the strongest; yet Muhammadans form, as we have seen (p. xx), a sixth part of its population[1]. As to Buddhism, we have indicated (pp. 53–61) that its relationship to Brāhmanism was in some respects similar to that of Christianity to Judaism; and although it is true that, in contrast to Christianity,

---

[1] It may startle some to learn from p. xx of this Introduction that England is the greatest Muhammadan power in the world, and that our Queen has probably more than double as many Muslim subjects as the ruler of the Turkish Empire. Roughly estimating the present population of the globe at thirteen hundred millions, the Buddhists along with the Confucianists (disciples of *Kūng-fū-tsze*, see p. 4, note 1) and Tauists (of *Lau-tsze*) would comprise about 490 millions; Christians, 360 millions; Muslims or Muhammadans, 100 millions; and Brāhmanical Hindūs and Semi-Hindūs, 185 millions. Of other creeds, the Jews comprise about 8 or 9 millions; Jainas, Pārsīs, and Sikhs together about 3 or 4 millions. The Fetish-worshippers of Africa, America, and Polynesia probably make up the remaining 153 millions. The census of 1872 showed that there were only 318,363 converts to Protestant Christianity in all India. The religion of Christians, Buddhists, and Muslims is missionary; that of Jews, Hindūs, and Pārsīs, non-missionary. Without the missionary spirit there can be no continued vitality and growth; and this spirit is part of the very essence of Christianity, whose first missionary was Christ Himself.

which, originating among Semitic Jews afterwards spread among the Āryans of Europe, Buddhism originated with the Aryans of India and afterwards spread among Turanian races (see p. 4, Lecture I, and p. 5, note 1); still India was most undoubtedly the original home of this most popular system—the nominal creed of the majority of the human race. Moreover, it may be gathered from a perusal of the dramas (such as the Mālatī-mādhava, p. 480), that Hindūism and Buddhism coexisted and were tolerant of each other in India till about the end of the eighth century of our era. A reference, too, to pp. 128–132 will show that the Buddhistic philosophy and Buddhistic ideas have left a deep impression on Hindūism, and still linger everywhere scattered throughout our Eastern Empire, especially among the Jainas[1] (see p. 128); and Buddhism is to this day, as is well known, the faith of our fellow-subjects in Ceylon, Pegu, and British Burmah, being also found in outlying districts of India, such as Chittagong, Darjeeling, Assam, Nepāl, Bhotan, and Sikkim.

It is one of the aims, then, of the following pages to indicate the points of contact between Christianity and the three chief false religions of the world, as they are thus represented in India[2].

---

[1] According to the last census the number of Buddhists and Jainas in India amounts to nearly three millions (2,629,200). Sir George Campbell's Report gives 86,496 as the number of Buddhists in the Bengal provinces. Although Jainism has much in common with Buddhism, it is nevertheless a very different system. The Jainas always call themselves and are considered Hindūs (see p. 130, note 1). According to Rājendralāla Mitra, the Jaina scriptures are comprised in fifty different works, collectively called the *Sūtras*, and sometimes the *Siddhāntas*, and classed in two different ways: 1st, under the two heads of *Kalpa-sūtra* and *Āgama*, five works coming under the former, and forty-five under the latter head: 2ndly, under eight different heads, viz. 1. eleven *Aṅgas;* 2. twelve *Upāṅgas;* 3. four *Mūla-sūtra;* 4. five *Kalpa-sūtra;* 5. six *Ćheddas;* 6. ten *Payannas;* 7. *Nandi-sūtra;* 8. *Anuyoga-dvāra-sūtra.* Some of them have a four-fold commentary, under the names *Ṭīkā*, *Niryukti*, *Ćūrṇī*, and *Bhāshya*, constituting with the original the five-fold (*pañćāṅga*) Sūtra. They are partly in Sanskṛit, partly in Māgadhī Prākṛit, and the total of the fifty works is said to amount to 600,000 Ślokas (see Notices of Sanskrit MSS. No. VIII. p. 67).

[2] Of course, the religion of ancient Persia, sometimes called Zoroastrianism—a most important and interesting creed (see p. 4)—is also represented, but the Pārsīs are numerically insignificant (see note, p. xviii).

This common ground is to be looked for more in Brāhmanism than in Buddhism, and even than in Islām. In proof of which I refer the reader to pp. 53–60 for a summary of Buddhism; to pp. 36, 324, and to p. 12, note 1, for a summary of Hindūism both popular and esoteric; to pp. 22, 228, for the Hindū account of the creation of the world[1]; to pp. 32, 394, for that of the deluge; to pp. 5–8 for the Hindū and Muhammadan doctrine of revelation and inspiration; to p. 146, note 1, for the Hindū conception of original sin; to p. 333, note 1, for the Hindū theory of the gradual depravation of the human race; to p. 31, note 1, and to p. 251, for that of sacrifices and sacramental acts[2]; to pp. 247–249, 279, for that of the mystical efficacy of water in cleansing from sin[3] (compare also

---

[1] Professor Banerjea ('Indian Antiquary,' Feb. 1875) thinks that the Hindū account of the creation of the world preserves traces of the revelation made in the Bible of the Spirit brooding on the surface of the waters; and that the theory of the Nāgas, who were half serpents half men, dwelling in the lower regions (see p. 430), confirms the Biblical account of the Serpent, which was originally perhaps a species corresponding to the Nāga, before the sentence was pronounced by which it became a creeping reptile. Compare the story of the eldest of the five sons of Āyus (of the lunar race), called Nahusha, cursed by Agastya to become a serpent, for excessive pride, in having, after gaining by penance the rank of Indra, compelled the Ṛishis to bear his litter on their backs, and then kicked some of them (Manu VII. 41; Vishṇu-purāṇa, p. 413; Mahā-bh. V. 343).

[2] The Hindūs have two roots for 'to sacrifice,' *hu* (=an older *dhu*= θυ) and *yaj*. The first is restricted to oblations of clarified butter in fire; the latter is applied to sacrificing, and honouring the gods with sacrifices generally. A third root, *su*, is used for offering libations with the juice of the Soma-plant, especially to the god Indra—the oldest form of sacrifice in India (note 1, p. 31). The idea of sacrifice is ingrained in the whole Hindū system. It is one of the earliest that appears in their religious works, and no literature—not even the Jewish—contains so many words relating to sacrifice as Sanskṛit. It is remarkable that the food offered to the gods, when appropriated and eaten by the priests, and the rice distributed by them to the people, are called *prasāda* (?=εὐχαριστία).

[3] Bathing in sacred rivers—especially in the Ganges and at particular Tīrthas, such as Haridvār, Prayāga—purifies the soul from all sin. Hence dying persons are brought to the river-side, leaves of the Tulasī plant being often put in their mouths. Hence also Ganges water (as well as other consecrated liquid) was used in the inauguration (*abhisheka*) of kings (see p. 515, and cf. Rāmāyaṇa II. xv. 5) and in the administration of oaths.

p. 284, line 9 from bottom); to pp. 201, 246, for that of regeneration or second birth; to pp. 278, 279, for that of atonement and expiation; to pp. 321–336 for the Hindū theory of incarnation and the need of a Saviour; to p. 324 for that of the triple manifestation or Hindū Triad; to pp. 104–106, 247 (with note 2), 251, for the Hindū and Muhammadan teaching as to the religious duties of prayer, ablutions, repetitions of sacred texts, almsgiving, penance, &c.; to p. 252, note 1, for the actual practice of these duties at the present day; to pp. 104–106 for the infliction of self-mortifications, fasting, &c.; and, lastly, to pp. 282–294, 440–448, 457–462, for examples of moral and religious sentiments.

Lest, however, it should be inferred that, while advocating perfect fairness and impartiality in comparing all four religious systems, I have aimed in the present work at lowering in the slightest degree the commanding position occupied by our own faith, or written anything to place Christianity in an unfavourable light in relation to the other systems of the world, I conclude this Introduction by adverting to some principal points which, in my opinion, constitute the distinctive features of our own religion, separating it decisively from all the other creeds as the only divine scheme capable of regenerating the entire human race.

It seems to me, then, that in comparing together these four systems—Christianity, Islām, Brāhmanism, and Buddhism—the crucial test of the possession of that absolute divine truth which can belong to one only of the four, and which—if supernaturally communicated by the common Father of mankind for the good of all His creatures—must be intended to prevail everywhere, ought to lie in the answer to two questions: 1st, What is the ultimate object at which each aims? 2ndly, By what means and by what agency is this aim to be accomplished?

1. Let us begin with Buddhism, because as a religious system it stands lowest; not indeed deserving, or even claiming, to be called a religion at all in the true sense of the word (see p. 57), though it is numerically the strongest of all the four creeds. With regard, then, to the first question:

The object aimed at by pure Buddhism is, as we have shown at p. 57, *Nirvāṇa*, the being blown out like a flame—in other words—utter annihilation. It is true that the S'ramaṇas or Bhikshukas, 'ascetics and religious mendicants,' alone can be said to aim directly at Nirvāṇa (see pp. 57, 58). The Upāsakas or laymen think only of the effect of actions on the happiness or misery of future states of being. But, if personality and the remembrance of previous existences are not preserved, how can death be regarded in any other light than absolute extinction?

2. Brāhmanism rises to a higher level, for here there is a theoretical craving after union with the Supreme Spirit, as the grand aim and object of the system (see p. 500). This union, however, really means identification with or absorption into the One only self-existing Being, as the river blends with the ocean; so that Brāhmanism really ends in destroying man's personality, and practically, if not theoretically, lands its disciples in the same absolute extinction aimed at by Buddhists. In fact, the higher and more esoteric the teaching of both these systems, the more evidently do they exhibit themselves in their true colours as mere schemes for getting rid of the evils of life, by the extinction of all activity, individuality, self-consciousness, and personal existence.

3. Let us now turn to Islām. The end which Muhammad set before the disciples of the Kurān was admission to a material paradise (*jannat*[1]), described as consisting of shaded gardens, abounding with delicious fruits, watered by flowing streams (*anhār*), filled with black-eyed Hūrīs, and replete with exquisite corporeal enjoyments. It is certainly true that spiritual pleasures and the favour of God are also said to form part of its delights, and that the permanence of man's personality is implied. But a holy God is still immeasurably removed from His creatures, and intimate union with Him, or even admission to His presence, is not the central idea of beatitude.

4. In contrast to Brāhmanism, Buddhism, and Islām, the one object aimed at in Christianity is, emphatically, such an *access to* and *union with* a holy God as shall not only secure the permanence of man's own individual will, energy, and personality, but even intensify them.

Perhaps, however, it is in the answer to the second question that the great difference between the four systems is most apparent.

How, and by what means is the object aimed at by each system avowedly effected? In replying to this, let us reverse the order, and commence with our own religion.

---

[1] Muslims believe there are seven (or eight) heavens representing degrees of felicity, and seven hells (*jahannam*), the seventh or deepest of which is for hypocrites, the sixth for idolaters, the third for Christians.

1. Christianity asserts that it effects its aim through nothing short of an entire change of the whole man, and a complete renovation of his nature. The means by which this renovation is effected may be described as a kind of *mutual transfer* or *substitution,* leading to a reciprocal interchange and co-operation between God and man's nature acting upon each other. Man—the Bible affirms—was created in the image of God, but his nature became corrupt through a taint, derived from the fall of the first representative man and parent of the human race, which taint could only be removed by a vicarious death.

Hence, the second representative man—Christ—whose nature was divine and taintless, voluntarily underwent a sinner's death, that the taint of the old corrupted nature transferred to him might die also. But this is not all. The great central truth of our religion lies not so much in the fact of Christ's death as in the fact of His *continued life* (Rom. viii. 34). The first fact is that He of His own free will died; but the second and more important fact is that He rose again and lives eternally, that He may bestow life for death and a participation in His own divine nature in place of the taint which He has removed.

This, then, is the reciprocal exchange which marks Christianity and distinguishes it from all other religions—an exchange between the personal man descended from a corrupt parent, and the personal God made man and becoming our second parent. We are separated from a rotten root, and are grafted into a living one. We part with the corrupt will, depraved moral sense, and perverted judgment inherited from the first Adam, and draw re-creative force—renovated wills, fresh springs of wisdom, righteousness, and knowledge[1]—from the ever-living divine stem of the

[1] It has been objected to Christianity that it discourages increase of knowledge; but the only knowledge it condemns is the empty knowledge which 'puffeth up' (1 Cor. viii. 1, 2). 'God is Light' or knowledge itself. The more a Christian man becomes Godlike, the more he aims at increase of light, whether in religion or science. It is said of Christ that 'in Him are hid all the treasures of wisdom and knowledge' (Col. ii. 3). Truth must be one, and all truth is declared to come by Him, as well as grace (St. John i. 17). Other religious systems, on the contrary, are interpenetrated with so much that is false in every branch of knowledge, that a simple lesson in geography tends to undermine every thoughtful person's faith in such creeds.

second Adam, to which, by a simple act of faith, we are united. In this manner is the grand object of Christianity effected. Other religions have their doctrines and precepts of morality, which, if carefully detached from much that is bad and worthless, may even vie with those of Christianity. But Christianity has, besides all these, what other religions have not—a personal God, ever living to supply the free grace or regenerating Spirit by which human nature is re-created and again made Godlike, and through which man, becoming once again 'pure in heart,' and still preserving his own will, self-consciousness, and personality, is fitted to have access to God the Father, and dwell in His presence for ever.

2. In Islām, on the contrary, Muhammad is regarded as the prophet of God and nothing more. He claimed no combination of divinity with humanity[1]. Even his human nature was not held

---

[1] He did not even pretend to be the founder of a new religion, but simply to have been commissioned to proclaim Islām (p. xliv) and its cardinal doctrine—the unity of the Godhead—which dogma the Kurān constantly affirms with great beauty of language (chap. ii. 256, xxiv. 36). God (Allāh) in the Kurān has one hundred names, indicative of his attributes, of which 'the merciful,' 'the compassionate' occur most frequently. But God, Muhammad maintained, begetteth not, nor is begotten. In chap. ii. of the Kurān, we read: 'To God belongeth the east and the west; therefore whithersoever ye turn yourselves to pray, there is the face of God; for God is omnipresent and omniscient. They say, "God hath begotten children." God forbid.' Nevertheless, Muhammad did not deny that Christ was a prophet and apostle. He merely claimed to be a later and greater prophet himself. The Kurān (lxi. 6) has the following: 'Jesus, the son of Mary, said, "O children of Israel, verily I am the apostle of God, sent unto you, confirming the law which was declared before me, and bringing good tidings of an apostle who shall come after me, whose name shall be Ahmad" (=Muhammad, in Greek περικλύτος, the Muslim doctors making out that παράκλητος ought to be so written).' But although thus arrogantly claiming to be the successor of Christ, any sharing (*shirk*) of God's divinity was utterly abhorrent from his whole teaching. He did not even rest his own claims on miracles (*āyat, karāmat*), which he constantly excused himself from working. It is said that some doubters once asked him to give them a sign by turning the hill Safā into gold, but he declined to do so on the ground that God had revealed to him that if after witnessing the miracle, they remained incredulous, they would all be destroyed. The only sign of his mission to which he pointed was the Kurān itself, declaring himself to be as untaught as a child just born (*ummīy*), or in other words a wholly

to be immaculate, nor did he make any pretence to mediatorial or vicarious functions. He died like any other man[1], and he certainly did not rise from the grave that his followers might find in him perpetual springs of divine life and vivifying power, as branches draw sap and energy from a living stem. Nor do Muslims believe him to be the source of any re-creative force, capable of changing their whole being. Whatever the theory as to God's mercy propounded in the Kurān, heaven is practically only accessible to Muslims through the strict discharge of religious duties

---

unlettered person, to whom a composition in marvellously beautiful language was revealed. It is, however, quite true that Muhammad's biographers afterwards attributed various miracles to their prophet. For instance, it is handed down by tradition that taking a bar of iron he struck a huge rock with such force that it fell shivered to pieces, and the blow created a light which flashed from Medina to Madain in Persia. On the night called *lailat ul mi'rāj* he ascended to heaven from Jerusalem on a fabulous mule named Burāk. He split the moon (by a miracle called *shakk ul kamar*). He healed the eye of a soldier. He turned a stick into a sword. He put his fingers over empty vessels, and fountains of water flowed into them. He fed 130 men on the liver of a sheep. He fed a million people on a few loaves and a lamb, and many fragments were left. He once, by prayer to God, brought back the sun in the heavens when it had nearly set. On his entrance into Mecca (Makkah) he was saluted by mountains and trees, which said, 'Peace be to thee, O prophet of God!'

Here, again, in contrast to the above, it is to be noted that about ninety names are applied in the Bible to Christ Himself as the God-Man, and that Christians appeal to the personal Christ, as the one miracle of miracles, and to His personal resurrection as the sign of signs; while Christ Himself appealed to no book except the Old Testament; nor did he write any book or direct any book to be written; and attributed more importance to His own *personal* example, words, and works (ἔργα) than to the wonders He performed, rebuking a constant craving after signs (σημεῖα). We may also note that the artless unaffected simplicity and total absence of what may be called *ad captandum* glitter of style in the language of the New Testament, contrast remarkably with the studied magniloquence of parts of Muhammad's pretended revelation. See on the subject of miracles a valuable little work by the Rev. G. Renaud, called, 'How did Christ rank the proofs of His mission?' (Hatchards, 1872.)

[1] He is supposed, however, not to have died a natural death, but to have been poisoned by a Jewess.

which God as an absolute sovereign and hard task-master imposes[1]. If these religious exercises are really more than a lifeless form,

[1] Muhammad sets forth faith in Islām and in his own mission, repentance, the performance of prayer, fasting, alms, pilgrimages, and the constant repetition of certain words (especially parts of the Kurān), as infallible means of obtaining paradise. In one place, suffering, perseverance, walking in the fear of God, and attachment to Him are insisted on. See Sale's Kurān, xxix. 1–7, iv. 21, xviii. 31, xx. 71, xxi. 94, xxii. 14, xxiii. 1. Yet it must be admitted that the Kurān elsewhere maintains that good works have no real meritorious efficacy in procuring paradise, and that the righteous obtain entrance there through God's mercy alone. Indeed, every action in Islām is done 'in the name of God, the merciful, the compassionate' (*b'ismillāh ar-rahmān ar-rahīm*). But it must be noted that the Kurān is by no means systematic or consistent. It was delivered in detached portions according to the exigences of the moment, and being often confused and contradictory, had to be explained and developed by traditional teaching. These traditions are called *Sunnah*, and a Sunnī is one who obeys the laws of Muhammad founded not only on the Kurān but on the traditions as interpreted by four great doctors or leaders of Islām, viz. Shāfi-'ī, Hanīfa, Mālik, and Hanbal, each of whom is the leader of a sect. It should be noted that the *Shī'as*—a name derived from *shī'at*, a party of persons forming a sect—are opposed to the Sunnīs, like Protestants to Roman Catholics. They reject the traditions of the Sunnīs, having separated from them about 363 years after Muhammad's Hijra (A. D. 985) under one of the 'Abbāssī Khalīfs (descendants of 'Abbās, Muhammad's uncle, who ruled as Khalīfs over Baghdad and Persia from A. D. 749 to 1258). They do not call themselves Shī'as, but *'Adlīyah*, 'the rightful society,' and deny the Khalīfate of the first three successors of Muhammad, Abūbakr, Omar, and Othmān (the first two being Muhammad's fathers-in-law and the third his son-in-law), who ruled at Medina. The Shī'as regard these three as usurpers of the successorship (Khalīfate), which they declare belonged only to another son-in-law, the fourth Khalīf, 'Alī (husband of the prophet's daughter Fātima, and father of Hasan and Husain), whom they regard as the first of their true Imāms, and who ruled with his sons at Kūfa. The Turks, Egyptians, and Indian Muhammadans are mostly Sunnīs, while the Persians are Shī'as. This doctrine of the Shī'as, which may be called the protesting form of Islām, is no doubt more spiritual than the original system of Muhammad. As it developed itself in Persia, it was influenced in some measure by the ancient religion of Zoroaster, which preceded it in that country. There the Shī'a tenets ultimately gave birth to a kind of spiritual philosophy called Sūfī-ism—so similar to the Indian Vedānta (see p. 36 of this volume) that it is said

the life-giving principle which animates them is not supposed to come from Muhammad. Nevertheless, candour compels us to admit that in one notable point every true Muslim sets the Christian a good example. The word Islām means 'complete submission to the will of God,' and a Muslim is one who submits himself to that will without a murmur. The same candour, however, also suggests the inquiry whether the submission of the adherent of Islām may not be that of an abject slave, dreading the displeasure of a stern master, rather than of a loving child depending on its Father for life and breath and all things.

3. As to Brāhmanism, we must, in fairness, allow that, according to its more fully developed system, the aim of union with God is held to be effected by faith in an apparently personal god, as well as by works and by knowledge. And here some of the lines of Brāhmanical thought seem to intersect those of Christianity. But the apparent personality of the various Hindū gods melts away, on closer scrutiny, into a vague spiritual essence. It is true that God becomes man and interposes for the good of men, causing a seeming combination of the human and divine—and an apparent interchange of action and even loving sympathy between the Creator and His creatures. But can there be any real interaction or co-operation between divine and human personalities when all personal manifestations of the Supreme Being—gods as well as men—ultimately merge in the Oneness of the Infinite, and nothing remains permanently distinct from Him? It must be admitted that most remarkable language is used of Kṛishṇa (Vishṇu), a supposed form of the Supreme, as the source of all life and energy (see

---

to be based upon two ideas, viz. 1. Nothing really exists but God; all besides is illusion. 2. Union with God is the highest object of human effort (see p. 113 of this volume). The Shī'as keep with great solemnity the anniversary of the murder of Husain, son of 'Alī, on a particular day in the Muharram (or first month of their lunar year). Hasan is supposed to have been poisoned by his wife, but Husain was killed at Karbalā by Yazīd, son of the first Umayyad Khalīf (commonly called Mu'āviya), who, instigated by Muhammad's favourite wife 'Ā-isha (daughter of Abūbakr), opposed the succession of 'Alī's descendants, assumed the government, and transferred the Khalīfate to Damascus. Hence the Shī'as perform pilgrimages to Karbalā, rather than to Mecca. The *Wahābīs* are a recent fanatical sect, founded by a man named Wahāb. They may be described as puritanical reformers, seeking to bring back Islām to its original purity.

pp. 144–148, and see also pp. 456, 457); but if identified with the One God he can only, according to the Hindū theory, be the source of life in the sense of giving out life to reabsorb it into himself. If, on the other hand, he is held to be only an incarnation or manifestation of the Supreme Being in human form, then by a cardinal dogma of Brāhmanism, so far from being a channel of life, his own life must be derived from a higher source into which it must finally be merged, while his claim to divinity can only be due to his possessing less of individuality as distinct from God than inferior creatures.

4. Finally, in Buddhism—as we have shown at p. 57—the extinction of personality and cessation of existence, which is the ultimate aim of this system, is effected by suppression of the passions, self-mortification, and abstinence from action. Buddha is no god, but only the ideal of what every man may become. He cannot, therefore, of course, be a source of even temporary life, when he is himself extinct. It is only in its high morality that Buddhism has common ground with Christianity. And can the only motive to the exercise of morality supplied by Buddhism—viz. on the one hand, the desire for non-existence; and, on the other, the hopes and fears connected with innumerable future existences—which existences are unconnected by conscious identity of being—be anything better than mere superstitious delusion?

It is refreshing to turn from such unsatisfying systems, however interspersed with wise and even sublime sentiments, to the living, energizing Christianity of European nations, however lamentably fallen from its true standard, or however disgraced by the inconsistencies and shortcomings of nominal adherents—possessors of its name and form without its power.

In conclusion, let me note one other point which of itself stamps our religion as the only system adapted to the requirements of the whole human race—the only message of salvation intended by God to be gradually pressed upon the acceptance of all His intelligent creatures, whether male or female, in all four quarters of the globe—I mean the position it assigns to women in relation to the stronger sex. It is not too much to affirm that the evils arising from the degradation of women, or at least the assumption of their supposed inferiority in the great religious systems of the East, constitute the principal bar to the progress and elevation of Asiatic nations. I refer the reader for evidence of this, as well as for fuller information on similar points, to pp. 257–259, 435–440 of the present volume.

It is, perhaps, almost impossible, as well as unreasonable, to expect the natives of India generally to look at such a question from a European stand-point. Nevertheless, those enlightened Hindūs and philanthropic Englishwomen who are now interesting themselves in the spread of female education throughout the East, may adduce good authority from India's own sacred books for striving to elevate the wives of India to a higher position than that they occupy in the present day. They have only to quote such passages as those referred to at p. 437, notes 1, 3, and p. 438 of this volume. To these may be added the remarkable definition of a wife given in Mahā-bhārata I. 3028 &c., of which I here offer a nearly literal version:

A wife is half the man, his truest friend—
A loving wife is a perpetual spring
Of virtue, pleasure, wealth; a faithful wife
Is his best aid in seeking heavenly bliss;
A sweetly-speaking wife is a companion
In solitude; a father in advice;
A mother in all seasons of distress;
A rest in passing through life's wilderness.

No wonder if, when sentiments like these are found in the sacred literature of India[1], a hope is dawning that inveterate prejudices may eventually give way, and that both Hindūs and Muslims may one day be brought to confess that one of the most valuable results of Christianity is the co-ordination of the sexes, and one of its most precious gifts the restoration of woman to man, not only as the help most meet for him—not only as his best counsellor and companion—but as his partner in religious privileges, and his equal, if not his superior, in religious capacities.

---

[1] Still more ancient and weighty authorities than the Mahā-bhārata are the Taittirīya-brāhmaṇa III. 3, 3, 1 (see p. 28 of this volume), and Manu IX. 45, 130 (pp. 288, 273 of this volume), which also assert that 'a wife is half of a man's self,' that 'a husband is one person with his wife,' and that 'a daughter is equal to a son.' The Ardha-nārī form of S'iva (see p. 325, note 1) seems to point to the same truth.

## *Modern Religious Sects of the Hindūs.*

Some account of these will be found in p. 127, note 1, and p. 327, note 2 of the present volume. They are fully described by Professor H. H. Wilson in vol. i. of his works edited by Dr. Rost. The three great sects are, *A*. The *Vaishṇavas*, who worship Vishṇu, as the chief god of the Tri-mūrti (p. 324). *B*. The *Śaivas*, who exalt S'iva. *C*. The *Śāktas*, adorers of the female deity Devī (generally regarded as S'iva's wife). Each sect is distinguished by different practices, and sectarian marks on the forehead (called *Tilaka*). All three are subdivided into numerous sub-sects, each of which again has two classes of persons under it—the clerical or monastic, and the lay.

*A*. The *Vaishṇavas* have six principal subdivisions, viz. 1. *Rāmānujas* or *Śrī-sampradāyins*, founded by the reformer *Rāmānuja*, who flourished in the South of India towards the latter part of the twelfth century; they have two perpendicular white lines drawn from the root of the hair to each eyebrow, and a connecting streak across the root of the nose. They draw their doctrines from Vedānta works, the Vishṇu and other Purāṇas, and are remarkable for the scrupulous preparation and privacy of their meals. A sect called *Rāmāvats* differ little from them. 2. *Rāmānandas*, founded by *Rāmānanda*, disciple of Rāmānuja, and numerous in Gangetic India; they worship Rāma-ćandra and Sītā. 3. Followers of *Kabīr*, the most celebrated of the twelve disciples of Rāmānanda, whose life is related in their favourite book the *Bhakta-mālā*. He lived about the end of the fourteenth century, and is said to have been a Muslim by birth. The *Kabīr-pathins* (or °*panthīs*) are found in Upper and Central India; they believe in one God, and do not observe all the Hindū ceremonies, yet pay respect to Vishṇu (Rāma) as a form of the Supreme Being. 4. *Vallabhāćāryas* or *Rudra-sampradāyins*, founded by *Vallabhāćārya*, who was born in 1479, and had great success in controversies with the S'aivas. He left behind 84 disciples. They draw their doctrines from the Bhāgavata-purāṇa and works of Vallabha. 5. *Mādhvas* or *Brahma-sampradāyins*, founded by *Madhvāćārya* (p. 127, note). They are found especially in the South of India, and although Vaishṇavas, exhibit a leaning towards S'iva. 6. *Vaishṇavas of Bengal*, founded by *Ćaitanya*, regarded as an incarnation of Kṛishṇa. They are distinguished by *bhakti* or devotion to Kṛishṇa, whose name they constantly repeat.

*B*. The *Śaivas* are generally distinguished by a horizontal Tilaka mark on the forehead, and by rosaries of Rudrāksha berries. The temples dedicated to S'iva in his symbol of the Liṅga (see p. 325, note 1) are numerous, but the doctrines of the great S'aiva teachers, such as S'aṅkara (p. 327, note 2), are too austere and philosophical for the mass of the people (p. 326). Earlier subdivisions of S'aivas are the *Raudras*, who have the Tri-śūla (p. 325, note 3) marked on their foreheads; the *Ugras*, who have the Ḍamaru on their arms; the *Bhāktas*, who have the Liṅga on their foreheads; the *Jaṅgamas*, who have that symbol on their heads; and the *Pāśupatas* (p. 127, note), who have it marked on other parts of their bodies. Some more modern subdivisions are, 1. *Daṇḍins* or mendicant staff-bearers; 2. *Daś-nāmī-daṇḍins*, divided into ten classes, each bearing a name of one of the ten pupils of the four disciples of S'aṅkara; 3. *Yogins* (or Jogīs), who cultivate absorption into S'iva by suppressions of breath, fixing the eyes, and eighty-four postures (see p. 103); 4. *Jaṅgamas*, called Liṅgavats (commonly Liṅgā-īts), as wearing the Liṅga on their person; 5. *Paramahansas*, who are solely occupied with meditating on Brahma; 6. *Aghorins* or *Aghora-pathins*, who propitiate S'iva by terrific and revolting austerities; 7. *Ūrdhva-bāhus*, who extend one or both arms over the head and hold them in that position for years; 8. *Ākāśa-mukhins*, who keep their necks bent back looking up at the sky. The S'aivas sometimes carry a staff with a skull at the top, called *Khaṭvāṅga*.

*C.* The *Śāktas* have two principal subdivisions, given pp. 502, 503. They aim at acquiring mystical powers by worshipping the S'akti.

Of the other sects named in p. 327, note 2, the *Gāṇapatyas* and *Sauryas* can scarcely now be regarded as important. The *Bhāgavatas* are said to be a division of the Vaishṇavas, and advocate faith in Bhagavat or the Supreme Being as the means of beatitude (according to S'āṇḍilya, p. 137, 2). They are sometimes called *Pañća-rātras*, as their doctrines are taught in the *Nārada-pañćarātra*.

A form of Vishṇu (Kṛishṇa), called *Viṭhṭhal* or *Viṭhobā*, is the popular god at Pandharpur in Mahā-rāshṭra, and the favourite of the celebrated Marāṭhī poet Tukārāma. The followers of Dādū (*Dādū-pathins*), a famous ascetic who lived at Jaipur about A. D. 1600, are also devoted to Vishṇu.

With regard to the *Sikhs* (Sanskṛit *Śishyāḥ*), disciples of *Nānak Shāh*, born near Lahore, A. D. 1469 (p. 327, note 2), this great reformer seems to have owed much to Kabīr, who preceded him. Their *grantha* or sacred books are written in old Pañjābī, and employ a modification of the Nāgarī character, called *Gurumukhī*. Their holy city is Umritsur.

Mendicant devotees who voluntarily undergo penances and austerities, and are variously called *Sannyāsīs* (often of the S'aiva sect), *Vairāgīs* (often of the Vaishṇava sect), *Yogīs* (or Jogīs, see p. 104), *Nāgas* (for *Nagnas*, naked devotees), and *Fakīrs* (which last name ought properly to be restricted to Muhammadans), form a large class in India.

There is an interesting sect of Syrian Christians in Travancore and Cochin, who have a bishop under the patriarch of Antioch, and trace back their foundation to St. Thomas, about A. D. 50, and to a colony which, 300 years afterwards, immigrated from Syria.

# INDIAN WISDOM.

## LECTURE I.

### *The Hymns of the Veda.*

IN the following Lectures I propose to offer examples of the most remarkable religious, philosophical, and ethical teachings of ancient Hindū authors, arranging the instances given in regular sequence according to the successive epochs of Sanskṛit literature. In attempting this task I am conscious of my inability to do justice in a short compass to the richness of the materials at my command. An adequate idea of the luxuriance of Sanskṛit literature can with difficulty be conveyed to occidental scholars. Perhaps, too, the severe European critic will be slow to acquiesce in any tribute of praise bestowed on compositions too often marked by tedious repetitions, redundant epithets, and far-fetched conceits; just as the genuine Oriental, nurtured under glowing tropical skies, cannot easily be brought to appreciate the coldness and severe simplicity of an educated Englishman's style of writing. We might almost say that with Hindū authors excellence is apt to be measured by magnitude, quality by quantity, were it not for the striking thoughts and noble sentiments which often reward the student who will take the trouble to release them from their surplusage of words; were it not also, that with all this tendency to diffuseness, it is certainly a fact that nowhere do we find the art of condensation so successfully cultivated as in some departments of Sanskṛit literature. Probably the very prolixity natural to Indian writers led to the opposite extreme of brevity, not merely by a law of reaction, but by the necessity for providing the memory with aids and restoratives when oppressed and debilitated by too great a burden. However that may be, every student of Sanskṛit will certainly note in its literary productions a singular inequality both as to quantity and quality; so that in studying Hindū literature continuously we are liable to be called upon to pass from the most exuberant verbosity to the most obscure brevity; from sound wisdom to little better than puerile unwisdom; from subtle reasoning to transparent sophistry; from high morality—often expressed in impressive language worthy of Christianity itself—to precepts implying a social condition scarcely compatible with the lowest grade of culture and civilization.

Such being the case, it will be easily understood that, although my intention in these Lectures is to restrict myself to selections from the best writings only, it does not therefore follow that every example given will be put forth as a model of style or wisdom. My simple object is to illustrate continuously the development of Hindū thought; and it will conduce to a better appreciation of the specimens I offer if I introduce them by brief descriptions of the portions of literature to which they belong.

To give order and continuity to the subject it will be necessary to begin with that foundation of the whole fabric of Hindū religion and literature—the Veda.

Happily this word 'Veda' has now a familiar sound among Englishmen who take an interest in the history and literature of their Indian fellow-subjects, so that I need say but little on a subject which is really almost trite, or at least has been already elucidated by many clear and able writers. Indeed, most educated persons are beginning to be conscious of the duty of studying fairly and without prejudice the other religions of the world. For may it not be maintained that the traces of the original truth imparted to mankind should be diligently sought for in every religious system, however corrupt, so that when any fragment of the living rock is discovered[1], it may (so to speak) at once be converted

---

[1] Surely we should study to be absolutely fair in our examination of other religions, and avoid all appearance of a shadow of misrepresentation in our description of them, endeavouring to take a just and comprehensive view, which shall embrace the purest form of each false system, and not be confined to those corruptions, incrustations, and accretions which in all religions tend to obscure, and even to conceal altogether, what there is of good and true in them. Missionaries would do well to read 'An Essay on Conciliation in Matters of Religion, by a Bengal Civilian,' published in Calcutta in 1849. Let them also ponder the words of Sir William Jones, in his 'Discourse on the Philosophy of the Asiatics' (vol. iii. p. 242, &c., of his Works). This great Orientalist there maintains that our divine religion, the truth of which is abundantly proved by historical evidence, has no need of such aids as many think to give it by asserting that wise men of the heathen world were ignorant of the two Christian maxims which teach us to do to others as we would they should do unto us, and to return good for evil. The first exists in the sayings of Confucius, and the spirit of both may be traced in several Hindū precepts. One or two examples will be found in the Hitopadeśa, and Sir W. Jones' is the following: *Su-jano na yāti vairam para-hita-buddhir vināśa-kāle 'pi Ćhede 'pi ćandana-taruḥ surabhayati mukhaṃ kuṭhārasya,* 'A good man who thinks only of benefiting his enemy has no feelings of hostility towards him even at the moment of being destroyed by him; (just as) the sandal-tree at the moment of being cut down sheds perfume on the edge of the axe.' Sir W. Jones affirms that this couplet was written three centuries B. C. It is given by Boehtlingk in his 'Indische Sprüche.' Professor Aufrecht, in his late article on the S'ārn̄gadhara-paddhati, mentions a similar verse in that Anthology attributed to an author Ravi-gupta. The Persian poet Sādī of Shīrāz has a maxim taken from the Arabs, 'Confer benefits on him who has injured thee.' Again, 'The men of God's true faith grieve not the hearts e'en of their foes' (chap. ii. story 4). Hāfiz is also quoted by Sir W. Jones thus:

'Learn from yon Orient shell to love thy foe,
And store with pearls the hand that brings thee woe.
Free, like yon rock, from base vindictive pride,
Imblaze with gems the wrist that rends thy side.

into a fulcrum for the upheaving of the whole mass of surrounding error? At all events, it may reasonably be conceded that if nothing true or sound can be shown to underlie the rotten tissue of decaying religious systems, the truth of Christianity may at least in this manner be more clearly exhibited and its value by contrast made more conspicuous.

If, then, a comparison of the chief religions[1] of the world, and an attempt to sweep away the incrustations which everywhere obscure the points of contact between them, is becoming every day more incumbent upon us, surely Brāhmanism, next to Judaism and Christianity, has the first claim on our attention, both from its connection with the religion of ancient Persia (said to have acted on Judaism during the captivity), and from its close relationship to Buddhism, the faith of about thirty-one per

---

Mark where yon tree rewards the stony shower
With fruit nectareous or the balmy flower.
All nature calls aloud, "Shall man do less
Than heal the smiter and the railer bless?"'

In S'ārṅgadhara's Anthology a sentiment is given from the Mahābhārata, which is almost identical with St. Matt. vii. 3—*Τί δὲ βλέπεις τὸ κάρφος τὸ ἐν τῷ ὀφθαλμῷ τοῦ ἀδελφοῦ σου, τὴν δὲ ἐν τῷ σῷ ὀφθαλμῷ δοκὸν οὐ κατανοεῖς.*

[1] These are eight in number, as shown by Professor Max Müller in his 'Science of Religion,' viz. 1. Judaism, 2. Christianity, 3. Brāhmanism, 4. Buddhism, 5. Zoroastrianism, 6. Islām; and the systems of the Chinese philosophers, viz. 7. Confucius (a Latinized form of Kūng-fū-tsze, 'the sage of the family of Kūng'), 8. Lau-tsze ('aged master or sage'); and these eight rest on eight sets of books, viz. 1. the Old Testament, 2. the New Testament, 3. the Veda, 4. the Tri-piṭaka, 5. the Zand-Avastā, 6. the Kurān, 7. the five volumes or Kīng (viz. Yi, Shū, Shī, Li-ki, Chūn-tsiu) and the four Shū or books, some of which were written by the philosopher Mencius (Mang-tsze), 8. the Tau-te-Kīng ('book of reason and virtue'); and are in seven languages, viz. 1. Hebrew, 2. Greek, 3. Sanskṛit, 4. Pāli, 5. Zand, 6. Arabic, and 7, 8. Chinese. Of these eight religions only four (the second, third, fourth, and sixth) are *numerically* important at the present day.

cent of the human race[1]. Now it is noteworthy that the idea of a direct revelation, though apparently never entertained in a definite manner by the Greeks and Romans[2], is perfectly familiar, first, to the Hindūs; secondly, to the Pārsīs, as representing the ancient Zoroastrian Persians; thirdly, to all the numerous races who have adopted the religion founded by Muhammad[3], and by

---

[1] Rather more than two-thirds of the human race are still unchristianized (see note, p. xxxv). Christianity and Buddhism, the two most prevalent religions of the world, and in their very essence the two most opposed to each other, though, at the same time, the two which have most common ground in their moral teaching, have both been rejected by the races which gave them birth; yet both, when adopted by other races, have acquired the greatest number of adherents. Christianity, originating with a Semitic race, has spread among Āryans; Buddhism, originating among Hindū Āryans, has spread chiefly among Turanian races. Buddhism was driven out of India into Ceylon and still continues there. Thence it passed into Burmah, Siam, Tibet, China, and Japan. It does not seem to have become established in China till the first century of our era, and did not reach Japan till much later. The form it has assumed in these countries deviates widely from the system founded by the great Indian Buddha, and its adoption by the masses of the people is after all more nominal than real. The ancient superstitious belief in good and evil spirits of all kinds (of the sun, wind, and rain; of the earth, mountains, rivers, trees, fields, &c., and of the dead) appears to prevail everywhere among the Chinese people, while the more educated are chiefly adherents of the old moral and philosophical systems taught by Kūng-fū-tsze (Confucius) and Lau-tsze. The latter taught belief in one universal spirit called *Tau*, 'the way,' and his disciples are therefore styled Tau-ists.

[2] Numa Pompilius is, however, supposed to have derived his inspirations from the prophetic nymph Aegeria; as the Greek poets are imagined to have owed theirs to the Muses.

[3] The name of the great Arabian Pseudo-prophet popularly spelt Mohammed, means 'the highly praised' or 'praiseworthy.' We very naturally call the religion he founded Mohammedanism, but he laid no claim to be a founder. Islām is a word denoting 'submission to the will and ordinances of God,' whose absolute unity Mohammed claimed as a prophet to have been commissioned to proclaim.

him called Islām. Let us beware, however, of supposing that the Veda occupies exactly the position of a Bible to the Hindūs, or that it is to them precisely what the Avastā is to the Pārsīs or the Kurān to Muslims. Such a notion must lead to some confusion of thought in studying these very different religious systems. For the word Avastā probably signifies 'the settled text' delivered by Zoroaster (properly Zarathustra, and in Persian Zardusht), which was written down and accompanied with its commentary and paraphrases in Pahlavī[1]; as in the Hebrew sacred writings, the Old Testament was furnished with its accompaniments of Chaldee translations and paraphrases called Targums.

Again, the word Kurān means emphatically 'the reading' or 'that which ought to be read by every one[2],' and is applied to a single volume, manifestly the work of one author, which, according to Muhammad, descended entire from heaven in the night called Al Kadr[3], in the month called Ramazān, though alleged to have been revealed to him by the angel Gabriel at different times, and chapter by chapter. In fact, Muhammad affirmed that, being himself illiterate, he was specially directed and miraculously empowered by God to commit the revelation to writing for the spread of the true faith. (See Introd. xli–xliii.)

---

[1] Pahlavī is a later Iranian dialect which followed on Zand and the old Persian of the inscriptions, and led to Parsī or Pāzand and the Persian of Firdausī. The word Zand at first denoted commentary, and was afterwards applied to the language.

[2] قرآن *qur'ān*, 'reading,' is the verbal noun of the Arabic root *qara'a*, 'to read.' In the 96th chapter of the Kurān the command is twice repeated, 'Read, in the name of thy Lord,' 'Read, by thy most beneficent Lord, who taught the use of the pen.'

[3] That is, 'the night of *qadr* or power.' The 97th chapter of the Kurān begins thus, 'Verily we sent down the Kurān in the night of Al Kadr.' See Sale's translation.

The word Veda, on the other hand, means 'knowledge,' and is a term applied to divine *unwritten* knowledge, imagined to have issued like breath from the Self-existent[1], and communicated to no single person, but to a whole class of men called Ṛishis or inspired sages. By them the divine knowledge thus apprehended was transmitted, not in writing, but through the ear, by constant oral repetition through a succession of teachers, who claimed as Brāhmans to be its rightful recipients. Here, then, we have a theory of inspiration higher even than that advanced by the Pseudo-prophet Muhammad and his followers, or by the most enthusiastic adherents of any other religion in the world. It is very true that this inspired knowledge, though its very essence was held to be mystically bound up with Śabda or 'articulate sound' (thought to be eternal), was ultimately written down, but the writing and reading of it were not encouraged. It was even prohibited by the Brāhmans, to whom alone all property in it belonged. Moreover, when at last, by its continued

[1] In Manu I. 3 the Veda is itself called 'self-existent.' There are, however, numerous inconsistencies in the accounts of the production of the Veda, which seem not to have troubled the Brāhmans or interfered with their faith in its divine origin. One account makes it issue from the Self-existent, like breath, by the power of A-dṛishṭa, without any deliberation or thought on his part; another makes the four Vedas issue from Brahman, like smoke from burning fuel; another educes them from the elements; another from the Gāyatrī. A hymn in the Atharva-veda (XIX. 54) educes them from Kāla or 'Time.' The Śatapatha-brāhmaṇa asserts that the Creator brooded over the three worlds, and thence produced three lights, fire, the air, and the sun, from which respectively were extracted the Ṛig, Yajur, and Sāma-veda. Manu (I. 23) affirms the same. In the Purusha-sūkta the three Vedas are derived from the mystical victim Purusha. Lastly, by the Mīmāṉsakas the Veda is declared to be itself an eternal sound, and to have existed absolutely from all eternity, quite independently of any utterer or revealer of its texts. Hence it is often called *śruta*, 'what is heard.' In opposition to all this we have the Ṛishis themselves frequently intimating that the Mantras were composed by themselves.

growth, it became too complex for mere oral transmission, then this Veda resolved itself, not into one single volume, like the Kurān, but into a whole series of compositions, which had in reality been composed by a number of different poets and writers at different times during several centuries.

There is this great difference, therefore, between the Kurān and the Veda, that whereas the reading of the former is regarded as a sacred duty, and constantly practised by all good Muslims, the Veda, even after it had been committed to writing, became absolutely a sealed book to the masses of Hindūs, and with the exception of some of the later Vedic works, called Upanishads, is to this day almost entirely unread even by the learned, however much it may be venerated and its divine authority as an infallible guide nominally upheld[1].

Of what, then, does this Veda consist? To conduce to clearness in arranging our examples we may regard it as separating itself into three quite distinct divisions, viz.

1. *Mantra* or prayer and praise embodied in texts and metrical hymns.

2. *Brāhmaṇa* or ritualistic precept and illustration written in prose.

3. *Upanishad*, 'mystical or secret doctrine' appended to the aforesaid Brāhmaṇa, in prose and occasional verse.

---

[1] The absolute and infallible authority of the Veda is held to be so manifest as to require no proof, and to be entirely beyond the province of reason or argument. Manu even extends this to Smṛiti (II. 10), where he says, 'By *śruti* is meant the Veda, and by *smṛiti* the books of law; the contents of these must never be questioned by reason.' Nevertheless, the want of familiarity with the Mantras of the Ṛig-veda is illustrated by the native editions of Manu. That published in Calcutta with the commentary of Kullūka is a scholarlike production, but almost in every place where the Mantras of the Ṛig-veda are alluded to by Manu (as in VIII. 91, XI. 250, 252, 253, 254) errors disfigure the text and commentary.

To begin, then, with the Mantra portion. By this is meant those prayers, invocations, and hymns which have been collected and handed down to us from a period after the Indian branch of the great Indo-European race had finally settled down in Northern India, but which were doubtless composed by a succession of poets at different times (perhaps between 1500 and 1000 years B.C.). These compositions, though very unequal in poetical merit, and containing many tedious repetitions and puerilities, are highly interesting and important, as embodying some of the earliest religious conceptions, as well as some of the earliest known forms, of the primitive language of that primeval Āryan race-stock from which Greeks, Romans, Kelts, Teutons, Russians, and Poles are all offshoots.

They are comprised in five principal Saṃhitās or collections of Mantras, called respectively Ṛik, Atharvan, Sāman, Taittirīya, and Vājasaneyin. Of these the Ṛig-veda-saṃhitā — containing one thousand and seventeen hymns — is the oldest and most important, while the Atharva-veda-saṃhitā is generally held to be the most recent, and is perhaps the most interesting. Moreover, these are the only two Vedic hymn-books worthy of being called separate original collections[1]; and to these, therefore, we shall confine our examples.

[1] The Atharva-veda (admirably edited by Professors Roth and Whitney) does not appear to have been recognized as a fourth Veda in the time of Manu, though he mentions the revelation made to Atharvan and Aṅgiras (XI. 33). In book XI, verse 264, he says, *Ṛićo yajūṉshi ćānyāni sāmāni vividhāni ća, esha jñeyas tri-vṛid vedo yo vedainaṃ sa veda-vit.* The Sāma-veda and the two so-called Saṃhitās or collections of the Yajur-veda (Taittirīya and Vājasaneyin or Black and White) all borrow largely from the Ṛik, and are merely Brahmanical manuals, the necessity for which grew out of the complicated ritual gradually elaborated by the Hindū Āryans. A curious allusion to the Sāma-veda occurs in Manu IV. 123 &c., 'The Ṛig-veda has the gods for its deities, the Yajur-veda has men for its objects, the Sāma-veda has

To what deities, it will be asked, were the prayers and hymns of these collections addressed? This is an interesting inquiry, for these were probably the very deities worshipped under similar names by our Āryan progenitors in their primeval home somewhere on the table-land of Central Asia, perhaps in the region of Bokhara, not far from the sources of the Oxus[1]. The answer is: They worshipped those physical forces before which all nations, if guided solely by the light of nature, have in the early period of their life instinctively bowed down, and before which even the more civilized and enlightened have always been compelled to bend in awe and reverence, if not in adoration.

To our Āryan forefathers in their Asiatic home God's power was exhibited in the forces of nature even more evidently than to ourselves. Lands, houses, flocks, herds, men, and animals were more frequently than in Western climates at the mercy of winds, fire, and water, and the sun's rays appeared to be endowed with a potency quite beyond the experience of any European country. We cannot be surprised, then, that these forces were regarded by our Eastern progenitors as actual manifestations, either of one deity in different moods or of separate rival deities contending for supremacy. Nor is

---

the Pitṛis, therefore its sound is impure.' Kullūka, however, in his commentary is careful to state that the Sāma-veda is not really impure, but only apparently so. This semblance of impurity may perhaps result from its association with deceased persons and its repetition at a time of A-śauća. The Sāma-veda is really a mere reproduction of parts of the Ṛik, transposed and scattered about piece-meal, only seventy-eight verses in the whole Sāma-veda being, it is said, untraceable to the present recension of the Ṛik. The greatest number of its verses are taken from the ninth Maṇḍala of the Ṛik, which is in praise of the Soma plant, the Sāma-veda being a collection of liturgical forms for the Soma ceremonies of the Udgātṛi priests, as the Yajus is for the sacrifices performed by the Adhvaryu priests.

[1] Professor Whitney doubts this usual assumption (Lectures, p. 200).

it wonderful that these mighty agencies should have been at first poetically personified, and afterwards, when invested with forms, attributes, and individuality, worshipped as distinct gods. It was only natural, too, that a varying supremacy and varying honours should have been accorded to each deified force—to the air, the rain, the storm, the sun, or fire—according to the special atmospheric influences to which particular localities were exposed, or according to the seasons of the year when the dominance of each was to be prayed for or deprecated.

This was the religion represented in the Vedas and the primitive creed of the Indo-Āryans about twelve or thirteen centuries before Christ. The first forces deified seem to have been those manifested in the sky and air. These were at first generalized under one rather vague personification, as was natural in the earliest attempts at giving shape to religious ideas. For it may be observed that all religious systems, even the most polytheistic, have generally grown out of some undefined original belief in a divine power or powers controlling and regulating the universe. And although innumerable gods and goddesses, gifted with a thousand shapes, now crowd the Hindū Pantheon, appealing to the instincts of the unthinking millions whose capacity for religious ideas is supposed to require the aid of external symbols, it is probable that there existed for the first Āryan worshippers a simpler theistic creed: even as the thoughtful Hindū of the present day looks through the maze of his mythology to the conception of one divine self-existing being, one all-pervading spirit, into whose unity all visible symbols are gathered, and in whose essence all entities are comprehended.

In the Veda this unity soon diverged into various ramifications. Only a few of the hymns appear to contain the simple conception of one divine self-existent omnipresent Being, and even in these the idea of one God present in all nature is somewhat nebulous and undefined[1]. Perhaps the most ancient and beautiful deification was that of Dyaus[2], 'the sky,' as Dyaush-pitar, 'Heavenly Father' (the Zeus or Ju-piter of the Greeks and Romans). Then, closely connected with Dyaus, was a goddess A-diti, 'the Infinite Expanse,' conceived of subsequently as the mother of all the gods. Next came a development of the same conception called Varuṇa, 'the Investing Sky,' said to answer to Ahura Mazda, the Ormazd of the ancient Persian (Zand) mythology, and to the Greek Οὐρανός—but a more spiritual conception, leading to a worship which rose to the nature of a belief in the great Πατὴρ ἡμῶν ὁ ἐν

---

[1] Though vaguely stated in the Veda, it was clearly defined in the time of Manu; see the last verses of the twelfth book (123–125): 'Him some adore as transcendently present in fire; others in Manu, lord of creatures; some as more distinctly present in Indra, others in pure air, others as the most high eternal Spirit. Thus the man who perceives in his own soul, the supreme soul present in all creatures, acquires equanimity towards them all, and shall be absorbed at last in the highest essence.' In the Purusha-sūkta of the Ṛig-veda (X. 90), which is one of the later hymns, probably not much earlier than the earliest Brāhmaṇa, the one Spirit is called Purusha. The more common name in the later system is *Brahman*, neut. (nom. *Brahmă*), derived from root *bṛih*, 'to expand,' and denoting the universally expanding essence or universally diffused substance of the universe. For it is evident that this later creed was not so much monotheistic (by which I mean the belief in one god regarded as a personal Being external to the universe, though creating and governing it) as pantheistic; Brahman in the neuter being 'simple infinite being'—the only real eternal essence—which, when it passes into actual manifested existence, is called Brahmā, when it develops itself in the world, is called Vishṇu, and when it again dissolves itself into simple being, is called S'iva; all the other innumerable gods and demigods being also mere manifestations of the neuter Brahman, who alone is eternal. This appears to be the genuine pantheistic creed of India to this very day.

[2] From *dyu* or *dyo*, the same as the Old German Tiu or Ziu, who, according to Professor Max Müller, afterwards became a kind of Mars (whence Tues-day). For Dyaush-pitar see Ṛig-veda VI. 51. 5.

τοῖς οὐρανοῖς. This Varuṇa, again, was soon thought of in connection with another vague personification called Mitra (= the Persian *Mithra*), 'god of day.' After a time these impersonations of the celestial sphere were felt to be too vague to suit the growth of religious ideas in ordinary minds. Soon, therefore, the great investing firmament resolved itself into separate cosmical entities with separate powers and attributes. First, the watery atmosphere—personified under the name of Indra, ever seeking to dispense his dewy treasures (*indu*), though ever restrained by an opposing force or spirit of evil called Vṛitra; and, secondly, the wind—thought of either as a single personality named Vāyu, or as a whole assemblage of moving powers coming from every quarter of the compass, and impersonated as Maruts or 'Storm-gods.' At the same time in this process of decentralization—if I may use the term—the once purely celestial Varuṇa became relegated to a position among seven secondary deities of the heavenly sphere called Ādityas (afterwards increased to twelve, and regarded as diversified forms of the sun in the several months of the year), and subsequently to a dominion over the waters when they had left the air and rested on the earth.

Of these separately deified physical forces by far the most favourite object of adoration was the deity supposed to yield the dew and rain, longed for by Eastern cultivators of the soil with even greater cravings than by Northern agriculturists. Indra, therefore—the Jupiter Pluvius of early Indian mythology—is undoubtedly the principal divinity of Vedic worshippers, in so far at least as the greater number of their prayers and hymns are addressed to him.

What, however, could rain effect without the aid of heat? A force the intensity of which must have impressed an Indian mind with awe, and led him to invest the possessor of it with divine attributes. Hence the other great god of Vedic worshippers, and in some respects the most important in his connection with sacrificial rites, is Agni (Latin *Ignis*), 'the god of fire.' Even Sūrya, 'the sun' (Greek ἥλιος), who was probably at first adored as the original source of heat, came to be regarded as only another form of fire. He was merely a manifestation of the same divine energy removed to the heavens, and consequently less accessible. Another deity, Ushas, 'goddess of the dawn,'—the ἠώς of the Greeks,—was naturally connected with the sun, and regarded as daughter of the sky. Two other deities, the Aśvins, were fabled as connected with Ushas, as ever young and handsome, travelling in a golden car and precursors of the dawn. They are sometimes called Dasras, as divine physicians, 'destroyers of diseases;' sometimes Nāsatyas, as 'never untrue.' They appear to have been personifications of two luminous points or rays imagined to precede the break of day. These, with Yama, 'the god of departed spirits,' are the principal deities of the Mantra portion of the Veda[1].

But here it may be asked, if sky, air, water, fire, and the sun were thus worshipped as manifestations of the supreme universal God of the universe, was not the earth also an object of adoration with the early Hindūs? And it should be stated that in the earlier system the earth under the name of Pṛithivī, 'the broad one,' *does* receive divine honours, being thought of as the mother of all beings. Moreover, various deities were regarded as the progeny resulting from the fancied union of earth with

[1] It should be observed that there is no trace in the Mantras of the Tri-mūrti or Triad of deities (Brahmā, Vishṇu, and Śiva) afterwards so popular. Nor does the doctrine of transmigration, afterwards an essential element of the Hindū religion, appear in the Mantra portion of the Veda. Caste is only clearly alluded to in one hymn (the Purusha-sūkta), generally allowed to be a comparatively modern composition.

Dyaus, 'heaven.' This imaginary marriage of heaven and earth was indeed a most natural idea, and much of the later mythology may be explained by it. But it is remarkable that as religious worship became of a more selfish character, the earth, being more evidently under man's control, and not seeming to need propitiation so urgently as the more uncertain air, fire, and water, lost importance among the gods, and was rarely addressed in prayer or hymn.

It may conduce to a better appreciation of the succeeding hymns if it be borne in mind that the deified forces addressed in them were probably not represented by images or idols in the Vedic period, though, doubtless, the early worshippers clothed their gods with human form in their own imaginations[1].

I now commence my examples with a nearly literal translation of the well-known sixteenth hymn of the fourth book of the Atharva-veda, in praise of Varuṇa or 'the Investing Sky[2]:'

---

[1] See Dr. Muir's Sanskṛit Texts, vol. v. p. 453.

[2] Ably translated by Dr. Muir (Sanskṛit Texts, vol. v. p. 63) and by Professor Max Müller. It may be thought that in giving additional translations of this and other hymns I am going over ground already well trodden; but it should be borne in mind that as the design of these Lectures is to illustrate *continuously* the development of Hindū knowledge and literature by a selection of good examples rendered into idiomatic English, I could not, in common justice to such a subject, exclude the best passages in each department of the literature merely because they have been translated by others. I here, however, once for all acknowledge with gratitude that, while making versions of my own, I have derived the greatest assistance from Dr. Muir's scholarlike translations and poetical paraphrases (given in his Texts), as well as from Professor Max Müller's works and those of Professor A. Weber of Berlin. It must be understood that my examples are not put forth as offering rival translations. They are generally intended to be as literal as possible consistently with the observance of English idiom, and on that account I have preferred blank verse; but occasionally they are paraphrases rather than

The mighty Varuṇa, who rules above, looks down
Upon these worlds, his kingdom, as if close at hand.
When men imagine they do ought by stealth, he knows it.
No one can stand or walk or softly glide along
Or hide in dark recess, or lurk in secret cell,
But Varuṇa detects him and his movements spies.
Two persons may devise some plot, together sitting
In private and alone; but he, the king, is there—
A third—and sees it all. This boundless earth is his,
His the vast sky, whose depth no mortal e'er can fathom.
Both oceans[1] find a place within his body, yet
In that small pool he lies contained. Whoe'er should flee
Far, far beyond the sky, would not escape the grasp
Of Varuṇa, the king. His messengers descend
Countless from his abode—for ever traversing
This world and scanning with a thousand eyes its inmates.
Whate'er exists within this earth, and all within the sky,
Yea all that is beyond, king Varuṇa perceives.
The winkings[2] of men's eyes, are numbered all by him.
He wields the universe, as gamesters handle dice.
May thy destroying snares cast sevenfold round the wicked,
Entangle liars, but the truthful spare, O king![3]

I pass from the ancient Āryan deity Varuṇa to the more thoroughly Indian god Indra (see p. 13).

The following metrical lines bring together various scattered texts relating to this Hindū Jupiter Pluvius[4]:

---

translations, sentences and words being here and there omitted or transposed, or fragments joined together, so as to read like one continuous passage. In fact, it will be seen that my main design has been to offer English versions of the text for general readers and for those students and educated men who, not being necessarily Sanskṛitists, are desirous of some insight into Hindū literature.

[1] That is, air and sea.

[2] The winking of the eye is an especial characteristic of humanity, distinguishing men from gods; cf. Nala V. 25, Māgha III. 42.

[3] Compare Manu VIII. 82: 'A witness who speaks falsely is fast bound by the snares of Varuṇa.' These snares are explained by Kullūka to be 'cords consisting of serpents' (*pāśaiḥ sarpa-rajjubhiḥ*).

[4] The texts which furnish the basis of these and the succeeding verses

Indra, twin brother of the god of fire,
When thou wast born, thy mother Aditi
Gave thee, her lusty child, the thrilling draught
Of mountain-growing Soma—source of life
And never-dying vigour to thy frame.
Then at the Thunderer's birth, appalled with fear,
Dreading the hundred-jointed thunderbolt—
Forged by the cunning Tvashṭṛi—mountains rocked,
Earth shook and heaven trembled. Thou wast born
Without a rival, king of gods and men—
The eye of living and terrestrial things.
Immortal Indra, unrelenting foe
Of drought and darkness, infinitely wise,
Terrific crusher of thy enemies,
Heroic, irresistible in might,
Wall of defence to us thy worshippers,
We sing thy praises, and our ardent hymns
Embrace thee, as a loving wife her lord.
Thou art our guardian, advocate, and friend,
A brother, father, mother, all combined.
Most fatherly of fathers, we are thine
And thou art ours; oh! let thy pitying soul
Turn to us in compassion, when we praise thee,
And slay us not for one sin or for many.
Deliver us to-day, to-morrow, every day.
Armed for the conflict, see! the demons come—
Ahi and Vṛitra, and a long array
Of darksome spirits. Quick, then, quaff the draught
That stimulates thy martial energy,
And dashing onward in thy golden car,
Drawn by thy ruddy, Ṛibhu-fashioned[1] steeds,
Speed to the charge, escorted by the Maruts.
Vainly the demons dare thy might; in vain
Strive to deprive us of thy watery treasures.
Earth quakes beneath the crashing of thy bolts.
Pierced, shattered, lies the foe—his cities crushed,
His armies overthrown, his fortresses
Shivered to fragments; then the pent-up waters,

will be found in the 5th volume of Dr. Muir's work, and there will also be found a complete poetical sketch of Indra (pp. 126–139).

[1] The Ṛibhus (Greek Ὀρφεύς) were the celestial artists of the Veda.

Released from long imprisonment, descend
In torrents to the earth, and swollen rivers,
Foaming and rolling to their ocean home,
Proclaim the triumph of the Thunderer.

Let us proceed next to the all-important Vedic deity Agni, 'god of fire,' especially of sacrificial fire. I propose now to paraphrase a few of the texts which relate to him:

Agni, thou art a sage, a priest, a king,
Protector, father of the sacrifice.
Commissioned by us men thou dost ascend
A messenger, conveying to the sky
Our hymns and offerings. Though thy origin
Be threefold, now from air and now from water,
Now from the mystic double Araṇi[1],
Thou art thyself a mighty god, a lord,
Giver of life and immortality,
One in thy essence, but to mortals three;
Displaying thine eternal triple form,
As fire on earth; as lightning in the air,
As sun in heaven. Thou art a cherished guest
In every household—father, brother, son,
Friend, benefactor, guardian, all in one.
Bright, seven-rayed god! how manifold thy shapes
Revealed to us thy votaries! now we see thee,
With body all of gold, and radiant hair
Flaming from three terrific heads, and mouths
Whose burning jaws and teeth devour all things.
Now with a thousand glowing horns, and now
Flashing thy lustre from a thousand eyes,
Thou'rt borne towards us in a golden chariot,
Impelled by winds, and drawn by ruddy steeds,
Marking thy car's destructive course, with blackness.
Deliver, mighty lord, thy worshippers.
Purge us from taint of sin, and when we die,
Deal mercifully with us on the pyre.
Burning our bodies with their load of guilt,
But bearing our eternal part on high
To luminous abodes and realms of bliss,
For ever there to dwell with righteous men.

---

[1] Two pieces of the wood of the Ficus religiosa used for kindling fire.

The next deity is Sūrya, 'the Sun[1],' who, with reference to the variety of his functions, has various names—such as Savitṛi, Aryaman, Mitra, Varuṇa, Pūshan, sometimes ranking as distinct deities of the celestial sphere. As already explained, he is associated in the minds of Vedic worshippers with Fire, and is frequently described as sitting in a chariot drawn by seven ruddy horses (representing the seven days of the week), preceded by the Dawn. Here is an example of a hymn (Ṛig-veda I. 50) addressed to this deity, translated almost literally:

Behold the rays of Dawn, like heralds, lead on high
The Sun, that men may see the great all-knowing god.
The stars slink off like thieves, in company with Night,
Before the all-seeing eye, whose beams reveal his presence,
Gleaming like brilliant flames, to nation after nation.
With speed, beyond the ken of mortals, thou, O Sun,
Dost ever travel on, conspicuous to all.
Thou dost create the light, and with it dost illume
The universe entire; thou risest in the sight
Of all the race of men, and all the host of heaven.
Light-giving Varuṇa! thy piercing glance doth scan
In quick succession all this stirring, active world,
And penetrateth too the broad ethereal space,
Measuring our days and nights and spying out all creatures.
Sūrya with flaming locks, clear-sighted god of day,
Thy seven ruddy mares bear on thy rushing car.
With these thy self-yoked steeds, seven daughters of thy chariot,
Onward thou dost advance. To thy refulgent orb
Beyond this lower gloom and upward to the light
Would we ascend, O Sun, thou god among the gods.

As an accompaniment to this hymn may here be mentioned the celebrated Gāyatrī. It is a short prayer to the Sun in his character of Savitṛi or 'the Vivifier,' and is the most sacred of all Vedic texts. Though not always understood, it is to this very day used by every Brāhman throughout India in his daily devotions. It occurs in

[1] Yāska makes Indra, Agni, and Sūrya the Vedic Triad of gods.

Ṛig-veda III. 62. 10[1], and can be literally translated as follows:'

Let us meditate (or, we meditate) on that excellent glory of the divine Vivifier. May he enlighten (or stimulate) our understandings. [*Tat Savitur vareṇyam bhargo devasya dhīmahi, Dhiyo yo naḥ praćodayāt.*]

May we not conjecture, with Sir William Jones, that the great veneration in which this text has ever been held by the Hindūs from time immemorial, indicates that the more enlightened worshippers adored, under the type of the visible sun, that divine light which alone could illumine their intellects?

I may here also fitly offer a short paraphrase descriptive of the Vedic Ushas, the Greek 'Ηώς, or 'Dawn:'

Hail ruddy Ushas, golden goddess, borne
Upon thy shining car, thou comest like
A lovely maiden by her mother decked,
Disclosing coyly all thy hidden graces
To our admiring eyes; or like a wife
Unveiling to her lord, with conscious pride,
Beauties which, as he gazes lovingly,
Seem fresher, fairer each succeeding morn.
Through years on years thou hast lived on, and yet
Thou'rt ever young. Thou art the breath and life
Of all that breathes and lives, awaking day by day
Myriads of prostrate sleepers, as from death,
Causing the birds to flutter from their nests,
And rousing men to ply with busy feet
Their daily duties and appointed tasks,
Toiling for wealth or pleasure or renown.

Before leaving the subject of the Vedic deities I add a few words about Yama, 'the god of departed spirits.' It appears tolerably certain that the doctrine of metempsychosis has no place in the Mantra portion of the Veda[2],

---

[1] Note that the Ṛishi or author was Viśvāmitra, a *Kshatriya.*

[2] In Maṇḍala I. 164. 32, *bahu-prajāḥ* is explained by *bahu-janma-bhāk*, 'subject to many births,' but it may mean 'having abundant offspring.'

nor do the authors of the hymns evince any sympathy with the desire to get rid of all action and personal existence, which became so remarkable a feature of the theology and philosophy of the Brāhmans in later times. But there are many indirect references to the immortality of the soul and a future life, and these become more marked and decided towards the end of the Ṛig-veda. One of the hymns in the last Maṇḍala is addressed to the Pitṛis or fathers, that is to say, the spirits of departed ancestors who have attained to a state of heavenly bliss, and are supposed to occupy three different stages of blessedness,—the highest inhabiting the upper sky, the middle the intermediate air, and the lowest the regions of the atmosphere near the earth. Reverence and adoration are always to be offered them, and they are presided over by the god Yama, the ruler of all the spirits of the dead, whether good or bad. The earlier legends represent this god as a kind of first man (his twin sister being Yamī) and also as the first of men that died. Hence he is described as guiding the spirits of other men who die to the same world. In some passages, however, Death is said to be his messenger, he himself dwelling in celestial light, to which the departed are brought, and where they enjoy his society and that of the fathers. In the Veda he has nothing to do with judging or punishing the departed (as in the later mythology), but he has two terrific dogs, with four eyes, which guard the way to his abode. Here are a few thoughts about him from various hymns in the tenth Maṇḍala of the Ṛig-veda:

> To Yama, mighty king, be gifts and homage paid.
> He was the first of men that died, the first to brave
> Death's rapid rushing stream, the first to point the road
> To heaven, and welcome others to that bright abode.
> No power can rob us of the home thus won by thee.
> O king, we come; the born must die, must tread the path

That thou hast trod—the path by which each race of men,
In long succession, and our fathers, too, have passed.
Soul of the dead! depart; fear not to take the road—
The ancient road—by which thy ancestors have gone;
Ascend to meet the god—to meet thy happy fathers,
Who dwell in bliss with him. Fear not to pass the guards—
The four-eyed brindled dogs—that watch for the departed.
Return unto thy home, O soul! Thy sin and shame
Leave thou behind on earth; assume a shining form—
Thy ancient shape—refined and from all taint set free.

Let me now endeavour, by slightly amplified translations, to convey some idea of two of the most remarkable hymns in the Ṛig-veda. The first (Maṇḍala X. 129), which may be compared with some parts of the 38th chap. of Job, attempts to describe the mystery of creation thus:

In the beginning there was neither nought nor aught,
Then there was neither sky nor atmosphere above.
What then enshrouded all this teeming Universe?
In the receptacle of what was it contained?
Was it enveloped in the gulf profound of water?
Then was there neither death nor immortality,
Then was there neither day, nor night, nor light, nor darkness,
Only the Existent One breathed calmly, self-contained.
Nought else than him there was—nought else above, beyond.
Then first came darkness hid in darkness, gloom in gloom.
Next all was water, all a chaos indiscreet,
In which the One lay void, shrouded in nothingness.
Then turning inwards he by self-developed force
Of inner fervour and intense abstraction, grew.
And now in him Desire, the primal germ of mind,
Arose, which learned men, profoundly searching, say
Is the first subtle bond, connecting Entity
With Nullity. This ray that kindled dormant life,
Where was it then? before? or was it found above?
Were there parturient powers and latent qualities,
And fecund principles beneath, and active forces
That energized aloft? Who knows? Who can declare?
How and from what has sprung this Universe? the gods
Themselves are subsequent to its development.
Who, then, can penetrate the secret of its rise?

Whether 'twas framed or not, made or not made; he only
Who in the highest heaven sits, the omniscient lord,
Assuredly knows all, or haply knows he not.

The next example is from the first Maṇḍala of the Ṛig-veda (121). Like the preceding, it furnishes a good argument for those who maintain that the purer faith of the Hindūs is properly monotheistic:

What god shall we adore with sacrifice?[1]
Him let us praise, the golden child that rose
In the beginning, who was born the lord—
The one sole lord of all that is—who made
The earth, and formed the sky, who giveth life,
Who giveth strength, whose bidding gods revere,
Whose hiding-place is immortality,
Whose shadow, death; who by his might is king
Of all the breathing, sleeping, waking world—
Who governs men and beasts, whose majesty
These snowy hills, this ocean with its rivers
Declare; of whom these spreading regions form
The arms; by whom the firmament is strong,
Earth firmly planted, and the highest heavens
Supported, and the clouds that fill the air
Distributed and measured out; to whom
Both earth and heaven, established by his will,
Look up with trembling mind; in whom revealed
The rising sun shines forth above the world.
Where'er let loose in space, the mighty waters
Have gone, depositing a fruitful seed
And generating fire, there *he* arose,
Who is the breath and life of all the gods,
Whose mighty glance looks round the vast expanse
Of watery vapour—source of energy,
Cause of the sacrifice—the only God
Above the gods. May he not injure us!
He the Creator of the earth—the righteous
Creator of the sky, Creator too
Of oceans bright, and far-extending waters.

---

[1] In the text this question is repeated at the end of every verse. A literal translation will be found in Muir's Sanskṛit Texts, vol. iv. p. 16.

Let me now give a few verses (not in regular order and not quite literally translated) from the celebrated Purusha-sūkta, one of the most recent of the hymns of the Ṛig-veda (Maṇḍala X. 90). It will serve to illustrate the gradual sliding of Hindū monotheism into pantheism, and the first foreshadowing of the institution of caste, which for so many centuries has held India in bondage:

The embodied spirit[1] has a thousand heads,
A thousand eyes, a thousand feet, around
On every side enveloping the earth,
Yet filling space no larger than a span[2].
He is himself this very universe,
He is whatever is, has been, and shall be.
He is the lord of immortality.
All creatures are one-fourth of him, three-fourths
Are that which is immortal in the sky.
From him, called Purusha, was born Virāj,
And from Virāj was Purusha produced[3]
Whom gods and holy men made their oblation.
With Purusha as victim they performed
A sacrifice. When they divided him,
How did they cut him up? what was his mouth?
What were his arms? and what his thighs and feet?

---

[1] According to the Upanishads and the Tattva-samāsa the all-pervading self-existent spirit is called Purusha, *puri śayanāt*, from dwelling in the body.

[2] Dr. Muir translates (literally), 'He overpassed the earth by a space of ten fingers.' The Kaṭha Upanishad (II. 4. 12) says that Purusha, 'the soul,' is of the measure of a thumb (*aṅgushṭha-mātraḥ*).

[3] This is tantamount to saying that Purusha and Virāj are in substance the same. Virāj, as a kind of secondary creator, is sometimes regarded as male, sometimes as female. Manu (I. 11) says that Purusha, 'the first male,' was called Brahmā, and was produced from the supreme self-existent Spirit. In I. 32 he says that Brahmā (see Kullūka's commentary), having divided his own substance, became half male, half female, and that from the female was produced Virāj, and that from Virāj was born Manu—the secondary progenitor and producer of all beings.

The Brāhman was his mouth, the kingly soldier[1]
Was made his arms, the husbandman his thighs,
The servile S'ūdra issued from his feet.

I close my examples of the Mantras with slightly amplified versions of two hymns—one in praise of Time, personified as the source of all things, taken from the Atharva-veda; the other addressed to Night, from the Ṛig-veda[2].

The following is the hymn to Time (Atharva-veda XIX. 53). A few verses at the end are omitted, one or two lines transposed, and a few inserted from the next hymn on the same subject:

Time, like a brilliant steed with seven rays,
And with a thousand eyes, imperishable,
Full of fecundity, bears all things onward.
On him ascend the learned and the wise.
Time, like a seven-wheeled, seven-naved car, moves on.
His rolling wheels are all the worlds, his axle
Is immortality. He is the first of gods.
We see him like an overflowing jar;
We see him multiplied in various forms.
He draws forth and encompasses the worlds;
He is all future worlds; he is their father;
He is their son; there is no power like him.
The past and future issue out of Time,
All sacred knowledge and austerity.
From Time the earth and waters were produced;
From Time, the rising, setting, burning sun;
From Time, the wind; through Time the earth is vast;
Through Time the eye perceives; mind, breath, and name
In him are comprehended. All rejoice
When Time arrives—the monarch who has conquered
This world, the highest world, the holy worlds,
Yea, all the worlds—and ever marches on.

---

[1] The second caste or Kshatriya is here called Rājanya. By 'husbandman' in the next line is of course meant the third or Vaiśya caste.

[2] Both literally translated into prose by Dr. Muir, Texts, vol. v. p. 408, vol. iv. p. 498.

The hymn to Night is my last example. It is taken from the tenth Maṇḍala of the Ṛig-veda (127):

The goddess Night arrives in all her glory,
Looking about her with her countless eyes.
She, the immortal goddess, throws her veil
Over low valley, rising ground, and hill,
But soon with bright effulgence dissipates
The darkness she produces; soon advancing
She calls her sister Morning to return,
And then each darksome shadow melts away.
Kind goddess, be propitious to thy servants
Who at thy coming straightway seek repose,
Like birds who nightly nestle in the trees.
Lo! men and cattle, flocks and wingëd creatures,
And e'en the ravenous hawks, have gone to rest.
Drive thou away from us, O Night, the wolf;
Drive thou away the thief, and bear us safely
Across thy borders. Then do thou, O Dawn,
Like one who clears away a debt, chase off
This black, yet palpable obscurity,
Which came to fold us in its close embrace.
Receive, O Night, dark daughter of the Day,
My hymn of praise, which I present to thee,
Like some rich offering to a conqueror.

## LECTURE II.

### *The Brāhmaṇas and Upanishads.*

HAVING thus endeavoured to gain an insight into portions of the Vedic Mantras, turn we now to the second division of the Veda, called Brāhmaṇa, or ritualistic precept and illustration. This division stands to the Mantra portion in a relation somewhat resembling that of the Talmud to the Mosaic code and of the Hadīs or Sunna to the Kurān. There is, however, a noteworthy difference; for the Mosaic code alone contains the true revelation of divine law for the Jew, and the Kurān is supposed to do the same for Muslims, whereas the Brahmaṇas are as much Veda and Śruti—as much revelation, according to the Hindū idea of revelation—as the Mantras.

In fact, in their relation to caste and the dominance of the Brāhmans, these Brāhmaṇas are even more important than the Hymns. When, however, we are asked to explain the contents of the Brāhmaṇas, we find it difficult to define their nature accurately. It is usual to consider them as a body of ritualistic precepts distributed under two heads of *Vidhi* and *Artha-vāda*, that is, rules and explanatory remarks. They are really a series of rambling and unsystematic prose compositions (the oldest of which may have been written seven or eight centuries B.C.), intended to serve as ceremonial directories for the use of the priests in the exercise of their craft, prescribing rules for the employment of the Mantras at sacrifices, speculating as to the meaning and effect of certain verses and metres, and giving detailed explanations of the origin, import, and conduct of the sacrifices, with the occasional addition of controversial remarks (*nindā*) and illustrations in the shape of legends and old stories. The great diffuseness of these compositions made them practically useless as directories to the ritual, until they themselves were furnished with guides in the form of Sūtras or aphoristic rules, to be afterwards described.

Each of the Saṃhitās or collections of Mantras has its own Brāhmaṇas. Thus the Ṛig-veda has the Aitareya-brāhmaṇa and the Kaushītaki- (or Śāṅkhāyana-) brāhmaṇa. The two collections of the Yajur-veda have the Taittirīya-brāhmaṇa and the Śatapatha-brāhmaṇa[1], which last, belonging to the Vājasaneyi-saṃhitā, is perhaps one of the most complete and interesting of these productions. The Sāma-veda has eight Brāhmaṇas, of which the best known are the Prauḍha or Pañća-viṉśa, the Tāṇḍya, and the Shaḍ-viṉśa. The Atharva-veda has also a Brāhmaṇa, called Go-patha[2].

Though much of the matter contained in these treatises is little better than mere silly sacerdotalism, yet they furnish valuable materials to any one interested in tracing out the growth of Brāhmanism and many curious and interesting legends.

One of the most remarkable of these legends, as introducing the idea of human sacrifice, is called 'the Story of Śunaḥśepa' in the Aitareya-brāhmaṇa[3] (Haug's edition, VII. 13; cf. Ṛig-veda I. 24. 12, &c., V. 2. 7). It has been well translated by more than one scholar. I here give a metrical epitome of part of the story:

---

[1] Edited, with the Vājasaneyi-saṃhitā, by Professor A. Weber of Berlin.

[2] This Brāhmaṇa must be less ancient than others, as, according to some, the Atharva-veda was not recognized as a part of S'ruti, 'revelation,' at the time of the composition of the more ancient Brāhmaṇas.

[3] Professor H. H. Wilson conjectured that this Brāhmaṇa was written about six centuries B. C. It is sometimes called Āśvalāyana-brāhmaṇa.

King Hariśćandra had no son; he asked
Great Nārada, the sage, 'What benefit
Comes from a son?' then Nārada replied—
'A father by his son clears off a debt[1],
In him a self is born from self. The pleasure
A father has in his own son exceeds
All other pleasures. Food is life, apparel
Is a protection, gold an ornament,
A loving wife the best of friends, a daughter
An object of compassion[2], but a son
Is like a light sent from the highest heaven.
Go then to Varuṇa, the god, and say—
"Let but a son be born, O king, to me,
And I will sacrifice that son to thee."'
This Hariśćandra did, and thereupon
A son was born to him, called Rohita.
One day the father thus addressed his son—
'I have devoted thee, my son, to him
Who granted thee to me, prepare thyself
For sacrifice to him.' The son said, 'No,'
Then took his bow and left his father's home.

The story goes on to relate that Varuṇa, being disappointed of his promised victim, punished Hariśćandra by afflicting him with dropsy. Meanwhile

For six long years did Hariśćandra's son
Roam in the forest; there one day he met
A famished Brāhman hermit, Ajīgarta,
Half dead with hunger in the wilderness.
The hermit was attended by his wife
And three young sons; then Rohita addressed him—
'O Brāhman, I will give a hundred cows
For one of these thy sons.' The father answered—
Folding his arms around his eldest boy—
'I cannot part with him.' The mother then

---

[1] A man is in debt to his forefathers till he has a son, because the happiness of the dead depends on certain ceremonies (called S'rāddha) performed by sons.

[2] Those who have lived in the East will perhaps understand why the birth of a daughter is here described as a calamity.

Clung to her youngest child and weeping said—
'I cannot part with him.' Then S'unaḥśepa,
Their second son, said, 'Father, I will go[1].'
So he was purchased for a hundred cows
By Rohita, who forthwith left the forest,
And taking him to Hariśćandra said—
'Father, this boy shall be my substitute.'
Then Hariśćandra went to Varuṇa
And prayed, 'Accept this ransom for my son.'
The god replied, 'Let him be sacrificed,
A Brāhmaṇ is more worthy than a Kshatriya.'

Upon that, the sacrifice with the intended victim was prepared. Four great Ṛishis officiated as priests, but they could not find any one willing to bind the boy to the sacrificial post. His father Ajīgarta, who had followed his son to the place of sacrifice, then came forward and said—

'Give me a hundred cows and I will bind him.'
They gave them to him, and he bound the boy.
But now no person would consent to kill him.
Then said the father, 'Give me yet again
Another hundred cows and I will slay him.'
Once more they gave a hundred, and the father
Whetted his knife to sacrifice his son.
Then said the child, 'Let me implore the gods,

[1] The Brāhmaṇa merely states that they agreed together upon selling the middle son. This idea of the voluntary offer of himself on the part of S'unaḥśepa may however be borrowed from the Rāmāyaṇa, where the story is thus related (I. 61, 62):

Ambarīsha, king of Ayodhyā, performed a sacrifice, but the victim being stolen by Indra, he is told by the priest that either the victim itself must be recovered, or a human victim substituted in its place. Ambarīsha wanders over the earth in search of the real victim, and meets at last with a Brāhman named Ričīka, to whom he offers a hundred thousand cattle for one of his sons. Ričīka refuses to let his eldest son go, and his wife will not part with the youngest. Upon this the middle son, S'unaḥ-śepa, volunteers to go, and is accepted. When about to be offered up as a sacrifice he is saved by Viśvāmitra, who teaches him a prayer to Agni, and two hymns to Indra and Vishṇu.

Haply they will deliver me from death.'
So S'unaḥśepa prayed to all the gods
With verses from the Veda, and they heard him.
Thus was the boy released from sacrifice,
And Hariśćandra was restored to health.

As a sequel to the preceding legend I extract the following curious passages from the Aitareya-brāhmaṇa, Book II. (Haug, 1–8), not in order and not quite literally:

The gods killed a man for their victim. But from him thus killed the part which was fit for a sacrifice went out and entered a horse. Thence the horse became an animal fit for being sacrificed. The gods then killed the horse, but the part fit for being sacrificed went out of it and entered an ox. The gods then killed the ox, but the part fit for being sacrificed went out of it and entered a sheep. Thence it entered a goat. The sacrificial part remained for the longest time in the goat, thence it became pre-eminently fit for being sacrificed[1].

The gods went up to heaven by means of sacrifice. They were afraid

---

[1] This is curious as indicating that human sacrifice, if it prevailed to any extent, was superseded by the sacrifice of animals, here enumerated in the regular order of their fitness for sacrifice according to some supposed inherent efficacy in each class. Such sacrifices were held to be propitiatory, though one object of a Hindū's oblations was to afford actual nourishment to the gods, food being a supposed necessity of their being. The Aśva-medha, or 'horse-sacrifice,' was a very ancient ceremony, hymns 162 and 163 in Maṇḍala I. of the Ṛig-veda being used at this rite. It was regarded as the chief of all animal sacrifices, and in later times its efficacy was so exaggerated that a hundred horse-sacrifices entitled the sacrificer to displace Indra from the dominion of heaven. Some think that the horse was not actually immolated, but merely bound to the post. Mr. Hardwick, in his valuable work, 'Christ and other Masters,' gives some interesting remarks on the five heads of Hindū sacrifices (vol. i. p. 324). The five heads are—1. *Agni-hotra*, burnt-offerings and libations of butter on fire every morning and evening (see p. 251); 2. *Darśa-pūrṇamāsa*, half-monthly sacrifices at new and full moon; 3. *Ćāturmāsya*, sacrifices every four months; 4. *Aśva-medha* and *paśu-yajña*, sacrifices of animals; 5. *Soma-yajña*, offerings and libations of the juice of the Soma or moon-plant (to Indra especially). Goats are still offered to Kālī, but Buddhism tended to abolish animal sacrifice in India.

that men and sages, after having seen their sacrifice, might inquire how they could obtain some knowledge of sacrificial rites and follow them. They therefore debarred them by means of the Yūpa (or post to which the victim was fastened), turning its point downwards. Thereupon the men and sages dug the post out and turned its point upwards, Thus they became aware of the sacrifice and reached the heavenly world.

The following lines may serve to give an outline of another curious legend in the Aitareya-brāhmaṇa (Haug's edition, I. 23), written perhaps seven or eight centuries B.C.:

> The gods and demons were engaged in warfare.
> The evil demons, like to mighty kings,
> Made these worlds castles; then they formed the earth
> Into an iron citadel, the air
> Into a silver fortress, and the sky
> Into a fort of gold. Whereat the gods
> Said to each other, 'Frame we other worlds
> In opposition to these fortresses.'
> Then they constructed sacrificial places,
> Where they performed a triple burnt oblation.
> By the first sacrifice they drove the demons
> Out of their earthly fortress, by the second
> Out of the air, and by the third oblation
> Out of the sky. Thus were the evil spirits
> Chased by the gods in triumph from the worlds.

I next give a metrical version of part of a well-known legend in the Śatapatha-brāhmaṇa (Professor Weber's edition, I. 8. 1. 1), which represents the Indo-Āryan tradition of the flood as it existed in India many centuries before the Christian era, perhaps not much later than the time of David:

> There lived in ancient time a holy man,
> Called Manu [1], who by penances and prayers

---

[1] According to the later mythology this Manu was not the first Manu, held to be the author of the well-known Code, but the seventh or Manu (Vaivasvata) of the present period, regarded as a progenitor of the human race, and represented as conciliating the favour of the Supreme Being by his piety in an age of universal depravity.

Had won the favour of the lord of heaven.
One day they brought him water for ablution;
Then, as he washed his hands, a little fish
Appeared and spoke in human accents thus—
'Take care of me and I will be thy saviour.'
'From what wilt thou preserve me?' Manu asked.
The fish replied, 'A flood will sweep away
All creatures, I will rescue thee from that.'
'But how shall I preserve thee?' Manu said.
The fish rejoined, 'So long as we are small
We are in constant danger of destruction;
For fish eats fish; so keep me in a jar;
When I outgrow the jar, then dig a trench
And place me there; when I outgrow the trench,
Then take me to the ocean, I shall then
Be out of reach of danger.' Having thus
Instructed Manu, straightway rapidly
The fish grew larger; then he spake again—
'In such and such a year the flood will come;
Therefore construct a ship and pay me homage.
When the flood rises, enter thou the ship,
And I will rescue thee.' So Manu did
As he was ordered, and preserved the fish,
Then carried it in safety to the ocean;
And in the very year the fish enjoined
He built a ship and paid the fish respect,
And there took refuge when the flood arose.
Soon near him swam the fish, and to its horn
Manu made fast the cable of his vessel.
Thus drawn along the waters Manu passed
Beyond the northern mountain. Then the fish,
Addressing Manu, said, 'I have preserved thee;
Quickly attach the ship to yonder tree.
But, lest the waters sink from under thee;
As fast as they subside, so fast shalt thou
Descend the mountain gently after them.'
Thus he descended from the northern mountain.
The flood had swept away all living creatures;
Manu alone was left. Wishing for offspring,
He earnestly performed a sacrifice.
In a year's time a female was produced.

She came to Manu, then he said to her,
'Who art thou?' She replied, 'I am thy daughter.'
He said, 'How, lovely lady, can that be?'
'I came forth,' she rejoined, 'from thine oblations
Cast on the waters; thou wilt find in me
A blessing, use me in the sacrifice.'
With her he worshipped and with toilsome zeal
Performed religious rites, hoping for offspring.
Thus were created men, called sons of Manu.
Whatever benediction he implored
With her, was thus vouchsafed in full abundance.

We shall see hereafter that the fish which figures in this story is declared, in the Mahābhārata, to be an incarnation of Brahmā, the creator, who assumed this form to preserve the pious Manu from perishing in the waters.

The Brāhmaṇas express belief in a future life more positively than the Mantras. They also assert that a recompense awaits all beings in the next world according to their conduct in this. But the doctrine of transmigration, which became afterwards an essential element of the Hindū religion, is not developed[1]. There is a remarkable passage in the Śatapatha-brāhmaṇa (X. 4. 3. 9), some idea of which may be gained from the following lines:

The gods lived constantly in dread of death—
The mighty Ender—so with toilsome rites
They worshipped and performed religious acts
Till they became immortal. Then the Ender
Said to the gods, 'As ye have made yourselves
Imperishable, so will men endeavour
To free themselves from me; what portion then
Shall I possess in man?' The gods replied,
'Henceforth no being shall become immortal
In his own body; this his mortal frame
Shalt thou still seize; this shall remain thy own.
He who through knowledge or religious works
Henceforth attains to immortality
Shall first present his body, Death, to thee.'

[1] See the third of Professor Weber's Indische Streifen, and compare note 1, p. 68.

I add one other passage extracted from the Aitareya-brāhmaṇa (Dr. Haug's edition, III. 44):

The sun never sets nor rises. When people think to themselves the sun is setting, he only changes about (*viparyasyate*) after reaching the end of the day, and makes night below and day to what is on the other side. Then when people think he rises in the morning, he only shifts himself about after reaching the end of the night, and makes day below and night to what is on the other side. In fact, he never does set at all. Whoever knows this that the sun never sets, enjoys union and sameness of nature with him and abides in the same sphere. [*Atha yad enam prātar udetīti manyante rātrer eva tad antam itvā atha ātmānaṃ viparyasyate, ahar eva avastāt kurute rātrīm parastāt. Sa vai esha na kadāćana nimroćati. Na ha vai kadāćana nimroćaty etasya ha sāyujyaṃ sarūpatāṃ salokatām aśnute ya evaṃ veda.*]

We may close the subject of the Brāhmaṇas by paying a tribute of respect to the acuteness of the Hindū mind, which seems to have made some shrewd astronomical guesses more than 2000 years before the birth of Copernicus.

## *The Upanishads.*

I come now to the third division of the Veda, called Upanishad, or mystical doctrine (*rahasya*). The title Upanishad (derived from the root *sad* with the prepositions *upa* and *ni*[1]) implies something mystical that underlies or is beneath the surface. And these Upanishads do in fact lie at the root of what may be called the philosophical side of Hindūism. Not only are they as much *śruti*, or revelation, as the Mantra and Brāhmaṇa, but they are practically the only Veda of all thoughtful Hindūs in the present day.

There appear, in real truth, to be two sides to almost every religious system. Perhaps the one religion of the world that offers the same doctrines both to the learned

[1] According to native authorities *upa-ni-shad* means 'to set ignorance at rest by revealing the knowledge of the supreme spirit.'

and unlearned is Christianity. Its deeper truths may be mysteries, but they are not restricted to any single class of men; they are open to the reception of all, and equally to be apprehended by all. The case is different with other religions. We know that the Greeks and Romans had their so-called mysteries reserved only for the initiated. Even the Kurān is held to possess an exoteric or evident meaning called *ẓahr*, and an esoteric, deeper significance called *baṭn;* and in later times a mystical system of pantheistic philosophy called Sūfī-ism was developed in Persia out of this esoteric teaching.

Very similar too is the Hindū idea of Veda or sacred knowledge. It is said to possess two quite distinct branches. The first is called Karma-kāṇḍa, which, embracing both Mantra and Brāhmaṇa, is for that vast majority of persons who are unable to conceive of religion except as a process of laying up merit by external rites. For these the one God, although really without form, assumes various forms with the sole object of lowering himself to the level of human understandings. The second branch of the Veda, on the other hand, is called Jṅāna-kāṇḍa, and is reserved for that select few who are capable of the true knowledge[1].

What then, it will be asked, is this true knowledge? The answer is that the creed of the man who is said to possess the true Veda is singularly simple. He believes in the unity of all being. In other words, that there is but one real Being in the universe, which Being also constitutes the universe. This, it will be said, is simple pantheism, but it is at least a pantheism of a very spiritual kind; for this one Being is thought of as the great universal Spirit, the only really existing Soul, with which all seem-

---

[1] The one implies action, the other cessation from all action. This division of the Veda is recognized by Manu, see XII. 88.

ingly existing material substances are identified, and into which the separate souls of men, falsely regarded as emanations from it, must be ultimately merged.

This, then, is the pantheistic doctrine everywhere traceable in some of the more ancient Upanishads, though often wrapped up in mystic language and fantastic allegory. A list of about 150 of these treatises has been given, but the absence of all trustworthy historical records in India makes it impossible to fix the date of any of them with certainty. Some of the more ancient, however, may be as old as 500 years before Christ. These are appended to the Āraṇyakas—certain chapters of the Brāhmaṇas so awe-inspiring and obscure that they were required to be read in the solitude of forests. Properly each Brāhmaṇa had its Āraṇyakas, but the mystical doctrines they contained were so mixed up with extraneous subjects that the chapters called Upanishads appear to have been added with the object of investigating more definitely such abstruse problems as the origin of the universe, the nature of deity, the nature of the soul, and the reciprocal connection of spirit and matter.

It is interesting to trace the rudiments of the later philosophy amid the labyrinth of mystic language, fanciful etymologies, far-fetched analogies, and puerile conceits, which bewilder the reader of the Upanishads. Moreover it is instructive to mark the connection of these treatises with the Brāhmaṇas, manifested by the frequent introduction of legendary matter and allusions to sacrificial rites. The language of both, though occasionally archaic, is less so than that of the Mantras, and differs little from classical Sanskṛit.

The following are some of the most important Upanishads:—the Aitareya Upanishad and Kaushītaki-brāhmaṇa Upanishad[1] of the Ṛig-veda; the Taittirīya

[1] Edited and translated for the Bibliotheca Indica by Professor Cowell.

belonging to the Taittirīya-saṃhitā of the Yajur-veda; the Bṛihad-āraṇyaka attached to the Śatapatha-brāhmaṇa of the Vājasaneyi-saṃhitā of that Veda and the Īśa or Īśāvāsya forming an actual part (the 40th chapter) of this latter Saṃhitā (this being the only instance of an Upanishad attached to a Saṃhitā rather than a Brāhmaṇa); the Ćhāndogya and Kena[1] belonging to the Sāma-veda; the Praśna, Muṇḍaka, Māṇḍukya, and Kaṭha belonging to the Atharva-veda. In some of these works (written generally in prose in the form of dialogues with occasional variations in verse) striking thoughts, original ideas, and lofty sentiments may be found scattered here and there, as I hope now to show. I commence my examples with a nearly literal translation of about half of a very short Upanishad—the Īśa[2]:

Whate'er exists within this universe
Is all to be regarded as enveloped
By the great Lord, as if wrapped in a vesture.
Renounce, O man, the world, and covet not
Another's wealth, so shalt thou save thy soul.
Perform religious works, so may'st thou wish
To live a hundred years; in this way only
May'st thou engage in worldly acts, untainted.
To worlds immersed in darkness, tenanted
By evil spirits, shall they go at death,
Who in this life are killers of their souls.
There is one only Being who exists
Unmoved, yet moving swifter than the mind;
Who far outstrips the senses, though as gods
They strive to reach him; who himself at rest
Transcends the fleetest flight of other beings;
Who, like the air, supports all vital action.
He moves, yet moves not; he is far, yet near;
He is within this universe, and yet
Outside this universe; whoe'er beholds

[1] Also called Talava-kāra, and also assigned to the Atharva-veda.

[2] This has been well edited and translated into prose by Dr. Röer. Sir W. Jones translated the Īśa, but by no means literally.

All living creatures as in him, and him—
The universal Spirit—as in all,
Henceforth regards no creature with contempt.
The man who understands that every creature
Exists in God alone, and thus perceives
The unity of being, has no grief
And no illusion. He, the all-pervading,
Is brilliant, without body, sinewless,
Invulnerable, pure, and undefiled
By taint of sin. He also is all-wise,
The Ruler of the mind, above all beings,
The Self-existent. He created all things
Just as they are from all eternity.

Next we may pass to a few passages selected from different portions of the Bṛihad-āraṇyaka Upanishad—a long and tedious but important work:

In this universe there was not anything at first distinguishable. But indeed it was enveloped by Death, and Death is Voracity—that is to say—the desire to devour (I. 2. 1).

As the web issues from the spider, as little sparks proceed from fire, so from the one Soul proceed all breathing animals, all worlds, all the gods, and all beings (II. 1. 20).

Being in this world we may know the Supreme Spirit; if there be ignorance of him, then complete death ensues; those who know him become immortal (IV. 4. 14).

When a person regards his own soul as truly God, as the lord of what was and is to be, then he does not wish to conceal himself from that Soul (IV. 4. 15).

That Soul the gods adore as the light of lights (*jyotishām̐ jyotiḥ*) and as the immortal life (IV. 4. 16).

Those who know him as the life of life, the eye of the eye, the ear of the ear, and the mind of the mind, have comprehended the eternal pre-existing Spirit (IV. 4. 18).

By the mind is he to be perceived, in him there is no variation. Whoever sees variation in him obtains death after death (IV. 4. 19).

Infinitely full (or pervasive) is that Spirit (regarded as independent of all relation); infinite too is this Spirit (in his relations and attributes). From the infinite is drawn out the infinite. On taking the infinite from the infinite, there remains the infinite (V. 1).

'I am Brahma.' Whoever knows this, 'I am Brahma,' knows all. Even the gods are unable to prevent his becoming Brahma (I. 4. 10).

Man indeed is like a lofty tree, the lord of the forest. His hair is like the leaves, his skin the external bark. From his skin flows blood as sap from the bark; it issues from his wounded body like sap from a stricken tree. If a tree be cut down, it springs up anew from the root. From what root does mortal man grow again when hewn down by death? [Cf. Job xiv. 7–10.] The root is Brahma, who is knowledge and bliss (III. 9. 28).

The Ćhāndogya Upanishad of the Sāma-veda has some interesting passages. In the seventh chapter occurs a dialogue between Nārada and Sanat-kumāra, in which the latter, in explaining the nature of God, asserts that a knowledge of the four Vedas, Itihāsas, Purāṇas, and such works, is useless without the knowledge of Brahma, the universal Spirit (VII. 1. 4):

The knowledge of these works is a mere name. Speech is greater than this name, Mind than Speech, Will than Mind, Sensation (or the capacity of feeling) is greater than Mind, Reflection is higher than Sensation, Knowledge than Reflection, Power than Knowledge, and highest of all stands Prāṇa or Life. As the spokes of a wheel are attached to the nave, so are all things attached to Life [1].

This Life ought to be approached with faith and reverence, and viewed as an Immensity which abides in its own glory. That Immensity extends from above and from below, from behind and from before, from the south and from the north. It is the Soul of the universe. It is God himself. The man who is conscious of this divinity incurs neither disease, nor pain, nor death.

But lest the deity might from this description be confounded with space, it is afterwards stated that he is inconceivably minute, dwelling in a minute chamber of the heart; and lest this should lead to the notion of his

---

[1] Cf. the hymn to Prāṇa, Atharva-veda XI. 4 (Muir's Texts, vol. v. p. 394). It begins thus, 'Reverence to Prāṇa, to whom this universe is subject, who has become the lord of all, on whom all is supported.' The text of this Veda has been edited in a masterly manner by Professors W. D. Whitney and R. Roth.

being finite, he is afterwards declared to be the Envelope of all creation.

In another part of the work (VI. 10) human souls are compared to rivers:

These rivers proceed from the East towards the West, thence from the ocean they rise in the form of vapour, and dropping again they flow towards the South and merge into the ocean.

Again (VIII. 4), the supreme Soul is compared to a bridge which cannot be crossed by disease, death, grief, virtue, or vice:

Crossing this bridge, the blind cease to be blind, the wounded to be wounded, the afflicted to be afflicted, and on crossing this bridge nights become days; for ever refulgent is the region of the universal Spirit.

Here is a portion of a passage in the Ćhāndogya Upanishad (VI. 2) which has some celebrity as containing the well-known Vedāntist formula *ekam evādvitīyam:*

In the beginning there was the mere state of being (τὸ ὄν)—one only without a second. Some, however, say that in the beginning there was the state of non-being (τὸ μὴ ὄν)—one only without a second. Hence out of a state of non-being would proceed a state of being. But, of a truth, how can this be? How can being (τὸ ὄν) proceed out of non-being? In the beginning, then, there was the mere state of being—one only without a second. It willed[1], 'I shall multiply and be born.' It created heat. That heat willed, 'I shall multiply and be born.' It created water. The water willed, 'I shall multiply and be born.' It created aliment. There-

[1] I follow Dr. Röer here. Subjoined are the divided Sanskrit words of the fragment taken from the original text:—*Sad eva idam agre āsīd, ekam eva advitīyam. Tad ha eke āhur asad eva idam agre āsīd, ekam eva advitīyam, tasmād asataḥ saj jāyeta. Kutas tu khalu syād iti, katham asataḥ saj jāyeta iti. Sat tv eva idam agre āsīd ekam eva advitīyam. Tad aikshata bahu syām prajāyeya iti, tat tejo asṛijata. Tat teja aikshata bahu syām prajāyeya iti, tad apo asṛijata. Tā āpa aikshanta bahvaḥ syāma prajāyemahi iti tā annam asṛijanta. Tasmād yatra kva ća varshati tad eva bhūyishṭham annam bhavati. Sā iyaṃ devatā aikshata, aham imās tisro devatā jīvena ātmanā anupraviśya nāma-rūpe vyākaravāṇi iti.*

fore, wherever rain falls much aliment is produced. That deity willed, 'Entering these three divinities in a living form, I shall develop name and form.'

In the Muṇḍaka Upanishad[1] there are some interesting passages. The following is from the second section of the second Muṇḍaka (5):

Know him, the Spirit, to be one alone. Give up all words contrary to this. He is the bridge of immortality.

The following remarkable passage from the third Muṇḍaka (1. 1–3) is quoted by the Sāṅkhyas in support of their doctrine of a duality of principle, but is also appealed to by Vedāntists. It rests on a Mantra of the Ṛig-veda (I. 164. 20), explained by Sāyaṇa in a Vedāntic sense[2]:

Two birds (the Paramātman and Jīvātman or supreme and individual souls) always united, of the same name, occupy the same tree (abide in the same body). One of them (the Jīvātman) enjoys the sweet fruit of the fig (or fruit of acts), the other looks on as a witness. Dwelling on the same tree (with the supreme Soul), the deluded (individual) soul, immersed (in worldly relations), is grieved by the want of power; but when it perceives the Ruler, separate (from worldly relations) and his glory, then its grief ceases. When the beholder sees the golden-coloured maker (of the world), the lord, the soul, the source of Brahmā, then having become wise, shaking off virtue and vice, without taint of any kind, he obtains the highest identity (Röer's edition, p. 305).

---

[1] The name Muṇḍaka is derived from Muṇḍ, 'to shave,' because he who understands the doctrine of this Upanishad is 'shorn' of all error.

[2] Subjoined is the Mantra:—*Dvā suparṇā sayujā sakhāyā samānaṃ vṛiksham parishasvajāte, Tayor anyaḥ pippalam svādv atty an-aśnann anyo abhićākaśīti*, 'two birds associated together as friends inhabit the same tree. The one of them tastes the sweet fig, the other looks on without enjoying.' S'aṅkara, commenting on the Upanishad, explains *sakhāyā* by *samāna-khyātau*, 'of the same name.' He also remarks that the Pippala or Aśvattha, 'holy fig-tree,' having roots above and branches bent downwards, is allegorical, and that each tree, springing from an unperceived root, is emblematic of the body, which really springs from and is one with Brahma. In the Kaṭha VI. 1 and Bhagavad-gītā XV. 1–3 the same tree is said to typify the universe. It is supposed to be the male of the Vaṭa or Banyan (Ficus Indica).

Here are two or three other examples from the same Upanishad:

As the spider casts out and draws in (its web), as from a living man the hairs of the head and body spring forth, so is produced the universe from the indestructible Spirit (I. 1. 7).

As from a blazing fire consubstantial sparks proceed in a thousand ways, so from the imperishable (Spirit) various living souls are produced, and they return to him too (II. 1. 1).

As flowing rivers are resolved into the sea, losing their names and forms, so the wise, freed from name and form, pass into the divine Spirit, which is greater than the great. He who knows that supreme Spirit becomes spirit (III. 2. 8, 9).

One of the most ancient and important Upanishads is the Kaṭha. It enjoys considerable reputation in India, and is also well known by Sanskṛit students in Europe. It opens with the story of Naćiketas.

He was the pious son of a sage who had given all his property to the priests, and who, in a fit of irritation, devoted this son to Death.

Naćiketas is described as going to Death's abode, and there, having propitiated Yama, he is told to choose three boons. The youth chose for the first boon, that he might be restored to life and see his reconciled father once more; for the second, that he might know the fire by which heaven is gained. When asked to name the third boon, he addresses the god of death thus,—

Some say the soul exists after death, others say it does not exist. I request, as my third boon, that I may be instructed by thee in the true answer to this question.

Death tries to put him off, intreating him to choose any other boon than this; but the youth persisting in his demand to be enlightened as to the mysteries of the next world, Yama at length gives way and enlarges upon the desired theme in the following manner (Vallī II):

The good, the pleasant, these are separate ends,
The one or other all mankind pursue;

But those who seek the good, alone are blest;
Who choose the pleasant miss man's highest aim.
The sage the truth discerns, not so the fool.
But thou, my son, with wisdom hast abandoned
The fatal road of wealth that leads to death.
Two other roads there are all wide apart,
Ending in widely different goals—the one
Called ignorance, the other knowledge—this,
O Naćiketas, thou dost well to choose.
The foolish follow ignorance, but think
They tread the road of wisdom, circling round
With erring steps, like blind men led by blind.
The careless youth, by lust of gain deceived,
Knows but one world, one life; to him the Now
Alone exists, the Future is a dream.
The highest aim of knowledge is the soul;
This is a miracle, beyond the ken
Of common mortals, thought of though it be,
And variously explained by skilful teachers.
Who gains this knowledge is a marvel too.
He lives above the cares—the griefs and joys
Of time and sense—seeking to penetrate
The fathomless unborn eternal essence.
The slayer thinks he slays, the slain
Believes himself destroyed, the thoughts of both
Are false, the soul survives, nor kills, nor dies;
'Tis subtler than the subtlest, greater than
The greatest, infinitely small, yet vast,
Asleep, yet restless, moving everywhere
Among the bodies—ever bodiless—
Think not to grasp it by the reasoning mind;
The wicked ne'er can know it; soul alone
Knows soul, to none but soul is soul revealed.

In the third Vallī (3, 4, &c.) of the same Upanishad the soul is compared to a rider in a chariot, the body being the chariot, the intellect the charioteer, the mind the reins, the passions or senses the horses, and the objects of sense the roads. The unwise man neglects to apply the reins; in consequence of which the passions, like unrestrained vicious horses, rush about hither and thither, carrying the charioteer wherever they please[1].

In the fifth Vallī (11) the following sentiment occurs:

As the sun, the eye of the whole world, is not sullied by the defects of the (human) eye or of external objects, so the inner soul of all beings is not sullied by the misery of the world.

I now add a few extracts from one of the most modern of these treatises, called Śvetāśvatara[2], which may serve to show how epithets of the Supreme Being are heaped together by the writers of the Upanishads without much order and often with apparent contradiction:

Him may we know, the ruler of all rulers,
The god of gods, the lord of lords, the greater
Than all the greatest, the resplendent being,
The world's protector, worthy of all homage.
Of him there is not cause nor yet effect.
He is the cause, lord of the lord of causes,
None is there like him, none superior to him,
His power is absolute, yet various,
Dependent on himself, acting with knowledge,
He the one god is hidden in all beings,
Pervades their inner souls and rules their actions,
Dwelling within their hearts, a witness, thinker,
The singly perfect, without qualities.
He is the Universe's maker, he
Its knower, soul and origin of all,
Maker of time, endowed with every virtue,
Omniscient, lord of all embodied beings,

---

[1] Compare Manu II. 88, 'In the restraint of the organs running wild among objects of sense, which hurry him away hither and thither, a wise man should make diligent effort, like a charioteer restraining restive steeds.' So Plato in the Phaedrus (54, 74) compares the soul to a charioteer (the reason) driving a pair of winged steeds, one of which (the will) is obedient to the rein, and tries to control its wild and vicious yoke-fellow (the appetite): Τριχῇ διειλόμην ψυχὴν ἑκάστην, ἱππομόρφω μὲν δύο τινὲ εἴδη, ἡνιοχικὸν δὲ εἶδος τρίτον, κ. τ. λ.

[2] Of the Yajur-veda, though sometimes found (according to Colebrooke) in Atharva-veda collections. See Weber's Indische Studien I. 420–439.

Lord of the triple qualities, the cause
Of man's existence, bondage and release,
Eternal, omnipresent, without parts,
All knowing, tranquil, spotless, without blame,
The light, the bridge of immortality,
Subtler than what is subtlest, many-shaped,
One penetrator of the universe,
All-blest, unborn, incomprehensible,
Above, below, between, invisible
To mortal eyes, the mover of all beings,
Whose name is Glory, matchless, infinite,
The perfect spirit, with a thousand heads,
A thousand eyes, a thousand feet, the ruler
Of all that is, that was, that is to be,
Diffused through endless space, yet of the measure
Of a man's thumb, abiding in the heart,
Known only by the heart, whoever knows him
Gains everlasting peace and deathlessness [1].

I close these extracts from the Upanishads by a metrical version of part of the first chapter of a short Upanishad called Maitrāyaṇi or Maitrāyaṇīya, belonging to the Black Yajur-veda [2]:

In this decaying body, made of bones,
Skin, tendons, membranes, muscles, blood, saliva,
Full of putrescence and impurity,
What relish can there be for true enjoyment? [3]
In this weak body, ever liable
To wrath, ambition, avarice, illusion,
To fear, grief, envy, hatred, separation

[1] Most of these epithets will be found in the following sections of the S'vetāśvatara Upanishad VI. 7, 8, 11, 17, 19, IV. 14, 17, 19, &c. Compare the extract from the Purusha-sūkta given at p. 24.

[2] Also called Maitrāyaṇī, Maitrāyaṇa, Maitrī, and Maitri. Under the latter name it has been well edited and translated for the Bibliotheca Indica by Professor E. B. Cowell. It is in seven chapters, the first of which was translated into prose by Sir W. Jones, but without any name. My version is partly based on his, but I have consulted Professor Cowell's more accurate translation.

[3] Compare Manu VI. 77.

From those we hold most dear, association
With those we hate; continually exposed
To hunger, thirst, disease, decrepitude,
Emaciation, growth, decline, and death,
What relish can there be for true enjoyment?
The universe is tending to decay,
Grass, trees, and animals spring up and die.
But what are they? Earth's mighty men are gone,
Leaving their joys and glories; they have passed
Out of this world into the realm of spirits.
But what are they? Beings greater still than these,
Gods, demigods, and demons, all have gone.
But what are they? for others greater still
Have passed away, vast oceans have been dried,
Mountains thrown down, the polar star displaced,
The cords that bind the planets rent asunder,
The whole earth deluged with a flood of water,
E'en highest angels driven from their stations.
In such a world what relish can there be
For true enjoyment? deign to rescue us;
Thou only art our refuge, holy lord[1].

---

[1] The following sentiment occurs in the text before the concluding line: *Andhodapāna-stho bheka iva aham asmin saṃsāre:*

Living in such a world I seem to be
A frog abiding in a dried-up well.

Compare some of the Stoical reflections of Marcus Aurelius, given by the Rev. F. W. Farrar in his 'Seekers after God:'

'Oil, sweat, dirt, filthy water, all things disgusting—so is every part of life.'

'Enough of this wretched life, and murmuring, and apish trifles.'

'All the present time is a point in eternity. All things are little, changeable, perishable.'

# LECTURE III.

## *The Systems of Philosophy.*

I MUST now advert in a general way to the six systems of philosophy which grew out of the Upanishads. They are sometimes called the six Śāstras or bodies of teaching, sometimes the Shaḍ Darśanas or six Demonstrations. They are—

1. The Nyāya, founded by Gotama.
2. The Vaiśeshika, by Kaṇāda.
3. The Sāṅkhya, by Kapila.
4. The Yoga, by Patañjali.
5. The Mīmāṉsā, by Jaimini.
6. The Vedānta, by Bādarāyaṇa or Vyāsa.

They are delivered in Sūtras or aphorisms, which are held to be the basis of all subsequent teaching under each head[1].

It is as impossible however to settle the date of any of them with certainty as it is to determine the period of the

---

[1] These Sūtras are often so brief and obscure as to be absolutely unintelligible without a commentary. They are commonly called 'aphorisms,' but really are mere memorial suggestions of the briefest possible kind, skilfully contrived for aiding the recollection of the teachers of each system. Probably the first to comment upon the Sūtras thus delivered was the author of them himself. He was followed by a vast number of other commentators in succeeding generations (generally a triple set), and by writers who often embodied in treatises or compendiums of their own the tenets of the particular school to which they were attached. The most celebrated of all commentators is the great S'aṅkara Āćārya, a native of Malabar, who lived probably between 650 and 740 A.D., and wrote almost countless works, including commentaries on the Upanishads, Vedānta-sūtras, and Bhagavad-gītā.

composition of any single work in Sanskṛit literature. Moreover, it is scarcely practicable to decide as to which of the six systems of philosophy preceded the other in point of time. All we can say is, that about 500 years before the commencement of the Christian era a great stir seems to have taken place in Indo-Āryan, as in Grecian minds, and indeed in thinking minds everywhere throughout the then civilized world. Thus when Buddha arose in India, Greece had her thinker in Pythagoras, Persia in Zoroaster, and China in Confucius. Men began to ask themselves earnestly such questions as—What am I? whence have I come? whither am I going? How can I explain my consciousness of personal existence? What is the relationship between my material and immaterial nature? What is this world in which I find myself? Did a wise, good, and all-powerful Being create it out of nothing? or did it evolve itself out of an eternal germ? or did it come together by the combination of eternal atoms? If created by a Being of infinite wisdom, how can I account for the inequalities of condition in it—good and evil, happiness and misery? Has the Creator form, or is he formless? Has he any qualities or none?

Certainly in India no satisfactory solution of questions such as these was likely to be obtained from the prayers and hymns of the ancient Indo-Āryan poets, which, though called Veda or 'knowledge' by the Brāhmans, did not even profess to furnish any real knowledge on these points, but merely gave expression to the first gropings of the human mind, searching for truth by the uncertain light of natural phenomena[1].

---

[1] The second aphorism of the Sāṅkhya-kārikā states distinctly that Ānuśravika or knowledge derived from S'ruti—the revelation contained in the Veda—is ineffectual to deliver from the bondage of existence.

Nor did the ritualistic Brāhmaṇas contribute anything to the elucidation of such topics. They merely encouraged the growth of a superstitious belief in the efficacy of sacrifices and fostered the increasing dependence of the multitude on a mediatorial caste of priests, supposed to be qualified to stand between them and an angry god. Still these momentous questions pressed for solution, and the minds of men finding no rest in mere traditional revelation and no satisfaction in mere external rites, turned inwards, each thinker endeavouring to think out the great problems of life for himself by the aid of his own reason. Hence were composed those vague mystical rationalistic speculations called Upanishads, of which examples have been already given. Be it remembered that these treatises were not regarded as antagonistic to revelation, but rather as completory of it. They were held to be an integral portion of the Veda or true knowledge; and, even more —they so rose in the estimation of thoughtful persons that they ended by taking rank as its most important portion, its grandest and noblest utterance, the apex to which all previous revelation tended. Probably the simple fact was, that as it was found impossible to stem the progress of free inquiry, the Brāhmans with true wisdom determined on making rationalistic speculation their own, and dignifying its first development in the Upanishads with the title of Veda. Probably, too, some of their number (like Jāvāli) became themselves infected with the spirit of scepticism, and were not to be restrained from prosecuting free philosophical investigations for themselves.

There are not wanting, however, evident indications that the Kshatriyas or second caste were the first introducers into India of rationalistic speculation. We shall presently point out that the great Buddha was a Kshatriya, and the Ćhāndogya Upanishad (V. 3) has a remarkable passage which, as bearing upon this point, I here abridge (Röer's edition, p. 315):

A youth called S'vetaketu (the son of a Brāhman named Gautama) repaired to the court of the king of Pañćāla, Pravāhaṇa, who said to him, 'Boy, has thy father instructed thee?' 'Yes, sir,' replied he. 'Knowest thou where men ascend when they quit this world?' 'No, sir,' replied he. 'Knowest thou how they return?' 'No, sir,' replied he. 'Knowest thou why the region to which they ascend is not filled up?' 'No, sir,' replied he. 'Why then saidst thou that thou hadst been instructed?' The boy returned sorrowful to his father's house and said, 'The king asked me certain questions which I could not answer.' His father said, 'I know not the answers.' Then he, Gautama, the father of the boy, went to the king's house. When he arrived, the king received him hospitably and said, 'O Gautama, choose as a boon the best of all worldly possessions.' He replied, 'O king, thine be all worldly possessions; tell me the answers to the questions you asked my son.' The king became distressed in mind (knowing that a Brāhman could not be refused a request) and begged him to tarry for a time. Then he said, 'Since you have sought this information from me, and since this knowledge has never been imparted to any other Brāhman before thee, therefore the right of imparting it has remained with the Kshatriyas among all the people of the world.'

This story certainly appears to favour the supposition that men of the caste next in rank to that of Brāhmans were the first to venture upon free philosophical speculation. However that may be, it was not long before Brāhmanism and rationalism advanced hand in hand, making only one compact, that however inconsistent with each other, neither should declare the other to be a false guide. A Brāhman might be a rationalist, or both rationalist and Brāhman might live together in harmony, provided both gave a nominal assent to the Veda, maintained the inviolability of caste, the ascendancy of Brāhmans, and their sole right to be the teachers both of religion and philosophy. But if a rationalist asserted that any one might be a teacher, or might gain emancipation for himself irrespectively of the Veda or caste observances, he was at once excommunicated as a heretic and infidel. It is evident that a spirit of free inquiry had begun to show itself even during the Mantra period and had become common enough in Manu's time. In the second book of his Laws (verse 11) it is declared:

The Brāhman who resorting to rationalistic treatises (*hetu-śāstra*) shall contemn the two roots of all knowledge (viz. *śruti* and *smṛiti*), that man is to be excommunicated (*vahish-kāryaḥ*) by the righteous as an atheist (*nāstika*) and reviler of the Vedas.

Such heretics, however, soon became numerous in India by the simple law of reaction; for it may with truth be asserted that the Buddhist reformation, when it first began to operate, was the result of a reaction from the tyranny of Brāhmanism and the inflexible rigour of caste. Like the return swing of a pendulum, it was a rebound to the opposite extreme—a recoil from excessive intolerance and exclusiveness to the broadest tolerance and comprehensiveness. It was the name for unfettered religious thought, asserting itself without fear of consequences and regardless of running counter to traditional usages, however ancient and inveterate.

According to this view, the lines of free inquiry which ended in the recognized schools of philosophy cannot be regarded as having sprung directly out of Buddhism; nor did the latter owe its origin to them. Buddhism and philosophy seem rather to have existed contemporaneously[1]. Buddhism was for the bold and honest free-thinker who cared nothing for maintaining a reputation for orthodoxy, while the schools of philosophy were the homes of those rationalists who sacrificed honesty at the shrine of ecclesiastical respectability. Doubtless the orthodox philosopher usually went through the form of denouncing

---

[1] The Sāṅkhya Sūtras I. 27–47 refer to certain Buddhistic tenets, but, as remarked by Dr. Muir, these may be later interpolations, and so prove nothing as to the priority of Buddhism.

all Buddhist heretics; but except in the three points of a nominal assent to the Veda, adherence to caste, and a different term for final emancipation, two at least of the systems, viz. the *Vaiśeshika* and *Sāṅkhya*, went almost to the same length with Buddhism, even to the practical if not ostensible ignoring of a supreme intelligent creator. It is curious, too, that Gotama or Gautama, the name of the supposed orthodox Brāhman founder of the *Nyāya*, was also a name of the heretical Kshatriya who founded Buddhism.

In fact, not the extremest latitudinarian of the present day could possibly be allowed such liberty of thought as was conceded to the free-thinkers of India, provided they neutralized their heterodoxy by nominally accepting the Veda, or at least its Upanishad portion, and conforming to *Hindū Dharma*—that is, to the duties of caste, involving of course the recognition of Brāhmanical ascendancy.

It would be difficult then, I think, to refer Hindū rationalism to any one special person or school as its founder. Not that Kapila, Gautama, and the great Buddha of the sixth century B.C., were myths. Some men of vigorous intellect and enlightened views doubtless arose who gathered together and formulated the floating free thought of the day; and some one of them, like the Buddha, became a rallying point for the increasing antipathy to sacerdotal domination, a kind of champion of reason and liberator of mind from the tyranny of traditional opinions. It may without hesitation be affirmed that such leaders of rationalistic inquiry once lived in India. I commence, then, with a brief notice of the celebrated Buddha.

## *Buddhism.*

Some particulars in the life of the great Buddha are known with tolerable certainty. He is described as the son of a king, *Śuddhodana*, who reigned in *Kapila-*

*vastu*, the capital of a country at the foot of the mountains of Nepāl[1]. He was therefore a prince of the Kshatriya or military caste, which of itself disqualified him in the eyes of the Brāhmans from setting up as a religious teacher. His proper family or tribal name was Śākya, and that of his race or clan Gautama or Gotama[2]; for it is well known that this great reformer never arrogated to himself an exclusive right to the title Buddha, 'enlightened,' or claimed any divine honours or even any special reverence. He is said to have entered on his reforming mission in the district of Magadha or Behār[3] about the year 588 B.C., but he taught that other philosophers (Budhas) and even numerous Buddhas—that is, perfectly enlightened men—had existed in previous periods of the world. He claimed to be nothing but an example of that perfection in knowledge to which any man might attain by the exercise of abstract meditation, self-control, and bodily mortification. Gentle, however, and unassuming as the great reforming Ascetic was, he aimed at the grandest

---

[1] His mother's name was Māyā or Māyā-devī, daughter of king Suprabuddha. The Buddha had also a wife called Yaśodharā and a son Rāhula and a cousin Ānanda.

[2] Gautama is said to have been one of the names of the great Solar race to which king Śuddhodana belonged. The titles Sinha and Muni are often added to Śākya, thus Śākya-sinha, 'the lion of the Śākyas;' Śākya-muni, 'the Śākya-saint.' His name Siddhārtha, 'one whose aims have been accomplished,' was either assumed, like Buddha, as an epithet in after life, or, as some say, was given by his parents, 'whose prayer had been granted,' something in the same manner as *Deva-datta*, Θεοδώρητος, Theodore. Śramaṇa, meaning 'ascetic,' is sometimes affixed to Gautama. He is also styled Bhagavat, 'the adorable,' and Tathā-gata or Su-gata, 'one who has gone the right way.' Every Buddhist may be a *Śramaṇa* (see p. 57) for the more rapid attainment of Nirvāṇa.

[3] He is said to have given lectures to his disciples in a garden belonging to a rich and liberal householder, named Sudatta or Anātha-piṇḍāda, in the city of Śrāvastī, somewhere in the district now called Oude, north of the Ganges.

practical results. He stood forth as the deliverer of a priest-ridden, caste-ridden nation,—the courageous reformer and innovator who dared to attempt what doubtless others had long felt was necessary, namely, the breaking down of an intolerable ecclesiastical monopoly by proclaiming absolute free trade in religious opinions and the abolition of all caste privileges [1]. It may be taken as a fixed law of human nature that wherever there arise extravagant claims to ecclesiastical authority on the one side, there will always arise Buddhas on the other—men who, like the Buddha of India, become rapidly popular by proclaiming

---

[1] Bauddhas or Buddhists believe that after immense intervals of time (Kalpas) men with perfect knowledge, entitled to be called supreme Buddhas, come into the world to teach men the true way to Nirvāṇa, which gradually fades away from their minds in the lapse of ages and has again to be communicated by another perfect teacher. The Buddha foretold that one of his followers was to be the next supreme Buddha. An ascetic who has arrived at the stage when there is only one more birth, before attaining to the rank of a Buddha, is called by Buddhists *Bodhi-sattva*, 'one who has the essence of perfect wisdom in him.' Few, of course, attain to be supreme Buddhas—completely enlightened teachers—though all may ultimately reach *Nirvāṇa*. Candidates for *Nirvāṇa* are called Arhats, i. e. 'venerables.'

Dr. Muir, at the end of the second volume of his Texts, gives a most interesting metrical translation of part of the *Lalita-vistara*, a legendary history in prose and verse of the Buddha's life. The prose of this history is in Sanskṛit, but the Gāthās or songs interspersed with it are in a kind of mixed dialect, half Sanskṛit, half Prākṛit. The passage translated describes Buddha as a deliverer and redeemer in terms which almost assimilate his character to the Christian conception of a Saviour. Professor Max Müller, in his Sanskṛit Literature (p. 79), has drawn attention to a passage from *Kumārila Bhaṭṭa*, according to which the following words, claiming the functions of a kind of vicarious redeemer, are ascribed to Buddha :—'Let all the evils (or sins) flowing from the corruption of the fourth or degenerate age (called *Kali*) fall upon me, but let the world be redeemed.' Bishop Claughton is reported to have said in a recent lecture, that there is nothing out of Christianity equal to Buddhism in a moral point of view.

general religious equality, universal charity and toleration, and whose followers develop their doctrines to a point beyond that intended by themselves. In fact, a sort of Buddhism capable of being pushed to the extremest point of Nihilism is a not unlikely terminus of all lines of uncontrolled thought, whose starting-point is the sense of freedom produced by the breaking loose of reason from the unnatural restraints which sacerdotal dogmatism delights to impose. It is a remarkable proof of the enchaining power of caste, that notwithstanding the popularity and attractive features of Buddhism, its universal toleration and benevolence, its recognition of the common brotherhood of mankind, its reverence for every form of organized existence—so that not only every human being, but every living creature however insignificant, has a right to respect and tender treatment—its inculcation of the virtues of self-sacrifice, purity, truthfulness, gentleness of speech, humility, patience, and courage—this wonderful system which originated in India and adapted itself so completely in most of its doctrines to Indian tastes and habits of thought, should have been in the end unsuccessful in its contest with Brāhmanism.

But though the religion of India at the present day is certainly not Buddhism, yet it is equally certain that this rejected system has left a deep impress on the Hindū mind, and has much in common with Hindūism generally; while its attractiveness to the Oriental character is notably evidenced, by its having during a period of about two thousand four hundred years so commended itself to Eastern nations as to number at this moment, according to recent calculations, about four hundred and fifty-five millions of nominal adherents. Therefore, before quitting the subject of the great Indian reformer, it will not be irrelevant if I indicate briefly the principal points of his teaching.

Let me begin by directing attention to its most marked

feature. The Buddha recognized no supreme deity[1]. The only god, he affirmed, is what man himself can become. In Brāhmanism God becomes man; in Buddhism man becomes a god. Practically, however, Buddhists are subject to a formidable god in *Karman*, 'act.' But this is a god to be got rid of as soon as possible, for action leads to continual existence, carried on through innumerable bodies till acts are adequately rewarded or punished; and that all existence is an evil is a fundamental dogma of Buddhism. Hence the great end of the system is *Nirvāṇa*, 'the being blown out' or non-existence. From this statement it might be supposed that all good actions as well as bad are to be avoided. But this is not exactly the case. Certain acts, involving abnegation of self and suppression of evil passions, are supposed very inconsistently to contribute to the great end of *Nirvāṇa* or non-existence. According to the best authorities[2], the Buddha regarded men as divided into two classes—first, those who are still attached to the world and worldly life; secondly, those who by self-mortification are bent on being delivered from it. The first class are Upāsakas or 'laymen,' the second are Śramaṇas or 'ascetics[3].' These last are rather monks or friars than priests. Of priests and clergy in our sense the Buddhist religion has none. In real fact Buddhism ought not to be called a religion at all, for where there is no god there can be no need of sacrifice or propitiation

[1] With Buddhists, as indeed with Brāhmans, the gods are merely superior beings, subject to the same law of dissolution as the rest of the universe. Certainly the Buddha himself never claimed to be worshipped as a god, nor is he so worshipped, though his memory is revered and the relics of him are inclosed in shrines, and even a kind of prayer in his honour is uttered or turned round in a wheel to act as a charm. Strictly, a Buddhist never prays; he merely contemplates.

[2] For a full account see the article 'Buddha' in Chambers' Cyclopaedia.

[3] They are also called Śrāvakas as hearers of Buddha and Mahā-śrāvakas as great hearers. When mendicants they are Bhikshus or Bhikshukas.

or even of prayer, though this last is practised as a kind of charm[1] against diseases, worldly evils and malignant demons, and as having, like other acts, a kind of mechanical efficacy. Both classes, however, laymen and ascetics, must equally practise certain virtues to avoid greater misery, either in future births or in one of the 136 hells; for the passing through repeated births, even in the most degraded forms of life, is not sufficient punishment for the effacement of demerit without the endurance of terrific torments in numerous hells[2].

Ten moral prohibitions are given. Five are for all, viz. Kill not. Steal not. Commit not adultery. Lie not. Drink no strong drink. The other five are for the ascetics who have commenced the direct pursuit of Nirvāṇa, viz. Eat no food out of season. Abstain from dances, theatres, songs, and music. Use no ornaments or perfumes. Abstain from luxurious beds. Receive no gold nor silver. Again, there are still more severe precepts for those who are not merely commencing a religious life, but have actually renounced the world. These persons are sometimes called Bhikshus or Parivrājakas, 'religious mendicants.' They must dress only in rags sewed together with their own hands, and covered with a yellow cloak. They must eat only one meal daily, and that before noon, and only what may be collected from door to door in a wooden bowl. For a part of the year they must live in the woods with no other shelter than a tree, and with no furniture but a carpet on which they must sit, and never lie down

[1] These Buddhist prayers are called Dhāraṇīs and are used, like the Brāhmanical Mantras, as charms against evil of all kinds. It should be noted that Buddhists believe in a kind of devil or demon of love, anger, evil, and death, called Māra, who opposed Buddha and the spread of his religion. He is supposed to send forth legions of evil demons like himself.

[2] See note 2, p. 66. There are also numerous Buddhist heavens. One of these, called Tushita, was inhabited by S'ākya-muni as a Bodhi-sattva before he came into the world as a Buddha.

during sleep. Besides these prohibitions and injunctions there are six transcendent perfections of conduct which lead to the other shore of Nirvāṇa (Pāram-itās, as they are called), and which are incumbent on all, viz. 1. Charity or benevolence (*dāna*). 2. Virtue or moral goodness (*śīla*). 3. Patience and forbearance (*kshānti*). 4. Fortitude (*vīrya*). 5. Meditation (*dhyāna*). 6. Knowledge (*prajñā*)[1]. Of these, that which especially characterizes Buddhism is the perfection of benevolence and sympathy displayed towards all living beings, and carried to the extreme of avoiding injury to the most minute animalculae and treating with tenderness the most noxious animals. Even self-sacrifice for the good of such animals and of inferior creatures of all kinds is a duty. It is recorded of the Buddha himself that in former existences he frequently gave himself up as a substituted victim in the place of doves and other innocent creatures to satisfy the appetites of hawks and beasts of prey; and on one occasion, meeting with a famished tigress unable to feed her cubs, he was so overcome with compassion that he sacrificed his own body to supply the starving family with food[2].

These rules of conduct include many secondary precepts; for instance, not only is untruthfulness prohibited, but all offensive and bad language; not only is patience enjoined, but the bearing of injuries, resignation under misfortune, humility, repentance, and the practice of confessing sins, which last appears to have been regarded as possessing in itself some kind of expiatory efficacy[3].

---

[1] Four others are sometimes added, making—7. *Upāya*, 'expediency.' 8. *Bala*, 'power.' 9. *Praṇidhi*, 'circumspection.' 10. *Jñāna*, 'knowledge of universal truth.' See Lalita-vistara by Rājendralāl Mitra, p. 7.

[2] Modern Buddhism is not so tender to animals as Jainism, and in China animal food is eaten.

[3] In the edicts of Piya-dasi (Sanskṛit Priya-darśi), supposed to be the same as Aśoka, one of the Buddhist kings of Magadha, who lived in the

The following is an abridged version of Buddha's outburst of joy at having achieved, by the knowledge of truth, emancipation from the troubles of life and solved for himself the great problem of existence[1]:

> See what true knowledge has effected here!
> The lust and anger which infest the world,
> Arising from delusion, are destroyed
> Like thieves condemned to perish. Ignorance
> And worldly longings, working only evil,
> By the great fire of knowledge are burnt up
> With all their mass of tangled roots. The cords
> And knots of lands and houses and possessions,
> And selfishness, which talks of 'self' and 'mine,'
> Are severed by the weapons of my knowledge.
> The raging stream of lust which has its source
> In evil thoughts, fed by concupiscence,
> And swollen by sight's waters, are dried up
> By the bright sun of knowledge; and the forest
> Of trouble, slander, envy, and delusion,
> Is by the flame of discipline consumed.
> Now I have gained release, and this world's bonds
> Are cut asunder by the knife of knowledge.

---

third century B.C., the people are commanded to confess their sins publicly every five years. Four great Buddhist councils were held, viz. 1. by Ajāta-śatru, king of Magadha after the Buddha's death (which occurred, according to the opinion of the generality of scholars, about 543 B.C.); 2. by Kālāśoka, a century later; 3. by Aśoka, 246 or 247 B.C.; 4. by Kanishka, king of Kashmīr, 143 B.C. At the first council all the teachings and sayings of the Buddha, who appears never to have written anything, were collected into three sets of books, called Tri-piṭaka, 'the three baskets or collections,' which form the Buddhist sacred scriptures. These three collections are—1. the Sūtra-piṭaka, collected by Ānanda, the Buddha's cousin, containing all the maxims and discourses of S'ākya-muni, and by no means brief like the Brāhmanical Sūtras; 2. the Vinaya-piṭaka, containing books on morals and discipline; 3. the Abhidharma-piṭaka, on metaphysics and philosophy (see Introduction, xxxii. note 1). Professor Kern, in his recent learned dissertation on Buddha, makes the date of Buddha's death 388 B.C.

[1] The original text is given by Professor Banerjea, Dialogues, p. 198.

Thus I have crossed the ocean of the world,
Filled with the shark-like monsters of desire,
And agitated by the waves of passion—
Borne onward by the boat of stern resolve.
Now I have tasted the immortal truth—
Known also to unnumbered saints of yore—
That frees mankind from sorrow, pain, and death.

This imperfect sketch of Buddhism in its earliest and purest phase may conduce to the better understanding of the other lines of Indian rationalism, which differed from it in pretending to accept the authority of the Veda.

These lines were before described as six in number, but they are practically reducible to three, the *Nyāya*, the *Sāṅkhya*, and the *Vedānta*. They all hold certain tenets in common with each other and to a certain extent also (especially the Sāṅkhya) with heretical Buddhism.

A common philosophical creed, as we have already hinted, must have prevailed in India long before the crystallization of rationalistic inquiry into separate systems. If not distinctly developed in the Upanishads, it is clearly traceable throughout Manu[1]; and as it is not only the faith of every Indian philosopher at the present day, but also of the greater number of thinking Brāhmans, whether disciples of any particular philosophical school or not, and indeed of the greater number of educated Hindūs, whether nominal adherents of Vishṇu or Śiva or to whatever caste they may belong—its principal features may be advantageously stated before pointing out the chief differences between the six systems.

1. In the first place, then, rationalistic Brāhmanism—as I propose to call this common faith—holds the eternity of soul, both retrospectively and prospectively[2]. It looks

[1] See Manu XII. 12, 15–18.

[2] Plato appears to have held the same: *Ψυχὴ πᾶσα ἀθάνατος, τὸ γὰρ ἀεικίνητον ἀθάνατον*, Phaed. 51. And again: *Ἐπειδὴ δὲ ἀγένητόν ἐστι, καὶ ἀδιά-*

upon soul as of two kinds: *a.* the supreme Soul (called variously *Paramātman, Brahman,* &c.); *b.* the personal individuated soul of living beings (*jīvātman*)[1]; and it maintains that if any entity is eternal it cannot have had a beginning, or else it must have an end. Hence the personal soul of every human being, just as the supreme Soul, has existed everlastingly and will never cease to exist[2].

2. In the second place this creed asserts the eternity of the matter or substance constituting the visible universe, or of that substance out of which the universe has been evolved; in other words, of its substantial or material cause[3]. It is very true that one system (the Vedānta)

---

φθορον αὐτὸ ἀνάγκη εἶναι, Phaed. 52. And again: Τοῦτο δὲ οὔτ' ἀπόλλυσθαι οὔτε γίγνεσθαι δυνατόν. Cicero expresses it thus: *Id autem nec nasci potest nec mori,* Tusc. Quaest. I. 23. Plato, however, seems to have given no eternity to individual souls, except as emanations from the divine; and in Timaeus 44 he distinguishes two parts of the soul, one immortal, the other mortal.

[1] All the systems, as we shall see, are not equally clear about the existence of a supreme Soul. One at least practically ignores such a soul. With regard to the *Sūtrātman,* see the Lecture on the Vedānta. The Buddhist also believes that all souls have existed from the beginning of a cycle, but, in opposition to the Brāhman, holds that their end is *Nirvāṇa.*

[2] The Muslims have two words for eternity: 1. ازل *azl,* 'that eternity which has no beginning' (whence God is called *Azalī,* 'having no beginning'); and 2. ابد *abd,* 'that eternity which has no end.'

[3] The term for substantial or material cause is *samavāyi-kāraṇa,* literally, 'inseparable inherent cause;' in the Vedānta *upādāna-kāraṇa* is used. With regard to the word 'matter,' see note, p. 64. Though the Greek philosophers are not very definite in their views as to the eternity of matter or its nature, yet they seem to have acquiesced generally in the independent existence of some sort of primordial substance. Plato appears to have held that the elements before the creation were shapeless and soulless, but were moulded and arranged by the Creator (Timaeus 27) out of some invisible and formless essence (ἀνόρατον εἶδός τι καὶ ἄμορφον, Timaeus 24). Aristotle in one passage describes the views of older philosophers who held that primeval substance was affected and made to undergo changes by some sort of affections like the Sāṅkhya

identifies soul with this substance by asserting that the world was not made out of gross particles of matter, but out of soul itself, as its illusory material cause; but to affirm that the universe (τὸ πᾶν) is a part of the one only existing soul is of course equivalent to maintaining the eternal existence of both. In real truth a Hindū philosopher's belief in the eternity of the world's substance, whether that substance has a real material existence or is simply illusory, arises from that fixed article of his creed, '*Ex nihilo nihil fit,*' *nāvastuno vastu-siddhiḥ.* In other words, *A-sataḥ saj jāyeta kutas,* 'how can an entity be produced out of a nonentity?'[1]

---

Guṇas, whence all the universe was developed: Τῆς μὲν οὐσίας ὑπομενούσης τοῖς δὲ πάθεσι μεταβαλλούσης, τοῦτο στοιχεῖον καὶ ταύτην τὴν ἀρχήν φασιν εἶναι τῶν ὄντων, Metaph. I. 3. (See Wilson's Sāṅkhya-kārikā, p. 53.) Aristotle adds his own opinion, 'It is necessary there should be a certain nature (φύσις)—either one or more—out of which other entities are produced.'

[1] Οὐδὲν γίνεται ἐκ τοῦ μὴ ὄντος, 'nothing is produced out of nothing.' All the ancient philosophers of Greece and Rome seem also to have agreed upon this point, as Aristotle affirms (περὶ γὰρ ταύτης ὁμογνωμόνουσι τῆς δόξης ἅπαντες οἱ περὶ φύσεως). Lucretius (I. 150) starts with laying down the same principle:—'Principium hinc nobis exordia sumet Nullam rem e nihilo gigni divinitus unquam.' Aristotle, in the third chapter of the first book of his Metaphysics, informs us that Thales made the primitive substance out of which the universe originated water, Anaximenes and Diogenes made it air, Heracleitus made it fire, Empedocles combined earth, air, fire, and water. Anaximander, on the other hand, regarded the primordial germ as an indeterminate but infinite or boundless principle (τὸ ἄπειρον). Other philosophers affirmed something similar in referring everything back to a confused chaos. Parmenides made Desire his first principle, and Hesiod, quoted by Aristotle, says poetically,—

> 'First indeed of all was chaos; then afterwards
> Earth with her broad breast (cf. Sanskṛit *pṛithivī*);
> Then Desire (ἔρος), who is pre-eminent among all the Immortals.'

Lastly, the Eleatics, like the Indian Vedāntists, were thoroughly pantheistic, and held that the universe was God and God the universe; in other words, that God was τὸ ἕν, or the only one existing thing. With all these accounts compare the Ṛig-veda hymn on the creation, translated on p. 22.

3. In the third place, the soul, though itself sheer thought and knowledge, can only exercise thought, consciousness, sensation, and cognition, and indeed can only act and will when connected with external and material objects of sensation[1], invested with some bodily form[2] and joined to mind (*manas*), which last (viz. mind) is an internal organ of sense (*antaḥ-karaṇa*)[3]—a sort of inlet of

---

[1] It is difficult to find any suitable word to express what the Hindūs mean by material objects. There seems, in real truth, to be no proper Sanskṛit word equivalent to 'matter' in its usual English sense. *Vastu*, as applied to the 'one reality,' is the term for the Vedāntist's universal Spirit; *dravya* stands for soul, mind, time, and space, as well as the five elements; *mūrtti* is anything which has definite limits, and therefore includes mind and the four elements, but not *ākāśa*, 'ether;' *pradhāna* is the original producer of the Sāṅkhya system; *padārtha* is used for the seven categories of the Vaiśeshika. What is here meant is not necessarily a collection of material atoms, nor, again, that imperceptible substance propounded by some as lying underneath and supporting all visible phenomena (disbelieved in by Berkeley), and holding together the attributes or qualities of everything, but rather what is seen, heard, felt, tasted, and touched, which is perhaps best denoted by the Sanskṛit word *vishaya*, the terms *samavāyi-kāraṇa* and *upādāna-kāraṇa* being generally used for the substantial or the material cause of the universe.

[2] All the systems assign to each person two bodies: *a.* an exterior or gross body (*sthūla-śarīra*); *b.* an interior or subtle body (*sūkshma-śarīra* or *liṅga-śarīra*). The last is necessary as a vehicle for the soul when the gross body is dissolved, accompanying it through all its transmigrations and sojournings in heaven or hell, and never becoming separated from it till its emancipation is effected. The Vedānta affirms the existence of a third body, called *kāraṇa-śarīra* or causal body, described as a kind of inner rudiment or latent embryo of the body existing with the soul, and by some regarded as primeval ignorance united with the soul in dreamless sleep. The Platonists and other Greek and Roman philosophers seem to have held a similar doctrine as to a subtle material envelope investing the soul after death, serving as its ὄχημα or vehicle. See Plato, Timaeus 17. This is like the idea of a deceased person's ghost or shade (εἴδωλον, umbra, imago, simulacrum). Cf. Virgil, Aeneid, VI. 390, 701.

[3] *Manas* is often taken as the general term applicable to all the mental powers, but *Manas* is properly a subdivision of *antah-karana*, which is

thought to the soul—belonging only to the body, only existing with it, and quite as distinct from the soul as any of the external organs of the body[1]. The supreme Soul (variously called *Paramātman*, *Brahman*, neut., &c.) has thus connected itself in successive ages with objects and forms, becoming manifest either as Brahmā the creator or in the form of other gods, as Vishṇu and Śiva (see note 1, p. 12), or again in the form of men.

4. Fourthly, this union of the soul with the body is productive of bondage, and in the case of human souls, of misery, for when once so united the soul begins to apprehend objects through the senses, receiving therefrom painful and pleasurable impressions. It also becomes conscious of personal existence and individuality; then it commences acting; but all action, whether good or bad, leads to bondage, because every act inevitably entails a consequence, according to the maxim, *Avaśyam eva bhoktavyaṃ kṛitaṃ karma śubhāśubham*, 'the fruit of every action good or bad must of necessity be eaten.' Hence, if an act be good it must be rewarded, and if bad it must be punished[2].

---

divided into *Buddhi*, 'perception or intellection;' *Ahan-kāra*, 'self-consciousness;' and *Manas*, 'volition or determination;' to which the Vedānta adds a fourth division, *Ćitta*, 'the thinking or reasoning organ.'

[1] This idea of the mind agrees to a great extent with the doctrine of Lucretius, stated in III. 94, &c.:

> 'Primum animum dico (mentem quem saepe vocamus)
> In quo consilium vitae regimenque locatum est,
> Esse hominis partem nihilo minus ac manus et pes
> Atque oculi partes animantis totius extant.'

The remainder of his description of the mind is very interesting in connection with the Hindū theory.

[2] In the Pańća-tantra (II. 135, 136) we read: 'An evil act follows a man, passing through a hundred thousand transmigrations; in like manner the act of a high-minded man. As shade and sunlight are ever closely joined together, so an act and the agent stick close to each other.'

5. Fifthly, in order to accomplish the entire working out of these consequences or 'ripenings of acts' as they are called (*karma-vipākāḥ*[1]), it is not enough that the personal soul goes to heaven or to hell. For all the systems contend that even in heaven or hell merit or demerit, resulting from the inexorable retributive efficacy of former acts, continues clinging to the soul as grease does to a pot after it has been emptied. The necessity for removal to a place of reward or punishment is indeed admitted[2]; but this is not effectual or final. In order that the consequences of acts may be entirely worked out, the soul must leave heaven or hell and return to corporeal existence. Thus it has to pass through innumerable bodies, migrating into higher, intermediate or lower forms, from a god[3] to a demon, man, animal, or plant, or even

[1] Bad consequences are called *Dur-vipāka*. Some of these, in the shape of diseases, &c., are detailed by Manu (XI. 48–52). Thus any one who has stolen gold in a former life will suffer from whitlows on his nails, a drinker of spirits will have black teeth, and the killer of a Brahman, consumption. In the S'abda-kalpa-druma, under the head of *Karma-vipāka*, will be found a long catalogue of the various diseases with which men are born as the fruit of evil deeds committed in former states of existence, and a declaration as to the number of births through which each disease will be protracted, unless expiations (*prāyaśćitta*) be performed in the present life, as described in the eleventh book of Manu.

[2] The twenty-one hells (*Narakas*) are enumerated in Manu IV. 88–90. One is a place of terrific darkness; another a pit of red-hot charcoal; another a forest whose leaves are swords; another is filled with fetid mud; another is paved with iron spikes. These are not to be confounded with the seven places under the earth, of which Pātāla is one, the abode of a kind of serpent demon. The Buddhists have one hundred and thirty-six hells in the interior of the earth, with regular gradations of suffering. Hindūs and Buddhists have also numerous heavens. The former make six regions rising above earth, the seventh; viz. *bhūr* (earth), *bhuvar*, *svar*, *mahar*, *janar*, *tapaḥ*, *satya*.

[3] The gods themselves are only finite beings. They are nothing but portions of the existing system of a perishing universe. In fact, they are represented as actually feeding on the oblations offered to them (see

a stone, according to its various shades of merit or demerit[1].

6. Sixthly, this transmigration of the soul through a

---

Bhagavad-gītā III. 11); they go through penances (see Manu XI. 221); they are liable to passions and affections like men and animals, and are subject, as regards their corporeal part, to the same law of dissolution, while their souls obey the same necessity of ultimate absorption into the supreme soul. The following occurs in the Sāṅkhya-kārikā (p. 3 of Wilson):—'Many thousands of Indras and other gods have, through time, passed away in every mundane age, for time cannot be overcome.' Muir's Texts, vol. v. p. 16.

[1] According to Manu XII. 3, *Śubhāśubha-phalaṃ karma mano-vāg-deha-sambhavaṃ karma-jā gatayo nṛīṇām uttamādhama-madhyamāḥ*, 'an act either mental, verbal, or corporeal bears good or evil fruit; the various transmigrations of men through the highest, middle, and lowest stages are produced by acts.' This triple order of transmigration is afterwards (XII. 40, &c.) explained to be the passage of the soul through deities, men, and beasts and plants, according to the dominance of one or other of the three Guṇas, goodness, passion, or darkness. And each of these three degrees of transmigration has three sub-degrees. The highest of the first degree is Brahmā himself, the lowest of the lowest is any *sthāvara* or 'stationary substance,' which is explained to mean either a vegetable or a mineral; other lowest forms of the lowest degree are in an upward order worms, insects, fish, reptiles, snakes, tortoises, &c. Again, in VI. 61, 63, we read: Let the man who has renounced the world reflect on the transmigrations of men caused by the fault of their acts (*karma-dosha*); on their downfall into hell and their torments in the abode of Yama; on their formation again in the womb and the glidings of the soul through ten millions of other wombs. Again, in XII. 54, 55, &c.: Those who have committed great crimes, having passed through terrible hells for many series of years, at the end of that time pass through various bodies. A Brahman-killer enters the body of a dog, boar, ass, camel, bull, goat, sheep, stag, bird, &c. The violator of the bed of a Guru migrates a hundred times into the forms of grasses, shrubs, plants, &c. In I. 49, XI. 143–146, it is clearly implied that trees and vegetables of all kinds have internal consciousness (*antaḥsañjñā*), and are susceptible of pleasure and pain. The Buddhists have also a triple series of transmigrations, borrowed doubtless from the Brāhmans. The highest is called *Mahā-yāna*, the lowest *Hīna-yāna*. Buddha is said to have pointed out to his followers a broom which he affirmed had formerly been a novice who had neglected to sweep out the assembly-hall.

constant succession of bodies, which is as much a fixed and peremptory doctrine of Buddhism as of Hindūism[1], is to be regarded as the root of all evil. Moreover, by it all the misery, inequality of fortune and diversity of character in the world is to be explained[2]. For even great

[1] The doctrine of metempsychosis, however, does not appear to have taken hold of the Hindū mind when the Mantras were composed. There seems at least to be no allusion to it in the Ṛig-veda, see note, p. 20. It begins to appear, though not clearly defined, in the Brāhmaṇas, and is fully developed in the Upanishads, Darśanas, and Manu. A passage in the S'atapatha-brāhmaṇa (XI. 6. 1. 1), quoted by Professor Weber and Dr. Muir, describes animals and plants as revenging in a future state of existence injuries and death inflicted on them by men in this life.

In Greece and Rome the doctrine of transmigration seems never to have impressed itself deeply on the popular mind. It was confined to philosophers and their disciples, and was first plainly taught by Pythagoras, who is said to have asserted that he remembered his own previous existences. He was followed by Plato, who is supposed by some to have been indebted to Hindū writers for his views on this subject. In the Timaeus (72, 73) he affirms his opinion that those who have lived unrighteously and effeminately will, at their next birth, be changed to women; those who have lived innocently but frivolously will become birds; those who have lived without knowledge of the truths of philosophy will become beasts; and those whose lives have been marked by the extreme of ignorance and folly will become fishes, oysters, &c. He sums up thus: Κατὰ ταῦτα δὴ πάντα τότε καὶ νῦν διαμείβεται τὰ ζῶα εἰς ἄλληλα, νοῦ καὶ ἀνοίας ἀποβολῇ ἢ καὶ κτήσει μεταβαλλόμενα. Virgil, in the sixth book of the Aeneid (680–751), describes the condition of certain souls, which, after going through a sort of purgatory for a thousand years in the lower regions, again ascend to earth and occupy new bodies.

The Jews seem to have known something of the doctrine, if we may judge by the question proposed to our Lord: 'Who did sin, this man (i. e. in a former life) or his parents, that he was born blind?' John ix. 2.

[2] Among Greek philosophers, Aristotle, in the eleventh book of his Metaphysics (ch. 10), goes into the origin of evil, and his view may therefore be compared with that of Hindū philosophers. He recognizes good as a paramount principle in the world, but admits the power of evil, and considers matter (ὕλη) as its prime and only source, much in the same way as the Gnostics and other early Christian philosophical sects, who, like Indian philosophers, denied the possibility of anything being pro-

genius, aptitude for special work, and innate excellence are not natural gifts, but the result of habits formed and powers developed through perhaps millions of previous existences. So again, sufferings of all kinds—weaknesses, sicknesses, and moral depravity—are simply the consequences of acts done by each soul, of its own free will, in former bodies, which acts exert upon that soul an irresistible power called very significantly *Adṛishṭa*, because felt and *not seen*.

Thus the soul has to bear the consequences of *its own acts only*. It is tossed hither and thither at the mercy of a force set in motion by itself alone, but which can never be guarded against, because its operation depends on past actions wholly beyond control and even unremembered [1].

7. Seventhly and lastly, from a consideration of these essential articles of Hindū Rationalism it is plain that the

---

duced out of nothing, and repudiated the doctrine that God could in any way be connected with evil. They, therefore, supposed the eternal existence of a sluggish, inert substance, out of which the world was formed by God, but which contained in itself the principle of evil.

[1] The absence of all recollection of acts done in former states of existence does not seem to strike the Hindūs as an objection to their theory of transmigration. Most of the systems evade the difficulty by maintaining that at each death the soul is divested of mind, understanding, and consciousness. See Mullens' Essay, p. 386. The Garbha Upanishad (4) attributes the loss of memory to the pain and pressure suffered by the soul in the act of leaving the womb. The mythology, however, records cases of men who were gifted with the power of recollecting former existences. In the Phaedo of Plato (47) Cebes is described as saying to Socrates, 'According to that doctrine which you are frequently in the habit of advancing, if it is true, that all knowledge is nothing else than reminiscence (ὅτι ἡμῖν ἡ μάθησις οὐκ ἄλλο τι ἢ ἀνάμνησις τυγχάνει οὖσα), it is surely necessary that we must at some former time have learned what we now remember. But this is impossible, unless our soul existed somewhere before it came into this human form.' Cicero, in Tusc. Quaest. I. 24, says, speaking of the soul, 'Habet primam memoriam, et eam infinitam rerum innumerabilium, quam quidem Plato recordationem esse vult superioris vitae.' Cf. S'akuntalā, Act V. 104 'Can it be that the dim

great aim of philosophy is to teach a man to abstain from every kind of action; from liking or disliking, from loving or hating, and even from being indifferent to anything.

The living personal soul must shake off the fetters of action and getting rid of body, mind, and all sense of separate personality, return to the condition of simple soul.

This constitutes *Pramā* or *Jñāna*, the true measure of all existing difficulties—the right apprehension of truth—which, if once acquired by the soul, confers upon it final emancipation, whether called *Mukti*, *Moksha*, *Niḥśreyasa*, *Apavarga*, or *Nirvāṇa*[1]. This, in short, is the summum bonum of philosophical Brāhmanism; this is the only real bliss,—the loss of all personality and separate identity by absorption into the supreme and only really existing Being—mere life with nothing to live for, mere joy with nothing to rejoice about, and mere thought with nothing upon which thought is to be exercised[2].

Having thus attempted to set forth the common tenets of Indian philosophy, I must next indicate the principal points in which the systems differ from each other[3].

---

memory of events long past, or friendships formed in other states of being, flits like a passing shadow o'er the spirit?' Virgil (Aeneid VI. 714) wisely makes the souls who are to occupy new bodies upon earth throng the banks of Lethe that they may drink a deep draught of oblivion from its waters.

[1] *Nirvāṇa*, 'the being blown out,' is, as we have seen, the Buddhist expression for liberation from existence. The other terms are used by rationalistic Brāhmanism. Two of the Darśanas, however, as we have seen, practically ignore a supreme Being.

[2] Mr. Hardwick has well shown that the great boon conferred by the Gospel, in contradistinction to these false systems, is the recognition of man's responsible free agency and the permanence of his personality. 'Not to be' is the melancholy result of the religion and philosophy of the Hindūs. See 'Christ and other Masters,' vol. i. p. 355. Christianity satisfies the deepest want of man's religious life, viz. to know and love God as a person. See Canon Liddon's 'Elements of Religion,' p. 36.

[3] These were explained in lectures to my highest class only.

# LECTURE IV.

## *The Nyāya.*

WE begin with the Nyāya of Gotama or Gautama, with its supplement, the Vaiśeshika, not because this is first in order of time (see p. 48), but because it is generally the first studied, and much of its terminology is adopted by the other systems[1].

The word Nyāya signifies 'going into a subject,' that is, investigating it analytically. In this sense of 'analysis,' Nyāya is exactly opposed to the word San̄khyā, 'synthesis.' It is common to suppose that the Nyāya is chiefly concerned with logic; but this is merely one part of a single topic. The fact rather is that this system was intended to furnish a correct method of philosophical inquiry into *all the objects and subjects* of human knowledge, including, *amongst others*, the process of reasoning and laws of thought. The Nyāya proper differs from its later development, the Vaiśeshika, by propounding sixteen topics in its first Sūtra. The first topic of these sixteen is *Pra-*

---

[1] The Nyāya Sūtras, consisting of five books, with the commentary, were printed at Calcutta in 1828, under the title of Nyāya-sūtra-vṛitti. Four of the five books were edited and translated by the late Dr. Ballantyne. He also published the Nyāya compendium, called Tarka-sangraha. A favourite text-book of this system is the Bhāshā-paricċheda, with its commentary, called Siddhānta-muktāvalī. This has been edited and translated by Dr. Röer. The Vaiśeshika Sūtras, consisting of ten books, have quite recently been edited and translated in a scholarlike manner by Mr. A. E. Gough, one of my most distinguished Boden scholars, and now Anglo-Sanskrit Professor in the Government College, Benares. Professor E. B. Cowell's edition of the Kusumāñjali, a Nyāya treatise proving the existence of a God, is an interesting work.

*māṇa*, that is, the means or instruments by which *Pramā* or the right measure of any subject is to be obtained. Under this head are enunciated the different processes by which the mind arrives at true and accurate knowledge.

These processes are declared in the third Sūtra of the first book to be four, viz.

a. *Pratyaksha*, 'perception by the senses.' b. *Anumāna*, 'inference.' c. *Upamāna*, 'comparison.' d. *Śabda*, 'verbal authority' or 'trustworthy testimony,' including Vedic revelation.

The treatment of the second of these, viz. inference, possesses more interest for Europeans, as indicating that the Hindūs have not, like other nations, borrowed their logic and metaphysics from the Greeks.

Inference is divided in Sūtra I. 32 into five Avayavas or 'members.'

1. The *pratijñā* or proposition (stated hypothetically).
2. The *hetu* or reason.
3. The *udāharaṇa* (sometimes called *nidarśana*) or example (equivalent to the major premiss).
4. The *upanaya* or application of the reason (equivalent to the minor premiss).
5. The *nigamana* or conclusion (i.e. the *pratijñā* or 'proposition' re-stated as proved).

This method of splitting an inference or argument into five divisions is familiarly illustrated by native commentators thus:

1. The hill is fiery; 2. for it smokes; 3. whatever smokes is fiery, as a kitchen-hearth (or, inversely, not as a lake, which is invariably without fire); 4. this hill smokes; 5. therefore this hill is fiery.

Here we have a combination of enthymeme and syllogism, which seems clumsy by the side of Aristotle's more concise method; the fourth and fifth members being repetitions of the second and first, which, therefore, appear superfluous. But it possesses some advantages when regarded, not as a syllogism, but as a full and complete rhetorical statement of an argument.

Perhaps the most noticeable peculiarity in the Indian method, stamping it as an original and independent analysis of the laws of thought, is the use of the curious terms, *Vyāpti*, 'invariable pervasion' or 'concomitance;' *Vyāpaka*, 'pervader' or 'invariably pervading attribute;' and *Vyāpya*, 'invariably pervaded.' These terms are employed in making a universal affirmation or in affirming universal distribution; as, for example, 'Wherever there is smoke there is fire.' 'Wherever there is humanity there is mortality.' In such cases an Indian logician always expresses himself by saying that there is an invariably pervading concomitance of fire with smoke and of mortality with humanity.

Similarly, fire and mortality are called the pervaders (*Vyāpaka*), smoke and humanity the pervaded (*Vyāpya*). The first argument would therefore be thus briefly stated by a *Naiyāyika:* 'The mountain has invariably fire-pervaded smoke, therefore it has fire.'

To show the importance attached to a right understanding of this technical expression *Vyāpti*, and to serve as a specimen of a Naiyāyika writer's style, I now make an abridged extract from Śan·kara-miśra's comment on the fourteenth Sūtra of the first daily lesson of the third book of the Vaiśeshika Sūtras (Gough, p. 86):

It may be asked, What is this invariable concomitance? (*Nanu keyaṃ vyāptiḥ.*) It is not merely a relation of co-extension. Nor is it the relation of totality. For if you say that invariable concomitance is the connection of the middle term with the whole of the major term (*kṛitsnasya sādhyasya sādhana-sambandhaḥ*), such connection does not exist in the case of smoke, &c. [for although fire exists wherever smoke exists, smoke does not always exist where fire exists, not being found in red-hot iron]. Nor is it natural conjunction; for the nature of a thing is the thing's proper mode of being. Nor is it invariable co-inherence of the major, which is absent only when there is absolute non-existence of that of which the middle is predicated; for volcanic fire must always be non-existent in a kitchen-hearth, though smoky. Nor is it the not being a subject of incompatibility with the predicate. Nor is it the possession of a form determined by the same connection as something else; as, for instance, the being fiery is not determined by connection with smoke, for the being fiery is more extensive. We proceed, then, to state that invariable concomitance is a connection requiring no qualifying term or limitation (*an-aupādhikaḥ sambandhaḥ*)[1]. It is an extensiveness co-extensive with the predicate (*sādhya-vyāpaka-vyāpakatvam*). In other words, invariable concomitance is invariable co-inherence of the predicate[2].

The second head or topic of the Nyāya is *Prameya*, by which is meant all the objects or subjects of *Pramā*—those points, in short, about which correct knowledge is to be obtained. This topic includes all the most important subjects investigated by Indian philosophy. The Prameyas are twelve, as given in the ninth Sūtra; thus,—

1. Soul (*ātman*). 2. Body (*śarīra*). 3. Senses (*indriya*). 4. Objects of sense (*artha*). 5. Understanding or intellection (*buddhi*). 6. Mind (*manas*). 7. Activity (*pravṛitti*). 8. Faults (*dosha*). 9. Transmigration (*pretya-bhāva*). 10. Consequences or fruits (*phala*). 11. Pain (*duḥkha*). 12. Emancipation (*apavarga*).

In his first topic Gautama provides for hearing opposing disputants who desire to discuss fairly any of these Prameyas which form his second topic.

With regard to his fourteen other topics, they seem to be not so much philosophical categories as an enumeration of the regular stages through which a controversy is likely

---

[1] Hence, 'the mountain is smoky because it has fire' is not *vyāpti*, but *ati-vyāpti*, because the upādhi or qualification *ārdrendana-jāta*, 'produced by wet wood,' must be added to make the argument correct. When the middle term (fire) and the major (smoke) are made co-extensive then the fault of *ati-vyāpti* is removed.

[2] It would be difficult to convey to a general reader any idea of the terseness with which the use of long compounds enables all this to be expressed in the original Sanskṛit. Of course the obscurity of the style is proportionably great, and the difficulty of translation enhanced. Mr. Gough, however, is not responsible for every word of the above.

to pass. In India argument slides into wrangling disputation even more easily than in Europe, and these remaining topics certainly illustrate very curiously the captious propensities of a Hindū disputant, leading him to be quick in repartee and ready with specious objections in opposition to the most conclusive logic.

There is, first, the state of *Saṃśaya*, or 'doubt about the point to be discussed.' Next, there must be a *Prayojana*, or 'motive for discussing it.' Next, a *Dṛishṭānta*, or 'familiar example,' must be adduced in order that a *Siddhānta*, or 'established conclusion,' may be arrived at. Then comes an objector with his *Avayava*, or 'argument' split up, as we have seen, into five members. Next follows the *Tarka*, or 'refutation (*reductio ad absurdum*) of his objection,' and the *Nirṇaya*, or 'ascertainment of the true state of the case.' But this is not enough to satisfy a Hindū's passion for disputation. Every side of a question must be examined—every possible objection stated—and so a further *Vāda*, or 'controversy,' takes place, which of course leads to *Jalpa*, 'mere wrangling,' followed by *Vitaṇḍa*, 'cavilling;' *Hetv-ābhāsa*, 'fallacious reasoning [1];' *Ćhala*, 'quibbling artifices;' *Jāti*, 'futile replies;' and *Nigraha-sthāna*, 'the putting an end to all discussion' by a demonstration of the objector's incapacity for argument.

The above are Gotama's sixteen topics. After enumerating them he proceeds to state how deliverance from the misery of repeated births is to be attained; thus,—

> Misery, birth, activity, fault, false notions; on the removal of these in turn (beginning with the last), there is the removal also of that which precedes it; then ensues final emancipation.

---

[1] As an example of fallacious argument may be taken the sixteenth Aphorism of the third book of the Vaiśeshika Sūtras, *yasmād vishāṇī tasmād aśvaḥ*, 'because this has horns, therefore it is a horse;' or the next Sūtra, *yasmād vishāṇī tasmād gauḥ*, 'because it has horns, therefore it is a cow,' which last is the fallacy of 'undistributed middle.'

That is to say, from false notions comes the fault of liking, disliking, or being indifferent to anything; from that fault proceeds activity; from this mistaken activity proceed actions involving either merit or demerit, which merit or demerit forces a man *nolens volens* to pass through repeated births for the sake of its reward or punishment. From these births proceed misery, and it is the aim of philosophy to correct the false notions at the root of this misery.

A Naiyāyika commentator, Vātsyāyana, thus comments on the foregoing statement (Banerjea, p. 185):

From false notion proceed partiality and prejudice; thence come the faults of detraction, envy, delusion, intoxication, pride, avarice. Acting with a body, a person commits injury, theft, and unlawful sensualities,—becomes false, harsh, and slanderous. This vicious activity produces demerit. But to do acts of charity, benevolence, and service with the body; to be truthful, useful, agreeable in speech, or given to repetition of the Veda; to be kind, disinterested, and reverential—these produce merit (*dharma*). Hence merit and demerit are fostered by activity. This activity is the cause of vile as well as honourable births. Attendant on birth is pain. That comprises the feeling of distress, trouble, disease, and sorrow. Emancipation is the cessation of all these. What intelligent person will not desire emancipation from all pain? For, it is said, food mixed with honey and poison is to be rejected. Pleasure joined with pain is to be avoided.

I pass at once to the most important part of the Nyāya system, its supplement:

## *The Vaiśeshika.*

We now come to the *Vaiśeshika* development of the Nyāya, attributed to an author Kaṇāda[1]. This is not

[1] This was probably a mere nickname, meaning 'Feeder on Atoms.' He is also called Ulūka. Gautama, the author of the Nyāya proper, had also a nickname, *Aksha-pāda*, 'eye-footed,' having his eyes always fixed in abstraction on his feet, or supernaturally gifted with eyes in his feet, because too absent to see with those in his head.

so much a branch of this system as a supplement to it, extending the Nyāya to physical inquiries, which it does very imperfectly, it is true, and often with strange fancies and blunders; but, nevertheless, with occasional exactness and not unfrequently with singular sagacity. It is certainly the most interesting of all the systems, both from its more practical character and from the parallels it offers to European philosophical ideas. It begins by arranging its inquiries under seven *Padārthas*, which, as they are more properly categories (i. e. an enumeration of certain general properties or attributes that may be predicated or affirmed of existing things[1]), are now the generally received categories of *Naiyāyikas*. They are as follow: 1. Substance (*dravya*). 2. Quality or property (*guṇa*). 3. Act or action (*karman*). 4. Generality or community of properties (*sāmānya*). 5. Particularity or individuality (*viśesha*). 6. Co-inherence or perpetual intimate relation (*samavāya*). 7. Non-existence or negation of existence (*abhāva*)[2].

---

[1] Thus man is a substance, so also is a chair and a stone; whiteness, blackness, breadth, and length, though very different things, are yet all qualities, &c.

[2] It is interesting to compare the ten Aristotelian categories. They are: 1. Οὐσία, 'Substance.' 2. Ποσόν, 'How much?' 'Quantity.' 3. Ποιόν, 'Of what kind?' 'Quality.' 4. Πρός τι, 'In relation to what?' 'Relation.' 5. Ποιεῖν, 'Action.' 6. Πάσχειν, 'Passiveness' or 'Passivity.' 7. Ποῦ, 'Where?' 'Position in space.' 8. Πότε, 'When?' 'Position in time.' 9. Κεῖσθαι, 'Local situation.' 10. Ἔχειν, 'Possession.' Mr. J. S. Mill, in his Logic, declares that this enumeration is both redundant and defective. Some obj cts are admitted and others repeated under different heads. 'It is like,' he says, 'a division of animals into men, quadrupeds, horses, asses, and ponies.' Action, passivity, and local situation ought not to be excluded from the category of relation, and the distinction between position in space and local situation is merely verbal. His own enumeration of all existing or describable things is as follows: 1. 'Feelings or states of consciousness.' Even the external world is only known as conceived by the mind. 2. 'The minds' which experience those feelings. 3. 'The bodies,'

Kaṇāda, however, the author of the Sūtras, enumerated only six categories. The seventh was added by later writers. This is stated in the fourth Sūtra of book I; thus (Gough's translation, p. 4):

The highest good results from knowledge of the truth which springs from particular merit, and is obtained by means of the similarity and dissimilarity of the categories, substance, attribute, action, generality, particularity, co-inherence.

The commentator adds:

In this place there is mention of six categories, but in reality non-existence is also implied by the sage as another category.

The seven categories are all subdivided.

Let us begin with the first category of *Dravya* or 'substance.' The fifth Sūtra makes the following enumeration of nine Dravyas:

Earth (*pṛithivī*), water (*āpas*), light (*tejas*), air (*vāyu*), ether (*ākāśa*), time (*kāla*), space (*diś*), soul (*ātman*), the internal organ, mind (*manas*) are the substances.

The commentator adds:

If it be objected, there is a tenth substance, darkness (*tamas*), why is it not enumerated? for it is recognized by perception, and substantially belongs to it, because it is possessed of colour and action; and because devoid of odour, it is not earth; and because it possesses dark colour, it is not water, &c.: we reply that it is not so, because it is illogical to imagine another substance, when it is necessarily produced by non-existence of light.

It should be stated that of these substances the first four (earth, water, light, and air) and the last (mind) are held to be atomic, and that the first four are both eternal and non-eternal—non-eternal in their various compounds,

---

supposed to excite feelings or sensations. 4. 'The successions and co-existences, the likenesses and unlikenesses' between these feelings. Further, he shows that all possible propositions affirm or deny one or other of the following properties or facts: 1. Existence, the most general attribute. 2. Co-existence. 3. Sequence or Succession. 4. Causation. 5. Resemblance. See Chambers' Cyclopaedia, under the article 'Categories.'

eternal in their ultimate atoms, to which they must be traced back[1].

Next follows the second category of 'quality.' The sixth Sūtra enumerates seventeen qualities or properties which belong to or are inherent in the nine substances:

Colour (*rūpa*), savour (*rasa*), odour (*gandha*), tangibility (*sparśa*), numbers (*saṅkhyāḥ*), extensions (*parimāṇāni*), individuality (*pṛithaktva*), conjunction (*saṃyoga*), disjunction (*vibhāga*), priority (*paratva*), posteriority (*aparatva*), intellections (*buddhayaḥ*), pleasure (*sukha*), pain (*duḥkha*), desire (*iććhā*), aversion (*dvesha*), volitions (*prayatnāḥ*) are (the seventeen) qualities.

The commentator Śan·kara-miśra adds seven others, which, he says, are implied, though not mentioned, making twenty-four in all. They are:

Gravity (*gurutva*), fluidity (*dravatva*), viscidity (*sneha*), self-reproduction (*sanskāra*, implying—*a.* impetus as the cause of activity; *b.* elasticity; *c.* the faculty of memory), merit, demerit, and sound.

In point of fact the Nyāya goes more philosophically and more correctly than the other systems into the

---

[1] According to the Platonic school, substances (*οὐσίαι*) are ranged under two heads—*a. νοηταὶ καὶ ἀκίνητοι*; *b. αἰσθηταὶ καὶ ἐν κινήσει*: *a.* perceptible by the mind and immovable; *b.* perceptible by the senses and in motion. Aristotle, in his Metaphysics (XI. I), seems to divide substances into three classes—*a.* those that are cognizable by the mind, immovable, unchangeable, and eternal; *b.* those cognizable by the senses and eternal; *c.* those cognizable by the senses and subject to decay, as plants and animals. *Οὐσίαι δὲ τρεῖς· μία μὲν, αἰσθητή· ἧς ἡ μὲν ἀΐδιος, ἡ δὲ φθαρτὴ, ἣν πάντες ὁμολογοῦσιν, οἷον τὰ φυτὰ καὶ τὰ ζῶα· ἡ δ᾽ ἀΐδιος. Ἄλλη δὲ ἀκίνητος.* In another place (VII. 8) he defines substance as the essence or very nature of a thing (*τό τι ἦν εἶναι*). Again, in illustration (IV. 8), he says that whatever may be the cause of being is a substance, as soul in an animal (*ἡ ψυχὴ τῷ ζώῳ*); and again, as many inherent parts in anything as define and indicate *what it is*, e. g. superficies, a line, number, and that essence of which the formal cause (*ὁ λόγος*) is the definition; and, thirdly, he says that earth, fire, water, &c., and all bodies and all animals consisting of these are substances. See the Rev. J. H. M'Mahon's useful translation, published by Bohn.

qualities of all substances. The twenty-four which it enumerates may be regarded as separating into two classes, according as they are the sixteen qualities of material substances or the eight properties of soul. These eight are intellection, volition, desire, aversion, pleasure, pain, merit, and demerit.

The third category, *Karman*, 'act' or 'action,' is thus divided in Sūtra I. 1. 7:

Elevation (literally throwing upwards), depression (throwing downwards), contraction, dilatation, and going (or motion in general) are the (five kinds of) acts. [*Utkshepaṇam avakshepaṇam ākuñćanam prasāraṇam gamanam iti karmāṇi.*]

The fourth category, *Sāmānya*, 'generality,' is said to be twofold, viz. higher (*para*) and lower (*apara*); the first being 'simple existence,' applicable to genus; the second being 'substantiality,' applicable to species.

The fifth category, *Viśesha*, 'particularity,' belongs to the nine eternal substances of the first category, viz. soul, time, place, ether, and the five atoms of earth, water, light, air, and mind, all of which have an eternal ultimate difference, distinguishing each from the other.

The sixth category, *Samavāya*, 'co-inherence' or 'intimate relation,' is of only one kind. This relation appears to be that which exists between a substance and its qualities, between atoms and what is formed out of them, or between any object and the general idea connected with it, and is thought to be a real entity, very much in accordance with the Platonic realism of the Middle Ages. It is the relation between a jar and the earth which composes it, between a cloth and its threads, between the idea of round and any round thing, between a whole and its parts, between a genus or species and its individuals, between an act and its agent, between individuality and eternal substance.

In connection with this sixth category may be mentioned the Nyāya theory of causation. Sūtra I. 2. 1, 2 states—

From non-existence of cause (*kāraṇa*) is non-existence of effect (*kārya*), but there is not from non-existence of effect non-existence of cause.

In the Tarka-saṅgraha a cause is declared to be 'that which invariably precedes an effect which otherwise could not be,' and three kinds of causes are enumerated, viz.

*a.* Co-inherence cause, or that resulting from intimate and constant relation—perhaps best rendered by 'substantial cause' (*samavāyi-kāraṇa*), as threads are the substantial cause of cloth. This corresponds to the material cause of Aristotle. *b.* Non-substantial cause (*a-samavāyi-kāraṇa*), as the putting together of the threads is of cloth. This corresponds to the formal cause. *c.* Instrumental cause (*nimitta-kāraṇa*), as the weaver's tools, the loom, or the skill of the weaver himself, &c. are of cloth. This corresponds to the efficient cause[1].

As to the seventh category of non-existence or negation, four kinds are specified, viz.

*a.* Antecedent (or the non-existence of anything before it began to exist, as a jar not yet made). *b.* Cessation of existence (as of a jar when it is smashed to pieces). *c.* Mutual non-existence (as of a jar in cloth). *d.* Absolute non-existence (as of fire in a lake).

Without dwelling longer on the seven categories we

---

[1] Aristotle's four causes are—1. Material cause, i. e. the matter (ὕλη) from which anything is made, as marble of a statue, silver of a goblet. 2. Formal cause, i. e. the specific form or pattern according to which anything is made, as a drawing or plan is the formal cause of the building of a house. 3. Efficient cause, i. e. the origin of the principle of motion (ὅθεν ἡ ἀρχὴ τῆς κινήσεως), as the energy of a workman is the prime mover in producing any work. 4. Final cause, i. e. the purpose for which anything is made, the motive for its production, or the end served by its existence. According to Dr. Ballantyne (Lecture on the Nyāya, p. 23), Aristotle's final cause has a counterpart in the Naiyāyika's *prayojana*, i. e. motive, purpose, or use. The writer in Chambers' Cyclopaedia, under the head of 'Cause,' shows that these causes of Aristotle and the Nyāya should rather be called the aggregate of *conditions* necessary to the production of any work of man.

must briefly indicate how the views of the *Nyāya* and *Vaiśeshika*, as to the external world and the nature of soul, differ from those of the other systems. First, then, as to the formation of the world. This is supposed to be effected by the aggregation of *Aṇus* or 'atoms.' These are innumerable and eternal, and are eternally aggregated, disintegrated, and redintegrated by the power of Adṛishṭa. According to Kaṇāda's Sūtras (IV. 1) an atom is 'something existing, having no cause, eternal' (*sad akāraṇavan nityam*). They are, moreover, described as less than the least, invisible, intangible, indivisible, imperceptible by the senses; and—what is most noteworthy in distinguishing the Vaiśeshika system from others—as having each of them a *Viśesha* or eternal essence of its own. The combination of these atoms is first into an aggregate of two, called *Dvy-aṇuka*. Three of them, again, are supposed to combine into a *Trasa-reṇu*, which, like a mote in a sunbeam, has just sufficient magnitude to be perceptible [1].

According to Colebrooke's statement of the Vaiśeshika theory the following process is supposed to take place in the aggregation of atoms to form earth, water, light, and air:

Two earthly atoms concurring by an unseen peculiar virtue (*a-dṛishṭa*), or by the will of God, or by time, or by other competent cause, constitute a double atom of earth; and by concourse of three binary atoms a tertiary atom is produced, and by concourse of four triple atoms a quaternary atom, and so on to a gross, grosser, or grossest mass of earth; thus great

---

[1] The binary compound only differs from the single atom by number, and not by measure, size, or perceptibility. Both are infinitesimal, and, being joined, can only produce an infinitesimal result (like multiplied fractions). It is the tertiary compound which first introduces magnitude and causes measure, just as a jar's measure is caused by that of its two halves. See Professor Cowell's translation of the Kusumāñjali, p. 66.

earth is produced; and in like manner great water from aqueous atoms, great light from luminous, and great air from aerial[1].

From the Tarka-saṅgraha we may continue the account thus:

*a.* Earth possesses the property of odour, which is its distinguishing quality. It is of two kinds, eternal and non-eternal—eternal in the form of atoms (*paramāṇu-rūpā*), non-eternal in the form of products (*kārya-rūpā*). The non-eternal character of aggregated earth is shown by the want of permanence in a jar when crushed to powder. When aggregated it is of three kinds, organized body (*śarīra*), organ of sense (*indriya*), and unorganic mass (*vishaya*). The organ connected with it is the nose or sense of smell (*ghrāṇa*), which is the recipient of odour. *b.* Water possesses the property of being cool to the touch. It is also of two kinds, eternal and non-eternal, as before. Its organ is the tongue or taste (*rasana*), the recipient of savour, which is one of the qualities of water.

---

[1] As these Lectures were delivered before classical scholars I thought it superfluous, at the time of their delivery, to indicate all the obvious points of comparison between Indian and European systems. Reference might here, however, be made to the doctrines of Epicurus, especially as expounded by Lucretius, who begins his description of the coalescing of atoms or primordial seeds to form the world and various material objects thus:

'Nunc age, quo motu genitalia materiai
Corpora res varias gignant, genitasque resolvant
Et qua vi facere id cogantur, quaeve sit ollis
Reddita mobilitas magnum per inane meandi
Expediam.' (II. 61–64.)

Nearly the whole of the second book of Lucretius might be quoted. It is full of interest in connection with the Vaiśeshika system. Cicero's criticisms on the Epicurean theory are also interesting in relation to this subject. In his De Natura Deorum (II. 37) he says, 'If a concourse of atoms could produce a world (*quod si mundum efficere potest concursus atomorum*), why not also a portico, a temple, a house, a city, which are much less difficult to form?' We might even be tempted to contrast some of the discoveries of modern chemists and physicists with the crude but shrewd ideas of Indian philosophers prosecuting their investigations more than 2000 years ago without the aids and appliances now at every one's command.

*c.* Light is distinguished by being hot to the feel[1]. It is similarly of two kinds, and its organ is the eye (*ćakshus*), the recipient of colour or form, which is its principal quality. *d.* Air is distinguished by being sensible to the touch. It is similarly of two kinds, and is colourless. Its organ is the skin (*tvać*), the percipient of tangibility. *e.* Ether is the substratum of the quality of sound. It is eternal, one, and all-pervading. Its organ is the ear (*śrotra*), the recipient of sound[2].

The great commentator Śaṅkarāćārya (quoted by Professor Banerjea, p. 62) states the process thus:

'At the time of creation action is produced in aerial atoms, which is dependent on A-dṛishṭa. That action joins its own atom with another. Then from binaries, by gradual steps, is produced the air. The same is the case with fire. The same with water. The same with earth. The same with organized bodies[3]. Thus is the whole universe produced from atoms[4].'

With regard to the question whether God or the supreme Soul is to be regarded as having taken part in the bringing together and arranging of these atoms, it should be noted that although the name of *Iśvara* is

---

[1] Light and heat are regarded by Naiyāyikas as one and the same substance. Curiously enough, gold is described as mineral (*ākara-ja*) light.

[2] Professor H. H. Wilson has observed (Sāṅkhya-kārikā, p. 122) that something like the Hindū notion of the senses and the elements partaking of a common nature is expressed in the dictum of Empedocles:

Γαίῃ μὲν γὰρ γαῖαν ὀπώπαμεν, ὕδατι δ' ὕδωρ,
Αἰθέρι δ' αἰθέρα δῖαν, ἀτὰρ πυρὶ πῦρ ἀΐδηλον.

'By the earthy element we perceive earth; by the watery, water; by the aerial element, the air of heaven; and by the element of fire, devouring fire.' Plato, Repub. VI. 18, has the following: Ἀλλ' ἡλιοειδέστατόν γε οἶμαι τῶν περὶ τὰς αἰσθήσεις ὀργάνων, 'I regard it (the eye) as of all the organs of sense possessing most likeness to the sun.' See Muir's Texts V. 298.

[3] In Manu (I. 75–78) and the Sāṅkhya and the Vedānta the order of the elements is ether, air, light or fire, water, and earth. See p. 93.

[4] Compare Cicero, De Natura Deorum II. 33, 'Since there are four sorts of elements, the continuance of the world is caused by their reciprocal action and changes (*vicissitudine*). For from the earth comes water; from water arises air; from air, ether; and then conversely in regular order backwards, from ether, air; from air, water; from water, earth, the lowest element.

introduced once into Gotama's Sūtras[1], it is not found in Kaṇāda's[2]. Probably the belief of both was that the formation of the world was simply the result of *Adṛishṭa*, or 'the unseen force, which is derived from the works or acts of a previous world,' and which becomes in Hindū philosophy a kind of god, if not the only god (see p. 69). Later Naiyāyika writers, however, affirm the existence of a supreme Soul, *Paramātman*, distinct from the *Jīvātman*, or 'human soul;' and this supreme Soul is described as eternal, immutable, omniscient, without form, all-pervading, all-powerful, and, moreover, as the framer of the universe.

Thus the Tarka-saṅgraha states (Ballantyne, p. 12):

The seat of knowledge is the soul (*ātman*). It is twofold, the living soul (*jīvātman*) and the supreme soul (*paramātman*). The supreme soul is lord, omniscient, one only, subject to neither pleasure nor pain, infinite and eternal.

Indeed the Nyāya is held by some to be the stronghold of Theism.

As to the living individual souls of corporeal beings, the Nyāya view is that they are eternal, manifold[3],

---

[1] The Sūtra is IV. 5. 19, and is as follows. Some one suggests, 'God is the (sole) cause, because we see that the acts of men are occasionally unattended by their fruits' (*īśvaraḥ kāraṇam purusha-karmāphalya-darśanāt*). The next Aphorism is an answer to this suggestion, and seems to assert that God was *not* the cause of the universe; thus, 'Not so, because in the absence of men's acts the fruit is not produced.' The next Aphorism runs thus: 'It (man's agency?) is not the (sole) cause, because that is caused by that.' The word 'sole,' however, is introduced by the commentator, and all three Aphorisms seem designedly obscure.

[2] According to Banerjea, p. 62; but the commentators say it is implied in the third Sūtra.

[3] According to the Vaiśeshika-sūtra III. 2. 20, *Vyavasthāto nānā*, 'because of its circumstances (or conditions), soul is manifold.' The commentator adds, 'Circumstances are the several conditions; as, one is rich, another mean; one is happy, another unhappy; one is of high, another of low birth; one is learned, another reads badly. These circumstances evincé a diversity and plurality of souls.'

eternally separate from each other and distinct from the body, senses, and mind, yet capable of apprehension, volition (or effort), desire, aversion, pleasure, pain, merit, and demerit.

In the Vaiśeshika Aphorisms (III. 2. 4) other characteristic signs (*lingāni*) of the living soul are given, such as the opening and shutting of the eyes, the motions of the mind and especially life[1]. The commentator, in commenting upon this, describes the soul as the 'governor or superintendent over the body.' Here is the passage (Gough, p. 110):

> Vitality is a mark of the existence of the soul; for by the word 'life' the effects of vitality, such as growth, the healing of wounds and bruises, are implied. For as the owner of a house builds up the broken edifice or enlarges a building which is too small, so the ruler of the body effects by food, &c., the increase and enlargement of the body, which is to him in the stead of a habitation, and with medicine and the like causes what is wounded to grow again and mutilated hands or feet to heal. Thus a superintendent of the body (*dehasya adhishṭhātā*) is proved like a master of a house.

It should be added that souls are held to be infinite, ubiquitous, and *diffused everywhere throughout space*, so that a man's soul is as much in England as in Calcutta, though it can only apprehend and feel and act where the body happens to be.

The Nyāya idea of the mind or internal organ (*Manas*) is that it, like the soul, is a Dravya or 'eternal substance.' Instead, however, of being diffused everywhere like the soul, it is atomic, like earth, water, fire, and air. Indeed, if it were infinite, like the soul, it might be united with all subjects at once, and all apprehensions might be contemporaneous, which is impossible. It is therefore regarded as a mere atom or atomic inlet to the soul, not allowing

---

[1] Plato (Phaedrus 52) defines soul as τὸ αὐτὸ αὑτὸ κινοῦν, quoted by Cicero, Tusc. Quaest. I. 23.

the latter to receive more than one thought or conception at a time. So in Nyāya-sūtra I. 3. 16, and in Vaiśeshika VIII. 1. 22, 23, it is affirmed as follows:

'The characteristic of the mind is that it does not give rise to more than one notion simultaneously.' 'Ether, in consequence of its universal pervasion, is infinitely great, and so likewise is soul. In consequence of non-existence of that universal pervasion, the internal organ (mind) is an atom [1].'

In regard to the authority to be accorded to the Veda, the views of the Nyāya appear by no means unorthodox. Gautama, in his Aphorisms (II. 58–60, 68), declares plainly that the Veda is not false, that it is not chargeable either with self-contradiction or tautology, and that it is an instrument of true knowledge. Similarly, the third Aphorism of Kaṇāda may be regarded as a kind of confession of faith in the Veda, intended apparently, like that of Gautama, to counteract imputations of heterodoxy.

In further proof of the Theism claimed for the Nyāya I here give a short passage from the Kusumāñjali, a Naiyāyika treatise by Udayana Āćārya, which will serve as a specimen of the sort of arguments employed to prove the existence of a personal God (Īśvara) in opposition to atheistical objectors. This work has been ably edited and translated by Professor E. B. Cowell [2]. The following is merely the opening of the fifth chapter, with a portion of Hari-dāsa's comment:

An omniscient and indestructible Being is to be proved from the existence of effects, from the combination of atoms, from the support of the

---

[1] The theory propounded by Lucretius was that the mind is composed of exceedingly subtle atoms; he says (III. 180) of it, 'Esse aio persubtilem atque minutis Perquam corporibus factum constare.' As to ether, see note 2, p. 93.

[2] I have referred to his edition and to Dr. Muir's extracts in the appendix to the third volume of his Texts.

earth in the sky, from traditional arts, from belief in revelation, from the Veda, from its sentences, and from particular numbers.

Comment: The earth must have had a maker, because it is an effect like a jar. Combination is an action, and therefore the action which produced the conjunction of two atoms at the beginning of a creation must have been accompanied by the volition of an intelligent being. Again, the world depends upon some being who wills to hinder it from falling, like a stick supported by a bird in the air. Again, the traditional arts (*pada*) now current, as that of making cloth, &c., must have proceeded from an independent being. Again, the knowledge derived from the Veda is derived from a virtue residing in its cause, because it is true knowledge[1], (this virtue consisting in the Veda's being uttered by a fit person, and therefore necessarily implying a personal inspirer.)

From this brief statement of the distinctive features of the Nyāya school it is clear that this system, at least in its Vaiśeshika cosmogony, is dualistic in the sense of assuming the existence of gross material *eternal atoms*, side by side either with *eternal souls* or with the supreme Soul of the universe. It sets itself against any theory which would make an impure and evil world spring from a pure and perfect spirit. Nor does it undertake to decide positively what it cannot prove dialectically,—the precise relation between soul and matter.

---

[1] Those who wish to pursue the argument should consult Professor Cowell's translation. It is interesting to compare Cicero, De Natura Deorum (II. 34): 'But if all the parts of the universe are so constituted that they could not be better for use or more beautiful in appearance, let us consider whether they could have been put together by chance or whether their condition is such that they could not even cohere unless divine wisdom and providence had directed them (*nisi sensu moderante divinâque providentiâ*).'

# LECTURE V.

## *The Sāṅkhya.*

THE Sāṅ-khya[1] philosophy, though possibly prior in date, is generally studied next to the Nyāya, and is more peremptorily and categorically dualistic (*dvaita-vādin*). It utterly repudiates the notion that impure matter can originate from pure spirit, and, of course, denies that anything can be produced out of nothing.

The following are Aphorisms, I. 78, 114–117, propounding its doctrine of evolution, which may not be altogether unworthy of the attention of Darwinians:

There cannot be the production of something out of nothing (*nāvas-tuno vastu-siddhiḥ*); that which is not cannot be developed into that which is. The production of what does not already exist (potentially) is

---

[1] Kapila, the reputed founder of this school (sometimes fabled as a son of Brahmā, sometimes as an incarnation of Vishṇu and identified with the sage described in the Rāmāyaṇa as the destroyer of the sixty thousand sons of Sagara, who in their search for their father's horse disturbed his devotions), was probably a Brāhman, though nothing is known about him. See Mahā-bhārata XII. 13703. The word *Kapila* means 'of a tawny brown colour,' and may possibly have been applied as a nickname, like Aksha-pāda and Kaṇāda. He is the supposed author of two works, viz. *a.* the original Sāṅ-khya Sūtras, sometimes called *Sāṅ-khya-pravaćana*, comprising 526 aphorisms in six books; *b.* a short work called the Tattva-samāsa or 'Compendium of Principles' (translated by Dr. Ballantyne). The original Sūtras are of course accompanied with abundant commentaries, of which one of the best known is the Sāṅ-khya-pravaćana-bhāshya, by Vijñāna-bhikshu, edited with an able and interesting preface by Dr. Fitz-Edward Hall. A very useful and popular compendium of the doctrines of this system, called the Sāṅ-khya-kārikā, was edited and translated by Professor H. H. Wilson.

impossible, like a horn on a man (*nāsad-utpādo nṛi-śṛiṅgavat*); because there must of necessity be a material out of which a product is developed; and because everything cannot occur everywhere at all times (*sarvatra sarvadā sarvāsambhavāt*); and because anything possible must be produced from something competent to produce it[1].

'Thus,' remarks a commentator, 'curds come from milk, not water. A potter produces a jar from clay, not from cloth. Production is only manifestation of what previously existed.' Aphorism 121 adds, 'Destruction is a resolution of anything into its cause.'

In the Sāṅkhya, therefore, instead of an analytical inquiry into the universe as actually existing, arranged under topics and categories, we have a synthetical system propounded, starting from an original primordial *tattva* or 'eternally existing essence[2],' called *Prakṛiti* (a word meaning 'that which evolves or produces everything else').

---

[1] See the note on the dogma *Ex nihilo nihil fit*, p. 63. We are also here reminded of Lucretius I. 160, &c.:

> *Nam si de Nihilo fierent ex omnibu' rebus*
> *Omne genus nasci posset; nil semine egeret;*
> *E mare primum homines, e terrâ posset oriri*
> *Squammigerum genus et volucres; erumpere caelo*
> *Armenta, atque aliae pecudes: genus omne ferarum*
> *Incerto partu culta ac deserta teneret:*
> *Nec fructus iidem arboribus constare solerent,*
> *Sed mutarentur: ferre omnes omnia possent.*

'If things proceed from nothing, everything might spring from everything, and nothing would require a seed. Men might arise first from the sea, and fish and birds from the earth, and flocks and herds break into being from the sky; every kind of beast might be produced at random in cultivated places or deserts. The same fruits would not grow on the same trees, but would be changed. All things would be able to produce all things.'

[2] It is usual to translate *tat-tva*, 'that-ness,' by 'principle;' but such words as 'essence,' 'entity,' and in some cases even 'substance,' seem to convey a more definite idea of its meaning. It corresponds to the barbarous term 'quiddity' (from *quid est?*), discarded by Locke and modern English philosophers. Certainly 'nature' is anything but a good equivalent for *Prakṛiti*, which denotes something very different from matter

It is described by Kapila in his sixty-seventh Aphorism as 'a rootless root[1],' *amūlam mūlam*, thus:

From the absence of a root in the root, the root (of all things) is rootless.

Then he continues in his sixty-eighth Aphorism:

Even if there be a succession of causes (one before the other) there must be a halt at some one point; and so Prakṛiti is only a name for the primal source (of all productions).

Beginning, then, with this original eternal germ or element, the Sān·khya reckons up synthetically, whence its name of 'Synthetic enumeration[2],' twenty-three other

---

or even the germ of mere material substances. It is an intensely subtle original essence wholly distinct from soul, yet capable of evolving out of itself consciousness and mind as well as the whole visible world. *Prakaroti iti prakṛiti* is given as its derivation in the Sarva-darśana-sangraha, p. 147, where *pra* seems to stand for 'forth,' not 'before.' The commentator on the Sān·khya-kārikā (p. 4) uses the word *padārtha* as applicable to all the twenty-five Tattvas. A Vedāntist would not regard *tat-tva* as an abstract noun from *tat*, 'that,' but would say it meant 'truth,' and in its etymology contained the essence of truth, viz. *tat tvam*, 'that art thou.'

[1] In a passage in the Timaeus (34) Plato propounds a theory of creation in allegorical and not very intelligible language, which the reader can compare with the Sān·khyan view: Ἐν δ' οὖν τῷ παρόντι χρὴ γένη διανοηθῆναι τριττά, τὸ μὲν γιγνόμενον, τὸ δ' ἐν ᾧ γίγνεται τὸ δ' ὅθεν ἀφομοιούμενον φύεται τὸ γιγνόμενον. καὶ δὴ καὶ προσεικάσαι πρέπει τὸ μὲν δεχόμενον μητρί, τὸ δ' ὅθεν πατρί, τὴν δὲ μεταξὺ τούτων φύσιν ἐκγόνῳ. διὸ δὴ τὴν τοῦ γεγονότος ὁρατοῦ καὶ πάντως αἰσθητοῦ μητέρα καὶ ὑποδοχὴν μήτε γῆν μήτε ἀέρα μήτε πῦρ μήτε ὕδωρ λέγωμεν, μήτε ὅσα ἐκ τούτων μήτε ἐξ ὧν ταῦτα γέγονεν· ἀλλ' ἀνόρατον εἶδός τι καὶ ἄμορφον, πανδεχές. 'For the present, therefore, we ought to consider three things, that which is produced, that in which it is produced, and that from which a thing is produced, having a natural resemblance. And especially it is proper to compare that which receives to the mother, that from which it receives to the father, and the nature which is between these to the child. Then, as to this mother and receptacle of things created which are visible and altogether perceptible, we cannot term it either earth, air, fire, or water, nor any one of their compounds, nor any of the elements from which they were produced, but a certain invisible and shapeless essence, which receives all things,' &c. Compare note 3, p. 62.

[2] Hence Sir W. Jones called the Sān·khya the Numeral philosophy. It

Tattvas or 'entities,' which are all productions of the first, evolving themselves out of it as naturally and spontaneously as cream out of milk or milk out of a cow.

The twenty-fifth entity is *Purusha,* 'the soul,' which is neither producer nor produced, but eternal, like Prakṛiti. It is quite distinct from the producing or produced elements and creations of the phenomenal world, though liable to be brought into connection with them. In fact, the object of the Sāṅkhya system is to effect the liberation of the soul from the fetters in which it is involved by union with Prakṛiti. It does this by conveying the Pramā or 'correct knowledge' of the twenty-four constituent principles of creation, and rightly discriminating the soul from them; its *Pramāṇas,* or 'means of obtaining the correct measure of existing things,' being reduced from four (see p. 72) to three, viz. *Drishṭa, Anumāna,* and *Āpta-vaćana,* 'perception by the senses, inference, and credible assertion or trustworthy testimony.'

The third Aphorism of the Sāṅkhya-kārikā thus reckons up the catalogue of all existing entities:

> The root and substance of all things (except soul) is Prakṛiti. It is no production. Seven things produced by it are also producers. Thence come sixteen productions. Soul, the twenty-fifth essence, is neither a production nor producer.

Hence it appears that from an original *Prakṛiti* (variously called *Mūla-prakṛiti,* 'root-principle;' *Amūlam mūlam,* 'rootless root;' *Pradhāna,* 'chief one;' *A-vyakta,* 'unevolved evolver;' *Brahman,* 'supreme;' *Māyā,* 'power of illusion[1]'), seven other producers are evolved, and as so evolved are regarded as Vikāras or 'productions.' The first production of the original producer is *Buddhi,* commonly

---

has been compared partly with the metaphysics of Pythagoras, partly (in its Yoga) with the system of Zeno; also with that of Berkeley.

[1] According to Gauḍapāda's commentary on Sāṅkhya-kārikā, 22.

called 'intellect or intellectual perception' (and variously termed *Mahat*, from its being the *Great* source of the two other internal faculties, Ahaṅkāra and Manas or 'self-consciousness and mind'). Third in order comes this *Ahaṅkāra*, the 'I-making' faculty, that is, self-consciousness or the sense of individuality (sometimes conveniently termed 'Ego-ism'), which produces the next five principles, called *Tanmātras* or 'subtle elementary particles,' out of which the grosser elements (*Mahā-bhūta*) are evolved [1]. These eight constitute the producers.

Then follow the sixteen that are productions only; and first in order, as produced by the *Tanmātras*, come the five grosser elements already mentioned, viz.

a. *Ākāśa* [2], 'ether,' with the distinguishing property of sound, or, in other words, the substratum of sound (which sound is the *vishaya* or object for a corresponding organ of sense, the ear). b. *Vāyu*, 'air,' with the property of tangibility (which is the *vishaya* for the skin). c. *Tejas* or *jyotis*, 'fire or light,' with the property of form or colour (which is the *vishaya* for the eye). d. *Apas*, 'water,' with the property of savour or taste (which is the *vishaya* for the tongue). e. *Pṛithivī* or *bhūmi*, 'earth,' with the property of odour or smell (which is the *vishaya* for the nose).

Each of these elements after the first has also the property or properties of the preceding besides its own.

---

[1] These Tanmātras appear nearly to correspond to the πρῶτα στοιχεῖα of Plato (Theaet. 139), or rather to the στοιχεῖα στοιχείων, 'elements of elements' (Theaet. 142), and to the ῥιζώματα of Empedocles.

[2] Ākāśa, as shown elsewhere (see p. 115, note 3), must not be exactly identified with the modern 'ether,' though this word is usually taken as its nearest possible equivalent. In some of its properties and functions it more corresponds with the *inane*, 'vacant space,' of Lucretius. *Quapropter locus est intactus Inane, vacansque* (I. 335). At any rate, one synonym of *ākāśa is śūnya*. Cicero, De Nat. Deorum II. 40, seems to identify *ether* with sky or space, which stretches to the remotest point and surrounds all things. The Rāmāyaṇa, II. 110. 5, makes Brahmā spring from ether, but the Epic and Purānic accounts of ākāśa are very inconsistent. Some say that it was created and is perishable, others that

Next follow the eleven organs produced, like the Tanmātras, by the third producer, Ahan·kāra, viz. the five organs of sense, the five organs of action [1], and an eleventh organ standing between these two sets, called *Manas*, 'the mind,' which is an internal organ of perception, volition, and action.

The eight producers, then, with the five grosser elements, ether, air, fire, water, earth, and with the eleven organs, constitute the true elements and constituent substances of the phenomenal world. As, however, the most important of the producers, after the mere unintelligent original germ, is the third, called *Ahan·kāra*, 'self-consciousness or individuality,' it is scarcely too much to maintain that, according to the Sān·khya view, the whole world of sense is practically created by the individual Ego [2], who is, nevertheless, quite distinct from the soul, as this soul is supposed to possess in itself no real consciousness of separate individuality, though deluded by it.

It should also be noted that, according to the Sān·khya theory, Prakṛiti, though a subtle elementary essence, is yet to be regarded as consisting of three ingredients or constituent principles in equipoise, called Guṇas. These are *Sattva*, *Rajas*, and *Tamas*, 'goodness or purity, passion or activity, and darkness or ignorance.'

Thus Kapila (Aphorism 61) affirms as follows:

Prakṛiti is the state of equipoise (*Sāmyāvasthā*) of goodness, passion, and darkness.

---

it was not created and is eternal. See Muir's Texts IV. 119, Mahā-bhārata XII. 6132.

[1] The five organs of sense or perception (*buddhīndriyāṇi*) are, ear, skin, eye, nose, tongue; those of action (*karmendriyāṇi*) are, larynx, hand, foot, and the excretory and generative organs.

[2] This idea of personal individual creation is what chiefly distinguishes the Sāṅkhya from the pantheism of the Vedānta, which denies all real personal individuality. It has also led to the Sān·khya system being compared to the theory of Berkeley.

Evidently, then, these three constituents of the primal elementary germ are really themselves elementary substances, and not qualities, although they are called Guṇas and although such expressions as goodness, purity, &c. convey more the notion of a quality than of any actual substance. According to the Sāṅkhya-pravaćana-bhāshya:

> These Guṇas are not like the 'qualities' of the Vaiśeshika. They are substances possessing themselves qualities or properties, such as conjunction, disjunction, lightness, motion, weight, &c. The word Guṇa, therefore, is employed because these three substances form the triple cord by which the soul, like an animal (*purusha-paśu*), is bound[1].

It is plain, indeed, that as one meaning of the word Guṇa is 'rope' or 'cord,' the Sāṅkhya three Guṇas may be supposed to act like a triple-stranded rope, binding and confining souls in different degrees[2]. In point of fact, goodness, passion, and darkness are imagined to be the actual substances of which Prakṛiti is constituted, just as trees are the constituents of a forest. Moreover, as they are the ingredients of Prakṛiti, so they make up the whole world of sense evolved out of Prakṛiti. Except, however, in the case of the original producer, they are not conjoined in equal quantities. They form component parts of everything evolved, but in varying proportions, one or other being in excess. In other words, they affect everything in creation unequally; and as they affect man, make him divine and noble, thoroughly human and selfish, or bestial and ignorant, according to the predominance of goodness,

---

[1] Aristotle (Metaph. I. 3) describes primordial substance as undergoing changes through different affections, something after the manner of the Sāṅkhya Guṇas. See note 3, p. 62.

[2] Manu states the doctrine of the three Guṇas very similarly (XII. 24, 25, &c.): 'One should know that the three Guṇas (bonds or fetters) of the soul are goodness, passion, and darkness; (bound) by one or more of these, it continues incessantly attached to forms of existence. Whenever any one of the three Guṇas predominates wholly in a body, it makes the embodied spirit abound in that Guṇa.'

passion, or darkness respectively. The soul, on the other hand, though bound by the Guṇas, is itself wholly and entirely free from such constituent ingredients (*nir-guṇa*). It stands twenty-fifth in the catalogue of Tattvas, and is to be wholly distinguished from the creations evolved by the three evolvers, *Prakṛiti*, *Buddhi*, and *Ahaṅkāra*. It has, in short, nothing whatever in common with the world-evolver, Prakṛiti, except eternal existence.

But although *Prakṛiti* is the sole originator of creation, yet, according to the pure Sāṅkhya, it does not create for itself, but rather for each individual soul which comes into connection or juxtaposition with it, like a crystal vase with a flower. Souls, indeed, exist eternally separate from each other and from the world-evolver Prakṛiti; and with whatever form of body they may be joined, they are held to be all intrinsically equal, and each retains its individuality, remaining one and unchanged through all transmigrations[1]. But each separate soul is a witness of the act of creation without participating in the act. It is a looker on, uniting itself with unintelligent *Prakṛiti*, as a lame man mounted on a blind man's shoulders, for the sake of observing and contemplating the phenomena of creation, which *Prakṛiti* herself is unable to observe. In the Sāṅkhya-kārikā (19) we read:

> The soul is witness, solitary, bystander, spectator, and passive. For its contemplation of *Prakṛiti* the union of both takes place, as of the halt and blind; by that union a creation is formed.

It appears, too, that all Prakṛiti's performances are

---

[1] This *separate* eternal existence of innumerable individual souls is the great feature distinguishing the Nyāya and Sāṅkhya from the Vedānta, which holds the oneness of all soul. And yet it would seem that each soul must be regarded as universally diffused both in Sāṅkhya and Nyāya (see p. 86); for unless the soul is all-pervading it cannot be eternal. All Hindūs hold that nothing can be eternal that is divisible into parts; and all things have parts except the infinite (soul) and the infinitesimal (atoms).

solely for the benefit of soul, who receives her favours ungratefully. Thus, in the Sān·khya-kārikā 59, 60, we have the following:

As a female dancer, having exhibited herself to a spectator, desists from the dance, so does Prakṛiti desist, having manifested herself to soul. By various means Prakṛiti, endowed with qualities (*guṇavat*), acting as a benefactress, accomplishes without profit to herself the purpose of soul, who is devoid of qualities (*aguṇa*) and makes no return of benefit.

In fact, Prakṛiti is sometimes reproached with boldness in exposing herself to the gaze of soul, who takes no interest whatever in the sight. There is something to a European mind very unreal, cloudy, and unpractical in all this. Certainly no one can doubt that the Sān·khya view of the soul is inferior to that of the Nyāya, which ascribes to it, when joined to mind, activity, volition, thought, and feeling (see p. 86). Obviously, too, its view of all existing things is even more atheistical than that of the earliest Naiyāyikas. For if the creation produced by the Evolver, Prakṛiti, has an existence of its own independent of all connection with the particular Purusha to which it is joined, there can be no need for an intelligent Creator of the world or even of any superintending power [1].

Here are two or three of Kapila's Aphorisms bearing upon the charge of atheism brought against him. An objection is made that some of his definitions are inconsistent with the supposed existence of a supreme Lord (*Īśvara*). To this he replies in the ninety-second and following Aphorisms, thus:

(They are not inconsistent) because the existence of a supreme Lord is unproved (*Īśvarāsiddheḥ*). Since he could not be either free (from desires and anxieties) or bound by troubles of any kind, there can be no proof of his existence. Either way he could not be effective of any

---

[1] I presume this is the reason why in a catalogue of MSS. just edited by Rājendralāl Mitra the Sān·khya is styled the Hylotheistic philosophy.

creation. (That is, if he were free from anxieties he could have no wish to create; and if he were bound by desires of any kind, he would then be under bondage, and therefore deficient in power.)

The commentary of Gauḍa-pāda on Sān·khya-kārikā 61 ought, however, to be here quoted:

The Sān·khya teachers say, 'How can beings composed of the three Guṇas proceed from Īśvara (God), who is devoid of Guṇas? Or how can they proceed from soul, equally devoid of qualities? Therefore they must proceed from Prakṛiti. Thus from white threads white cloth is produced; from black threads, black cloth;' and so from Prakṛiti, composed of the three Guṇas, the three worlds composed of the three Guṇas are produced. God (Īśvara) is free from Guṇas. The production of the three worlds composed of the Guṇas from him would be an inconsistency.

Again, with reference to the soul, we have the following in Kapila's ninety-sixth Aphorism:

'There is a ruling influence of the soul (over Prakṛiti) caused by their proximity, just as the loadstone (draws iron to itself).' That is, the proximity of soul to Prakṛiti impels the latter to go through the steps of production. This sort of attraction between the two leads to creation, but in no other sense is soul an agent or concerned in creation at all[1].

Notwithstanding these atheistical tendencies, the Sān·khya evades the charge of unorthodoxy by a confession of faith in the Veda. Hence in Aphorism 98 we have—

The declaration of the meaning of the texts of the Veda is an authority, since the author of them knew the established truth.

And it should be noted that some adherents of the Sān·khya maintain the existence of a supreme Soul[2], called

---

[1] It is stated in Kapila's fifty-eighth Aphorism, quoted by Dr. Ballantyne, that the bondage of the soul caused by its union with Prakṛiti is after all merely nominal, and not real, because it resides in the mind, and not in the soul itself (*vān·mātraṃ na tu tattvaṃ ćitta-sthiteḥ*). See Mullens' Essay, p. 183.

[2] Or, according to Professor E. B. Cowell, 'personified Sum of existence.' Elphinstone's India, p. 126, note.

Hiraṇya-garbha, and of a general ideal phenomenal universe with which that supreme Soul is connected and into which all the subcreations of inferior souls are by him gathered. Nor can it be affirmed that the Sāṅkhya proper commits itself to a positive denial of the existence of a supreme Being, so much as to an ignoring of what the founder of the school believed to be incapable of dialectic demonstration. As, however, the original World-evolver only evolves the world for the sake of the spectator, soul, this is practically an admission that there can be no realization of creation without the union of Prakṛiti with Purusha, the personal soul. In all probability Kapila's own idea was that every Purusha, though he did not himself create, had his own creation and his own created universe comprehended in his own person[1]. It may easily be supposed that this union of Purusha and Prakṛiti began soon to be compared to that of male and female; and it may be conjectured that the idea of the production of the universe by the male and female principles associating together, which was symbolized by the Ardha-nārī form of Śiva, and which lies at the root of the whole later mythology of India, was derived mainly from the Sāṅkhya philosophy.

It was not indeed to be expected that the uneducated masses could make anything of a metaphysical mysticism which could not be explained to them in intelligible language. How could they form any notion of a primordial eternal energy evolving out of itself twenty-three other elements or substances to form a visible world for the soul, described as apathetic, inactive, devoid of all qualities, and a mere indifferent spectator, though in close contact

[1] Something after the manner of Berkeley, who held that the 'without' was all within, though he believed in the real existence of external objects produced by other minds and wills.

with the individual Evolver and deluded by its self-consciousness? But they could well understand the idea of a universe proceeding from Prakṛiti and Purusha as from mother and father. Indeed the idea of a union between the female principle, regarded as an energy, and the male principle, is of great antiquity in Hindū systems of cosmogony. In the Ṛig-veda and Brāhmaṇas there are various allusions, as we have already seen, to a supposed union of Earth and Heaven, who together produce men, gods, and all creatures [1].

Buddhism, moreover, which represented many of the more popular philosophical ideas of the Hindūs perhaps as early as the sixth century B.C., has more in common with the Sān-khya philosophy than with any of the other systems.

Even the cosmogony of Manu, although a compound of various theories, presents a process of evolution very similar, as we shall see hereafter, to that of the Sān-khya.

Again, the antiquity and prevalence of Sān-khyan ideas is proved by the frequent allusions to them in the great Indian epic poem, called Mahā-bhārata [2]; and the permanence of their popularity till at least the first century of our era is indicated by the fact that the celebrated philosophical poem called Bhagavad-gītā attempts to reconcile the Sān-khya with Vedāntist views [3].

Perhaps, however, the extensive prevalence of Sān-khyan

---

[1] See Muir's Texts, vol. v. pp. 22, 23.

[2] In the Sabhā-parvan (Muir, vol. iv. p. 173) Kṛishṇa is described as undeveloped Prakṛiti, the eternal creator (*esha prakṛitir a-vyaktā kartā ćaiva sanātanaḥ*). On the other hand, in the Vana-parvan (1622, &c., Muir, vol. iv. p. 195) the god S'iva is declared to be the cause of the causes of the world (*loka-kāraṇa-kāraṇam*), and therefore superior and antecedent to Pradhāna and Purusha. Again, in S'ānti-parvan 12725, 12737, 13041, &c., the sons of Brahmā are called Prakṛitayaḥ.

[3] See Lecture VII on the Eclectic School and Bhagavad-gītā.

ideas in India is best shown by the later cosmogony and mythology. In those repositories of the popular Hindū creed, the Purāṇas and Tantras, Prakṛiti becomes a real Mother of the universe. It is true that in some of the Purāṇas there is occasional confusion and perversion of Sān-khyan doctrines. Thus, for example, in the Vishṇu-purāṇa I. 2. 22, we have the following:

'There was neither day nor night, neither sky nor earth; there was neither darkness nor light nor anything else. There was then the One, Brahma, the Male, possessing the character of Pradhāna (*prādhānika*)[1].' And further on: 'The principles or elements, commencing with Mahat, presided over by Purusha and under the influence of Pradhāna, generated an egg, which became the receptacle of Vishṇu in the form of Brahmā.'

But generally in the later mythology, especially as represented by the Tantras, the Sān-khya principle of Prakṛiti takes the form of female personifications, who are thought of as the wives or creative female energies of the principal male deities, to whom, on the other hand, the name Purusha, in the sense of the supreme Soul or the supreme Male, is sometimes applied[2]. This is especially the case with the Śakti or female energy of Śiva, worshipped by a vast number of persons as the true *Jagadambā*, or 'Mother of the universe.'

These proofs of the ancient popularity of the Sān-khya and its influence on the later mythology may help us to understand that, although in modern times there are comparatively few students of the Sān-khya among the Paṇḍits of India, there is still a common saying current everywhere (which will be found in Mahā-bhārata, Śānti-parvan, 11676), *Nāsti Sān-khya-samaṃ jñānaṃ nāsti Yoga-samam balam*, 'there is no knowledge equal to the Sān-khya and no power equal to the Yoga.'

---

[1] Compare the Ṛig-veda hymn, translated at p. 22 of this book.

[2] Vishṇu or Kṛishṇa is called Purushottama, and the name Purusha is equally given to Brahmā and Śiva.

## *The Yoga.*

The Yoga, commonly regarded as a branch of the Sān-khya, is scarcely worthy of the name of a system of philosophy, though it has undoubted charms for the naturally contemplative and ascetical Hindū, and lays claim to greater orthodoxy than the Sankhya proper by directly acknowledging the existence of Īśvara or a supreme Being[1]. In fact, the aim of the Yoga is to teach the means by which the human soul may attain complete union with the supreme Soul. This fusion (*laya*) or union of individual with universal spirit may be effected even in the body. According to Patañjali, the author of the system, the very word *Yoga* is interpreted to mean the act of 'fixing or concentrating the mind in abstract meditation,' and this is said to be effected by preventing the modifications of *Ćitta* or the thinking principle [which modifications arise through the three Pramāṇas, perception, inference, and verbal testimony, as well as through incorrect ascertainment, fancy, sleep, and recollection], by the constant habit (*abhyāsa*) of keeping the mind in its unmodified state—a state clear as crystal when uncoloured by contact with other substances—and by the practice of *Vairāgya*—that is, complete suppression of the passions. This *Vairāgya* is only to be obtained by *Īśvara-praṇidhāna* or the contemplation of the supreme Being, who is defined to be a particular Purusha or Spirit unaffected by works, afflictions, &c., and

[1] The Yoga was propounded by Patañjali (of whom nothing is known, except that he was probably not the same person as the author of the Mahā-bhāshya) in Aphorisms called the Yoga-sūtra, a work in four books or chapters, two of which, with some of the commentary of Bhoja-rājā or Bhoja-deva, were translated by Dr. Ballantyne. Other commentators were Vāćaspati-miśra, Vijñāna-bhikshu, and Nāgoji-bhaṭṭa.

having the appellation *Praṇava* or *Om*. The repetition of this monosyllable is supposed to be attended with marvellous results, and the muttering of it with reflection on its meaning[1] is said to be conducive to a knowledge of the Supreme and to a prevention of all the obstacles to Yoga. The eight means of mental concentration are—1. *Yama*, 'forbearance,' 'restraint.' 2. *Niyama*, 'religious observances.' 3. *Āsana*, 'postures[2].' 4. *Prāṇāyāma*, 'suppression of the breath' or 'breathing in a peculiar way.' 5. *Pratyāhāra*, 'restraint of the senses.' 6. *Dhārāṇa*, 'steadying of the mind.' 7. *Dhyāna*, 'contemplation.' 8. *Samādhi*, 'profound meditation,' or rather a state of religious trance, which, according to the Bhagavad-gītā (VI. 13), is most effectually attained by such practices as fixing the eyes intently and incessantly on the tip of the nose, &c.[3] The system of Yoga appears, in fact, to be a mere contrivance for getting rid of all thought, or at least for concentrating the mind with the utmost intensity upon nothing in particular. It is a strange compound of mental and bodily exercises, consisting in unnatural restraint, forced and painful postures, twistings and contortions of the limbs, suppressions of the breath, and utter absence of mind. But although the Yoga of Patañjali professes to effect union with the universal Spirit by means such as these, it should be observed that far more severe austerities and self-imposed physical mortifications are

---

[1] *Om* is supposed to be composed of the three letters A, U, M, which form a most sacred monosyllable (*ekākshara*), significant of the supreme Being as developing himself in the Triad of gods, Brahmā, Vishṇu, and Śiva. See Bhagavad-gītā VIII. 13, and especially Manu II. 83, 84.

[2] One of these postures is called *paryan̄ka-bandhana* or *paryan̄ka-granthi*, 'bed-binding' or 'bed-knot,' and is performed by sitting on the hams with a cloth fastened round the knees and back. See line 1 of the Mṛić-ćhakaṭikā.

[3] See the account of the Bhagavad-gītā, p. 142 of this volume.

popularly connected with the Yoga system. All Hindū devotees and ascetics, especially those who, as forming a division of the Śaiva sect, identify the terrific god Śiva with the supreme Being, are commonly called Yogins or Yogīs, and indeed properly so called, in so far as the professed object of their austerities is union with the Deity[1].

The variety and intensity of the forms of austerity practised by such Yogīs in India would appear to surpass all credibility were they not sufficiently attested by trustworthy evidence. A few illustrations may not be out of place here, or at least may be instructive, especially as bearing upon an interesting field of inquiry, viz. first, how is it that faith in a false system can operate with sufficient force upon a Hindū to impel him to submit voluntarily to almost incredible restraints, mortifications of the flesh, and physical tortures? and secondly, how is it that an amount of physical endurance may be exhibited by an apparently weakly and emaciated Asiatic, which would be impossible in a European, the climate and diet in the one case tending to debilitate, in the other to invigorate?

In the Śakuntalā (Act VII. verse 175) there is a description of an ascetic engaged in Yoga, whose condition of fixed trance and immovable impassiveness had lasted so long that ants had thrown up a mound as high as his waist without being disturbed, and birds had built their nests in the long clotted tresses of his tangled hair. This may be thought a mere flight of poetical fancy, but a Mohammedan traveller, whose narrative is quoted by Mr. Mill (British India, I. 355), once actually saw a man in India standing motionless with his face turned towards the sun. The same traveller, having occasion to revisit

---

[1] The name Fakīr or Faqīr, sometimes given to Hindū devotees, ought to be restricted to Muslims. It is an Arabic word, meaning 'poor,' 'indigent.'

the same spot sixteen years afterwards, found the very same man in the very same attitude. Such men have been known to fix their gaze on the sun's disk till sight has been extinguished. This is paralleled by a particular form of austerity described in Manu VI. 23, where mention is made of the *Pañća-tapās*, a Yogī who, during the three hottest months (April, May, and June), sits between four blazing fires placed towards the four quarters, with the burning sun above his head to form a fifth. In fact, a Yogī was actually seen not long ago (Mill's India, I. 353) seated between four such fires on a quadrangular stage. He stood on one leg gazing at the sun while these fires were lighted at the four corners. Then placing himself upright on his head, with his feet elevated in the air, he remained for three hours in that position. He then seated himself cross-legged and continued bearing the raging heat of the sun above his head and the fires which surrounded him till the end of the day, occasionally adding combustibles with his own hands to increase the flames.

Again, in the Asiatic Monthly Journal for March, 1829, an account is given of a Brāhman who, with no other apparatus than a low stool, a hollow bamboo, and a kind of crutch, poised himself apparently in the air, about four feet from the ground, for forty minutes. This actually took place before the governor of Madras. Nor does there appear to be any limit to the various forms of austerity practised by Hindū devotees. We read of some who acquire the power of remaining under water for a space of time quite incredible; of others who bury themselves up to the neck in the ground, or even below it, leaving only a little hole through which to breathe; of others who keep their fists clenched for years till the nails grow through the back of their hands; of others who hold one or both arms aloft till they become immovably fixed in that position and withered to the bone; of others who roll their bodies for thousands of miles to some place of pilgrimage; of others who sleep on beds of iron spikes. One man was seen at Benares (described in the Asiatic Researches, vol. v. p. 49) who was alleged to have used such a bed for thirty-five years. Others have been known to chain themselves for life to trees; others, again, to pass their lives, heavily chained, in iron cages. Lastly, the extent to which some Indian ascetics will carry fasting far exceeds anything ever heard of in Europe, as may be understood by a reference to the rules of the lunar penance given by Manu (VI. 20, XI. 216–220). This penance is a kind of fast which consists in diminishing the consumption of food every day by one mouthful for the waning half of the lunar month, beginning with fifteen mouthfuls at the full moon until the quantity is reduced to 0 at the new moon, and then increasing it in like manner during the fortnight of the moon's increase.

Of course all these mortifications are explicable by their connection with the fancied attainment of extraordinary sanctity and supernatural powers.

As a conclusion to the subject of Yoga, I quote a remarkable passage from Professor Banerjea (Dialogues, pp. 69, 70):

The Yogī may not see or hear what passes around,—he may be insensible to external impressions, but he has intuition of things which his neighbours cannot see or hear. He becomes so buoyant, or rather so sublimated by his Yoga, that gravitation, or, as Bhāskarāćārya calls it, the attractive power of the earth, has no influence on him. He can walk and ascend in the sky, as if he were suspended under a balloon. He can by this intuitive process inform himself of the mysteries of astronomy and anatomy, of all things in fact that may be found in any of the different worlds. He may call to recollection the events of a previous life. He may understand the language of the brute creation. He may obtain an insight into the past and future. He may discern the thoughts of others. He may himself vanish at pleasure, and, if he choose to do so, enter into his neighbour's body and take possession of his living skin.

By these and other doctrines of Hindū philosophy we are often reminded that the human mind repeats itself according to the sentiment expressed in Ecclesiastes i. 9, 'The thing that hath been, it is that which shall be; and that which is done is that which shall be done: and there is no new thing under the sun.' Certainly almost all extravagant ideas now current seem to have their counterpart, if not their source, in the East. The practisers of self-imposed superstitious restraints and mortifications, not to speak of the votaries of animal magnetism, clairvoyance, and so-called spiritualism, will find most of their theories represented or rather far outdone by corresponding notions existing in this Yoga system invented by the Hindūs considerably more than 2000 years ago, and more or less earnestly believed in and sedulously practised up to the present day.

# LECTURE VI.

## *The Pūrva-mīmāṉsā and Vedānta.*

OUR next subject is the Mīmāṉsā of Jaimini [1], which is sometimes connected with the Vedānta, this latter being called the *Uttara-mīmāṉsā* or *Brahma-mīmāṉsā*—as founded on the Upanishads or latter part of the Vedas —while Jaimini's system is styled the *Pūrva-mīmāṉsā* or *Karma-mīmāṉsā*, as concerned with the Mantras and Brāhmaṇas only. It is more usual, however, to indicate the opposition of the two systems to each other by calling the one Mīmāṉsā and the other Vedānta. In fact, Jaimini's system, like the Yoga, cannot suitably be called a subdivision of any other system, for it is in real truth not a system of philosophy, but rather of *ritualism*. It does not concern itself, like the other systems, with investigations into the nature of soul, mind, and matter, but with a correct interpretation of the ritual of the Veda and the solutions of doubts and discrepancies in regard to Vedic texts caused by the discordant explanations of opposite schools. Its only claim to the title of a philosophy consists in its *mode* of interpretation, the topics being

---

[1] Jaimini, as usual, enunciated his doctrines in aphorisms. His work called the Mīmāṉsā-sūtra or Jaimini-sūtra is in twelve books. It has been partly edited and translated by Dr. Ballantyne. A commentary on it was written by S'abara-svāmin, which is being published in the Bibliotheca Indica, and this again was commented on by the celebrated Mīmāṉsā authority, Kumārila (also styled Kumārila-bhaṭṭa, Kumārila-svāmin), whose work was again followed by numerous other commentaries and treatises. A compendious explanation of the system, called *Jaiminīya-nyāya-mālā-vistara*, was written by Mādhavāćārya. Jaimini must have been a learned Brāhman, but nothing is known as to the date of his life.

arranged according to particular categories (such as authoritativeness, indirect precept, &c.), and treated according to a kind of *logical method*, commencing with the proposition to be discussed, the doubt arising about it, the *Pūrva-paksha* or primâ facie and wrong view of the question, the *Uttara-paksha* or refutation of the wrong view, and the conclusion. The main design of the whole system appears to be to make a god of ritualism. Hence it consists chiefly of a critical commentary on the Brāhmaṇa or ritual portion of the Veda in its connection with the Mantras, the interpretation given being an exposition of the obvious literal sense and not of any supposed occult meaning underlying the text, as in the Upanishads and Vedānta. Jaimini was, in point of fact, the opponent of both rationalism and theism. Not that he denied a God, but the real tendency of his teaching was to allow no voice or authority to either reason or God. The Veda was to be everything. A supreme Being might exist, but was not necessary to the system. The Veda, said Jaimini, is itself authority and has no need of an Authorizer. His first Aphorism states the whole aim and object of his system, viz. a desire to know duty (*dhrama-jijñāsā*). When amplified, it may be thus stated:

> Understand, O student, that, after studying the Veda with a preceptor, a desire to know *Dharma* or duty is to be entertained by thee.

The fifth Aphorism asserts the strange doctrine of an original and perpetual connection between a word and its sense. It is thus paraphrased:

> The connection of a word with its sense is contemporaneous with the origin of both. In consequence of this connection, the words of the Veda convey unerring instruction in the knowledge of duty.

But it is to be understood that *Dharma* or duty consists in the performance of the ritual acts prescribed by the Veda because they are so prescribed, without reference to the will or approval of any personal god, for Dharma is itself the bestower of reward. Some recent Mīmāṉsakas, however, maintain that Dharma ought to be performed as an offering to a supreme Being, and that it is to be so performed as a means of emancipation. Even a verse of the Bhagavad-gītā is quoted in support of this view. Kṛishṇa, regarded by his worshippers as a manifestation of the supreme lord of the universe, says to Arjuna,—

> Whatever thou doest, whatever thou eatest, whatever thou sacrificest, whatever thou givest away, whatever austerity thou practisest, do that as an offering to me (IX. 27). (See Lecture VII on the Eclectic School and Bhagavad-gītā, p. 143 of this volume.)

Some singular speculations occur in Jaimini's system. As he maintains the inherent authority of the Veda, without any dependence on an eternal Authorizer or Revealer, so he asserts its own absolute eternity, and declares that only eternally pre-existing objects are mentioned in it. This theory is supported by affirming that sound is eternal, or rather that an eternal sound underlies all temporary sound. From Aphorism 18 we gather the following:

> Sound must be eternal, because its utterance [exhibition] is intended to convey a meaning to others. If it were not eternal it would not continue till the hearer had learned its sense, and thus he would not learn the sense, because the cause had ceased to exist.
>
> If, on the other hand (says a commentator), it continues to exist for any period, however short, after ceasing to be perceived, it is impossible to assign any other instant at which there is any evidence of the discontinuance of its existence, whence its eternity is inferred [1].

This eternity of sound is further pretended to be established by the two following short passages, one from the Ṛig-veda (VIII. 64. 6) and one from Smṛiti, with which I close this brief notice of the Mīmāṉsā:

---

[1] See Muir's Texts, vol. iii. pp. 53, 57; Dr. Ballantyne's Mīmāṉsā-sūtra, p. 23.

'Send forth praises, O Virūpa, with an eternal voice.'

'An eternal voice, without beginning or end, was uttered by the self-existent[1].'

Let me conclude these remarks on the singular theory of the eternity of sound by observing that the Chinese are said to have a saying, 'The echoes of a word once uttered vibrate in space to all eternity.'

## *The Vedānta.*

Of orthodox systems there only remains the Vedānta of Vyāsa or Bādarāyaṇa[2]; but this is in some respects the most important of all the six, both from its closer con-

---

[1] The whole text of the Ṛig-veda (VIII. 64. or 75. 6) is, *Tasmai nūnam abhidyave vāćā Virūpa nityayā, vrishṇe ćodasva sushṭutim*, 'send forth praises to this heaven-aspiring and prolific Agni, O Virūpa, with an eternal voice.' Nitya, though taken by the Mīmāṇsakas in the sense of 'eternal,' probably means only 'unceasing.' Dr. Muir's Texts, vol. iii. p. 51. The text from Smṛiti has only as yet been found in Mahā-bhārata, S'ānti-parvan 8. 533, *An-ādi-nidhanā nityā vāg utsṛishṭā svayam-bhuvā.*

[2] The reputed author of this system, Bādarāyaṇa, is very loosely identified with the legendary person named Vyāsa, who is supposed to have arranged the Vedas and written the Mahā-bhārata, Purāṇas, and a particular Dharma-śāstra or law-book. No doubt the name Vyāsa, 'arranger,' was applied as a kind of title to various great writers or compilers, and in this sense it seems to have been given to the founder of the Vedānta system. He propounded his views, as usual, in Sūtras, but Bādarāyaṇa's Aphorisms are generally called Brahma-sūtra, or sometimes S'ārīraka-sūtra, and the system itself is variously styled Brahma-mīmāṇsā and S'ārīraka-mīmāṇsā (investigation into the supreme Soul or embodied Spirit). The text of the Sūtras and the celebrated commentary by S'an-karāćārya have been edited in the Bibliotheca Indica by Dr. Röer, and a portion translated by Professor Banerjea. Dr. Ballantyne also edited and translated a portion of the Sūtras and commentary and a popular compendium called the Vedānta-sāra. A vast number of other commentaries and treatises on the Vedānta exist.

formity to the pantheistic doctrines propounded in the Upanishads, on which treatises as forming the end of the Veda it professes to be founded, and from its greater adaptation to the habits of thought common among thinking and educated Hindūs, as much in present as in former periods. The pantheism pervading the Upanishads and leading directly to the Vedānta system has already been illustrated by a selection of examples.

The following simple confession of a Vedāntist's faith can be added from the Ćhāndogya Upanishad (III. 14):

> All this universe (τὸ πᾶν) indeed is Brahma; from him does it proceed; into him it is dissolved; in him it breathes[1]. So let every one adore him calmly.

Here, then, we have presented to us a different view of the origin of the world. In the Nyāya it was supposed to proceed from a concurrence of innumerable eternal atoms; in the Sān̄khya from one original eternal element called Prakṛiti; both operating independently, though associated with eternal souls and, according to one view, presided over by a supreme Soul. But in the Vedānta there is really no material world at all, as distinct from the universal Soul. Hence the doctrine of this school is called *A-dvaita*, 'non-dualism.' The universe exists but merely as a form of the one eternal essence (τὸ ἕν). He is the all-pervading Spirit, the only really existing substance (*vastu*). Even as early as the Ṛig-veda the outlines of this pantheistic creed, which became more definite in the Upanishads and Vedānta, may be traced. The germ of the Vedānta is observable in the Purusha-sūkta, as we

---

[1] This is expressed in the text by one compound, *taj-jalān*, interpreted as equivalent to *taj-ja, tal-la, tad-ana*. The whole text is *sarvaṃ khalv idam brahma taj-jalān iti śānta upāsīta*. The philosophy of the Sūfīs, alleged to be developed out of the Kurān (see p. 36), appears to be a kind of pantheism very similar to that of the Vedānta.

have already shown by the example given at p. 24. The early Vedāntic creed has the merit of being exceedingly simple. It is comprised in these three words, occurring in the Ćhāndogya Upanishad (see p. 41), *Ekam evādvitīyam*, 'one only Essence without a second;' or in the following line of nine short words, *Brahma satyaṃ jagan mithyā jīvo brahmaiva nāparaḥ*, 'Brahma is true, the world is false, the soul is only Brahma and no other.'

As the Nyāya has much in common with the practical philosophy of Aristotle, which gave to things and individuals, rather than to ideas, a real existence, so the Vedānta offers many parallels to the idealism of Plato [1]. Bādarāyaṇa's very first Aphorism states the object of the whole system in one compound word, viz. *Brahma-jijñāsā*,

---

[1] Plato does not always state his theory of ideas very intelligibly, and probably modified them in his later works. He seems, however, to have insisted on the doctrine that mind preceded and gave rise to matter, or, in other words, that the whole material world proceeded from or was actually produced by the Creator according to the idea or pattern of a world existing eternally and for ever the same in his own mind. In the Timaeus (10) he says: 'To discover the Maker and Father of this universe (τοῦ παντός) is difficult, and, when he has been discovered, it is impossible to describe him to the multitude. According to which of two patterns (πρὸς πότερον τῶν παραδειγμάτων) did he frame the world? According to one subsisting for ever the same? Or according to one which was produced? Since, then, this universe is beautiful and its Artificer good, he evidently looked in modelling it to an eternal (ἀΐδιον) pattern.' Similarly, Plato seems to have held that the human mind has existing within it certain abstract ideas or ideal forms which precede and are visibly manifested in the actual concrete forms around us. For example, the abstract ideas of goodness and beauty are found pre-existing in the mind, and, as it were, give rise to the various good and beautiful objects manifested before our eyes. In the same manner all circular things must have been preceded by some ideal circular form existing as an eternal reality. For, according to Plato, these abstract ideas had a real, eternal, unchanging existence of their own, quite separate from and independent of the ever-varying concrete objects and appearances connected with them.

'Brahma-inquisitiveness,' i. e. the desire of knowing Brahman (neut.), or the only really existing being.

Here we may quote a portion of Śankarāćārya's commentary (Röer's edition, pp. 29 and 43):

The knower of Brahma attains the supreme good and supreme object of man (*param purushārtham*=τὸ ἀγαθόν, τὸ ἄριστον, summum bonum).

A really existing substance (*vastu*) cannot alternately be thus and not thus, cannot (optionally) be and not be. The knowledge of a substance just as it is in reality (i. e. true knowledge) is not dependent on a man's own personal notions (*na purusha-buddhy-apeksham*)[1]. It depends on the substance itself. To say of one and the same post that it is either a post or a man or something else is not true knowledge (*tattva-jñānam*). It is a false notion (*mithyā-jñānam*)[2]. That it is a post is alone the truth, because it is dependent on the substance itself (*vastu-tantratvāt*). Thus the proving of an existing substance is dependent on the substance itself. Thus the knowledge of Brahma is dependent on the substance itself (not on the notion a man may form of Brahma), because it relates to a really existing substance (*bhūta-vastu-vishayatvāt*).

In the second Aphorism Brahma[3] is defined to mean 'that from which the production of this universe results.'

Śan-kara adds a fuller definition, thus (Röer's edition, p. 38):

---

[1] S'an-kara appears here to argue against a doctrine like that ascribed to Protagoras, πάντων μέτρον ἄνθρωπος, 'the individual man is the standard of all things.'

[2] One of Plato's causes of mistaken notion is that when two persons or things have been seen and their forms impressed on the mind, they are yet, owing to imperfect observation, mistaken the one for the other: 'It remains that I may form a false notion in this case, when knowing you and Theodorus and having the impression of both of you on that waxen tablet of the mind (ἐν ἐκείνῳ τῷ κηρίνῳ) made by a seal ring as it were, seeing you both from a distance and not sufficiently distinguishing you, I fit the aspect of each to the impression of the other, changing them like those that put their shoes on the wrong feet: τότε δὴ συμβαίνει ἡ ἑτεροδοξία καὶ τὸ ψευδῆ δοξάζειν,' Theaet. 122. Compare Banerjea's translation of the Brahma-sūtra, p. 2.

[3] The name *Brahman* is in fact derived from the root *bṛih* or *vṛih*, 'to grow and expand,' and therefore means literally the one essence which grows or expands. *Vṛiksha*, 'a tree,' is from the same root.

Brahma is that all-knowing, all-powerful Cause from which arises the production, continuance, and dissolution of the universe, which (universe) is modified by name and form, contains many agents and patients (*kartṛi-bhokṭṛi-saṃyukta*), is the repository (*āśraya*) of actions and effects, and in the form of its arrangement cannot be conceived even by the mind.

The Aphorisms which follow, as far as the 28th, proceed to define and describe the character of God as the supreme Soul of the universe. I here give a summary[1] of the most interesting of them, with portions of the commentary:

That the supreme Being is omniscient follows from the fact that he is the source of the Veda (*śāstra-yonitvāt*). As from that Being every soul is evolved, so to that same Being does every soul return. How can souls be merged into Prakṛiti?[2] for then the intelligent would be absorbed in the unintelligent. He, the supreme Being, consists of joy. This is clear from the Veda, which describes him as the cause of joy; for as those who enrich others must be themselves rich, so there must be abundant joy with him who causes others to rejoice. Again, he, the one God, is the light (*jyotis*). He is within the sun and within the eye. He is the ethereal element (*ākāśa*)[3]. He is the life and the breath of life (*prāṇa*). He is the life with which Indra identified himself when he said to Pratardana, 'I am the life, consisting of perfect knowledge. Worship me as the life immortal[4].'

From other portions of the Aphorisms it appears that the τὸ ἕν, or one universal essence called Brahma, is to the external world what yarn is to cloth, what milk to curds,

---

[1] See Dr. Ballantyne's translation, and that of Professor Banerjea.

[2] The Prakṛiti or Pradhāna of the Sāṅkhya system.

[3] Professor Banerjea considers that the word 'ether' is not a good rendering for *ākāśa*, which pervades everything. There is ākāśa in our cups and within our bodies, which are surely not ethereal. One of the synonyms of ākāśa is *śūnya*, and this may be compared in some respects to the 'inane' or space of Lucretius (I. 330):

*Nec tamen undique corporeâ stipata tenentur*
*Omnia naturâ; namque est in rebus inane.*

'And yet all things are not on all sides held and jammed together in close and solid parts; there is a space (or void) in things.'

[4] This is from the Kaushītaki-brāhmaṇa Upanishad, chapter 3. See Professor E. B. Cowell's translation.

what earth to a jar, and gold to a bracelet. He is both creator and creation[1], actor and act. He is also Existence, Knowledge, and Joy (*Saċ-ċid-ānanda*), but is at the same time without parts, unbound by qualities (*nir-guṇa*, see p. 95), without action, without emotion, having no consciousness such as is denoted by 'I' and 'Thou[2],' apprehending no person or thing, nor apprehended by any, having neither beginning nor end, immutable, the only real entity.

This is surely almost tantamount to asserting that pure Being is identical with pure Nothing, so that the two extremes of Buddhistic Nihilism and Vedāntic Pantheism, far as they profess to be apart, appear in the end to meet.

I add two or three extracts from Śan-karāćārya's comment on Sūtra II. I. 34[3]:

It may be objected that God is proved not to be the cause of the universe. Why? From the visible instances of injustice (*vaishamya*) and cruelty (*nairghṛiṇya*). Some he makes very happy, as the gods, &c.; some very miserable, as the brutes, &c.; and some in a middling condition, as men, &c. Being the author of such an unjust creation, he is proved to be subject to passions like other persons—that is to say, to partiality and prejudice—and therefore his nature is found wanting in

---

[1] A true Vedāntic spirit is observable in the Orphic hymns when they identify Zeus with the universe; thus, 'Zeus is the ether; Zeus is the earth; Zeus is the heaven; Zeus is all things.' Orphic. Fragm. IV. 363, VI. 366. Compare also Virgil, Aeneid VI. 724, &c.:

> 'Principio caelum ac terras, camposque liquentes
> Lucentemque globum Lunae, Titaniaque astra,
> Spiritus intus alit, totamque infusa per artus
> Mens agitat molem et magno se corpore miscet.'

[2] As shown by Professor Banerjea, Śan-kara compares the second person *Thou* with darkness, because there cannot be a real Thou. So Śan-kara affirms that 'Thou' and 'I' are as opposed as darkness and light. Plato speaks similarly of darkness and light in connection with nonentity and real entity. Sophist. 254.

[3] Quoted by Professor Banerjea and Mr. Mullens, and translated by them. Dialogues, p. 120, &c. Essay on Hindū Philosophy, p. 190. The Aphorism is, *Vaishamya-nairghṛiṇye na sāpekshatvāt tathāhi darśayati.*

spotlessness. And by dispensing pain and ruin, he is chargeable with malicious cruelty, deemed culpable even among the wicked. Hence, because of the instances of injustice and cruelty, God cannot be the cause of the universe. To this we reply: Injustice and cruelty cannot be charged upon God. Why? Because he did not act independently (*sāpekshatvāt*). God being dependent (*sāpekshaḥ*) creates this world of inequalities. If you ask on what he is dependent, we reply, on merit and demerit (*dharmādharmau*). That there should be an unequal creation, dependent on the merit and demerit of the souls created, is no fault of God. As the rain is the common cause of the production of rice and wheat, but the causes of their specific distinctions as rice and wheat are the varying powers of their respective seeds; so is God the common cause in the creation of gods, men, and others; but of the distinctions between gods, men, and others, the causes are the varying works inherent in their respective souls.

In commenting on the next Aphorism (35), he answers the objection, 'How could there be previous works at the original creation?' The objection and reply are thus stated[1]:

The supreme Being existed at the beginning, one without a second (see p. 113). Hence, before the creation there could be no works in dependence on which inequalities might be created. God may be dependent on works after distinctions are made. But before the creation there could be no works caused by varying instruments, and therefore we ought to find a uniform creation (*tulyā sṛishṭiḥ*). We reply: This does not vitiate our doctrine, because *the world is without beginning* (*anāditvāt saṃsārasya*). The world being without beginning, nothing can prevent works and unequal creations from continuing in the states of cause and effect, like the seed and its plant (*vījāṅkura-vat*).

Other objections to the Vedānta theory are thus treated by Śaṅkara:

How can this universe, which is manifold, void of life, impure, and irrational, proceed from him who is one, living, pure, and rational? We reply: The lifeless world can proceed from Brahma, just as lifeless hair can spring from a living man. But in the universe we find him who enjoys and him who is enjoyed; how can he be both? We reply: Such are the changes of the sea. Foam, waves, billows, bubbles are not different from the sea. There is no difference between the universe and

[1] The original Sūtra is, *Na karmāvibhāgād iti ćen nānāditvāt.*

Brahma. The effect is not different from its cause. He is the soul; the soul is he. The same earth produces diamonds, rock-crystal, and vermilion. The same sun produces many kinds of plants. The same nourishment is converted into hair, nails, &c. As milk is changed into curds, and water into ice, so is Brahma variously transformed without external aids. So the spider spins its web from its own substance. So spirits assume various shapes.

Such a creed as this does not necessarily imply what the later Vedāntists teach—that the world is all Māyā, 'a mere illusion.' This illusion theory, now so popular among Indian philosophers, receives little countenance in the Upanishads, being rather imported from Buddhism. A true Vedāntist, though he affirms that Brahma alone is real, allows a *vyāvahārika*, 'practical existence' to souls, the world, and Īśvara, as distinguished from *pāramārthika*, 'real,' and *prātibhāsika*, 'apparent or illusory existence.' How, indeed, can it be denied that external things exist, when we see them before our eyes and feel them at every instant? But how, on the other hand, can it be maintained that an impure world is the manifestation of a pure spiritual essence? To avoid this difficulty, the supreme Spirit is represented as ignoring himself by a sort of self-imposed ignorance, in order to draw out from himself for his own amusement the separate individuated souls and various appearances, which, although really parts of his own essence, constitute the apparent phenomena of the universe. Hence the external world, the living souls of individual men, and even Īśvara, the personal God, are all described as created by a power which the Vedāntist is obliged, for want of a better solution of his difficulty, to call A-vidyā [1], generally translated 'Ignorance,' but perhaps better rendered by 'False knowledge' or 'False notion.'

Of this power there are two distinct forms of operation,

[1] Something like the Ἀγνοία of Plato. See Banerjea's translation of the Sūtras, p. 3.

viz. 1. that of envelopment (*āvaraṇa*), which, enveloping the soul, causes it to imagine that it is liable to mundane vicissitudes—that it is an agent or a patient; that it rejoices or grieves, &c.—as if a person under a delusion were to mistake a rope for a snake: 2. that of projection (*vikshepa*), which, affecting the soul in its state of pure intelligence, raises upon it the appearance of a world, producing first the five subtile elements and drawing out from them seventeen subtile bodies (also called *linga-śarīra*, comprising the five organs of sense, the five organs of action, the five vital airs, with *buddhi* and *manas*), and the five gross elements in the same order as in the Sāṅkhya (see p. 93). Hence the soul mistakes itself for a mere mortal, as it mistook the rope for a snake[1].

By reason of A-vidyā, then, the Jīvātman, or 'personal soul of every individual,' mistakes the world, as well as its own body and mind, for realities, just as a rope in a dark night might be mistaken for a snake. The moment the personal soul is set free from this self-imposed Ignorance by a proper understanding of the truth, through the Vedānta philosophy, all the illusion vanishes and the identity of the Jīvātman and of the whole phenomenal universe with the Paramātman, or 'one only really existing spirit,' is re-established[2].

Let me here introduce a version of part of a short Vedāntic tract in verse, called *Ātma-bodha*, 'knowledge of soul,' attributed to the great Śaṅkarāćārya. It is highly esteemed as an exposition of Vedāntic doctrines, and has therefore been inserted by Dr. Häberlin in his anthology of shorter poems[3]. The following metrical lines

---

[1] See Ballantyne's Lecture on the Vedānta-sāra, p. 25. Reference may also be made to the Vedānta-paribhāshā, a text book of the most modern Vedāntic school.

[2] See the passage from the Muṇḍaka Upanishad, quoted p. 42.

[3] There is also a Tamil version and commentary translated by the

may serve as a specimen of some of the ideas contained in this well-known epitome of Hindū pantheistic philosophy:

Knowledge alone effects emancipation.
As fire is indispensable to cooking,
So knowledge is essential to deliverance (2).
Knowledge alone disperses ignorance,
As sunlight scatters darkness—not so acts;
For ignorance originates in works (3).
The world and all the course of mundane things
Are like the vain creation of a dream[1],
In which Ambition, Hatred, Pride, and Passion
Appear like phantoms mixing in confusion.
While the dream lasts the universe seems real,
But when 'tis past the world exists no longer (6).
Like the deceptive silver of a shell[2],
So at first sight the world deludes the man
Who takes mere semblance for reality (7).
As golden bracelets are in substance one
With gold, so are all visible appearances
And each distinct existence one with Brahma (8).
By action of the fivefold elements[3]
Through acts performed in former states of being,
Are formed corporeal bodies, which become
The dwelling-place of pleasure and of pain (11).
The soul inwrapped in five investing sheaths[4]
Seems formed of these, and all its purity
Darkened, like crystal laid on coloured cloth (14).
As winnowed rice is purified from husk,
So is the soul disburdened of its sheaths
By force of meditation[5], as by threshing (15).

---

Rev. I. F. Kearns, Madras, 1867. I have consulted the Tamil commentary as given by Mr. Kearns.

[1] Cf. Shakspeare's 'We are such stuff As dreams are made on, and our little life Is rounded with a sleep.' Tempest, Act iv. Scene 1.

[2] That is, the mother-of-pearl oyster (*śukti*).

[3] This is called *Pańćī-kṛita* or *Pańćī-karaṇa*, the production of the body, and indeed of the whole world, by the action of the five elements (see p. 93), being a dogma of the Vedānta.

[4] See the remarks, p. 123.

[5] *Yukti* seems here to be equivalent to *yoga*. It may also mean 'argument,' 'reasoning.'

The soul is like a king whose ministers
Are body, senses, mind, and understanding[1].
The soul is wholly separate from these,
Yet witnesses and overlooks their actions (18).
The foolish think the Spirit acts, whereas
The senses are the actors, so the moon
Is thought to move when clouds are passing o'er it (19).
When intellect and mind are present, then
Affections, inclinations, pleasures, pains
Are active; in profound and dreamless sleep
When intellect is non-existent, these
Exist not; therefore they belong to mind (22).
As brightness is inherent in the sun,
Coolness in water, warmness in the fire,
E'en so existence, knowledge, perfect bliss[2],
And perfect purity inhere in soul (23).
The understanding cannot recognize
The soul, nor does the soul need other knowledge
To know itself[3], e'en as a shining light
Requires no light to make itself perceived (27, 28).
The soul declares its own condition thus—
'I am distinct from body, I am free
From birth, old age, infirmity, and death.
I have no senses; I have no connection
With sound or sight or objects of sensation.
I am distinct from mind, and so exempt

---

[1] The soul is supposed by Vedāntists to have three conditions besides the conditions of pure intelligence, viz. waking, dreaming, and profound or dreamless sleep (*su-shupti*). While awake, the soul, associated with the body, is active and has to do with a real creation. While dreaming, it has to do with an unreal or illusory world. When profoundly and dreamlessly asleep, it is supposed to have retired by the channel of some of the pericardial arteries into the perfect repose of union with the supreme Soul. See Vedānta-sūtra III. 2. 1–10.

[2] Hence the Vedāntist's name for the one universal Spirit, *Saććid-ānanda*.

[3] The celebrated Hindū maxim *Atmānam ātmanā paśya*, 'know (see) thyself by thyself,' or 'know the soul by the soul,' has, therefore, a deeper philosophical meaning than the still more celebrated Greek precept γνῶθι σεαυτόν, attributed to Thales.

From passion, pride, aversion, fear, and pain.
I have no qualities[1], I am without
Activity, and destitute of option[2],
Changeless, eternal, formless, without taint,
For ever free, for ever without stain.
I, like the boundless ether, permeate
The universe within, without, abiding
Always, for ever similar in all,
Perfect, immovable, without affection,
Existence, knowledge, undivided bliss,
Without a second, One, supreme am I' (31–35).
The perfect consciousness that 'I am Brahma'
Removes the false appearances projected
By Ignorance[3], just as elixir, sickness (36).
The universal Soul knows no distinction
Of knower, knowledge, object to be known.
Rather is it enlightened through itself
And its own essence, which is simple knowledge (40).
When contemplation rubs the Araṇi[4]
Of soul, the flame of knowledge blazing up
Quickly consumes the fuel ignorance (41).
The saint[5] who has attained to full perfection
Of contemplation, sees the universe
Existing in himself, and with the eye
Of knowledge sees the All as the One Soul (46).
When bodily disguises[6] are dissolved,
The perfect saint becomes completely blended
With the one Soul, as water blends with water,
As air unites with air, as fire with fire (52).
That gain than which there is no greater gain,
That joy than which there is no greater joy,
That lore than which there is no greater lore,
Is the one Brahma—this is certain truth (53).

---

[1] The epithet *nir-guṇa*, 'quality-less,' so commonly applied to the supreme Being in India, will be better understood by a reference to p. 95.

[2] *Nir-vikalpa* may perhaps be translated, 'destitute of all reflection,' or perhaps, 'free from all will.'

[3] *Avidyā-vikshepān*, 'the projections of ignorance.' See p. 119.

[4] See note, p. 18.

[5] Yogin, see p. 102.

[6] *Upādhi*, a term for the illusive disguises assumed by Brahma.

That which is through, above, below, complete,
Existence, wisdom, bliss[1], without a second[2],
Endless, eternal, one—know that as Brahma (55).
That which is neither coarse nor yet minute,
That which is neither short nor long, unborn,
Imperishable, without form, unbound
By qualities, without distinctive marks,
Without a name—know that indeed as Brahma (59).
Nothing exists but Brahma, when aught else
Appears to be, 'tis, like the mirage, false[3] (62).

With regard to the five sheaths (*pañća-kośa*) alluded to in the fourteenth verse of the Ātma-bodha, it must be noted that in the Vedānta the individuated soul, when separated off from the supreme Soul, is regarded as enclosed in a succession of cases (*kośa*) which envelope it and, as it were, fold one over the other, 'like the coats of an onion[4].' The first or innermost sheath is called the *Vijñāna-maya-kośa* or 'sheath composed of mere intellection,' associated with the organs of perception. This gives the personal soul its first conception of individuality. The second case is called the *Mano-maya* or 'sheath composed of mind,' associated with the organs of action. This gives the individual soul its powers of thought and judgment. The third envelope is called the *Prāṇa-maya* or 'breathing sheath,' i. e. the sheath composed of breath and the other vital airs associated with the organs of action. The fourth case is called the *Anna-maya* or 'covering supported by food,' i. e. the corporeal form or gross body; the three preceding sheaths, when combined together, constituting the subtile body. A fifth case, called *Ānanda-maya* or 'that composed of supreme bliss,' is also named, although not admitted by all. It must be regarded as the innermost of all, and ought therefore, when five are enumerated, to be placed before

---

[1] *Sać-ćid-ānandam.* [2] *A-dvayam.*

[3] *Mithyā yathā maru-marīćikā.*

[4] As remarked by Dr. Ballantyne, Lecture on the Vedānta-sāra, p. 29.

the Vijñāna-maya. Moreover, a collective totality of subtile bodies is supposed to exist, and the soul, which is imagined to pass through these subtile bodies like a thread, is called the *Sūtrātman*, 'thread-soul' (occasionally styled the *Prāṇātman*), and sometimes identified with Hiraṇya-garbha.

Of course the Vedānta theory, if pushed to its ultimate consequences, must lead to the neglect of all duties, religious and moral, of all activity, physical or intellectual, and of all self-culture. If everything (τὸ πᾶν) be God, then you and he and I must be one. Why should any efforts be made for the advancement of self or for the good of others? Everything we have must be common property. According to the Bṛihad-āraṇyaka Upanishad (IV. 5):

> Where there is anything like duality there one sees another, one smells another, one tastes another, one speaks to another, one hears another, one minds another, one regards another, one knows another; but where the whole of this (τὸ πᾶν) is one spirit, then whom and by what can one see? whom and by what can one smell? whom and by what can one taste? to whom and by what can one speak? whom and by what can one hear? whom and by what can one mind? whom and by what can one regard? whom and by what can one know?

This Indian pantheism is paralleled by some phases of modern German thought, as described by Dean Mansel in the following extract from one of his Essays lately published:

> With German philosophers the root of all mischief is the number two—Self and Not-self, Ego and Non-ego. The pantheist tells me that I have not a real distinct existence and unity of my own, but that I am merely a phenomenal manifestation, or an aggregate of many manifestations of the one infinite Being. If [then] we shrink from Nihilism, there remains the alternative of Pantheism. The instincts of our nature plead against annihilation and maintain, in spite of philosophy, that there must really exist something somewhere. Granting that something exists, why is that something to be called Ego? What qualities can it possess which shall make it *I* rather than *Thou*, or any one being rather than any other being? I am directly conscious of the existence of a self. But this consciousness

is a delusion. This self is but the phenomenal shadow of a further self, of which I am not conscious. Why may not this also be a shadow of something further still? Why may there not be a yet more remote reality, which is itself neither self nor not-self, but the root and foundation, and at the same time the indifference of both? This ultimate existence, the one and sole reality, is then set up as the deity of philosophy, and the result is pure pantheism.

Perhaps it may not be out of place here to contrast with Indian ideas Aristotle's grand conception of the nature of God as propounded in the eleventh book of his Metaphysics[1]. In chapter vii of that book Aristotle says (not, however, quite in the order here given):

The principle of life is in God; for energy of mind constitutes life, and God is this energy. He, the first mover, imparts motion and pursues the work of creation as something that is loved (κινεῖ δὲ ὡς ἐρώμενον). His course of life (διαγωγή) must be similar to what is most excellent in our own short career. But he exists for ever in this excellence, whereas this is impossible for us. His pleasure consists in the exercise of his essential energy, and on this account vigilance, wakefulness, and perception are most agreeable to him. Again, the more we examine God's nature the more wonderful does it appear to us. He is an eternal (ἀΐδιον) and most excellent (ἄριστον) Being. He is indivisible (ἀδιαιρετός), devoid of parts (ἀμερής), and having no magnitude (μέγεθος), for God imparts motion through infinite time, and nothing finite, as magnitude is, can have an infinite capacity. He is a being devoid of passions and unalterable (ἀπαθὲς καὶ ἀναλλοίωτον)[2].

---

[1] This work has been well translated by the Rev. J. H. M'Mahon.

[2] Hence, according to the translator, Aristotle's idea of God is that he is a Being whose essence is love, manifested in eternal energy, the final cause of this energy being the happiness of his creatures, in which he himself participates for ever. Aristotle, again, warns his disciples against regarding God's nature through the medium of their own subjectivity. There is a celebrated passage in book XI, chap. viii, in which he says that traditions have been handed down representing the heavens as gods, and the divine essence (τὸ θεῖον) as embracing the whole of nature; and these traditions, he affirms, are kept up to win over the multitude and secure obedience to the laws and for the sake of general expediency. On that account gods are described as existing in the form of man (ἀνθρωποειδεῖς), or even as taking the shape of animals.

Before quitting the subject of the Vedānta philosophy it should be stated that in many points the Vedānta agrees with the Sān-khya. The order of creation in both is nearly the same, though the 'Originant' in one case is *Prakṛiti*, in the other *A-vidyā*, 'ignorance' (or 'false knowledge'). But even here an attempt is made by some to establish a community of ideas by identifying both *Prakṛiti* and *A-vidyā* with *Māyā* or 'illusion.' In both systems the gross elements proceed from subtile principles, imperceptible to sense, in the same order (see the Sān-khyan account of the elements, p. 93). In both there is a subtile as well as a gross body[1]. The nature of the soul in being incapable of cognition without the help of the mind or internal organ (*antaḥ-karaṇa*) is described in nearly similar language by both. Again, this internal organ (*antaḥ-karaṇa*) is held by both to stand between the organs of perception and those of action, as an eleventh organ partaking of the nature of each (see p. 94). But while the Sān-khya divides the internal organ into *Buddhi*, 'intellectual perception,' *Ahan-kāra*, 'self-consciousness,' and *Manas*, 'the reasoning mind,' the first being the great source of the others (see p. 93), the Vedānta propounds a fourth division, viz. *Ćitta* or 'the faculty of thought.' On the other hand, the Vedānta adds two Pramāṇas or 'instruments of true knowledge' (*An-upalabdhi*, 'non-perception' or 'negative proof,' and *Arthāpatti*, 'inference from circumstances') to the four admitted by the Nyāya (see p. 72), while the Sān-khya rejects the Nyāya *Upamāna*, and retains as its only three Pramāṇas, *Pratyaksha*, *Anumāna*, and *Śabda*.

---

[1] The gross body is sometimes called the nine-gated city of Brahma (*Brahma-pura*), from its being the abode of the soul and from its having nine openings.

## LECTURE VII.

### *Irregular Systems and Eclectic School.*

BEFORE passing to the Eclectic School I must notice briefly two heretical and irregular systems of philosophy, which probably grew out of Buddhism, or at least have much in common with it as well as with the six orthodox systems just described.

These two systems are, 1. that of the Jainas or Jains, 2. that of the Ćārvākas or Materialists. They are described in the celebrated Mādhavāćārya's work, called Sarva-darśana-sangraha, which is a concise description of various Hindū systems and sects, religious and philosophical, orthodox and heterodox, even including the science of applying quicksilver (*raseśvara*, regarded as a form of Śiva) or its preparations to various chemical and alchemical operations, and embracing also Pāṇini's theory of grammar [1].

---

[1] Mādhava lived in the fourteenth century. He was elder brother of Sāyaṇa, and associated with him in the commentary on the Ṛig-veda. (By Mr. Burnell, however, in his preface to the Vanśa-brāhmaṇa, he is identified with Sāyaṇa.) He was also prime minister in the court of Bukka I at Vijaya-nagara. He wrote many works (e.g. an introduction to the Mīmānsā philosophy, called Nyāya-mālā-vistara, a commentary on Parāśara's law-book, the Kāla-nirṇāya, &c.) besides the Sarva-darśana-sangraha, which treats of fifteen systems as follow: 1. *Ćārvāka-darśana*; 2. *Bauddha-d°*; 3. *Ārhata-d°*; 4. *Rāmānuja-d°*; 5. *Pūrṇa-prajña-d°*; 6. *Nakulīśa-pāśupata-d°*; 7. *Śaiva-d°*; 8. *Pratyabhijñā-d°*; 9. *Raseśvara-d°*; 10. *Aulūkya-d°*; 11. *Akshapāda-d°*; 12. *Jaimini-d°*; 13. *Pāṇini-d°*; 14. *Sānkhya-d°*; 15. *Pātañjala-d°*. The Vedānta is not included in the list. Rāmānuja, the founder of the fourth, was a Vaishṇava Reformer, who, according to H. H. Wilson, lived about the middle of the twelfth century. The fifth is the doctrine of Ānanda-tīrtha, surnamed Madhvāćārya, and also called Madhya-mandira, his epithet *Pūrṇa-prajña* merely meaning 'one whose knowledge is complete.' The sixth is the system of a branch of the Māhe-

*Jainism.*

Mādhava's account of the Jainas or Jains, whom he calls Ārhatas (from *arhat*, 'venerable,' applied to a Jina or chief saint), comes third in his list of sects, and naturally follows his exposition of the Bauddha doctrines. Jainism is, in fact, the only representative of Buddhistic ideas now left in India, and has so much in common with them that, having already gained some insight into Buddhism, we need only notice a few of the distinctive features of a system which is certainly its near relation, if not its actual descendant[1].

The Jainas, who are still found in great numbers in various parts of India[2], are divided into two principal sects or parties,—1. the Śvetāmbaras, 'clothed in white garments;' 2. the Dig-ambaras, 'sky-clad' or 'naked[3];'

---

śvaras, as shown by Professor E. B. Cowell (Colebrooke's Essays, I. pp. 431, 434). He conjectures that S'iva himself, called Nakulīśa, may have been the supposed founder of this sect, and points out that the Pāśupatas are worshippers of S'iva as *Paśu-pati*, 'master of all inferior creatures' (explained by some to mean 'lord of *paśu* or the soul entangled in the bonds of matter'). The eighth is like the sixth and that of the Māheśvaras, a form of S'aiva doctrine, but more pantheistic, the S'aivas maintaining that God is, in creating, *Karmādi-sāpeksha*, 'dependent on the acts &c. of individual souls,' while this eighth asserts that God's will is the only cause of creation; for it is said, 'He being independent (*nir-apekshaḥ*) and regarding no face but his own, threw all existences as a reflection on the mirror of himself.' Hence *pratyabhijñā* is defined as *pratimābhimukhyena jñānam*, 'recognition as of a visible object or image.' The tenth is the Vaiśeshika. See note, p. 76.

[1] I have consulted Professor E. B. Cowell's appendix to Colebrooke on the Jainas, H. H. Wilson's essay, an article in Chambers' Cyclopaedia and in the 'Indian Antiquary' for September 1873, and a dissertation on the Jainas in Tamil by a learned Jain, named S'āstram Aiyar, in the Rev. H. Bower's introduction to the Ćintāmaṇi, Madras, 1868. Professor Kern regards the Jains as having originally formed one sect with the Buddhists.

[2] They are most numerous in Gujerat and the west coast, but are found everywhere, especially in South Behār (Magadha), where they originated.

[3] Also called Muktāmbaras, Vi-vasanas. A nickname for an ascetic of both sects is Luñćita-keśa, 'one who tears out his hair.'

the latter, however, wear coloured garments, except while eating, and are required to carry peacocks' tails in their hands. These sects, though their doctrines rest on the same sacred books, called collectively Sūtras[1], differ in some unimportant matters, such as the clothing or non-clothing of their images, the number of their heavens, &c. They both agree with the Buddhists in rejecting the Veda of the Brāhmans. The principal point in the Jaina creed is the reverence paid to holy men, who, by long discipline, have raised themselves to divine perfection. The Jina or 'conquering saint,' who, having conquered all worldly desires, declares the true knowledge of the Tattvas, is with Jainas what the Buddha or 'perfectly enlightened saint' is with Buddhists. He is also called Jineśvara, 'chief of Jinas;' Arhat, 'the venerable;' Tīrtha-kara or Tīrthan-kara, 'the saint who has made the passage of the world;' Sarva-jña, 'omniscient;' Bhagavat, 'holy one.' Time with Jainas proceeds in two eternally recurring cycles or periods of immense duration, defying all human calculation: 1. the Utsarpiṇī or 'ascending cycle;' 2. the Avasarpiṇī or 'descending cycle.' Each of these has six stages. Those of the Utsarpiṇī period are bad-bad, bad, bad-good, good-bad, good, good-good time. In the Avasarpiṇī period the series begins with good-good and goes regularly backwards. In the first cycle the age and stature of men increases; in the other, decreases. We are now in the fifth stage of the Avasarpiṇī, i. e. in 'bad' time. When the two cycles have run out, a Yuga or 'age' is accomplished. Twenty-four Jinas or 'perfect saints' raised to the rank of gods have appeared in the present Avasarpiṇī cycle, twenty-four in the past Utsarpiṇī, and twenty-four will appear in the future[2]. The idols representing them

[1] See Introduction, p. xxxvi, note 1. They have also Purāṇas.

[2] The names are all given in the Abhidhāna-ćintāmaṇi, a well-known vocabulary of synonyms, by a learned Jain, named Hemaćandra, who is

are always, like that of the Buddha, in a contemplative posture, but have different animals, plants, and symbols accompanying them (such as a bull, elephant, horse, ape, a lotus, the moon), to serve as distinguishing characteristics. The first Jina of the present cycle lived 8,400,000 years, and attained a stature equal to the length of 500 bows (*dhanus*). The age and stature of the second was somewhat less, and so in a descending scale. The last two Jinas, Pārśva-nātha and Mahā-vīra, were probably real persons and are those principally revered by the Jainas of the present day [1], the first founder of the sect having been Pārśva-nātha, and its first active propagator, Mahā-vīra. In the same cycle there have lived twelve Ćakra-vartins, 'universal emperors,' nine divine personages called Bala-devas, nine called Vāsudevas, and nine others called Prativāsudevas, making a list of sixty-three divine persons in all [2].

With regard to the world, the Jainas affirm that, being formed of eternal atoms, it has existed and will exist

---

said to have lived in the twelfth century of our era. Those of the present cycle are, 1. Ṛishabha or Vṛishabha; 2. Ajita; 3. Sambhava; 4. Abhinandana; 5. Sumati; 6. Padmaprabha; 7. Su-pārśva; 8. Ćandra-prabha; 9. Pushpa-danta; 10. S'ītala; 11. S'reyas or S'reyāṉśa; 12. Vāsupūjya; 13. Vimala; 14. Ananta; 15. Dharma; 16. S'ānti; 17. Kunthu; 18. Ara; 19. Malli; 20. Muni-suvrata or Su-vrata; 21. Nimi; 22. Nemi; 23. Pārśva-nātha or Pārśva; 24. Vardhamāna or Mahā-vīra or Vīra. The last of these dwindled to the size of an ordinary man, and only lived forty, while the twenty-third lived a hundred years.

[1] Dr. Muir has kindly allowed me to read his abstract of Professor H. Kern's learned dissertation on the date of Buddha's death and the Aśoka inscriptions, written for a forthcoming number of the 'Indian Antiquary,' whence I gather that, notwithstanding the notable difference between the legends of S'ākya-muni and Jina Mahā-vīra, there are also striking points of resemblance. Mahā-vīra is said to have been the son of Siddhārtha, of the solar race, and to have died in 388 B.C., which is also Dr. Kern's date for the death of the Buddha S'ākya-muni.

[2] See their names in Hemaćandra's third chapter.

eternally. They believe that it has three divisions, viz. lower, middle, and upper, and that there are numerous hells and heavens. All existing things are arranged under the two great Tattvas of Jīva, 'living soul,' and A-jīva, 'inanimate objects.' Of living souls there are three kinds: a. *Nitya-siddha*, 'ever perfect,' as the Jina; b. *Muktātman*, 'liberated soul;' c. *Baddhātman*, 'bound soul,' or one bound by works and worldly associations. Material objects are sometimes classed under a Tattva called *Pudgala*, and some make seven, others nine Tattvas.

There are three 'gems' which together effect the soul's *Moksha*, 'liberation,' viz. *a.* right intuition (*samyag-darśana*); *b.* right knowledge (*samyag-jñāna*); *c.* right conduct (*samyak-ćaritra*). This last consists in observing five duties or vows of self-restraint (*Vratas*), thus: 1. Do not kill or injure; which Jainas carry to so preposterous an extreme that they strain water before drinking it, sweep the ground with a brush before treading on it, never eat or drink in the dark, and sometimes wear muslin before their mouths to prevent the risk of swallowing minute insects. Moreover, they never eat figs or any fruit containing seed, nor will they even touch flesh-meat with their hands. 2. Do not tell lies. 3. Steal not. 4. Be chaste and temperate in thought, word, and deed. 5. Desire nothing immoderately.

There are two classes of Jainas, as of Buddhists (see p. 57), viz. *Śrāvakas*, those who engage in lay or secular occupations, and *Yatis*, monks or ascetics, who are required to pluck out their hair or wear it cropped short. The latter are often collected in Maṭhas or 'monasteries,' being called *Sādhu* when not monastic. Jainas are sometimes called Syād-vādins, from their method of propounding seven modes of reconciling opposite views as to the possibility of anything existing or not existing (*sapta-bhaṅga-naya*, *syād-vāda*). It should be noted that they accord a sort of modified worship to the Hindū gods (especially Brahmā, Vishṇu, Śiva, and Gaṇeśa, as subordinate to the Jinas); and are even observers of caste, and claim to be regarded as Hindūs, though rejecting the Hindū Veda. In Western India the priests of Jaina temples are Brāhmans.

*The Ćārvākas.*

Nothing is known about Ćārvāka, the Pyrrho and Epicurus of India and founder of the materialistic school. His system is the worst form of all heresies, and therefore honoured with the first place in Mādhavāćārya's Sarva-darśana-sangraha. In the Śānti-parvan of the Mahā-bhārata (1410, &c.) there is a story of a Rākshasa named Ćārvāka, who, in the disguise of a mendicant Brāhman, reviled Yudhishṭhira during his triumphant entry into Hastinā-pura, and uttered profane and heretical doctrines. He was, however, soon detected, and the real Brāhmans, filled with fury, killed him on the spot. This legend may possibly rest on some basis of fact.

The creed of the Ćārvākas, who are sometimes called Lokāyatas or Lokāyatikas[1], is said to have been derived from the Vārhaspatya Sūtras (Aphorisms of Vṛihaspati). They reject all the Pramāṇas, or 'sources of true knowledge,' except Pratyaksha, 'perception by the senses' (see p. 72); they admit only four Tattvas or 'eternal principles,' viz. earth, air, fire, and water, and from these intelligence (*ćaitanya*) is alleged to be produced; they affirm that the soul is not different from the body; and, lastly, they assert that all the phenomena of the world are spontaneously produced, without even the help of Adṛishṭa (see p. 69). I sum up their views with a version of a passage in the Sarva-darśana-sangraha (Īśvara-ćandra Vidyāsāgara's edition,

[1] By some this name is given to a subdivision of the Ćārvākas. The name Ćārvāka is applied to any adherent of the materialistic school; see Vedānta-sāra, 82–85.

p. 6), setting forth the opinions of the Ćārvāka materialists according to the supposed teaching of Vṛihaspati[1]. The sentiments, it will be perceived, are worthy of the most sceptical, materialistic, and epicurean of European writers :

No heaven exists, no final liberation,
No soul, no other world, no rites of caste,
No recompense for acts; the Agnihotra[2],
The triple Veda, triple self-command[3],
And all the dust and ashes of repentance—
These yield a means of livelihood for men,
Devoid of intellect and manliness.
If victims slaughtered at a sacrifice
Are raised to heavenly mansions[4], why should not
The sacrificer immolate his father?
If offerings of food can satisfy[5]
Hungry departed spirits, why supply
The man who goes a journey with provisions?
His friends at home can feed him with oblations.
If those abiding in celestial spheres
Are filled with food presented upon earth,
Why should not those who live in upper stories
Be nourished by a meal spread out below?

[1] I have consulted Professor E. B. Cowell's appendix to Colebrooke's Essay, and Dr. Muir's prose translation as given by him in his article on 'Indian Materialists' (Royal Asiatic Society's Journal, vol. xix, art. xi). He compares a passage in the Vishṇu-purāṇa III. 18, which contains similar sentiments. Cf. also the speech of the rationalistic Brāhman Jāvāli, addressed to Rāma in the Rāmāyaṇa. [2] See note, p. 32.

[3] *Tri-daṇḍa*, 'control over thoughts, words, and actions,' denoted by the three Daṇḍas or staves carried by ascetics. See Manu XII. 10, 11.

[4] This, as Dr. Muir points out, refers to Manu V. 42, where it is stated that animals duly sacrificed are conveyed to mansions of supreme felicity. Cf. Mahā-bhārata, Āśvamedhika-parvan 793 &c.

[5] This is a hit at the S'rāddha, one of the most important of all Hindū religious acts, when oblations of cakes and libations of water are made to the spirits of deceased fathers, grandfathers, and progenitors. The strict observance of these ceremonies at regular intervals is at least an evidence of the strength of filial feeling among Hindūs. Respect for parents and their memory has all the sanction of religion, and is even more insisted on as a religious duty than in Europe.

While life endures let life be spent in ease
And merriment[1]; let a man borrow money
From all his friends and feast on melted butter.
How can this body when reduced to dust
Revisit earth? and if a ghost can pass
To other worlds, why does not strong affection
For those he leaves behind attract him back?
The costly rites enjoined for those who die
Are a mere means of livelihood devised
By sacerdotal cunning—nothing more.
The three composers of the triple Veda
Were rogues, or evil spirits, or buffoons.
The recitation of mysterious words
And jabber[2] of the priests is simple nonsense.

### *The Eclectic School represented by the Bhagavad-gītā.*

As a fitting conclusion to the subject of Indian philosophy let me endeavour to give some idea of one of the most interesting and popular works in the whole range of Sanskṛit literature, called Bhagavad-gītā, the Song of Bhagavat—that is, the mystical doctrines (*Upanishadaḥ*[3]) sung by 'the adorable one'—a name applied to Kṛishṇa when identified with the supreme Being. This poem, abounding in sentiments borrowed from the Upanishads, and commented on by the great Vedāntic teacher Śankarāćārya, may be taken to represent the Eclectic school of Indian philosophy. As the regular systems or Darśanas were more or less developments of the Upanishads, so the Eclectic school is connected with those mystical treatises

---

[1] 'Let us eat and drink, for to-morrow we die,' 1 Cor. xv. 32. See Dr. Muir's note. Compare such Horatian precepts as Epod. XIII. 3, &c.

[2] Two curious Vedic words, *jarbharī* and *turpharī*, are given in the text as specimens of what I suppose modern scoffers might call 'Vedic slang.' They occur, as Dr. Muir points out, in Ṛig-veda X. 106. 6, and Nirukta XIII. 5. For their explanation see Böhtlingk and Roth and my Sanskṛit-English Dictionary.

[3] At the end of each chapter the name of the chapter is given in the plural; thus, *Iti śrī-bhagavad-gītāsu upanishatsu*, &c. See note 1, p. 138.

through the Śvetāśvatara Upanishad[1] of the Black Yajur-veda (see p. 45). This latter is doubtless a comparatively modern work, but whether composed before or after the Bhagavad-gītā, certain it is that the design of both appears to be the same. They both aim at reconciling the conflicting views of different systems, and both do so by attempting to engraft the Sān-khya and Yoga upon Vedānta doctrines[2]. Although, therefore, the order of creation and much of the cosmogony and other Sān-khya views are retained in both, the paramount sovereignty of the supreme Soul of the universe (Brahma) as the source and ultimate end of all created things, and yet wholly independent of all such creations, is asserted by both.

Some extracts from the Śvetāśvatara, describing the character and attributes of this supreme Being, who is everything and in everything, have already been given at p. 45. The following are additional extracts from the first and third chapters (Röer, pp. 50, 55, 58):

This (absolute Brahma) should be meditated on as eternal and as abiding in one's own soul; for beside him there is nothing to be known (*nātaḥ paraṃ veditavyaṃ hi kiñcit*). As oil in seeds (*tileshu*), butter in cream, water in a river, and fire in wood, so is that absolute Soul perceived within himself by a person who beholds him by means of truth and by austerity.

---

[1] The name of this Upanishad is derived from a sage, Śvetāśvatara, who, at the end of the work (VI. 21), is said to have taught the doctrine of Brahma to the most excellent of the four orders. It has been translated by Dr. Röer into English, and nearly all by Professor Weber into German (Indische Studien I. 422–429). The author must have been a Śaiva (not a Vaishṇava, like the author of the Bhagavad-gītā), as he identifies Rudra with the supreme Being. According to Wilson, *Śveta*, 'white,' *Śvetāśva*, 'white-horsed,' *Śveta-śikha*, 'white-haired,' and *Śveta-lohita*, 'white-blooded,' were names of four disciples of Śiva. Weber suspects here a mission of Syrian Christians, and thinks that both the Upanishad and the Gītā, the latter especially, may have borrowed ideas from Christianity.

[2] See Dr. Röer's introduction for a full explanation of this.

He is the eye of all, the face of all, the arm of all, the foot of all.

Thou art the black bee (*nīlaḥ pataṅgaḥ*), the green bird with red-coloured eye, the cloud in whose womb sleeps the lightning, the seasons, the seas. Without beginning thou pervadest all things by thy almighty power; for by thee are all the worlds created.

The following, again, is an example of a passage occurring in the fourth chapter (5), which is decidedly Sāṅ-khyan in its tone:

The one unborn (individual soul), for the sake of enjoyment, lies close to the One unborn (*Prakṛiti*), which is of a white, red, and black colour [answering evidently to the three Sāṅ-khyan Guṇas], which is of one and the same form, and produces a manifold offspring. Then the other unborn (or eternal soul) abandons her (*Prakṛiti*) whose enjoyment he has enjoyed.

Let us now turn to the Bhagavad-gītā. The real author of this work is unknown. It was at an early date dignified by a place in the Mahā-bhārata, in which poem it lies imbedded, or rather inlaid like a pearl [1], contributing with other numerous episodes to the mosaic-like character of that immense epic. The Bhagavad-gītā, however, is quite independent of the great epic; and it cannot be questioned that its proper place in any arrangement of Sanskṛit literature framed with regard to the continuous development and progress of Hindū thought and knowledge should be at the close of the subject of philosophy. The author was probably a Brāhman and nominally a

[1] It has been interpolated into the Bhīshma-parvan of the Mahā-bhārata and is divided into eighteen chapters or into three sections, each containing six lectures, commencing at line 830 of the twenty-fifth chapter of the Parva, and ending at line 1532. Such is the estimation in which the work is held both in Asia and Europe, that it has been translated into Hindī, Telugu, Kanarese, and other Eastern languages, and is also well known by European translations, of which that of Sir C. Wilkins, published in London in 1785, was the first. Mr. J. C. Thomson's edition and translation, published, with an elaborate introduction, by Stephen Austin in 1855, is, on the whole, a very meritorious production, and I am glad to acknowledge my obligations to it.

Vaishṇava, but really a philosopher whose mind was cast in a broad and comprehensive mould. He is supposed to have lived in India during the first or second century of our era[1]. Finding no rest for his spirit in any one system of philosophy, as commonly taught in his own time; much less in the corrupt Brāhmanism which surrounded him, he was led to make a selection from the various schools of rationalistic and dogmatic thought, so as to construct a composite theory of his own. This he did with great perspicuity and beauty of language, interweaving various opinions into one system by taking, so to speak, threads from the Sān-khya, Yoga, and Vedānta, as well as from the later theory of Bhakti or 'faith in a supreme Being[2].' With these threads he weaves, as it were, a woof of many-coloured hues of thought, which are shot across a stiff warp of stern uncompromising pantheistic doctrines, worthy of the most decided adherent of the Vedānta school[3]. Of these cross threads the most conspicuous are those of the Sān-khya system, for which the author of the Gītā has an evident predilection. The whole composition is skilfully thrown into the form of a dramatic poem or dialogue, something after the manner

[1] Some consider that he lived as late as the third century, and some place him even later, but with these I cannot agree.

[2] The Aphorisms of S'āṇḍilya, the editing of which was commenced by Dr. Ballantyne and continued by Professor Griffith, his successor at Benares, deny that knowledge is the one thing needful, and insist on the subjection of knowledge to the higher principle of *Bhakti*, 'faith in God.' The first Aphorism introduces the inquiry into the nature of faith, thus, *Athāto bhakti-jijñāsā*. Professor Weber and others think that the introduction of πίστις and ἀγάπη into the Hindū system is due to the influence of Christianity.

[3] The predominance of pantheistic doctrines, notwithstanding the attempt to interweave them with portions of the Sān-khya and Yoga systems, is denoted by the fact that the Vedāntists claim this poem as an exponent of their own opinions.

of the book of Job or a dialogue of Plato[1]. The speakers are the two most important personages in the Mahā-bhārata, Arjuna and Kṛishṇa. Arjuna is perhaps the real hero of that epic. He is the bravest, and yet the most tender-hearted of the five sons of Pāṇḍu. The god Kṛishṇa, who is identified with Vishṇu[2], and in this philosophical dialogue is held to be an incarnation of the supreme Being himself, had taken human form as the son of Devakī and Vasudeva, who was brother of Kuntī, wife of Pāṇḍu. Hence the god was cousin of the sons of Pāṇḍu, brother of Dhṛitarāshṭra, the sons of these brothers being of course related as cousins to each other. In the great war which arose between the two families, each contending for the kingdom of Hastināpura[3], Kṛishṇa refused to take up arms on either side, but consented to act as the charioteer

---

[1] It is, however, styled an Upanishad, or rather a series of Upanishads, because, like the Upanishads, it reveals secret and mystical doctrines. For instance, at the close of the dialogue (XVIII. 63), Kṛishṇa says, 'I have thus communicated to you knowledge more secret than secret itself' (*iti me jñānam ākhyātaṃ guhyād guhyataraṃ mayā*).

[2] Professor Weber (Indische Studien I. 400) thinks that Brāhmans may have crossed the sea to Asia Minor at the beginning of the Christian era, and on their return made use of Christian narratives to fabricate the story of their deified hero, Kṛishṇa, whose very name would remind them of Christ. The legends of the birth of Kṛishṇa and his persecution by Kaṇsa, remind us, says Weber, too strikingly of the corresponding Christian narratives to leave room for the supposition that the similarity is quite accidental. According to Lassen, the passages of the Mahā-bhārata in which Kṛishṇa receives divine honours are later interpolations, and the real worship of Kṛishṇa is not found before the fifth or sixth century. Dr. Lorinser, as we shall presently see, thinks he can trace the influence of Christianity throughout the Bhagavad-gītā. The legend of S'veta-dvīpa in the Mahā-bhārata (XII. 12703) certainly favours the idea of some intercourse with Europe at an early date. The legends relating to Kṛishṇa are found detailed at full in the tenth book of the Bhāgavata-purāṇa and its Hindī paraphrase, the Prem Sāgar.

[3] See the epitome of this great epic in a subsequent Lecture.

of Arjuna and to aid him with his advice. At the commencement of the Bhagavad-gītā the two contending armies are supposed to be drawn up in battle array, when Arjuna, struck with sudden compunction at the idea of fighting his way to a kingdom through the blood of his kindred, makes a sudden resolution to retire from the combat, confiding his thoughts to Kṛishṇa thus (I. 28–33):

> Beholding these my relatives arrayed
> Before my eyes in serried line of battle,
> Preparing for the deadly fray, my limbs
> Are all relaxed, my blood dries up, a tremor
> Palsies my frame, the hairs upon my skin
> Bristle with horror, all my body burns
> As if with fever, and my mind whirls round,
> So that I cannot stand upright, nor hold
> The bow Gāṇḍīva slipping from my hand.
> I cannot—will not fight—O mighty Kṛishṇa.
> I seek not victory, I seek no kingdom.
> What shall we do with regal pomp and power,
> What with enjoyments or with life itself,
> When we have slaughtered all our kindred here?

Kṛishṇa's reply to this speech is made the occasion of the long philosophical and theological dialogue which, in fact, constitutes the Bhagavad-gītā, the main design of which undoubtedly is to exalt the duties of caste above all other obligations, including the ties of friendship and affection, but at the same time to show that the practice of these duties is compatible with all the self-mortification and concentration of thought enjoined by the Yoga philosophy, as well as with the deepest devotion to the supreme Being, with whom Kṛishṇa claims to be identified[1]. As

[1] There is a sect among the Hindūs called Gāṇapatyas, who identify Gaṇapati or Gaṇeśa with the supreme Being. Their doctrines are embodied in the Gaṇeśa-purāṇa, but they have a poem called the Gaṇeśa-gītā, which is identical in substance with the Bhagavad-gītā, the name of Gaṇeśa being substituted for that of Kṛishṇa.

Arjuna belongs to the military caste, he is exhorted to perform his duties as a soldier. Again and again is he urged to fight, without the least thought about consequences, and without the slightest question as to the propriety of slaughtering his relations, if only he acts in the path of duty. Hence we have the following sentiments repeated more than once (III. 35, XVIII. 47, 48):

> Better to do the duty of one's caste[1],
> Though bad and ill-performed and fraught with evil,
> Than undertake the business of another,
> However good it be. For better far
> Abandon life at once than not fulfil
> One's own appointed work; another's duty
> Brings danger to the man who meddles with it.
> Perfection is alone attained by him
> Who swerves not from the business of his caste.

Remembering the sacred character attributed to this poem and the veneration in which it has always been held throughout India, we may well understand that such words as these must have exerted a powerful influence for the last 1800 years; tending, as they must have done, to rivet the fetters of caste-institutions which, for several centuries preceding the Christian era, notwithstanding the efforts of the great liberator Buddha, increased year by year their hold upon the various classes of Hindū society, impeding mutual intercourse, preventing healthy interchange of ideas, and making national union almost impossible.

Before proceeding to offer further examples, we may remark that as the Bhagavad-gītā is divided into three sections, each containing six chapters, so the philosophical teaching is somewhat distinct in each section.

---

[1] Compare S'akuntalā, verse 133, 'Verily the occupation in which a man is born, though it be in bad repute, must not be abandoned.' The words used (*saha-jaṃ karma*) are the same as those in the Bhagavad-gītā.

The first section dwells chiefly on the benefits of the Yoga system, pointing out, however, as we have already observed, that the asceticism of the Yoga ought to be joined with action and the performance of regular caste duties, and winding up with a declaration that the grand end and aim of all asceticism is to attain that most desirable pantheistic state which enables a man to see God in everything and everything in God. Arjuna is exhorted as a member of the soldier-caste to dismiss all doubt about the propriety of fighting and killing his relations, by an argument drawn from the eternal existence of the soul, which is nobly expressed thus (II. 11, &c.)[1]:

The wise grieve not for the departed, nor for those who yet survive.
Ne'er was the time when I was not, nor thou, nor yonder chiefs, and ne'er
Shall be the time when all of us shall be not; as the embodied soul
In this corporeal frame moves swiftly on through boyhood, youth, and age,
So will it pass through other forms hereafter—be not grieved thereat.
The man whom pain and pleasure, heat and cold affect not, he is fit
For immortality; whatever is not cannot be, whatever is
Can never cease to be. Know this—the Being that spread this universe
Is indestructible. Who can destroy the Indestructible?
These bodies that inclose the everlasting soul, inscrutable,
Immortal, have an end; but he who thinks the soul can be destroyed,
And he who deems it a destroyer, are alike mistaken; it
Kills not, and is not killed; it is not born, nor doth it ever die;
It has no past nor future—unproduced, unchanging, infinite; he
Who knows it fixed, unborn, imperishable, indissoluble,
How can that man destroy another, or extinguish aught below?
As men abandon old and threadbare clothes to put on others new,
So casts the embodied soul its worn-out frame to enter other forms.
No dart can pierce it; flame cannot consume it, water wet it not,
Nor scorching breezes dry it—indestructible, incapable
Of heat or moisture or aridity, eternal, all-pervading,
Steadfast, immovable, perpetual, yet imperceptible,
Incomprehensible, unfading, deathless, unimaginable[2].

---

[1] I have endeavoured to give a more literal version than the well-known one of Dean Milman, though I have followed him in some expressions.

[2] Compare the passage from the Kaṭha Upanishad, translated p. 44.

The duty of Yoga or 'intense concentration of the mind on one subject' (viz. the supreme Being, here identified with Kṛishṇa), till at last the great end of freedom from all thought, perfect calm, and absorption in the Deity are obtained, is enjoined with much force of language in the second and sixth books, from which I extract the following examples, translated nearly literally, but not quite according to the order of the text:

That holy man who stands immovable,
As if erect upon a pinnacle [1],
His appetites and organs all subdued,
Sated with knowledge secular and sacred,
To whom a lump of earth, a stone, or gold [2],
To whom friends, relatives, acquaintances,
Neutrals and enemies, the good and bad,
Are all alike, is called 'one yoked with God.'
The man who aims at that supreme condition
Of perfect yoking [3] with the Deity
Must first of all be moderate in all things,
In food, in sleep, in vigilance, in action,
In exercise and recreation. Then
Let him, if seeking God by deep abstraction,
Abandon his possessions and his hopes,
Betake himself to some secluded spot [4],
And fix his heart and thoughts on God alone.
There let him choose a seat, not high nor low,
And with a cloth or skin to cover him,
And Kuśa grass beneath him, let him sit
Firm and erect, his body, head, and neck
Straight and immovable, his eyes directed
Towards a single point [5], not looking round,

---

[1] *Kūṭa-sthaḥ* (VI. 8) may mean 'standing erect like a peak.'

[2] Tersely expressed in Sanskṛit by *sama-loshṭāśma-kāñćanaḥ* VI. 8.

[3] I use these expressions as kindred words to the Sanskṛit *yukta* and *yoga*. 'Joined' and 'junction' are also cognate expressions.

[4] Cf. Matt. vi. 6, 'But thou, when thou prayest, enter into thy closet, and when thou hast shut thy door, pray to thy Father which is in secret.'

[5] The text (VI. 13) says, 'fixing his eyes on the tip of his nose' (*samprekshya nāsikāgram*). See p. 103.

Devoid of passion, free from anxious thought,
His heart restrained, and deep in meditation.
E'en as a tortoise draws its head and feet
Within its shell, so must he keep his organs
Withdrawn from sensual objects. He whose senses
Are well controlled attains to sacred knowledge,
And thence obtains tranquillity of thought.
Without quiescence there can be no bliss.
E'en as a storm-tossed ship upon the waves,
So is the man whose heart obeys his passions,
Which, like the winds, will hurry him away.
Quiescence is the state of the Supreme.
He who, intent on meditation, joins
His soul with the Supreme, is like a flame
That flickers not when sheltered from the wind.

I pass now to the second division of this poem, in which the pantheistic doctrines of the Vedānta are more directly inculcated than in the other sections. Kṛishṇa here in the plainest language claims adoration as one with the great universal Spirit, pervading and constituting the universe. I extract portions from different parts of this section without observing the order of the text, which contains much tautology, as well as repetitions of similar ideas in different language:

Whate'er thou dost perform, whate'er thou eatest,
Whate'er thou givest to the poor, whate'er
Thou offerest in sacrifice, whatever
Thou doest as an act of holy penance,
Do all as if to me, O Arjuna (IX. 27)[1].

[1] Compare 1 Cor. x. 31, 'Whether therefore ye eat, or drink, or whatsoever ye do, do all to the glory of God.' Dr. Lorinser, expanding the views of Professor Weber and others concerning the influence of Christianity on the legends of Kṛishṇa, thinks that many of the sentiments of the Bhagavad-gītā have been directly borrowed from the New Testament, copies of which, he thinks, found their way into India about the third century, when he believes the poem to have been written. He even adopts the theory of a parallel in the names of Christ and Kṛishṇa. He seems, however, to forget that fragments of truth are to be found in all religious systems, however false, and that the Bible, though a true revela-

I am the ancient sage[1], without beginning,
I am the Ruler and the All-sustainer[2],
I am incomprehensible in form,
More subtle and minute than subtlest atoms[3];
I am the cause of the whole universe;
Through me it is created and dissolved;
On me all things within it hang suspended,
Like pearls upon a string[4]. I am the light
In sun and moon, far, far beyond the darkness[5];
I am the brilliancy in flame, the radiance
In all that's radiant, and the light of lights[6],

---

tion, is still in regard to the human mind, through which the thoughts are transfused, a thoroughly Oriental book, cast in an Oriental mould, and full of Oriental ideas and expressions. Some of his comparisons seem mere coincidences of language, which might occur quite naturally and independently. In other cases, where he draws attention to coincidences of ideas—as, for example, the division of the sphere of self-control into thought, word, and deed in chap. XVII. 14–16, &c., and of good works into prayer, fasting, and alms-giving—how could these be borrowed from Christianity, when they are also found in Manu, which few will place later than the fifth century B. C.? Thus a *Tri-daṇḍin* (Manu XII. 10) is explained to mean 'a triple commander,' who commands his thoughts, words, and actions (see note 3, p. 133); the same division is found in Manu II. 192, 236. Professor Cowell has pointed out that it occurs still earlier than Manu, in the Black Yajur-veda VI. 1. 7, and its Āraṇyaka X. 1. 10, and in the Aitareya-brāhmaṇa III. 28. Plato also has the same in his Protagoras (p. 348), and it is found in the Zand Avastā (Gāthā Ahunavaiti III. 3). Nevertheless, something may be said for Dr. Lorinser's theory. His German translation (1869) is rich in notes, pointing out parallels. See also the 'Indian Antiquary' for October 1873.

[1] *Kaviḥ purāṇaḥ* VIII. 9. 'Kavi' in Vedic Sanskṛit means 'wise,' and is an epithet applied to most of the gods, especially to Agni. The meaning 'poet' belongs to later Sanskṛit. [2] *Sarvasya dhātā* VIII. 9.

[3] *Aṇor aṇīyān* VIII. 9. Compare p. 82 of this volume.

[4] VII. 7. Dr. Lorinser compares Rom. xi. 36, 'Of him, and through him, and unto him, are all things.' John i. 3, 'All things were made by him; and without him was not anything made that was made.'

[5] *Prabhāsmi śaśi-sūryayoḥ* VII. 8. *Tamasaḥ parastāt* VIII. 9. Cf. 1 John i. 5, 'God is light, and in him is no darkness at all.' See Ṛig-veda I. 50. 10.

[6] *Jyotishāṃ jyotiḥ* XIII. 17. Cf. Bṛihad-āraṇyaka Upanishad, quoted p. 39 of this volume.

The sound in ether, fragrance in the earth,
The seed eternal of existing things [1],
The life in all, the father, mother, husband,
Forefather, and sustainer of the world,
Its friend and lord. I am its way [2] and refuge,
Its habitation and receptacle,
I am its witness. I am Victory
And Energy; I watch the universe
With eyes and face in all directions turned [3].
I dwell, as Wisdom, in the heart of all [4].
I am the Goodness of the good, I am
Beginning, Middle, End, eternal Time,
The Birth, the Death of all [5]. I am the symbol A
Among the characters [6]. I have created all
Out of one portion of myself. E'en those
Who are of low and unpretending birth [7],
May find the path to highest happiness,
If they depend on me; how much more those
Who are by rank and penance holy Brāhmans
And saintly soldier-princes like thyself.
Then be not sorrowful; from all thy sins

---

[1] *Sarva-bhūtānāṃ vījam* VII. 10, X. 39. Cf. John i. 3, 'All things were made by him.'

[2] *Gati* IX. 18. Cf. John xiv. 6, 'I am the way.'

[3] *Viśvato-mukha*, 'facing in all directions,' IX. 15.

[4] *Jñānaṃ hṛidi sarvasya nishṭhitam* XIII. 17. Cf. 2 Cor. iv. 6.

[5] Compare Rev. i. 17, 18, 'I am the first and the last; and have the keys of hell and of death.' Mr. Mullens draws attention to parallel descriptions of the supreme Ruler in the Greek Orphic hymns: 'Zeus was the first and Zeus the last; Zeus is the head; Zeus, the centre; from Zeus have all things been made; Zeus is the breath of all things; Zeus is the sun and moon,' &c. See his Essay, p. 193, and cf. note 1, p. 116. Cf. also an inscription said to exist in a temple of Athene, Ἐγώ εἰμι πᾶν τὸ γεγονὸς καὶ ὂν καὶ ἐσόμενον.

[6] *Aksharāṇām a-kāro 'smi* X. 33. Compare Rev. i. 8, 'I am Alpha and Omega.'

[7] *Pāpa-yonayaḥ*, 'base-born,' IX. 32. The text states who these are, viz. Women, Vaiśyas, and Śūdras. This is significant in regard to the Hindū estimate of the female sex. A woman's religion is thought to consist in obedience first to her father and then to her husband, with attention to domestic duties. See Manu II. 67. But the joining of

I will deliver thee[1]. Think thou on me,
Have faith in me, adore and worship me[2],
And join thyself in meditation to me;
Thus shalt thou come to me, O Arjuna;
Thus shalt thou rise to my supreme abode,
Where neither sun nor moon have need to shine,
For know that all the lustre they possess is mine[3].

I come now to chapter XI, called 'the Vision (or Revelation) of the Universal Form' (*viśva-rūpa-darśanam*). Arjuna filled with awe at the discovery of the true nature of Kṛishṇa, acting as his charioteer, addresses him thus:

Most mighty Lord supreme, this revelation
Of thy mysterious essence and thy oneness
With the eternal Spirit, clears away
The mists of my illusions. Show me then
Thy form celestial, most divine of men[4],
If haply I may dare to look upon it.

---

Vaiśyas with Śūdras is curious (cf. p. 159. 6). Brāhmans, Kshatriyas, and Rājarshis, i.e. holy personages—half princes, half saints—are by birth and rank fitted for religious exercises, and more likely to reach heaven.

[1] *Ahaṃ tvāṃ sarva-pāpebhyo moćayishyāmi mā śućaḥ.* Cf. Matt. ix. 2, 'Be of good cheer; thy sins be forgiven thee.' A sense of original corruption seems to be felt by all classes of Hindūs, as indicated by the following prayer used after the Gāyatrī by many religious persons:

*Pāpo 'ham pāpa-karmāham pāpātmā pāpa-sambhavaḥ,*
*Trāhi mām, puṇḍarīkāksha sarva-pāpa-hara Hare,*

'I am sinful, I commit sin, my nature is sinful, I am conceived in sin,
Save me, O thou lotus-eyed Hari, the remover of sin.'

[2] The original is, *Man-manā bhava mad-bhakto mad-yājī māṃ namaskuru* IX. 34. Cf. Prov. xxiii. 26, 'My son, give me thine heart.'

[3] *Na tad bhāsayate sūryo na Śaśāṅkaḥ* XV. 6. *Yad āditya-gataṃ tejo yać ćandramasi tat tejo viddhi māmakam* XV. 12. Cf. Rev. xxi. 23, 'The city had no need of the sun, neither of the moon, to shine in it: for the glory of God did lighten it.' Cf. also Mahā-bhārata III. 1745, &c., *Na tatra sūryāḥ somo vā dyotate na ća pāvakaḥ, Svayaiva prabhayā tatra dyotante puṇya-labdhayā*, 'there (in Indra's heaven) the sun shines not, nor the moon nor fire; there they (righteous men) shine by their own glory acquired by their own merit.'

[4] *Purushottama*, 'most excellent of men,' a common name for Kṛishṇa.

To this Kṛishṇa replies:

Thou canst not bear to gaze upon my shape
With these thy human eyes, O son of Pāṇḍu,
But now I gift thee with celestial vision;
Behold me in a hundred thousand forms,
In phases, colours, fashions infinite.

Here follows the description of Kṛishṇa's supernatural transformation[1]:

Thus having said, the mighty Lord of all
Displayed to Arjuna his form supreme,
Endowed with countless mouths and countless eyes,
With countless faces turned to every quarter,
With countless marvellous appearances,
With ornaments and wreaths and robes divine,
With heavenly fragrance and celestial weapons.
It was as if the firmament were filled,
All in an instant, with a thousand suns,
Blazing with dazzling lustre, so beheld he
The glories of the universe collected
In the one person of the God of gods[2].

Arjuna, with every hair on his body bristling with awe, bows his head at this vision, and folding his hands in reverence, gives utterance to a passionate outburst of enthusiastic adoration, which I here abridge:

I see thee, mighty Lord of all, revealed
In forms of infinite diversity.
I see thee like a mass of purest light,
Flashing thy lustre everywhere around.

---

[1] The idea of this, Dr. Lorinser considers borrowed from the Gospel narrative of the transfiguration. It is certainly very instructive to contrast the simplicity of the Gospel scene: 'His face did shine as the sun, and his raiment was white as the light,' Matt. xvii. 2, Mark ix. 3.

[2] In the Udyoga-parva of the Mahā-bhārata (4419–4430) Kṛishṇa reveals his form in the same way to the assembled princes, who are obliged to close their eyes at the awful sight, while the blind Dhṛita-rāshṭra is gifted with divine vision that he may behold the glorious spectacle (4437).

I see thee crowned with splendour like the sun,
Pervading earth and sky, immeasurable,
Boundless, without beginning, middle, end,
Preserver of imperishable law,
The everlasting Man[1]; the triple world
Is awe-struck at this vision of thy form,
Stupendous, indescribable in glory.
Have mercy, God of gods; the universe
Is fitly dazzled by thy majesty,
Fitly to thee alone devotes its homage.
At thy approach the evil demons flee,
Scattered in terror to the winds of heaven.
The multitude of holy saints[2] adore thee—
Thee, first Creator[3], lord of all the gods,
The ancient One[4], supreme Receptacle
Of all that is and is not, knowing all,
And to be known by all. Immensely vast,
Thou comprehendest all, thou art the All (XI. 40).
To thee earth's greatest heroes must return,
Blending once more with thy resplendent essence,
Like mighty rivers rushing to the ocean (XI. 28).
To thee be sung a thousand hymns of praise
By every creature and from every quarter,
Before, above, behind. Hail! Hail! thou All!
Again and yet again I worship thee.
Have mercy, I implore thee, and forgive,
That I, in ignorance of this thy glory,
Presumed to call thee Friend; and pardon too
Whate'er I have too negligently uttered,
Addressing thee in too familiar tones.
Unrivalled God of gods, I fall before thee
Prostrate in adoration, thou the Father

---

[1] *Sanātanaḥ purushaḥ* (XI. 18) may be translated 'the eternal Spirit.'

[2] *Maharshis*, great saints and Siddhas, XI. 21. Cf. parts of the Te Deum. The Siddhas are semi-divine beings supposed to possess great purity, called Sādhyas in the earlier mythology (Manu I. 22). Siddhas and Sādhyas are sometimes confused, though mentioned separately in the text.

[3] Cf. John viii. 58, 'Before Abraham was, I am.'

[4] *Purushaḥ purāṇaḥ*, 'the most ancient person,' XI. 38. Cf. Daniel vii. 9, 'The Ancient of days did sit.'

Of all that lives and lives not; have compassion,
Bear with me, as a father with a son,
Or as a lover with a cherished one.
Now that I see thee as thou really art,
I thrill with terror! Mercy! Lord of lords,
Once more display to me thy human form,
Thou habitation of the universe[1].

Many other remarkable passages might be adduced in connection with the first two divisions of the subject-matter of the Bhagavad-gītā. I note the following:

He who has brought his members under subjection, but sits with foolish mind thinking in his heart of sensual things, is called a hypocrite (*mithyā-ćāra*). (III. 6. Cf. Matt. v. 28.)

Many are my births that are past; many are thine too, O Arjuna. I know them all, but thou knowest them not. (IV. 5. Cf. John viii. 14.)

For the establishment of righteousness am I born from time to time. (IV. 8. Cf. John xviii. 37, 1 John iii. 3.)

I am dearer to the wise than all possessions, and he is dear to me. (VI. 17. Cf. Luke xiv. 33, John xiv. 21.)

The ignorant, the unbeliever, and he of a doubting mind perish utterly. (IV. 40. Cf. Mark xvi. 16.)

In him are all beings, by him this universe was spread out. (VIII. 22. Cf. Acts xvii. 28.)

Deluded men despise me when I have taken human form. (IX. 11. Cf. John i. 10.)

In all the Vedas I am to be known. (XV. 15. Cf. John v. 39.)

As many uses as there are in a reservoir filled with waters coming from all parts (for bathing, washing, or drinking), so many does a knowing Brāhman find in all the Vedas. (II. 46. Mr. Thomson compares the various uses made of texts from our own sacred Scriptures.)

The next is suggestive of the doctrine that the condition of the soul for a future state is determined before death:

Whatever a man's state of mind be at the moment when he leaves the

---

[1] XI. 45, 46. Dr. Lorinser compares the awe of our Lord's disciples, Matt. xvii. 6, 'They fell on their face, and were sore afraid.' Also of Simon Peter, Luke v. 8, 'When Simon Peter saw it, he fell down at Jesus' knees, saying, Depart from me; for I am a sinful man, O Lord.'

body to that condition does he always go, being made to conform to that. (VIII. 6. Cf. Eccles. xi. 3. This is the dying Saṇskāra which delays the passage to heaven.)

A similar passage occurs in the Ćhāndogya Upanishad:

Man is a creature of intelligence (*kratu-maya*), whatever ideas he forms in this life, he becomes so when he departs to another, therefore he should reflect (on God, III. 14. 1).

The next is a paraphrase of XVI. 12–16. It may be compared with Luke xii. 17–20:

Entangled in a hundred worldly snares,
Self-seeking men, by ignorance deluded,
Strive by unrighteous means to pile up riches.
Then, in their self-complacency, they say,
'This acquisition I have made to-day,
That I will gain to-morrow; so much pelf
Is hoarded up already, so much more
Remains that I have yet to treasure up.
This enemy I have destroyed, him also
And others in their turn I will dispatch.
I am a lord; I will enjoy myself;
I'm wealthy, noble, strong, successful, happy;
I'm absolutely perfect; no one else
In all the world can be compared to me.
Now I will offer up a sacrifice,
Give gifts with lavish hand and be triumphant.'
Such men, befooled by endless, vain conceits,
Caught in the meshes of the world's illusion,
Immersed in sensuality, descend
Down to the foulest hell of unclean spirits.

I add a few lines from chapter III, in which Kṛishṇa exhorts Arjuna to energetic action by an argument drawn from the example set by himself in his own everlasting exertions for the good of the world (cf. John v. 17). The order of the text is not observed in the following version, and the sentiment in lines 6, 7, is from chapter II. 47:

Perform all necessary acts, for action
Is better than inaction, none can live
By sitting still and doing nought; it is
By action only that a man attains

Immunity from action. Yet in working
Ne'er work for recompense; let the act's motive
Be in the act itself. Know that work
Proceeds from the Supreme. I am the pattern
For man to follow; know that I have done
All acts already, nought remains for me
To gain by action, yet I work for ever
Unweariedly, and this whole universe
Would perish if I did not work my work (III. 19).

The third division of the poem, comprising the six last chapters, aims particularly at interweaving Sāṅkhya doctrines with the Vedānta, though this is done more or less throughout the whole work. It accepts the doctrine of a supreme presiding Spirit (called *Param Brahma* or *Adhyātmam*, XIII. 12, VIII. 1), as the first source of the universe, but asserts the eternal existence of Prakṛiti and Purusha —that is, of an original eternal element and soul—both emanating from the supreme Being (then regarded as *Parā Prakṛiti*, 'supreme Prakṛiti'). It maintains the individuality and personality of souls, and affirms that the body (*kshetra*) and all the world of sense is evolved out of Prakṛiti by the regular Sāṅkhyan process, through Buddhi, Ahaṅkāra, the five subtile elements, the five grosser elements, and the eleven organs, including mind. Thus, in XIII. 19 and in VII. 4–6, we read:

Learn that *Prakṛiti* and *Purusha* also are both of them without beginning. And know that the Vikāras, or 'productions,' and the Guṇas (see p. 95) are sprung from Prakṛiti.

Earth, water, fire, air, ether, mind, intellect, and egoism, into these eight is my Prakṛiti divided. This Prakṛiti is the inferior one, but learn my superior Prakṛiti to be other than this. Understand that all things are produced from this other Prakṛiti.

Again, in VII. 12–14, Kṛishṇa, speaking of the three Guṇas, says:

Know that all the three Guṇas, whether Sattva, Rajas, or Tamas (cf. p. 94), proceed only from me. I am not in them, but they in me.

All this universe, deluded by these three conditions consisting of the

Guṇas, does not recognize me, the imperishable Being, superior to them all.

For this divine illusion (*Māyā*, i. e. 'illusory creation'), consisting of the three Guṇas, caused by me, is difficult to be passed over. Those only are delivered from it who have recourse to me.

The eclecticism of the Bhagavad-gītā will be sufficiently apparent from these examples. I close my brief survey of this celebrated poem by three or four passages (taken from chapter III. 27, chapter XIII. 29, 31), which form a fit conclusion to the subject, as they contain the gist of the whole argument, viz. that it is Arjuna's duty as a soldier to act like a soldier and to do the work of his caste, regardless of consequences; and that this may be done consistently with adhesion to the Vedāntic dogma of the soul's real inactivity and state of passionless repose:

All actions are incessantly performed
By operation of the qualities
Of Prakṛiti; deluded by the thought
Of individuality, the soul
Vainly believes itself to be the doer.
The soul existing from eternity,
Devoid of qualities, imperishable,
Abiding in the body, yet supreme,
Acts not, nor is by any act polluted.
He who perceives that actions are performed
By Prakṛiti alone, and that the soul
Is not an actor, sees the truth aright.

Kṛishṇa's last advice may be thus summed up:

Act then and do thine own appointed task,
In every action my assistance ask,
Do all with heart and soul absorbed in me,
So shalt thou gain thine end and be from trouble free.

Arjuna's conclusion may be thus paraphrased:

Eternal One! thy glory just beheld
Has all illusion from my soul dispelled;
Now by thy favour is my conscience clear,
I will thy bidding do and fight without a fear.

To any one who has followed me in tracing the outline

of this remarkable philosophical dialogue, and has noted the numerous parallels it offers to passages in our sacred Scriptures, it may seem strange that I hesitate to concur in any theory which explains these coincidences by supposing that the author had access to the New Testament or that he derived some of his ideas from the first propagators of Christianity. Surely it will be conceded that the probability of contact and interaction between Gentile systems and the Christian religion in the first two centuries of our era must have been greater in Italy than in India. Yet, if we take the writings and recorded sayings of three great Roman philosophers, Seneca, Epictetus, and Marcus Aurelius, we shall find them full of resemblances to passages in our Scriptures, while there appears to be no ground whatever for supposing that these eminent Pagan writers and thinkers derived any of their ideas from either Jewish or Christian sources. In fact, the Rev. F. W. Farrar, in his interesting and valuable work, 'Seekers after God,' has clearly shown that 'to say that Pagan morality kindled its faded taper at the Gospel light whether furtively or unconsciously, that it dissembled the obligation and made a boast of the splendour, as if it were originally her own, is to make an assertion wholly untenable.' He points out that the attempts of the Christian Fathers to make out Pythagoras a debtor to Hebraic wisdom, Plato an 'Atticizing Moses,' Aristotle a picker up of ethics from a Jew, Seneca a correspondent of St. Paul, were due 'in some cases to ignorance, and in some to a want of perfect honesty in controversial dealing.'

His arguments would be even more conclusive if applied to the Bhagavad-gītā, the author of which was probably contemporaneous with Seneca. It must, indeed, be admitted that the flashes of true light which emerge from the mists of pantheism in the writings of Indian philosophers, must spring from the same source of light as the Gospel itself; but it may reasonably be questioned whether there could have been any actual contact of the Hindū systems with Christianity without a more satisfactory result in the modification of pantheistic and anti-Christian ideas. In order that the resemblances to Scripture in the writings of Roman philosophers may be compared with those just noted, I subjoin a few instances from 'Seekers after God,' and Dr. Ramage's 'Beautiful Thoughts:'

1. Seneca. 'God comes to men: nay, what is nearer, comes into men.' 'A sacred spirit dwells within us, the observer and guardian of all our evil and our good.' Cf. 1 Cor. iii. 16. 'Let him who hath conferred a favour hold his tongue.' 'In conferring a favour nothing should be more avoided than pride.' Cf. Matt. vi. 3. 'If you wish to be loved, love.' 'Expect from another what you do to another.' 'We are all wicked; therefore whatever we blame in another we shall find in our own bosom.' 'A good man is God's disciple and imitator and His true offspring, whom that magnificent Father doth, after the manner of severe parents, educate hardly.' 'God is nigh to thee, He is with thee, He is in thee.' 'Temples are not to be built for God with stones piled on high; He is to be consecrated in the breast of each.' 'What a foolish thing it is to promise ourselves a long life, who are not masters of even to-morrow!' 'Live with men as if God saw you.' 'Other men's sins are before our eyes; our own behind our back.' 'The greater part of mankind are angry with the sinner and not with the sin.' 'The severest punishment a man can receive who has injured another, is to have committed the injury.'

2. Epictetus. 'If you always remember that in all you do in soul or body God stands by as a witness, in all your prayers and your actions you will not err; and you shall have God dwelling with you.' 'How should a man grieve his enemy? By preparing himself to act in the noblest manner.' Cf. Rom. xii. 20.

3. Marcus Aurelius. 'The best way of avenging thyself is not to become like the wrong-doer.' 'Men exist for the sake of one another. Teach them or bear with them.' Cf. 2 Thess. iv. 15, Col. iii. 13. 'In the morning when thou risest unwillingly let these thoughts be present, "I am rising to the work of a human being. Why, then, am I dissatisfied if I am going to do the things for which I exist and for which I was brought into the world?" Dost thou exist, then, to take thy pleasure, and not for action or exertion? Dost thou not see the little birds, the ants, the spiders, the bees working together to put in order their several parts of the universe?' Cf. Prov. vi. 6.

# LECTURE VIII.

## *Smṛiti—The Vedāṅgas.*

HITHERTO we have been engaged in describing briefly and illustrating by selected examples the three divisions of the Veda, viz. Mantra, Brāhmaṇa, and Upanishad, and the six Darśanas or systems of philosophy developed out of the third of these divisions. All three portions of the Veda come under the head of *Śruti*, 'audition,' or *Śruta*,—that which is directly heard or revealed—the eternal voice of divine knowledge heard[1] by certain holy men called Ṛishis, and by them orally transmitted; or if committed to writing, then written down exactly as heard, without any intervention of human authorship. We now pass from Śruti and the six Darśanas to the second great head of Sanskṛit literature, called *Smṛiti*, 'recollection' or that which is remembered and handed down by tradition (as distinguished from 'audition'). This is believed to be founded on Śruti, 'direct revelation,' as its primary basis, and only possesses authority in so far as it is in harmony with such revealed truth[2]. The very essence of Smṛiti, however, is considered to be that it was delivered *memoriter* by human authors and put into the form of human composition. In its widest acceptation, Smṛiti may be said to include six principal subjects or departments, viz. I. *six Vedāṅgas*, 'limbs for supporting the Veda,' or, in other

---

[1] The expression generally used is that the Ṛishis *saw* the hymns, *ṛishi* being fancifully connected with *dṛishi*, as if from root *dṛiś;* but the terms *Śruti* and *Śruta*, taken in connection with the theory of the eternity of sound, indicate that the ear was the channel of communication.

[2] If *Veda-vāhya*, it is declared to be *nishphala*. Manu XII. 95.

words, helps to aid the student in reading, understanding and applying it to sacrificial rites (and hence called *Pravaćana*, Manu III. 184): they are—1. Kalpa, 'ceremonial directory,' comprising rules relating to the Vedic ritual and the whole complicated process of sacrifices, which rules are called Śrauta-sūtra, because they are *Vedic*, and relate directly to the application of the Mantra and Brāhmaṇa portion of Śruti, being especially guides to the Brāhmaṇas; 2. Śikshā, 'the science of pronunciation;' 3. Ćhandas, 'metre;' 4. Nirukta, 'exposition of difficult Vedic words;' 5. Vyākaraṇa, 'grammar;' 6. Jyotisha, 'astronomy,' including arithmetic and mathematics, especially in connection with astrology. Of these Vedāṅgas, 1. and 6. are for employing the Veda at sacrifices, 2. and 3. are for reading, 4. and 5. for understanding it. II. The *Smārta-sūtra*, a comprehensive term for such rules as do not relate to *Śrauta* or *Vedic* ceremonies, which were usually on a grand scale and public in their character, but rather to religious acts of a private and personal kind, falling naturally under two divisions, viz. *a*. family or domestic rites (*gṛihya*) performed at stated periods; *b*. conventional usages and every-day practices (*samayāćāra*); on which account these Smārta Sūtras must be separated into two classes, *a*. Gṛihya-sūtra, *b*. Sāmayāćārika-sūtra. III. The *Dharma-śāstras* or 'Law-books,' and especially the *Laws of Manu*, and other so-called inspired law-givers—supposed to have grown out of the Smārta Sūtras. IV. The *Itihāsas* or 'legendary poems,' under which head I place as portions of Smṛiti the two great epic poems called Rāmāyaṇa and Mahā-bhārata, and then, for convenience, as following and depending on these, but not as properly Smṛiti, the artificial poems (Kāvyas) and erotic poems and the dramas, almost all of which in their subject-matter are closely connected with the two great epics. V. The *eighteen Purāṇas* or ancient legendary histories and traditions, with their train of eighteen inferior Purāṇas (*Upa-purāṇa*) and subsequent Tantras. VI. The *Nīti-śāstras* or ethical and didactic writings of all kinds, including collections of fables and moral precepts.

I propose now to take these six divisions of post-Vedic literature in order, beginning with I. the Vedāṅgas.

## I. *The Vedāṅgas.*

They are six in number. Let us consider them (not quite according to the Hindū order) in the following sequence: 1. *Kalpa*; 2. *Śikshā*; 3. *Ćhandas*; 4. *Nirukta*; 5. *Vyākaraṇa*; 6. *Jyotisha.*

### *The Vedāṅgas—Kalpa*, 'ceremonial directory.'

In the first place, then, as regards *Kalpa*; this denotes, as we have seen, a kind of ceremonial directory or rubric put forth in the form of short aphoristic Sūtras or rules, called *Śrauta*, because serving as guides for the application of the Mantra and Brāhmaṇa portion of Śruti to the conduct of sacrificial rites. There are Śrauta Sūtras for each of the five Saṃhitās of the Veda. Thus, for the Ṛig-veda there are the *Āśvalāyana*, *Śāṅkhāyana*, and *Śaunaka* Śrauta Sūtras; for the Sāma-veda, the *Maśaka*, *Lāṭyāyana*, and *Drāhyāyaṇa*; for the Taittirīya or Black Yajur-veda, the *Āpastamba*, *Baudhāyana*, *Satyāshāḍha Hiraṇya-keśin*, *Mānava*, *Bhāradvāja*, *Vādhūna*, *Vaikhānasa*, *Laugākshi*, *Maitra*, *Kaṭha*, and *Vārāha*; for the Vājasaneyi or White Yajur-veda there is only the *Kātyāyana*[1]; for the Atharva-veda only the *Kauśika*.

I should remark here that the word *Sūtra* (derived from the root *Siv*, 'to sew') means properly 'string,' and that this name was applied to any series[2] of rules or

---

[1] Edited by Professor Weber to complete the series of his great edition of the White Yajur-veda with its Brāhmaṇa (the S'atapatha).

[2] *Sūtra* in the singular may denote a whole collection of rules.

aphorisms, either because they were, figuratively, strung together, or because they were written on leaves held together by strings [1]. It is perhaps essential to the true nature of a Brāhmanical Sūtra that it should be a rule or dogma expressed as briefly as possible. In the grammatical Sūtras not a single letter is allowed which can by any contrivance be dispensed with, and moreover in these Sūtras letters and syllables are often used symbolically, like algebraic signs, to indicate ideas which would otherwise require a whole sentence or more to express them at full. In the philosophical Sūtras, as we have already seen, great brevity and a rigid economy of words is also practised, the aim being to furnish the shortest possible suggestive memorial sentences as an aid to the memory of both teachers and learners in an age when books were scarce and paper and printing unknown (see note, p. 48). This extreme conciseness is not always maintained, especially in later Sūtra works, but it generally holds good that the older the Sūtra the greater its curtness and elliptical obscurity, so that without a commentary or a key to their interpretation these ancient aphorisms are quite unintelligible. In later times, as books became more common, the necessity for elaborate and overstrained conciseness was gradually removed [2], and rules and aphorisms, though still strung together in Sūtra style, were more fully and explicitly and even sometimes metrically stated [3]. In fact, these later Sūtra works may be regarded as simple collections of formulated precepts or dogmas adapted to serve as convenient manuals to particular systems of teaching, whether in ritual, philosophy, law, or grammar. If Sanskṛit scholars are asked to state the age of the

[1] This last is the theory of the late Professor Goldstücker.

[2] This relaxation led at last to the very opposite extreme of prolixity, as in the Buddhist Sūtras.

[3] In some Sūtra works there is an occasional admixture of S'lokas.

oldest Sūtra works, they are again obliged to confess their inability to fix any precise date. The most ancient are probably not older than the fifth or sixth century B.C., and the time of the compilation of the most recent is perhaps not far removed from the commencement of the Christian era. I have placed the Kalpa Sūtras first because they are probably oldest, being closely connected with the Brāhmaṇa or ritual portion of Śruti, and thence called Śrauta.

The following translation of the first ten Sūtras of Kātyāyana's Śrauta-sūtra, which belong to the Śatapatha-brāhmaṇa and White Yajur-veda (see Weber's edition), will give some idea of the nature of these rules. To make each aphorism intelligible, additional matter has to be introduced from the commentary of Yājṅika-deva. This I have done parenthetically in the examples here given. I have also given the original text of the Sūtras in italics:

1. Now, therefore, the right (of engaging in sacrificial acts is about to be laid down in the following rules). [*Athāto 'dhikāraḥ.*]

2. (Sacrificial) acts (like the Agni-hotra, &c.) are attended with recompense (such as the attainment of heaven, of wealth, of a son, &c.) [*Phala-yuktāni karmāṇi.*]

3. (According to the primâ facie view of the matter there must be a right) of all (creatures, e. g. of men, even though blind, dumb, lame, or deaf, of gods, of Ṛishis, and of animals, but not of plants, to engage in sacrificial acts), without distinction, (because all such creatures are capable of desiring recompense.) [*Sarveshām aviśeshāt.*]

4. But (according to the orthodox view, the right belongs) to human beings (only), because (they only, as the Veda declares, have) the power of undertaking (sacrificial acts, and not to gods, Ṛishis, and animals). [*Manushyāṇāṃ vārambha-sāmarthyāt.*]

5. Cripples, those ignorant of the Veda, eunuchs, and S'ūdras (are to be) excepted. [*Anga-hīnāśrotriya-shaṇḍha-śūdra-varjam.*]

6. (The right belongs) to Brāhmans, Kshatriyas[1], and Vaiśyas (but not to S'ūdras), according to the Vedic precept. [*Brāhmaṇa-rājanya-vaiśyānāṃ śruteḥ.*]

---

[1] The word *Rājanya* is used here and in the Purusha-sūkta for Kshatriya, see p. 24.

7. A woman also (has the right), since there is no difference (between her and her husband in regard to the desire for heaven). [*Strī ćāviśeshāt.*]

8. And since it is so seen (in the Veda). [*Darśanāć-ća.*]

9. (According to one view, the right belongs) to a man of the Rathakāra[1] ('chariot-maker') caste, (so far as regards the rite) of placing the sacred fire (on the sacrificial ground, on the score of this caste being reckoned among the first three classes). [*Rathakārasyādhāne.*]

10. (But according to the orthodox view) it is settled (that the Rathakāra is not to be reckoned among the first three classes). [*Niyataṃ ća.*]

## *The Vedāṅgas—Śikshā,* 'phonetic directory.'

The next Vedāṅga in our list is *Śikshā* or the science of proper pronunciation, especially as teaching the laws of euphony peculiar to the Veda. This comprises the knowledge of letters, accents, quantity, the right use of the organs of articulation, and phonetics generally. One short comparatively modern treatise on phonetics, consisting in one recension of thirty-five and in another of fifty-nine verses (ascribed to Pāṇini), and a chapter of the Taittirīyāraṇyaka are regarded as the representatives of this subject; but the Vedic Prātiśākhyas and other works on Vedic phonetics may be included under it[2], and it will be convenient so to regard them. These Prātiśākhyas are grammatical, or rather phonetic, treatises written in the Sūtra style (some of them perhaps of a more recent date than Pāṇini[3]), regulating the euphonic combination of letters and their peculiar pronunciation according to the

---

[1] This mixed caste, held to be the offspring of a Māhishya by a Karaṇī, is also called Saudhanvana. It appears to have enjoyed some religious privileges, perhaps because the Ṛibhus were Ratha-kāras, see note, p. 17. Cf. Ṛig-veda III. 60. 4.

[2] A number of works bearing the name of *Śikshā,* and dealing with phonetics and other kindred subjects, have been recently brought to notice. See Haug on *the Vedic Accent* (Munich, 1874.)

[3] The late Professor Goldstücker, in his work on Pāṇini, decides that all the Prātiśākhyas must have been posterior to Pāṇini; but this opinion is shared by few other scholars.

practice of the different Śākhās, 'branches,' of the Vedas, in those traditional versions of the Vedic texts handed down by different families. The Prātiśākhyas do not undo words in the same way as the Vyākaraṇa, but take actually formed words as they occur in the hymns, and teach the phonetic changes they undergo, the mode of pronouncing the accents, &c. In fact they show how the Pada text is converted by a process of euphonic combination into the Saṃhitā.

Since the chief virtue of the Vedic texts was in their oral repetition, and since so much importance was attached to the proper pronunciation and accentuation of every syllable, it may be easily supposed that these phonetic manuals were of great value to persons who had to repeat Mantras every day as an essential part of their religious exercises. They probably served as guides and aids to the memory, both for teachers in instructing their pupils and for pupils in learning to recite the Veda. Four Prātiśākhyas are extant, viz.: 1. one to the Śākala-śākhā of the Ṛig-veda, ascribed to Śaunaka[1]; 2. another to a Śākhā of the Taittirīya or Black Yajur-veda[2]; 3. another to a Śākhā of the Mādhyandinas, of the family of the Vājasaneyins or 'followers of the White Yajur-veda,' whence this is called the Vājasaneyi-prātiśākhya[3]; it is ascribed to an author, Kātyāyana, probably identical with the writer of the Vārttikas or 'supplementary rules' to Pāṇini; 4. an Atharva-veda-prātiśākhya, called Śaunakīyā Ćaturādhyāyikā[4], 'Śaunaka's treatise in four chapters.' No Prātiśākhya has yet been found to the Sāma-veda.

[1] Edited and translated into French by M. Adolphe Regnier, and into German by Professor Max Müller.

[2] Edited, with its commentary, and translated by Professor William D. Whitney.

[3] Edited and translated by Professor Weber in the 'Indische Studien.'

[4] Also edited, with a most valuable English translation and notes, by Professor William D. Whitney.

The relative age of the Prātiśākhyas in their present form is an open question. That to the Ṛig-veda has been by some confidently declared the oldest, though written in Ślokas with occasional admixture of other metres.

I here translate the fifth and sixth Sūtras of this Prātiśākhya, as they contain a statement of some of the points which form the subject of the work:

Heaviness (i.e. prosodial length), lightness (i.e. prosodial shortness), equality, shortness, longness, and prolation (of vowels), elision, augmentation, and change, original form, non-change of Visarga into a sibilant, regular order, the mixed tone, high tone, low tone, breath and sound[1], and both (combined),—all this must be accurately understood by one who reads (or repeats) the words of the Veda.

[*Gurutvaṃ laghutā sāmyaṃ hrasva-dīrgha-plutāni ća* ı
*Lopāgama-vikārāś-ća prakṛitir vikramaḥ kramaḥ* ıı
*Svaritodātta-nīćatvaṃ śvāso nādas tathobhayam* ı
*Etat sarvaṃ ća vijñeyaṃ ćhando-bhāshām adhīyatā* ıı]

The first Atharva-veda-prātiśākhya states the subject of the treatise (Whitney, p. 9), and gives a fourfold division of all the parts of speech in its first Sūtra, thus:

The two qualities of the four kinds of words—noun (*nāma*), verb (*ākhyāta*), preposition (*upasarga*), and particle (*nipāta*)—as euphonically joined and as separate words, are here the subject (*prātijñam*).

That is to say, the design of the Prātiśākhya is to form a Saṃhitā out of a Pada text. In fact, it supposes all the words of the Veda to be separated from each other (as they are in the Pada), and then teaches how they are to be euphonically connected, as they must be in the Saṃhitā[2].

The second chapter introduces a number of rules of

---

[1] We learn from the Atharva-veda-prātiśākhya I. 12, 13, that in the surd consonants there is mere breath, and in the sonant, sound.

[2] In the *Krama* text the 1st word is recited with the 2nd, that is repeated with the 3rd, that with the 4th, &c. In the *Jaṭā*, the 1st word and 2nd, 2nd and 1st, and 1st and 2nd again; next the 2nd and 3rd, 3rd and 2nd, and 2nd and 3rd, and so on. In the *Ghana*, the 1st and 2nd, 2nd and 1st, 1st and 2nd again, 3rd; then 3rd, 2nd, 1st, 1st, 2nd, 3rd; then the 2nd begins a new Ghana.

Sandhi, which will be familiar to the students of Pāṇini's Grammar. The first Sūtra consists of one word, which must be amplified thus (Whitney's edition, p. 72):

(The following rules are to be understood as of force when the separate words of the disjointed text are put together) in the Saṃhitā [Saṃhitā-yām].

Then follow the rules, of which I subjoin three or four examples (II. 10, 11, 18, 19, III. 20):

Before *ś*, *n* becomes *ṅ* [*na-kārasya śa-kāre ṅakāraḥ*].

Also before a sonant palatal (as before *j*) [*ća-vargīye ghoshavati*].

After the preposition *ud*, there is elision of the letter *s* of the roots *sthā* and *stambh* [*lopa udaḥ sthā-stambhoḥ sa-kārasya*].

There is elision of *R* before *r* [*rephasya rephe*].

When *r* is elided (the preceding vowel is lengthened) [*ra-lope*].

The Vājasaneyi-prātiśākhya (I. 27) gives a still more complete enumeration of the parts of speech, thus:

Words are made up of inflected verbal bases [i. e. bases having the personal endings, technically called *tiṅ*], nouns derived from verbs by Kṛit affixes, nouns derived from nouns by Taddhita affixes and four kinds of compounds (Avyayī-bhāva, Tatpurusha, Dvandva, Bahu-vrīhi). [*Tiṅ-kṛit-taddhita-ćatushṭaya-samāsāḥ śabda-mayam.* See Professor Max Müller's Ancient Sanskṛit Literature, p. 164.]

## *The Vedāṅgas—Ćhandas,* 'metre.'

This Vedāṅga is imperfectly represented by the *Ćhandaḥ-śāstra* ascribed to Piṅgala or Piṅgala-nāga, which may be as old as the second century B.C., and treats of Prākṛit as well as Sanskṛit metres, including only a few Vedic. Other works on metres are the Nidāna-sūtra in ten Prapāṭhakas and the Śruta-bodha. In truth, prosody, like every other subject in Sanskṛit literature, affords field for almost endless investigation. It is a complete study in itself, and its importance in the estimation of the Hindūs is shown by the excessive cultivation and elaboration bestowed upon their whole metrical system. A knowledge of the metre of each hymn of the Veda was considered essential to the right use and proper recitation of the Mantras. Hence we find Sāyaṇa, in his introduction to the first hymn of the Ṛig-veda, quoting the following precept:

He who shall cause any one to repeat (*adhyāpayet*) or shall himself repeat (any hymn of the Veda) without having acquainted himself with the name of the Ṛishi to whom it was revealed, the metre (*ćhandas*) in which it was written, the deity to whom it was addressed, and its right application (*yoga*), is the worst of sinners (*pāpīyān*).

Again, immediately afterwards, he adds:

Any one who makes use of (a hymn) without knowing the Ṛishi, the metre, the deity, the right interpretation according to the Brāhmaṇas (*brāhmaṇārtha*), and the accents is called 'a Mantra-thorn' (*mantra-kaṇṭaka*, as destroying or obstructing its efficacy).

In the ninth verse of the Purusha-sūkta of the Ṛig-veda (see p. 24) the metres are said to have sprung from Purusha himself, thus:

From that universal sacrifice sprang the Ṛić and Sāman verses, the metres, and the Yajus (*ćhandāṉsi jajñire tasmād yajus tasmād ajāyata*).

The Taittirīya-saṃhitā VII. 1. 1. 4 &c. describes the creation of several metres by Prajāpati (Muir, vol. i. p. 15):

Prajāpati desired 'may I be propagated.' He formed the Trivṛit from his mouth. After it were produced the deity Agni, the metre Gāyatrī, &c.

In Manu IV. 99, 100, we have the following:

Let not a man repeat the Veda without clear pronunciation (of the letters, accents, &c., *svara-varṇādi*, Kullūka). Let him always be careful to recite it as composed in metre (*ćhandas-kṛitam*).

It is remarkable that in Pāṇini's Grammar the usual name for the Veda is Ćhandas (see p. 179).

From the importance thus assigned to the metrical structure of the hymns we shall be prepared to find frequent allusions to the subject of metres in the Brāhmaṇas. In fact, these treatises attach a kind of mystical efficacy to their right use, and whole chapters of the Upanishads enlarge on the same fanciful theme. The Gāyatrī is held in especial veneration, the most sacred text of the Ṛig-veda being in this metre. (See p. 20.)

The following passage is from the Śatapatha-brāhmaṇa I. 2, 5, 6, &c. (Muir's Texts, vol. iv. p. 123):

The gods having placed Vishṇu to the east surrounded him with metres (*ćhandobhir abhitaḥ paryagṛihṇan*); saying, 'On the south side, I surround thee with the Gāyatrī metre; on the west I surround thee with the Trishṭubh metre; on the north I surround thee with the Jagatī.' Having thus surrounded him with metres, they placed Agni on the east, and thus they went on worshipping and toiling. By this means they acquired this whole earth (*tena imāṃ sarvāṃ pṛithivīṃ samavindanta*).

Again, in the fourteenth Brāhmaṇa of the Bṛihad-āraṇyaka Upanishad we read (Röer, p. 254):

The *Ṛićaḥ*, *Yajūṇshi*, and *Sāmāni* are eight syllables (*ashṭāv aksharāṇi*); the second Pāda (*padam*) of the Gāyatrī consists of eight syllables (*ashṭāksharam*). This Pāda of the Gāyatrī represents that nature of the three Vedas. Whoever knows this Pāda of the Gāyatrī conquers all that is conquerable by the knowledge of the three Vedas.

Hence we cannot be surprised that some of the most sacred metres, especially the Gāyatrī, were in the end personified and invested with divine functions. Our present purpose and limits do not admit of our giving schemes of even the commonest forms of Sanskṛit metre, whether Vedic or Post-vedic. They will be found enumerated in the third edition of my Sanskṛit Grammar, pp. 388–392[1]. Let me merely observe that great licence is allowed in Vedic prosody, so that in the Gāyatrī, which may be regarded as consisting either of three divisions of eight syllables each (whence it is called *tri-padā*) or of six feet of four syllables each, the quantity of each syllable is very irregular, although the second, fourth, and sixth feet generally contain two iambics.

Of Post-vedic metres we have so great a variety that it becomes necessary to arrange them under classes and orders, genera and species. In truth, the elaboration of

---

[1] See also Colebrooke's Essay on Sanskṛit and Prākṛit metres and Professor Weber's articles in the 'Indische Studien.'

every kind of complicated metre is carried to an extent quite beyond the ordinary practice of poetical composition in other languages. 'A Hindū poet,' says Dr. Yates, 'may proceed to any length he pleases, within the limits of *a thousand syllables to the half-line*,' or quarter-stanza. The Daṇḍaka metre (of which a specimen occurs in the drama called Mālatī-mādhava, Act V[1]) offers more than any other an almost incredible capability of expansion. It will admit, indeed, of the stanza extending 27 × 4 to 999 × 4 syllables. But the commonest form of metre, chiefly found in epic poetry—the Anushṭubh or Śloka—is short and easy. It consists of four half-lines of eight syllables each or two lines of sixteen syllables each, the last two feet of each line being iambics (see my Sanskṛit Grammar, p. 288). The Indra-vajrā (with its Upendra-vajrā variety) is also a common metre, and one of the most rhythmical. It nearly corresponds to one occurring in Horace's fourth Ode:

> Vūlcānŭs ārdēns ŭrĭt ōffĭcīnās,
> Trăhūntquĕ sīccās māchĭnaē cărīnās.

But to make the Latin agree with the Sanskṛit metre we must suppose the first syllable of *machinae* and of *urit* to be short. It might be represented in an English line thus, 'Dṓwn cōmes thĕ rāin ānd wĭth ĭt cōmes thĕ thūndēr,' an emphasis being placed on the first syllable.

### *The Vedān·gas—Nirukta*, 'exposition.'

The object of this Vedān·ga is etymological explanation or interpretation of difficult Vedic words. Doubtless, numerous works devoted to this object once existed, but all have perished except one, which is now the typical

[1] Beginning *Praćalita-kari-kṛitti*, &c. It has fifty-four syllables to the quarter-verse. This specimen is translated in the Asiatic Researches, vol. x. p. 456.

representative of the whole class[1]. This is a compilation, accompanied with an exposition, by an author named Yāska, who, according to the best authorities, lived before Pāṇini[2], probably about 400 years B.C., or about 1800 years before Sāyaṇa. His work consists first of three bare lists or catalogues of words in five chapters: viz. *a*. The *Naighaṇṭuka* in three chapters of synonyms or rather of collections of words said to have the same meaning as some one word of known signification given at the end, one such collection being called a Nighaṇṭu. The synonyms in each collection vary from two (III. 22) to one hundred and twenty-two (II. 14), and can scarcely be called synonyms in the strict sense. For example, when it is said that *vartate*, 'he turns;' *loṭate*, 'he rolls;' *sarpati*, 'he creeps;' *sravati*, 'he flows;' *sraṉsate*, 'he drops;' *plavate*, 'he swims;' *ḍīyate*, 'he flies;' *patati*, 'he falls,' and 122 other words are all synonyms of *gamati*, 'he goes,' or *gati*, 'going,' this must be understood very widely as intending to include all forms and varieties of motion. Again, in I. 12, we have a collection of 101 words, which are all said to be synonyms of water (*udaka*), but it is obvious that the only attribute most of these have in common is, that they are varieties of fluids, including, for example, nectar (*amṛita*) and clarified butter (*havis*). Seeing, therefore, that many of the words brought together are old Vedic words of doubtful meaning, quite unknown to classical Sanskṛit, and seeing that a complete explanation of the gradations and modifications of sense under each head of synonyms is wanting, the practical utility of these lists is of course very small indeed. *b*. The

---

[1] No less than seventeen Nairuktikas or 'interpreters of the Veda' are mentioned by name as having preceded Yāska. See Dr. Muir's article on the interpretation of the Veda, p. 321.

[2] Pāṇini himself implies (IV. I. 112) that the name Yāska means a descendant of Yaska.

*Naigama*, a collection of 278 separate words (*padāni*) occurring in the Veda (*nigama*), all in one chapter of three sections. *c.* The *Daivata* or 151 words relating to deities and religious or sacrificial acts, in one chapter of six short sections. Whether these collections were drawn up by Yāska himself or by some previous compiler is not certain, but there is no doubt that the second and most important part of the work, viz. the Nirukta or 'explanation' of the words in these lists, is his own composition. Although, therefore, the term Nirukta is sometimes applied to the lists of words, it more properly belongs to Yāska's explanation of them, which occupies twelve chapters. The first of the twelve is a kind of introduction, which contains some interesting discussions of philological questions and a sort of summary or sketch of grammar; the following two chapters are an imperfect exposition of the Naighaṇṭuka or 'lists of synonymous words,' the deficiency of which has been to a certain extent supplied by Durga, a commentator on Yāska; the next three chapters explain the Naigama or 'single Vedic words,' and the last six the Daivata or 'deities addressed in the hymns.' Thus the three collections with their explanations occupy seventeen chapters. The value of the work[1] consists in its being the oldest extant commentary on the Veda. When words are explained, Vedic passages are quoted in illustration, and the author often enters into curious etymological investigations, which possess great interest from their universally admitted antiquity, but are difficult to understand from the extreme brevity and obscurity of their style.

I here abridge some valuable remarks from Dr. John Muir's article on the 'Interpretation of the Veda,' in the Royal Asiatic Society's Journal (vol. ii. new series, p. 320):

The Nirukta makes frequent reference to the Brāhmaṇas, and alludes

[1] It has been ably edited by Professor Roth.

to various schools of Vedic interpretation which existed anterior to its author, such as the Nairuktas or 'etymologists,' the Aitihāsikas or 'legendary writers,' and the Yājñikas or 'ritualists.' Yāska supplies specimens of the mode of explaining the hymns adopted by different schools of interpreters. Thus we are told (Nirukta XI. 29, 31) that the Nairuktas understood Anumati, Rākā, Sinīvālī, and Kuhū to be goddesses, while the Yājñikas took them for the new and full moons. The gods called Aśvins were a great enigma. The Nirukta (XII. 1) gives the following answers to the question who they were: 'Heaven and Earth,' say some; 'Day and Night,' say others; 'the Sun and Moon,' say others; 'two Kings, performers of holy acts,' say the Aitihāsikas. Again, Nirukta (VI. 13) tells us that Aurṇabhāva understood Nāsatyau (an epithet of the Aśvins) as 'true, not false.' Agrāyaṇa took it to mean 'leaders of truth' (*satyasya praṇetārau*); while Yāska himself suggests that it may mean 'nose-born' (*nāsikā-prabhavau*). Again, we are informed (Nirukta III. 8) that some understood the five peoples (*pañća-janāḥ*) mentioned in Ṛig-veda X. 53. 4 to be the Gandharvas, Pitṛis, gods, Asuras, and Rakshases; whilst Aupamanyava took them for the four castes and the Nishādas. So, again, Kātthakya understood Narāśaṇsa to designate 'sacrifice,' but S'ākapūṇi took it for a name of Agni (Nir. VIII. 4. 5). In like manner, Yāska's predecessors were not agreed as to what was meant by Vishṇu's three steps in Ṛig-veda I. 22. 17; S'ākapūṇi maintaining that they were planted on the earth, the atmosphere, and the sky respectively; and Aurṇabhāva that the hill over which the sun rises, the meridian, and the hill where he sets, were the localities referred to. One of these predecessors (Kautsa) had the audacity to assert that Vedic exposition was useless, as the hymns were obscure, unmeaning, or mutually contradictory. As instances of obscurity he cites the texts in which the words *amyak* (Ṛig-veda I. 169. 3), *yādriśmin* (V. 44. 8), *jārayāyi* (VI. 12. 4), and *kāṇukā* (VIII. 66. 4) occur. In regard to this charge, Yāska replies that it is not the fault of the post that the blind man does not see it. In the Nirukta-pariśishṭa the 'four defined grades or stages of speech' referred to in Ṛig-veda I. 164. 45, are said to be explained by the Rishis as meaning the four mystic words, *om, bhūh, bhuvaḥ, svar;* by the grammarians, as denoting nouns, verbs, prepositions, and particles; by the ritualists, as the hymns, liturgical precepts, Brāhmaṇas, and ordinary language; by the etymologists, as the Ṛig, Yajush, Sāman, and the current language; by others, as the speech of serpents, birds, reptiles, and the vernacular; by the spiritualists, as that of beasts, musical instruments, wild animals, and soul.

It is evident from the above remarks that great difference of opinion existed among expositors of the Veda even in Yāska's time, considerably more than 2000 years ago, and that the objections of sceptics and rationalists had to be met and answered by orthodox theologians like himself. He commences his own exposition thus (I. 1):

The traditional collection of words has been thus traditionally repeated. That must now be explained. They call this traditional collection the Nighaṇṭus. [*Samāmnāyaḥ samāmnātaḥ sa vyākhyātavyas tam imaṃ samāmnāyaṃ nighaṇṭava ity āćakshate.*]

Perhaps as good an example of Yāska's condensed style as can be offered is a passage quoted and explained by Professor Goldstücker from Roth's edition, I. 3. It is interesting as showing that, for the better interpretation of the Veda, Yāska aimed at giving some sort of exposition of grammar and grammatical science as then understood:

(The ancient grammarian) S'ākaṭāyana says that prepositions when not attached (to nouns or verbs) do not express meanings; but Gārgya says that they illustrate (or modify) the action which is expressed by a noun or verb, and that their senses are various (even when detached). Now they express that sense which inheres in them; that is, that which modifies the sense of a noun or verb. The preposition *ā* is in the sense of limit; *pra* and *parā* express the reverse of that; *abhi*, direction towards; *prati*, the reverse of that; *ati* and *su*, superiority; *nir* and *dur*, the reverse of these two; *ni* and *ava*, the act of taking down; *ud*, the reverse of these two; *sam*, combining together; *vi* and *apa*, the reverse of that; *anu*, similarity or being after; *api*, conjunction; *upa*, the being appended; *pari*, being all around; *adhi*, being above or supremacy: thus they express various meanings, and these must be taken into consideration. [*Na nirbaddhā upasargā arthān nir-āhur iti Śākaṭāyano, nāmākhyātayos tu karmopasaṃyoga-dyotakā bhavanty uććāvaćāḥ padārthā bhavantīti Gārgyas, tad ya eshu padārthaḥ prāhur ime taṃ nāmākhyātayor artha-vikaraṇam; ā ity arvāg-arthe, pra parety etasya prātilomyam; abhīty ābhimukhyam, pratīty etasya prātilomyam; ati su ity abhipūjitārthe, nir dur ity etayoḥ prātilomyaṃ; ny aveti vinigrahārthīyā, ud ity etayoḥ prātilomyaṃ; sam ity ekībhāvaṃ, vy apety etasya prātilomyam; anv iti sādṛiśyāparabhāvam; apīti saṃsargaṃ; upety upajanam; parīti sarvato-bhāvam; adhīty uparibhāvam aiśvaryaṃ vaivam uććāvaćān arthān prāhus ta upekshitavyāḥ.*]

There is a still more interesting passage on the subject of derivation a little further on in the same chapter (I. 12):

So these four kinds of words have been enumerated, nouns (*nāman*), verbs (*ākhyāta*), prepositions (*upasarga*), and particles (*nipāta*). S'ākaṭāyana affirms that nouns are derived from verbs, and on this point there is an agreement of the etymologists (*nairukta-samayaḥ*). But Gārgya and some of the grammarians say that not all (nouns are derived from verbs). For if all nouns came from verbs, then whatever performs the same action ought to have the same name. Thus, if *aśva*, 'a horse,' were derived from the root *aś*, 'to pass through,' then every one who passes along a road ought to be called *aśva*; and if *tṛiṇa*, 'a blade of grass,' were derived from the root *tṛid*, 'to pierce,' then everything that pierces ought to be called *tṛiṇa*. Again, if all nouns were derived from verbs, then everything would have as many names as there are states with which it could be connected. Thus, *sthūṇā*, 'a post,' might be called *dara-śayā*, 'hole-sleeper,' because resting in a hole, or *saṅ-janī*, 'joiner together,' because things are joined by being attached to it. [Yāska ends by taking the side of S'ākaṭāyana. See Professor Max Müller's Ancient Sanskṛit Literature, p. 165.]

The thirteenth and fourteenth chapters, commonly called the Nirukta-pariśishṭa, are thought to be the work of a more recent author than Yāska. There are numerous classical glossaries by later lexicographers, e.g.:

The Amara-kosha (sometimes called Tri-kāṇḍa, 'having three chapters'), by the Bauddha Amara-siṇha, probably not later than A.D. 500; the Abhidhāna-ratna-mālā, by Halāyudha; the Abhidhāna-ćintāmaṇi, by the Jaina Hema-ćandra; the Viśva-prakāśa, by Maheśvara; the Dharaṇi; the Medinī; the Hārāvalī, &c.

### *The Vedān·gas—Vyākaraṇa*, 'grammar.'

This word *Vy-ā-karaṇa* means literally 'undoing,' and is applied first to linguistic analysis and then generally to grammar, but especially to Pāṇini's grammar[1]. It is the opposite to *Saṉskaraṇa*, 'putting together,' whence the formed language is called *Saṉskṛita*, 'constructed.' Strictly, the great Vyākaraṇa of Pāṇini can scarcely be regarded as a Vedān·ga, seeing that it only treats of the

[1] No Paṇḍit would use Vyākaraṇa except for Sanskṛit grammar, and a man's Sanskṛit scholarship is often summed up by describing him as knowing 'the Vyākaran.'

Vedic idiom exceptionally. The grammatical Sūtras which preceded his time and which have nearly all perished must have constituted the Vyākaraṇa division of works ancillary to the study of the Veda[1]. Nevertheless, the grammar of Pāṇini, which is the great standard of correct Sanskṛit, is usually taken to represent this Vedāṅga, and as it is one of the most remarkable literary works that the world has ever seen, and as no other country can produce any grammatical system at all comparable to it, either for originality of plan or for analytical subtlety, a brief description of its characteristic features may be introduced here.

Little or nothing is known of Pāṇini, the author of the grammar. He is described as a descendant of Paṇin and grandchild of an inspired legislator named Devala. His mother's name was Dākshī (whence he is called Dāksheya), and Śalātura in the Gandhāra country (Kandahar), north-west of Attock on the Indus, is said to have been his birth-place (whence his name Śālāturīya). He belonged, therefore, to the North-western or Western school. As, however, in later times he became more and more an object of reverence, he was at last actually canonized by his admirers, that is to say, exalted to the rank of a Ṛishi or inspired Muni. Hence he is fabled to have *seen* rather than composed his grammar, which was declared to have been supernaturally revealed to him, the first fourteen

[1] Pāṇini himself mentions several grammarians as having preceded him, such as Āpiśali, Kāśyapa, Gārgya, Gālava, Ćākravarmaṇa, Bhāradvāja, Śākaṭāyana, Śākalya, Senaka, and Sphoṭāyana. The Uṇādi-sūtras (commented on by Ujjvala-datta), giving the affixes, commencing with *uṇ*, for the formation of words whose meaning has deviated from accordance with their etymology, and whose root is not always clear, are thought by some to be anterior to Pāṇini. Possibly he may have made a list of them himself. At any rate, he mentions the *affixes* in III. 3. 1, III. 4. 75. Śāntanava's Phiṭ-sūtras on accent are probably later than Pāṇini. They have been well edited by Professor Kielhorn. I believe Dr. Bühler has found part of a work which claims to be Śākaṭāyana's grammar.

Sūtras especially having been communicated, according to the legend, by the god Śiva. It is of course quite impossible to fix with certainty at what period Pāṇini lived. The late Professor Goldstücker thought he had good grounds for deciding that the great grammarian preceded Buddha. This would place him in the sixth century B. C. Other scholars, whose opinions are entitled to respect, consider that an earlier date cannot be assigned to him than the middle of the fourth century B. C.

His work—perhaps the most original of all productions of the Hindū mind—is sometimes called the Ashṭādhyāyī, sometimes Ashṭakam Pāṇinīyam, because it consists of eight lectures (Adhyāyas), each of which is again subdivided into four chapters (Pādas). In these eight Adhyāyas are contained 3996 Sūtras or Aphorisms[1]. The first Adhyāya explains the technical terms used in the grammar and the rules for their interpretation and application[2]. A root is called Dhātu, and a crude base Prātipadika, but a root never appears without some appendage (*anubandha*) in the shape of indicatory syllables or letters (technically called *it*) which do not really form part of the root, but merely denote certain peculiarities in its inflection, conjugation, &c. Similar indicatory letters and syllables (*it*) are attached either at the beginning or end of all affixes, augments, &c.[3] The case affixes are called *sup*,

[1] Three or four of these are supposed to be later additions. In the excellent edition of Professor Böhtlingk there are 3997, including the fourteen Śiva Sūtras. Pāṇini is also the supposed author of the oldest Dhātu-pāṭha or dictionary of roots with their Anubandhas.

[2] A rule giving the key to Pāṇini's Sūtras and their application is called a Paribhāshā; one which explains the technical terms is a Sañjñā.

[3] For example, the root *nid* is called *nidi* to show that a nasal is inserted in conjugation, thus, *nindāmi*, *nindasi*, &c. The affix *maya* is called *mayaṭ* to show that its feminine is *mayī*. Sometimes these *Its* or *Anubandhas* serve to distinguish two roots or affixes, which, although similar in sound, have different senses; for example, the root *dā*, 'to

and the personal endings or terminations of verbs *tiṅ*. Between the latter and the root a conjugational syllable is inserted, called *vikaraṇa*. The third chapter of the first Adhyāya treats of the proper use of the active voice (*Parasmai-pada*) and middle or reflexive voice (*Ātmane-pada*). The second Adhyāya explains compound words. The third, fourth, and fifth Adhyāyas enumerate the various affixes and their meanings. Those belonging to verbs occupy the third Adhyāya; those affixed to nouns, the fourth and fifth. The sixth, seventh, and eighth Adhyāyas treat of the changes which roots and affixes undergo by augments and substitutions of various kinds. For brevity and economy of words nothing can be more successful than the system in which all this immense and intricate subject is explained. The Sūtras of Pāṇini are indeed a perfect miracle of condensation, their main design apparently being to aid the memory of teachers rather than learners by the briefest possible suggestions. When a single letter can be saved every other consideration is sacrificed to this paramount object; and to attain a greater amount of abridgment than could be effected by the use of ordinary words an arbitrary symbolical language is coined, the key to which must be acquired before the rules themselves can be rendered intelligible[1]. Perhaps the closing Sūtra of the whole work may be taken as the best instance of the consummate brevity attained. It consists of two letters, as follows: *a a*. This is said to mean:

---

give,' is called *ḍudāñ*, while *dā*, 'to divide,' is called *dāp*; the affix *vat*, meaning 'like,' is called *vati*, while the affix *vat*, meaning 'possessed of,' is called *vatup*. Sometimes the only use of these Anubandhas is to enable Pratyāhāras to be formed; thus the case-ending of the accusative dual is called *auṭ* merely for the sake of forming the Pratyāhāra *suṭ*.

[1] For example, *śyan* stands for the characteristic of roots of the fourth class, *yak* for the passive, *ṇić* for the causal, *san* for the desiderative, *yaṅ* for the intensive.

Let short *a* be held to have its organ of utterance contracted, now that we have reached the end of the work in which it was necessary to regard it as otherwise.

Here is one from the sixth Adhyāya (I. 77): *Iko yaṇ aći.* This, of course, is not Sanskṛit, but a kind of grammatical algebra. *Ik* is a symbol standing for the four vowels *i*, *u*, *ṛi*, *lṛi*, and gifted with an imaginary genitive case *ikaḥ* (here changed to *iko*). *Yaṇ* is a symbol for the letters *y*, *v*, *r*, *l*; and *ać* (supposed to possess a locative case *aći*) represents all the vowels. The rule at full is:

The letters *y*, *v*, *r*, *l* take the place of *i*, *u*, *ṛi*, *lṛi*, short or long, respectively, when followed by any dissimilar vowel.

Moreover, an aphorism which stands at the head of a series and is hence called an *Adhikāra* or 'governing rule' is never repeated, but must be supplied after the whole series till the influence (*anuvṛitti*) of this governing Sūtra is supposed to cease, such cessation being called *nivṛitti.* Thus the seventy-fourth Sūtra of the third chapter of Adhyāya I is *ṇićaś-ća*, which must be interpreted thus:

And after a verbal base ending in the causal affix (*ṇić*) the Ātmane-pada must come when the result of the action returns to the agent.

Of course nearly all the matter necessary to make this rule intelligible has to be supplied from other rules, and especially from the Adhikāra rule 12, which is separated by sixty-two intervening Sūtras.

In short, a careful examination of Pāṇini's grammar will dispose the student to appreciate Colebrooke's remark that 'the endless pursuit of exceptions and limitations so disjoins the general precepts, that the reader cannot keep in view their intended connection and mutual relation. He wanders in an intricate maze, and the clue of the labyrinth is continually slipping from his hand.'

In point of fact, however, this grammar ought not to be examined from a European point of view at all.

We must not forget that an Indian Paṇḍit's ideas of grammar are very different from our own. Europeans are apt to look on a grammar of any kind as a necessary evil, only to be tolerated because indispensable to the attainment of a desired end beyond. With us the grammar of a language is in most cases a mere passage to its literature, a dreary region to be traversed as soon as possible. A Paṇḍit, on the other hand, regards grammar as we should regard the natural sciences. It is with him a something to be studied and elaborated for its own sake. According to the late Professor Goldstücker, 'Pāṇini's work is indeed a kind of natural history of the Sanskṛit language[1].' It gives an account of the linguistic facts and phenomena as it finds them, tracing them out as they occur without regard to any scientific or methodical arrangement of materials. Thus the prolongation of vowels is dealt with as a fact, and is followed out through a whole chapter in order to trace all the instances in which such a lengthening takes place, whether in declension or conjugation or the composition of words. Hence the rules of declension and conjugation do not follow each other in their usual order according to the European system, but are scattered about in a disjointed and often very perplexing manner, so that it becomes necessary to search for and put together Aphorisms in widely separated parts of the work to enable the statement of some grammatical law or process to be completed.

Pāṇini's grammar was criticized and its deficiencies supplied by the celebrated Kātyāyana, who is called Vārttika-kāra, as author of the Vārttikas or 'supplementary rules and annotations.' He must have lived some time after Pāṇini, perhaps in the century following. Some, however, believe the two grammarians to have been con-

[1] See Chambers' Cyclopaedia, article Pāṇini.

temporaneous. Kātyāyana again was criticized by his rival Patañjali, who generally supports Pāṇini against the composer of the supplementary rules. To Patañjali we owe one of the most wonderful grammatical works that the genius of any country has ever produced, viz. the Mahā-bhāshya or 'great commentary[1],' written not so much to explain Pāṇini as to defend such of his Aphorisms as had been criticized by Kātyāyana. He was probably not the same person as the author of the Yoga philosophy. According to some, his mother's name was Goṇikā ; he was born at Gonarda in the east of India, and he lived for some time in Kashmīr, where his work was well known. According to Professor Goldstücker, he wrote between 140 and 120 B.C.[2]; but Professor Weber places him about 25 years after Christ. These three men, Pāṇini, Kātyā-

[1] The whole of this great work has been lately edited by two Paṇḍits at Benares. See the able article on it by Professor Weber in the last volume of the 'Indische Studien.' A copy has been kindly sent to me by Professor A. E. Gough. Patañjali's additions to the Vārttikas are called *Ishṭis* or Desiderata. He is also the author of many Kārikās or memorial verses on grammar. A compendium of such verses was also made by Bhartṛi-hari.

[2] See the 'Indian Antiquary' for February 1873. See also an article on Patañjali in Chambers' Cyclopaedia, where it is well said that 'Patañjali's method is analogous to that of other classical commentaries; it establishes, usually by repetition, the correct reading of the text in explaining every important or doubtful word, in showing the connection of the principal parts of the sentence, and in adding such observations as may be required. Frequently Patañjali attaches his own critical remarks to the emendations of Kātyāyana, often in support of the views of the latter, but not seldom, too, in order to refute his criticisms and to defend Pāṇini; while, again, at other times, he completes the statement of one of them by his own additional rules.' Rāmkṛishṇa Gopal Bhāṇḍārkar, writing in the 'Indian Antiquary' for October 1872, states his opinion that Patañjali lived when Pushpamitra was reigning at Pāṭali-putra, and 'that he probably wrote the third chapter of his Bhāshya between 144 B.C. and 142 B.C.' Professor Weber, however, controverts this conclusion.

yana, and Patañjali, compose the great Indian triumvirate of grammarians, from whose authority there is no appeal in anything which relates to Vyākaraṇa. About one hundred and fifty grammarians and commentators followed in their footsteps, each criticizing or commenting on his predecessors. Among these may be mentioned Kaiyaṭa or Kaiyyaṭa, who commented on Patañjali in a work called the Bhāshya-pradīpa, and was himself commented on by Nāgojī-bhaṭṭa in the Bhāshya-pradīpoddyota[1]. One of the best of the more modern commentaries on Pāṇini is Vāmana's Kāśikā Vṛitti, so called because composed at Kāśī or Benares. A grammarian named Bhaṭṭoji-dīkshita attempted to arrange the Aphorisms on a plan more in accordance with modern ideas. His useful work is called the Siddhānta-kaumudī[2]. A second and greater simplification of Pāṇini is the Madhyama-kaumudī, and a still greater is the Laghu-kaumudī of Varada-rāja[3], which is in fact a kind of abridgment of the Siddhānta-kaumudī, current in the north-west of India.

Vopadeva, a grammarian who is said to have flourished about the latter half of the thirteenth century at the court of Hemādri, king of Deva-giri (Dowlatābād), wrote a grammar for beginners on a system of his own, called the Mugdha-bodha[4], which is much valued as an authority in Bengal, and referred to by many native commentators, such, for example, as Bharata-mallika or Bharata-sena, who therefore called his commentary on the Bhaṭṭi-kāvya, Mugdha-bodhinī.

Vopadeva's arrangement and many of his technical

---

[1] This Nāgojī-bhaṭṭa was also the author of a grammatical work called Paribhāshendu-śekhara, lately edited at Bombay, with a translation, by Professor F. Kielhorn.

[2] A new edition of this was published not long ago in India.

[3] This was edited and translated by Dr. Ballantyne.

[4] It has been edited like Pāṇini by Professor Böhtlingk.

terms and symbolical expressions (including the technical forms of his affixes) differ from those of Pāṇini, and the only allusion to Vedic peculiarities is in the last Sūtra of the work (XXVI. 220), which is as follows:

Manifold forms and irregularities are allowed in the Veda. [*Bahulam brahmaṇi,* which corresponds to Pāṇini's often repeated *bahulaṃ ćhandasi,* II. 4. 39, II. 4. 73, &c. Cf. also Pāṇini's *vyatyayo bahulam,* 'opposition to the usual rule is frequent in the Veda,' III. 1. 85.]

In fact, Vopadeva [1] does not aim at the completeness of Pāṇini. He omits all notice of the accents, and his treatment of the laws of euphonic combination is by no means exhaustive. In his explanation of declension and conjugation he is more satisfactory, and he gives numerous useful examples and paradigms, but usually contents himself with general rules, and does not, like Pāṇini, trouble himself to trace out minute particulars or examine into every corner of an intricate subject with a view to a careful search for all possible exceptions. Professor Böhtlingk has given an analysis of the Mugdha-bodha in the preface to his excellent edition of the work. Vopadeva's first chapter explains technical terms; the second treats of euphonic laws; the third, of declension; the fourth,

[1] It is very necessary to know the commonest of Vopadeva's technical expressions, as they are not only occasionally used by some native commentators, but are also employed in some instances by European expounders of Sanskṛit grammar. They often deviate from Pāṇini's system. For example, the memorial terminations usually given for verbs are those of Vopadeva (VIII. 1); *dhu* stands for dhātu, 'a root;' *vri* for vṛiddhi; *kva* for the terminations of the singular; *vva* for bahu-vaćana, those of the plural; *li* for lin·ga, a nominal base; *lidhu* for nominal verbs; *śup* and *up* for the characteristic *u* of the eighth class of roots; *tum* and *ćatum* instead of Pāṇini's *tumun,* for the Kṛit affix *tum* forming the infinitive; *śāna* (not *śānać*) for the termination of the present participle Ātmane; *śri* for the pronominals (called Sarva-nāman by Pāṇini); *samāhāra* for Pāṇini's *pratyāhāra* (see my Sanskṛit-English Dictionary). Nevertheless, Vopadeva adopts a great number of Pāṇini's technical terms.

of the formation of feminines; the fifth, of the use of the cases; the sixth, of compound words; the seventh, of Taddhita affixes; the eighth, of technical terms applicable to verbs and of roots of the first class; the ninth and tenth, of roots of the second and third classes; the eleventh to the seventeenth, of roots of the fourth to the tenth classes, one chapter being devoted to each class; the eighteenth, of causal verbs; the nineteenth, of desideratives; the twentieth, of intensives; the twenty-first, of nominals; the twenty-second, of the use of the Parasmai-pada; the twenty-third, of the use of the Ātmane-pada; the twenty-fourth, of passives, impersonals, and reflexive verbs; the twenty-fifth, of the use of the tenses and moods; the twenty-sixth, of Kṛit affixes and of affixes added to roots to form participles, &c.

I conclude by observing that a popular grammar called the *Kātantra* (or *Kalāpa*) is being well edited for the Bibliotheca Indica by Professor J. Eggeling.

### *The Vedāṅgas—Jyotisha*, 'astronomy.'

This Vedāṅga should rather be called 'the astronomical or astrological calendar.' Strictly speaking, it is represented by a short tract, consisting of thirty-six verses, in a comparatively modern style, to which scholars cannot assign a date earlier than 300 years B. C. According to the best authorities, no genuine Sūtras on astronomy have as yet been discovered. The object of the Jyotisha Vedāṅga is to fix the most auspicious days and seasons for commencing sacrifices. This treatise, brief and unsatisfactory as it is, nevertheless deserves attention as embodying some of the most ancient astronomical ideas, among which may be mentioned the measure of a day by thirty Muhūrtas or hours of forty-eight minutes, the division of the zodiac into twenty-seven parts or lunar asterisms (the first of which is Kṛittikā), and the traditional place of the solstitial points, from which the attempt has been repeatedly made (by Jones, Davis, Colebrooke, Pratt, and others) to deduce a date for the treatise itself, as well as for the whole Vedic literature.

The following is Colebrooke's translation of verses seven and eight of the Jyotisha tract[1], which verses have been the subject of much controversy in relation to their bearing on the determination of dates from a comparison of the present position of the solstitial points :

The sun and moon turn towards the north at the beginning of S'ravishṭhā (=Dhanishṭhā), but the sun turns towards the south in the middle of the constellation over which the serpents preside; and this (turn towards the south and towards the north) always happens in the months of Māgha and S'rāvaṇa. [*Prapadyete Śravishṭhādau sūrya-ćandramasāv udak, Sārpārdhe dākshiṇārkas tu, māgha-śrāvaṇayoḥ sadā.*] In the northern passage an increase of day and decrease of night take place amounting to a Prastha (or thirty-two Palas) of water; in the southern, both are reversed (i.e. the days decrease and the nights increase), and the difference amounts, by the journey, to six Muhūrtas. [*Gharma-vṛiddhir apām prasthaḥ kshapā-hrāsa udag-gatau, Dakshiṇe tau viparyastau shaṇ-muhūrty ayanena tu.*]

Whatever may be the value of these verses in an astronomical point of view, it is clear that a superstitious belief in the importance of choosing auspicious days and lucky moments for the performance of rites and ceremonies, whether public or domestic, began to show itself

[1] See Professor E. B. Cowell's new edition of Colebrooke's Essays, republished by his son, Sir T. E. Colebrooke, p. 98; and see especially Professor Whitney's valuable notes on this point (p. 126). The latter shows that the date derivable from the statement made in the Jyotisha has a necessary uncertainty of about four centuries (from the 14th to the 10th B.C.), and he claims that the actual uncertainty is still greater—that, in fact, the statement is worth nothing as yielding any definite date at all. Weber had before pointed out that the difference of six Muhūrtas between the longest and shortest day or night is accurate only in the extreme north-western corner of India.

very early in India, and that it grew and strengthened simultaneously with the growth of priestcraft and the elaboration of a complex ritual. The influence of the sun upon the atmosphere and soil made itself so manifest that it was only natural to infer that similar influences belonged to the moon, planets, and stars; and the personification and deification of all the most conspicuous luminaries which resulted from the supposed power inherent in their rays, of course intensified the superstitious feeling of dependence upon their favourable aspects for the success, not only of religious acts, but of all the affairs of life. Pernicious as such superstitious ideas were in their effect on the mind and all mental progress, they were nevertheless productive of good in impelling the acute Hindū to study the movements of the heavenly bodies, and stimulating him to undertake arithmetical and mathematical investigations. In all probability, astronomical and mathematical science had an independent origin in India. It is at least certain that they were cultivated with some success at a very early epoch, though of course very roughly in the absence of all optical and mechanical appliances. We have already given an example from the Aitareya-brāhmaṇa, which contains certain shrewd guesses at scientific truth in regard to the sun (see p. 35).

In some of the earliest hymns of the Veda the Nakshatras or lunar mansions[1] are mentioned in connection with the moon (see Ṛig-veda I. 50. 2). Moreover,

---

[1] For the twenty-seven Vedic Nakshatras see my Sanskṛit-English Dictionary (also Appendix). The word *Nakshatra* at first meant a star or asterism in general; then it was applied to the selected series of asterisms through or near which the moon passes; and finally it was loosely used for the part of the moon's path, the 27th or 28th of the zodiac, marked by each asterism. In the later mythology the lunar mansions were fabled as the twenty-seven daughters of Daksha and wives of the moon.

some of the phases of the moon, such as *Anumati*, 'the moon one digit less than full,' *Rākā*, 'the full moon,' *Kuhū* (or *Gungu*), 'the new moon,' and *Sinīvālī*, 'the first thin crescent preceding or following new moon,' are personified (see Ṛig-veda II. 32. 8), so that we are justified in inferring that the movements of the moon in the zodiac and its use as the time-measurer and month-maker (*māsa-kṛit*)[1] were studied and noted by the Hindūs perhaps as early as 1400 years B.C. The twenty-seven lunar mansions implied a lunar division of the zodiac into twenty-seven equal parts of 13° 20′ to each part. Such a division (into twenty-seven or twenty-eight parts) is shared by other Asiatic peoples, as the Arabs and Chinese, and the question where it originated has provoked much discussion, without leading to any definite and certain results[2]. The names of the Indian months have certainly been taken from the asterisms in which the moon was supposed to be full at different times of the year, and, what is still more significant, the names of some of these lunar asterisms have clearly been derived from ancient·

---

[1] This is a Vedic name of the moon. A root *mā*, 'to measure,' meaning also 'the measurer,' is first applied to the moon in Sanskṛit and then to a lunation or period measured by one revolution of the moon. Something similar has happened in the cognate Āryan languages. At least we know that the words for 'month' are generally derived from the moon, our word 'month' being nothing but *moonth.* In Ṛig-veda X. 85. 2 occurs the following: *Atho nakshatrāṇām eshām upasthe Soma āhitaḥ*, 'Soma is deposited in the lap of these Nakshatras.'

[2] The various opinions and the arguments by which they have been supported have been lately reviewed by Professor Whitney in his 'Oriental and Linguistic Studies,' vol. ii. pp. 341–421. He regards the matter as still unsettled. The solar signs of the zodiac and much of the later astronomy, with many astronomical terms (such as *horā*=ὥρα; *kendra*=κέντρον; *dṛikāna*, the third of a zodiacal sign=δέκανος; *liptā*, the minute of a degree=λεπτός), were borrowed from the Greeks.

Vedic deities, like the Aśvins[1], &c. In the Yajur-veda and Brāhmaṇas occur the expressions Nakshatra-darśa and Gaṇaka, applied to observers of the heavens, either as astronomers or astrologers[2]; and the adjustment of the lunar to the solar year by the insertion of a thirteenth or intercalary month (*mala-māsa*, *malimluća*, *adhimāsa*, sometimes called *Purushottama*) is probably alluded to in an ancient hymn (Ṛig-veda I. 25. 8), and frequently in more recent parts of the Veda. (Vājasaneyi-saṁhitā 22. 30, Atharva-veda V. 6. 4, &c.)

Whatever conclusions we may arrive at as to the original source of the first astronomical ideas current in the world, it is probable that to the Hindūs is due the invention of algebra[3] and its application to astronomy and geometry. From them also the Arabs received not only

---

[1] The names of the months are Māgha (from the Nakshatra *Maghā*), Phālguna (from *Phalgunī*), Ćaitra (from *Ćitrā*), Vaiśākha (from *Viśākhā*), Jyaishṭha (from *Jyeshṭhā*), Āshāḍha (from *Ashāḍhā*), Śrāvaṇa (from *Śravaṇa*), Bhādrapada or Bhādra (from *Bhadra-padā*), Āśvina (from *Aśvinī*), Kārttika (from *Kṛittikā*), Mārgaśīrsha, commonly called Agrahāyaṇa (from *Mṛiga-śiras*), Pausha (from *Pushya*). I have arranged these names so as to correspond as nearly as possible with our months, *Māgha* representing January—February, and the others continuing in regular order; but practically the Hindū calendar generally begins with Vaiśākha, this being considered the first month in the year.

[2] Of course astronomy and astrology were mixed up together, and the progress of the former was impeded in India by its subservience to the latter.

[3] The name Algebra (from the Arabic *al jabr*, 'the reduction of parts to a whole or of fractions to integers') shows that Europe received algebra like the ten numerical symbols from the Hindūs through the *Arabs*. The Sanskṛit word for algebra, *Vīja-gaṇita*, means 'calculation of seeds,' 'calculation of original or primary elements,' i.e. analysis. If the Greeks did not receive their first ideas of algebra from the Hindūs, it may at least be taken as proved (from all that Colebrooke has so ably written on the subject), that the Hindūs were certainly not indebted to the Greeks, but invented their system independently.

their first conceptions of algebraic analysis, but also those invaluable numerical symbols and decimal notation now current everywhere in Europe, which have rendered untold service to the progress of arithmetical science. It will not, therefore, be irrelevant if I introduce here a short account of the chief Hindū astronomical and mathematical works with a few illustrative extracts.

By some authorities nine principal astronomical treatises, called Siddhāntas, are named, viz. the *Brahma-siddhānta*, *Sūrya-s°*, *Soma-s°*, *Vṛihaspati-s°*, *Garga-s°*, *Nārada-s°*, *Parāśara-s°*, *Pulastya-s°*, *Vasishṭha-s°*; by others five, viz. the *Pauliśa-s°*, *Romaka-s°*[1], *Vāsishṭha-s°*, *Saura-s°*, and *Brāhma-s°* or *Paitāmaha-s°*, and these five, sometimes called collectively the Pañća-siddhāntikā, are said to be the original Siddhāntas. Whether the Sūrya-s° is the same as the Saura-s° appears somewhat doubtful, but this treatise, fabled to have been revealed by Sūrya 'the Sun' himself, is perhaps the best known of all Hindū astronomical works both in India and Europe[2].

The earliest Hindū astronomer whose name has come down to us is Ārya-bhaṭa, who lived, according to Colebrooke, about the fifth century of our era. Others place him, or another astronomer of his name, in the third century. Ārya-bhaṭa is the author of three works, the Āryabhaṭīya, Daśa-gītikā, and Āryāshṭa-śata, and is said to have asserted a diurnal revolution of the earth on its axis, to have known the true theory of the causes of lunar and solar eclipses, and noticed the motion of the

---

[1] This title Romaka-s° points to an exchange of ideas on astronomical subjects between India, Greece, and Rome.

[2] It has been well edited by Dr. Fitz-Edward Hall, and there are two translations of it, one published in America with notes (by Professor Whitney), and another by Bāpudeva S'āstrī.

solstitial and equinoctial points[1]. Professor Kern has just published an edition of the *Āryabhaṭīya.*

After Ārya-bhaṭa came the astronomer Varāha-mihira, who lived about the sixth century of our era, and was born at Ujjayinī. He wrote a work on nativities called Vṛihaj-jātaka, another well-known astrological work called Bṛihat-saṃhitā (recently translated by Professor Kern[2], an extract from which is given p. 189), and a summary of the five original Siddhāntas called Pañća-siddhāntikā.

Next to Ārya-bhaṭa and Varāha-mihira lived Brahmagupta (probably towards the end of the sixth century), who wrote the Brahma-siddhānta, containing the chapters on arithmetic (*gaṇita*) and algebra (*kuṭṭaka*[3]) in Colebrooke's Indian Algebra.

Fourth and last of celebrated astronomers and mathematicians came Bhāskara or Bhāskarāćārya, who is supposed to have lived in the twelfth century and composed a well-known book called the Siddhānta-śiromaṇi, containing the treatises on algebra (*Vīja-gaṇita*) and arithmetic (*Līlāvatī*[4]), translated by Colebrooke.

I proceed now to select specimens of the contents of the above works. The first extract gives the Indian division of time taken from the Sūrya-siddhānta (I. 11–13), Bhāskara's Siddhānta-śiromaṇi (I. 19, 20), and other works with their commentaries (Burgess, pp. 5, 6). It illustrates very curiously the natural taste of the Hindūs for hyperbole, leading them to attempt almost infinite calculations

---

[1] According to Brahma-gupta, as quoted by the writer of the article Sanskṛit Literature in Chambers' Cyclopaedia, which I have consulted.

[2] For the Journal of the Royal Asiatic Society.

[3] *Kuṭṭaka* properly means a 'pulverizer' or 'multiplier.'

[4] *Līlāvatī*, 'delightful by its elegance,' is merely the name of the chapter on arithmetic (*pāṭī-gaṇita*, divided into *vyakta-gaṇita*, 'distinct computation,' and *avyakta-g°*, 'indistinct'). The name is also applied to a supposed 'charming woman,' to whom instruction in arithmetic is given.

of inconceivable periods in the one direction, and infinitesimal subdivisions of the most minute quantities in the other. Without any reliable chronology in regard to the precise dates of any great events in their own history, they yet delight in a kind of chronology or 'science of time,' making time past, present, and future a subject of the most elaborate and minute computations. Hence we find them heaping billions upon millions and trillions upon billions of years, and reckoning up ages upon ages, Aeons upon Aeons, with even more audacity than modern geologists and astronomers. In short, an astronomical Hindū ventures on arithmetical conceptions quite beyond the mental dimensions of any one who feels himself incompetent to attempt the task of measuring infinity. Here is the time-table enumerating the subdivisions of what is called *real* and *unreal* time:

'That which begins with respirations (*prāṇa*) is called real (*mūrta*) time; that which begins with atoms (*truṭi*) is called unreal (*amūrta*) time. Ten long syllables (*gurv-akshara*) make one respiration (*prāṇa*, *asu*); six respirations make one Vināḍī (also called *pala* or *vighaṭikā* of twenty-four seconds); sixty Vināḍīs = one Nāḍī or Nāḍikā (also called *daṇḍa*, *ghaṭī*, *ghaṭikā* of twenty-four minutes); sixty Nāḍīs = one day (a sidereal day and night); thirty sidereal days = one civil (*sāvana*) month; a civil month consists of thirty sunrises; a lunar month of thirty lunar days (*tithi*); a solar (*saura*) month is determined by the entrance of the sun into a sign of the zodiac.' And now with regard to unreal time: 'One hundred atoms (*truṭi*) = one speck (*tatpara*); thirty specks = one twinkling (*nimesha*); eighteen twinklings = one bit (*kāshṭhā*); thirty bits = one minute (*kalā*); thirty minutes = one half-hour (*ghaṭikā*); two half-hours = one hour (*kshaṇa*); thirty hours = one day.' This makes the atom $\frac{1}{33750}$ of a second.

Considerable variations occur in Manu and the Purāṇas. According to Manu (I. 64) thirty Kalās = one Muhūrta or hour of forty-eight minutes. The Vishṇu-purāṇa (Wilson, p. 22) makes the atom = $\frac{1}{2110}$ of a second, and goes back beyond an atom to a Paramāṇu or infinitesimal atom, which it makes = $\frac{1}{38000}$ of a second. All, however, agree in dividing the day into thirty hours, just as the month is divided into thirty Tithis or lunar days, and the year into three hundred and sixty days, an intercalary month being inserted once in five years, which is thought to be the most ancient Hindū method of computing time[1]. The Sūrya-siddhānta then proceeds, like Manu (I. 68. 71), to reckon up vast periods of time through ages[2] (*yuga*) and great ages (*mahā-yuga*), till it arrives at an Aeon (*kalpa*), the total duration of which is said to be 4,320,000,000 years. In verse 24 we read (Burgess, p. 12):

One hundred times four hundred and seventy-four divine years passed while the All-wise was employed in creating the animate and inanimate creation, plants, stars, gods, demons, and the rest.

Further on we have the division of a circle, which corresponds with our own:

Sixty seconds (*vikalā*) make a minute (*kalā*), sixty minutes make a degree (*bhāga*), thirty degrees make a sign (*rāśi*), twelve signs make a revolution (*bhagaṇa*).

The following is the measurement of the earth:

Twice 800 *yojanas* are the diameter of the earth; the square root of ten times the square of that is the earth's circumference.

According to Bhāskara the earth's diameter is 1581 *yojanas*, so that if the *yojana* is reckoned at about four and a half English miles (which is given as one estimate of its length, though its value varies), the calculation in both cases is not very far from accurate.

---

[1] Almanacs and horoscopes (*Janma-patra*) are called *Pañćāṅga*, as treating of five things, viz. solar days (commonly called Vāras, from the days of the week, Āditya-v°, Soma-v°, Maṅgala-v°, Budha-v°, Guru-v°, S'ukra-v°, S'ani-v°), lunar days (Tithis), the twenty-seven Nakshatras, the twenty-seven Yogas, the eleven Karaṇas.

[2] There are properly four Yugas or ages in every Mahāyuga, viz. *Kṛita*, *Tretā*, *Dvāpara*, and *Kali*, named from the marks on dice, the Kṛita being the best throw of four points, and the Kali the worst of one point.

At the commencement of Sūrya-siddhānta, Chapter II, we have a strange theory of planetary motion (p. 47):

Forms of time (*kālasya mūrtayaḥ*) of invisible shape (*adṛiśya-rūpāḥ*) stationed in the zodiac (*bhagaṇāśritāḥ*), called conjunction (*śīghroćća*), upper apsis (*mandoćća*), and node (*pāta*), are causes of the motion of the planets. The planets attached to these Beings by cords of air are drawn away by them with the right and left hand, forward or backward, according to nearness, toward their own place. A wind, moreover, called *Pravaha*, impels them towards their own apices (*ućća*); being drawn away forward and backward, they proceed by a varying motion.

In the previous Chapter (29, 34) the following statement occurs:

In an age (*yuga*) the revolutions of the sun, Mercury (*Budha*), and Venus (*Śukra*), and of the conjunctions of Mars (*Mangala*, *Bhauma*) Saturn (*Śani*), and Jupiter (*Vṛihaspati*), moving eastward, are four million, three hundred and twenty thousand. Of the asterisms, one billion, five hundred and eighty-two million, two hundred and thirty-seven thousand, eight hundred and twenty-eight.

I next give a portion of a remarkable passage from Varāha-mihira's *Bṛihat-saṃhitā* or 'complete system of natural astrology' (see Dr. Kern's translation, p. 433, of vol. iv. of the Royal Asiatic Society's Journal):

An astrologer ought to be of good family, friendly in his appearance, and fashionable in his dress; veracious and not malignant. He must have well-proportioned, compact, and full limbs, no bodily defect, and be a fine man, with nice hands, feet, nails, eyes, chin, teeth, ears, brows, and head, and with a deep and clear voice; for generally one's good and bad moral qualities are in unison with one's personal appearance. As to mathematical astronomy, he must know the divisions of the heaven and of time, in ages, years, half-years, seasons, months, half-months, days, watches, hours, half-hours, minutes, respirations, moments, subdivisions of a moment, &c., as taught in the five Siddhāntas (see p. 185). He must know the reason why there are four kinds of months—the solar (*saura*), natural (*sāvana*), stellar (*nākshatra*), and lunar (*ćāndra*) months—and how it happens that there are intercalary months and subtractive days. He must know the beginning and end of the Jovian cycle of sixty years, of the lustrums, years, days, hours, and their respective lords. He must foretell the moment of commencement and separation, the direction, measure, duration, amount of obscuration, colour and place of the eclipses of sun and moon; also the future conjunctions and hostile encounters of the nine planets[1]. He must be skilful in ascertaining the distance of each planet from the earth, expressed in *yojanas;* further, the dimensions of their orbits and the distance of the places on earth, in *yojanas.* He ought to be clever in geometrical operations and in the calculation of time. If, moreover, he knows how to speak pithily, because he thoroughly understands all sorts of captious questions; if the science he expounds, by being put to the test by his own exertion and unceasing study, has become more refined—like gold is rendered purer by being put on the touchstone, by purification in fire, and by careful workmanship—then he may be said to be a scientific man. It has been said: 'How can one who solves no difficulty, nor answers any question, nor teaches his pupils, be styled a scientific man?' And thus it has been said by the great seer Garga: 'The king who does not honour a scholar accomplished in horoscopy and astronomy comes to grief.' 'As the night without a light, as the sky without the sun, so is a king without an astrologer; like a blind man he erreth on the road.' 'No one who wishes for well-being should live in a country where there is no astrologer.' 'No one that has studied astrology can go to the infernal regions.' 'A person who, without knowing the science, exercises the profession of an astrologer is a wicked man and a disgrace to society. Consider him to be a mere star-gazer. But such a one as properly knows horoscopy, astronomy, and natural astrology, him ought the king to honour and his service he ought to secure.'

With regard to Colebrooke's translation of Bhāskara's work on algebra (*Vīja-gaṇita*), the following extract is taken from the translator's introduction (p. xxii):

The motions of the moon and sun were carefully observed by the Hindūs, and with such success that their determination of the moon's synodical revolution is a much more correct one than the Greeks ever achieved. They had a division of the ecliptic into twenty-seven and twenty-eight parts, suggested evidently by the moon's period in days, and seemingly their own. It was certainly borrowed by the Arabs[2]. They

---

[1] The nine planets are the Sun and Moon, Mercury, Venus, Mars, Jupiter, Saturn, with Rāhu and Ketu or the ascending and descending nodes.

[2] The Arabs, however, appear to have adopted the division of the zodiac into twenty-eight segments. Professor Whitney thinks that the Arabs did not borrow their lunar zodiac from the Hindūs. See p. 183 and the authorities there referred to.

were particularly conversant with the most splendid of the primary planets; the period of Jupiter being introduced by them, in conjunction with those of the sun and moon, into the regulation of their calendar in the form of the cycle of sixty years, common to them and the Chaldeans.

We may add that from certain expressions in Bhāskara's work (see p. 106, Banerjea's Dialogues, p. 69[1]), it is inferred that some idea of the laws of gravitation was formed by Hindū astronomers as early as the twelfth century of our era. The precession of the equinoctial points (*vishuvat, krānti-pāta*) was well known to Bhāskara, and the effect of the moon in causing tides seems to have been suspected much earlier (cf. Raghu-vanśa V. 61).

The points in which Hindū algebra appears particularly distinguished from the Greek are (Colebrooke, p. xvi):

In addition to a better and more comprehensive algorithm (or notation): 1st. The management of equations involving more that one unknown term. 2nd. The resolution of equations of a higher order, in which, if they achieved little, they had at least the merit of the attempt and anticipated a modern discovery in the solution of biquadratics. 3rd. General methods for the solution of indeterminate problems of first and second degrees, in which they went far, indeed, beyond Diophantus, and anticipated discoveries of modern algebraists. 4th. Application of algebra to astronomical investigation and geometrical demonstration, in which they hit on some matters re-invented in later times. One of their anticipations of modern discoveries is the demonstration of the noted proposition of Pythagoras concerning the square of the base of a rectangular triangle being equal to the squares of the two legs containing the right angle.

As to the notation or algorithm of algebra, Colebrooke remarks (p. x):

The Hindū algebraists use abbreviations and initials for symbols. They distinguish negative quantities by a dot, but have not any mark, besides the absence of the negative sign, to discriminate a positive quantity. No marks or symbols indicating operations of addition or multiplication &c. are employed; nor any announcing equality or relative magnitude

---

[1] See also the 'Indian Antiquary' for July 1872, p. 224.

(greater or less)[1]. But a factum is denoted by the initial syllable of a word of that import, subjoined to the terms which compose it, between which a dot is sometimes interposed. A fraction is indicated by placing the divisor under the dividend, but without a line of separation. The symbols of unknown quantity are not confined to a single one, but extend to ever so great a variety of denominations, and the characters used are initial syllables of the names of colours, excepting the first, which is the initial of *yāvat-tāvat* (applied to the *first* unknown quantity, i.e. 'so much' of the unknown as this coefficient number). Colour, therefore, means unknown quantity or the symbol of it. Letters are likewise employed as symbols, either taken from the alphabet or else initial syllables of words signifying the subjects of the problem. Initials of the terms for square and solid respectively denote those powers. An initial syllable is in like manner used to mark a surd root (see the next extract and succeeding examples).

The following is from the Vīja-gaṇita (chap. vi):

This is analysis by equation comprising several colours. In this the unknown quantities are numerous, two and three or more, for which *yāvat-tāvat* and the several colours are to be put to represent the values. They have been settled by the ancient teachers of the science, viz. black (*kāla*), blue (*nīla*), yellow (*pīta*), red (*lohita*), green (*haritaka*), white (*śveta*), variegated (*ćitra*), tawny (*kapila*), tan-coloured (*piṅgala*), grey (*dhūmra*), pink (*pāṭala*), mottled (*śavala*), blackish (*śyāmala*), another kind of black (*mećaka*), &c. Or letters (that is, *k* &c.) are to be employed as names of the unknown. [In practice the initial syllables of the above words are used thus, *yā, kā, nī, pī, lo.*]

I here give some of the Sanskṛit equivalents for terms in arithmetic and algebra:

An absolute quantity which has specific form is *rūpa* (applied in the singular to a unit, in the plural to an integer number, and often expressed by the first syllable *rū*). A surd or irrational number is *karaṇī* (often denoted by the first syllable *ka*). A nought or cipher is *śūnya, ća*; a fraction which has a cipher for its denominator *ća-hara*; minus *ṛina, kshaya* (negative quantity); plus *dhana, sva* (positive quantity). A result or product is *bhāvita* (often expressed by the first syllable *bhā*;

[1] The sign of equality was first used by Robert Recorde (because, he said, 'No two things can be more equal than a pair of parallels'), and those of relative magnitude by Harriot.—Colebrooke.

hence the product of two unknown quantities is expressed by *yā. kā bhā*, or *kā. nī bhā;* so also the square of the first unknown quantity multiplied by the cube of the second is thus abbreviated, *yā va. kā gha, bhā*).

It may be interesting to note the system of numeration increasing in decuple proportion given in chapter II of the Līlāvatī. This method, with the invention of the nine numerical figures (*anka*) and of the nought (*śūnya*) and of the decuple value assigned to each according to its position in the series, is thought to be of divine origin:

Unit (*eka*), ten (*daśa*), hundred (*śata*), thousand (*sahasra*), ten thousand (*ayuta*), a hundred thousand (*laksha*, commonly called 'a lac'), million (*prayuta*), ten millions (*koṭi*, commonly called 'a krore'), a hundred millions (*arbuda*), a thousand millions (*abja* or *padma*), ten thousand millions (*kharva*), a hundred thousand millions (*nikharva*), a billion or million of millions (*mahā-padma*), ten billions (*śanku*), a hundred billions (*jaladhi* or *samudra*), a thousand billions (*antya*), ten thousand billions (*madhya*), a hundred thousand billions (*parārdha*).

I add four specimens of problems from the Līlāvatī and Vīja-gaṇita (Colebrooke, pp. 24, 124, 191, 269, 272):

1. Out of a swarm of bees, one-fifth part settled on a Kadamba blossom; one-third on a S'ilīndhra flower; three times the difference of those numbers flew to the bloom of a Kuṭaja. One bee, which remained, hovered about in the air. Tell me, charming woman, the number of bees.

2. How many are the variations of form of the (ten-armed) god S'ambhu (S'iva) by the exchange of his ten attributes held reciprocally in his several hands, viz. the rope (*pāśa*), the hook for guiding an elephant (*ankuśa*), the serpent, the hour-glass-shaped drum (*ḍamaru*), the human skull, the trident (*triśūla*), the club shaped like the foot of a bedstead (*khaṭvānga*), the dagger, the arrow, the bow? And those of (the four-armed) Hari (Vishṇu) by the exchange of the mace, the discus (*ćakra*), the lotus, and the conch (*śankha*)? Answer 3,628,800; 24.

3. Eight rubies, ten emeralds, and a hundred pearls, which are in thy ear-ring, my beloved, were purchased by me for thee at an equal amount; and the sum of the rates of the three sorts of gems was three less than half a hundred: tell me the rate of each, auspicious woman.

4. What four numbers are such that the product of them all is equal to twenty times their sum? The answer to this last is: Here let the first number be *yā* 1; and the rest be arbitrarily put 5, 4, and 2. Their sum is *yā* 1, *rū* 11, and multiplied by 20, *yā* 20, *rū* 220. Product of all the quan-

tities, *yā* 40. Statement for equation, $\begin{array}{l} y\bar{a}\ 40,\ r\bar{u}\ \ 0 \\ y\bar{a}\ 20,\ r\bar{u}\ 220 \end{array}$. Hence by the first analysis, the value of *yā* is found 11, and the numbers are 11, 5, 4, 2.

I should mention here that attached to each Veda there are certain works called *Pariśishṭa* or 'Supplements,' intended to supply directions omitted in the Śrauta Sūtras, &c. There are also the *Anukramaṇī* or 'Indices,' giving the first words of every hymn, the metre, the names of the authors and of the deities addressed, the number of verses, &c.

There are also Upa-vedas or 'secondary Vedas,' which, however, have really little or no connection with either the Veda or Smṛiti. They are, 1. *Āyur-veda*, 'the science of life' or medicine (regarded as belonging to the Atharva-veda, and by some to the Ṛig-veda); 2. *Gāndharva-veda*, 'the science of music' (as a branch of the Sāma-veda); 3. *Dhanur-veda*, 'the science of archery' or military art (connected with the Yajur-veda); 4. *Sthāpatya-veda*, 'the science of architecture,' including the Śilpa-śāstra:

As to 1, Two great medical writers are *Ćaraka* and *Su-śruta*, whose works treat of anatomy, physiology, materia medica, pharmacy, surgery (*śalya*), toxicology (*visha*), omens, and the evil influence of planets and demons (*bhūta*) in causing diseases. (See Wilson's Essays, vol. i. pp. 269–276, 380–393.) Su-śruta's work, in six books, has been well edited at Calcutta by Srī Madhusūdana Gupta. As to 2, Works on music treat of notes, scales, melodies, singing, musical instruments, and sometimes of dancing. Six primary modes or modifications of melody, called Rāgas, are enumerated, which are personified, and each of them married to five or sometimes six Rāgiṇīs. The chief musical works are the *Saṅgīta-ratnākara*, by Śārṅga-deva; the *Saṅgīta-darpaṇa*, by Dāmodara; and the *Saṅgīta-dāmodara*, by Śubhaṅ-kara. As to 3, This science is by some ascribed to Viśvāmitra, by others to Bhṛigu. As to 4, Some assert that there are sixty-four treatises on the sixty-four Śilpas or 'mechanical arts,' such as architecture, sculpture, carpentry, jewellery, farriery, &c. The principal work on architecture is the *Māna-sāra*, 'essence of measurement,' in fifty-eight chapters, giving rules for the construction of buildings, temples, ornamental arches (*toraṇa*), &c. Other works, by celebrated Sthapatis or 'architects,' describe the soil suited for building and rites in honour of the *Vāstu-purusha*, 'spirit presiding over sites.'

# LECTURE IX.

## II. *The Smārta Sūtras or Traditional Rules.*

IN our classification of Smṛiti or Post-vedic literature, at the commencement of the last Lecture, we placed the Smārta Sūtras under the second head, and pointed out that they were to a great extent the source of the subsequent law-books which form, in our arrangement, the third head of Smṛiti. We also observed that the term *Smārta-sūtra* is a general expression for collections of aphoristic rules which are distinguished from the Śrauta-sūtra of the Kalpa Vedāṅga, because they do not relate to Śrauta or Vedic ceremonies, but rather to *Gṛihya* or 'domestic rites' and *Samayāćāra* or 'conventional every-day practices.' Hence the Smārta Sūtras are commonly subdivided into, a. *Gṛihya Sūtras*, and b. *Sāmayāćārika Sūtras*. It will be desirable, therefore, before commencing our survey of Manu's celebrated Law-book, to advert briefly to these sources from which some of its materials were derived, and especially to the Gṛihya Sūtras[1]. Of these there are collections of different schools attached to each Veda. Thus to the Ṛig-veda belong the *Āśvalāyana*[2] and *Śāṅkhāyana* Gṛihya Sūtras; to the Sāma-veda those of *Gobhila*[2]; to the Vājasaneyi-saṃhitā or White Yajur-veda those of *Pāraskara*; to the Taittirīya or Black Yajur-

---

[1] Probably, however, Manu owes more to the Sāmayāćārika than to the Gṛihya Sūtras, although these latter are now best known to us by printed editions. We find that the authors of Gṛihya Sūtras have often the same name as the authors of law-books.

[2] There are also, as we have seen, Āśvalāyana S'rauta-sūtra under the head of 'Kalpa,' and probably each school had all three sets of Sūtras complete, though they are seldom all preserved. The Āśvalāyana Gṛihya

veda those of *Kāṭhaka*, *Baudhāyana*, *Bhāradvāja*, *Āpastamba*[1], the *Maitrāyaṇīya*, *Mānava* (which last have perished, though some of their Kalpa-sūtras have been preserved, see p. 213), &c.

In fact, every Brāhmanical family or school (*ćaraṇa*[2]) had probably its own traditional recension (*śākhā*, p. 161) of the Mantra and Brāhmaṇa portion of the Vedas as well as its own Kalpa, Gṛihya, and Sāmayāćārika Sūtras; and even at the present day the domestic rites of particular families of Brāhmans are performed in accordance with the Sūtras of the Veda of which they happen to be adherents.

Since these Gṛihya and Sāmayāćārika Sūtras are older than Manu, they are probably as old as the sixth century B. C., but possibly the works we possess represent comparatively recent collections of the original texts.

It has been already pointed out that the Śrauta Sūtras are a kind of rubric for the more public solemn sacrifices (Jyotishṭoma, Agnishṭoma, Aśva-medha, &c.) enjoined by the Veda. The subject of the Gṛihya is rather that indicated by Manu when he says (III. 67):

> Let the householder observe domestic rites with the sacred fire kindled at his marriage (called *Gārhapatya*) according to rule, and perform the five devotional acts and the daily domestic oblations. [*Vaivāhike 'gnau kurvīta gṛihyaṃ karma yathā-vidhi Pañća-yajña-vidhānaṃ ća paktiṃ* (=*pākam*) *ćānvāhikīṃ gṛihī*.]

---

Sūtras and part of the Pāraskara have been edited and translated into German by Professor Stenzler (Leipzig, 1864, 1865), and the former have also been edited by Paṇḍits for the Bibliotheca Indica (Calcutta, 1869). The Gobhilīya Gṛihya Sūtras are being edited for the Bibliotheca Indica.

[1] The Āpastambas appear to have preserved all three sets of Sūtras complete, for there are also Āpastamba S'rauta-sūtra and Sāmayāćārika-sūtra. According to Professor Bhāṇḍārkar there are numbers of Brāhmans in the south of India who are adherents of the Black Yajur-veda and who receive *dakshiṇā* or 'fees' from rich men for repeating it with the Āpastamba Sūtras.

[2] A work called the *Ćaraṇa-vyūha* gives catalogues of these schools.

Indeed the word Gṛihya means 'household,' and these Sūtras do in fact give rules for the five diurnal acts of domestic devotion called *Mahā-yajña* (or *Pañća-yajña*, four of them being also *Pāka-yajña*, Manu II. 86), as well as for the domestic ceremonies named *Saṉskāras*, common to all the three higher classes, and not restricted to Brāhmans. The twelve Saṉskāras are described at p. 246. They are generally performed at the one domestic hearth, instead of with all the three fires (called collectively *Tretā*) of the *Vitānas* or 'hearths used at public sacrifices.'

I proceed to give a brief account of Āśvalāyana's Gṛihya Sūtras of the Ṛig-veda, making one prefatory remark that the Hindū race affords perhaps the only example of a nation who, although apparently quite indifferent to the registering of any of the great facts of their political life, or even to the recording of any of the most remarkable events of their history—as, for example, the invasion of the Greeks under Alexander the Great—nevertheless, at a very early period, regulated their domestic rites and customs according to definite prescribed rules, which were not only written down, but preserved with religious care, and are many of them still in force. Moreover, as this race belongs to the same original race-stock as ourselves, the antiquity of their customs must of necessity invest them with great interest in our eyes.

The domestic oblations called Pāka-yajña (Manu II. 86, 143) are distinguished from the Vaitānika[1] in the first two Sūtras, thus (Stenzler's edition, I. 1. 2):

---

[1] Kullūka, on Manu V. 84, derives *vitāna* from *vitan*, 'to spread out,' and explains *Vaitānika* to be those S'rauta oblations which are performed when the Gārhapatya fire is spread over both the Āhavanīya and Dakshiṇa hearths (*vaitānam śrauto homaḥ gārhapatya-kuṇḍa-sthān agnīn āhavanīyādi-kuṇḍeshu vitatya kriyate*). See also Manu VI. 9. There is much difference of opinion as to the exact meaning of *pāka-yajña*. Stenzler translates it by 'Koch-opfer,' and thinks it means an oblation offered

The Vaitānika oblations (performed with all the three sacred fires[1]) have been explained (in the S'rauta-sūtra), we will now describe those (performed with the) domestic (fire only). There are three kinds of Pāka-yajña, viz. those that are offered in fire (such as oblations of butter, &c.); those that are presented without being offered in fire; those that are offered to the supreme Being (*Brahmaṇi*) in the feeding of Brāhmans (*Brāhmaṇa-bhojane*).

Book I. ii. enumerates the gods to whom oblations are to be offered, such as Agni, Indra, Soma, Heaven and Earth, Yama, Varuṇa, the Viśve Devāḥ (cf. Manu III. 90, 121), Brahman, &c. These, it will be observed, are generally Vedic deities. The third prescribes the mode of preparing the place where oblations are to be made.

The fourth commences with the following Sūtra:

The ceremonies of tonsure (*ćaula*=*ćūḍā-karman*), investiture with the sacred cord (*upanayana*), shaving the beard (*go-dāna*) and marriage must be performed during the northern course of the sun (*udag-ayane*), in the light half of the month (*āpūryamāṇe pakshe*), and under an auspicious constellation (*kalyāṇe nakshatre*).

These Sanskāra ceremonies are then described (beginning with marriage), and whenever Mantras or texts of the Veda have to be repeated during the performance of each rite, the first word or words of the several texts are cited. Thus before the marriage ceremony an oblation of clarified butter is to be offered with repetition of the text: *Tvam*

---

on the domestic fire when the daily food is cooked. Some of the commentators, on the other hand, interpret *pāka* by 'small,' 'simple,' and some by 'good.' In Manu II. 86 four Pāka-yajñas or 'domestic oblations' are mentioned (which Kullūka explains by *Vaiśvadeva-homa, bali, nitya-śrāddha*, and *atithi-bhojana*), thus identifying them with four of the Mahā-yajñas, see p. 203. Seven different kinds of Pāka-yajña will be found enumerated in my Sanskṛit-English Dictionary.

[1] In Manu III. 100, 185, five sacred fires are mentioned, and a Brāhman who keeps them all burning, called a *Pañćāgni* (=*Agnihotrin*), is regarded as peculiarly pious. They are, 1. *Dakshiṇa* (*Anvāhārya-paćana* in the Brāhmaṇas); 2. *Gārhapatya*; 3. *Āhavanīya*; 4. *Sabhya*; 5. *Āvasathya*. The three first fires are the most important and are collectively called *Tretā*. Agnihotrīs are still met with in India.

*Aryamā bhavasi yat kanīnām*, &c., 'thou art Aryaman in relation to maidens' (Ṛig-veda V. 3. 2).

The fifth Chapter prescribes the due selection of a wife after proper inquiry as to family and condition. Sūtra 3 says:

A man ought to marry a woman who is possessed of intelligence, beauty, good character, and auspicious marks, and who is free from disease. (Compare the directions Manu III. 4–10.)

The sixth Chapter specifies and describes the eight forms of marriage, called *Brāhma*, *Daiva*, *Prājāpatya*, *Ārsha*, *Gāndharva*, *Āsura*, *Paiśāća*, and *Rākshasa*. They are also enumerated by Manu (III. 21), but not quite in the same order, and by Yājñavalkya (I. 58, 61). Manu (III. 27–34) describes them more fully than Āśvalāyana.

Book I. vii. prescribes a common marriage ceremony:

West of the (sacred) fire a stone (for grinding corn and condiments, such as is used by women in all households) is placed, and north-east a water-jar. The bridegroom offers an oblation, standing, looking towards the west, and taking hold of the bride's hands while she sits and looks towards the east. If he wishes only for sons, he clasps her thumbs and says, 'I clasp thy hands for the sake of good fortune;' the fingers alone, if he wishes for daughters; the hairy side of the hand along with the thumbs, if he wishes for both (sons and daughters). Then, whilst he leads her towards the right three times round the fire and round the water-jar, he says in a low tone, 'I am he, thou art she; thou art she, I am he; I am the heaven, thou art the earth; I am the Sāman, thou art the Ṛić. Come; let us marry, let us possess offspring; united in affection, illustrious, well disposed towards each other (*sumanasyamānau*), let us live for a hundred years.' Every time he leads her round he makes her ascend the mill-stone, and says, 'Ascend thou this stone, be thou firm as a stone' (*aśmeva tvaṃ sthirā bhava*). Then the bride's brother, after spreading melted butter on the joined palms of her hands, scatters parched grains of rice on them twice. Then, after pouring the oblation of butter on the fire, some Vedic texts are recited. Then the bridegroom unlooses the two braided tresses of hair, one on each side of the top of the bride's head, repeating the Vedic text, 'I loose thee from the fetters of Varuṇa with which the very auspicious Savitṛi has bound thee' (Ṛig-veda X. 85. 24[1]). Then he causes her to step seven steps towards the

[1] The text in the original is *Pra tvā muñćāmi Varuṇasya pāśād yena*

north-east quarter, saying to her, 'Take thou one step (*ekapadī bhava*) for the acquirement of sap-like energy (*ishe*); take thou two steps for strength (*ūrje dvipadī bhava*); take thou three steps for the increase of wealth (*rāyas-poshāya*); take thou four steps for well-being (*māyobhavyāya*); take thou five steps for offspring (*prajābhyaḥ*); take thou six steps for the seasons (*ṛitubhyaḥ*); take thou seven steps as a friend (*sakhā saptapadī bhava*[1]); be faithfully devoted to me; may we obtain many sons! may they attain to a good old age!' Then bringing both their heads into close juxtaposition, some one sprinkles them with water from the jar. He should then remain for that night in the abode of an old Brāhman woman whose husband and children are alive. When the bride sees the polar star and Arundhatī and the seven Ṛishis, let her break silence and say, 'May my husband live and may I obtain children.'

In Book I. viii. 12, 13, 14, we have the following:

When he (the bridegroom) has completed the marriage ceremonial he should give the bride's dress to one who knows the Sūryā-sūkta (Ṛigveda X. 85), and food to the Brāhmans; then he should make them pronounce a blessing on him. [*Ćarita-vrataḥ sūryā-vide vadhū-vastraṃ dadyāt | annam brāhmaṇebhyaḥ | atha svasty-ayanaṃ vāćayīta.*]

Book I. ix. directs that after the marriage (*pāṇi-grahaṇa*) the first duty of the bridegroom is to attend to the kindling and maintaining of the household fire. The tenth Chapter prescribes the performance of the rite called *Sthālīpāka*, which appears to have been an oblation of rice, &c., cooked in a kind of caldron. The eleventh gives the rules for the ritual of animal sacrifice (*paśu-kalpa*), and the twelfth for the *Ćaitya-yajña*, which seems to have been a ceremonial performed at monuments, accompanied with offerings, perhaps to the memory of deceased persons. The thirteenth, fourteenth, fifteenth, sixteenth, and seventeenth Chapters prescribe certain domestic ceremonies connected with the birth and treatment of children, which

---

*tvābadhnāt Savitā suśevaḥ.* It is from the well-known Sūryā-sūkta (X. 85), describing the marriage ceremony of Sūryā, the youthful daughter of the Sun, united to Soma, the Moon.

[1] Sakhā is Vedic for Sakhī. See Scholiast on Pāṇini IV. 1. 62.

are included under the Saṇskāras enjoined in the second Book of Manu. They are as follow:

*Garbha-lambhana*, a rite performed on the first signs of conception, and *Puṇsavana*, one that takes place on the first indication of the conception of a living male (cf. Manu II. 27).

*Sīmantonnayana*, 'arranging the parting of the mother's hair,' observed in the fourth, sixth, or eighth month of pregnancy.

*Hiraṇya-madhu-sarpishām prāśanam*, 'feeding an infant with honey and clarified butter from a golden spoon' before cutting the navel-string at birth=*jāta-karman* (Manu II. 29).

*Anna-prāśana*, 'feeding an infant with rice' between the fifth and eighth month (Manu II. 34).

*Ćaula* (=*ćūḍā-karman*), 'tonsure' or shaving the hair except one lock on the crown, performed in the third year (cf. Manu II. 35).

In Book I. xix. we have precise directions in regard to investiture (*upanayana*) with the sacred thread (*yajño-pavīta*),—a ceremony of great importance, supposed to confer on the recipients (like the Christian rite of baptism) a second spiritual birth. This is enjoined for a Brāhman in his eighth year, for a Kshatriya in his eleventh, and for a Vaiśya in his twelfth, though the time may be extended in each case. These are therefore the three twice-born (*dvi-ja*) classes. (Cf. Manu II. 36–38.) The twenty-second gives rules for the guidance of the young Brāhman as a Brahma-ćārin or 'student of the Veda' in the house of his preceptor after investiture by him. It begins thus:

'Thou art now a Brahma-ćārī, take care to wash out thy mouth daily with water (=*upa-spṛiś*, *ā-ćam* in Manu II. 51, 53), do thy appointed work (*karma kuru*), sleep not in the day-time (*divā mā svāpsīḥ*, cf. *divā-svapna*, Manu VII. 47), obey thy preceptor, study the Veda (*Vedam adhīshva*); every morning and evening go out to beg for alms; every evening and morning collect fuel for the fire.' The period of studentship is to last for twelve years or until the student has acquired a knowledge of the Vedas (*grahaṇāntam*; cf. Manu III. 1, II. 53–60).

The fourth and fifth Chapters of the second Book prescribe the Ashṭakā and Anvashṭakya Śrāddha ceremonies.

The subject of Book II. vii. viii. is Vāstu-parīkshā, 'examination of soil and situation' before fixing on a site, or laying the foundation of a house, thus:

A piece of ground (should be chosen) which does not contain saline soil, and the title to which is not likely to involve legal disputes, and which is well stocked with plants and trees, and where there is plenty of Kuśa grass and Vīraṇa (fragrant grass). All thorny shrubs and plants with milky sap should be rooted out. A hole should be dug knee-deep and filled again with the excavated earth. If the earth when restored to the hole appears more than enough to fill it, the soil is excellent; if just enough, it is fairly good; if too little, it is bad. [*Adhike praśastaṃ same vārttaṃ nyūne garhitam*, VIII. 3.] At sunset the hole should be filled with water and allowed to stand all night. If in the morning it is still full of water, the soil is excellent; if it is moist, the soil is fairly good; if dry, bad. White, sweet-tasting, sandy soil is good for Brāhmans, red for Kshatriyas, yellow for Vaiśyas.

Book II. x. prescribes a solemn entrance into the new house (*gṛiha-prapadana*), after having stored it with seed-grain. The owner is then to cause the adjacent land belonging to him to be ploughed up and sown at the right season, and, standing at a particular spot with his back to the wind, he is to offer oblations, repeating a hymn of the Ṛig-veda (IV. 57), part of which I here translate freely:

May the land's Lord be present as our friend!
So shall we prosper[1]. May the god accord us
Cattle and horses, nourishment and food!
By gifts like these he manifests his favour.
God of the land! bestow on us sweet water.
To us may every herb be sweet as honey!
To us may sky and atmosphere and rain
Be kind! and may the god who owns the soil
Be gracious! may we fearlessly approach him!
For us may oxen plough auspiciously[2]!

---

[1] Lit. 'with the Lord of land as our friend,' &c. [*Kshetrasya patinā vayaṃ hiteneva jayāmasi.*]

[2] *Śunam=sukham.*

May peasants labour happily! may ploughshares
Draw every furrow smoothly! may the ploughmen[1]
Follow the oxen joyfully! May he,
The rain-god, water happily the earth
With sweetest showers! may the god of air
And sun[2] bestow on us prosperity!

The first Chapter of the third Book prescribes the five solemn offerings or devotional acts which every twice-born man is required to perform every day. These correspond to the five *Mahā-yajñāḥ* of Manu III. 69–71, sometimes called the five Sacraments. They are acts of homage directed—1. to the gods; 2. to all beings; 3. to departed ancestors; 4. to the Ṛishis or authors of the Veda; 5. to men (1. *deva-yajña*, 2. *bhūta-y°*, 3. *pitṛi-y°*, 4. *brahma-y°*, 5. *manushya-y°*). The first is performed by an oblation (*homa*) to the gods offered on the domestic fire; the second by an offering (*bali*) to animals and all creatures; the third by pouring out water to the spirits of the departed; the fourth by repetition of the Veda; the fifth by gifts to men and hospitality to guests (cf. Manu III. 81, &c., where, however, they are not given in the same order).

The second and third Chapters treat of the fourth diurnal act of devotion (*brahma-yajña*), and direct the twice-born man how he is to conduct his private devotions, and how and what he is to repeat to himself (*svādhyāya-vidhi*):

He is to go in an easterly or northerly direction outside his place of abode, wearing his sacrificial cord (*yajñopavīta*) over his shoulder; he is first to bathe, and, having rinsed out his mouth (*āćamya*), to sit down on Kuśa grass placed so that the points are directed towards the east (Manu II. 75), and to repeat the sacred syllable *om*, the three Vyāhṛitis (*bhūr*, *bhuvaḥ*, *svar*), and the Sāvitrī (or *Gāyatrī*, see p. 20; cf. Manu II. 75–77, 79). Then he is to repeat, for as long a time as he may think proper, portions of some of the Ṛić, Yajus, Sāman, Atharvāṅgiras, Brāhmaṇas, Kalpas, Gāthās, Nārāśaṇsīs, Itihāsas, and Purāṇas[3] (see note, p. 252.)

---

[1] *Kīnāśāḥ*. [2] This is the native interpretation of S'unā-sīrā. See Wilson.
[3] The modern Brahma-yajña of pious Brāhmans is based on this Sūtra.

With regard to this subject, see p. 252 of this volume.

Book III. vii. declares that if a twice-born man, being in good health, allows himself to fall asleep while the sun is setting, he is to pass the remainder of the night in an upright position, without uttering a word, and at sun-rise to repeat five verses, from the fourth to the eighth inclusive, of Ṛig-veda X. 37, beginning, 'With whatever light, O sun, thou dispellest the darkness.' [*Yena sūrya jyotishā bādhase tamo*, &c.] Again, if the sun should rise while he is asleep, he is to continue standing and silent during the day, and to repeat the last four verses of the same hymn (cf. Manu II. 219–222). The eighth, ninth, and tenth Chapters prescribe the ceremonies to be performed by a twice-born man whose period of studentship with his preceptor is completed, and who is about to return (*samāvartamāna*) home, and become a householder:

He is to procure various articles for himself and his preceptor (at any rate for the latter), such as a necklace, two ear-rings, a suit of clothes, a parasol, a pair of shoes, a staff, a turban, perfumes, &c. (cf. Manu II. 245, 246). Having completed his studies and received permission from his preceptor to depart, and having inquired what fee (*artha*) he is to pay, he must perform an ablution (*snāna*). He is then to make certain vows of purity, after which he becomes elevated to the condition of a Snātaka (cf. Manu III. 4) or Brāhman who, after purification, has passed from the first stage of life—that of a student—to the second stage or that of a householder (*griha-stha*).

The fourth Book is perhaps the most interesting. In the first four Chapters it prescribes the funeral rites to be performed at the burning of dead bodies[1], and gives some directions as to the subsequent Śrāddha ceremonies:

When a man dies, a piece of ground is to be excavated in a *Śmaśāna*

---

[1] See the article 'Über Todtenbestattung,' by Professor Max Müller in vol. ix of the Zeitschrift der Deutschen Morgenländischen Gesellschaft, in which a portion of this division of the Āśvalāyana Gṛihya Sūtras is translated into German. With regard to the importance of the following extracts as bearing upon Satī (*Suttee*), see p. 258 of this volume.

or 'burning-ground' south-east or south-west of his abode. His relations are to carry the fires and the sacrificial implements (*yajña-pātrāṇi*) to the excavated place. Those of them who are most advanced in years (*pravayasaḥ*) are to walk behind in single file—the men separated from the women—bearing the corpse, the hair and nails of which have all been cut off or clipped, and leading the sacrificial animal, either a cow or a black she-goat. The remaining relations and connexions are to follow with their garments and sacrificial cords hanging down (*adho-nivītāḥ*), and their hair dishevelled—the elder in front, the younger behind. When they reach the prepared ground, the performer of the ceremony is to sprinkle water on it with a branch of the S'amī tree, repeating Ṛig-veda X. 14. 9:

'Depart (ye evil spirits), slink away from here; the Fathers (his departed ancestors) have made for him this place of rest, distinguished (*vyaktam*) by days (*ahobhir*), waters (*adbhir*), and bright lights (*aktubhiḥ*)[1].'

Then he is to deposit the fires around the margin of the excavated place—the Āhavanīya fire to the south-east, the Gārhapatya to the north-west, and the Dakshiṇa to the south-west (see note, p. 198). Then some one who understands what is required, is to collect a heap of fire-wood and pile it up inside the sacrificial ground (*antar-vedi*). Next, a layer of Kuśa grass is to be spread over the heap along with the black skin of the goat and the clipped hair, and the dead body is to be placed upon it with the feet towards the Gārhapatya fire and the head towards the Āhavanīya. North of the body his wife is to be made to lie down (on the funeral pile), along with the bow of the dead man if he was a soldier (*Kshatriya*). Then either her husband's brother (*devaraḥ*), who is in the place of a husband to her (*patisthānīyaḥ*), or a pupil, or an old servant causes her to rise up, repeating the words of Ṛig-veda X. 18. 8:

'Rise up, O woman (*udīrshva nāri*), come back to the world of life; thou art lying by a dead man; come back. Thou hast sufficiently fulfilled the duty of a wife and mother (*janitvam*) to the husband who wooed thee (*didhishos*) and took thee by the hand.' (See note 2, p. 258.)

Next, the brother-in-law is to take back the bow, repeating Ṛig-veda X. 18. 9:

'I take the bow out of the hand of the dead man for our own protection, for our glory, and for our strength; remain thou there, we will remain here as heroes, (so that) in all battles we may conquer our foes.'

---

[1] The meaning of this is not very clear. I understand it as denoting that the ground is open and well exposed to daylight and well sprinkled with water and surrounded with the fires.

Then he is to place the various sacrificial implements and portions of the sacrificial animal in the two hands and on different parts of the body of the corpse. This being done, he is to order the three fires to be kindled (*agnīn prajvālayati*). If the Āhavanīya fire reaches the dead man first, then his spirit is borne to heaven; if the Gārhapatya, then his spirit is taken to the middle region (*antariksha-loka*); if the Dakshiṇa, then it remains in the world of mortals (*manushya-loka*). When all three reach him together, this is the most auspicious sign of all. While the body is burning, portions of hymns of the Ṛig-veda (such as X. 14. 7, 8, 10, 11, X. 16. 1–4, X. 17. 3–6, X. 18. 11, X. 154. 1–5) are to be repeated.

The following are examples of some of the verses:

Open thy arms, O earth, receive the dead
With gentle pressure and with loving welcome.
Enshroud him tenderly, e'en as a mother
Folds her soft vestment round the child she loves (X. 18. 11).
Soul of the dead! depart; take thou the path—
The ancient path—by which our ancestors
Have gone before thee; thou shalt look upon
The two kings, mighty Varuṇa and Yama,
Delighting in oblations; thou shalt meet
The Fathers and receive the recompense
Of all thy stored-up offerings above.
Leave thou thy sin and imperfection here;
Return unto thy home once more; assume
A glorious form. By an auspicious path
Hasten to pass the four-eyed brindled dogs—
The two road-guarding sons of Saramā;
Advance to meet the Fathers who, with hearts
Kindly disposed towards thee, dwell in bliss
With Yama; and do thou, O mighty god,
Intrust him to thy guards [1] to bring him to thee,
And grant him health and happiness eternal (X. 14. 7–11) [2].

When a dead body is burnt by one who knows and can repeat these verses properly, then it is certain that the soul (invested with a kind of subtile body [3]) rises along with the smoke to heaven (*sahaiva dhūmena svargaṃ lokam etīti ha vijñāyate*).

---

[1] These are the four-eyed watch-dogs mentioned before.

[2] Part of this has been freely rendered in a version given p. 22.

[3] The eighth Sūtra of Chapter IV states that a hole ought to be dug

Then the performer of the ceremony is to repeat the verse (Ṛig-veda X. 18. 3)

> We living men, survivors, now return
> And leave the dead; may our oblations please
> The gods and bring us blessings! now we go
> To dance and jest and hope for longer life.

After this they are to move to a spot where there is a pool of still water, dip themselves once, cast a handful of water into the air, pronouncing the name of the dead man and that of his family (e. g. 'O Devadatta Kāśyapa, this water is for thee'); then coming out of the water, they are to put on other clothes and to sit down till the stars appear or else till the sun is quite invisible, when they are to proceed homewards, the younger ones walking first, the elder behind. Before entering the house they are (for purification) to touch a stone, fire, cow-dung, grains of barley, oil, and water. During one night they are not to cook any food, but to eat only what is already prepared, and for three nights they are not to touch anything containing salt.

Book IV. v. prescribes the gathering together the bones and ashes of the deceased (*sañćayana*, Manu V. 59):

This is to take place after the tenth day of the dark half of the month, on an odd day (i.e. the eleventh, thirteenth, fifteenth, &c.), and under a single Nakshatra (i.e. not under one like Ashāḍhā, which is both *pūrvā* and *uttarā*).

The bones and ashes of a man are to be placed in an undecorated funeral vase or long vessel (*alakshaṇe kumbhe*), and those of a woman in a female vase (of a fuller shape, supposed to resemble the female figure). A hole is to be excavated and the bones thus collected in a vessel are to be placed in it, while Ṛig-veda X. 18. 10 is repeated:

'Go to thy mother Earth, the Widely-extended (*uru-vyaćasam*), the Broad, the Auspicious; may she be to thee like a young maiden, soft as wool (*ūrṇa-mradā*), to a pious person! may she protect thee from the embrace of the goddess of corruption!' (*Nirṛiter upasthāt.*)

Then earth is to be scattered over the excavation, and Ṛig-veda X. 18. 11, 12 are to be repeated (see p. 206 for verse 11). Lastly, a cover or

---

north-eastward of the Āhavanīya fire and strewn with the plants Avakā and Śīpāla; and the commentator adds that the soul of the dead man, invested with its vehicular subtile body (called *ātivāhika* and sometimes *adhishṭhāna* and distinct from the *linga* or *sūkshma*, being *angushṭha-mātra*, 'of the size of a thumb'), waits in this hole until the gross body is burnt, and then emerging, is carried with the smoke to heaven.

lid is to be placed over the vase or long vessel and the hole is to be filled up with earth, so that the vessel is quite hidden from view, while Ṛig-veda X. 18. 13 is repeated:

'I raise up the earth around thee for a support, placing this cover on thee without causing injury. May the Fathers guard this funereal monument for thee! May Yama establish a habitation for thee there!'

This being accomplished, the relations are to return home, without looking about, and after they have performed an ablution they are to offer the first S'rāddha to the deceased person separately (*ekoddishṭa*).

Book IV. vii. prescribes four kinds of *Śrāddha,* i. e. offerings to deceased persons and Pitṛis or ancestors generally: 1. *Pārvaṇa,* 'monthly,' to ancestors for three generations on the days of conjunction or new moon (cf. Manu III. 282; those to ancestors generally being called *Nitya,* 'constant,' 'daily,' and others *Ashṭakā,* as performed on the eighth day of certain months); 2. *Kāmya,* 'voluntary,' performed for some object of desire (as the obtaining of a son); 3. *Ābhyudayika,* performed as thank-offerings on occasions of family rejoicing (as at the Saṉskāras) or for increase of prosperity, &c. (*Vṛiddhi-pūrta*); 4. *Ekoddishṭa,* 'special,' having reference to one person recently deceased, and not to ancestors generally. It is repeated annually on the anniversary of his death. (Those which are occasional are sometimes called *Naimittika.*) To these funeral ceremonies Brāhmans are to be invited. They are to be feasted, and gifts presented to them. The guests are to be made to sit down with their faces towards the North, and water is to be poured into their hands with Kuśa grass and Sesamum seed (*tila,* cf. Manu III. 223). Cakes of rice (*piṇḍa*) and libations of water are to be offered with the auspicious exclamation Svadhā. There is also another Śrāddha called *Daiva,* in honour of the Viśve Devāḥ, 'deities collectively,' or of a particular troop of deities, ten in number. Hence some distinguish eight kinds of Śrāddha (see p. 253); and the Nirṇaya-sindhu, twelve.

A fuller description of these solemn Śrāddhas is given

by Manu III. 123–286, and in verse 202 the meaning of the term Śrāddha is explained as follows :

Mere water (*vāry api*) offered with faith (*śraddhayā*) to the Pitṛis in silver or plated (*rājatānvitaiḥ*) vessels procures imperishable bliss (*akshayāyopakalpate*).

I close my account of the Āśvalāyana Gṛihya Sūtras by remarking that the rules relating to funeral ceremonies in the fourth Book, of which an abstract has just been given, possess great interest in their connexion with the eighteenth hymn of the tenth Maṇḍala of the Ṛig-veda. Although the Sūtras direct that the texts of this hymn are to be used, yet the rite must have undergone considerable modifications since the period when the hymn was composed.

It may be gathered from a study of the text of the hymn, that at the early period when the Āryan race first settled on the plains of Hindūstān, there was not the same prolonged and elaborate observance of funeral rites, which in later times was converted into an excuse for the ostentatious and costly feasting of priests and guests (see p. 255). But there was no less solemnity in the conduct of the ceremonial, no less exhibition of grief for the dead in the tender treatment of his remains, and no less affectionate respect for his memory,—a feeling cherished as a religious duty, more tenaciously in India than in Europe.

We notice, too, even at that early epoch an evident belief in the soul's eternal existence and the permanence of its personality hereafter, which notably contrasts with the later ideas of transmigration, absorption into the divine essence, and pantheistic identification with the supreme Soul of the universe.

We learn also from this same hymn that the body in ancient times was not burnt but buried ; nor can we discover the slightest allusion to the later practice of Satī or cremation of the widow with her husband.

The corpse of the deceased person was deposited close to

a grave dug ready for its reception, and by its side his widow, if he happened to be a married man, seated herself, while his children, relatives, and friends ranged themselves in a circle round her. The priest stood near at an altar, on which the sacred fire was kindled, and having invoked Death, called upon him to withdraw from the path of the living, and not to molest the young and healthy survivors, who were assembled to perform pious rites for the dead, without giving up the expectation of a long life themselves. He then placed a stone between the dead body and the living relations, to mark off the boundary line of Death's domain, and offered up a prayer that none of those present might be removed to another world before attaining to old age, and that none of the younger might be taken before the elder. Then the widow's married female friends walked up to the altar and offered oblations in the fire; after which the widow herself withdrew from the inner circle assigned to the dead, and joined the survivors outside the boundary-line, while the officiating priest took the bow out of the hand of the deceased, in order to show that the manly strength which he possessed during life, did not perish with him, but remained with his family. The body was then tenderly laid in the grave with repetition of the words of the hymn already translated, 'Open thy arms, O Earth, receive the dead,' &c. (see p. 206). The ceremony was concluded by the careful closing of the tomb with a stone slab. Finally a mound of earth was raised to mark and consecrate the spot[1].

With regard to the Sāmayāćārika Sūtras little remains to add to what has already been stated. Not many collections of this third class of Sūtras (as distinguished

---

[1] A fuller account of the whole rite will be found in Professor Stenzler's 'Rede über die Sitte,' which I have consulted throughout.

from the Śrauta and Gṛihya) have been preserved. Were they better known to us, we should probably find that they furnished materials for Manu's compilation, even more than the Gṛihya Sūtras appear to have done. It is for this reason that, as introductory to the Dharma-śāstras or Law-books, they are sometimes called Dharma-sūtras. Since 'conventional, every-day practices' constitute the proper subject of these Sūtras, and it is clear that conventional usages may often come under the head of Gṛihya or 'domestic rites,' it may easily be understood that the Sāmayāćārika not unfrequently go over the same ground as the Gṛihya Sūtras. For instance, we find them both giving rules for the Saṉskāras &c. (see p. 246). Perhaps the best known Sāmayāćārika Sūtras are those of Āpastamba belonging to the Black Yajur-veda (see note 1, p. 196). An account of these will be found in Professor Max Müller's 'Ancient Sanskṛit Literature' (p. 100, &c.), and in No. 732 of Rājendralāla Mitra's MSS. They commence as follows:

1. Therefore let us now explain the Sāmayāćārika duties. [*Athātaḥ sāmayāćārikān dharmān vyākhyāsyāmaḥ.*]

2. These agreements which were made by men who knew the law are an authority. [*Dharma-jña-samayaḥ pramāṇam.*]

3. And the Vedas (are an authority). [*Vedāś-ća.*]

## III. *The Dharma-śāstras or Law-books—Manu.*

At least forty-seven independent Law-books[1] are enumerated, and of these at least twenty are still extant and are mentioned by Yājñavalkya (I. 3–5), as follow:

1. That of Manu. 2. Yājñavalkya (second in importance to Manu). 3. Atri. 4. Vishṇu. 5. Hārīta. 6. Uśanas. 7. Aṅgiras. 8. Yama. 9. Āpastamba. 10. Saṃvarta. 11. Kātyāyana. 12. Vṛihaspati. 13. Parā-

[1] Professor Stenzler enumerates forty-six, Dr. Röer forty-seven. The names of the authors of some of these law-books are the same as those of some of the Gṛihya Sūtras, e. g. Āpastamba, Pāraskara, and Baudhāyana. The same men may have been authors of both Sūtras and Dharma-śāstras.

śara. 14. Vyāsa. 15. S'an-kha. 16. Likhita. 17. Daksha. 18. Gotama or Gautama. 19. Sātātapa. 20. Vasishṭha. There is also a Law-book, the joint production of S'an-kha and Likhita; and others ascribed to Nārada, Bhṛigu, &c. (see the end of Lecture X); and Kullūka, the commentator on Manu, mentions the names of Baudhāyana, Medhātithi, Govinda-rāja, &c.

Let us first endeavour to gain some idea of the character of the most celebrated and ancient of these books commonly called 'the Code of Manu.'

This well-known collection of laws and precepts is perhaps the oldest and most sacred Sanskṛit work after the Veda and its Sūtras. Although standing in a manner at the head of Post-vedic literature, it is connected with the Veda through these Sūtras, as the philosophical Darśanas are through the Upanishads. Even if not the oldest of Post-vedic writings (see note, p. 215), it is certainly the most interesting, both as presenting a picture of the institutions, usages, manners, and intellectual condition of an important part of the Hindū race at a remote period, and as revealing the exaggerated nature of the rules by which the Brāhmans sought to secure their own ascendancy, and to perpetuate an organized caste-system in subordination to themselves. At the same time it is in other respects perhaps one of the most remarkable books that the literature of the whole world can offer, and some of its moral precepts are worthy of Christianity itself.

Probably the compilation we now possess is an irregular compendium of rules and maxims by different authors, which existed unwritten for a long period of time, and were handed down orally. An original collection is alluded to by commentators under the titles Vṛiddha and Vṛihat, which is said to have contained 100,000 couplets, arranged under twenty-four heads in one thousand chapters; whereas the existing Code contains only 2685 verses. Possibly abbreviated versions of old collections were made at successive periods, and additional matter inserted, the present text merely representing the latest compilation.

At any rate we must guard against a supposition that the expression 'Code,' often applied to this collection, is intended to denote a systematic arrangement of precepts which existed as actual laws in force throughout one country. It is probable that the whole of India was never under one government. Some few powerful monarchs are known to have acquired sovereignty over very extensive territories, and were then called Ćakra-vartins, but we must beware of imagining that Manu's Law-book is a record of national ordinances and institutions prevalent over the whole of such territories. No doubt ultimately it worked its way to acceptance with the entire Hindū community; and certainly in the end it not only secured for itself a high place in popular estimation and a degree of reverence only second to that accorded to the Veda, but it became, moreover, the chief authority as a basis of Hindū jurisprudence. Originally, however, its position must have been different. It merely represented certain rules and precepts (perhaps by different authors) current among a particular tribe, or rather school of Brāhmans called Mānavas, who probably lived in the North-western region between the rivers Sarasvatī and Dṛishadvatī (see p. 216), not far from Delhi and the scene of the great social conflict described in the Mahābhārata[1]. This tribe seems to have belonged to the Taittirīyakas, 'adherents of the Black Yajur-veda;' and their Mantras, Brāhmaṇa, and Śrauta Sūtras are still extant[2], but their

[1] The inference deducible from II. 17, 18, that the Mānavas lived in the region of the earliest Āryan settlements, must have weight in determining the antiquity of the Code and its value as representing the ancient social life of the Hindūs before their advance into the Dekhan.

[2] A counterpart of a MS. of a commentary on part of the Mānava-kalpa-sūtra has been edited by the late Professor Goldstücker.

Gṛihya and Sāmayāćārika Sūtras appear to have perished. In all probability, too, many of the rules, as we have them presented to us, were simply theoretical,—inserted to complete an ideal of what ought to constitute a perfect system of religious, ceremonial, moral, political, and social duties. Who the real compiler and promulgator of the Institutes was, is not known. He was probably a learned Brāhman of the Mānava school.

We must, of course, make a due allowance for the mythical element in the Code, as, for instance, when a divine sage named Manu[1] (or Svāyambhuva—'sprung from the great self-existent Being') is made to say (I. 58–60) as follows:

The god (Brahmā) having framed this system of laws himself, taught it fully to me in the beginning. I then taught it to Marīći and the nine other sages, my offspring (of whom Bhṛigu is one, cf. I. 35). Of these (my sons) Bhṛigu is deputed by me to declare the Code to you (Ṛishis) from beginning to end, for he has learned from me to recite the whole of it. Then the great sage, Bhṛigu, having been thus appointed by Manu

---

[1] This name of the supposed divine progenitor of all beings is derived from the root *man*, which means 'to think' or 'reason' (and especially according to the Hindū theory, 'to think upon and understand the Veda,' whence the desiderative form *Mīmāṇsā* from the same root, signifying 'investigation of the meaning of the Veda'). Bhṛigu states (I. 61) that Manu sprang from Svayambhū, and that six other Manus descended from him; whereas Manu himself (I. 33–36) declares that he was created by Virāj, the male power produced by Brahmā, and that being so created he produced the ten Maharshis or Prajāpatis, who again produced seven Manus. The name, however, is generic. In every Kalpa or interval from creation to creation there exist fourteen successive Manus, whence each whole period is called a *Manv-antara*, described as innumerable in I. 80. In the present creation there have been as yet seven Manus: 1. Manu *Svāyambhuva*, the supposed author of the Code, who produced the ten Prajāpatis or 'patriarchs' for peopling the universe; 2. *Svārоćisha*; 3. *Auttami*; 4. *Tāmasa*; 5. *Raivata*; 6. *Ćākshusha*; 7. *Vaivasvata*, son of the Sun, the Manu of the present period, regarded as a kind of Indian Adam or Noah (see note, p. 32). According to some, this last Manu was the author of the Code, and therefore, as progenitor of the Solar line of kings, a Kshatriya.

to promulgate his laws, addressed all the Ṛishis with a pleased mind, saying, 'Listen!'

Manu, therefore, is supposed to speak in his own person as far as I. 60. After that, Bhṛigu is the speaker, and the closing verse of the whole Code (XII. 126) describes it as *Mānavaṃ Śāstram Bhṛigu-proktam*, 'enunciated by Bhṛigu;' while in XI. 243 Prajāpati or Brahmā himself is declared to have created it by the power of austerity (*tapasā*).

We need hardly, however, explain that these are merely ideal personages, introduced dramatically like Kṛishṇa in the Bhagavad-gītā; or rather perhaps are later additions, designed to give an air of antiquity and divine authority to the teaching of the Code.

The work in its present form can scarcely, I think, be assigned to a date earlier or later than the fifth century B.C.[1] Strictly speaking, or at least according to European

[1] Sir W. Jones held that Manu's book was drawn up in about the year 1280 B.C. Mr. Elphinstone placed it 900 years B.C. Possibly some parts of it may represent laws and precepts which were current among the Mānavas at the latter date, but no one would now assign so early a date to the actual compilation of the Code. Nor can it, I think, reasonably be placed later than the fifth century B.C. The gods mentioned are chiefly Vedic, and the fourfold caste system is that of the Purusha-sūkta (see p. 24). There is no direct allusion to Buddhism, though many of Manu's precepts are decidedly Buddhistic, having frequent parallels in the Dhamma-pada, which indicate that Buddhistic ideas were gaining ground in the locality represented by the Code. Nor is there any allusion to Satī, nor to the worship of Vishṇu and S'iva, which, from a statement of Megasthenes, may be inferred to have prevailed in India soon after Alexander's invasion. Nor is there any mention of the stories of the Mahābhārata and Rāmāyaṇa. At the same time the former Epic often contains verses identical with those of Manu. These are probably either taken from Manu or derived from a common source. Possibly, however, portions of the Mahābhārata may be older than Manu. Certainly in III. 232 occur the words *Dharma-śāstra*, *Ākhyāna*, *Itihāsa*, *Purāṇa*, and *Khila*, as titles of sacred works, and Kullūka explains *Itihāsa* by *Mahā-bhārata*, but these words may refer to the older works, which were the sources of the present compilations.

notions, it is, as I have already hinted, no orderly codification of national statutes and customs, but rather an unsystematic compilation from previous sources[1], which, by blending civil and criminal law with religious, moral, and ceremonial precepts, philosophical doctrines, and metaphysical theories, confounds the ordinances of government with the obligations of religion, domestic life, and private morals. It is in twelve Chapters or Books.

In verse 6 of Book II we have a statement as to the 'root' or basis of all law (*dharma-mūlam*). This is declared to be (1) the whole Veda (*Vedo 'khilaḥ*), (2) the traditional law (*Smṛiti*), (3) morality (*Śīlam*) of those who know the Veda, and (4) the practices and customs (*āćāraḥ*), established from time immemorial, of good men. In matters indifferent a man is free to follow his own inclination (*ātma-tushṭi*).

Again, in verses 107, 108 of Book I it is said:

In this (Code) appears the whole system of law, with definitions of good and bad actions, and the traditional practices (*āćāra*) of the four classes, which usages are held to be eternal (*śāśvataḥ*, since they reach back to a period beyond the memory of man). Traditional practice (*āćāra*) is equivalent to supreme law (*paramo dharmaḥ*), since it is so pronounced by the Veda and by Smṛiti (*Smārta*).

This Law-book, therefore, is a metrical compendium of rules of Smṛiti, Śīla, and Āćāra, most of which had been previously collected and propounded under the name of Gṛihya and Sāmayāćārika Sūtras. At the end of Book I a summary of subjects is given, but we may more conveniently examine the contents of the twelve books under six principal heads, viz. 1. Veda, 'sacred knowledge' and religion; 2. Vedānta or Ātma-vidyā, as terms for philosophy

[1] An evidence in favour of the supposition that more than one person may have had a hand in the Code is deducible from the emphasis laid upon certain maxims which are especially ascribed to Manu himself, such, for example, as V. 41, 131; VI. 54; VIII. 124, 168, 279, 339; IX. 158, 182, 239; X. 63, 78, all of which introduce some phrase like *Manur abravīt*.

in general; 3. Āćāra; 4. Vyavahāra; 5. Prāyaś-ćitta; 6. Karma-phala.

It will be found that after eliminating the purely religious and philosophical precepts the greater number of rules propounded fall under the third head of *Āćāra*, 'established practices,' which are described (II. 17, 18) as *Sad-āćāra*, 'approved practices,' sanctioned by the Veda and Smṛiti, if they are those which prevailed between the two sacred rivers, Sarasvatī and Dṛishadvatī, in the region called Brahmāvarta. The word Āćāra is, in truth, a very wide term, including under it all the observances of caste, regarded as constituting the highest law and highest religion—such observances, for instance, as the division of a Brāhman's life into four periods, the conduct of a student in the house of his preceptor, investiture with the sacred cord, the five diurnal devotional acts, the domestic ceremonies of marriage, funeral rites, the various modes of gaining subsistence (*vṛitti*), the rules of diet, the laws concerning women, and, in short, all the observances of private morality and social economy[1].

The fourth head, *Vyavahāra*, 'practices of law and kingly government,' embraces the procedure of legal tribunals and all the rules of judicature and civil and criminal law.

The fifth head of *Prāyaś-ćitta*, 'penitential exercises,' comprehends all the rules of penance and expiation.

The sixth head, *Karma-phala*, 'recompenses or consequences of acts,' is concerned not so much with rules of conduct as with the doctrine of transmigration; the unavoidable effect of acts of all kinds being to entail repeated births through numberless existences until the attainment of final beatitude.

All these rules apply especially to the highest class,

---

[1] In Book V. 4 there is a curious passage which attributes Death's power over Brāhmans to four causes, viz. 1. omitting to repeat the Veda, 2. neglect of Āćāra, 3. idleness, 4. sins of diet.

viz. Brāhmans, whose ascendancy in the social scale is in fact the first Āćāra, which must be accepted as *paramo dharmaḥ*, 'the highest law and highest religion.'

It is only natural that, since the precepts included under these six heads were framed by Brāhmans, they should have been framed with especial reference to the life of Brāhmans, the regulations for which engross six Books, and are besides introduced everywhere throughout the other six. But as the Brāhman could not be supported in his priority of rank without the strong arm of the Kshatriya or military class, a large portion of the work is devoted to the definition of the Kshatriya's duties and an exaggerated delineation of the kingly character and office, while the Vaiśyas and Śūdras, though essential to Manu's Ćāturvarṇya or fourfold social system [1], and the mixed classes are little noticed. (See p. 234, &c.)

---

[1] 'Caste' is quite a modern word, and is supposed to be a corruption of the Portuguese *casta*, 'a race.' Manu's word for the four classes is *varṇa*, 'colour,' which suggests some original distinction of colour as marking the dominant races. The later term for caste is *jāti*, 'birth,' corrupted into *jāt*. Of Manu's four castes the Brāhmans alone remain, though the Rājputs claim to be descendants of the ancient Kshatriyas. The mixed castes of the present day are almost innumerable, each separate trade forming a separate one. In Bengal there are the Rajaks, 'washermen,' the Tāntīs, 'weavers,' the Kaṇsāris, 'braziers,' the Jāliyās, 'fishermen,' the Surīs, 'spirit sellers;' besides low and servile castes, such as the Bāgdis, Bediyās, Ḍoms, Hāḍis. Moreover, we find castes within castes, so that even the Brāhmans are broken up and divided into numerous races, which again are subdivided into numerous tribes, families, or subcastes. There are the Kānyakubja Brāhmans, the Sārasvata, the Gauḍa or Gauṛ (Gor), the Maithila, the Utkala, the Drāviḍa, the Karṇāṭa, the Mahārāshṭra, the Gurjara, &c., all of which races are subdivided into a greater or less number of tribes and families, forming, as it were, subcastes, which do not intermarry. It is said that in Bengal religion was once at so low an ebb that a king, named Ādiśūra (*Ādīśvara*), sent to the Rājā of Kanyākubja or Kanouj for some high-caste Brāhmans to revive it. These were accordingly sent, and, having settled in Bengal, became

Hence, after an account of the creation of the world in the first Book, the four stages of a Brāhman's life are the first and only subjects treated of in regular order in the second, third, fourth, fifth, and sixth Books; the sixth being devoted to the duties of the last two stages of anchorite (*vāna-prastha*) and religious mendicant (*bhikshu*). The fifth Book contains, moreover, rules and regulations about food, the killing of animals, purification after defilement, the duties of wives and the position of women generally. The seventh and eighth Books propound the rules of government and judicature, principally, of course, for the guidance of the second great class or Kshatriyas, from which the king was chosen. The ninth Book con-

divided into one hundred and fifty-six tribes, of which one hundred were called Vārendra and fifty-six Rāḍha or Rāṛh, as belonging to the district of Rāḍhā in the West of Bengal. Of the former eight, and of the latter six, are regarded as Kulīna or 'noble.' Kullūka, the commentator on Manu, was a Vārendra Brāhman. The six Kulīna Rāṛh tribes are called Banerjea (Bandyopādhyāya), Mukhurjea (Mukhopādhyāya), Ćaturjea (Ćaṭṭopādhyāya), Gānguli, Goshāla, Kanjalāla. The caste which in Bengal now comes next in rank to the Brāhman is the Vaidya or Baidya, 'medical' (=Ambashṭha, Manu X. 8); and the Kanouj Brāhmans, when they settled in Bengal, brought with them a number of Kāyasthas or 'writers,' from whom sprang the present numerous Kāyastha or 'writer-caste,' subdivided into various tribes, such as Gos (Ghosha), Bose (Vasu), Mitra, De, Datta, Pālita, Dāsa, Sena, &c. After them come the Nava S'āk or 'nine divisions,' viz. Gopa, Mālī, Tailī, Tantrī, Modaka, Varajī ('betel-grower'), Kulāla, Karmakāra, Nāpita. See Professor Cowell's Colebrooke's Essays II. 169. The power of caste and the effect of contact with Europeans in weakening it, are illustrated by the following extract from Dr. Hunter's valuable work on Orissa: 'Elderly Uriyas have more than once deplored to me the hopeless degeneracy of their grown-up sons, many of whom have actually no objection to wearing English shoes. In 1870 a Uriya Brāhman held the post of sub-inspector of police in Purī itself, within the shadow of Jagan-nāth, although a leather belt formed part of his uniform. Five years ago a Brāhman who accidentally touched leather would have had to choose between public expiation or degradation and expulsion from caste.' Vol. ii. p. 147.

tains further precepts on the subject of women, husband and wife, their offspring, and the law of inheritance and division of property. At the end (221, &c.) there are additional rules of government for kings and a few precepts which have direct reference to the two remaining principal castes—the Vaiśyas and Śūdras—the former comprising agriculturists and merchants; the latter, slaves and servants. The tenth Book treats of the mixed classes, arising out of intermarriage between the four original principal castes. It also describes the employments to which the several classes are restricted, and states the occupations permitted to Brāhmans, Kshatriyas, Vaiśyas, and Śūdras in times of great exigency and distress. There are some verses at the end (122–129) which are interesting as treating directly of the duties and position of Śūdras. The eleventh Book gives rules for expiation and penance (*prāyaś-ćitta*), both for sins committed in this life—especially sins against caste—and for the effects of offences perpetrated in previous bodies, as shown in congenital diseases, &c. (XI. 48, 49). The twelfth continues the subject of the recompenses or consequences of acts (*karma-phala*), good or bad, as leading to reward in heaven or punishment in various hells (XII. 75, 76), and to triple degrees of transmigration (see p. 280). It closes with directions as to the best means of obtaining final beatitude and absorption into the universal Essence.

From this outline of the contents of the so-called Code of Manu we may perceive that the most diversified topics are introduced, some of which are quite out of the province of a mere code of laws or even of a collection of social and moral precepts. In the next Lecture I propose examining the contents more in detail.

# LECTURE X.

## *The Dharma-śāstras or Law-books—Manu continued.*

THE Code of the Mānavas, which we have assigned in its present form to about the fifth century B.C. (see p. 215), and which for convenience we may call 'Manu's Law-book,' is a metrical version of the traditions (*smṛiti*) of the Mānavas, probably before embodied in their Gṛihya and Sāmayāćārika Sūtras (p. 214), the metre being Anushṭubh or that of the common Śloka [1] (p. 166). My aim in the present Lecture will be to analyze and arrange in a connected manner the contents of the Code [2], offering prose translations of selected passages and pointing out in a general way the characteristic features of (1) its sacred knowledge and religion, (2) its philosophy, (3) its *Āćāra* or 'social rules and caste organization,' (4) its *Vyavahāra* or 'criminal and civil laws and rules of government,' (5) its system of *Prāyaś-ćitta* or 'penance,' (6) its system of *Karma-phala* or 'future recompenses of acts done in this life.' In the next Lecture I propose to give specimens of

---

[1] The use of the common Epic S'loka throughout the *whole* work is one reason for regarding it as Post-vedic, but we must not forget that the Anushṭubh metre is found even in the Veda (see X. 85, X. 90, &c.)

[2] I have used the Calcutta edition, which has the excellent commentary of Kullūka-bhaṭṭa. I have always consulted Sir W. Jones' translation, and I owe much to Dr. Johaentgen's tract *Über das Gesetzbuch des Manu.* When Kullūka lived is not known, but he describes himself in his modest preface (written in the S'ārdūla-vikrīḍita metre) as a Brāhman, the son of Bhaṭṭa-divākara, of the Vārendra tribe of Gauḍa (Gauṛ) or Bengal, and as having fixed his abode at Benares. I did not read Mr. Talboys Wheeler's analysis till my own was completed.

the most striking passages, under the last four heads, in a metrical English version.

I. First, then, as to its religious teaching. We may notice that this generally agrees with the later Vedic period, especially that represented by the Purusha-sūkta and some of the Brāhmaṇas.

'Divinely revealed knowledge' in general is called *Veda* (IV. 125, &c.); sometimes *Trayī vidyā* (IV. 125); sometimes *Brahman* (nom. neut. *brahma,* I. 23, II. 81, VI. 83, in which last passage this title is also applied to the Vedānta or Upanishads); sometimes *Śruti* (as distinguished from Smṛiti, II. 10); sometimes *Ćhandāṅsi* (when the metrical Mantras are especially intended, IV. 95–97, III. 188); once *Ārsha* (neut., XII. 106), and even *Vāć,* 'word,' described as a Brāhman's weapon (XI. 33).

The three Vedas are mentioned by name in I. 23, IV. 123, 124, XI. 264, and their Saṃhitā in XI. 77, 200, 258, 262. In I. 23 we read that Brahmā milked out the triple Veda (*trayam brahma*), Ṛik, Yajus, and Sāman from Fire, Air, and the Sun, for the complete performance of sacrifice; and in II. 77 he is said to have milked out the sacred text called Sāvitrī (= Gāyatrī, p. 20) from the three Vedas[1]. The Brāhmaṇa portion of the Veda does not seem to be directly mentioned, except under the name of Brahma, as distinguished from the Mantra portion, called Ćhandas (IV. 100). The eternity and infallible authority of the Veda and the duty and expiatory efficacy of a complete knowledge of all three Vedas (XI. 262) are insisted

[1] See note, p. 9. In XI. 265 the three Vedas are said to be included in the triliteral Om. In IV. 125, Om, the Vyāhṛitis (viz. Bhūḥ, Bhuvaḥ, Svar), and the Sāvitrī text are described as extracted from the three Vedas. In III. 185, a Brāhman who understands the application of some portion of the Yajur-veda is called *Tri-ṇāćiketa,* and one skilled in some part of the Ṛig-veda a *Tri-suparṇa,* though it is clear from Kullūka's remarks that the exact meaning of these words was not known in his time.

on in the strongest language. In illustration, I here give a version of a passage in Book XII. 94, &c.:

The Veda is of patriarchs and men,
And e'en of gods, a very eye eternal,
Giving unerring light; it is beyond
All finite faculties, nor can be proved
By force of human argument—this is
A positive conclusion. Codes of laws
Depending on the memory of men—
Not grounded on the Veda—heresies
And false opinions, all are held to be
Barren and worthless and involved in darkness.
Whatever doctrine rests not on the Veda
Must pass away as recent, false, and fruitless.
The triple world and quadruple distinction
Of classes and of Āśramas[1], with all
That has been, is, and ever will be, all
Are through the Veda settled and established.
By this eternal Veda are sustained
All creatures; hence we hold it as supreme—
Chief instrument of happiness to man.
Command of armies, regal dignity,
Conduct of justice and the world's dominion
He merits who completely knows the Veda.
As with augmented energy the fire
Consumes e'en humid trees, so he who knows
This book divine burns out the taint of sin
Inherent in his soul through former works.
For he who apprehends the Veda's truth,
Whatever be his Order, is prepared
For blending with the great primeval Spirit,
E'en while abiding in this lower world.

The inferior relationship of the Sāma-veda to the two others is remarkable. The Ṛig-veda is said to be most concerned with the gods, the Yajur-veda with the religious rites of men, and the Sāma-veda with those of the Pitṛis

[1] That is, the four orders or stages of life (of student, householder, anchorite, and mendicant) into which a Brāhman's life is divided.

(IV. 124). Hence the sound of the latter is described as impure (*a-śući*, see note, p. 9).

In unison with this, an order of precedence is prescribed in III. 145. The preference at a Śrāddha is directed to be given to a priest called Bahv-ṛića (elsewhere Hotṛi), who has made the Ṛig-veda his special study; then to one who has studied all the branches (*Śākhānta-ga*) and especially the Yajur-veda, and who is called Adhvaryu; and lastly to a Sāma-veda priest, who is styled Ćhando-ga (= Udgātṛi).

It is clear that when the Code was compiled the Atharva-veda had not yet been generally accepted as a fourth Veda, though it must have existed, as there is express allusion (XI. 33) to the revelation[1] made to *Atharvan* and *An̄giras*.

I annex three other remarkable examples of the estimation in which the Veda was held:

A Brāhman by retaining the Ṛig-veda in his memory incurs no guilt, though he should destroy the three worlds (XI. 261).

This Veda is the refuge (*śaraṇa*) of those who do not understand it (*ajñānām*) as well as those who do (*vijānatām*), of those who seek heaven and of those who seek immortality (*ānantyam*, VI. 84).

When there is (apparent) contradiction of two precepts in the Veda (*śruti-dvaidham*) both are declared to be law; both have been justly promulgated (*samyag-uktau*) by ancient sages as valid law. Thus, there is a Vedic precept, (enjoining the sacrifice to be performed) when the sun has risen, and before it has risen, and when neither sun nor stars are visible (*samayādhyushite*). Wherefore the oblation to fire (*yajñaḥ=agni-hotra-homaḥ*) may be made at all times (II. 14, 15).

The doctrine of the Upanishads is directly mentioned in VI. 29 and alluded to elsewhere, thus:

He should study the Upanishad portion of the Veda (*aupanishadīḥ śrutīḥ*) for the sake of attaining union with the universal Spirit.

Let the whole Veda be studied (or repeated) by a twice-born man along with the Upanishads. [*Vedaḥ kritsno 'ahigantavyaḥ sa-rahasyo dvi-janmanā*, II. 165; cf. also II. 140, XI. 262.]

He should continually repeat (*japet*) that part of the Veda (*brahma*)

---

[1] Described by Kullūka as consisting of charms and incantations.

which is on the subject of sacrifice (*adhiyajñam*), and that relating to the deities (*adhidaivikam*), and that relating to soul (*ādhyātmikam*), and that declared in the Upanishads (*Vedāntābhihitam*, VI. 83).

The Kalpa Sūtras are probably referred to in II. 140.

A knower of Nirukta (see p. 166) is reckoned among the Brāhmans who compose a Parishad in XII. 111, but no reference is made to Yāska, nor is it likely that his work then existed (see p. 167).

In I. 11. 50 the name Brahman is applied to the supreme Being (=*Brahmā*, Kullūka); in XII. 50 the Creator of the universe is called Brahmā (see note 1, p. 12); in XI. 243, XII. 121, Prajāpati. In I. 6 the supreme Spirit is termed Svayambhū, 'the Self-existent;' in I. 10, Nārāyaṇa. In XII. 121 the names Vishṇu and Hara occur; but generally the gods named belong more to the Vedic than to the Epic and Purānic period. For instance, in Book IX. 303 we have the following list of deities:

Of Indra, Sūrya, Vāyu (or Māruta), Yama, Varuṇa, Ćandra, Agni, and Pṛithivī, let the king emulate the power and conduct.

There is no allusion to the Post-vedic Tri-mūrti or popular worship of Brahmā, Vishṇu, and Śiva, nor to the still more recent worship of the Śakti—that is to say, 'the energy' represented by the wives of the deities, especially by Durgā, wife of Śiva. Nor, again, is there any recognition of that principle of *bhakti* or 'faith' in Kṛishṇa, as supreme Lord of the universe, which was a subsequent development of Hindū religious thought (p. 137).

The doctrine of transmigration is, however, fully stated, and, as a consequence of this, the hells described in the Code (IV. 88–90, XII. 75, 77), though places of terrible torture, resolve themselves into merely temporary purgatories, while the heavens (IV. 182, 260, VI. 32, II. 244) become only steps on the road to union with Brahma.

The three worlds (*trailokya*, *loka-traya*) alluded to in XI. 236, 261, are probably the heavens, atmosphere, and earth.

What must strike every one as singular in regard to the religion of the Code is the total absence of allusion to public and congregational services or teaching in temples. Public sacrifices are certainly mentioned, but the chief rites of religion were evidently of a domestic kind, and the priests, whatever their ancient functions may have been, were at the time of the composition of the Code more like domestic chaplains (see p. 238). Little, too, is said about idols[1]—certainly nothing to countenance the adoration of them or to encourage Brāhmans to undertake the care of idol-temples, nor are there directions as to offering rice, flowers, and perfumes at idol-shrines, which oblations (*naivedya*) are commonly presented before images in temples at the present day.

II. In the second place, as to the philosophy of Manu's Law-book. It is plain from a passage already quoted (p. 52 of this volume), that a love for rationalistic speculations (*hetu-śāstra*) and a spirit of free scepticism were beginning to show themselves in India at the time the Code was compiled; and it is possible that Buddha's adherents, though not mentioned by name, were pointed at with reprobation under the designation *Nāstikāḥ*, 'atheists' (= *Ćārvāka*, Kullūka II. 11), and *Pāshaṇḍinaḥ*, 'heretics' (= *Śākya-bhikshu-kshapaṇakādi*, Kullūka IV. 30, I. 118).

[1] It is very doubtful whether idolatry was at all commonly practised at the time of the compilation of the Code. We have already seen that there is no satisfactory proof of the existence of idols in the Vedic period. See p. 15 of this volume. In Manu III. 152 a Devalaka, 'attendant on an idol' (=*pratimā-paricāraka*), is directed to be shunned. Certainly in II. 176, the Brāhman student is enjoined to perform *devatābhyarćanam*, 'worship of the deities,' and this is interpreted by Kullūka to mean *pratimādishu hari-harādi-deva-pūjanam*, 'doing homage to Vishṇu and S'iva before images,' &c., but whether Manu really intended to denote *pratimā* by *devatā* is questionable. In IX. 285, however, the accidental breaker of images (*pratimānām bhedakaḥ*) is directed to repair them and pay a fine.

The Code itself may have been an attempt to stem the current of opinion which was setting in the direction of Buddhism and rationalistic Brāhmanism. The compiler, however, thought it necessary to adopt some of the current philosophical theories, and accordingly we find them interspersed throughout the work, though more directly stated at the beginning and end. They are of that vague and misty kind which probably prevailed at the period preceding the crystallization of the various systems into distinct schools. The words Sāṅkhya, Yoga, Nyāya, Vaiśeshika, and Mīmāṉsā do not occur as designations of philosophical systems. We notice indeed a strong leaning towards the Sāṅkhyan line of thought, though we find only a confused statement of some leading ideas of that system, without any mention of its twenty-five Tattvas. The growth of pantheistic ideas, as foreshadowed in the Purusha-sūkta of the Ṛig-veda (see p. 24), is also traceable. All existing things are said to emanate from Brahma, the one self-existent Spirit, to whom all things must also return. Ātma-vidyā, equivalent to Brahma-vidyā and to the Vedānta doctrine, is directed to be studied in VII. 43, and Vedāntic ideas pervade the whole twelfth Book, which, however, may possibly be due to later additions. Still more remarkable is the attention directed to be given to the study of Ānvīkshikī, 'logic' (VII. 43 = *tarka-vidyā*); and although the Nyāya and Mīmāṉsā had evidently not become schools, we find from XII. 111 that a Parishad or 'assembly of twelve Brāhmans,' competent to decide on disputed points of law, includes a Haituka (= *nyāya-jña*) and a Tarkin (= *mīmāṉsaka*, Kullūka). Moreover, in XII. 106, it is declared that he only understands the Veda who investigates it by the rules of Tarka (= *mīmāṉsādi-nyāya*), agreeably to Vedic doctrine—all of which precepts are, of course, inconsistent with the reprobation of Haitukas in II. 11, IV. 30; as well as with a precept in II. 10, where Śruti and Smṛiti are affirmed to be *a-mīmāṉsye*, 'not to be reasoned about.'

The cosmogony adopted presents us with a compound of both the Sāṅkhya and Vedānta theories of creation before they had diverged into distinct systems. There is, however, in Book I a synthetical scheme advanced which, though a confusion of two separate statements, one made by Manu himself (I. 14, &c.), the other by Bhṛigu (I. 74, &c.), certainly more accords with the Sāṅkhyan doctrine than with any other (see p. 100). I here abridge the account, commencing I. 5:

This universe first existed only in darkness (*tamo-bhūtam*), imperceptible, undefinable, as if immersed in sleep (*prasuptam*). Then the Self-existent (*Svayam-bhū*, described by the same epithet as the Sāṅkhyan *Prakṛiti*, viz. *A-vyakta*, 'undiscerned' or 'undeveloped'), having willed to produce various beings from his own substance, first with a thought created the waters, and placed on them a productive seed or egg (*vīja* or *aṇḍa*). Then he himself was born in that egg in the form of Brahmā. Next he caused the egg to divide itself, and out of its two divisions framed the heaven above and the earth beneath. Afterwards, having divided his own substance, he became half male, half female (I. 32), and from that female produced Virāj (see note 3, p. 24), from whom was created Manu, the secondary progenitor of all beings. Then he (Brahmā, according to Kullūka on I. 14) from the supreme Soul (*Ātman*) drew forth *Manas* (=*Mahat* or *Buddhi*, 'Intellect,' as explained by Kullūka on I. 74, 75[1], in which passage *Manas* is the principle of thought and stands for both Buddhi and Ahaṅ-kāra). Next to that came Ahaṅ-kāra, and, after that, the Tan-mātras or 'subtile principles of the elements.' From these seven active principles (called 'the seven Purushas,' I. 19)—viz. Mahat or Buddhi (called *Manas* in I. 14, 74, 75), Ahaṅ-kāra, and the five subtile elements—were evolved the five gross or material elements (*mahā-bhūta*), the organs of sense, and the whole world of sense. (Compare the Sāṅkhyan doctrine at pp. 93, 94.)

It is curious to compare Strabo XV. 59 (see p. 281).

All this confusion and obscurity in the account of the

[1] But according to I. 14 (Kullūka) *Manas* must be distinguished from *Buddhi*, and regarded as a product of Ahaṅ-kāra, as in the Sāṅkhya system.

creation is symptomatic of diversity of authorship. Of the two narratives, that of Bhṛigu is the simplest. But both (I. 14 and I. 74) make 'the principle of thought' the first product—that which is and is not (*sad-asad-ātmakam*)—to which belongs a real existence, and yet not eternity, because it is a product; (see Sāṅkhya-pravaćana V. 56.) I now abridge what follows according to Bhṛigu's statement:

The first Manu Svāyambhuva produced six other Manus, and these seven Manus (see note, p. 214), each in his own period, were the creators of all things (I. 61–63).

In order to show the duration of a Manv-antara or Manu-period, the divisions of time from a moment to a day of Brahmā (12,000,000 years) are specified (I. 64–73):

A Manu-period consists of seventy-one times the 12,000 years, which constitute an age of the gods (I. 79). Each Mahā-yuga or great age of the world is subdivided into four Yugas or ages, viz. 1. Kṛita, 2. Tretā, 3. Dvāpara, and 4. Kali, each decreasing in excellence; and the life of man lasts for 400 years in the first, 300 years in the second, 200 years in the third, and 100 years in the present or Kali age[1].

In I. 87–101 the account of the creation is concluded by a description of the origin of the four castes from the mouth, arm, thigh, and foot of Brahmā, and the pre-eminence assigned to Brāhmans (see extracts, pp. 240, 241).

In the twelfth Book the leaning towards a Sāṅkhyan line of thought is again conspicuous. In 24–38 we have a description of the three Guṇas of the Sāṅkhya, viz. Sattva, Rajas, and Tamas, all three of which are said to pervade, and one or other of which predominate in every mortal frame (see note 2, p. 95). In XII. 24 it is asserted that these three form the constituent substances of *ātman* (self or soul), and that the first developed principle—Mahat or Buddhi—is also pervaded by them. Again, the triple degrees of transmigration, highest, middle, and

[1] We find it constantly implied in Hindū writings that the natural term of human life in the present age is 100 years.

lowest, through gods, men, and beasts, are supposed to result from acts done under the dominance of these three Guṇas (see note 1, p. 67). We have also the three Pramāṇas of the Sāṅkhya philosophy clearly laid down in XII. 105:

Three means of attaining true knowledge or three standards of truth, viz. perception by the senses (*pratyaksha*), inference (*anumāna*), and the Veda (*Śabda*) or various books founded on it—these three must be known thoroughly by one wishing for a clear idea of duty (see pp. 72, 92 of this volume).

Although, however, the germ of the Sāṅkhya is clearly traceable, there is an evident commingling of pantheistic ideas, tending towards the Vedānta, in the frequent declaration that all existing things emanate from, and will ultimately be absorbed into Brahma, 'the universal Spirit.' The distinction between the Jīvātman and Paramātman (see p. 62) is recognized in VIII. 91, which verse Kullūka explains by a reference to the Vedic allegory of the two birds (quoted p. 42 of this volume). Nevertheless, we miss in Manu what we find in the later philosophical schools, a clear definition of the subtile body, as composed of the subtile elements, and a plain statement of its relationship to the individual soul and of its accompanying the soul through all its transmigrations. The survival of this soul over the dissolution of the gross body is indeed plainly implied; but Manu's doctrine is that if a man has been wicked the soul clothed in a kind of body, composed of coarse and impure elements, undergoes along with it torment in hell for a time (XII. 21); whereas, if a man has been virtuous, the soul invested in a kind of ethereal and shining body (*kha-śarīrin*), composed of pure elementary particles of air, wind, and fire, enjoys bliss in heaven with it for a certain period (IV. 243, III. 93, II. 82, XII. 20); after which both the wicked and the virtuous are born again.

Nor do we find any precise definition of Brahman (neut.)

as pure absolute Spirit,—the only really existing entity,—according to the Vedānta doctrine. Brahma seems rather to be regarded as a kind of shining ethereal essence, out of which the universe was evolved and into which it becomes absorbed (cf. II. 28, IV. 232, VI. 79, 81, 85, XII. 123-125).

III. Thirdly, as to the Āćāra, 'rules and precepts of conduct,' and social legislation of the Mānavas.

The organization of classes in I. 87-91 is so simple that this simplicity, if it be not merely theoretical, bears witness to the antiquity of a considerable portion of the Code. According to Book X. 3, 4, there are only four pure classes (*varṇāḥ*, p. 218), as follows:

The Brāhman (or priestly class), the Kshatriya (or military class), and the Vaiśya (or agricultural class) constitute the three twice-born (*dvi-jāti* or *dvi-ja*) classes (as obtaining a second spiritual birth through investiture with the sacred thread, see p. 246); the Śūdra (or servile class) is once-born (*eka-jāti*), and constitutes the fourth class; there is no fifth class.

From priority of birth, from superiority of origin (in being sprung from the mouth of the Creator), from possession of the Veda (*niyam-asya* [=*vedasya*] *dhāraṇāt*, i. e. from the right of studying, teaching, and expounding it), and from a distinction in the reception of the sacrificial thread (as the most important of the twelve Sanskāras or 'purificatory rites,' specified in II. 27, &c.), the Brāhman is the lord (*prabhu*) of all the classes (X. 3. See p. 240).

The only allusion in the Veda to this fourfold division is in the Purusha-sūkta (Ṛig-veda X. 90. 12), which, as we have seen (p. 24), is one of its most recent hymns.

A similar division into classes or professions is found to have prevailed in almost all countries [1].

---

[1] Megasthenes (according to Strabo's India, 39), the Greek ambassador of Seleukos Nikator (Alexander's successor between the Euphrates and Indus, B.C. 312) at the court of Sandrokottos (Ćandra-gupta) in Pāṭali-putra (Παλίβοθρα), divided the Hindū people into seven classes, viz. philosophers, husbandmen, shepherds, tradesmen or artificers, soldiers, spies or overseers (ἔφοροι), and councillors of state (see note 2, p. 244); perhaps because Herodotus divided the inhabitants of Egypt into seven, viz. priests, soldiers, cowherds, swineherds, tradesmen, interpreters, and pilots;

In the same tenth Book of Manu, however, we have a more developed social system depicted, and a number of mixed castes (*varṇa-sankaraḥ, sankara-jātīyāḥ*, X. 12) are described as resulting from the intermarriage of the pure classes[1]:

---

but Diodorus and Plato made only five divisions, and Strabo only three. From Plato's Timaeus (6) it appears that a similar division of professions existed among the Athenians. *Πρῶτον μὲν τὸ τῶν ἱερέων γένος, ἀπὸ τῶν ἄλλων χωρὶς ἀφωρισμένον, μετὰ δὲ τοῦτο τὸ τῶν δημιουργῶν, ὅτι καθ' αὑτὸ ἕκαστον ἄλλῳ δὲ οὐκ ἐπιμιγνύμενον δημιουργεῖ, τότε τῶν νομέων καὶ τὸ τῶν θηρευτῶν, τότε τῶν γεωργῶν· καὶ δὴ καὶ τὸ μάχιμον γένος ᾔσθησαί που τῇδε ἀπὸ πάντων τῶν γενῶν κεχωρισμένον, οἷς οὐδὲν ἄλλο πλὴν τὰ περὶ τὸν πόλεμον ὑπὸ τοῦ νόμου προσετάχθη μέλειν.* Again, from a passage in Herodotus (I. 101), it is inferred that a similar distinction existed among the Medes. In Malcolm's History of Persia (I. 205) the Persian monarch Jamshīd is said to have divided the Persians into four classes. Mr. Mill also points out an instructive passage in Plato's Republic (II. 11), in which, describing the simplest form of a political association, he makes it to consist of four or five classes of men: *Εἴη δ' ἂν ἥ γε ἀναγκαιοτάτη πόλις ἐκ τεττάρων ἢ πέντε ἀνδρῶν.* Finally, we read in Millar's Historical View of the English Government (I. 11) that the Anglo-Saxons were originally divided into four great classes—artificers and tradesmen, husbandmen, soldiers, and clergy.

[1] Mr. W. F. Sinclair gives some interesting information (in the February and March numbers of the 'Indian Antiquary') in regard to the various subdivisions or sub-castes of Brāhmans, and adds a list of forty mixed castes, now found in the Dekhan. With regard to the Brāhmans, he places at the head the *Chitpāvan* (i. e. I presume, *Ćitta-pāvana*, 'heart-purifiers') or *Konkanasth* (=*Konkaṇa-stha*) Brāhmans, to whom the notorious Nāna Sāhib of Bithūr belonged. Then come the *Deśasth* (=*Deśa-stha*) or *Ṛigvedī* Brāhmans, who claim for themselves descent from the Ṛishis, and therefore the highest rank; then the *Yajur-vedī*, who are chiefly engaged in trade; and then the *Devrukh* (?), who are mostly agricultural. There are also in the Dekhan *Telangī* (i. e. *Telingī*, from Sanskṛit *tri-linga*) Brāhmans, from the Karṇāṭak, chiefly engaged in trade; Kanouj Brāhmans (from Hindūstān), who are often Sipāhīs in native regiments or *employées* upon the railway, and some other tribes. With regard to the forty mixed castes enumerated by Mr. Sinclair, I here subjoin some of them as given by him, with a few notes of my own—*Prabhūs* (Sanskṛit *prabhu*), who are the highest, and divided into *Kāyasth* and *Pataṇe* (?); *Sonārs* (=*Suvarṇa-kāra*) or goldsmiths, a

By unlawful intermarriage of the classes (*vyabhićāreṇa varṇānām*), by their marrying women who ought not to be married, and by neglect of their own duties, mixed classes are produced (X. 24).

These have a great variety of names, such as Mūrdhā-vasikta, Māhishya, Karaṇa or Kāya-stha, Ambashṭha or Vaidya, Āyogava, Dhigvaṇa, Pukkasa, Ćaṇḍāla (see p. 237), and are restricted to particular occupations. Still the superiority of the Brāhmans in the Hindū lawyer's scheme is the hinge on which the whole social system turns. In fact, the state of society depicted is that of pure and unmitigated Brāhmanism,—a state of things which, if it really admitted of the amount of Brāhmanical arrogance described as existing, would more than account for the Buddhist reaction. The Brāhmans are made to constitute the great central body around which all other classes and orders of beings revolve like satellites. Not only are they invested with the highest dignity and importance, but they are bound together, and their position secured by the most stringent rules; while the other three classes of soldiers, agriculturists, and servants are made powerless for combined resistance by equally stringent regulations, one class being separated from the other by insurmountable lines of demarcation.

---

subdivision of whom are the *Ratha-kāra* Sonārs, who claim to be of Brāhman race (cf. note 1, p. 160); *Vāṇīs* (Banias, Banians=Baniyās, Sanskṛit *baṇik*), who are grocers and grain-dealers, and are distinguished by great reverence for animal life; *Bhāṭiyās* or cloth and cotton merchants; *Khattrīs*, who claim Rājput (=*Kshatriya*) descent, but are dealers in cloth, gold and silver lace, &c.; *Vaiśyas*, who claim to be a remnant of the original Vaiśyas, and are traders; *Mārvāḍī*, merchants; *Simpīs* or tailors; *Sūtars* (=*Sūtra-dhāra*) or carpenters; *Sikalgars* (*Saiqal-gar*), turners and weapon-sharpeners; *Lohārs* (=*Loha-kāra*) or smiths; *Telīs* (=*Tailī*, from *Tailin*) or oilmen; *Koshṭīs* and *Sālīs* or weavers; *Kumbhārs* (=*Kumbha-kāra*) or potters; *Kolīs*, who are Bhistīs or water-bearers; *Parīts* or washermen; *Loṇārīs* (=*Lavaṇa-kārin*) or preparers of salt and lime and charcoal; *Rangārīs* (=*Ranga-kārin*) or dyers; *Chambhārs* (=*Ćarma-kārin*) or leather-cutters and shoe-makers, &c.

We must, however, guard against supposing that a Brāhman claimed to take the lead merely in the character of a priest. To understand more clearly the nature of Brāhmanical ascendancy we must ask ourselves the question, What physical and moral forces led to the first movements which ended in the crystallization of social distinctions into the caste-system?

It seems probable, then, that the formation of hard lines of separation between the classes was more the result of gradual and natural adjustment than of preconcerted plan. There can be little doubt that when the Āryan Hindūs came into India as immigrants and conquerors, they were without any systematic arrangement of classes. Their first seat was in the Pañjāb, around the five chief affluents of the Indus and in the neighbourhood of Delhi. This was a productive plain watered by rivers [1]. Hence it happened that, although in their primeval abode, somewhere in Central Asia, they were probably half nomad, half agricultural, they became, when fairly settled in Hindūstān, a nation of agriculturists [2]. The soil, too, being fertile, yielded more than enough to supply the necessities

[1] By degrees they spread themselves over the whole region called by Manu (II. 21, 22) Āryāvarta, 'the abode of Āryas,' i. e. the great central plains (Madhya-deśa), extending from the western to the eastern sea, and bounded on the north and south by the Himālaya and Vindhya mountains. Only in this region were the three first classes allowed to dwell, but Śūdras might sojourn wherever they liked. (See Manu II. 21-24.)

[2] The very name Ārya is, as every one now knows, connected with the root 4 *ṛi=ar*, whence *aratrum*, 'a plough' (cf. Sanskṛit *aritra*). It is curious to note how Brāhmans, after their segregation as the dominant class, sought to depreciate agriculture. Manu (X. 84) says, 'Some think that agriculture (*kṛishi*) is an excellent thing, but it is a mode of existence blamed by the good, because the iron-mouthed ploughshare wounds the earth and the creatures living in it.' Mr. W. F. Sinclair informs us in the 'Indian Antiquary,' that in the Dekhan the cultivators of the soil are by the modern races of Brāhmans considered pure Śūdras.

of the cultivators. Hence the surplus produce enabled a large non-agricultural population to spring up. Some of these applied themselves to trade and the improvement of mechanical arts; others were enabled to devote themselves to one of three occupations: 1. mental and religious culture; 2. military exercises; 3. domestic service[1]. It was, indeed, absolutely necessary that the cultivators who were called Vaiśyas, because they 'settled down' on the soil and gradually acquired an hereditary right to its occupation[2], should have a class of military men above them, with leisure either to cultivate arms, and so defend the land thus occupied from the attacks of other invaders, or to undertake the cares of government, and so protect

---

[1] The same happened in the fertile plains of Egypt and Mesopotamia.

[2] In modern times they are called Ryots, from the Arabic رعية *ra''īyat*, 'protected people' (root رعي 'to pasture, guard'). The Hindū term Vaiśya is more expressive of their original condition. It is derived from the root *viś*, 'to enter into,' 'sit down on,' 'settle down on,' 'occupy' (whence *veśa*, 'an abode'), cognate with *vicus*, 'a village,' and *οἶκος*, 'an abode,' and our affix 'wick' at the end of names of towns, denoting originally a settlement or station of cultivators. Hence the root *viś*, when used as a substantive, means 'a man of the people.' The Vaiśyas were allowed to become merchants if they preferred trading to agriculture; but the only provision for classes of artisans and mechanics, is from the mixed classes. This indicates that Manu's division belongs to an early period, before the industrial and mechanical arts had acquired much importance, though they must have been considerably advanced even in Vedic times (as shown by Dr. Muir, Texts V. 450–472). The Hindū village system of the present day seems to have been developed out of that represented in Manu's Code. Almost everywhere are found bodies of agriculturists who have settled on the soil from time immemorial, and formed themselves into little republics presided over by a half-elective, half-hereditary headman, and a number of village officials (properly twelve, e.g. watchman, accountant, priest, schoolmaster, doctor, barber, astrologer, &c.), the lands around the village forming a sort of jurisdiction, and disputes being settled by gatherings of the villagers under trees, while various low-caste menials who have no interest in the soil are attached to the community.

property from the dangers incident to anarchy. These ultimately received the name *Kshatriya.* But in the earliest times, as represented by the Vedic hymns, they were called *Rājanya,* 'the kingly class.' (See the Purusha-sūkta, translated p. 24, and see p. 25, note 1.) Doubtless, when this class first arose they must have constituted the most powerful order of society; and so, indeed, practically they must have always remained, notwithstanding the intellectual superiority of the Brāhmanical class[1]. That the close interdependence of the two higher classes was recognized by the Brāhmans themselves is shown by the following:

A Kshatriya cannot thrive without a Brāhman, nor a Brāhman without a Kshatriya. The Brāhman and the Kshatriya when assoaiated together prosper in this world and the next (IX. 322).

It was also necessary that there should be a class willing to perform personal domestic service. These were called Śūdras; and this class was probably made up to some extent of the remnants of the Turanian tribes, who were conquered by the Āryan Hindūs, and who were mostly driven southwards[2]. But, although servants, they

[1] The name Kshatriya comes from *kshatra,* 'dominion,' which is probably from root 1 *kshi*=κτάομαι, 'to possess, rule.' It is fancifully derived from *kshatāt tra,* 'preserving from injury,' in Raghu-vaṉśa II. 53. Manu X. 119 says, 'While defending the Vaiśyas by his arms (*śastreṇa vaiśyān rakshitvā*) he may raise from them the rightful revenue (*dharmyam āhārayed balim*),' which was really taken from the soil in kind.

[2] It may be questioned whether Śūdra (though found in the Purusha-sūkta, Ṛig-veda X. 90. 12) is a genuine Sanskṛit word. At least no satisfactory etymology is given for it, and this favours the idea of its denoting some pre-Āryan race. The fanciful derivation from *Śuć,* 'to grieve,' and *dru,* 'to run,' is hardly worth noticing. Besides the Turanian races who partially blended with the Āryans there were doubtless other aboriginal tribes who occupied the hills and outlying districts and who were called Mlećchas, as constituting those more barbarous and uncultivated communities who stood aloof and would not amalgamate with the Āryans. *Mlećcha-deśa* is defined to be a country where the four classes do not dwell. In Manu X. 44 a number of degraded tribes are mentioned, such as

were neither slaves nor serfs. They merely occupied the lowest step in the social organization. It is true that in theory (X. 129) they were debarred from any superfluous accumulation of wealth, yet, in point of fact, they sometimes rose to affluence, and even became kings[1]:

As a S'ūdra, without censuring others, performs lawful acts, so, without being censured, he obtains exaltation in this world and the next (X. 128).

Again, the gradual assumption of superiority over the Kshatriyas, Vaiśyas, and Śūdras, by a class of men who called themselves Brāhmans[2], seems to have been

---

Paundrakas, Odras, Dravidas, Kāmbojas, Yavanas, S'akas, Pāradas, Ćīnas, Kirātas, &c. As these were probably powerful warlike tribes, they are declared by Manu to be outcaste Kshatriyas. It is clear that the mountaineer Kirātas were a martial race; nor could they have been greatly despised, for Arjuna lived among them and adopted their style of life in order to learn archery from S'iva, regarded as their god. See my account of the Kirātārjunīya and the 'Indian Antiquary' for June, 1874, p. 178. The most degraded outcastes were men called Ćāṇḍālas or Ćaṇḍālas (children of a S'ūdra man and a Brāhmaṇī); they were expelled from towns, where they could not even walk except by day; they wore only dead men's clothes, rusty iron ornaments, &c. (X. 51–56).

[1] Professor Cowell, in a note to Elphinstone's India, p. 18, well shows that the condition of a S'ūdra was very superior to that of the helot, slave, and serf of the Greek, Roman, and feudal system. The Purāṇas record dynasties of S'ūdra kings, and even Manu notices these. In II. 238 it is said, 'A believer in Scripture may receive pure knowledge even from a S'ūdra.' In modern times cultivators of the soil are in some places regarded as S'ūdras. There are occasional passages in the Mahābhārata depreciating caste and even Vedic knowledge in comparison with moral character; cf. the Rāja-dharma of the S'ānti-parvan 2955.

[2] According to some scholars the original meaning of *brahman* was 'prayer,' or rather 'devotional spirit pervading and filling the soul' (root *bṛih* or *vṛih*). Hence it came afterwards to mean Veda, 'sacred knowledge,' in which sense it is often used by Manu. Similarly, *brahman* and *brāhmaṇa* meant originally 'a prayer-offerer,' and afterwards 'religious teacher,' the signification 'priest' not having been attached to these words till sacrificial ideas had fully developed themselves in the Hindū mind. It is a mistake to suppose that Brāhmaṇa and priest are convertible terms. Brāhmans are rather 'men of the first class.'

due to the operation of a law of intellectual development, such as has been common among all nations in their progress towards civilization, in all periods of the world's history. Those who were intellectually superior took advantage of that growth of religious cravings which generally accompanies political growth, and formed themselves into a fraternity of religious teachers, who afterwards became priests. Religion, or a sense of dependence upon God and a desire to propitiate Him, has always formed a marked feature of the Hindū character. Hence in India, the fraternity of priests multiplied with unusual rapidity; so that a considerable number of the sacerdotal class were thrown out of employment and forced to engage in secular occupations. In this manner it came to pass that although all priests were properly Brāhmans, all Brāhmans were by no means necessarily priests. Nor was it likely that with the partial secularization of the Brāhmans the complicated Vedic ceremonial could be long maintained. Some public sacrifices, such as the Agnishṭoma, were still performed, but the more intricate rites enjoined by the Brāhmaṇas and occasionally practised in ancient times, lasting for long periods, and requiring for their efficacious performance a staff of sixteen different orders of priests[1], fell into partial if not entire desuetude. It was found, however, indispensable to the retention of power over the other classes that some sacerdotal offices should be maintained. In proportion, indeed, to the neglect of high ceremonial observances was there an increased strictness in exacting a knowledge of the Veda, and the discharge of domestic rites for which a priest's teaching and superintendence were required.

In II. 84, 85, it is declared that all Vedic rites, oblations

---

[1] See their names all given in my Sanskṛit-English Dictionary under Ṛitv-ij, p. 181, col. 1.

to fire, and solemn sacrifices gradually pass away (*ksharanti*), but that the act of repeating the Veda, especially the repetition of the Gāyatrī with the four mystic syllables, is ten times better than the appointed sacrifice (see pp. 252, 253).

Manu is careful to assign distinct functions and titles to the priests qualified for these duties; thus we read:

Some Brāhmans are intent on knowledge (of the supreme Spirit), others are intent on acts of austerity (*tapo-nishṭhāḥ*), others on acts of austerity and repetition of the Veda combined, and others on sacrificial rites (III. 134).

He who is selected for the office of preparing the sacred fire, for conducting the Pāka-yajña (see note, p. 197) and performing the Agnishṭoma[1] and other sacrifices, is called the *Ṛitv-ij* of his employer (II. 143).

He who having invested his pupil with the sacred thread afterwards instructs him in the whole Veda, with the rules of ceremonial (*sakalpam*[2]) and the Upanishads, is called an *Āćārya* (II. 140).

He who, for the sake of a livelihood, gives instruction in one part only of the Veda or in the Vedāṅgas (such as grammar, &c.) is called an *Upādhyāya* or sub-teacher (II. 141).

The Brāhman who performs the Saṉskāra ceremonies on conception &c. according to rule, and who feeds the child with rice (i. e. performs the *anna-prāśanam* in the sixth month, see II. 34 and p. 201 of this volume), is called a *Guru*[3] (II. 142).

Manu, however, found it necessary to conciliate the Kshatriya class. The most exalted eulogies were lavished

---

[1] The Agnishṭoma is a protracted sacrifice of five days' duration, performed by one who is desirous of obtaining heaven. It is either a part or a modification of the Jyotishṭoma, and in ancient times required sixteen priests.

[2] That is, probably, 'the Kalpa Sūtras.'

[3] The title Guru, however, appears to have been applied in a general way to all spiritual preceptors, cf. p. 245. It is sometimes used alone as a distinctive epithet of Prabhā-kara, a teacher of the Mīmāṉsā, often named in conjunction with Kumārila, to denote whom the title Bhaṭṭa is generally employed in the same way. According to Yājñavalkya I. 34, a Guru is one who imparts the Veda, while an Āćārya is one who invests with the Yajñopavīta or 'sacred thread.' Similarly in the Pañjāb the teachers of the Grantha (Granthīs) are called Gurus.

on kings; but Brāhmans were to act as their advisers and to have much of the judicial authority and interpretation of the laws in their own hands, and were always theoretically superior in rank—a circumstance which led in the end to jealousies, feuds, and even internecine warfare between the first two classes. Certain privileges also naturally fell to the Vaiśyas, and both they and the Kshatriyas were equally with the Brāhmans entitled to the appellation *Dvi-ja*, 'twice-born.' Their whole status, however, depended upon various domestic rites, to the due conduct of which the superintendence of Brāhmans was indispensable. Yet, in spite of the importance and dignity thus attached to the priestly office, a Brāhman, according to Manu's Code, was by *birth* and *divine right*—not by profession or self-elevation—at the head of all creatures. He was born a Brāhman and did not become one. He not only inherited superiority as his birthright, but was created a leader of mankind—a sort of deity in human shape—by the fiat of the great Creator himself.

He is declared, in Book I. 87, to have proceeded from the mouth of Brahmā, as the Kshatriya did from his arm, the Vaiśya from his thigh, and the Śūdra from his foot. Manu's theory, in short, was that the distinction of caste and the inherent superiority of one class over the three others was as much a law of nature and a matter of divine appointment, as the creation of separate classes of animals, with insurmountable differences of physical constitution, such as elephants, lions, horses, and dogs.

That the Brāhmans assumed a pre-eminence nothing short of divine, is clear from numerous passages. I select the following:

Since the Brāhman sprang from the most excellent part, since he has the priority arising from primogeniture (*jyaishṭhyāt*), and since he possesses the Veda, he is by right the lord (*prabhu*) of this whole creation (I. 93. See also p. 231 of this volume).

A Brāhman, whether learned or unlearned, is a mighty divinity (*daivatam mahat*), just as fire is a mighty divinity, whether consecrated (*praṇīta*) or unconsecrated (IX. 317).

Even when Brāhmans employ themselves in all sorts of inferior occupations (*an-ishṭeshu*), they must under all circumstances be honoured, for they are to be regarded as supreme divinities (*paramaṃ daivatam*, IX. 319).

From his high birth alone (*sambhavenaiva*) a Brāhman is regarded as a divinity even by the gods (*devānām api*). His teaching must be accepted by the rest of the world as an infallible authority (*pramāṇam*), for the Veda (*brahma*) itself is the cause (of its being so accepted, XI. 84).

Consistently with the divine nature thus ascribed to the Brāhman, he is declared to possess powers of the most tremendous and awe-inspiring character:

Let not a king, although fallen into the greatest distress (through a deficiency of revenue), provoke Brāhmans to anger (by taking revenue from them), for they, if once enraged, could instantly (by pronouncing curses and mystical texts) destroy him with all his army and retinue.

Who, without bringing destruction on himself, can provoke those men, by whose imprecation (*abhiśāpena*, Kullūka) all-devouring fire was created, and by whom the undrinkable ocean was swallowed [1], and the wasted moon restored to its full size [2] (*āpyāyitaḥ=paśćāt pūritaḥ*, IX. 313, 314)?

---

[1] This seems to refer to the legend of Agastya, who is said to have swallowed the ocean and was afterwards raised to be regent of the star Canopus. Much, however, of the detail of this legend must be later.

[2] This refers to the legend of Ćandra, 'the Moon,' afflicted with consumption for fifteen days by his father-in-law, Daksha, because of his (the Moon's) partiality for Rohiṇī, one of Daksha's daughters, some of whom had become his wives. On the Moon's repentance, his wasted strength and size were restored. Manu IX. 129 states that Daksha gave ten of his daughters to Dharma, thirteen to Kaśyapa, and twenty-seven to Soma, the Moon. The legend of Daksha's daughters is found (like many other of Manu's allusions) in the Taittirīya-saṃhitā, ii. 3, 5: 'Prajāpati had thirty-three daughters—he gave them to king Soma; among them he only went to Rohiṇī. The others jealous returned [to their father]: he went after them, he sought them again; but he [the father] did not give them again to him. He said to him, "Take an oath that you will go to them alike, then I will give them to you again." He

What king would gain increase of revenue by oppressing those who, if angry, could create other worlds and guardians of worlds (*loka-pālān*), and could create new gods and mortals (IX. 315)?

A Brāhman, well skilled in the law, need not make any representation to the king (if he has received an injury), for, by his own power (*sva-vīryeṇa*), he may punish (*śishyāt*) those who injure him. His own power is stronger than the power of the king, therefore by his own might may a Brāhman chastise (*nigrihṇīyāt*) his foes. He may, without hesitation, make use of (as magical formularies) the sacred texts (*śrutīḥ*) revealed to Atharvan and Aṅgiras (*Atharvāṅgirasīḥ*, see note, p. 9); for the uttering of texts (*vāk=abhićāra-mantroććāraṇam*) is the weapon (*śastram*) of a Brāhman; with that he may destroy his foes (XI. 31-33).

The crime of striking and killing a Brāhman involves, of course, terrible consequences, thus:

He who merely assails a Brāhman with intent to kill him will continue in hell (*narakam*) for a hundred years, and he who actually strikes him, a thousand years (XI. 206. Compare also IV. 165, where it is said that the hell to which he will be consigned, and where he will be made to wand erabout incessantly, is called *Tāmisra*, 'profound darkness').

As many particles of dust (*pāṇśūn*) as the blood of a Brāhman absorbs from the soil, so many thousands of years must the shedder of that blood abide in hell (XI. 207).

The above may be thought an exaggeration of the powers and status claimed by the highest order of Hindū society, and doubtless the compiler of the Code often draws an ideal picture of a condition of things which never actually existed, and was never likely to exist; much in the same manner as we in England maintain that our king can do no wrong. Yet in the matter of the Brāhman we are compelled to accept the colouring as, in the main, truthful. Only recently there appeared in a leading journal a report of a sermon preached by a converted Brāhman, in which the preacher asserted that the Brāhmans of the present day pretend to 'dethrone the Creator and put themselves in

took an oath; he gave them back to him. He only out of them went to Rohiṇī. Him, the king [Soma], consumption attacked. This is the origin of the Rāja-yakshma.'

his place. Moreover, that he himself (the preacher) had claimed and received divine honours and had seen believers (among his own fellow-countrymen) greedily drink the water in which his feet had been washed[1].'

It may be asked how did the Brāhman, laden with all this weight of dignity and theoretically debarred from all other occupations, except studying and teaching the Veda, and performing religious rites, contrive to support himself? The answer is that he took care to provide for his own material comforts[2] by making the efficacy of all repe-

---

[1] The Rev. Nārāyan S'eshādri (a Marāṭhī name derived from the serpent-like folds of the serpent S'esha, Vishṇu's seat), who preached on Easter Sunday, April 5, 1874 (in a Presbyterian Church in Kensington Park Road), a sermon, the report of which appeared in the next day's 'Daily News.' He embraced the Christian faith on September 13, 1843. He had to give up father, mother, three brothers, and three sisters. Such is the condition of Brāhmanical society that a man must renounce all former associations when converted. I subjoin a further portion of the matter reported as preached. 'He had been emptied of Hindooism. This creed dealt largely in the marvellous; for instance, it is said that one great saint drank up all the ocean in three sips, and was afterwards seated among the constellations on account of this feat. But there was a philosophic as well as a popular form of Hindooism. There were atheistical and theistical forms, the latter having as many advocates in India as it had in this country, in Germany, and in the United States. He dwelt at length on the pantheistic notion of Brahm, which ignored man's responsibility. Man's sins, in fact, became God's sins; and gradually the preacher had become convinced that this was blasphemy.'

[2] This appears to hold good even in the present day; for Professor Rāmkṛishṇa Bhāṇḍārkar, writing in the 'Indian Antiquary' for May, 1874, remarks that repetition of the Veda for *dakshiṇā* still prevails in Gujarāt and to a much greater extent in the Marāṭhī country and Tailangana. 'Numbers of Brāhmans go about to all parts of the country in search of *dakshiṇā*, and all well-to-do natives patronize them according to their means, by getting them to repeat portions of their Veda, which is mostly the Black Yajush, with Āpastamba for their Sūtra. Hardly a week passes here in Bombay in which no Tailanga Brāhman comes to ask me for *dakshiṇā*.'

titions of the Veda and all sacrificial rites depend upon the gifts (*dakshiṇāḥ*) with which they were accompanied:

A sacrifice performed with trifling presents (*alpa-dakshiṇaḥ*) destroys the organs of sense, fame, heaven, life, reputation, offspring, cattle; therefore let no man undertake a sacrifice who has not plenty of money to make liberal gifts (XI. 40).

Let a man, according to his ability, give wealth to Brāhmans who know the Vedas and keep apart from the world. By so doing he obtains heaven when he dies (XI. 6).

A king, even though dying (from want), must not receive taxes from a Brāhman learned in the Vedas, nor must he allow such a Brāhman dwelling in his country to pine away with hunger. Of that king in whose territory a Brāhman learned in the Vedas wastes with hunger, the whole kingdom will in a short time be wasted with famine (VII. 133, 144).

All that exists in this universe is the Brāhmans' property (I. 100).

Moreover, when the increase of the Brāhmanical class compelled the secularization of many of its members, they were allowed to engage in the occupations of the other classes. This was at first only permitted under circumstances of exigency and distress. Some verses in XII. 71, X. 75, 76, 80–82, lay down the law on this point:

A Brāhman who swerves from his own peculiar duty is, on departing this life, born again as a vomit-eating demon called Ulkā-mukha (XII. 71).

Repetition (or study) of the Veda (*adhyayanam*), expounding it (or literally, teaching others to repeat it, *adhyāpanam*), sacrificing (*yajanam*) and assisting others to sacrifice (*yājanam*), giving (*dānam*) and receiving gifts (*pratigrahaḥ*) are the six legitimate acts[1] (*shaṭ-karmāṇi*) of a Brāhman. Of these six acts, three are the means of his subsistence, viz. assisting at sacrifices, teaching the Veda, and receiving presents from a pious giver (*viśuddhāt*). These three privileges (*dharmāḥ*) are limited to Brāhmans, and do not extend to Kshatriyas (X. 75–77). Hence a Brāhman is called *Tri-karman*, 'one who engages in three acts.'

The most proper occupation for the Brāhman is teaching and expounding the Veda (*vedābhyāsaḥ*); for a Kshatriya, defending the people; for a Vaiśya, agriculture, keeping cattle, and trade (*vārtā-karma*[2]). Yet a

---

[1] Called the 'six privileges.' A particular tribe of Konkan Brāhmans is said to be excluded from these privileges because its members eat fish.

[2] This word *vārtā-karman*, as may be gathered from Kullūka's commentary on these three verses, includes *kṛishi*, *go-raksha*, and *bāṇijya*. The caste-division of Megasthenes (note 1, p. 231) separates these three.

Brāhman, unable to subsist by his proper employment, may live by the duty of a soldier, for that is the next in dignity. If it be asked, how is he to live if unable to subsist by either of these occupations? the answer is that he may adopt the mode of life of a Vaiśya (X. 80–82. See also X. 101, 102. Cf. note 2, p. 235).

Here are some of the rules by which the whole existence of a Brāhman from the cradle to the grave was regulated:

Every Brāhman was supposed to pass through four Āśramas or 'Orders,'—that is to say, his life was divided into four stages or periods according as he became successively, 1. Religious student (*brahma-ćārin*); 2. Householder (*gṛiha-stha*); 3. Anchorite or hermit (*vānaprastha*); 4. Religious mendicant (*bhikshu* or *parivrājaka* or *sannyāsin*). For the regulation of his life in the first two of these periods the most minute instructions are spread over the 2nd, 3rd, 4th, and 5th Books with much wearisome detail and repetition [1].

To begin with the religious student. The young Brāhman is to reside with his preceptor (*guru*) until he has gained a thorough knowledge of the three Vedas. This residence may continue for thirty-six years, or for half that time, or for a quarter of it, according to his capacity for acquiring the requisite instruction (cf. Gṛihya Sūtras, p. 201). He may even be a student for life (*naishṭhika*, III. 1, II. 243).

He is of course to go through all the twelve Saṇskāras or 'purificatory rites' (II. 27, &c.). They are supposed to purify a man from the taint of sin derived from his parents (*gārbhikam enas*), and are enjoined, with certain variations, on all the three first classes alike; some being performed before the birth of a male child, and some during the first year after birth. I here enumerate them:

---

[1] It is interesting to find that Megasthenes (Strabo XV. 1, 59), three centuries B.C., had noted that Brāhmans, even from the time of conception (ἤδη δ' εὐθὺς καὶ κυομένους), were under the care of learned men, and lived for thirty-seven years as philosophers before becoming householders.

1. *Garbhādhāna* or *Garbha-lambhana*, 'the ceremony on conception' (p. 201); 2. *Puṉsavana* (p. 201); 3. *Sīmantonnayana* (p. 201); 4. *Jāta-karman* (p. 201); 5. *Nāma-karman* or *Nāma-karaṇa*, 'the ceremony of giving a name' on the tenth or twelfth day after birth (Manu II. 30); 6. *Nish-kramaṇa*, 'taking out the child' in the fourth month to see the sun (II. 34); 7. *Anna-prāśana* (p. 201); 8. *Ćūḍā-karman* or *Ćaula* (p. 201); 9. *Upanayana* (p. 201); 10. *Keśānta*, 'cutting off the hair,' performed on a Brāhman in his sixteenth year, on a Kshatriya in his twenty-second, on a Vaiśya in his twenty-fourth (Manu II. 65); 11. *Samāvartana*, performed on the student's return home after completing his studies with his preceptor (pp. 204, 249); 12. *Vivāha*, 'marriage.' This last is the principal purificatory rite for women; but they are allowed some of the others, provided there is an omission of the Mantras or Vedic texts, with which all the Saṉskāras were accompanied (II. 66, 67).

It is noteworthy that marriage is the twelfth Saṉskāra, and hence a religious duty incumbent upon all, completing the purification and regeneration of the twice-born:

Of the above twelve rites, 1, 2, 3, and 10 are little observed. The other eight are more worthy of attention; 8 and 9 are of considerable legal importance even in the present day, and 7 is still practised. 7 and 12 are said to be the only rites allowed to Śūdras. Other Saṉskāras, practised in some parts of India, are mentioned, such as *Karṇa-vedha*, 'boring the ears;' and occasionally the imparting of the Sāvitrī or 'sacred Vedic text' (=Gāyatrī, p. 20), which ought to be performed at Upanayana, is reserved for a separate ceremony four days later.

But the most important of the above Saṉskāras is *Upanayana*, 'investiture with the sacred cord,' already described in the Gṛihya Sūtras (p. 201). This cord, which is a thin coil of three threads, commonly called the *Yajñopavīta* or 'sacrificial thread,' is worn over the left shoulder and allowed to hang down diagonally across the body to the right hip, and the wearing of it by the three twice-born classes was the mark of their second birth [1]. A third birth is mentioned for Brāhmans (II. 169):

The first birth is from the natural mother; the second from the binding

---

[1] It is still worn, but the word *Yajñopavīta* for 'the sacred thread' has been corrupted into Jane-o. In Bengālī it is called *Poitā* for *Pavitra*.

on of the girdle (*mauñji-bandhane*); the third is at initiation into sacrificial rites (as the *jyotishṭoma*, &c.), according to a precept of the Veda.

There was some difference in the kind of thread worn, according to the class of the wearer. In II. 44 we read:

The sacred cord of a Brāhman must be of cotton (*kārpāsa*), so as to be put on over his head in a coil of three threads (*tri-vṛit*); that of a Kshatriya of flax or hemp (*śaṇa*); that of a Vaiśya of wool (*āvika*).

[In the previous two verses Manu intimates that a Brāhman must also have a girdle (*mekhalā*) either of Muñja grass or of Kuśa grass. From II. 169, 170, it might be inferred that the girdle and sacrificial thread are equivalent, but II. 174 clearly distinguishes them. The leather mantle, thread, girdle, staff, and under clothing are, all five, prescribed at the time of Upanayana, and the binding on of the girdle seems to complete the rite.]

The ceremony of investiture begins by the youth's standing opposite the sun and walking thrice round the fire. Then girt with the thread, he asks alms from the assembled company. This begging for alms still constitutes part of the rite, and indicates that the youth undertakes to provide himself and his preceptor (*guru, āćārya*) with food (p. 201). The Guru then initiates him into the daily use of the Sāvitrī or holy prayer in the three-measured Gāyatrī (pp. 20, 165), preceded by three suppressions of breath (*tribhiḥ prāṇāyāmaiḥ*), the triliteral syllable *Om*, and three Vyāhṛitis or mystical words, *Bhūr Bhuvaḥ Svar* [1], and admits him to the privilege of repeating the three Vedas, and of performing other religious rites, none of which are allowed before investiture (II. 171, 173). The Guru or Āćārya is thus his spiritual father.

Purifications, ablutions, and libations (called Savanas) are enjoined on Vānaprasthas or 'hermits' (p. 260) at all the three Sandhyās [2], that is, at the three divisions of the

---

[1] The utterance of these three mystical words, meaning 'earth, the middle region, and heaven' (note 2, p. 66), together with the awful syllable *Om* (pp. 103, 222), is supposed to be attended with marvellous and mysterious effects (see II. 76, 79, 83, 84). Note the sacredness attached to the number three.

[2] See Book VI. 22, 24, and compare Kullūka, *savaneshu snāyāt, prātar-*

day—sunrise, noon, and sunset—but on Brahma-ćārins and Gṛiha-sthas at the two Sandhyās of sunrise and sunset only, when the Gāyatrī (p. 20) is by all means to be repeated. Thus, in II. 222, we have:

Let him constantly observe the two Sandhyās according to rule, sipping water, with all his organs controlled and with fixed attention, repeating the Gāyatrī prayer (*japyam*, which ought to be repeated).

The young Brāhman is also every day to bathe; to offer oblations of water (*tarpaṇa*) to the gods, holy sages (*Ṛishis*) generally, and departed ancestors (*Pitṛis*); to reverence the deities [according to Kullūka, *Devatā* = *pratimā*, the images of the deities]; and to offer an oblation of fuel to the sacred fire (II. 176). But in V. 88 he is forbidden to perform the regular offerings of water to deceased persons, till his studentship is completed. He is to abstain from meat, perfumes, unguents, sensuality, wrath, covetousness, dancing, music, gambling, detraction of others, falsehood, impurity of all kinds, and is never to injure any being (II. 177–179).

Every day, too, both morning and evening, he is to go round the neighbouring villages begging for food for himself and his preceptor and collecting fuel for the maintenance of the sacred fire (II. 187).

He is always to pay the most profound respect to his religious teacher (*guru*), as well as to his parents and to all persons older than himself:

By reverencing his mother he gains this terrestrial world; by rever-

---

*madhyandina-sāyam savaneshu trishu devarshi-pitṛi-tarpaṇam kurvan.* Sandhyā often means 'twilight,' but is applied to morning and evening twilight and to the change from midday to afternoon. With reference to the Hindū and Mohammedan custom of performing religious rites three times a day, we may compare a passage in Daniel, who 'kneeled upon his knees three times a day, and prayed, and gave thanks before his God,' Dan. vi. 10. And David says, 'Evening, and morning, and at noon, will I pray, and cry aloud,' Ps. lv. 17.

encing his father, the middle world; by constant attention to his spiritual master (*guru*), the celestial world of Brahmā (II. 233).

A youth who habitually salutes and constantly reveres the aged, prospers in four things, life, knowledge, fame, and strength (II. 121).

In short, even Christians may learn from Hindūs, as indeed from Oriental nations generally[1], 'to love, honour, and succour their father and mother, to submit themselves to all their governors, teachers, spiritual pastors and masters, and to order themselves lowly and reverently to all their betters;' and, moreover, to extend the duty of 'hurting nobody by word or deed' to animals and the whole inferior creation[2].

On completing his studies the young Brāhman is to give some valuable present to his preceptor. He is then to perform the proper Saṉskāra ceremony of ablution (*snāna*) on the occasion of his solemn return to his own home (*samāvartana*), as already described (see pp. 204, 246):

Let not a student who knows his duty make a present to his spiritual master before the ceremony on his return; but when, being permitted by his preceptor, he is about to perform the requisite ablution (*snāsyan*), let him offer him some valuable article (*gurv-artham*, such as a field, gold, a jewel, cow, horse, &c.) as a gift to the best of his ability (II. 245, 246).

The young Brāhman's return to his own house is made an occasion of festivity; he is decked with flowers and receives a present of a cow (III. 3). He is then to select a wife of the same class with himself, endowed with auspicious marks (*lakshaṇa*), and thereupon he enters the second Āśrama, and becomes a householder (*gṛiha-stha*). Some curious directions for his guidance in choosing a wife are given (III. 8–10):

Let him not marry a girl with reddish hair, nor one with a superfluity of limbs (as, for instance, one with six fingers), nor one who is sickly, nor

---

[1] Notably from the Chinese as well as from the Hindūs.

[2] I am told, however, that, notwithstanding the strict rules of *a-hiṉsā*, the 'Society for Prevention of Cruelty to Animals' might find work to do in some parts of India.

one with either too little or too much hair, nor one who talks too much, nor one who is red-eyed, nor one named after a constellation, a tree, or a river, nor one with a barbarous name (*antya*=*mlećcha*), or the name of a mountain, a bird, a snake, a slave, or any frightful object. But let him marry a woman without defective or deformed limbs, having an agreeable name, whose gait is like that of a flamingo (*haṉsa*) or elephant [1], whose hair and teeth are moderate in quantity, and whose whole body is soft.

We have seen that marriage is a Saṉskāra. Hence it is a religious duty and a purificatory rite (p. 246).

It is clear from III. 12–15, IX. 45, 101, that, as a general rule, a twice-born man is expected to have one wife only; but polygamy is not illegal, and he might take other wives of classes different from his own, being careful to settle their precedence according to the order of these classes (IX. 85). A Brāhman might thus have four wives, one from his own class and one from each of the three classes below him; a Kshatriya three; and a Vaiśya two. But the sons of inferior wives are degraded and called Apasadaḥ (X. 10). Nevertheless, if there be four wives of a Brāhman in the order of the classes, and sons are born to all four wives, there is a rule for dividing the inheritance between them (IX. 149).

Manu's eight forms of marriage are specified in the Gṛihya Sūtras (see p. 199). Of these the first four, viz. that of Brahmā (which is described as 'the gift of a daughter to a man learned in the Veda'), the Devas (*daiva*), Ṛishis (*ārsha*), and Prajāpatis (*prājāpatya*), are the most approved for a Brāhman. The Gāndharva marriage ('from affection without any nuptial rite') and Rākshasa ('marrying a girl carried off as a prize in war') were allowable for Kshatriyas; the Āsura and Paiśāća were prohibited.

A description has been given of one of the oldest marriage rites (p. 199), as well as of the ceremony on commencing residence in a new house (p. 202). The house-

---

[1] That is, having a kind of rolling gait, corresponding to Homer's εἰλίποδας.

holder is to fulfil every day all his domestic religious duties (*gṛihyaṃ karma*), some of which, such as the morning and evening oblation (*agnihotra*, *sāyam-prātar-homa*), are to be performed with the fire of the nuptial ceremony maintained ever afterwards (*vaivāhike 'gnau*, III. 67, see p. 31).

He is especially to perform the five *Mahā-yajñāḥ*, great devotional acts[1] (III. 70, &c.): viz. 1. towards the divine Ṛishis, by repetition and teaching of the Veda (*Brahma-yajña*); 2. towards departed fathers (*Pitṛi-y°*), by the Śrāddha ceremonies; 3. towards the gods (*Deva-y°*), by oblations (*homa*[2]) to Fire, Prajāpati, Heaven and Earth, Indra, Soma, &c. (85–89); 4. towards all creatures (*Bhūta-y°*), including good and evil spirits supposed to people the air, by the *bali* or offering of rice-grains &c. generally scattered on the house-top or outside the door for animals to devour (91); 5. towards men, by hospitality (*Manushya-y°*). A description of all five has already been given (p. 203).

---

[1] The Musalmans have also five principal devotional acts, but these are not all diurnal. They are—1. Prayer (*namāz*) five times a day, practically reduced to three times, morning, midday, and evening. 2. Alms-giving (*zakāt*). 3. Fasting (*roza*), especially keeping the great fast during the ninth month, Ramazān (رمضان), once a year. 4. Pilgrimage to Mecca (*haj*) once in a lifetime. 5. Confession of faith (*shahādat*), i. e. repeating the *tawhīd* or 'declaration of faith in the unity of God:' 'there is no god but God, and Muhammad is the apostle of God.' A Hājjī is a pilgrim who has performed the Haj. There is no duty of pilgrimage among the five necessary devotional acts prescribed by Manu, but the Hindū system has, nevertheless, its Haj. Purī, in Orissa (the abode of Jagan-nāth), is described by Mr. Hunter as the Jerusalem of India. It is really only one of the Indian Meccas. Other great places of pilgrimage (*Tīrthas*) are Hari-dvār, in the Himālaya (one of the most celebrated), where the Ganges is supposed to have descended from the head of S'iva on to the earth; Ćitrakūṭ, in Bundelkhand, Rāma's first abode after his banishment; Jvālā-mukhī, in the Pañjāb, where Satī, wife of S'iva, burned herself, and her presence is thought to be denoted by gas flaming from the ground.

[2] The *homa* or 'oblation of butter' was the peculiar offering to the god of fire, as the Soma juice was to Indra, the rain-god. See note, p. 31.

The last four are sometimes called Pāka-yajňas (II. 86). Of these five, the first, viz. repetition of the Veda (*Brahma-yajňa, japa-y°, svādhyāya*[1], III. 81, II. 85, 86), and espe-

[1] It seems to me that Sir W. Jones' usual translation of this and similar words by '*reading* and *studying* the Veda,' conveys a somewhat wrong idea. The words generally used to denote the performance of the Brahma-yajňa rather imply 'going over inaudibly to one's self,' 'repeating or muttering texts in a low tone of voice.' It is doubtful whether the Veda was ever read or studied as we should read a book in the present day. Neither the word Veda nor any of the words connected with it imply truth written down like our word 'Scripture;' and for a long period the writing of it was discouraged, if not prohibited. The very object of the long residence with a Guru (see p. 245) was to learn to repeat the sacred texts by heart, not to study them. Indeed, very little mention of writing is made in Manu. Even written evidence is not alluded to as it is in Yājňavalkya. In connection with the repetition of the Veda at the present day I here give the substance of an interesting article by Professor Bhāṇḍārkar in the 'Indian Antiquary' for May, 1874. Every Brāhmanic family is devoted to the study of a particular Veda or S'ākhā of a Veda, and its family domestic rites are performed in accordance with the Sūtra of that Veda. In Northern India the favourite Veda is the White Yajur-veda in its Mādhyandina S'ākhā, but the study has almost died out except at Benares. (According to Mr. Burnell the Black Yajur-veda is the favourite in the Telugu country.) Brāhmans of each Veda are divided into two classes—Gṛihasthas, who are devoted to worldly avocations, and Bhikshukas, who study the sacred texts and perform religious rites. Both classes have to repeat the Sandhyā-vandana or 'morning and evening prayers' (see p. 248), which principally consist of the Gāyatrī (see p. 20), recited five, ten, twenty-eight, or a hundred and eight times. Besides these prayers, many perform daily the Brahma-yajňa, incumbent on all alike on certain occasions. This for Ṛig-vedī Brāhmans consists of—1. Part of Ṛig-veda I. 1. 2. Aitareya-brāhmaṇa I. 1. 3. Portions of the Aitareya-āraṇyaka (1–5). 4. The opening text or a portion of the White Yajur-veda. 5. Of the Sāma-veda. 6. Of the Atharva-veda. 7. Of the Āśvalāyana Kalpa-sūtra. 8. Of the Nighaṇṭu. 9. Of the Nirukta. 10. Of the Ćhandas. 11. Of the Jyotisha. 12. Of the S'ikshā. 13. Of Pāṇini. 14. Of Yājňavalkya's Smṛiti. 15. Of the Mahābhārata. 16. Of Kaṇāda's Sūtra. 17. Of Jaimini's Mīmāṇsā. 18. Of Bādarāyaṇa's Vedānta-sūtra. This course of Svādhyāya is based on Āśvalāyana's Sūtra III. 23 (given at p. 203 of this volume). No. 1 corresponds to his Ṛić;

cially of the Gāyatrī text, is regarded as the most efficacious; and a peculiar virtue is attributed to its being repeated in a low tone or even mentally:

The Japa-yajña or 'repetition of the Veda' is declared to be ten times superior to the Vidhi-yajña (or appointed oblations at the changes of the moon, called *Darśa* and *Paurṇamāsa*, see note, p. 31); a hundred times superior, if it is muttered in a low voice (*upāṇśu*); and a thousand times superior, if it is only mentally repeated (*mānasaḥ*, II. 85).

The four Pāka-yajñas, even when accompanied with the Vidhi-yajña, are not together worth a sixteenth part of the Japa-yajña (II. 86).

A Brāhman becomes fit for beatitude by simple repetition of the Veda, whether he perform other rites or not; of this there is no doubt (II. 87).

Let him habitually repeat (*abhyaset=japet*) the Veda at the right season without weariness, for that is called his highest duty (*paro dharmaḥ*); every other duty is called subordinate (*upa-dharmaḥ*, IV. 147).

The filial piety of the Hindūs is notably manifested in the importance attached to the *Śrāddhas*, sometimes reckoned as twelve in number (the three principal being *Nitya*, 'daily;' *Pārvaṇa*, 'monthly;' *Ekoddishṭa*, 'special,' p. 208), consisting of an offering of water (*udaka-dāna*, *tarpaṇa*) and cakes of rice-meal, &c. (*piṇḍa*) to a deceased father, grandfather, and great grandfather, and to fore-

---

4, 5, 6 to his Yajur, Sāman, and Atharvāṅgiras; 2, 3 to his Brāhmaṇas &c. Those Bhikshukas who have studied the whole Veda follow Āśvalāyana's precept *yāvan manyeta tāvad adhītya*. Some of them are also Yājñikas, skilled in the performance of sacred rites, and some are Vaidikas, whose sole occupation in life is to learn the Vedas by heart in the Saṃhitā, Pada, Krama, Jaṭā, and Ghana arrangement of the texts (see p. 162) without making a single mistake in the Sandhi changes or even in the accents. The Ṛig-vedīs pronounce the accents differently from the Taittirīyas, while the Mādhyandinas indicate the accents by movements of the right hand. In addition to the Mantra portion of the Veda, the Ṛig-vedīs learn to recite the Brāhmaṇa portion and the Vedāṅgas, including the Kalpa and Gṛihya Sūtras. At a public recitation the first place is given to Ṛig-vedīs, the second to Yajur-vedīs, and the third to Sāma-vedīs (cf. p. 223). As the Black and White Yajur-vedīs are liable to quarrel about precedence, they are not generally invited to recital-meetings (*Mantra-jārgaras*) together.

fathers and progenitors (*Pitṛis*) collectively, on which offerings they are supposed really to feed (III. 237). The custom was probably very ancient, as the Pitṛis are addressed with the utmost reverence in the Ṛig-veda (VI. 52. 4, VII. 35. 12, X. 14. 7, 8, &c. See p. 21 of this volume).

The actual funeral, when the bodies of all deceased persons (except those of infants up to two years old, cf. p. 302) are burnt, is described at p. 205. The offering to deceased fathers at the Śrāddha is the key to the Hindū law of inheritance. It furnishes the principal evidence of kinship, on which the title to participate in the patrimony is founded, no power of making wills being recognized in Manu or any other authoritative code of Hindū jurisprudence (see p. 270). The *Gotra* or family is in fact a corporate body bound together by what may be called *Sapiṇḍa*ship (*Sapiṇḍatā*) and *Samānodaka*ship (*Samānodaka-bhāva*, Manu V. 60). All who offer the funeral cake (*piṇḍa*) and water (*udaka*) together are Sapiṇḍas and Samānodakas to each other, and a kind of intercommunion and interdependence is thus continually maintained between the dead and living members of a family—between past, present, and future generations. Practically, however, the closeness of the interconnexion extends only to three generations on each side, so that if we imagine a clasp connecting two short chains of three links each, this will represent the householder uniting father, grandfather, and great grandfather, on the one side, with son, grandson, and great grandson on the other—in all seven persons connected by the Piṇḍa (Manu V. 60). The first three are supposed to be dependent on the living paterfamilias for their happiness, and even for their support, through the constant offering of the sacred cakes and water; and he himself, the moment he dies, becomes similarly dependent on the three succeeding generations.

The connexion of *Samānodaka*ship lasts longer, and

ends only when the family names are no longer known (V. 60).

The object of such Śrāddhas is twofold, viz. first, the re-embodying of the soul of the deceased in some kind of form after cremation of the corpse, or simply the release of the subtile body which is to convey the soul away (see p. 206). Secondly, the raising him from the regions of the atmosphere, where he would have otherwise to roam for an indefinite period among demons and evil spirits to a particular heaven or region of bliss. There he is eventually half deified among the shades of departed kinsmen. Manu, however, is not clear as to the precise effect of the Śrāddha. He merely states that its performance by a son or the nearest male kinsman is necessary to deliver a father from a kind of hell called *Put*[1], and that the spirits of the departed (Pitṛis) feed on the offered food (III. 237).

Special Śrāddhas such as these (p. 208), which form to this very day the most important religious rite among the Hindūs, are accompanied with much feasting and costly gifts to the Brāhmans invited to assist at their celebration[2] (III. 145). The performance of the first Śrāddha is more particularly marked by largesses of all kinds, and sometimes, it is said, costs a rich man a sum equivalent to several thousand pounds[3]. It should take place the day after mourning expires, and then at intervals during twelve successive months, this monthly ceremony being called by Manu *Anvāhārya* (III. 123). Afterwards it

[1] See Manu IX. 138. Whence a son who performs the rite is called *Put-tra*, 'the rescuer from Put.' This explains the desire of every Hindū for the birth of a son rather than a daughter; but it seems inconsistent that the Śrāddha should have an effect irrespective of deeds done during life.

[2] In Book III. 145 we have *yatnena bhojayeć ćhrāddhe bahv-ṛićam veda-pāragam*, see p. 209. Manu, however, discouraged too much feasting (*vistara*), and limited the number of guests, see III. 125, 126.

[3] That of the Bengālī millionaire, Ramdoolal Dey, cost £50,000, according to Mr. Wheeler.

should be performed on all anniversaries of a father's death. Other Śrāddhas are described at p. 208.

It is curious to learn from III. 150–168 Manu's idea of the persons to be excluded from these ceremonies (viz. thieves, spirit-drinkers, atheists, men with diseased nails or teeth, dancers, physicians, &c., see note, p. 275).

At some Śrāddhas the old Dharma-śāstras, Ākhyānas, Itihāsas, and Purāṇas were recited (III. 232, note, p. 215).

With reference to the subject of diet, it is clear from V. 15. 5, &c., that as a general rule the eating of flesh (*mān̲sa*) and of fish (*matsya*) by twice-born men was prohibited; that the drinking of spirituous liquor was included among the five great sins (see p. 274); and that many other kinds of food, such as garlic, onions, leeks (*laśuna, gṛiñjana, palāṇḍu*), mushrooms (*kavaka, ćhatrāka*), and carnivorous birds (*kravyādāḥ pakshiṇaḥ*, V. 11), were forbidden. But it is an argument for the antiquity of Manu's Law-book that it directs flesh-meat (*āmisha*) to be eaten at some of these Śrāddhas (III. 123, IV. 131). I annex a few interesting passages which bear upon the killing of animals for sacrifice and the eating of flesh-meat under certain circumstances:

Never let a Brāhman eat the flesh of cattle unconsecrated with Mantras, but let him eat it only when hallowed with texts of the Veda (IV. 36).

On a solemn offering to a guest (*madhu-parka*) at a sacrifice, and in holy rites to departed ancestors or to the gods—on these occasions and no other may cattle be slain (V. 41).

As many hairs as grow on any animal, so many similar deaths shall one who slays it unnecessarily (*vṛithā*) endure hereafter from birth to birth. By the Self-existent himself were animals created for sacrifice, which was ordained for the welfare (*bhūtyai*) of all this universe; therefore slaughter of animals for sacrifice is no slaughter (V. 38, 39)[1].

In eating meat (*mān̲sa-bhakshane*) and in drinking wine (*madye*) there is no crime (provided it be on a lawful occasion, V. 56).

---

[1] This is another indication of the priority of at least part of Manu's Code to the general spread of Buddhism, which reformation led to the almost total abolition of animal sacrifice in India.

Hospitality is enjoined on the householder, in the strongest language, as a religious duty (see also p. 287):

No guest (*atithi*) who arrives in the evening, brought by the setting sun (*sūryoḍhaḥ*), must be dismissed. Whether he arrives in season or out of season, let him be allowed to sojourn in the house and be well entertained.

A Brāhman sojourning in a house and not honoured takes to himself all the merit of the householder's good deeds (III. 100).

Let the householder not eat anything himself till he has made his guest eat. The honouring of a guest confers wealth, reputation, life, and heaven (III. 105, 106. Compare also IV. 29).

An oblation (of food) in the fire of a Brāhman's mouth delivers (the offerer) from great guilt (III. 98).

With regard to the householder's wife and the condition of women as depicted by Manu, we may observe that their position is one of entire subordination, amounting, in theory, to a complete abnegation of what in these days would be called 'women's rights.' But although it is certain that the inferiority of woman is a fixed Oriental dogma which no contact with Europeans is likely entirely to eradicate, yet it must be borne in mind that the practice does not always conform to the theory. The influence of Hindū mothers in their own families, and the respect paid to them by their children, have always been great; and it is one indication of the antiquity of Manu's Code that, although some of its precepts pronounce women unfit for independence, and debarred from the study of the Veda, others concede to them an amount of freedom to which they became strangers in times subsequent to the influx of Mohammedan customs [1]. In some cases a girl, if unmarried for three years, is even allowed to choose her own husband [2], when she is called Svayam-varā (IX. 90, 92). It is very true that Manu distinctly directs (V. 162,

[1] The seclusion of Hindū women is chiefly due to the introduction of Muslim customs when the Mohammedans invaded India.

[2] Girls of the Kshatriya class sometimes chose their own husbands, as we know from the story of Nala and other episodes of the Mahābhārata.

IX. 47, 65) that no second husband is to be allowed to widows, but he nowhere alludes to that exaggerated devotion which induced the Satī or 'devoted wife' to burn herself with her husband's body—a custom which from about the time of Alexander's invasion [1], more than 300 years B.C., till the year 1829, has led to the sacrifice of innumerable lives, and has left a blot on the annals of our own administration [2].

---

[1] It is clear from Strabo XV. 30 and 62 that Satī prevailed in India about the time of Alexander. Strabo says that the Kathaei (=Kanyā-kubja or perhaps Kshatriya), a tribe in the Pañjāb, in order to prevent wives poisoning their husbands, made a law that they should be burnt with them when they died (*συγκατακαίεσθαι τεθνεῶσι τοῖς ἀνδράσι τὰς γυναῖκας*), and that some wives burnt themselves voluntarily (*ἀσμένας*). Compare also Diodorus Siculus (XIX. 33), who describes how, after the battle between Antiochus and Eumenes, one of the wives of the Indian general Κητεὺς (=Ketu or Khatrī?) burnt herself, after contending with the other for the honour. But Arrian makes no mention of any Satī. He only describes (VII. 2, 3) how Κάλανος (perhaps=Sanskṛit Kalyāṇa), one of a sect of Indian wise men who went naked, burnt himself upon a pile. The description is like that of the self-cremation of the ascetic S'ara-bhaṅga in Rāmāyaṇa III. 9. Cf. Cicero, Tusc. Disp. II. 22 and de Divin. I. 23. The following is a portion of the latter passage: 'Est profecto quiddam etiam in barbaris gentibus praesentiens, atque divinans: siquidem ad mortem proficiscens Calanus Indus, cum adscenderet in rogum ardentem, O praeclarum discessum, inquiet, e vitâ!' The idea of Satī seems to have been borrowed by the Hindūs from the Scythians (Herod. IV. 71). A similar custom prevailed among the Thracians (Herod. V. 5). Cf. also Propertius III. 13, 'Ardent victrices, et flammae pectora praebent, Imponuntque suis ora perusta viris.' Mādrī, wife of Pāṇḍu, became a Satī (Mahā-bhārata, Ādi-parva 4896). Compare Dr. Rost's edition of Wilson's Works, vol. ii. pp. 270–309.

[2] The practice of Satī was for a long time thought to be so intimately connected with the religious belief of the Hindūs, that our Government did not venture to put a stop to it. It was known to be enjoined in the Brahma-purāṇa and Codes of Vyāsa, Aṅgiras, &c.; and such authorities as Colebrooke (see his life by his son, p. 287) and H. H. Wilson (in 1828) gave their opinion against interference, although it was ascertained that neither the Veda nor Manu directed or even hinted at concremation of the

Indeed, the marriage of widows is even spoken of as practised, though reprehended (IX. 66–68); and a damsel given away in marriage may be re-betrothed, if her husband die before she is actually married (69).

The following passages will be sufficient to fill up the picture of Hindū domestic life (see also p. 288):

Day and night must women be made to feel their dependence on their husbands. But if they are fond of worldly amusements (*vishayeshu sajjantyaḥ*), let them be allowed to follow their own inclinations (IX. 2).

Even if confined at home by faithful guardians they are not (really) guarded; but those women who guard themselves by their own will (*ātmānam ātmanā yās tu raksheyuḥ*) are well guarded (IX. 12).

Let not (a husband) eat with his wife, nor look at her eating (IV. 43).

Women have no business to repeat texts of the Veda (*nāsti strīṇāṃ kriyā mantrair*), thus is the law established (IX. 18).

Domestic rites are to be performed in common with a wife (*sādhāraṇo dharmaḥ patnyā saha*), so it is ordained in the Veda (IX. 96).

No sacrifice is permitted to women separately (from their husbands), no religious observance (*vratam*), no fasting (*uposhitam*). As far as a wife obeys her husband so far is she exalted in heaven (V. 155).

A husband must continually be revered (*upaćaryaḥ*) as a god (*deva-vat*) by a virtuous wife (V 154).

A virtuous wife who remains unmarried after the death of her husband goes to heaven, even though she have no son (V. 160).

---

living wife with the dead husband. To Raghu-nandana (according to Dr. F. Hall) is due the alteration of the last word of a Ṛig-veda text (X. 18. 7, see p. 209) on which the authority for Satī was made to rest: *Anaśravo 'namīvāḥ su-ratnā ā rohantu janayo yonim agre*, 'without tears, without sorrow, bedecked with jewels, let the wives go up to the altar first,' where *agneḥ*, 'of fire,' was substituted for *agre*, 'first.' (Compare pp. 205, 209, 210.) It is true that our Government adopted a middle course, and prohibited the burning of the widow, except under strict regulations, and except with her own full consent; and officials were to be present to see the rules enforced; but I have been informed by a distinguished friend (Mr. Seton-Karr) who held high offices in India, that, in consequence of our half-sanction, the number of widows actually returned as burnt, rose in one year to 800, while in other years (between 1815 and 1828) it varied from 300 to 600. Lord William Bentinck passed a law in 1829 (Reg. xvii) which suppressed the practice with entire success and without difficulty.

We have already indicated that in the third and fourth periods of his life a Brāhman, according to Manu, is to become first an anchorite (*vānaprastha*) and then a religious mendicant (*bhikshu* or *parivrājaka*). It is indeed wholly improbable that all Brāhmans conformed to this rule, but the second verse of the sixth Book prescribes that when the father of a family perceives his hair to be turning grey, or as soon as his first grandchild is born, and after he has paid his three debts[1], he is to retire to a forest and there as a hermit to practise austerities:

Having taken up his sacred fire (*agni-hotram*) and all the domestic utensils for making oblations to it, and having gone forth from the town to the forest, let him dwell there with all his organs of sense well restrained (VI. 4).

With many kinds of pure food let him perform the five Mahā-yajńas or 'devotional rites' (VI. 5).

Let him also offer the Vaitānika oblations with the (three sacred) fires according to rule (see p. 197, note 1, p. 198).

Let him roll backwards and forwards on the ground, or stand all day on tiptoe (*prapadaiḥ*), let him move about by alternately standing up and sitting down, going to the waters to bathe at the three Savanas (sunrise, sunset, and midday, VI. 22. See last line of p. 247).

Let him practise the rules of the lunar penance (VI. 20. See p. 106).

In the hot weather let him be a Pańća-tapās (VI. 23. See p. 105).

Let him offer libations (*tarpayet*) to the gods and Pitṛis, performing ablutions at the three Savanas (VI. 24).

Having consigned the three sacred fires (*vaitānān*) to his own person (by swallowing the ashes) according to prescribed rules, let him remain without fire, without habitation, feeding on roots and fruits, practising the vow of a Muni (i. e. the *Mauna-vrata* of perpetual silence, VI. 25).

Book VI. 33 directs him for the fourth period of his life to wander about as a Bhikshu or Parivrājaka, 'religious mendicant' (*ćaturtham āyusho bhāgam parivrajet*). Here are a few rules for the regulation of this final stage of his existence, when he is sometimes called a *Sannyāsin*,

[1] These three debts (*trīṇi ṛiṇāni*) are, 1. to the gods, 2. to the Pitṛis, 3. to the Ṛishis. The 1st is liquidated by sacrifices, the 2nd by begetting a son for performance of the S'rāddha, the 3rd by repetition of the Veda.

'one who has given up the world;' sometimes a *Yati*, 'one who has suppressed his passions[1]:'

Let him remain without fire, without habitation (*a-niketaḥ*); let him resort once a day to the town for food, regardless of hardships, resolute, keeping a vow of silence (*muni*), fixing his mind in meditation (VI. 43).

With hair, nails, and beard well clipped, carrying a bowl (*pātrī*), a staff (*daṇḍī*), and a pitcher (*kusumbhavān*), let him wander about continually, intent on meditation and avoiding injury to any being (VI. 52).

In this manner, having little by little (*śanaiḥ śanaiḥ*) abandoned all worldly attachments (*saṅgān*), and freed himself from all concern about pairs of opposites[2] (*dvandva*), he obtains absorption into the universal Spirit (*brahmaṇy avatishṭhate*, VI. 81).

IV. Let us now note, in the fourth place, the chief characteristics of Manu's ordinances of government and judicature (*vyavahāra*), and a few of the most remarkable civil and penal laws and rules of evidence[3]. The treatment of these subjects, which ought to constitute the most

---

[1] I find that some of M. Barth's remarks in the 'Revue Critique' for June 13, 1874, bear on what I have stated with regard to Manu's ordinances in the preceding pages: 'Si nous remontons plus haut, aux livres védiques, aux plus anciens comme aux plus modernes, nous trouvons la nation Indienne divisée en un grand nombre de petites principautés, où domine le principe ethnique de la peuplade et du clan. Cette organisation qui n'avait certainement pas beaucoup changé à l'époque du Buddha, s'accorde encore moins avec le système de Manu, qui suppose une certaine uniformité et l'existence de grands états. La plupart de ces peuplades avaient sans doute un état social analogue : de temps immémorial elles étaient divisées en 4 classes. . . . Mais il est difficile de préciser le degré de rigueur de cette division. Encore à une époque relativement récente (Ćhāndog. Up. iv. 4. 2) la plus jalouse, et la plus fermée de ces classes, celle des Brâhmanes, ne paraît pas très scrupuleuse quant à la pureté du sang. Je ne puis donc voir autre chose dans la théorie officielle de la caste qu'une sorte de thème convenu dont il faut faire usage avec la plus grande prudence, thème dont la donnée fondamentale a dû, parce qu'elle était consacrée par une tradition sainte, se prêter successivement, et d'une façon plus ou moins artificielle à l'explication d'états de société bien différents.'

[2] Such as honour and dishonour (*mānāpamāna*), joy and sorrow, &c.

[3] I have here consulted Elphinstone's and Mill's India.

important department of a code of laws, is only commenced by Manu in the second half of his work, and is chiefly comprised in one quarter of it, viz. the seventh, eighth, and ninth Books. As the state of society depicted in the first six Books is of a simple and primitive character, recognizing only four principal divisions of the people, so the only form of government prescribed in the seventh Book is of a paternal and patriarchal description. The king is to rule by divine right, and, though a despot, to act like a father[1] towards his subjects (*varteta pitṛi-van nṛishu*, VII. 80). That he was treated as a kind of divinity is evident:

The Creator created a king for the protection of the whole world by drawing forth eternal particles (*mātrāḥ śāśvatīḥ*) from the essence of Indra, Anila (Wind), Yama (god of justice), Sūrya (Sun), Agni (Fire), Varuṇa, Ćandra (Moon), and Kuvera (god of wealth, VII. 3, 4).

A king, even though a child, must not be treated with contempt, as if he were a mortal; he is a great divinity in human shape (VII. 8).

He is directed to appoint seven or eight ministers (VII. 54) and to consult them first apart, and then collectively, as a kind of council. His prime minister (VII. 58) is to be a Brāhman[2], and in him he is to place implicit confidence (59). He is to have a standing army (VII. 102, 103), commander-in-chief (VII. 65), and an ambassador (*dūtaḥ*) of great knowledge and abilities (VII. 63). The following is very significant:

Determination not to retreat in battle (*sangrāmeshu anivartitvam*), protection of the people, and obedience (*śuśrūshā*) to Brāhmans is the highest duty of kings, and secures their felicity in heaven (VII. 88).

The king's mode of life and the distribution of his time

---

[1] Compare S'akuntalā, Act V: *Tvayi parisamāptam bandhu-kṛityam prajānām*, 'in thee (the king) is comprehended the whole duty of a kinsman towards thy subjects.' Δεσπότης is said to be=Sanskṛ *dāsa-pati*, 'lord of conquered races.'

[2] This rule was followed by S'ivajī in the constitution of the Marāṭhī empire, and the Peshwa or chief of the eight Pradhānas, 'principal ministers,' ultimately superseded S'ivajī's weak successors and usurped the supremacy.

are carefully regulated (VII. 145, &c.) He is to rise in the last watch of the night, then to hold a court, then to assemble his council and deliberate on the affairs of his kingdom and all the eightfold business of kings (VII. 154); after that, to engage in manly exercises, then to dine, taking care that his food is not poisoned (VII. 218), and then to regulate his family; after that, he is allowed some relaxation; then he is to review his troops; then to perform religious exercises; and lastly, being himself well armed, to receive the report of his spies (*ćāra*), informers and secret emissaries (*praṇidhi*), who are regarded as of great importance[1]. He is to conclude the day by a frugal meal and musical recreations, and to go to bed early (VII. 225)[2]. The rules for diplomacy and war show that India was divided into a number of unequal states. Intrigues are to be carried on with the leaders of the enemy, and negotiation is declared to be better than force (VII. 197, 198). In battle the king is to set an example of personal bravery (VII. 87). The chief weapon is the bow (VII.

[1] In IX. 256 a king is called *ćāra-ćakshuḥ*, 'spy-eyed.'

[2] The royal office was no sinecure. This is evident from the Mahabhārata and Daśa-kumāra-ćarita as well as from Manu. It appears that the day and night were each divided into eight portions of one hour and a half each, reckoned from sunrise, and thus distributed. Day—1. the king being dressed is to audit accounts; 2. he is to pronounce judgments in appeals; 3. he is to breakfast; 4. he is to receive and make presents; 5. he is to discuss political questions with his ministers; 6. he is to amuse himself; 7. he is to review his troops; 8. he is to hold a military council. Night—1. he is to receive the reports of his spies and envoys; 2. he is to dine; 3. he is to retire to rest after the perusal of some sacred work; 4 and 5. he is to sleep; 6. he is to rise and purify himself; 7. he is to hold a private consultation with his ministers and instruct his officers; 8. he is to attend upon the Purohita or 'family priest' for the performance of religious ceremonies (Wilson's Hindū Theatre, i. 209). Megasthenes (Strabo XV. 1, 55) says that the Indian king may not sleep in the day-time, but continues the whole day judging causes. Compare Macaulay's account of the daily life of Frederic the Great (Essays, p. 805).

74). Elephants, chariots, cavalry, and infantry form the *Ćatur-aṅga* or 'fourfold army[1],' and minute directions are given for its marching (VII. 187, &c.)

With regard to internal administration, it is clear from the Code that the country was partitioned into divisions governed by vicegerents, to whom the king delegated his own despotic powers, and whose authority was again delegated to other subordinate governors, who again divided their power by committing it to other rulers of townships in a regular chain, the highest governor ruling over a thousand towns, the next over a hundred, the next over twenty, the next over ten (cf. St. Luke xix. 17), and the lowest ruling over one town:

Let the lord of one town (*grāmikaḥ*) notify of his own accord, and in due order, to the lord of ten towns (*grāma-daśeśāya*) any crimes which have taken place in his own district, and the lord of ten to the lord of twenty; let the lord of twenty notify everything to the lord of a hundred, and the lord of a hundred to the lord of a thousand (VII. 116, 117).

Another important subject is revenue, which the monarch is to obtain from the following sources: 1. Taxes on the produce of land, which was probably held in common by village communities, though occasional grants may have been made to individuals, the king being theoretically the only absolute proprietor of the soil (*bhūmer adhipatiḥ*, VIII. 39)[2]. 2. Taxes on the produce of labour. 3. Taxes on certain metals and commodities added to capital stock. 4. Taxes on purchases and sales. 5. A kind of poll-tax. 6. Another kind paid in labour.

With regard to 1, the usual proportion of produce taken by the king was a sixth part, but in times of necessity

---

[1] In VII. 185 a sixfold (*shaḍ-vidha*) army is spoken of, the two other component parts being officers and attendants.

[2] In later times a sort of middle-man, to whom the name *Zamīndār* (introduced by the Mohammedans) is applied, acquired an ownership nearly absolute in the soil; or, at any rate, intervened between the Ryot or 'cultivator' and the king, receiving a share of the produce from the former and paying a stipulated proportion to the sovereign.

(as of war or invasion), he might even take a fourth of the crops. But, even though dying for want of money, he is never to receive a tax from a Brāhman conversant with the Veda (VII. 133)[1]. The following passages illustrate the above six heads of taxation:

1. A sixth, an eighth, or a twelfth part of grain may be taken by the king (according to the goodness or badness of the soil, VII. 130).

The king who, without giving protection, takes a sixth part of the grain as tax (*bali*) is declared to draw upon himself all the sins of all his subjects (VIII. 308).

A military king (*kshatriyaḥ*) who takes even a fourth part in a time of necessity (*āpadi*) while protecting his subjects to the utmost of his ability is freed from all culpability (X. 118).

2. Moreover, he may take a sixth part of the annual increase of trees (*dru*), meat, honey, clarified butter, perfumes, medicinal herbs, liquids, flowers, roots, and fruits, of leaves (*patra*), pot-herbs (*śāka*), grass, wicker-work (*vaidala*), hides, earthenware vessels, and all articles made of stone (VII. 131, 132).

3. Of cattle and gold and silver (*hiraṇyayoḥ*) added to the capital stock (*mūlād adhikayoḥ*), a fiftieth part may be taken by the king (VII. 130).

Of old treasures and precious metals in the earth the king may take one half, because he protects his subjects and is the paramount lord of the soil (VIII. 39).

4. Having well considered the rates of purchase and sale, the length of transit (*adhvānam*), with cost of food &c. on the journey (*saparivyayam*), the profit gained, and expense of insurance (*yoga-kshemam*), let him make merchants pay taxes on their commodities (VII. 127).

5. The king should cause the lower classes (*pṛithag-janam=nikṛishṭa-janam*, Kullūka) in his kingdom, who live by petty trading, to pay some small sum (per head) in the name of the annual tax (VII. 137).

6. The king should cause inferior artisans and artificers (such as black-smiths, &c.) and men of the servile class (*śūdrān*), who support themselves by their own labour, to work for one day in every month (VII. 138).

As regards the administration of justice, this is also to be performed by the king in person, aided by Brāhmans

[1] In S'akuntalā, Act II, Māṭhavya says to the king, 'Say you have come for the sixth part of their grain which they owe you for tribute.' The Mahā-bhārata allows secularized Brāhmans to be taxed. Strabo (XV. 1, 40) says, 'the whole land belongs to the king, but the Indians work it on condition of receiving the fourth part of the crops (ἐπὶ τετάρταις).'

or else by a Brāhman acting as his deputy, assisted by three others (VIII. 9, 10). In Book VII. 14 we read:

For the use of the king the great Creator (*Īśvaraḥ*) created in the beginning his own son Justice, composed of particles of his own divine essence, to act as the protector of all creatures (by wielding) the rod of punishment.

The terrible consequences of neglecting to wield this rod are described in VII. 20, &c. (see p. 289). The king is not to encourage litigation (*notpādayet kāryam*, VIII. 43). Nevertheless, he is to be ready every day to decide causes in the court (*sabhā*) when brought before him. The mode of conducting a trial is simple and patriarchal. In VIII. 23 we read:

Let the king, having seated himself on the judgment-seat, with his body suitably attired and his mind collected (*samāhitaḥ*), and having offered homage (*praṇamya*) to the gods who are guardians of the world, commence the trial of causes (*kārya-darśana*). (Cf. Strabo XV. 1, 55.)

The litigant parties are to be heard in person, and the plaintiff's accusation is to be made *vivâ voce*. The witnesses are to be examined by the judge, who is to observe their countenances carefully (VIII. 25, 26). In his decision the judge is to attend to local usage, established practice (*āćāra*), the decisions of former judges (VIII. 45, 46), and written codes of law (*śāstra*, VIII. 3).

Let me pass on to notice the broad features of the civil and criminal code. It is, of course, very desirable that the distinction between civil and criminal laws should be clearly marked out. They are, however, mixed together very confusedly in the eighteen heads or divisions of law given by Manu (Book VII . 4–7) as follows:

The eighteen titles or branches of law are: 1. recovery of debts (*rinādānam*); 2. deposits (*nikshepaḥ*); 3. sale of property by one who is not the rightful owner (*asvāmi-vikrayaḥ*); 4. engaging in business after joining partnership, association in trade (*sambhūya samutthānam*); 5. non-delivery of what has been given (*dattasyānapakarma*); 6. non-payment of wages (*vetanasya adānam*); 7. breach of contract (*saṃvido vyatikramaḥ*); 8. annulling of purchase or sale (*kraya-vikrayānuśayaḥ*); 9. disputes between the owner and tender of cattle or between master and servant (*vivādaḥ svāmipālayoḥ*); 10. the law respecting disputes about boundaries (*sīmā-vivāda-dharmaḥ*); 11, 12. the two kinds of assault, viz. blows and abuse, or assault with blows and assault with slander (*pārushye-daṇḍa-vāćike*); 13. theft and larceny (*steyam*); 14. robbery with violence (*sāhasam*); 15. adultery (*strī-saṅgrahaṇam*); 16. the law regulating (the duties of) husband and wife (*strī-pun-dharmaḥ*); 17. partition of patrimony or inheritance (*vibhāgaḥ*); 18. gambling with dice and betting on animals, such as fighting-cocks (*dyūtam āhvayaś-ća*).

The first nine of the above titles and the sixteenth and seventeenth belong to civil law; those from the eleventh to the fifteenth, and the eighteenth relate to criminal law; the tenth belongs partly to civil, partly to criminal. With reference to the whole arrangement of the subject, Mr. James Mill's History of India (vol. i. p. 195, &c.) has some valuable remarks, the substance of which I here give:

Though no arrangement would appear more natural than the division of laws into *civil* and *penal*, we find them here mixed together. Another obvious ground of division—the distinction between the laws about *persons* and the laws about *things*—which prevailed in Roman law and was transferred, rude as it was, to English, seems never to have occurred to Hindū lawyers in the time of Manu. The first nine of the heads in Manu's arrangement relate to contracts, but the division is rude and imperfect. It begins with 'Loans,' one of the most refined of contracts. The subject of 'purchase and sale' is divided into two parts, but one occupies the third place in the list, the other the eighth, and a number of heterogeneous subjects intervene. 'Partnership' occupies a middle place between two subjects, to neither of which it has any relation. 'Non-payment of wages' stands immediately before 'Breach of contract,' as a separate title, though it ought to be included under that head. In fact, this seventh head is so general that it comprehends the whole subject of contracts. When the subject of contracts is ended, the principal branches of criminal law are introduced. After these and some other topics follows the great subject of inheritance[1].

Under the head of *Civil Law* the most interesting of Manu's ordinances are on the important subject of *property*, whether acquired by possession or occupancy (*lābha*,

---

[1] In consulting Mr. James Mill I have found that some of his statements must be taken with considerable qualification, prejudiced as he appears to have been against everything Hindū.

*bhukti, bhoga*), by purchase (*kraya*), by contract (*saṃvid, vyavahāra*), by labour (*karma-yoga*), by donation (*prati-graha*), by inheritance (*dāya*). I note the following:

He who has acquired any property through the sale of it (*vikrayāt*) in the presence of a number (of buyers and sellers) justly obtains the right to that property by reason of having paid the purchase money (VIII. 201).

The property of infants who are heirs let the king hold in trust until the owner has completed his term of studentship or till he is of age (at sixteen, VIII. 27).

Let the king fix the rate of sale and purchase of all marketable commodities (*sarva-paṇyānām*), after having considered the distance (from which they have been imported), the remoteness of the place to which they are sent, the time they are kept, and the gain or loss upon them. Once in every five nights or once a fortnight he should fix the proper rate in the presence of those (who understand it, VIII. 401, 402).

A lost article, when found, should be guarded by trusty men. Any thieves convicted of stealing it should be condemned to be trampled to death by the royal elephant (VIII. 34).

It is evidence of a somewhat rude state of society that in certain cases a man is allowed to repent of a bargain and to have a contract annulled, thus:

When a man has bought or sold anything (not perishable, such as land or copper), and may afterwards repent, he may restore it or take it back within ten days (*antar-daśāhāt*, VIII. 222).

Marriage is regarded as a contract, but the same liberty of annulling is in this case not allowed:

If a man shall give away in marriage a girl who has any defects (*doshavatīm*) without notifying these defects, the king must fine him ninety-six Paṇas (*kuryād daṇḍam shaṇṇavatim paṇān*, VIII. 224).

The repetition of the nuptial texts (*pāṇigrahaṇikā mantrāḥ*) are the settled mark (*niyataṃ lakshaṇam*) of a marriage contract. Of those texts (the one) repeated on (making) the seventh step (viz. *sakhā sapta-padī bhava*, see p. 200, l. 7) is decided by the wise to be (the sign of) the completion (*nishṭhā*) of the contract (VIII. 227).

Throughout Eastern countries, especially in ancient times, the insecurity of property has led to two practices little resorted to by the peoples of modern Europe, viz. concealment of valuable articles and the habit of entrusting them for safety to the keeping of others. We can understand, therefore, the importance assigned in Manu's Law-book (Book VIII. 179, &c.) to the subject of 'deposits' or, according to legal phraseology, 'bailments.' This branch of law opens thus:

A wise man should make a deposit (*nikshepam nikshipet*) with a person of good family, of good conduct, acquainted with law, a speaker of truth, possessing numerous relations, wealthy and honourable (VIII. 179).

If a bailee (*nyāsa-dhārin*) fail to restore a deposit, and there are no witnesses, the judge is to cause secret agents (*praṇidhi*) to deposit gold with him, and should he fail to redeliver it, he is to be made to pay (*dāpyaḥ*) the equivalent of both deposits (VIII. 181–184).

Another proof of a primitive state of society may be found in the rules respecting interest and the premium paid for the use of borrowed property. This is sometimes allowed to be paid in kind[1]; as, for instance, when grain, fruit, wool, animals, &c., have been borrowed, showing that coined money was still uncommon as a general circulating medium. (Compare the mention of *nāṇaka*, 'coin,' in the later Code of Yājñavalkya II. 241.)

Interest on money (*kusīda-vṛiddhiḥ*) received all at once (and not by the month, &c.) must not exceed the double (of the sum lent)[2]; on grain (*dhānye*), fruit (*sade*), wool (*lave*), and beasts of burden (*vāhye*) it must not exceed five times the value (*pańćatā*, VIII. 151).

The rate of interest (*vṛiddhi*) is not only high, but varies according to the class of the man to whom anything is lent; but compound interest (*ćakra-vṛiddhi*) is not approved (VIII. 153):

A money-lender (*vārdhushikaḥ*) may take two per cent (*dvikaṃ śatam*) as interest per month from a Brāhman, three (*trikam*) from a Kshatriya, four (*ćatushkam*) from a Vaiśya, and five (*pańćakam*) from a Śūdra, in the order of the classes (VIII. 142).

In VIII. 156, 157, there is a law bottomry, which is

---

[1] Compare Deut. xxiii. 19, 20, 'Thou shalt not lend upon usury to thy brother; usury of money, usury of victuals, usury of anything that is lent upon usury: unto a stranger thou mayest lend upon usury,' &c.

[2] Principal doubled by accumulated interest is called in Marāṭhī *Dām-dupaṭ*. Even now a village Mahājan will take from 50 to 75 per cent.

interesting as showing that sea-voyages were undertaken in Manu's time.

The recovery of debts is enforced by stringent laws, and the debtor is not only made to pay what he owes, but an additional fine to the king, thus[1]:

When a debt has to be paid (*riṇe deye*) which is admitted to be just, the debtor owes a fine of five per cent (*pañćakaṃ śatam*) in addition, and ten per cent if it be repudiated (though it be just, VIII. 139).

The laws respecting herdsmen (*paśu-pāla*) and their employers (*svāmin*) are carefully laid down (VIII. 229, &c.) I note one instance (VIII. 232):

The herdsman himself must restore an animal that has been lost (*nashṭa*), or destroyed by vermin (*kṛimibhiḥ*), or killed by dogs, or has perished by falling into a hole (*vishame*) through want of his having exerted himself to save it (*hīnam purusha-kāreṇa*).

We may also observe that the hire of some kinds of agricultural labourers is directed to be paid in kind[2]:

That hired herdsman whose hire is paid with milk must be allowed by the owner of the cattle to milk the best cow out of ten (*daśato-varām*), unless he be paid with some other kind of food (VIII. 231).

The most important subject connected with property is the law of inheritance (*dāya*) treated of in the ninth Book of Manu's Code. And here we cannot fail to be struck with the remarkable circumstance that Hindū law does not allow the owner of property any testamentary power[3].

---

[1] No sanction, however, is given by Manu to the later practice of *Dharnā* or 'sitting at the door of a house to compel payment of a debt.' The person so sitting refuses to eat, and as long as he does so the debtor must abstain from food too, and if the suitor perishes the crime of his death falls on the debtor. Originally the person sitting in Dharnā, either on his own behalf or that of another, was a Brāhman. See H. H. Wilson's Glossary of Indian Terms.

[2] Paymetns in kind in aid of money wages are not unusual even in the present day. Even quite recently in British territory the land-tax was sometimes paid in kind, and is still so paid in some native states.

[3] Our Government made this legal by the Hindū Wills Act (xxi. of 1870). Certain peculiar documents, however, resembling wills, but bearing other titles, were previously recognized by our courts.

Indeed, a proper word for 'will' or 'testament' does not exist in the Sanskṛit language. It must be borne in mind that in a patriarchal state of society all family property was supposed to be held in common by a sort of joint ownership, the father or principal person in a household being regarded as a head partner.

In India, where customs become stereotyped for centuries, this primitive idea of a common title to the family property has continued to prevail up to recent times. The family is, as we have seen, a corporate society, whose bond of union is the sacred oblation offered in common by its living to its deceased members. On the death of a father the sons or nearest relatives succeed to the inheritance by simple right of *Sa-piṇḍa*ship, that is, by a right obtained through the common offering of rice-cakes (*piṇḍa*) and of water &c. to a deceased father, grandfather, and great grandfather at the Śrāddha ceremonies (see p. 254). It must be noted, however, that although the whole family has a joint-interest in the property, the estate cannot be divided during the lifetime of the parents, and even at their death the eldest son is allowed to take the father's place as chief manager of the family partnership, thus:

The eldest brother may take the paternal property (*pitryaṃ dhanam*) entirely (into his own hands). The rest of the family (*śeshāḥ*) may live under him (*tam upajīveyuḥ*) exactly as they lived under the father (IX. 105).

An eldest brother conducting himself as he ought (towards his younger brothers) is to be regarded by them as a mother and father (IX. 110).

Nevertheless, the brothers are allowed, if they like, to separate, and full directions are given in Book IX. 112 &c. for the partition of the family estate; a distinction being made according to merit as well as age, and some being, very unjustly according to our ideas, disqualified:

After the death of the father and mother, the brothers having assembled together may make a partition of the paternal property, but they have no power to do so during the lifetime of their parents (IX. 104).

Either let them live together (*sahavaseyuḥ*) or separately, from religious motives; since the number of religious rites (such as the five *Mahā-yajñāḥ*, see p. 251) are increased by separation of households, therefore separation is legal (IX. 111).

The portion taken out (of the estate) by the eldest son is a twentieth, along with the best of all the chattels; by the middle son, a fortieth; and by the youngest, an eightieth (IX. 112).

A deduction (*uddhāra*) being thus made, the remainder should be allotted among the brothers in equal shares; if no deduction is made they should share in the following manner: Let the eldest take a double share and the next born a share and a half (if they excel in learning and merit), and let the younger sons have a share each (IX. 116, 117).

Those brothers who are addicted to vicious habits (such as gambling, licentiousness, &c.) forfeit a right (*nārhanti*) to any share in the inheritance (IX. 214).

Impotent persons (*klīva*), those who have lost caste (*patita*), those who are blind, deaf, insane, paralyzed (*jaḍa*), dumb, defective in limb or sense, are also debarred from sharing (IX. 201).

But a wise heir will in common justice supply all such persons with food and raiment (*grāsāććhādanam*) to the best of his ability. Otherwise he is guilty of a great crime (IX. 202).

It must be observed that women are generally excluded from a direct title to share in the division of property:

Three persons are declared to have no property of their own (*a-dhanāḥ*), a wife, a son, and a slave. Whatever money they earn is his to whom they belong (VIII. 416).

Nevertheless, some marriage portions (*śulka*) or gifts received by a married woman at and after the nuptial ceremony, are regarded as her own peculiar property. These constitute what is still called *Strī-dhana*[1], 'a woman's (separate) wealth or dower,' which, according to Manu, is sixfold:

---

[1] Commonly written Stridhun. Mr. Herbert Cowell, in his Tagore Law Lectures for 1871 (p. 28), says, that although this property is supposed to belong exclusively to a wife, the husband has a concurrent power over it, so that he may use it in any exigency, without being held accountable for it. Strī-dhana is now, however, acquired 'by gift, by earnings, and by inheritance,' and the Dāyabhāga lays down that the husband has power over the wife's earnings and 'any presents she may receive from any other but kindred.'

Whatever was given over the nuptial fire (*adhy-agni*), whatever she receives while being led in procession from her father's to her husband's house (*adhyāvāhanikam*), a gift (from her husband) in token of affection (*prīti*), and a similar gift received from her brother, from her mother, from her father, all these are declared to be a woman's own property (IX. 194).

Those young girls, too, who are unmarried (*kanyāḥ*) at a father's death are directed (IX. 118) to receive an allotment out of the shares accruing to their brothers. The following also (IX. 130) is noteworthy:

A man's own son is even as himself, and a daughter is like a son. How, then (if he have no son), ought any one else than a daughter, who is part of his own person (*ātmani tishṭhantī*), to inherit his own property?

I pass on to a brief notice of Manu's *Criminal Code*. The three most conspicuous features of his penal laws are exactly those which mark the earliest forms of criminal legislation, viz. severity, inconsistency, and a belief in the supposed justice of the *lex talionis*, the latter leading to punishments which in later times would be considered unjustifiably disproportionate to the offences committed, and sometimes barbarously cruel[1]. Thus:

With whatever member of the body a low-born man may injure a superior, that very member of his must be mutilated (VIII. 279).

A once-born man insulting (*kshipan*) twice-born men with abusive language (*vāćā dāruṇayā*) must have his tongue cut (VIII. 270).

Should he mention their name and caste with insulting expressions (as,

---

[1] Mr. Mill on this point quotes Sir W. Jones, who is not, like himself, disposed to view everything Hindū in an unfavourable light. 'The cruel mutilations practised by the native powers are shocking to humanity.' We know what was said by our Lord about 'an eye for an eye and a tooth for a tooth,' Matt. v. 38. See Lev. xxiv. 20, Deut. xix. 21. Compare the laws of Draco and of the ancient Egyptians. Strabo (XV. 1. 54) says of the Hindūs, 'He who has given false testimony suffers mutilation of the extremities (ἀκρωτηριάζεται), and he who maims a limb is condemned to suffer maiming.'

'Hallo! there, Yajñadatta, vilest of Brāhmans'), a red-hot iron spike ten fingers long is to be thrust into his mouth (VIII. 271).

Should he, through arrogance, attempt to instruct a Brāhman in his duty (saying, 'you ought to do so and so'), the king is to have boiling oil poured into his mouth and ears (VIII. 272).

Thieves are to have their hands cut off, and then to be impaled on a sharp stake (IX. 276).

A goldsmith detected in committing frauds is to have his body cut to pieces with razors (IX. 292).

Perhaps the most objectionable feature in the penal code is not the cruel retaliation, which was probably more a matter of theory than actual practice, but the leniency with which Brāhmans are directed to be treated. It will be observed that a graduated scale is prescribed according to the rank of the offender and the class to which he belongs, thus:

A king must never kill a Brāhman, though he may be found guilty of all possible crimes (*sarva-pāpeshv api sthitam*); let him expel him from the kingdom unharmed in body and intact in all his property. There is no greater injustice on earth than the killing of a Brāhman. The king, therefore, must not harbour a thought about putting him to death (VIII. 380, 381).

A Kshatriya insulting a Brāhman must be fined a hundred Paṇas (*śataṃ daṇḍam arhati*); a Vaiśya doing the same must pay one hundred and fifty or two hundred Paṇas; a Śūdra doing the same must receive corporal punishment[1] (*badham arhati*, VIII. 267).

Five great crimes (*mahā-pātakāni*) are enumerated in Book XI. 54, which are described as entailing the highest degree of guilt, though certainly from a European point of view they cannot all be regarded as equally heinous:

1. Killing a Brāhman (*brahma-hatyā*); 2. drinking intoxicating liquor (*surā-pāna*); 3. stealing gold from a Brāhman (*steya*); 4. adultery with the wife of a Guru or spiritual teacher (*gurv-anganāgamaḥ*); and 5. associating with any one guilty of such sins.

Severe penances voluntarily performed, rather than

[1] *Badha* might be rendered 'capital punishment,' but Kullūka explains it by 'the lash.'

legal penalties judicially inflicted, are enjoined for some of these crimes (see p. 279); and they are declared in XI. 49 to involve rather singular consequences (*phala*) in future states of existence. Thus for 1. a man will suffer from consumption (*kshaya-rogitvam*) in a future life (see also XI. 73); for 2. he will have discoloured teeth; for 3. diseased nails (*kaunakhyam*)[1].

Moreover, in XII. 54–57, much more awful results are alleged to follow hereafter; inasmuch as those who are guilty of these great crimes are condemned to dwell for a vast number of years in terrible hells (*ghorān narakān*) before entering on new states of being. After protracted torture in one or other of these hells (see p. 225) a Brāhman-slayer (*brahma-hā*) must enter the body of a dog, boar, ass, camel, bull, goat, sheep, stag, bird, or outcaste Ćaṇḍāla, according to the degree of his guilt; a spirit-drinker will become a worm, insect, moth, &c.; a gold-stealer will pass a thousand times into the bodies of spiders, snakes, noxious demons, &c. (Compare p. 281.)

Some crimes in the second degree are the following:

Falsely asserting oneself to be of too high a caste, falsely accusing a Guru, forgetting texts of the Veda through neglect of repeating them (*brahmojjhatā*), giving false testimony (*kauṭa-sākshyam*), eating impure food, stealing deposits, incest, intercourse with women of the lowest class.

A long list of crimes in the third degree (*upapātaka*) is given in XI. 59–66. Some of them are:

Killing a cow (*go-badhaḥ*); neglect of repetition of the Veda (i. e. of the daily Brahma-yajña); neglect of the sacred fire; usury (*vārdhushyam*); selling a tank or garden or wife or child; neglecting investiture (*vrātyatā*); superintendence over mines of any kind (*sarvākareshv adhikāraḥ*); cutting down green trees for fuel; performing religious rites for selfish motives (*ātmārtham*); reading infidel books (*asać-ćhāstrādhi-*

---

[1] For this reason it is directed in Book III. 153, 154, that consumptive persons and persons with diseased nails (*ku-nakhin*) and discoloured teeth (*śyāva-dantaka*) ought to be excluded from S'rāddhas.

*gamanam*); addiction to music and dancing (*kauśīlavyasya kriyā*); atheism (*nāstikyam*).

For many of these crimes also voluntary penances constitute the only punishment. Thus the killer of a cow must undergo great hardships and make atonement by attending upon a herd, guarding them from injury, following them day and night in all weathers for three months, swallowing the dust raised by their hoofs, &c. (XI. 108–115).

Trial by ordeal (*divya*) is recognized by Manu, though the ten different forms of it are not all specified as in later works[1]:

Let him cause a man (whose veracity is doubted) to take hold of fire or dive under water (*apsu nimajjayet*), or touch the heads of his wife and sons one by one. The man whom flaming fire burns not and water forces not up (*āpo nonmajjayanti*), and who suffers no harm, must be instantly held innocent of perjury (VIII. 114, 115).

It remains to notice a few of the laws of evidence. Fearful denunciations are pronounced against those who deliver false testimony in a court of justice (VIII. 82). The strictest rules are also to be observed in selecting witnesses competent to give trustworthy evidence (see p. 290). At least three witnesses are required to establish a fact in dispute:

If a man is summoned (*kṛitāvasthaḥ*) by a creditor for a debt and denies it when questioned, he is to be proved guilty by three witnesses at least (*try-avaraiḥ sākshibhiḥ*) in the presence of a Brāhman appointed by the king[2] (VIII. 60).

---

[1] These ten forms (some of which are given by Yājñavalkya, see p. 300) are—1. *Tulā*, 'the balance;' 2. *Agni*, 'fire;' 3. *Jala*, 'water;' 4. *Visha*, 'poison;' 5. *Kośa*, 'drinking water in which an idol has been washed;' 6. *Taṇḍula*, 'ejecting chewed rice-grains;' 7. *Tapta-māsha*, 'taking a Māsha weight of gold out of heated oil;' 8. *Phāla*, 'holding a hot ploughshare;' 9. *Dharmādharma*, 'drawing concealed images of virtue and vice out of a vessel filled with earth;' 10. *Tulasī*, 'holding the leaves of holy basil.' This holy basil is said to be sacred to Vishṇu.

[2] Compare Yājñavalkya's rules about witnesses, which are a development of those of Manu. See p. 301.

Witnesses are to deliver their testimony *vivâ voce* and no directions are given about written documents which makes it probable that this kind of evidence though fully recognized by Yājñavalkya (see p. 300), wa not received, or at least not usual, at the early epoch whe Manu's Law-book was composed. If the testimony i contradictory, the judge is to decide by the majority o credible witnesses. If the number of witnesses is equal he is to be guided by the testimony of those who are mos distinguished for virtuous qualities (VIII. 73). A simila rule is propounded by Yājñavalkya (see p. 301). It is noteworthy point that women are, as a rule, debarred fron giving evidence, except for women (VIII. 68). Moreovei the distinctions between the credibility of witnesses mus strike a European mind as somewhat extraordinary an whimsical. A man who has male offspring is thought mor worthy of credence than a man who has female (VIII. 62) perhaps because he is supposed to have a greater stak in the common weal. A hungry or thirsty and tired per son is excluded from all right of bearing testimony (VIII 67). The reason for the following is not very clear:

In cases of robbery with violence (*sāhaseshu*), theft, and adulter (*steya-saṃgrahaṇeshu*), calumny and assault (*vāg-daṇḍayoḥ pārushye*), judge must not examine (the competence of) witnesses too strictly (*na parīksheta sākshiṇaḥ*, VIII. 72).

The following precept is calculated, I fear, to diminish the favourable impression which the laws of the Mānavas taken together and regarded relatively to circumstances must produce on a candid mind:

In certain cases a man stating a fact falsely from a pious motiv (*dharmataḥ*), even though he knows the truth, is not excluded fron heaven; such a statement they call divine speech.

Whenever the death of a Brāhman, Kshatriya, Vaiśya, or S'ūdra may result from speaking the truth, then an untruth may be told, for falsehood is in this case preferable to truth (VIII. 103, 104).

A similar precept occurs in Yājṅavalkya's Code, but an expiation is there prescribed. (See the examples, p. 301.)

V. I now turn to some of the Prāyaś-ćitta or 'penances' enjoined in the eleventh Book of Manu:

A twice-born man performing the *Prājāpatya* penance (i. e. that called after Prajāpati) must for three days eat only once in the morning, for three days only once in the evening, for three days food unsolicited (but given as alms), and for three days more nothing at all (XI. 211).

A twice-born man performing the penance called *Ati-kṛiććhra* ('very severe') must eat, as before (i. e. as described in the last), a single mouthful (*grāsam*) for three times three days, and for the last three days must fast entirely (XI. 213).

A Brāhman performing the penance called *Tapta-kṛiććhra* ('hot and severe') must swallow hot water, hot milk, hot clarified butter, and hot air, each of them for three days successively, after bathing and keeping his organs of sense all restrained (XI. 214).

The act of fasting for twelve days, performed by one whose heart is restrained, and whose mind is attentive, is called the *Parāka* penance, which removes all guilt (XI. 215).

Eating for one day the excrement and urine of a cow mixed with milk, curds, clarified butter and water boiled with Kuśa grass, and fasting entirely for a day and night is the penance called *Sāntapana* (XI. 212).

This last penance is to be performed by any one who does any voluntary act causing loss of caste (*jāti-bhraṉśa-karaṃ karma*); if the act be involuntary, the Prājāpatya is to be performed. (See XI. 124.)

The *Pańćagavya* penance consists in swallowing the five products of a cow mentioned above under the Sānta-pana penance. This is declared to be a sufficient atonement for having stolen food, a carriage, bed, chair, roots, flowers, or fruit (XI. 165). A variety of other curious penances and expiations are enumerated:

A twice-born man having, through infatuation, drunk intoxicating liquor, may (as an expiation) drink the same liquor when boiling hot (*agni-varnām*). If his body is completely scalded by this process he is absolved from guilt (XI. 90).

When the divine knowledge (*brahma*) which is in his body (*kāya-gatam*) is once immersed in spirituous liquor, his Brāhmanical rank departs and he descends to the condition of a Śūdra (XI. 97).

He who says 'hush' (*hūm*) to a Brāhman, or 'thou' to one who is his superior (in knowledge), must perform an ablution, eat nothing for the rest of the day, and appease the Brāhman's anger by prostrating himself at his feet (XI. 204).

If a Brāhman who has drunk the Soma-juice (at a Soma-sacrifice, see end of note 1, p. 9) smells the breath of a man who has been drinking spirituous liquor, he is absolved from the taint by thrice suppressing his breath under water and swallowing clarified butter (XI. 149).

One of the most severe penances is called *Ćāndrāyaṇa* or 'the lunar penance,' described in VI. 20, XI. 216–221. We have already given a short account of this (see p. 106), and have only here to note, as peculiar, some of the offences for which it is required to be performed:

The Ćāndrāyaṇa is declared to be an expiation for carrying off a man or woman, for seizing a field or house, and for taking without permission the water of a well or reservoir (XI. 163). It is also to be performed for acts which cause mixture of caste and exclusion from society (XI. 125).

The following will show that the greatest atoning efficacy is attached to a repetition of the Veda:

Having repeated (*japitvā*) the Sāvitrī (or Gāyatrī, see p. 20) three thousand times with a collected mind, and having drunk milk for one month in a cow-house, a Brāhman is delivered from the guilt of receiving gifts from wicked persons (*asat-pratigrahāt*, XI. 194).

Desiring to obtain absolution (*ćikīrshan apanodanam*) for all his sins great and small, he should repeat once a day for a year the text beginning *Ava* and that beginning *Yatkiṃ ćedam* (Ṛig-veda VII. 89. 5).

Having accepted a prohibited gift or eaten improper food, he is absolved by repeating for three days the texts (Ṛig-veda IX. 58) beginning *Tarat sa mandī dhāvati* (XI. 252, 253).

Although he be guilty of many crimes (*bahv-enāḥ*) he is absolved (*śudhyate*) by repeating (*abhyasya*) for a month the text beginning *Somā-rudrā* (Ṛig-veda VI. 74. 1, Atharva-veda VII. 42. 1) and the three texts beginning *Aryamaṇam varuṇam mitram*, &c. (Ṛig-veda IV. 2. 4), while performing ablution in a running stream (XI. 254).

By intently (*samāhitaḥ*) repeating three times the whole Saṃhitā (and Brāhmaṇa *Kullūka*) of the Ṛig, Yajur, and Sāma-veda with their Upanishads (*sa-rahasya*), he is absolved from all his sins (XI. 262).

VI. The sixth and last head is that of *karma-phala*, 'acts-recompenses.' I select a few passages illustrative of the most characteristic of all Hindū doctrines—that of the soul's transmigration through three stages of being, until a complete recompense of its acts is effected.

Book XII. 3, 9, 11, 39, 40, declares that the triple order of transmigration through the highest, middle, and lowest stages, results from good or bad acts, words, and thoughts produced by the influence of the three Guṇas, Sattva, Rajas, and Tamas (see note 1, p. 67); and that for sins of act, a man takes a vegetable or mineral form (*sthāvaratām*); for sins of word, the form of a bird or beast; for sins of thought, that of a man of the lowest caste; but that a triple self-command (p. 144, note 1, p. 291) leads to emancipation from all births and final beatitude:

Those who are endowed with the Sattva Guṇa ('purity') take the form of gods (*devatvam*), those who are filled with Rajas ('passion') become men, and those who are overwhelmed with Tamas ('darkness and ignorance') become beasts (XII. 40).

But in XII. 41, 50 each of the three orders of transmigration is described as divided into a threefold scale of being, the gradations and subdivisions of which proceed on principles which are not very consistent or intelligible:

1. *a.* Highest highest—Brahmā, the creator, Marīći, &c. *b.* Highest middle—Sacrificers (*yajvānaḥ*), Ṛishis, incarnate deities (*devāḥ=devatāḥ vigrahavatyaḥ*), regents of the stars, Pitṛis, Sādhyas, &c. *c.* Highest lowest—Ascetics, religious mendicants, Brāhmans, demigods borne in heavenly cars (*vaimānikāḥ*), those that preside over the lunar mansions, Daityas, &c. (XII. 48–50).

2. *a.* Middle highest—Gandharvas, Guhyakas, Yakshas, Apsarases, &c. *b.* Middle middle—Kings, Kshatriyas, the chaplains of kings (*purohitāḥ*), &c. *c.* Middle lowest—Club-fighters (*jhallāḥ*), prize-fighters (*mallāḥ*), actors, those who live by the use of weapons, gamblers, and drinkers (XII. 45–47).

3. *a.* Lowest highest—Dancers, birds (*suparṇāḥ=pakshiṇaḥ*), deceitful men, Rākshasas, Piśāćas, &c. *b.* Lowest middle—Elephants, horses, S'ūdras, despicable Mleććhas, lions, tigers, boars. *c.* Lowest lowest—Vegetables and minerals (*sthāvarāḥ=vṛikshādayaḥ*), worms, insects, fish, reptiles, tortoises, cattle, animals of various kinds (XII. 42–44).

It is curious to note the effect of apparently slight sins of commission and omission in degrading a man to lower conditions of being, or in exposing him to diseases:

Through speaking ill (*parīvādāt*) of his preceptor, a man will be born an ass; if he reviles him, a dog; if he uses his property without leave, a worm; if he envies him, an insect (II. 201).

If a man steal grain he shall be born a mouse; if brass, a gander; if water, a water-duck; if honey, a gad-fly; if milk, a crow; if syrup, a dog; if ghee, a weasel (XII. 62).

A Brāhman neglecting his own appointed caste duty (*dharmāt svakāt*) will be born as a vomit-eating demon; a Kshatriya, as a demon feeding on excrement and dead bodies; a Vaiśya, as a demon feeding on putrid carrion (*Ulkā-mukha, Kaṭa-pūtana*, and *Maitrāksha-jyotika*, XII. 71, 72).

A stealer of grain will be afflicted with dyspepsia (in a future existence); a stealer of the words (of the Veda, by repeating it without authority), with dumbness; a stealer of cloth, with leprosy; a horse-stealer, with lameness (XI. 51). Compare p. 275[1].

---

[1] It may be interesting to annex to this Lecture a few of the statements of Megasthenes (300 years B.C.) about the Brāhmans (Strabo XV. 1, 59): 'They practise the greatest austerities to prepare for death (ἀσκήσει πλείστῃ χρῆσθαι πρὸς τὸ ἑτοιμοθάνατον), which they hold to be birth to a real and happy life (γένεσιν εἰς τὸν ὄντως βίον καὶ τὸν εὐδαίμονα); they maintain that nothing of what happens to men is good or bad; that the world was created and is perishable; that it is spheroidal; that the God who made and rules it pervades every part of it; that water was the first element created; that besides the four elements there is a fifth (πρὸς τοῖς τέτταρσι στοιχείοις πέμπτη τίς ἐστι φύσις); and that the earth is in the centre of the universe. Besides, like Plato, they weave many fables (μύθους) about the immortality of the soul and punishments in hell. As to the Hindūs generally—they are ignorant of writing, have no written laws, and arrange everything from memory (XV. 53, 66). They do not employ slaves (54). They worship Jupiter Pluvius (τὸν ὄμβιον Δία), the river Ganges, and the gods of the country; those who live in the mountains worship Dionysos (=Śiva); those in the plains, Herakles (=Vishṇu, XV. 58, 69); they never drink wine except at sacrifices (53). It is not permitted to any one to marry a person of another caste, nor to change from one business or trade to another, nor to engage in many pursuits, unless he belong to the caste of philosophers (XV. 49). These philosophers are of two kinds, Brachmanes and Garmanes (Βραχμᾶνες, Γαρμᾶνες=Brāhmans and Śramaṇas or Buddhist ascetics, 59). Both practise endurance (καρτερίαν), and will remain a whole day in one posture without moving (60. Cf. also XV. 61, 63).'

# LECTURE XI.

## *The Law-books—Manu continued.*

I NOW endeavour to give, as literally as possible, a metrical version of some of Manu's most noteworthy precepts, selected from different parts of the Code, under the four heads of *Āćāra*, 'rules of conduct;' *Vyavahāra*, 'rules of government and judicature;' *Prāyaś-ćitta*, 'penance;' *Karma-phala*, 'rewards and punishments of acts.'

### *Āćāra*, 'rules of conduct.'

A Brāhman from exalted birth is called
A god among the gods, and is a measure
Of truth for all the world, so says the Veda (XI. 84).

Knowledge[1], descending from her home divine,
Said to a holy Brāhman, I am come
To be thy cherished treasure, trust me not
To scorners, but to careful guardians,
Pure, self-restrained, and pious; so in them
I shall be gifted with resistless power (II. 114, 115).

The man with hoary head is not revered
As aged by the gods, but only he
Who has true knowledge[2]; he, though young, is old (II. 156).

A wooden elephant, an antelope
Of leather, and a Brāhman without knowledge—
These are three things that only bear a name (II. 157).

As with laborious toil the husbandman,
Digging with spade beneath the ground, arrives
At springs of living water, so the man
Who searches eagerly for truth will find
The knowledge hidden in his teacher's mind (II. 118).

---

[1] In II. 117 knowledge is divided into three parts—1. *Laukika*, 'secular;' 2. *Vaidika*, 'Vedic;' 3. *Ādhyātmika*, 'spiritual' or that which relates to soul.

[2] Strabo XV. 1, 54, says of the Hindūs, Οὐδὲ τῇ ἡλικίᾳ τῶν γερόντων προνομίαν διδόασιν ἂν μὴ καὶ τῷ φρονεῖν πλεονεκτῶσι.

With pain the mother to her child gives birth,
With pain the father rears him ; as he grows
He heaps up cares and troubles for them both ;
Incurring thus a debt he ne'er can pay,
Though he should strive through centuries of time (II. 227).

Think constantly, O son, how thou mayest please
Thy father, mother, teacher—these obey.
By deep devotion seek thy debt to pay.
This is thy highest duty and religion (II. 228).

Who finds around him only wicked sons,
When called by fate to pass the gloom of death,
Is like a man who seeks to cross a flood
Borne on a raft composed of rotten wood (IX. 161).

Even though wronged, treat not with disrespect
Thy father, mother, teacher, elder brother (II. 226).

From poison thou mayest take the food of life,
The purest gold from lumps of impure earth,
Examples of good conduct from a foe,
Sweet speech and gentleness from e'en a child,
Something from all ; from men of low degree
Lessons of wisdom, if thou humble be (II. 238, 239).

Wound not another, though by him provoked,
Do no one injury by thought or deed,
Utter no word to pain thy fellow-creatures (II. 161).

Say what is true, speak not agreeable falsehood (IV. 138).

Treat no one with disdain[1], with patience bear
Reviling language ; with an angry man
Be never angry ; blessings give for curses (VI. 47, 48).

E'en as a driver checks his restive steeds,
Do thou, if thou art wise, restrain thy passions,
Which, running wild, will hurry thee away (II. 88).

When asked, give something, though a very trifle,
Ungrudgingly and with a cheerful heart,

---

[1] In IV. 135 the householder is especially warned against treating with contempt a Brāhman well versed in the Veda, a Kshatriya, and a serpent, because (says Kullūka) the first has the power of destroying him by his unseen power of magical texts and spells, the other two by their seen power (*dṛishṭa-śaktyā*). Cf. the passages relative to the power of the Brāhmans, translated p. 241.

According to thy substance; only see
That he to whom thou givest worthy be (IV. 227, 228).

Pride not thyself on thy religious works,
Give to the poor, but talk not of thy gifts.
By pride religious merit melts away,
The merit of thy alms by ostentation (IV. 236, 237).

None sees us, say the sinful in their hearts;
Yes, the gods see them, and the omniscient Spirit
Within their breasts. Thou thinkest, O good friend,
'I am alone,' but there resides within thee
A Being who inspects thy every act,
Knows all thy goodness and thy wickedness (VIII. 85, 91).

The soul is its own witness; yea, the soul
Itself is its own refuge; grieve thou not,
O man, thy soul, the great internal Witness (VIII. 84).

The Firmament, the Earth, the Sea, the Moon,
The Sun, the Fire, the Wind, the Night, and both
The sacred Twilights[1], and the Judge of souls[2],
The god of Justice, and the Heart itself—
All constantly survey the acts of men (VIII. 86).

When thou hast sinned, think not to hide thy guilt
Under a cloak of penance and austerity (IV. 198).

No study of the Veda nor oblation,
No gift of alms, nor round of strict observance
Can lead the inwardly depraved to heaven (II. 97).

If with the great Divinity who dwells
Within thy breast thou hast no controversy,
Go not to Ganges' water to be cleansed,
Nor make a pilgrimage to Kuru's fields (VIII. 92)[3].

Iniquity once practised, like a seed,
Fails not to yield its fruit to him who wrought it,
If not to him, yet to his sons and grandsons (IV. 173).

Contentment is the root of happiness,
And discontent the root of misery.
Wouldst thou be happy, be thou moderate (IV. 12).

Honour thy food, receive it thankfully,

---

[1] See the account of the Sandhyās, p. 248. [2] Yama, see p. 21.

[3] See note 1, p. 251.

Eat it contentedly and joyfully,
Ne'er hold it in contempt; avoid excess,
For gluttony is hateful, injures health,
May lead to death, and surely bars the road
To holy merit and celestial bliss (II. 54, 57).

Desire is not extinguished by enjoyment,
Fire is not quenched by offerings of oil,
But blazes with increased intensity (II. 94).

Shrink thou from worldly honour as from poison,
Seek rather scorn; the scorn'd may sleep in peace,
In peace awake; the scorner perishes (II. 162, 163).

Daily perform thy own appointed work
Unweariedly; and to obtain a friend—
A sure companion to the future world—
Collect a store of virtue like the ants
Who garner up their treasures into heaps;
For neither father, mother, wife, nor son,
Nor kinsman, will remain beside thee then,
When thou art passing to that other home—
Thy virtue will thy only comrade be (IV. 238, 239).

Single is every living creature born,
Single he passes to another world,
Single he eats the fruit of evil deeds,
Single, the fruit of good; and when he leaves
His body like a log or heap of clay
Upon the ground, his kinsmen walk away;
Virtue alone stays by him at the tomb
And bears him through the dreary trackless gloom (IV. 240–242)[1].

Thou canst not gather what thou dost not sow;
As thou dost plant the tree so will it grow (IX. 40).

Depend not on another, rather lean
Upon thyself; trust to thine own exertions.
Subjection to another's will gives pain;
True happiness consists in self-reliance (IV. 160).

Strive to complete the task thou hast commenced;
Wearied, renew thy efforts once again;

---

[1] Dr. Muir has pointed out that the expression *tamas tarati dustaram*, 'he crosses the gloom difficult to be passed,' may be taken from Atharva-veda IX. 5. 1, *tīrtvā tamāṉsi bahudhā mahānti.*

Again fatigued, once more the work begin,
So shalt thou earn success and fortune win (IX. 300).

Never despise thyself, nor yet contemn
Thy own first efforts, though they end in failure;
Seek Fortune with persistency till death,
Nor ever deem her hard to be obtained (IV. 137).

Success in every enterprise depends
On Destiny[1] and man combined, the acts
Of Destiny are out of man's control;
Think not on Destiny, but act thyself (VII. 205).

Be courteous to thy guest who visits thee;
Offer a seat, bed, water, food enough,
According to thy substance, hospitably;
Naught taking for thyself till he be served;
Homage to guests brings wealth, fame, life, and heaven (III. 106, IV. 29).

He who possessed of ample means bestows
His gifts on strangers while his kindred starve,
Thinks to enjoy the honey of applause,
But only eating poison dies despised—
Such charity is cruelty disguised (XI. 9).

He who pretends to be what he is not,
Acting a part, commits the worst of crimes,
For, thief-like, he abstracts a good man's heart (IV. 255).

Though thou mayest suffer for thy righteous acts,
Ne'er give thy mind to aught but honest gain (IV. 171).

So act in thy brief passage through this world
That thy apparel, speech, and inner store
Of knowledge be adapted to thy age,
Thy occupation, means, and parentage (IV. 18).

The man who keeps his senses in control,
His speech, heart, actions pure and ever guarded[2],
Gains all the fruit of holy study; he
Needs neither penance nor austerity (II. 160).

But if a single organ fail, by that defect
His knowledge of the truth flows all away
Like water leaking from a leathern vessel (II. 99).

Contentment, patience under injury,

---

[1] *Daiva* is here the Adṛishṭa described p. 69. [2] See note 1, p. 291.

Self-subjugation, honesty, restraint
Of all the sensual organs, purity,
Devotion[1], knowledge of the Deity[2],
Veracity, and abstinence from anger,
These form the tenfold summary of duty (VI. 92).

Long not for death, nor hanker after life;
Calmly expect thy own appointed time,
E'en as a servant reckons on his hire (IV. 45).

This mansion of the soul, composed of earth,
Subject to sorrow and decrepitude,
Inhabited by sicknesses and pains,
Bound by the bonds of ignorance and darkness,
Let a wise man with cheerfulness abandon (VI. 77).

Quitting this body, he resembles merely
A bird that leaves a tree. Thus is he freed
From the fell monster of an evil world[3] (VI. 78).

## *Duties of Women and Wives.*

In childhood must a father guard his daughter;
In youth the husband shields his wife; in age
A mother is protected by her sons—
Ne'er should a woman lean upon herself (V. 148, IX. 3).

A faithful wife who wishes to attain
The heaven of her lord, must serve him here
As if he were a god, and ne'er do aught
To pain him, whatsoever be his state,
And even though devoid of every virtue (V. 154, 156).

She who in mind, speech, body, honours him,
Alive or dead, is called a virtuous wife (V. 165).

Be it her duty to preserve with care
Her husband's substance; let her too be trusted
With its expenditure, with management
Of household property and furniture,
Of cooking and purveying daily food.

---

[1] Kullūka interprets *dhī* by 'knowledge of the sacred truth contained in the Śāstras.'

[2] *Vidyā*, 'knowledge of the supreme Spirit.'—Kullūka.

[3] *Kṛiććhrād grāhāt*=*saṃsāra-kashṭād grāhād iva.*

Let her be ever cheerful, skilled in all
Domestic work, and not too free in spending (V. 150).

Drink, bad companions, absence from her lord,
Rambling about, unseasonable sleep,
Dwelling in others' houses, let her shun—
These are six things which tarnish woman's fame (IX. 13).

Whatever be the character and mind
Of him to whom a woman weds herself,
Such qualities her nature must imbibe,
E'en as a river blending with the sea (IX. 22).

Women, united by the marriage tie
To men they love, in hope of virtuous offspring,
Worthy of honour, eminently blessed,
Irradiate the houses of their lords,
Like shining lights or goddesses of fortune (IX. 26).

Then only is a man a perfect man
When he is three—himself, his wife, his son—
For thus have learned men the law declared,
'A husband is one person with his wife' (IX. 45).

Fidelity till death, this is the sum
Of mutual duties for a married pair (IX. 101).

And if the wife survives, let her remain
Constant and true, nor sully her fair fame,
E'en by the utterance of another's name (V. 157).

## *Vyavahāra*, 'rules of government and judicature.'

The Lord of all in pity to our needs
Created kings, to rule and guard us here;
Without a king this world would rock with fear (VII. 3).

A king, e'en though a child, must not be treated
As if he were a mortal; rather he
Is a divinity in human shape (VII. 8).

The king, his council, and the royal city,
The country[1], treasure, army, and ally,
These are the seven members of a realm (IX. 294).

---

[1] For *rāshṭra* (=*deśa*) Yājñavalkya (I. 352) substitutes *jana*, 'the people.'

Dread of the rod alone restrains the bad,
Controls the good, and makes a nation happy (VII. 15).

The king must therefore punish fearlessly;
Else would the strong oppress the weak, the bad
Would wrong the good, and pierce them as with iron[1];
The crow would eat the consecrated rice,
The dog the burnt oblation; ownership
And rights of property would be subverted;
All ranks and classes would become confused,
All barriers and bridges broken down,
And all the world turned wrong side uppermost (VII. 20, 21, 24).

But let the monarch, ere he wield his rod,
Consider place and time, the written law
Of justice, and the measure of his strength (VII. 16).

Gamesters and public dancers, heretics,
Revilers of the Veda, infidels,
Sellers of liquor, men who interfere
In others' duties and neglect their own,
All such he should expel from his domain (IX. 225).

To women, children, crazy men, and fools,
The old, the poor, the sickly, and infirm
Let him be never harsh; if they do wrong
Let them be bound or punished tenderly[2] (IX. 230).

That king is equally unjust who frees
The guilty or condemns the innocent.
The wicked he must treat like thorny weeds,
They must be rooted out with active arm;
The good and virtuous let him shield from harm (IX. 252, 253).

Let not a king or judge promote disputes,
But if a suit be tried, let him with fairness
Adjudicate between the disputants (VIII. 43).

When Goodness, wounded by Iniquity,
Comes to a court of justice, and the judge

---

[1] The literal translation of the text here is 'the stronger would roast the weaker like fish on a spit' (*śūle matsyān ivāpakshyan durbalān balavattarāḥ*).

[2] The text says 'with a whip, twig, or rope.' It must be presumed that the whip and twig are intended to be used in the case of children only.

Extracts not tenderly the pointed dart,
That very shaft shall pierce him to the heart (VIII. 12).

Justice destroyed will ruin the destroyer;
Preserved, it will preserve. Beware, O judge,
Lest outraged justice overthrow the world (VIII. 15).

E'en as a hunter tracks the lurking-place
Of some poor wounded deer by drops of blood,
So must a king by strict investigation
Trace out the source of violated justice (VIII. 44).

Let him with full deliberation weigh
The evidence, the place, the mode, the time,
The facts, the truth, and his own frame of mind,
Firmly adhering to the rules of law (VIII. 45).

Just men and men of sense, whate'er their caste,
And those who know their duty and are free
From love of gain, may tender evidence;
The opposite must not be witnesses (VIII. 63).

Kings, priests, religious students, anchorites,
All interested men, friends, boon companions,
Foes, criminals, diseased and perjured men,
Low artisans and dancers, lunatics,
Old men, and children, drunkards, vagabonds,
Thieves, starving wretches, irritated persons,
A single witness—these are all excluded (VIII. 64–67).

Let women act as witnesses for women;
The twice-born classes for the twice-born; slaves
For slaves, and only lowest men for outcastes (VIII. 68).

The court must not be entered by a witness,
Unless he speak the truth without reserve;
For equally does he commit a crime,
Who tells not all the facts, or tells them falsely (VIII. 13).

A witness who gives evidence with truth
Shall be absolved from every sin, and gain
Exalted glory here and highest bliss above (VIII. 81, 83).

Headlong in utter darkness shall the wretch
Fall into hell, who in a court of justice
Answers a single question falsely; he
Shall be tormented through a hundred births (VIII. 82, 94).

And all the merit of his virtuous acts

Shall be transferred to dogs. Therefore be true,
Speak the whole truth without equivocation (VIII. 90, 101).

Let no considerate witness take an oath
Lightly, or in a trifling matter; he
Who does so shall incur eternal ruin (VIII. 111).

## *Prāyaś-ćitta*, 'penance and expiation.'

According to a man's sincerity
In penitent confession of his crime,
And detestation of the evil deed,
Shall he be pardoned and his soul released
From taint of guilt, like serpent from its skin (XI. 227, 228).

If he do wrong, 'tis not enough to say
I will not sin again; release from guilt
Depends on true contrition, which consists
In actual abstinence from sinful deeds (XI. 230).

Therefore, whatever fault a man commits,
Whether from ignorance or knowingly,
Let him, desiring quittance from his crime,
Beware how he offend a second time (XI. 232).

Revolving in his mind the certainty
Of retribution in a future state,
Let him be pure in thought, in word, in deed[1] (XI. 231).

By free confession, penitence, and penance,
By daily repetition of the Veda[2],
By the five holy acts[3], by giving alms,
By patience, and by bearing injuries,
The greatest sinner may obtain release (XI. 227, 245).

Whate'er is hard to cross, whate'er is hard
To have or do or be, may be attained
By penance—sins of heart and speech and act
May be burnt out; therefore be rich in penance (XI. 238, 241).

---

[1] Here and in another example below further instances occur of Manu's triple division of 'thought, word, and deed' (see note, p. 143). The same triple division is frequent in Buddhistic writings.

[2] *Khyāpanena, anutāpena, tapasā, adhyayena ća.*

[3] That is, the five Mahā-yajñas; see p. 251.

E'en as a clod of earth melts all away
Cast in a mighty lake, so every sin
Becomes effaced, merged in the triple Veda (XI. 263).
In penance all the bliss of gods and men
Is said to have its root, continuance, end[1] (XI. 234).

## *Karma-phala*, 'recompenses of acts.'

Innumerable souls, endued with form,
Issue like scintillations[2] from the substance
Of the great Self-existent, constantly
Impelling beings multiform to action (XII. 15).
Whate'er the act a man commits, whate'er
His state of mind, of that the recompense
Must he receive in corresponding body (XII. 81).
Action of every kind, whether of mind
Or speech or body, must bear fruit, entailing
Fresh births through multifarious conditions,
In highest, mean, and lowest transmigrations (XII. 3).
Souls gifted with the quality of goodness
Attain the state of gods; those filled with passion,
The state of men; and those immersed in darkness,
The state of beasts—this is the triple course (XII. 40).
Let all men ponder with attentive mind
The passage of the soul through diverse forms,
Of Brahmā, gods and men, beasts, plants, and stones,
According to their good or evil acts,
And so apply their minds to virtue only (XII. 22, 42, 50).
Just in proportion as a vital soul
Addicts itself to sensuality,
In that degree its senses shall become
Intensely keen in future transmigrations (XII. 73).
Reflect thou on man's manifold transitions
And passages through forms of being, caused
By faults of action[3], and his headlong fall
Down to the lower regions; then the torments

[1] A variety of penances will be found detailed at p. 278.
[2] Compare the extracts from the Upanishads, pp. 39, 43.
[3] *Avekṣheta gatīr nṛīṇām karma-dosha-samudbhavāḥ.*

Reserved for him by Yama; then in life
His partings from his loved ones and his meetings
With those he loves not; then the victory
Of sickness and decrepitude and death;
Then the soul's painful egress from the body,
And lastly its return to other forms,
Passing from womb to womb to undergo
Ten thousand millions of existences[1] (VI. 61–63).

Then do thou contemplate with fixed attention
The subtile essence of the Soul supreme,
Existing in the highest and the lowest—
Pervading every creature equally (VI. 65).

He who perceives the omnipresent God
Is nevermore enslaved by acts, but he
Who sees him not, can never be released (VI. 74).

Those who repeat their vicious acts are doomed
To misery, increasing more and more,
In forms becoming more and more debased (XII. 74).

They shall be born as despicable beasts,
Suffer the worst extremes of cold and heat,
Painful diseases, various kinds of terror (XII. 77, 80).

He who by firmness gains the mastery
Over his words, his mind, and his whole body,
Is justly called a triple-governor[2] (XII. 10).

Exerting thus a threefold self-command
Towards himself and every living creature,
Subduing lust and wrath, he may aspire
To that perfection which the good desire (XII. 11).

Every created being which exists
And yet is not eternal[3], is in Soul.

---

[1] *Yoni-koṭi-sahasreshu sṛitīś-ća antar-ātmanaḥ.*

[2] This is the Tri-daṇḍin (see note, p. 144). It is noticeable that the Indian ascetic, who is described by Arrian (VII. 2) as exciting the wonder of Alexander the Great by his *καρτερία*, is named *Δάνδαμις*, probably from the same root as *daṇḍa* (*dam*, 'to subdue,' in Intens.). By others he is called Mandanis (root *maṇḍ ?*).

[3] This seems to mean, as explained by Dr. Johaentgen, that to which belongs a real existence and yet not eternity, because it is a product. Cf. Sāṅkhya-pravaćana V. 56.

He who with fixed abstraction sees himself
And all things in the universal Self[1]
Cannot apply his soul to wickedness (XII. 118).

This universal Soul is all the gods,
Is all the worlds, and is the only source
Of all the actions of embodied spirits (XII. 119).

He is their ruler, brighter than pure gold,
Subtler than atoms, imperceptible,
Except by minds abstracted, all-pervading,
Investing all with rudiments of matter,
Causing all beings to revolve like wheels
In regular and constant revolution
Through birth and growth, decay and dissolution (XII. 122, 124).

The man who sees by means of his own soul
The universal Spirit present there,
Present in every creature everywhere,
With perfect equanimity may wait
Till he has reached the state of bliss supreme—
Complete absorption in the eternal essence (XII. 125).

### *The Code of Yājṅavalkya.*

The most important Law-book next to Manu is the Dharma-śāstra of Yājṅavalkya, which, with its most celebrated commentary, the Mitāksharā by Vijṅāneśvara, is at present the principal authority of the school of Benares and Middle India. It seems originally to have emanated from a school of the White Yajur-veda in Mithilā[2] or North Behar, just as we have seen (p. 213) that the Code of the Mānavas did from a school of the Black

---

[1] Dr. Johaentgen thinks that *Ātman* in these passages is wrongly translated 'the supreme Soul.' He believes that it denotes 'the whole self or soul' of man, regarded as an epitome of the universe, and he refers in confirmation of his view to Tattva-samāsa 56. See also Manu VIII. 84, translated p. 284.

[2] According to Dr. Röer, it is still the leading authority of the Mithilā school, but Colebrooke names other works as constituting the chief texts of this school.

Yajur-veda in the neighbourhood of Delhi. Book I. 2 makes the author say:

The chief of devout sages (Yājñavalkya), dwelling in Mithilā, having reflected for a moment, said to the Munis, 'Listen to the laws which prevail in the country where the black antelope is found' (cf. Manu II. 23).

Yājñavalkya's work[1] is much more concise than that of Manu, being all comprised in three books instead of twelve, which circumstance leads to the inference that it has suffered even more curtailment at the hands of successive revisers of the original text than the Code of the Mānavas. Like that Code, it seems to have been preceded by a Vṛiddha and a Vṛihad Yājñavalkya. The whole work, as we now possess it, is written in the ordinary Śloka metre. The first Book, consisting of 376 couplets, is chiefly on social and caste deities (*āćāra*); the second, consisting of 307 verses (which have been transferred almost word for word to the Agni Purāṇa), is mainly on administrative judicature and civil and criminal law (*vyavahāra*); the third, consisting of 335 verses, is principally on devotion, purification, expiation, penance (*prāyaś-ćitta*), &c. The Mitāksharā commentary follows the same arrangement, and is divided also into three parts.

As to the date of Yājñavalkya's Law-book, it has been conjecturally placed in the middle of the first century of our era. The period of its first compilation cannot, of course, be fixed with certainty, but internal evidence clearly indicates that the present redaction is much more recent than that of Manu's Law-book.

The following points have been noted by me:

---

[1] The edition I have used is the excellent one of Stenzler. I have consulted his preface and translation, and the translation of part of the Code made by Dr. Röer and W. A. Montriou, to which there is an instructive introduction.

1. Although Yājṅavalkya's Code must have represented the customs and practices prevalent in a district (Mithilā) situated in a different and more easterly part of India, yet nearly every precept in the first book, and a great many in the second and third, have their parallels in similar precepts occurring throughout the Code of the Mānavas.

2. Although generally founded on Manu, it represents a later stage of Hindū development. Its arrangement is much more systematic. It presents fewer repetitions and inconsistencies, and less confusion of religion, morality, and philosophy, with civil and criminal law.

3. In Book I. 3 the sources of law are expanded beyond those stated by Manu; although afterwards in I. 7 Manu's fourfold Dharma-mūlam (see p. 216) is adopted, thus:

'The Vedas, with the Purāṇas, the Nyāya, the Mīmāṇsa, the codes of law (*dharma-śāstra*), and the (six) Vedāṅgas are the fourteen repositories (*sthānāni*) of the sciences (*vidyānām*) and of law (*dharmasya*, I. 3).

'The Veda (*śruti*), traditional law (*smṛiti*), the practices of good men (*sad-āćāra*), and one's own inclination, are called the root of law' (I. 7).

4. Those of its precepts which introduce new matter evince a more advanced Brāhmanism and a stricter caste-organization; thus, for example, it is directed in I. 57 that a Brāhman must not have a S'ūdrā as a fourth wife, but only wives of the three higher classes, whereas in Manu (see p. 250) such a wife is permitted[1].

5. In I. 271, 272, there is an allusion to the shaven heads (*muṇḍa*) and yellow garments (*kashāya-vāsas*) of the Buddhists, which marks a period subsequent to the establishment and previous to the expulsion of Buddhism. It must be admitted, however, that there is no mention of the Buddhists by name.

6. In II. 185 the king is recommended to found and endow monasteries and to place in them Brāhmans learned in the Vedas.

7. In II. 241 mention is made of *Nāṇaka*, 'coined money,' both true and counterfeit (*akūṭa* and *kūṭaka*), whereas, although Manu speaks of weights of gold and silver, such as S'uvarṇas, Palas, Nishkas, Dharaṇas, and Purāṇas (VIII. 135–137), it is very doubtful whether any stamped coin was current in his day.

8. Written accusations and defences (*lekhya*) are required to be made (II. 6, 7), and written documents (*likhitam*) are allowed as evidence (II. 22); and in I. 318 grants of land and copper-plates, properly sealed, are mentioned.

9. The worship of Gaṇeśa, as the remover of obstacles, is expressly

---

[1] Later Codes limit Brāhmans to wives of their own classes only.

alluded to in I. 270, and *Graha-yajña* or 'offerings to the planets' are directed to be made in I. 294.

10. In III. 110 the author of the Code (Yājñavalkya) speaks of an Āraṇyaka or Upanishad (of the White Yajur-veda), which he had himself received from the Sun, and of a Yoga-śāstra, 'Yoga system of philosophy,' which he had himself delivered (to Patañjali[1]).

Some of these points seem decisive as to the lapse of a considerable period between Manu and Yājñavalkya, and lead us to agree with those who hesitate to refer the latter Code, in its present form, to an earlier epoch than the first century of our era[2]. On the other hand, some of the facts stated incline us to attribute a greater antiquity to portions of the work than that usually assigned to it.

I proceed to give specimens of the three divisions of Yājñavalkya's Code.

I. The following are from the first Book on *Āćāra* or 'social customs and immemorial practices.' Attention should be directed to the parallels in Manu at the end of several of the translated passages. The mention of four Vedas and the efficacy attributed to their repetition is noticeable:

Brāhmans, Kshatriyas, and Vaiśyas are called twice-born (*dvi-jāḥ*), since they are born once from their mothers and a second time through the binding on of the girdle (*Mauñji-bandhanāt*, I. 39. Cf. Manu II. 169, and see p. 247).

The Veda is more efficacious in effecting the final salvation of the twice-born (*dvijātīnāṃ niḥśreyasa-karaḥ paraḥ*) than sacrifices, than penances, and even than good works (I. 40. Cf. Manu II. 166).

---

[1] See p. 102 of this volume. Patañjali, who flourished, according to Lassen, about 200 B.C., is not, however, mentioned in the text.

[2] Some of Yājñavalkya's verses are found in the Pañća-tantra, the date of the oldest portions of which is usually referred to the fifth century of our era. In almost all Sanskṛit works the introduction of apposite verses from older sources, for the illustration of the original text, is common.

A twice-born man[1] who every day repeats the texts of the Ṛig-veda (*ṛićaḥ*) satiates the gods with honey and milk, and the fathers (*Pitṛīn*) with honey and butter (I. 41. Cf. Manu II. 107).

He who every day to the best of his ability repeats the texts of the Yajur-veda (*yajūnshi*) refreshes the gods with butter and nectar and the fathers with honey and butter (I. 42).

He who every day repeats the texts of the Sāma-veda (*sāmāni*) satiates the gods with Soma-juice and butter and the fathers as before (I. 43).

Twice-born men who every day to the best of their power repeat the texts of the Atharva-veda (*Atharvāngirasaḥ*, see p. 224) satiate the gods with marrow (*medasā*) and the fathers as before (I. 44).

He who every day to the best of his power repeats the sacred discussions (*vākovākyam*[2]), the Purāṇas, the Nārāśansīs[3], the sacred songs (*gāthikāḥ*), the Itihāsas, and the sciences (*vidyāḥ*), satiates the inhabitants of the skies (*divaukasaḥ*) with flesh, milk, rice, and honey, and the fathers as before (I. 45, 46).

The precept that the twice-born can take a S'ūdrā as a wife (cf. Manu III. 13, IX. 149) is not approved by me, since in that wife (*tatra*) he is himself born again (whence she is called *jāyā*, according to Manu IX. 8).

Three wives in the regular order (of the first three classes) may belong to a Brāhman, two to a Kshatriya, and one to a Vaiśya. A S'ūdra must only have one of his own class (I. 56, 57).

Once every year (the following persons) are to be honoured with a respectful offering (*argha*): a Snātaka (see p. 204), an Āćārya (see p. 239), a king, a friend, and a son-in-law, but a sacrificing priest at every sacrifice[4] (I. 110. Cf. Manu III. 119).

A traveller is to be treated as a guest, and also a Brāhman who knows the entire Veda. These two a householder, who wishes to obtain

---

[1] These following five verses are more explicit than Manu in describing the efficacy of the Brahma-yajña or Japa-yajña (see p. 252). They are based on S'atapatha-brāhmaṇa XI. 5, 6, 4–8, and on Āśvalāyana Gṛihya-sūtra III. 3. 2, &c.

[2] This might be translated 'dialogue.' It appears from S'atapatha-brāhmaṇa IV. 6, 9, 20, that some portions of Vedic tradition were called *vākovākyam* or *brahmodyam*.

[3] See this word in my Sanskṛit-English Dictionary. Compare the directions as to the *brahma-yajña* in the Āśvalāyana Gṛihya-sūtra, translated p. 203 of this volume.

[4] These six are also named in Pāraskara's Gṛihya-sūtra I. 1 (Stenzler) as worthy of the Argha.

the world of Brahman, must especially honour (I. 111. Cf. Manu I. 120, 130).

The success of every action depends on destiny and on a man's own effort; but destiny is evidently nothing but (the result) of a man's act in a former state of existence (I. 348. Cf. Manu VII. 205 and p. 286 of this volume).

Some expect the whole result from destiny or from the inherent nature (or force of a thing); some expect it from the lapse of time; and some, from a man's own effort: other persons of wiser judgment expect it from a combination of all these (I. 349).

II. The following are from the second section of Yājṅavalkya's Code on *Vyavahāra* or 'the administration of justice:'

Every day should a king, reflecting on his reward equal to that of sacrifices, personally investigate lawsuits in regular order surrounded by assessors[1] (I. 359. Cf. Manu VIII. 1).

---

[1] Colebrooke, in one of his Essays (Professor E. B. Cowell's edition, vol. ii. p. 490), gives an interesting account of the composition of an Indian court of justice, according to the rules of Hindū Law-books. The administration of justice, civil and criminal, is one of the chief duties of the Rājā or sovereign. Hence the king's court takes precedence of all. He is assisted by learned Brāhmans as assessors, one of whom acts as chief judge in his absence. It is not stationary, but follows him about. The second court, which is stationary, is that of the chief judge (*Prāḍ-vivāka*), appointed by the king, and assisted by three or more Brāhman assessors, not exceeding seven. The third court is that of the inferior judges for local trials. Besides these, there are country courts or assemblies of townsmen (*Pūga*), of traders, artisans, &c. (*Śreṇi*), and of kinsmen (*Kula*) for arbitration in small matters. The sovereign or supreme court (to which there is an appeal from all the others) is compared to a body consisting of various members, viz. 1. the king, 2. the chief judge, 3. the assessors, 4. the ministers of state, 5. the king's domestic priest, 6. the written law, 7. gold, fire and water (used for oaths and ordeals), 8. the accountant, 9. the scribe (*Kāyastha*), 10. the keeper of things in dispute and the enforcer of judgments, 11. the messenger, 12. the moderator of the court. The audience or bystanders are also regarded as a component part of the court, any one duly qualified to interpose with a suggestion or advice being at liberty to do so. All this is illustrated in a most interesting

A king, having duly corrected the castes, families, companies of artisans (*śreṇī*), schools, and communities of people that have swerved from the duty of their caste (*sva-dharmāt*, cf. p. 140), should place them in the right path (I. 360. Cf. Manu VIII. 41).

Let the king, keeping himself free from anger and covetousness, try lawsuits along with learned Brāhmans in accordance with the rules of written law (*dharma-śāstrānusāreṇa*, II. 1. Cf. Manu VIII. 1).

He should appoint as judges men well versed in the study of the Veda, conversant with the laws, speakers of truth, impartial to friend and foe (II. 2).

When any one, injured by others in any way contrary to law or usage, makes a representation to the king, this is a proper subject for a lawsuit (*vyavahāra-padam*, II. 5).

The charge, as made by the plaintiff, is to be put down in writing in presence of the defendant, marked with the year, month, half-month, day, names, caste, &c. (II. 6).

The answer to the charge is to be then written down in presence of the person who made the first representation; after which the plaintiff shall immediately cause to be committed to writing the proofs by which his accusation is supported (II. 6, 7).

Legal proof (*pramāṇam*) is of three kinds, viz. written documents (*likhitam*), actual possession (*bhuktiḥ*), and witnesses (*sākshiṇaḥ*). In the absence of any one of these, some one of the ordeals (*divyānyatamam*) is enjoined (II. 22. Cf. Manu VIII. 114).

The scales (*tulā*), fire, water, poison, drinking the water in which idols have been washed (*kośa*), these are the ordeals for the testing of innocence (II. 95. See note 1, p. 276).

There should be at least three witnesses, persons who act in accordance with the precepts of the Veda or traditional law and are of suitable caste (II. 69. Cf. Manu VIII. 60, and see p. 276 of this volume).

The judge should thus address the witnesses standing near the plaintiff (*vādin*) and defendant (*prativādin*), 'Whatever worlds are appointed for the worst criminals, for incendiaries, for murderers of women and children, these shall be the abode of him who gives false evidence' (*sākshyam anṛitam*, II. 73, 74. Cf. Manu VIII. 89).

---

manner by the ninth act of the drama called Mṛiććhakaṭikā, to which reference will be made in a subsequent Lecture. In the description of a court of justice there given, as Professor Cowell has remarked, the S'reshṭhin or 'chief of the merchants' and the Kāyastha or 'scribe' seem to sit as assessors with the judge.

Know that whatever merit has been acquired by thee through good actions in hundreds of former births shall become the property of him whom thou defeatest by false evidence[1] (II. 75. Cf. Manu VIII. 90).

In conflicting evidence (*dvaidhe*), that of the majority (*bahūnām*) must be taken; in the case of an equality of testimony, that of the virtuous persons; when these disagree, then the statements of the most virtuous must be taken (II. 78. Cf. Manu VIII. 73).

Whenever the evidence of a witness might occasion the death of a person of whatever class, the witness may tell an untruth. To obtain expiation (*pāvanāya*) after such false evidence twice-born men must offer an oblation (*ćaru*) to Sarasvatī (II. 83. Cf. Manu VIII. 104, 105).

When a murder or robbery has occurred (*ghātite 'pahṛite*) and no traces of it are found beyond the village, the blame must rest on the governor of the village (*grāma-bhartuḥ*), and the village must pay (II. 271, 272).

When a Brāhman is a thief, he must be marked with a hot iron and banished from the country (II. 270).

Housebreakers, stealers of horses and elephants, and those who commit murder with violence should be impaled (II. 273. Cf. Manu IX. 276, 280).

A stealer of clothes should have his hand cut off; cut-purses should have the thumb and fore-finger amputated (II. 274. Cf. Manu IX. 277).

The highest fine should be imposed on any one who knowingly gives a thief or murderer food, shelter, fire, water, advice, implements, or money (II. 276. Cf. Manu IX. 278).

Whoever falsifies scales, an edict, measures or coins, or does business with them so falsified should be made to pay the highest fine (II. 240. Cf. Manu IX. 232).

One who falsely practises as a physician must pay the first fine, if his deception be practised towards animals; the middle fine, if towards men; the highest fine, if towards any of the king's officers (II. 242. Cf. Manu IX. 284).

Any one who adulterates medicine, or oil, or salt, or perfumes, or corn, or sugar, or other commodities, should be made to pay sixteen Paṇas (II. 245. Cf. Manu VIII. 203, IX. 286, 291).

The highest fine should be imposed on those who, knowing the rise or fall in prices, combine to make a price of their own to the detriment of workmen and artisans (II. 249).

If a king has imposed any fine unjustly, he must give thirty times the

---

[1] In Manu the merit is said to be transferred to dogs, see p. 291.

amount to Brāhmans after having made an offering to Varuṇa (II. 307. Cf. Manu IX. 244).

III. The third Book gives various rules for *Prāyaś-ćitta*, 'penance, expiation, and purification.' Many of the laws are like those of Manu. It will suffice to note a few examples which have reference to funeral ceremonies:

A child under two years old must be buried, and no offering of water should be made to him. (The corpse of) any other deceased person should be accompanied by (a procession of) relations to the burning-place (*ā-śmaśānāt*, III. 1. See p. 204. Cf. Manu V. 68, 69, 103).

It is then to be burnt with common fire (*laukikāgninā*) while they repeat the hymn to Yama (*yama-sūktam*) and the sacred chant (*gāthām*, III. 2).

It is usual (for the relatives) to pour out a libation of water once (to the deceased), uttering his name and family, (and then) remaining silent (see p. 207).

But religious students and outcastes are not allowed to offer the oblations of water (III. 5. Cf. Manu V. 88).

The funeral oblation is not allowed for heretics (*pāshaṇḍin*), persons without any fixed station (*an-āśritāḥ*), thieves, women who have killed their husbands, or who have lived an independent life (*kāma-gāḥ*), or have been drunkards, or have committed suicide (*ātma-tyāginyaḥ*, III. 6. Cf. Manu V. 89, 90).

When the relatives have poured out water, have completed their ablutions, and have seated themselves on a spot covered with soft grass, (the elder ones) may repeat to the others some verses from the ancient Itihāsas, such as the following (III. 7):

> Does it not argue folly to expect
> Stability in man, who is as transient
> As a mere bubble and fragile as a stalk?
> Why should we utter wailings if a frame,
> Composed of five material elements,
> Is decomposed by force of its own acts,
> And once again resolved into its parts?
> The earth, the ocean, and the gods themselves
> Must perish, how should not the world
> Of mortals, light as froth, obey the law
> Of universal death and perish too (III. 8–11)?

After hearing verses of this kind they should return home, the younger ones leading the way, stopping solemnly outside the door of the house to chew leaves of the Nimb tree (*Nimba-patrāṇi*, III. 12).

After they have rinsed out their mouths and touched fire, water, cow-dung, white mustard-seed, and placed their feet on a stone, they should enter the house slowly (III. 13. Cf. the account of the funeral procession in the Gṛihya-sūtras, pp. 205–207).

Impurity caused by the ceremonies connected with touching a corpse (*śāvam āśauċam*) lasts for either three nights or ten nights (III. 18. Cf. Manu V. 59, 64).

Those who preserve this Law-book diligently in their memories shall obtain reputation in this world and shall go to heaven (III. 330).

He who repeats only three verses out of this Law-book at a S'rāddha causes perpetual satisfaction to his departed ancestors; of this there is no doubt. A Brāhman may obtain merit, a Kshatriya may become victorious, and a Vaiśya may become rich in corn and money by preserving this book in his memory (III. 332, 333).

## *The eighteen principal Codes posterior to Manu and Yājñavalkya.*

A list of eighteen of the most important of these has been given at p. 211. They are all extant in some form or other, as described by Colebrooke[1]. Little or nothing is known about the authorship of any one of them. They have arisen from the necessity of framing new laws or modifying old ones to suit particular localities and particular periods. In order to invest them with antiquity and authority, they are all eighteen ascribed, like the Codes of Manu and Yājñavalkya, to various mythical inspired sages. The fact is, that although Manu and Yājñavalkya still form the basis of Hindū jurisprudence, many of their laws are regarded by more recent Hindū legislators as only intended for the first three ages of the world, and therefore as having no force, or superseded by

[1] See Professor E. B. Cowell's edition of his Essays, vol. i. pp. 468–470. The works or their abridgments, ascribed to these eighteen inspired law-givers, have been all printed at Calcutta.

others, in the present fourth and more degenerate Kali-yuga (see note 2, p. 187). Thus the author of the work ascribed to Nārada[1] says:

Marriage with the widow of a deceased brother, the slaughter of cattle in entertaining guests, flesh-meat at funeral obsequies, and the entrance into the third order (or that of a Vānaprastha, 'hermit') are forbidden in the fourth age.

The following acts, allowed under certain circumstances by ancient law, are also forbidden in the fourth age:

Drinking any spirituous liquor, even at a religious ceremony[2]; the gift of a young married woman to another bridegroom if her husband should die while she is still a virgin; the marriage of twice-born men with women not of the same class; any intercourse with a twice-born man who has passed the sea in a ship; the slaughter of a bull at a sacrifice, &c.

And the author of Parāśara's Code[3] affirms:

The laws of various ages are different. Manu's Law-book belongs to the Kṛita age, Gautama's to the Tretā, that of S'an-kha and Likhita to the Dvāpara, and Parāśara's Code to the Kali age.

Many modern lawyers, however, regard the whole of Smṛiti, beginning with Manu, as one, and assert that the inconsistencies and contradictions it contains are all capable of explanation.

I here annex a few particulars relative to the eighteen principal Codes posterior to Manu and Yājñavalkya:

1. That attributed to *Atri*, one of Manu's ten Prajāpatis (I. 35), is in verse, and written in a perspicuous style. 2. That of *Vishṇu* is also in verse, and is regarded as an excellent treatise, an abridgment of which is also extant. 3. That of *Hārīta*, on the contrary, is in prose, but has been abridged in a metrical form. 4. That of *Uśanas* or S'ukra is in verse, and an abridgment is extant. 5. A short treatise of about seventy verses is ascribed to *An-giras*, one of Manu's Prajāpatis and Maharshis (I. 35). 6. A tract consisting of one hundred verses, commented on by

---

[1] Quoted by Sir W. Jones, vol. viii. p. 153.

[2] As, for example, the Sautrāmaṇī.

[3] Quoted by Professor Stenzler in his preface to Yājñavalkya.

Kullūka-bhaṭṭa, is mythically attributed to *Yama* (brother of Manu Vaivasvata), ruler of the world of spirits. 7. That of *Āpastamba* is in prose, but an abridgment in verse also exists. 8. *Saṃvarta's* Code has also a metrical abridgment. 9. *Kātyāyana's* law-treatise is full and perspicuous. 10. *Vṛihaspati's* has been abridged, and it is doubtful whether we possess the abridgment or the Code itself. 11. *Parāśara's* treatise is regarded by some as the highest authority for the Kali or fourth age of the world. It has been commented on by Mādhavāćārya. 12. A law-treatise is ascribed to the celebrated *Vyāsa*, son of Parāśara. 13, 14. Two separate tracts in verse by *Śaṅkha* and *Likhita* exist, but their joint treatise in prose is the one usually cited by Kullūka and others. It is supposed to be adapted to the Dvāpara age. 15. A Code in verse of no special interest is attributed to *Daksha*, one of Manu's ten Prajāpatis (I. 35). 16. A prose treatise written in a clear style bears the name of *Gautama*. It is held to have been written for the Tretā age. 17. Śātātapa's Code is chiefly on penance and expiation. There is an abridgment of it in verse. 18. The treatise attributed to Vaśishṭha, another of Manu's Prajāpatis (I. 35), is a mixture of prose and verse.

Of other codes ascribed to various mythical lawgivers in the Padma-purāṇa &c. it will be sufficient to mention those of Marīći, Pulastya, Bhṛigu, Nārada (Manu I. 35), Kaśyapa, Viśvāmitra, Gārgya, Baudhāyana, Paiṭhīnasi, Sumantu, Lokākshi, Kuthumi or Kuṭhumi, and Dhaumya.

Besides, there are a vast number of legal treatises and commentaries based on ancient codes by modern lawyers, whose works are current and more or less esteemed as authorities in different parts of India. They form five schools, of which I here give a brief account.

### *The Five Schools of Hindū Law.*

These are the schools of—1. Bengal, 2. Benares, 3. Mithilā (North Behār and Tirhut), 4. Madras (*Drāviḍa*), and 5. Bombay (*Mahā-rāshṭra*)[1]. There are certain books

[1] I have here consulted Mr. Herbert Cowell's Tagore Law Lectures, copies of which have always been kindly given to me by the Senate of the Calcutta University.

regarded as special authorities in each of these principal schools.

1. In Bengal both Manu and Yājñavalkya are of course held in great reverence as original sources of law. We have already noted that the best commentary on Manu is one called Manv-artha-muktāvalī, by Kullūka-bhaṭṭa (see p. 221). There is also a commentary by Medhātithi (partially lost, and completed by another author); another by Govinda-rāja; another by Dharaṇī-dhara, Bhāguri, and others. To Yājñavalkya belong at least four other commentaries besides the Mitāksharā, viz. that of Aparārka (which is the oldest of all); of Śūla-pāṇi (called the Dīpa-kalikā); of Deva-bodha, and of Viśva-rūpa. Śūla-pāṇi is also the author of a work on penance and expiation. The Mitāksharā of Vijñāneśvara[1] is, however, the principal commentary on Yājñavalkya (as before noticed). It is much studied in Bengal, but the chief authority in the Bengal school is a well-known work, somewhat different in character and principles, called the Dāya-bhāga or 'treatise on inheritance,' ascribed to Jīmūta-vāhana[2], by some thought to have been a prince of the house of Silāra, who either composed this work himself or caused it to be compiled rather earlier than the beginning of the sixteenth century. It should be stated that both the Mitāksharā and Dāya-bhāga are developments of, rather than commentaries on, Manu and Yājña-valkya. Although they profess to be based on these ancient books, they sometimes modify the laws there propounded to suit a more advanced social system. In other

---

[1] Vijñāneśvara belonged to a sect of Sannyāsins founded by Śaṅkarā-ćārya, and his commentary may have been written as early as the ninth century of our era.

[2] Translated by Colebrooke. Jīmūta-vāhana's work seems to have been called Dharma-ratna, and only the chapter on inheritance is preserved.

cases they discuss doubtful points and supply omissions; while they, in their turn, have been commented on by succeeding lawyers, whose works introduce still further modifications on various important points[1], thus:

Three principal commentaries on the Mitāksharā are named, viz. the Subodhinī of Viśveśvara-bhaṭṭa (thought by Colebrooke to be as old as the fourteenth century); a later work by Bālam-bhaṭṭa; and a third (called the Pratītāksharā) by Nanda-paṇḍita (who was also the author of the work on adoption called Dattaka-mīmāṉsā and of the Vaijayantī (see next page). The commentaries on the Dāya-bhāga are numerous. Some of these (published under the patronage of Prasanna Kumār Thākur) are, that of S'rīkṛishṇa-tarkālan-kāra, which, with a treatise by the same author called Dāya-krama-san-graha, is highly esteemed in Bengal; that of S'rī-nāthāćārya-ćūḍāmaṇi; that of Aćyuta-ćakravartin; and that of Maheśvara. Before any of these ought to be placed the works of a celebrated Brāhman (who lived at the beginning of the sixteenth century), named Raghu-nandana, in about twenty-seven books, on rites and customs and the times of their observance. His treatises, intended to comment on and support Jīmūta-vāhana, are called Smṛiti-tattva, Tithi-tattva, &c., the former including the Vyavahāra-tattva and Dāya-tattva[2].

2. As regards the school of Benares and Middle India it should be noted that the Mitāksharā of Vijñāneśvara is acknowledged as an authority, and studied by the adherents of this school, as it is to a certain extent by all five schools. But in the Benares school certain popular commentaries on the Mitāksharā, such as the Vīra-mitrodaya of Mitra-miśra and the Vivāda-tāṇḍava of Kamalākara, have great weight.

3. In the Maithila school or that of Mithilā (North Behār and Tirhut), besides the Code of Yājñavalkya with the

---

[1] The certainty we feel as to the accuracy of the texts of all important Sanskṛit works is due to the practice of writing commentaries, which always quote the words of the original, and so prevent changes. Again, the accuracy and genuineness of the best commentaries is secured by other commentaries on them.

[2] Printed at Calcutta in 1828. Raghu-nandana is often called Smārta-bhaṭṭāćārya.

Mitāksharā, the Vivāda-ćintāmaṇi and Vyavahāra-ćintāmaṇi of Vāćaspati Miśra[1] are much studied; also the Vivāda-ratnākara of Ćaṇḍeśvara (who lived about 1314) and the Vivāda-ćandra, composed by a learned female named Lakhimā-devī, who is said to have set the name of her kinsman, Misarū-miśra, to her own works.

4. In the Drāviḍian or South-Indian school, besides the Mitāksharā, as before, there is the Smṛiti-ćandrikā and Dattaka-ćandrikā of Devana-bhaṭṭa; Mādhavāćārya's commentary on Parāśara's Code (called Parāśara-smriti-vyākhyā); and Nanda-paṇḍita's commentary on Vishṇu's Code (called Vaijayantī), and on Parāśara's Code, and his treatise on the law of adoption called Dattaka-ćandrikā.

5. In the Western school (of Bombay and Mahā-rāshṭra), besides the Mitāksharā, certain treatises by Nīlakaṇṭha-bhaṭṭa, particularly one called Vyavahāra-mayūkha[2], have the most weight.

---

[1] Often called Miśra. His work has been translated by Prasanna Kumār Thākur, and printed at Calcutta in 1863. A copy was kindly sent to me by the translator.

[2] A translation of this by Mr. H. Borrodaile of the Bombay Civil Service was published at Surat at the Mission Press in 1827.

# LECTURE XII.

## IV. *The Itihāsas or Epic Poems—The Rāmāyaṇa*[1].

IN India, literature, like the whole face of nature, is on a gigantic scale. Poetry, born amid the majestic scenery of the Himālayas, and fostered in a climate which inflamed the imaginative powers, developed itself with Oriental luxuriance, if not always with true sublimity. Although the Hindūs, like the Greeks, have only two great epic poems[2]—the Rāmāyaṇa and Mahā-bhārata—yet to compare these vast compositions with the Iliad and the Odyssey, is to compare the Indus and the Ganges, rising in the snows of the world's most colossal ranges, swollen by numerous tributaries, spreading into vast shallows or branching into deep divergent channels, with the streams of Attica or the mountain-torrents of Thessaly. There is, in fact, an immensity of bulk about this, as about every other department of Sanskṛit literature, which to a European mind, accustomed to a more limited horizon, is absolutely bewildering.

---

[1] A portion of the matter of this Lecture and of that on the Mahā-bhārata was delivered by me as a public Lecture before the University of Oxford, on the 9th of May, 1862, and was afterwards published in a little work called 'Indian Epic Poetry,' which is now out of print.

[2] I am here speaking of that form of epic poetry which may be called natural and spontaneous as distinguished from artificial. Whether the Indian Epics (Itihāsas) or even the Iliad can be strictly said to answer Aristotle's definition of Epos, is another question. Artificial epic poems (Kāvyas) are not wanting in later Sanskṛit, and specimens will be given in a subsequent Lecture.

Nevertheless, a sketch, however imperfect, of the two Indian Epics can scarcely fail to interest Occidental scholars; for all true poetry, whether European or Asiatic, must have features of resemblance; and no poems could have achieved celebrity in the East as these have done, had they not addressed themselves to feelings and affections common to human nature, and belonging alike to Englishmen and Hindūs.

I propose, therefore, in the next three Lectures, to give a brief general idea of the character and contents of the Rāmāyaṇa and Mahā-bhārata[1], comparing them in some important particulars with each other, and pointing out the most obvious features of similarity or difference, which must strike every classical scholar who contrasts them with the Iliad and the Odyssey.

It is, of course, a principal characteristic of epic poetry, as distinguished from lyrical, that it should concern itself more with external action than internal feelings. It is this which makes Epos the natural expression of early national life. When centuries of trial have turned the mind of nations inwards, and men begin to speculate, to reason, to elaborate language and cultivate science, there may be no lack of refined poetry, but the spontaneous production of epic song is, at that stage of national existence, as impossible as for an octogenarian to delight in the giants and giant-killers of his childhood. The Rāmāyaṇa and Mahā-bhārata then, as reflecting the Hindū character in ancient times, may be expected to abound in stirring incidents of exaggerated heroic action.

Songs in celebration of great heroes were probably current in India quite as early as the Homeric poems in

---

[1] A more complete analysis of the Rāmāyaṇa and Mahā-bhārata was given by me at the end of the little work called 'Indian Epic Poetry,' and will probably be reprinted with additions hereafter.

Greece. No mention, indeed, is made of Rāma, Arjuna, and Yudhi-shṭhira in the hymns of the Ṛig-veda, but the deeds of Indra and other gods and heroes, who were supposed to protect the more civilized Āryas from the barbarous An-āryas, are there narrated and lauded, and it is in the songs composed in their praise that we may trace the foreshadowings of Indian epic poetry. Again, we know that Itihāsas, or legendary narratives, were recited orally at the period when the Gṛihya Sūtras and Manu were composed (see last line of p. 203; note, p. 215; and p. 256). Such narratives doubtless recounted the adventures of the popular heroes of the period, with all the warmth of colouring natural to writers whose imaginations were stimulated by an Eastern climate and environments; but it is scarcely credible that they could have achieved much popularity had they not rested on a basis of historical truth.

It is certainly likely that at some early date, not long after the first settlement of the Āryan races in the country of the five rivers, rival tribes of immigrants, called Kurus, advancing from that region towards the plains of Hindūstān, contended for supremacy. It is, moreover, probable that soon after their final occupation of the Gangetic districts, a body of invaders headed by a bold leader, and aided by the warlike but uncivilized hill-tribes, forced their way southwards into the peninsula of India as far as Ceylon. The heroic exploits of the chieftains in both cases would naturally become the theme of epic poetry, and the wild Aborigines of the Vindhya and neighbouring hills would be poetically converted into monkeys[1], while

---

[1] Strabo (XV. 29) relates that on a particular occasion a large number of monkeys came out of a wood and stood opposite the Macedonian troops, who seeing them apparently stationed in military array, mistook them for a real army and prepared to attack them as enemies.

the powerful pre-Āryan races of the south would be represented as many-headed ogres and blood-thirsty demons[1].

[1] We must be careful not to confound the great Drāviḍian races occupying the Madras Presidency and speaking Tamil, Telugu, Kanarese, and Malayālam, with the uncivilized aboriginal tribes found on the hills and in the jungles of India. The Drāviḍian races (probably symbolized by the Rāvaṇas and Vibhīshaṇas of epic poetry) were the precursors of the Sanskṛit-speaking Āryans, and possibly had their origin in the same districts of Central Asia, whence they immigrated by the same mountain-passes into the Pañjāb and Northern India. They may have partially amalgamated with the advancing Āryans, but were mostly driven southwards. There they attained a considerable independent civilization. Their languages, although eventually more or less intermingled with Sanskṛit words, are agglutinating (commonly called Turanian) in structure, and possess an extensive and important literature of their own. On the other hand, the hill-tribes and others (such as were symbolized by the monkey-armies of Hanumat)—the Goṇḍs of Central India, the Bhīls of the hills to the west of the Goṇḍs, the Khoṇḍs or Kus of the eastern districts of Goṇḍvāna and the ranges south of Orissa, the Santhāls and Kols of the hills to the west of Bengal, the Khāsias and Gāros of the eastern border—are the present representatives of numerous wild Tartar tribes who swarmed into India at various epochs, some of them probably coming from Chinese Tartary and Tibet, and taking the course of the Brahma-putra into Bengal. These speak an infinite number of different dialects and are almost all mutually unintelligible. If the term Turanian is to embrace races so widely separated by language and customs as the Drāviḍians and various hill-tribes of India, the sooner it is expelled from the vocabulary of philologists and ethnologists the better. At any rate, there must be two great classes of Turanian languages, the North and the South; the former comprising the three sisters Tungusic (or Mantchu), Mongol, and Turkish, besides Samoyedic and Finnish, while the latter takes in Tibetan, Siamese, Burmese, and the Drāviḍian languages; the monosyllabic Chinese standing, as it were, between the two. Perhaps the dialects of the Himālayan tribes have, of all hill-dialects, the best title to be ranked among the South Turanian class. Dr. Caldwell, in his valuable Comparative Grammar of the South-Indian Languages, has discussed the affiliation of the Drāviḍian family with great ability. He considers that the Drāviḍians were the first inhabitants of India, and that they were driven southwards by other invaders, who were afterwards subdued by the Āryans. The rude dialects

These races, who are called *An-ārya*, 'ignoble,' in opposition to *Ārya*, 'noble,' had been gradually driven southwards or towards the hills by the Āryan settlers. They probably made great resistance in the North at the time the Ṛig-veda was composed. They are there called Dasyus, Yātudhānas, &c., and described as monstrous in form, godless, inhuman, haters of Brāhmans, disturbers of sacred rites, eaters of human and horse flesh (Ṛig-veda X. 87, 16; Muir's Texts II. 435). In the epic poems they are generally called Rākshasas or evil demons, the relentless enemies of gods and good men and of all sacred rites[1].

---

of the more southern hill-tribes are partially connected with the Drāviḍian, especially the Tuḍa, Koṭa (two dialects of the Nīl-giri hills), Goṇḍ, and Khoṇḍ (Ku). The Ramūsies and most of the Korawars speak a patois of Telugu. The Male-arasars ('hill-kings') of the Southern Ghāts speak partly corrupt Malayālam and corrupt Tamil. The Lāmbādies, or gipsies, speak a dialect of Hindūstānī. Among the barbarous tribes of the South are included the Vedārs of the forests of Ceylon.

[1] In one place (Rāmāyaṇa III. i. 15) they are described as black, with woolly hair and thick lips. The following is from III. i. 22, &c.: 'Men-devouring Rākshasas of various shapes and wild-beasts dwell in this vast forest. They harass the devotees in the settlements. These shapeless and ill-looking monsters testify their abominable character by various cruel and terrific displays of it. These base-born wretches (*an-ārya*) perpetrate the greatest outrages. Changing their shapes and hiding in the thickets they delight in terrifying devotees. They cast away the sacrificial ladles and vessels (*śrug-bhāṇḍam*), pollute the cooked oblations, and defile the offerings with blood. They utter frightful sounds in the ears of the faithful.' Virādha, a Rākshasa, is said (Rāmāyaṇa III. vii. 5; Muir II. 427) to be 'like a mountain-peak, with long legs, a huge body, a crooked nose, hideous eyes, a long face, pendent belly, &c., like Death with an open mouth.' The Nishādas of the Purāṇas, though described as dwarfish, have similar features, and are no doubt intended for the same race. In the same way, in describing races unknown to the Greeks, such as the Cyclopes, Laestrygones, Centauri, &c., Homer and other Grecian writers are given to exaggeration, and relate the most absurd fables.

It is to the subjugation of these non-Āryan races by heroic Āryan leaders who were Kshatriyas, as well as to the rivalry between different tribes of the settlers themselves, that we owe the circumstances out of which the two great Epics arose. Whether the celebrated Āryan warriors of the Rāmāyaṇa and Mahā-bhārata were identical with those of the Itihāsas of which mention is made in the Gṛihya Sūtras and in Manu (III. 232) cannot be proved; but this much is clear, that the exploits of the three Rāmas, Arjuna, &c., became, soon after Manu's time, the theme of song, and that these heroes were in the first instance represented as merely men of great strength and prowess, whose powers, however extraordinary, were not more than human. The oral descriptions of their deeds and adventures by public reciters formed the original basis of the two great Epics, and were naturally the peculiar property of the Kshatriya and conquering class. Probably these narratives were in the first instance delivered in prose, which became gradually interspersed with the simplest forms of metre, such as that called Anushṭubh or Śloka[1].

It is easy indeed for the most cursory reader of the Rāmāyaṇa and Mahā-bhārata to trace a substratum or basis (*mūla*) of simple heroic narration underlying the mass of more recent accretions. But to what date is this first frame-work of the poems to be referred? And again—When occurred that first process of brāhmanizing which obscured and transformed its original character? And lastly—When was the structure completed and the

[1] The oldest part of the Mahā-bhārata has a section entirely in prose (see note 1, p. 372). The invention of the S'loka is attributed to Vālmīki, the reputed author of the Rāmāyaṇa, with the object doubtless of establishing his claims to be regarded as one of the earliest and most ancient of Indian poets. This metre is found in the Veda.

whole work moulded into a form similar to that we now possess?

With regard to the first of these questions, I have now to submit five reasons in support of the view that the earliest or pre-brāhmanical composition of both Epics took place at a period not later than the fifth century B.C., as follow:

1. The Rāmāyaṇa records no case of Satī. In the Mahā-bhārata, Mādrī, wife of Pāṇḍu, is made to immolate herself with her husband[1], and the four wives of Vasu-deva and some of Kṛishṇa's wives do the same[2]; but it is remarkable that none of the numerous widows of the slain heroes are represented as burning themselves in the same manner. This shows that the practice of Satī was beginning to be introduced in the North-west of India near the Pañjāb (where we know it prevailed about 300 years B.C.), but that it had not at the time of the earliest composition of the Rāmāyaṇa reached the more eastern districts. But if one Epic records no Satī, and the other only rare cases—notwithstanding the numerous opportunities for referring to the practice afforded by the circumstances of the plot—it follows that we ought to place the laying down of the first lines of both compositions before the third century B.C., when we know from Megasthenes that it prevailed generally even as far east as Magadha.

2. The first construction, or, so to speak, 'first casting' of the stories of Rāma and of the Pāṇḍavas as poems with definite plots, seems to have been pre-buddhistic quite as clearly as it was pre-brāhmanical—by which I mean, that it took place anterior to the actual establishment of Buddhism as a rival system. Only one direct mention of Buddha and Buddhism occurs in the Rāmāyaṇa, and the verses in which it occurs (II. cviii. 30–38), and in which Buddha is compared to a thief, are admitted to be an interpolation and not part of the original poem. Nor can it be proved that any such direct reference occurs in the original Mahā-bhārata. Nevertheless, there are numerous allusions (not bearing the stamp of later additions) in both Epics, especially the latter, to that development of rationalistic inquiry and Buddhistic scepticism, which we know commenced about 500 years B.C.[3]

---

[1] Ādi-parvan 4896. See also 3030. [2] Mausala-parvan 194, 249.

[3] Note particularly the infidel doctrines expressed by the Brāhman Jāvāli (see p. 353), and Book I. 12. of the Bengālī recension of the Rāmāyaṇa, where S'ramaṇas, or Buddhist mendicants, are mentioned (see also p. 133).

3. It is evident from the Aśoka inscriptions that the language of the mass of the people in Hindūstān in the third century B.C. was not pure Sanskṛit. It consisted rather of a variety of provincial Sanskritic dialects, to which the general name of Prākṛit is applied. If, then, the first redaction of these popular poems had taken place as late as the third century, is it likely that some forms of Prākṛit would not have been introduced into the dialogues and allowed to remain there, as we find has been done in the dramas, the oldest of which—the Mṛiććhakaṭikā—can scarcely be much later than the second century B.C.? It is true that the language of the original story of both Epics, as traceable in the present texts, is generally simple Sanskṛit, and by no means elaborate or artificial; but this is just what might have been understood by the majority of the people about five centuries B.C., before the language of the people had become generally prakriticized.

4. When the story of the poems was first put together in a continuous form, it is clear that the Dekhan and more westerly and southerly regions of India had not been occupied by the Āryans. But we know from the Aśoka inscriptions that the empire of the kings of Magadha and Pālibothra in the third century radiated in all directions, as inscriptions are found in the Pañjāb, at Delhi, in Kuttack, and as far west as Gujarāt.

5. The Greek writer, Dion Chrysostomos, who was born about the middle of the first century, and was especially honoured by the emperor Trajan, mentions (Or. LIII. 555) that records existed in his time of epic poems, recited by the Hindūs, which had been copied or translated from Homer. These statements, as Professor Lassen has shown (Ind. Alt. III. 346), must have been taken from the accounts of Megasthenes, who lived at the court of Ćandra-gupta (see note p. 231). They indicate that poems resembling the Iliad were current in India at least as early as the third or fourth century B.C., though it by no means follows that the Hindū poets borrowed a single idea from Homer[1].

---

[1] The passage in Dion Chrysostomos is as follows: *Ὁπότε καὶ παρ' Ἰνδοῖς ᾄδεσθαι φασὶ τὴν Ὁμήρου ποίησιν, μεταβαλόντων αὐτὴν εἰς τὴν σφετέραν διάλεκτόν τε καὶ φωνήν* (Reiske's Edit. p. 253). There seems too great a disposition among European scholars to regard the Hindūs as destitute of all originality. I cannot but agree with Professor Lassen that Megasthenes was mistaken, though obviously the story of the great war between the rival tribes, and that of the carrying off of Sītā by a South-Indian chief, have, of course, points of resemblance to the Iliad, which may have suggested the idea of plagiarism. The sufferings of king Dhṛita-rāshṭra are like those of Priam, and the lamentations of the wives of the slain heroes after the

These points seem to merit consideration in fixing 500 B.C. as an approximate date for the first or pre-brāhmanical and pre-buddhistic versions of the two poems. The names of the authors of these original versions appear to have perished, unless it be held (which seems highly improbable) that the story of Rāma must be assigned to Vālmīki from its very first existence as a Kāvya.

We come next to the second stage of their construction. We have suggested the fifth century B.C. as the probable date of the rise of Brāhmanism, as depicted in Manu (see p. 215), and with it of Buddhistic scepticism. The ambitious Brāhmans who aimed at religious and intellectual supremacy, gradually saw the policy of converting the great national Epics, which they could not suppress, into instruments for moulding the popular mind in accordance with their own pattern. Possibly, too, they may have hoped to turn them into important engines for arresting the progress of Buddhistic rationalism. Accordingly, I conjecture that in the fourth century B.C. they commenced re-constructing and remodelling the two great Epics. They proceeded, in short, to brāhmanize what was before the property of the Kshatriya or warrior caste. This process was of course committed to poets who were Brāhmans, and was not completed all at once. Those songs which described too plainly the independence of the military caste, were modified, obscured by allegory, and rendered improbable by monstrous fable and mythological embellishments. Any circumstance which appeared opposed to the Brāhmanical system, was speciously ex-

battles between the Pāṇḍavas and Kauravas are like those of Hecuba and Andromache, while the martial deeds of Arjuna and Duryodhana resemble those of Achilles and Hector. According to Professor Weber the passage in Dion contains the earliest notice by other writers of the Indian epic poems. He is, moreover, of opinion that the Indian poets really took ideas from Homer.

plained away, glossed over, or mystified[1]. If unbelievers, like Jāvāli, were brought on the scene, it was only that their arguments might be refuted, and their characters reprobated (see p. 354). The great Kshatriya dynasties were made to trace back their origin to Brāhmanical sages (see p. 346). Kings were allowed to undertake nothing except under the direction of Brāhman ministers[2]; while the great heroes themselves were not really Kshatriyas, or even human beings, but emanations of the Deity.

In the case of the Rāmāyaṇa, the unity of the story was never broken by calling in the aid of more than one author, whose name was Vālmīki, and who must have completed the task single-handed. Hence it never lost its character of a Kāvya, or poem, with a clear and coherent plot. On the other hand, the brāhmanizing of the story of the great war between the Pāṇḍavas and Kauravas seems to have attracted a succession of poets, who interwove their own compositions into the original texture of the work, so that its individuality, and even the name of its first author, disappeared under the constant accession of new matter. Hence we must suppose, in the

---

[1] Thus when Daśaratha kills a boy while hunting (see p. 250), the dying youth is made to explain that, although a hermit's son, he is no Brāhman, thereby relieving the king from the guilt of Brāhmanicide, which, according to Manu, was unpardonable either in this world or the next (Manu VIII. 381, XII. 55). Again, the account of the victory of the Kshatriya Rāma-ćandra over the Brāhman Paraśu-rāma—the mythical champion of the sacerdotal caste—is surrounded with a haze of mysticism (see p. 331, note 2; p. 349); while the episode which relates at full Viśvāmitra's quarrel with the great saint Vaśishṭha, and the success of the former, though a Kshatriya, in elevating himself to a Brāhman's rank, introduces the wildest hyperbole, with the manifest object of investing the position of a Brāhman with unapproachable grandeur, and deterring others from attempts in the same direction (see p. 363).

[2] King Daśaratha in the Rāmāyaṇa is described as surrounded by Brāhman ministers (see p. 342).

case of the Mahā-bhārata, more than one Brāhmanical redaction and amplification, which need not be assumed for the completion of the Rāmāyaṇa. Moreover, the great mass of ever-increasing materials under which the original story of the Pāṇḍavas became almost lost to view, and under which the title to the name Kāvya merged in that of a rambling Itihāsa, had to be adjusted and arranged by an imaginary compiler, called Vyāsa.

The first orderly completion, then, of the two poems in their brāhmanized form, may have taken place, I think, in the case of the Rāmāyaṇa about the beginning of the third century B.C., and in the case of the Mahā-bhārata (the original story of which is possibly more ancient than that of the Rāmāyaṇa) still later,—perhaps as late as the second century B.C. The posteriority of the brāhmanized Mahā-bhārata may be supported by the more frequent allusions it contains to the progress of Buddhistic opinions, and to intercourse with the Yavanas or Greeks, who had no considerable dealings with the Hindūs till two or three centuries after Alexander's invasion[1].

---

[1] A candid study of Professor Weber's writings, and especially of the reproduction of his views lately put forth in the 'Indian Antiquary,' has led me to modify to a certain extent the statements in my Lecture on 'Indian Epic Poetry,' delivered May 9, 1862; but I cannot agree in thinking that the work of Vālmīki is to be referred to as late a date as the beginning of the Christian era. Nor can I concur in the opinion that the Rāmāyaṇa is later than, and to a certain extent a copy of the Buddhist story of Rāma, called Daśaratha-jātaka, in which Rāma is represented as the brother of Sītā, and in which there are certain verses almost identical with verses in the present text of the Rāmāyaṇa. Nor do I think that the great Indian Epic has been developed out of germs furnished by this or any other Buddhistic legends. Still less can I give in my adhesion to the theory that the Hindū Epics took ideas from the Homeric poems; or to the suggestion of Mr. Talboys Wheeler, that the story of the Rāmāyaṇa was invented to give expression to the hostile feeling and contention between the Brāhmans and Buddhists of Ceylon, alleged to be represented by the Rākshasas.

It is, however, necessary to refer the final construction of both poems in their present form to a third and still later epoch, and even to assign portions of them to the early centuries of our own era, if we are to accept as integral parts of the two Epics such a supplement to the Rāmāyaṇa as the Uttara-kāṇḍa, and such additions to the Mahā-bhārata as the Bhagavad-gītā and Hari-vaṉśa, as well as those later episodes which identify Rāma and Kṛishṇa with the Supreme Being. And here again in this final construction of both poems, we must bear in mind, that the deification of Rāma represents an earlier stage of Vishṇu-worship than that of Kṛishṇa; and that the Rāmāyaṇa, as now presented to us, contains far fewer recent additions than the Mahā-bhārata.

My reasons, therefore, for placing the first Brāhmanical construction of the two Indian Epics in the third and second century B.C. respectively, and for commencing an account of epic poetry with the story of Rāma, rather than with that of Pāṇḍavas, will be clear. It must be remembered, however, that the priority of one poem over the other cannot be made to rest on any certain chronological basis. Indeed, the Mahā-bhārata describes a conflict between rude colonists in a district nearer to the earliest settlements of the Āryans, while the Rāmāyaṇa is concerned with a more established kingdom (Kośala), and a more civilized and luxurious capital city (Ayodhyā).

Before commencing our summary of either story it will be desirable to note more particularly when and how the doctrine of divine incarnation was imported into both poems, imparting to them that religious and sacred character which they have ever since retained, and which is a distinguishing feature in comparing them with the epic poetry of other nations. We know from the statements of Megasthenes, preserved in Strabo and Diodorus, that the worship of Vishṇu in his heroic incarnations prevailed in Hindūstān about 300 years before Christ (see note, p. 281). The deification of great men probably began with the desire of the Brāhmans to incorporate the most eminent Kshatriya heroes into their system. It proceeded, however, from necessity rather than from any wish to do honour to the warrior caste. The Buddhistic movement in India had broken down the Brāhmanical monopoly and introduced a rival principle. Some counteracting and equally popular expansion of religious creed seemed essential to the very existence of Brāhmanism, and it became absolutely necessary to present the people with deities of their own as a counter-attraction to Buddhism. Hence the previously human heroes Rāma and Kṛishṇa were exalted by the Brāhmans to divine rank, and even Buddha himself was, in the end, adopted into their system and represented as one of the ten incarnations of the god Vishṇu[1].

But the idea of divine incarnation had taken possession of the Hindū mind still earlier. It is probable that in that primeval country, where the ancestors of Greeks and Hindūs had their common home, men satisfied their first religious instincts by idealizing and worshipping, under no defined form and without precise ritual, the principal forces and energies of nature—the air, the rain, the wind, the storm, the fire, the sun—the elements on which, as an agricultural and pastoral race, their welfare depended. This was the earliest religion of nature which the Āryan family carried with them when they first left their home, and which they cherished in their wanderings; and in this we may trace the germ of their subsequent religious

[1] Heroism, undaunted bravery, and personal strength will always find worshippers in India. It is recorded that a number of Pañjābī Hindūs commenced worshipping the late John Nicholson, one of the bravest and noblest of men, under the name Nikkil Seyn. He endeavoured to put a stop to the absurdity, but they persisted in their worship notwithstanding.

systems. When they had settled down in new resting-places, their religious cravings naturally found utterance in prayers, hymns, and a simple form of ritual. Religion, or a sense of dependence on a higher Power, and a desire to realize his presence, grew with their growth and strengthened with their strength. But in all ages and countries the religion of the mass of mankind rapidly assumes an anthropomorphic character. A richly peopled mythology arose in India and Greece as naturally as poetry itself. The one was the offspring of the other, and was in fact the poetical expression of those high aspirations which marked the Āryan character. Soon the Hindū, like the Greek, unguided by direct revelation, personified and deified not only the powers of external nature, but all the internal feelings, passions, moral and intellectual qualities and faculties of the mind. Soon he began to regard every grand and useful object as a visible manifestation of the supreme Intelligence presiding over the universe, and every departed hero or benefactor as a mere reflection of the same all-wise and omnipresent Ruler. Hence, to give expression to the varied attributes and functions of this great Being, thus visibly manifested to the world, both Hindū and Greek peopled their pantheons with numerous divine and semi-divine creations, clothing them with male and female forms, and inventing in connexion with them various fanciful and often monstrous myths, fables, and allegories, which the undiscriminating multitude accepted as realities, without at all understanding the ideas they symbolized. In India we are able to trace back the development of these anthropomorphic ideas to their source in the Ṛig-veda, and thence follow them step by step through Manu, the epic poems, and Purāṇas. In the Ṛig-veda a god Vishṇu is often named as a manifestation of the Solar energy, or rather as a form of the Sun; and the point which distinguishes him from the others is his striding over the heavens in three paces, supposed to symbolize the three stages of the Sun's daily course in his rising, culminating, and setting (see note, p. 331). Subsequently he takes a foremost place among the twelve Ādityas, or twelve distinct forms of the Sun in the twelve months of the year. In the Brāhmaṇas he is identified with sacrifice (*Yajña*), and once described as a dwarf (*Vāmana;* Śatapatha-brāhmaṇa XIV. 1, 1, 6, I. 2, 5, 5). In Manu, Brahman, the universal Soul, is represented as evolving his essence in the form of Brahmā, the Creator of all things, and various other visible manifestations of the Deity are recognized, as in the Veda. In Book XII. 121, Vishṇu and Hara (= Śiva) are mentioned as present in the human body, the former imparting movement to its muscles, the latter bestowing strength.

In all this, however, there was not enough to satisfy the cravings of the human heart for a religion of faith in a personal god—a god sympathizing with humanity, and even with the lower forms of animal life, loving all his creatures, interested in their affairs, and ever at hand to assist them in their difficulties. Nor, on the other hand, was there sufficient to meet the demands of other constituent parts of man's complex nature for a religion of activity and good works; of austerity and subjugation of the passions; of contemplation and higher spiritual knowledge. Soon, therefore, the great Spirit of the universe began to be viewed still more anthropomorphically, through the medium of man's increasing subjectivity, as a Being who not only created man but condescended to human sympathies, and placed himself in the closest connexion with all his creatures, whether gods, men, or animals.

But first arose the inquiry why and how this great Being willed to create at all? To account for this it was conceived that when the universal and infinite Being

Brahma (*nom. case of the neut. Brahman*)—the only really existing entity, wholly without form and unbound and unaffected by the three Guṇas or by qualities of any kind (pp. 95, 116)—wished to create for his own entertainment the phenomena of the universe, he assumed the quality of activity (*rajas*) and became a male person as Brahmā (*nom. case masc.*) the Creator. Next, in the progress of still further self-evolution, he willed to invest himself with the second quality of goodness (*sattva*) as Vishṇu the Preserver, and with the third quality of darkness (*tamas*[1]) as Śiva the Destroyer. This development of the doctrine of triple manifestation (*tri-mūrti*), which appears first in the brāhmanized version of the Indian Epics, had already been adumbrated in the Veda in the triple form of fire (see p. 18), and in the triad of gods, Agni, Sūrya, and Indra (see note, p. 19); and in other ways[2].

In fact the Veda, rather than Manu, was the source of the later incarnations (see notes, pp. 329–331). It was the Vedic Vishṇu (connected with Sūrya, 'the Sun') who became Vishṇu the world-preserver, while Rudra (connected with Indra and the Maruts), the god of tempests, became the world-dissolver Śiva. Under the latter form, the Supreme Being is supposed to pass from the operation of creation and preservation to that of destruction, these three separate acts being assigned to separate deities who are themselves finite, and obey the universal law of dissolution at the end of a Kalpa (see note, p. 333), when they again become merged in simple Soul (*kevalātman*). But as

[1] In the Kumāra-sambhava II. 4, we have the following: *Namas trimūrtaye tubhyam prāk-sṛishṭeḥ kevalātmane Guṇa-traya-vibhāgāya paścād bhedam upeyushe*, 'Hail to thee of triple form, who before creation wast simple Soul, and afterwards underwent partition for the distribution of the three Guṇas.'

[2] The thirty-three gods (3 multiplied by 11) of the Ṛig-veda (*tribhir ekādaśair devebhir yātam*, I. 34, 11, I. 45, 2) point to the same idea of triple manifestation.

it was essential that even the god of dissolution should connect himself with humanity, and as, according to a fundamental dogma of Hindūism, all death leads to new life, all destruction to reproduction, it was natural that the latter operation should be chosen as the link of connexion, rather than the former. His function of destroyer is, therefore, interchanged with that of creator (note 2, p. 326); he himself is called Śiva, 'the Auspicious,' and his character is oftener typified by the reproductive Lin·ga (without necessary implication of sensual ideas) than by any symbol of destruction. Under this image, in fact, he is generally worshipped in India[1]. Nevertheless, he is also represented in human form, living in the Himālaya mountains along with his wife Pārvatī[2], sometimes in the act of trampling on and destroying demons, wearing round his black neck (*nīla-kaṇṭha*) a serpent and a necklace of skulls, and furnished with a whole apparatus of external emblems (such as a white bull on which he rides, a crescent, a trident[3], tiger's skin, elephant's skin, rattle,

[1] Twelve celebrated Lin·gas were set up, about the tenth century, in twelve great shrines, in twelve chief cities of India, of which Somnath was one. The representation of the generative organ is not offensive to delicacy even when surrounded by the Yoni, or female symbol. Quite enough, however, is implied to account for the degeneration of Śiva-worship in modern times, as expressed in the works called Tantras and in the practices of the Śāktas. The representation of Śiva as Ardha-nārī, half male, half female, symbolizes the unity of the generative principle. Some think the god Śiva with the Lin·ga (Phallus) was adopted by the Āryans from the aborigines. The word Śiva means 'auspicious,' and being first applied euphemistically to the god of tempests (Rudra) afterwards passed into the name of the god of destruction.

[2] The *śakti* or active energy of a deity is personified as his wife, and those who worship the female principle are called Śāktas. Pārvatī, daughter of the mountain, and worshipped under the name Durgā in Bengal, is the chief object of the adoration of Śāktas and Tāntrikas.

[3] This three-pronged symbol may denote creation, destruction, and regeneration. He has also three eyes (one of which is in his forehead),

noose, &c.), the exaggeration of which imparts a childish and grotesque character to Hindū symbolism when regarded from a European point of view. Again, Mahā-deva, or the great deity Śiva, is sometimes connected with humanity in one other personification very different from that just noted, viz. that of an austere naked ascetic, with matted hair[1] (*Dig-ambara, Dhūrjaṭi*), living in a forest apart from his consort, abiding in one spot fixed and immovable (*Sthāṇu*)—teaching men by his own example, first, the power to be acquired by penance (*tapas*), mortification of the body[2], and suppression of the passions; and, secondly, the great virtue of abstract meditation (*samādhi*), as leading to the loftiest spiritual knowledge (*jñāna*) and ultimately to union (*yoga*) or actual identification with the great Spirit of the universe (*Paramātman*)[3].

---

in allusion to either the three Vedas or time past, present, and future (whence he is called *Try-ambaka*), and five faces (whence his name *Pañćānana*); the crescent moon also symbolizing his power over the measurement of time. He is sometimes said to manifest himself under eight forms—ether, air, fire, water, earth, sun, moon, the sacrificing priest (whence his name *Ashṭa-mūrti*). His black throat was caused by the deadly poison churned out of the ocean, which would have destroyed the universe had he not swallowed it.

[1] The hair is so worn by S'iva-worshipping Yogīs (see p. 104).

[2] In Mahā-bhārata, Sauptika-parvan 769, Brahmā, the Creator, is represented as calling on S'iva to create living creatures; and the latter, to qualify himself for the task, undergoes a severe penance under water.

[3] In the character of 'lord of abstract meditation,' S'iva is called *Yogeśa, Yogin*. Indeed, in some of the Purāṇas the origin of the Yoga (see p. 104) is ascribed to S'iva. In Book I. 55 and III. 45–50 of the Kumāra-sambhava, and in the opening invocation or Nāndī of the Mṛićchakaṭikā, there is a description of S'iva's posture and whole appearance while engaged in profound meditation. He is seated on his hams in the posture called *paryanka-bandha* (p. 103, note 2), with his breath suppressed and his vision fixed on his nose. While in this situation the god of love attempted to inspire him with affection for Pārvatī, daughter of Himālaya, in order that a son might be born to S'iva for the destruction of the Daitya Tāraka, who had extorted, by his penances, so many

These three manifestations of Brahmā, Vishṇu, and Śiva, whose functions are sometimes interchanged[1], exhibit the three sides of Hindūism as developed in the epic poems, and still more unfolded in the subsequent Purāṇas. The first is the religion of activity and works, the second that of faith and love, the third that of austerity, contemplation, and spiritual knowledge. This last is regarded as the highest, because it aims at entire cessation of action and total effacement of all personal entity and identity by absorption into simple Soul.

In medieval times bitter rivalries and disputes sprung up between the upholders of these three doctrines expressed by the worship of Brahmā, Vishṇu, and Śiva[2]

---

boons from Brahmā, that the whole universe had become subject to him. S'iva, indignant at the interruption of his austerities, reduced Kāma (Love) to ashes by a flash from his eye. Pārvatī then herself followed S'iva's example, and commenced a course of penance, whereby she conciliated S'iva and became his wife. A son, Kārttikeya, 'god of war,' was then born, who killed Tāraka. This is the subject of the Kumāra-sambhava. The use of ashes rubbed upon the body and of Rudrāksha berries, to form rosaries, is of great importance in S'iva-worship.

[1] Thus, Vishṇu-worship (like S'iva-worship) is connected with the highest spiritual knowledge in the Bhagavad-gītā. See also note 2, p. 326. In some parts of India a saint *Dattātreya* is revered as combining the Hindū Triad in himself.

[2] Brahmā, 'the Creator,' however, is supposed to have done his work. Hence the worship of this manifestation fell into desuetude, and only in one place do traces of it continue, viz. Pushkara in Ājmīr (Rājputāna). Even the worship of the other two manifestations began in time to languish, until that of S'iva was revived by the great teacher and reformer S'an-karāćārya (sometimes described as an incarnation of S'iva) in the eighth century; and that of Vishṇu or Kṛishṇa by Rāmānuja in the twelfth, and by Vallabhāćārya at the end of the fifteenth. S'iva is now the favourite manifestation with Brāhmans and the better classes, as Kṛishṇa is with the others. Benares is a stronghold of S'iva-worship (whence his name Kāśī-nātha), but even there Kṛishṇa is the popular god of the lower orders. The chiefs of many monasteries in the south of India are to this day called S'an-karāćāryas. A popular festival, or rather fast (*upavāsa, vrata*), called S'iva-rātri, in honour of the god S'iva (under the form of the Lin-ga), is kept for a whole day and night, on

respectively. Each sect was jealous of the superiority of his own system, and particular Purāṇas were devoted to the exaltation of the one god or the other. But in the present day the strife of sects has generally given way to universal toleration, and a liberal school of theology has arisen in India. Most thinking men among the educated classes, whatever may be the form of religion to which they nominally incline, regard the names Brahmā, Rāma, Kṛishṇa, and Śiva as mere convenient symbols for different manifestations of the one Supreme Being, who may be worshipped under different external forms and by separate methods, according to the disposition,

---

the 14th of the dark half of the month Māgha (January—February). The spring festival (*utsava*), commonly called Hūlī or Holī, celebrated a few days before the full moon of Phālguna (February—March), and still more popular than the last, is said to be in honour of Kṛishṇa and the Gopīs dancing round fires. Their frolics are commemorated in a variety of sports and jokes. In some parts of India the Holī corresponds to the Dola-yātrā or 'swinging festival,' when figures of Kṛishṇa and his favourite wife Rādhā are swung in an ornamented swing. The Dīvālī (*dīpālī*) or 'festival of lights,' at the end of Aśvin and beginning of Kārtik (September—October), is in honour of Vishṇu's wife Lakshmī. Those who worship Durgā or Pārvatī, wife of S'iva, are called S'āktas (see note 2, p. 325). Besides the three principal sects of *Śaivas*, *Vaishṇavas*, and *Śāktas*, three other inferior ones are often named, viz. the *Gāṇapatyas* or worshippers of Gaṇa-pati or Gaṇeśa, the *Sauryas* or *Sauras*, worshippers of Sūrya, 'the sun,' and the *Bhāgavatas*, who are supposed to worship Bhagavat, 'the Supreme Being.' There are also the Sikhs of the Pañjāb, disciples of Guru Nānak Shah—born near Lahore—who in the reign of Baber, at the end of the fifteenth century, attempted to combine Hindūism with Islām, and promulgated about the time of our Reformation a book called the Ādi Grantha, 'first Book' (prohibiting idol-worship and teaching the unity of the Godhead pantheistically), as a kind of new Veda. He was succeeded by nine other Gurus, each of whom was in some way remarkable. The tenth, Govind, added another 'Book' to the first, and, meeting with persecution under Aurangzīb, converted the Sikhs from peaceable disciples of a peculiar teacher into a military nation and enemies of the Mogul empire. The Sikh chiefs formed themselves into confederacies called Misals, over whom Runjit Siṉh eventually became supreme.

circumstances, and preference (*ishṭi*) of his worshippers. They hold, in short, that there are three ways or means of salvation, 1. the way of works (*karman*), 2. that of faith (*bhakti*), 3. that of spiritual knowledge (*jñāna*); and heaven, they assert, may be reached by any one of these three roads or by a combination of all. The second, however, represents the popular side of the Indian creed, as of all religions, false or true.

It is as Vishṇu, then, that the Supreme Being, according to the Hindūs, exhibited his sympathy with human trials, his love for the human race, his respect for all forms of life, and his condescension towards even the inferior animals as integral parts of his creation. Portions of his essence, they assert, became incarnate in the lower animals, as well as in men, to rescue the world in great emergencies. Nine principal occasions have already occurred in which the god has thus interposed for the salvation of his creatures. A tenth has still to take place. These incarnations are briefly as follow[1]:

1. *Matsya*, the fish. In this Vishṇu became a fish to save the seventh Manu, the progenitor of the human race, from the universal deluge[2]. (See the story told p. 394.)

2. *Kūrma*[3], the tortoise. In this he descended to aid in recovering certain valuable articles lost in the deluge.

---

[1] It should be mentioned that the Bhāgavata-purāṇa gives twenty-two incarnations of Vishṇu. Muir's Texts IV. 156.

[2] The oldest version of this legend, which furnished the germ of the subsequent incarnation, is found in the S'atapatha-brāhmaṇa, as given pp. 32–34 of this volume. The legend is also told in Mahā-bhārata Vana-parvan 12747 &c., where the fish is represented as an incarnation of Brahmā; and in the Bhāgavata-purāṇa VIII. 24, 7, where it is identified with Vishṇu. Muir's Texts I. 208 &c.

[3] In S'atapatha-brāhmaṇa VII. 4, 3, 5, Prajāpati (or Brahmā) is said to have assumed the form of the tortoise: 'Having assumed the form of a tortoise, Prajāpati created offspring. That which he created he made (*akarot*); hence the word *kūrma*.' Muir's Texts IV. 27.

For this purpose he stationed himself as a tortoise at the bottom of the ocean, that his back might serve as a pivot for the mountain Mandara, around which the gods and demons twisted the great serpent Vāsuki. They then stood opposite to each other, and using the snake as a rope and the mountain as a churning-stick, churned the ocean[1] for the recovery of the Amṛita or 'nectar,' the goddess Lakshmī[2], and twelve other sacred things which had been lost in the depths.

3. *Varāha*, the boar. In this he descended to deliver the world from the power of a demon called Hiraṇyāksha, who had seized the earth and carried it down into the lowest depths of the sea. Vishṇu, as a boar, dived into the abyss, and after a contest of a thousand years, slew the monster and raised the earth[3]. In the earlier legends the universe is represented as a mass of water, and the earth being submerged, was upheaved by the tusks of the divine boar. According to some, the object of this incarnation was to recover the lost Vedas. It is noticeable that the first three incarnations are all connected with the tradition of a universal deluge.

---

[1] In this there appears to be an allegory, and the lesson that may be supposed to be taught is, that nothing valuable can be produced or recovered by man without great labour—without, as it were, stirring the lowest depths of his whole nature.

[2] Goddess of beauty, and wife of Vishṇu, a kind of Hindū Venus, Aphrodite (ἀφροδίτη, 'foam-born').

[3] The germs of the fable in the earlier literature are very simple. In Taittirīya-brāhmaṇa I. 1, 3, 5, we read: 'This universe was formerly water. Prajāpati, as a boar, plunged beneath. He found the earth below. Breaking off a portion of her he rose to the surface.' In S'atapatha-brāhmaṇa XIV. 1, 2, 11, occurs the following: 'The earth was formerly so large—*Emūsha*, a boar, raised her up' (Muir's Texts IV. 27). In the Rāmāyaṇa II. 110, Brahmā, not Vishṇu, is represented as taking the form of the boar: 'All was water only in which the earth was formed. Thence arose Brahmā. He, becoming a boar, raised up the earth,' &c. See Muir's Texts I. 53, IV. 36, &c.

4. *Nara-siṉha*, the man-lion. In this he assumed the shape of a creature, half man, half lion, to deliver the world from the tyranny of a demon called Hiraṇya-kaśipu, who had obtained a boon from Brahmā that he should not be slain by either god or man or animal. Hence he became so powerful that he usurped the dominion of the three worlds, and appropriated the sacrifices made to the gods. When his pious son Prahlāda praised Vishṇu, the demon tried to destroy the boy, but Vishṇu appeared out of a pillar in the form Nara-siṉha and tore Hiraṇya-kaśipu to pieces.

These first four incarnations are said to have taken place in the Satya or first age of the world.

5. *Vāmana*, the dwarf. In the second or Tretā age Vishṇu descended as a dwarf, to deprive the demon Bali (who resembles Rāvaṇa and Kaṉsa in the stories of Rāma and Kṛishṇa) of the dominion of the three worlds. Vishṇu presented himself before him as a diminutive man, and solicited as much land as he could step in three paces. When his request was granted he strided in two steps over heaven and earth, but out of compassion left the lower world or Pātāla in the demon's possession[1].

6. *Paraśu-rāma*, Rāma with the axe. In this Vishṇu was born as the son of the Brāhman Jamad-agni and descendant of Bhṛigu, in the second age, to restrain the Kshatriyas from arrogating dominion over the Brāhmanical caste. Paraśu-rāma is said to have cleared the earth twenty-one times of the Kshatriya class[2] (see p. 349).

---

[1] The germ of this incarnation in the Ṛig-veda. I quote one passage: 'Vishṇu strode over this (universe); in three places he planted his step' (I. 22, 17). Hence Vishṇu is called *Tri-vikrama*. See also p. 323 of this volume and Muir's Texts, vol. iv. p. 63. An account of the Dwarf incarnation is given in Rāmāyaṇa (Schlegel) I. 31, 2, and (Bombay ed.) I. 29, 2, &c. (Gorresio I. 32, 2). It is noticed in the Mahābhārata, S'ānti-parvan 12943 &c., Vana-parvan 484 &c.

[2] Though now regarded as the mythical type of Brāhmanism, arrayed

7. *Rāma* (commonly called Rāma-ćandra[1], 'the mild or moon-like Rāma'), the hero of the Rāmāyaṇa, son of king Daśaratha of the Solar race, and therefore a Kshatriya. Vishṇu took this form at the close of the second or Tretā age, to destroy the demon Rāvaṇa (see p. 345).

8. *Kṛishṇa*, 'the dark god'—the most popular of all the later deities of India[2]. This incarnation of Vishṇu, at the end of the Dvāpara or third age of the

---

in opposition to the military caste, he was probably, in the first instance, the hero of a quarrel caused by a Kshatriya's stealing a cow from a Brāhman named Jamad-agni. In revenge, his son Paraśu-rāma slew the Kshatriya, upon which the other Kshatriyas murdered Jamad-agni, and a fierce contest ensued between his son and the murderers. All this points to the historical fact of constant struggles between the two leading classes, and it may be inferred from the circumstance that Paraśu-rāma is described as fighting with (and conquered by) Rāma-ćandra, as well as with Bhīshma in the Mahā-bhārata, that the Kshatriyas held their own if they did not gain the upper hand. The story of Paraśu-rāma is told in the Vana-parvan 11071 &c., and in the Śānti-parvan 1707 &c.; also in the ninth book of the Bhāgavata and in the Padma and Agni Purāṇas. In the Vana-parvan 8679, Paraśu-rāma is described as struck senseless by Rāma-ćandra. The Udyoga-parvan 7142 &c. relates the long single combat between Paraśu-rāma and Bhīshma. They both repeatedly strike each other senseless. Ultimately they are persuaded by some Munis to leave off fighting. In Ādi-parvan 272–280, the destruction of the Kshatriyas by Paraśu-rāma is said to have taken place between the Tretā and Dvāpara ages. Muir's Texts I. 447. Tradition ascribes the formation of the Malabar coast to Paraśu-rāma, who is said to have compelled the ocean to retire and to have caused fissures in the western Ghāts by blows of his axe.

[1] The addition of Ćandra, to distinguish this Rāma from the other two, is only found in the later literature (see note 1, p. 362).

[2] Especially in Bengal. In the upper provinces (except at Mathurā or Muttra, Kṛishṇa's own city), Oude, Behār, and the greater part of Hindūstān Proper, the seventh incarnation, Rāma-ćandra, is principally worshipped. That Kṛishṇa-worship is comparatively modern is shown by the fact that in the old Buddhist Sūtras the gods reverenced at the time Buddhism arose are named, viz. Brahmā, Nārāyaṇa, Śiva, Indra, &c., but not Kṛishṇa.

world[1], as the eighth son of Vasu-deva and Devakī of the Lunar race, was for the destruction of the tyrant Kaṉsa, the representative of the principle of evil, corresponding to Rāvaṇa in the previous incarnation.

---

[1] The Kali-yuga or fourth age of the world was supposed to commence at the death of Kṛishṇa. Hence the events of the Mahā-bhārata must have taken place during the third or Dvāpara age, and those of the Rāmāyaṇa at the end of the second or Tretā age. From the gambling scene in the Second Act of the Mṛiććhakaṭikā, it is probable that the names of the four ages are connected with throws of dice; Kṛita being the best throw; Tretā, the throw of three or the second best throw; and Dvāpara, the throw of two or a worse throw; the worst of all being Kali. The Hindū notion appears to have been that gambling prevailed especially in the Dvāpara and Kali Yugas. In the episode of Nala, the personified Dvāpara enters into the dice, and the personified Kali into Nala himself, who is then seized with the fatal passion for play. The Hindū idea of a succession of four Yugas or ages, in which a gradual deterioration of the human race takes place, has its counterpart among the Romans in the Golden, Silver, Brazen, and Iron ages, as described in Ovid's Metamorphoses (I. 89 &c.). But the Hindū system of mundane periods is more elaborately extended, and perhaps agrees better with modern scientific theories (see p. 187, note 2). A Mahā-yuga or period of four ages comprises 12,000 years of the gods, which (according to the Vishṇu-purāṇa) are equal to 12,000 × 360 (the assumed number of days in an ordinary year), and therefore to 4,320,000 years of mortals, when another cycle of four ages is commenced. One thousand of these periods of four ages constitute a Kalpa or day of Brahmā = 4,320,000,000 human years (comprising under it fourteen Manv-antaras or periods presided over by fourteen successive Manus), after which there is a universal collapse (*pratisańćara, mahā-pralaya*) of all creation—including Brahmā, Vishṇu, S'iva, gods, demons, men, animals—into Brahman or simple being. In the present Kalpa or Aeon, six Manus have passed away, of whom the first was Svāyambhuva, the present or seventh being Vaivasvata. Manu's account is confused, and some think the periods of his four Yugas are no more than 4800, 3600, 2400, and 1200 ordinary years respectively (Manu I. 69–71). There is no allusion to mundane periods in the Ṛig-veda, but there is in the Aitareya-brāhmaṇa (VII. 15). The present Kali-yuga is reckoned to have begun February 18th, 3102 B.C. at midnight, on the meridian of Ujjayinī. Whitney's 2nd Series of Oriental Studies, p. 366; Muir's Texts I. 43; Weber's Indische Studien I. 286, 460.

The details of the later life of Kṛishṇa have been interwoven with the later portions of the Mahā-bhārata, but they do not belong to the plot, and they might be omitted without impairing its unity. He is certainly not the hero of the great Epic. He appears as a great chief who takes the part of the real heroes—the Pāṇḍavas[1]—and his claims to deification are often disputed. His earlier days and juvenile feats, though not found in the oldest parts of the Mahā-bhārata, may be gathered from the Hari-vanśa and Purāṇas, especially the tenth book of the Bhāgavata-purāṇa, from which we learn as follows:

Vasu-deva (a descendant of the Yadu who with Puru, as sons of Yayāti, formed the two branches of the lunar dynasty) had two wives, Rohiṇī and Devakī. The latter had eight sons, of whom the eighth was Kṛishṇa. It was predicted that one of these would kill Kansa, king of Mathurā and cousin of Devakī. He therefore imprisoned Vasu-deva and his wife, and slew their first six children. The seventh, Bala-rāma, was abstracted from Devakī's womb, transferred to that of Rohiṇī, and thus saved. The eighth was Kṛishṇa, born with black skin and the mark called *Śrī-vatsa* on his breast[2]. His father, Vasu-deva, escaped from Mathurā with the child, and, favoured by the gods, found a herdsman named Nanda—of the race of the Yādavas—whose wife, Yaśodā, had just had a son, whom Vasu-deva conveyed to Devakī, after substituting his own son in its place. Nanda took the infant Kṛishṇa and settled first in Gokula or Vraja, and afterwards in Vṛindāvana, where Kṛishṇa and Bala-rāma grew up together, roaming in the woods, and joining in the sports of the herdsmen's sons. While still a boy, Kṛishṇa destroyed the serpent Kāliya, and lifted up the mountain Govardhana on his finger to shelter the Gopīs from the wrath of Indra, who, enraged by their love for Kṛishṇa, tried to destroy them by a deluge. He is described as sporting constantly with these Gopīs or shepherdesses, of whom a thousand became his wives, though only eight are

---

[1] Later additions to the Mahā-bhārata make the Pāṇḍavas also incarnations of certain deities.

[2] The anniversary of the birth-day of Kṛishṇa, called Janmāshṭamī, because his birth is said to have occurred on the eighth day of the month Bhādra (August—September), is celebrated as a great festival. Professor Weber has lately published some valuable information on this subject.

specified, Rādhā being the favourite. Kṛishṇa built Dvārakā in Gujarāt, and thither transported the inhabitants of Mathurā after killing Kaṉsa.

According to some, Kṛishṇa is not an incarnation of Vishṇu, but Vishṇu himself; in which case, *Bala-rāma*, 'the strong Rāma[1],' born at the end of the Dvāpara or third age of the world, as son of Vasu-deva and Devakī, and elder brother of Kṛishṇa, is sometimes substituted for Kṛishṇa as the eighth incarnation of Vishṇu.

9. *Buddha*. According to the Brāhmans, Vishṇu assumed the form of the great sceptical philosopher, in the fourth age of the world, to delude the Daityas or demons into neglecting the worship of the gods, and thus exposing them to destruction.

10. *Kalki* or *Kalkin*, who is yet to appear at the close of the fourth or Kali age, when the world has become wholly depraved, for the final destruction of the wicked, for the re-establishment of righteousness upon the earth,

---

[1] This third Rāma, usually held to be the seventh son of Vasu-deva, and sometimes called *Halāyudha*, 'armed with a plough-shaped weapon,' sometimes *Musalin*, 'club-armed,' is the Hindū Hercules. In Mahābhārata I. 7308 (as well as in the Vishṇu-purāṇa), he is said to have been produced from a white hair of Vishṇu, as Kṛishṇa was from a black. Elsewhere he is said to be an incarnation of the great serpent S'esha, and in Anuśāsana-parvan 6163 he is regarded as a Nāga, or semi-divine being, half man, half serpent; and at his death (recorded in Mausala-parvan 117), a large Nāga is described as coming out of his mouth and entering the ocean. Diodorus Siculus, in his account of the Indians (II. 39), has the following: 'It is said that Hercules also (as well as Διονύσος, worshipped by the inhabitants of the mountains) lived amongst them; and, like the Greeks, they represent him with a club and lion's skin; and that in strength of body and bravery, he excelled all mortals, and purged the earth and sea from monsters (θηρίων). And that since he had numerous sons from his many wives, but only one daughter, when they were grown up, he divided the whole of India into equal parts, so that each of his sons should have a kingdom of his own, and his one daughter he made queen. And that he founded many cities, and among them the largest and most celebrated was Palibothra (Παλίβοθρα); and that after his death, he obtained divine honours.'

and the renovation of all creation with a return to a new age of purity (*satya-yuga*). According to some, he will be revealed in the sky, seated on a white horse, with a drawn sword in his hand, blazing like a comet[1].

Looking more closely at these ten incarnations, we may observe that in the first three Vishṇu is supposed to be present in the body of animals, and in the fourth to take the form of a being half animal, half human. This last may be regarded as a kind of intermediate link, the object of which is to prevent too great abruptness in connecting the Deity with the higher forms of worldly existence. From the mixed manifestation of half a lion, half a man, the transition is natural to that of a complete man. The divine essence passing into human forms commences with the smallest type of humanity, represented by a dwarf. Thence it rises to mighty heroes, who deliver the world from the oppression of evil demons and tyrants whose power increases with the deterioration of mankind during the four ages. In the tenth and final manifestation, which remains to be revealed, evil and wickedness are to be entirely rooted out. We see in all this the working of the Hindū idea of transmigration. Even in Manu's time it was an accepted dogma that the souls of men, popularly regarded as emanations from the Deity, might descend into the bodies of animals, or rise to those of higher beings. It was therefore an easy expansion of such a doctrine to imagine the divine Soul itself as passing through various stages of incarnation for the delivery of the world from the effects of evil and sin, and for the maintenance of order in the whole cycle of creation.

Let me introduce here a curious legend from the Bhāgavata-purāṇa X. lxxxix, which is also told at the end of the Prem Sāgar. I translate it (with a little amplifica-

---

[1] According to Vishṇu-purāṇa IV. 24, he is to be born as Kalki in the family of Vishṇu-yaśas, an ancient Brāhman of S'ambhala.

tion) as well illustrating the character of the three gods, Brahmā, Vishṇu, and Śiva, in their relationship to men :

The great sage Bhṛigu, one of the ten Maharshis or primeval patriarchs created by the first Manu (I. 35), was asked which god was the greatest. He said he would endeavour to ascertain, and first went to Brahmā; on approaching whom, he purposely omitted an obeisance. Upon this, the god reprehended him very severely, but was pacified by seasonable apologies. Next he entered the abode of S'iva, in Kailāsa, and omitted to return the god's salutation. The vindictive deity was enraged, and would have destroyed the sage, but was conciliated by his wife Pārvatī. Lastly, he repaired to Vaikuṇṭha, the heaven of Vishṇu, whom he found asleep with his head on Lakshmī's lap. To make a trial of his forbearance, he boldly gave the god a kick on his breast, which awoke him. Instead of showing anger, however, the god arose, and on seeing Bhṛigu, inquired tenderly whether his foot was hurt, and then proceeded to rub it gently. 'This,' said Bhṛigu, 'is the mightiest god; he overpowers by the most potent of all weapons—sympathy and generosity.'

## *The Rāmāyaṇa.*

I proceed now to give a brief account of Vālmīki's[1] poem, the Rāmāyaṇa (*Rāma-ayana*, 'the goings or doings

[1] Vālmīki is thought to have been born in that part of India which corresponds to Kośala, the chief town of which was Ayodhyā (reigned over by Daśaratha, Rāma's father), and which was close to the region of Videha, whose king, Janaka, was the father of Sītā, and whose connexion with Yājñavalkya is described in the Brāhmaṇa of the White Yajur-veda, and in some of the Mahā-bhārata legends. Vālmīki himself is believed to have been an adherent of the Black Yajur-veda, and it is certain that the story of Rāma was carefully preserved among the Taittirīyakas, and that Vālmīki interweaves their legends into his narrative. According to Mr. Cust (Calcutta Review XLV), Vālmīki resided on the banks of the Jumnā, near its confluence with the Ganges at Allahabad; and tradition has marked a hill in the district of Banda, in Bundelkund, as his abode. Some actually assert that he began life as a highway robber, but repenting of his misdeeds, betook himself to a hermitage, on this hill, where he eventually received Sītā, the wife of Rāma, when banished by her over-sensitive husband. There were born her two sons, Kuśa and Lava (sometimes combined into one compound, thus—*Kuśī-*

of Rāma'), which in its present form consists of about 24,000 stanzas, mostly in the common heroic Anushṭubh metre[1].

It should be noted in the first place that the purity of its text has been exposed to risks, which the longer Epic has escaped. Its story was more popular and attractive. It was shorter, and far less burdened with digressions; it had more unity of plot; its language was simpler and presented fewer difficulties. As a result of these circumstances it was more easily committed to memory. Hence it happened that, even after the final settlement of its text, it became orally current over a great part of India. We know from the fourth chapter of the first book that it had its minstrels and reciters like the Greek ῥαψῳδοί, and variations in the wording of the narratives became almost unavoidable. In process of time, as written copies of the poem multiplied, the unfettered flow of the common heroic metre facilitated slight alterations and interpolations by transcribers who sometimes aimed at being poets themselves. Hence we have at least three versions of the text of the poem: one belonging to Benares and the North-west; another, which is generally, though not always, more diffuse and open to suspicion of interpolations, peculiar to Calcutta and Bengal Proper; and a third,

---

*lavau*), who were taught to sing the poem descriptive of their unknown father's actions, and from whom are traced the proudest Rajput castes. The reviewer thinks it not unlikely that Vālmīki may have been contemporaneous with the heroes whom he describes.

[1] The metre in which the greater part of the Rāmāyaṇa and Mahā-bhārata is written is the common S'loka (see my Sanskṛit Grammar, 935), in which only five syllables out of sixteen in each line are really fixed. The others may be either long or short. The Indra-vajrā variety of Trishṭubh is however frequently used in the Mahā-bhārata; and in the Rāmāyaṇa, at the end of the chapters, we have often the Jagatī (Gram. 937, 941). The former of these has eleven syllables to the half-line, the latter twelve; and the quantity of every syllable being fixed, there is less simplicity and freedom of style.

to Western India (Bombay). These principal recensions, as well as all the known MSS., whatever may be their occasional variations[1], divide the poem into seven books, as follow:

1. *Bāla-kāṇḍa*, the section relating to the boyhood of Rāma. 2. *Ayodhyā-k°*, descriptive of the transactions in Ayodhyā and the banishment of Rāma by his father, king Daśaratha. 3. *Araṇya-k°*, narrating events in the forest-abode of Rāma after his banishment, including the carrying off of Sītā by Rāvaṇa. 4. *Kishkindhyā-k°*, detailing the occurrences at Kishkindhyā, the capital city of Rāma's ally Sugrīva. 5. *Sundara-k°*, 'the beautiful section,' giving an account of the miracles by which the passage of the straits and the arrival of the invading armies in Laṅkā (Ceylon) were effected. 6. *Yuddha-k°*, describing the actual war with Rāvaṇa in Laṅkā, the victory over his armies and his destruction by Rāma, the recovery of Sītā, the return to Ayodhyā, the reunion of the four brothers, and final coronation of Rāma. 7. *Uttara-k°*, narrating the concluding events of the history of Rāma after his coronation on returning to Ayodhyā—his sensitiveness to the gossip and

---

[1] Professor Weber shows that the variations now discovered in MSS. of the Rāmāyaṇa in different parts of India are so great, that it is no longer possible to talk of three recensions only. With regard to the Bengal (Gauḍa) recension, it may be observed that in that part of India, where there is less demand for MSS., learned men have been their own scribes, and have always tampered more freely with original texts than the unlearned copyists of the North. In 1806 and 1810 Carey and Marshman published the text and translation of two books out of the seven which complete this recension; but here and there they have followed the northern. Twenty years afterwards Augustus William Schlegel published the text of two books of the northern version, with a Latin translation of the first; and after another interval of twenty years Signor Gorresio, a learned Italian scholar, published, at the expense of king Charles Albert, a very beautiful and accurate edition of the Bengal recension, with an Italian translation, which I have generally followed in my summary of the narrative. The remainder of that particular recension, the editing of which was commenced by Schlegel, was left unprinted. More than ten years have elapsed since editions of the more reliable recension, with commentary, were put forth at Calcutta and Bombay. That of Calcutta is dated Saṃvat, 1917. Mr. R. Griffith's poetical translation of the Rāmāyaṇa, which has appeared since, deserves, and has received, the greatest commendation.

scandal of the citizens, his consequent banishment of Sītā to the hermitage of Vālmīki, notwithstanding the absolute certainty of her blameless conduct during her captivity in Rāvaṇa's palace, the birth of his twin sons, Kuśa and Lava, in the hermitage, his final reunion with her, and translation to heaven. All this supplement to the story has been dramatized by Bhava-bhūti in his Uttara-rāma-ćaritra, and the whole previous history in his Mahā-vīra-ćaritra.

We have already noted that the seventh Book, as well as the introductory chapters of the first, giving a summary of the plot, and the passages identifying Rāma with Vishṇu or the Supreme Being (such as VI. cii. 12, Gorresio), are in all probability comparatively modern appendages.

No suspicion, however, of interpolations and variations avails to impair the sacred character of the poem in the eyes of the natives[1]. Some idea of the veneration in which it is held may be formed from the verses at the end of the introductory chapter, which declare—

He who reads and repeats this holy life-giving Rāmāyaṇa is liberated from all his sins and exalted with all his posterity to the highest heaven.

Brahmā also, in I. 2, 40, is made to utter the following prophecy in the presence of the poet Vālmīki:

As long as the mountains and rivers shall continue on the surface of the earth, so long shall the story of the Rāmāyaṇa be current in the world. [*Yāvat sthāsyanti girayaḥ saritaś-ća mahītale Tāvad Rāmāyaṇa-kathā lokeshu praćarishyati.*]

The main story of the poem[2], although often interrupted by long episodes which have little bearing on the

---

[1] Weber has noted that in the Sarva-darśana-san̄graha (p. 72, l. 15) a passage is quoted from the Skanda-purāṇa which places the Mūla-rāmāyaṇa, 'original Rāmāyaṇa,' as a Śāstra after the four Vedas, the Bhārata, and the Pańća-rātraka. Some of the Sargas in the Uttara-kāṇḍa have no comment as being *prakshipta*.

[2] While writing my account of the Rāmāyaṇa, I have consulted an able article on this poem in the Calcutta Review (XLV), to which I am under great obligations. The author of the article is my friend Mr. R. N. Cust, a late distinguished member of the Bengal Civil Service.

plot, flows in a far more continuous and traceable course than that of the Mahā-bhārata. It may be divided into four principal parts or periods, corresponding to the chief epochs in the life of Rāma. I. The account of his youthful days; his education and residence at the court of his father Daśaratha, king of Ayodhyā; his happy marriage to Sītā; and his inauguration as heir-apparent or crown-prince. II. The circumstances that led to his banishment; the description of his exile and residence in the forests of Central India. III. His war with the giants or demons of the South for the recovery of his wife Sītā, carried off by their chief Rāvaṇa; his conquest and destruction of Rāvaṇa, and reunion with Sītā. IV. His return with Sītā to Ayodhyā; his restoration to the throne of his father; and his subsequent banishment of Sītā[1].

The poem opens with a description of Ayodhyā[2], and

---

[1] According to Professor Lassen the development of the story of Rāma may be divided into four stages. The first construction of the poem did not carry the narrative beyond the banishment of Rāma to the Himālaya and the circumstances which caused his wife Sītā and his brother Lakshmaṇa to follow him into exile. The second changed the place of banishment to the Godāvarī, and described the protection afforded to the hermits against the attacks of the aborigines. The third embraced the account of the first attempts to subdue the inhabitants of the Dekhan. The fourth amplification, which resulted from the knowledge gained by the Hindūs of the island of Ceylon, included the description of Rāma's expedition against Lan-kā. See Ind. Alt. II. p. 505.

[2] Although Ayodhyā is the base of operations in the Rāmāyaṇa, yet the poet carries us through a vast extent of country, conducting us now beyond the Sutlej into the Pañjāb, now across the Vindhya mountains into the Dekhan, and now across the Narmadā and Godāvarī to the most southern parts of India, even to the island of Ceylon. The geography of the poem, however, though far more interesting, and extending to wider points in every direction, than that of the Mahā-bhārata, is not always to be trusted. The river Sarayū is now called the Gogra.

an eulogium on Daśaratha and his ministers, of whom the most eminent were the two prime ministers Vasishṭha and Vāmadeva. Besides these, there were eight other counsellors (*amātyāḥ*), agreeably to the precept laid down by Manu (see p. 262 with note 2). These are of course all Brāhmans, and direct the affairs of the government. King Daśaratha has no son (VIII. 1)—a serious calamity in India, where a son is needed for the due performance of the Śrāddha (see p. 255 with note 1). The usual remedy for this misfortune was a great sacrifice, purposely cumbered with a most tedious and intricate ceremonial, not to be performed except by Brāhmans, who received in return enormous gifts. The Rākshasas were, of course, eagerly on the watch for any flaw, defect, or mistake. If any occurred, the whole ceremony was seriously obstructed, and its efficacy destroyed.

Ṛishyaśṛiṅga, therefore, a celebrated sage, is married to Daśaratha's daughter Śāntā, and induced to assist at the celebration of a great Aśva-medha or horse-sacrifice.

The episode in which the story of this sage is told is very curious:

It so happened, that in the neighbouring kingdom of Aṅga, now known as Bhagulpore, in Bengal, there had been a great dearth, and the king, Lomapāda, had been assured that the only chance of obtaining rain was to entice the ascetic Ṛishyaśṛiṅga from his retirement, and induce him to marry the king's daughter, or rather the adopted child of Lomapāda, and real daughter of Daśaratha. This ascetic was the son of Vibhāṇḍaka, a sainted mortal of frightful power, who had produced him apparently without a mother, and had brought him up alone in the wilderness, where he had never seen nor even heard of the fascinations of women. The plan was to send a party of young females, disguised as ascetics, and inveigle the great saint from his retreat. The description of the surprise and unsettlement of mind, the interruption of devotion, and heart's unrest, that befell the unhappy saint when he received his strange guests, is very singular. In the end, the ascetic is seduced from his hermitage, put on board a vessel on the Ganges, married to the king's daughter, and brought to Ayodhyā, to conduct the sacrifice [1].

The horse-sacrifice [2], therefore, was successfully performed. We are told that no oblation was neglected, nor any mistake committed; all was in exact conformity to the Veda (I. xiii. 10). The queen Kauśalyā, mother

---

[1] I have consulted here Mr. Cust's article in the Calcutta Review (XLV). He there remarks that 'we might laugh at the conceit of such a case being possible had not a modern traveller in the Levant, Mr. Curzon, assured us of the existence of a similar case in one of the convents of Mount Athos in the nineteenth century. He there found a monk in middle life who had never set eyes on women, nor had any notion of them beyond what could be formed from a black and hideous altar-picture of the Virgin Mary. The cruel traveller, by an accurate description of the many charms of the fair sisterhood, entirely destroyed the poor monk's peace of mind for the future.'

[2] The horse chosen for this purpose was let loose and allowed to roam about for a year. If no one was able to seize it during this period, it was deemed fit for sacrifice; but the seizure was sometimes effected by the god Indra, whose tenure of heaven was imperilled by the great power acquired by those who completed many Aśva-medhas. Another year was consumed in preparations for the sacrifice. The description of the ceremony, in I. xiii, is curious. Twenty-one Yūpas or sacrificial posts were erected, to which were tied various animals, and the horse. Near the latter the queens of Daśaratha watched for a whole night. The marrow (*vapā*) of the horse [*patatrin*=horse; according to the commentator, *purā aśvānām pakshāḥ santīti*] was then taken out and dressed, and the horse itself cut up and offered in the fire, and the king, smelling the smoke of the burning flesh, became absolved from his sins. Various other sacrifices seem to have accompanied the Aśva-medha, such as the Ćatushṭoma, Jyotishṭoma, Atirātra, Abhijit, &c. The *Pravargya* and *Upasad* are described in Aitareya-brāhmaṇa I. 18, 1, 23–25. Compare the Aśva-medha hymns of the Ṛig-veda (I. 162, 163) and the rules for this sacrifice given in S'atapatha-brāhmaṇa XIII. and Kātyāyana's Sūtras XX. 6, 78. An important part of the proceedings was the feasting and the largesses. King Daśaratha is described as giving to the priests a million cows, a hundred million pieces of gold, and four times as many pieces of silver.

of Rāma, and the other two queens, Sumitrā and Kaikeyī[1], remain with the slaughtered horse for one whole night (I. xiii. 36, 37). The gods, Brahmā, Vishṇu, and Śiva, along with Indra and his troop of Maruts, assemble to receive their shares of the sacrificial oblations, and being satisfied, promise four sons to Daśaratha (I. xiv. 9). The scene then changes to the abode of the gods, where a deputation of the deities waits on Brahmā, and represents to him that the universe is in danger of being destroyed by the chief of the Rākshasas or evil demons, called Rāvaṇa, who from his island-throne in Ceylon menaces earth and heaven with destruction. His power is described as so great that—

> Where he is, there the sun does not give out its heat; the winds through fear of him do not blow; the fire ceases to burn; and the ocean, crowned with rolling billows, becomes motionless (I. xiv. 17).

The secret of this power lay in a long course of austerity[2], which, according to the Hindū doctrine, gained for

---

[1] Of Daśaratha's three wives, the chief, Kauśalyā, is said to have been of his own race and country (probably so called from Kośala, the country of Daśaratha); the second, Kaikeyī, was the daughter of Aśva-pati, king of Kekaya, supposed to be in the Pañjāb (whence the king himself is sometimes called Kekaya); and the third, Sumitrā, was probably from Magadha or Behār. The father of the last is said to have been a Vaiśya. It is noticeable that Aśva-pati, king of Kekaya, is mentioned in the Brāhmaṇa of the White Yajur-veda as nearly contemporary with Janaka, father of Sītā.

[2] According to the Hindū theory (cf. p. 106), the performance of *tapas* or austerities of various kinds was like making deposits in the bank of heaven. By degrees an enormous credit was accumulated, which enabled the depositor to draw to the amount of his savings, without fear of his drafts being refused payment. The merit and power thus gained by weak mortals was so enormous, that gods as well as men were equally at the mercy of these all but omnipotent ascetics. Hence both Ṛishis and Rākshasas and even gods, especially Śiva (p. 326), are described as engaging in self-inflicted austerities, in order to set mere human beings an example,

him who persevered sufficiently, however evil his designs, superiority to the gods themselves, and enabled Rāvaṇa to extort from the god Brahmā this remarkable boon—that neither gods, genii, demons, nor giants should be able to vanquish him. As, however, in his pride, he scorned to ask security from man also, he remained vulnerable from this one quarter, if any mortal could be found capable of coping with him. While the discussion of the matter is carried on in heaven, Vishṇu joins the conclave, and at the request of the other gods, promises to take the form of man that he may kill Rāvaṇa, and consents to become incarnate for this purpose, in the family of Daśaratha, king of Ayodhyā (Oude), of the Solar dynasty.

It should be stated here that, according to the legendary history of India, two lines of rulers were originally dominant in the north of India, called Solar and Lunar, under whom numerous petty princes held authority and to whom they acknowledged fealty. Under the Solar dynasty the Brāhmanical system gained ascendancy more rapidly and completely than under the Lunar kings in the more northern districts, where fresh arrivals of martial tribes preserved an independent spirit among the population already settled in that district.

This Solar line, though practically commencing with

---

or perhaps not to be supplanted by them, or else not to be outdone in aiming at re-absorption into Brahma. In these cases it is incorrect (as remarked by Professor Banerjea) to translate *tapas* by 'penance,' if expiation for sin is thereby implied. It is simply self-inflicted pain and suffering, with a view to the acquisition of superhuman powers, or of final emancipation. The root *tap* signifies first 'to burn' and then 'to torment.' It is connected with Lat. *tepeo*. Also with Greek *τέφρα*, root *ταφ*, *θάπτω*, which last originally signified 'to burn,' not 'to bury,' dead bodies. As, however, 'penance' is derived from *poena*, 'pain,' it is perhaps a suitable equivalent for the Sanskṛit *tapas*.

Ikshvāku, is fabled to have derived its origin from the Sun, and even from an earlier source—the god Brahmā himself. Perhaps the object of the Brāhman poet or later constructor of the poem might have been to connect Rāma in his then acknowledged character of an incarnation of Vishṇu, with the solar Vishṇu of the Veda (see p. 323). However this may have been, nothing shows more clearly than the legendary pedigree of Rāma how the whole poem was subjected to a brāhmanizing process. We see from it that the most powerful line of Kshatriya kings is thus made to owe its origin to Brāhmanical sages of the greatest sanctity. I here abridge the genealogy:

Ikshvāku was the son of Manu Vaivasvata (i. e. the seventh Manu, or Manu of the present period). The latter was a son of Vivasvat or the Sun (commonly called Sūrya). The Sun again was a son of the Muni Kaśyapa, who was the son of the Ṛishi Marīći, who was the son of Brahmā. From Ikshvāku sprang the two branches of the Solar dynasty, viz. that of Ayodhyā or Oude, which may be said to have commenced in Kakutstha, the grandson of Ikshvāku (as the latter's son Vikukshi, father of Kakutstha, did not reign), and that of Mithilā, or Videha (North Behār and Tirhut), which commenced in another of Ikshvāku's sons, Nimi. Thirty-fifth in descent from Kakutstha came Sagara; fourth from him Bhagīratha; third from him Ambarīsha; and fifteenth from him Raghu, who was father of Aja, who was father of Daśaratha. Hence we have the following order of names: Brahmā, Marīći, Kaśyapa, Vivasvat or Sūrya, Vaivasvata, Ikshvāku [Vikukshi], Kakutstha [.................................], Sagara [. .], Dilīpa, Bhagīratha [. .], Ambarīsha [. . .], Nala [. . . . . . . . . .], Raghu, Aja, Daśaratha, Rāma.

This explains why Rāma is variously called Kākutstha, Rāghava, Dāśaratha, Dāśarathi, &c.[1]

[1] This list agrees with the usual one as exhibited in Prinsep's table; but there is considerable variation in the genealogy, as given in Rāmāyaṇa II. cx. and in the Raghu-vaṇśa. For instance, the son of Ikshvāku is said to be Kukshi, and his son Vikukshi; the son of Dilīpa is Bhagīratha, and his son is Kakutstha, and his son is Raghu. In the Raghu-vaṇśa, Raghu, father of Aja (V. 36), is said to be the son of Dilīpa (III. 13).

We are thus brought to the real commencement of the story—the birth of Rāma[1]. Four sons are born from the three wives of Daśaratha; the eldest, Rāma, possessing half the nature of Vishṇu, from Kauśalyā; the second, Bharata, possessing a fourth part, from Kaikeyī; and the other two, Lakshmaṇa and Śatru-ghna, sharing the remaining quarter between them, from Sumitrā. The brothers are all deeply attached to each other; but Lakshmaṇa (often called Saumitri) is especially the companion of Rāma, and Śatru-ghna of Bharata[2].

While yet striplings, Rāma and his brothers are taken by Viśvāmitra (see p. 363) to the court of Janaka, king of Mithilā or Videha[3]. He had a wonderful bow, once the

---

[1] In Schlegel's and the Bombay Rāmāyaṇa, the horoscope of Rāma's birth is given. His birthday is called *Rāma-navamī* (see p. 367, note 1), because he is said (I. xix. 1, 2, II. xv. 3) to have been born on the 9th Tithi of Caitra, about the vernal equinox, Jupiter being in Cancer (*Karkaṭa*). Weber thinks that the mention of the Zodiacal sign and the planet Jupiter is a proof of the late date to be assigned to the composition of the Rāmāyaṇa, or at least of this passage, seeing that the Hindūs obtained their knowledge of the signs and planets from the Greeks, and these latter only completed their Zodiac in the first century B.C. Weber, however, remarks that in the Rāmāyaṇa Ceylon is never called Tāmraparṇī or Siṇhala (by which name alone it was known to the Greeks), but always *Laṅkā*.

[2] Although in xix. the birth of Bharata is narrated after that of Rāma, he is supposed to have been born after the twins; and we read in I. xv. that the divine nectar containing the essence of the god Vishṇu was drunk by Sumitrā next to Kauśalyā. According to Schlegel, Bharata was eleven months junior to Rāma, and the twins only three months. Probably the mother of Bharata was higher in rank than Sumitrā, which would give him the precedence. Lakshmaṇa was to Rāma like another self (*Rāmasya Lakshmaṇo vahiḥprāṇa ivāparaḥ, na ća tena vinā nidrām labhate, na taṃ vinā mishṭam annam upānītam aśnāti*, I. xix. 20–22).

[3] It is evident that Mithilā (North Behār and Tirhut), situated quite towards the east, was an Āryan country at this time, for Janaka is described (Rām. I. 12) as conversant with all the Śāstras and Vedas. He is a frequent interlocutor in the Bṛihad-āraṇyaka.

property of Śiva, and had given out, that the man who could bend it should win his beautiful daughter Sītā[1]. On the arrival of Rāma and his brothers the bow is brought on an eight-wheeled platform, drawn by no less than 5000 men. Rāma not only bends the bow, but snaps it asunder with a concussion so terrible that the whole assembly is thrown to the ground, and the earth quivers as if a mountain were rent in twain.

Sītā thus becomes the wife of Rāma, and she remained his one wife—the type of wife-like devotion. Rāma also remained her faithful lord—the type of all that a husband ought to be in loving tenderness and fidelity[2].

On their way back to Ayodhyā, Daśaratha and his sons are met by Paraśu-rāma, and here we have introduced the curious episode of the conflict between the second Rāma and the previous incarnation of Vishṇu—who suddenly appears on the scene (though not till various strange omens and awful portents had given notice of his approach) to challenge the young son of Daśaratha. The object of this digression, which is clearly not part of the original story, seems to be, that the ex-incarnation of Vishṇu, as a Brāhman, may, by acknowledging himself justly superseded by the Kshatriya incarnation, give a

---

[1] Called Sītā because not born from a woman, but from a furrow (*sītā*) while Janaka was ploughing (I. lxvi. 14). This has given rise to a theory that the story of Rāma allegorizes the introduction of agriculture into the south of India. The name Sītā occurs in Taittirīya-brāhmaṇa II. 3, 10, 1–3, as applied to the daughter of Savitṛi, or Prajāpati, and as in love with the Moon, who on his part loves another daughter, S'raddhā, but in the end is brought to love Sītā. (See also Ṛig-veda IV. 57, 6, 7; Atharva-veda XI. 3, 12.) This is a variation of the older legend which represents Savitṛi as giving his daughter Sūryā in marriage to the Moon. This may account for the name *Rāma-ćandra*, 'moon-like Rāma,' which was ultimately given to the hero of the Rāmāyaṇa.

[2] In this respect he contrasts very remarkably with the five Pāṇḍavas —the heroes of the Mahā-bhārata—who had one wife between them as common property, besides others on their own private account.

Brāhmanical sanction to the deification of the second Rāma; but much mythological mysticism is mixed up with the narrative, with the apparent design of obscuring the actual facts of the Kshatriya hero's victory, which could not, if stated in plain language, be otherwise than mortifying to Brāhmanical pride. I here abridge the story as told in Rāmāyaṇa I. lxxiv. &c. (Schlegel; Muir's Texts, vol. iv. pp. 176, 177):

When the king and his son Rāma were returning home after the marriage of the latter to Sītā, he was alarmed by the ill-omened sounds uttered by certain birds, which, however, were counteracted, as the sage Vasishṭha assured the king, by the auspicious sign of his being perambulated by the wild animals of the forest. Then a hurricane shook the earth, uprooting the trees, and thick darkness veiled the sun. Finally, Paraśu-rāma appeared, fearful to behold, brilliant as fire, with his axe in his hand, and a bow on his shoulder. He was angry at the breaking of the bow of S'iva, of whom he was a disciple. Being reverently received, he proceeded to tell Rāma, Daśaratha's son, that he had heard of his success in breaking S'iva's bow, and had brought another bow, once the property of Vishṇu (I. lxxv. 13), which he asked Rāma to bend, and fit an arrow on the string, adding, that if he succeeded in bending it, he (Paraśu-rāma) would challenge him to single combat. Rāma replies that though his powers were slighted by his rival, he would give him a proof of his strength. Whereupon, he angrily snatches the bow from Paraśu-rāma, bends it, fits an arrow on the string, and tells his challenger that he will spare his life because he is a Brāhman, but will either destroy his supernatural power of movement, or deprive him of the abode in bliss he had acquired by his austerities. The gods now arrive to be witnesses of the scene. Paraśu-rāma becomes disheartened, loses his strength, and entreats not to be deprived of his faculty of moving in the air (lest he should be unable to fulfil his promise, made to Kaśyapa, to leave the earth every night). He then continues to say that by the bending of the bow he recognizes Rāma's divinity, and that he regards defeat by the lord of the three worlds as no disgrace. The second Rāma then shoots the arrow, and thereby in some mysterious manner destroys Paraśu-rāma's abode in the celestial world.

Daśaratha and his party now return to the capital, and preparations are made for the inauguration of Rāma as successor to the throne, when Kaikeyī, mother of his brother

Bharata, jealous of the preference shown to the son of Kauśalyā, demands of the king the fulfilment of a promise, made to her in former years, that he would grant her any two boons she asked. A promise of this kind in Eastern countries is quite inviolable; and the king being required to banish his favourite son Rāma for fourteen years to the forest of Daṇḍaka, and to instal Bharata, is forced to comply.

Rāma, therefore, with his wife Sītā and his brother Lakshmaṇa, is banished. They establish themselves in the forest near the river Godāvarī[1]. Meanwhile the heart-broken king pines away in inconsolable anguish. Here occurs a touching episode (II. lxiii). The king, in the midst of his despondency, confesses that his present bereavement is a punishment for a deed of blood committed by himself accidentally in his youthful days. Thus it happened: (I translate as nearly as I can word for word, in a metre resembling the sixteen-syllable heroic verse of the original, omitting portions here and there):

One day when rains refreshed the earth, and caused my heart to swell with joy,
When, after scorching with his rays the parchëd ground, the summer sun
Had passed towards the south; when cooling breezes chased away the heat,
And grateful clouds arose; when frogs and pea-fowl sported, and the deer
Seemed drunk with glee, and all the winged creation, dripping as if drowned,
Plumed their dank feathers on the tops of wind-rocked trees, and falling showers
Covered the mountains till they looked like watery heaps, and torrents poured
Down from their sides, filled with loose stones and red as dawn with mineral earth,
Winding like serpents in their course; then at that charming season I,
Longing to breathe the air, went forth, with bow and arrow in my hand,
To seek for game, if haply by the river-side a buffalo
Or elephant or other animal might cross, at eve, my path,
Coming to drink. Then in the dusk I heard the sound of gurgling water:
Quickly I took my bow, and aiming toward the sound, shot off the dart.

[1] The Daṇḍaka forest is described as beginning south of the Jumnā, and extending to the Godāvarī. The whole of that country was a wilderness, inhabited by savage tribes (Rākshasas), and infested by wild beasts.

A cry of mortal agony came from the spot,—a human voice
Was heard, and a poor hermit's son fell pierced and bleeding in the stream.
'Ah! wherefore then,' he cried, 'am I a harmless hermit's son struck down?
Hither to this lone brook I came at eve to fill my water-jar.
By whom have I been smitten? whom have I offended? Oh! I grieve
Not for myself or my own fate, but for my parents, old and blind,
Who perish in my death. Ah! what will be the end of that loved pair,
Long guided and supported by my hand? this barbëd dart has pierced
Both me and them.' Hearing that piteous voice, I Daśaratha,
Who meant no harm to any human creature, young or old, became
Palsied with fear; my bow and arrows dropped from my senseless hands;
And I approached the place in horror; there with dismay I saw,
Stretched on the bank, an innocent hermit-boy, writhing in pain and smeared
With dust and blood, his knotted hair dishevelled, and a broken jar
Lying beside him. I stood petrified and speechless. He on me
Fixed full his eyes, and then, as if to burn my inmost soul, he said,
'How have I wronged thee, monarch? that thy cruel hand has smitten me—
Me, a poor hermit's son, born in the forest: father, mother, child
Hast thou transfixed with this one arrow: they, my parents, sit at home
Expecting my return, and long will cherish hope—a prey to thirst
And agonizing fears. Go to my father—tell him of my fate,
Lest his dread curse consume thee, as the flame devours the withered wood.
But first in pity draw thou forth the shaft that pierces to my heart,
And checks the gushing life-blood, as the bank obstructs the bounding stream[1].'
He ceased, and as he rolled his eyes in agony, and quivering writhed
Upon the ground, I slowly drew the arrow from the poor boy's side.
Then with a piteous look, his features set in terror, he expired.
Distracted at the grievous crime, wrought by my hand unwittingly;
Sadly I thought within myself, how best I might repair the wrong.
Then took the way he had directed me towards the hermitage.
There I beheld his parents, old and blind; like two clipped wingless birds
Sitting forlorn, without their guide, awaiting his arrival anxiously,
And, to beguile their weariness, conversing of him tenderly.
Quickly they caught the sound of footsteps, and I heard the old man say,
With chiding voice, 'Why hast thou lingered, child? Quick give us both to drink
A little water. Long forgetful of us, in the cooling stream
Hast thou disported; come in—for thy mother yearneth for her son.
If she or I in ought have caused thee pain, or spoken hasty words,

---

[1] I have omitted the youth's statement that he is not a Brahman, but begotten by a Vaiśya on a Sūdrā woman (II. lxiii. 48, &c.).

Think on thy hermit's duty of forgiveness; bear them not in mind.
Thou art the refuge of us refugeless—the eyes of thy blind sire.
Why art thou silent? Speak! Bound up in thee are both thy parents' lives.'
He ceased, and I stood paralysed—till by an effort resolutely
Collecting all my powers of utterance, with faltering voice I said,
'Pious and noble hermit; I am not thy son; I am the king:
Wandering with bow and arrow by a stream, seeking for game, I pierced
Unknowingly thy child. The rest I need not tell. Be gracious to me.'
Hearing my pitiless words, announcing his bereavement, he remained
Senseless awhile; then drawing a deep sigh, his face all bathed in tears,
He spake to me as I approached him suppliantly, and slowly said,
'Hadst thou not come thyself, to tell the awful tale, its load of guilt
Had crushed thy head into ten thousand fragments. This ill-fated deed
Was wrought by thee unwittingly, O king, else hadst thou not been spared,
And all the race of Rāghavas had perished. Lead us to the place:
All bloody though he be, and lifeless, we must look upon[1] our son
For the last time, and clasp him in our arms.' Then weeping bitterly
The pair, led by my hand, came to the spot and fell upon their son.
Thrilled by the touch, the father cried, 'My child, hast thou no greeting for us?
No word of recognition: wherefore liest thou here upon the ground?
Art thou offended? or am I no longer loved by thee, my son?
See here thy mother. Thou wert ever dutiful towards us both.
Why wilt thou not embrace me? speak one tender word. Whom shall I hear
Reading again the sacred S'āstra in the early morning hours?
Who now will bring me roots and fruits to feed me like a cherished guest?
How, weak and blind, can I support thy aged mother, pining for her son?
Stay! Go not yet to Death's abode—stay with thy parents yet one day,
To-morrow we will both go with thee on the dreary way. Forlorn
And sad, deserted by our child, without protector in the wood,
Soon shall we both depart toward the mansions of the King of death.'
Thus bitterly lamenting, he performed the funeral rites; then turning
Towards me thus addressed me, standing reverently near—'I had
But this one child, and thou hast made me childless. Now strike down
The father: I shall feel no pain in death. But thy requital be
That sorrow for a child shall one day bring thee also to the grave.'

After narrating this affecting incident of his early life, king Daśaratha, struck with remorse, sickens and dies[2].

---

[1] This is literally translated. It is well known that blind people commonly talk of themselves as if able to see.

[2] His body is burnt with much pomp. We have already noted, as a

Soon afterwards the ministers assemble, and decide that Bharata shall assume the government (II. lxxix), but he declines to deprive his elder brother Rāma of his rightful inheritance, and declares his intention of setting out for the forest with a complete army (*ćatur-aṅga*) to bring Rāma back, and his determination to undergo in his place the appointed term of fourteen years' exile in the forest (II. lxxix. 8, 9).

After some trouble he discovers Rāma's retreat at Ćitra-kūṭa[1]. There and then he breaks the sad news of his father's death, and entreats him to return to Ayodhyā and assume the sovereignty (cii).

Next ensues a generous contest between the brothers; Bharata imploring Rāma to accept the throne, and Rāma insisting on the duty of fulfilling his father's vow (cvi, cvii).

Here occurs the episode in which the Brāhman Jāvāli, who is a sort of impersonation of scepticism, tries in a brief address (II. cviii) to instil atheistic and irreligious sentiments into Rāma, hoping to shake his resolution and induce him to accept the kingdom. His speech, which is full of interest as indicating the prevalence of infidel and materialistic doctrines at the time when the brahmanized version of the Rāmāyaṇa was completed, may be thus abridged:

---

proof of the antiquity of the poem, that his widows are not burnt with him (see p. 315).

[1] The isolated hill Ćitra-kūṭa is the holiest spot of the worshippers of Rāma, and is crowded with temples and shrines of Rāma and Lakshmaṇa. Every cavern is connected with their names; the heights swarm with monkeys, and some of the wild-fruits are still called Sītā-phal. It is situated on a river called the Piśunī, described as the Mandākinī (II. xcv), fifty miles south-east of the town of Bandah in Bundelkund, lat. 25. 12, long. 80. 47. The river is lined with ghats and flights of stairs suitable for religious ablutions. It is worthy of note that at some holy places all distinctions of caste are laid aside by the Hindūs.

You ought not by abandoning your paternal kingdom to enter upon a wrong road, beset with difficulties and troubles. Permit yourself to be enthroned in Ayodhyā. Daśaratha (your father) is dead and is now nothing to you, nor you to him. Any one who feels attachment for any other person is insane, since no one is anything to any other. I grieve for those who swerve not from virtue and justice; such persons suffer affliction here, and when they die incur annihilation. Men are careful to offer oblations to their progenitors, but what can a dead man eat? If an oblation eaten here by one person, passes into the body of another, then let a S'rāddha be offered to a man who is travelling abroad; he need not eat upon his journey (cf. the doctrine of the Ćārvākas, p. 132). The books composed by theologians (in which men are enjoined to) worship, give gifts, offer sacrifice, practise austerities, abandon the world, are mere artifices to draw forth gifts (*dāna-saṃvananā*). Make up your mind (*kuru buddhim*) that no one exists hereafter. Have regard only to what is visible and perceptible by the senses (*pratyaksham*). Cast everything beyond this behind your back (*pṛishṭhataḥ kuru*). (See Dr. Muir's article on Indian Materialists, Journal of the Asiatic Society, vol. xix. p. 303.)

Rāma's reply, in which he indignantly rebukes Jāvāli, is a noble vindication of religion and faith, but his reference to Buddhism and his designation of Buddha himself as a *Ćora* or thief (II. cviii. 33) must be regarded as interpolations [1].

In the end Bharata desists from pressing his brother to accept the throne, but only consents to take charge of the kingdom as a deposit. He bears away Rāma's shoes on his head in token of this (cxiii. 1), and takes up his abode outside Ayodhyā, at Nandi-grāma, until the return of the rightful king, never transacting any business without first laying it before the shoes (cxv). Before dismissing him, the forgiving Rāma entreats him not to indulge angry feelings towards his mother for having caused the family calamities, in these words:

Cherish thy mother Kaikeyī, show no resentment towards her (II. cxii. 27).

[1] Other allusions to rationalistic doctrines will be found scattered throughout the Rāmāyaṇa.

After Bharata's departure ten years of Rāma's banishment pass in moving from one hermitage to another. In the description of the quiet life of the exiles we find that their morning and evening devotions are never omitted, and that Sītā dutifully waits on her husband and brother-in-law, never eating till they have finished[1]. When they travel, Rāma walks first, Sītā in the middle, and Lakshmaṇa behind (III. xv. 1). At length they move westward to visit the hermitage of the sage Agastya, near the Vindhya mountains. He advises Rāma to live for the remainder of his exile in the neighbourhood of Janasthāna at Pañćavatī on the Godāvarī[2] (xix). This district is infested by Rākshasas, and, amongst others, by Rāvaṇa's sister, Śūrpa-ṇakhā, who becomes smitten with love for Rāma. He of course repels her, telling her that he is already married (xxiv. 1); but this only rouses the jealousy of Śūrpa-ṇakhā, who makes an attack on Sītā, and so infuriates the fiery Lakshmaṇa that he thoughtlessly cuts off her ears and nose[3] (xxiv. 22). Śūrpa-ṇakhā, smarting with pain and bent on revenge, repairs to her brother Rāvaṇa, the demon-monarch of Ceylon.

The description of Rāvaṇa (III. xxxvi; Bombay ed. xxxii) is as follows:

This mighty demon had ten faces, twenty arms, copper-coloured eyes, a huge chest, and bright teeth like the young moon. His form was as a thick cloud, or a mountain, or the god of death with open mouth. He had all the marks of royalty; but his body bore the impress of wounds inflicted by all the divine arms in his warfare with the gods. It was scarred by the thunderbolt of Indra, by the tusks of (Indra's) elephant Airāvata, and by the discus of Vishṇu. His strength was so great that he could agitate

---

[1] This custom remains unaltered to the present day. Compare Manu IV. 43: 'Let him not eat with his wife, nor look at her eating.'

[2] A spot now known as Nāsik, in the Bombay presidency.

[3] It was from this circumstance that Pañćavatī is now called Nāsik (*nāsikā*, 'the nose').

the seas and split the tops of mountains. He was a breaker of all laws, and a ravisher of other men's wives. He once penetrated into Bhogavatī (the serpent-capital of Pātāla), conquered the great serpent Vāsuki, and carried off the beloved wife of Takshaka. He defeated Vaiśravaṇa (i.e. his own brother Kuvera, the god of wealth), and carried off his self-moving chariot called Pushpaka. He devastated the divine groves of Ćitra-ratha, and the gardens of the gods. Tall as a mountain-peak he stopped with his arms the sun and moon in their course, and prevented their rising. The sun, when it passed over his residence, drew in its beams in terror. He underwent severe austerities in the forest of Gokarṇa for ten thousand years, standing in the midst of five fires (see p. 105) with his feet in the air; whence he was released by Brahmā, and obtained from him (among other boons, see p. 345) the power of taking what shape he pleased[1].

The better to secure the mighty Rāvaṇa's co-operation, Śūrpa-ṇakhā succeeds in inspiring him with a passion for Sītā (III. xxxviii. 17), whom he determines to carry off. Having with difficulty secured the aid of another demon, Mārīća,—who was the son of the Tāḍakā (I. xxvii. 8) formerly killed by Rāma,—Rāvaṇa transports himself and his accomplice in the aërial car Pushpaka to the forest near Rāma's dwelling. Mārīća then assumes the form of a beautiful golden deer, which so captivates Sītā (III.

---

[1] One cannot help comparing part of this description with Milton's portrait of Satan. The majestic imagery of the English poet stands out in striking contrast to the wild hyperbole of Vālmīki. It appears from III. liii (Gorresio) that Rāvaṇa was the son of Viśravas, who was the son of the sage Pulastya, who was the son of Brahmā. Hence Rāvaṇa was the brother of the god Kuvera (though by a different mother), and in verse 30 he calls himself his brother and enemy. Both he and Kuvera are sometimes called Paulastya. Vibhīshaṇa and Kumbha-karṇa were also brothers of Rāvaṇa, and, like him, propitiated Brahmā by their penances, and, like him, obtained boons, but the boon chosen by Vibhīshaṇa was that he should never swerve from virtue, and by Kumbha-karṇa (whose size was gigantic and appetite voracious) that he should enjoy deep sleep for long periods of time. (See Mahā-bhārata III. 15916.)

xlviii. 11) that Rāma is induced to leave her with Lakshmaṇa, that he may catch the deer for her, or kill it. Mortally wounded by his arrow, the deer utters cries for help, feigning Rāma's voice, which so alarms Sītā that she persuades Lakshmaṇa against his will to leave her alone and go to the assistance of his brother. Meanwhile Rāvaṇa approaches in the guise of a religious mendicant. All nature seems petrified with terror as he advances (III. lii. 10, 11); and when Sītā's eyes fall on the stranger, she starts, but is lulled to confidence by his mendicant's dress, and offers him food and water. Suddenly Rāvaṇa declares himself. Then throwing off his disguise he avows his intention to make her his queen. Sītā's indignation bursts forth, but her wrath is powerless against the fierce Rāvaṇa, who takes her up in his arms, places her in his self-moving car, and bears her through the sky to his capital. As Sītā is carried along, she invokes heaven and earth, mountains and streams (lv. 43). The gods and saints come to look on, and are struck with horror, but they stand in awe of the ravisher, and know that this is part of the plan for his destruction. All nature shudders, the sun's disk pales, darkness overspreads the heavens (lviii. 16–43). It is the short-lived triumph of evil over good. Even the great Creator Brahmā rouses himself, and exclaims, 'Sin is consummated' (III. lviii. 17).

Arrived in the demon-city, Rāvaṇa forces Sītā to inspect all the wonders and beauties of his capital (III. lxi), and then promises to make them hers, if she will consent to become his queen. Indignantly rejected, he is enraged, and delivers her over to the guardianship of a troop of Rākshasīs or female furies, who are described as horrible in appearance, and cannibal in their propensities (III. lxii. 29–38). Tormented by them, she seems likely to die of despair, but Brahmā in compassion sends Indra to her with the god of sleep[1], and a vessel containing celestial food (lxiii. 7, 8) to support her strength.

Terrible is the wrath of the usually gentle Rāma when on his return he finds that Sītā is carried off by Rāvaṇa (lxix). He and Lakshmaṇa at once set off on a long search, determined to effect her rescue. After many adventures, in the course of which they have a battle with a headless fiend called Kabandha, who opposes their progress, but is killed, and then restored to life by them (III. lxxiv), they make an alliance with Sugrīva, king of the monkeys (foresters), and assisted by Hanumat, one of the monkey-generals, and by Rāvaṇa's brother Vibhīshaṇa, invade Laṅkā, the capital of Rāvaṇa, in Ceylon (IV. lxiii).

To transport the army across the channel, a bridge is constructed under the direction of the monkey-general Nala, son of Viśva-karman:

Thousands of monkey bridge-builders, flying through the sky in every direction, tear up rocks and trees, and throw them into the water. In bringing huge crags from the Himālayas, some are accidentally dropped, and remain to this day monuments of the exploit. At length a pier[2] is formed twenty Yojanas long and ten wide (V. xcv. 11–15), by which the whole army crosses, Vibhīshaṇa taking the lead. The gods, Ṛishis, Pitṛis, &c., look on, and utter the celebrated prophecy—

'*As long as the sea shall remain, so long shall this pier* (setu) *endure, and the fame of Rāma be proclaimed*[3].'

---

[1] Similarly in the Odyssey (IV. 795) Minerva sends a dream to console and animate Penelope.

[2] The god of the ocean at first objected to a regular embankment (V. xciv. 8), though a pier (described as a *setu*) was afterwards constructed: the line of rocks in the channel is certainly known in India as Rāma-setu. In maps it is called 'Adam's bridge.' Everywhere in India are scattered isolated blocks, attributed by the natives to Rāma's bridge-builders. More than this, the hill Govardhana, near Muttra, and the whole Kymar range in Central India are firmly believed to have arisen from the same cause.

[3] 'In the midst of the arm of the sea is the island Ramesurum (Rāmeśvara), or the pillar of Rāma, of as great repute and renown as the pillars of the western Hercules. There to this day stands a temple of massive Cyclopean workmanship, said to have been built by the hero, the idol of

After various engagements, described with much wearisome exaggeration, the great battle between Rāma and Rāvaṇa takes place:

The gods assemble to take the side of the former, and all the demons and evil spirits back their own champion (VI. lxxxvii. 8). Rāvaṇa is mounted on a magic car, drawn by horses having human faces (*manushya-vadanair hayaiḥ*); and, in order that the two champions may fight on an equality, Indra sends his own car, driven by his charioteer Mātali, for the use of Rāma. Both armies cease fighting, that they may look on (xci. 2); but the gods and demons in the sky, taking the part of either warrior, renew their ancient strife[1]. The heroes now overwhelm each other with arrows. Rāma cuts off a hundred heads from Rāvaṇa successively; but no sooner is one cut off than another appears in its place[2] (xcii. 24), and the battle, which has already lasted seven days and seven nights without interruption, seems likely to be endlessly protracted, until Mātali informs Rāma that Rāvaṇa is not vulnerable in the head. Thereupon Rāma shoots off the terrible arrow of Brahmā[3], given to him by the sage Agastya, and the demon-king falls dead (xcii. 58).

---

which is washed daily with water from the Ganges. From the highest point is a commanding view of the ocean, and the interminable black line of rocks stretching across the gulf of Manaar. Thither, from all parts of India, wander the pilgrims, who are smitten with the wondrous love of travel to sacred shrines. From Chuteerkote (*Ćitra-kūṭa*), near the Jumnā, it is roughly calculated to be one hundred stages. We have conversed with some who have accomplished the great feat: but many never return; they either die by the way, or their courage and strength evaporate in some roadside hermitage. Whatever may be its origin, there is the reefy barrier, compelling every vessel from or to the mouths of the Ganges, to circumnavigate the island of Ceylon.' Calcutta Review, XLV.

[1] This is just what takes place in the Iliad before the great battle between Achilles and Hector, the gods taking their respective places on either side (Il. XX). It is interesting to compare the simple Homeric narrative with the wild improbabilities of the Indian poem.

[2] This reminds one of Hercules and the Hydra.

[3] Here called *paitāmaham astram*, and described as having the wind for its feathers, the fire and the sun for its point, the air for its body, and the mountains Meru and Mandara for its weight (VI. xcii. 45). It had the very convenient property of returning to its owner's quiver after doing its work. There appear to have been various forms of this unerring weapon.

Great portents and prodigies precede the fall of Rāvaṇa, and when the victory is consummated a perfect deluge of flowers covers the conqueror. The generous Rāma causes magnificent obsequies to be performed over the body of his enemy, which is duly consumed by fire[1], and then places Vibhīshaṇa on the throne of Lan-kā (VI. xcvii. 15). Rāma then sends Hanumat with a message to Sītā, and Vibhīshaṇa brings her into his presence in a litter (*śivikā*); but Rāma allows her to come before him on foot, that she may be seen by all the army.

The monkeys crowd round her, admiring her incomparable beauty, the cause of so much toil, danger, and suffering to themselves[2]. On seeing her, Rāma is deeply moved. Three feelings distract him—joy, grief, and anger (xcix. 19)—and he does not address his wife. Sītā, conscious of her purity, is hurt by his cold reception of her, and bursts into tears, uttering only the words, *hā āryaputra,* 'alas! my husband!' Rāma then haughtily informs her, that having satisfied his honour by the destruction of the demon who had wronged his wife, he can do no more. He cannot take her back, contaminated as she must certainly be (VI. c). Sītā asserts her innocence in the most dignified and touching language, and directs Lakshmaṇa to prepare a pyre, that she may prove her purity. She enters the flames, invoking Agni (ci); upon which all the gods with the old king Daśaratha appear, and reveal to Rāma his divine nature[3], telling him that he is Nārāyaṇa, and that Sītā is Lakshmī (cii). Agni, the god of fire, then presents himself, holding Sītā, whom he places in Rāma's arms unhurt[4]. Thereupon Rāma is overjoyed, and declares that he only consented to the ordeal that he might establish his wife's innocence in the eyes of the world (ciii). Daśaratha then blesses his son, gives him

---

[1] Contrast this with Achilles' treatment of the fallen Hector.

[2] The whole scene is very similar to that in Iliad III. 121, &c., where Helen shows herself on the rampart, and calls forth much the same kind of admiration.

[3] He never appears to be conscious of it, until the gods enlighten him. (See VI. cii. 10, cxix.) This is not the case with Kṛishṇa in the Mahābhārata. It is probable, as we have seen, that all these passages are later additions.

[4] The whole description of Sītā's repudiation by Rāma is certainly one of the finest scenes in the Rāmāyaṇa.

good advice, and returns to heaven (civ); while Indra, at the request of Rāma, restores to life all the monkeys killed during the war (cv).

Rāma and Lakshmaṇa, along with Vibhīshaṇa, Sugrīva, and the allies, now mount the self-moving car Pushpaka, which is described as containing a whole palace within itself, and set out on their return to Ayodhyā; Rāma, to beguile the way as they travel through the sky, recounting to Sītā all the scenes of their late adventures lying beneath their feet[1] (cviii). On their reaching the hermitage of Bharadvāja at Prayāga, the car is stopped; and the fourteen years of banishment having now expired (cix), Hanumat is sent forward to announce their return to Bharata. Rāma and the three brothers are now once more reunited, and, accompanied by them and by Sītā and the monkeys, who assume human forms (cxii. 28), he makes a magnificent entry into Ayodhyā. He is then solemnly crowned, associates Lakshmaṇa in the empire, and, before dismissing his allies, bestows on them splendid presents (cxii). Hanumat, at his own request, receives as a reward the gift of perpetual life and youth (cxii. 101). Every one returns happy and loaded with gifts to his own home, and Rāma commences a glorious reign at Ayodhyā (cxiii).

Such is a brief sketch of the Rāmāyaṇa, omitting the Uttara-kāṇḍa or supplementary chapters, which contain the concluding events in the life of Rāma (see p. 339). Much of the story, exaggerated as its later details are, probably rests, as we have already pointed out, on a foundation of historical truth.

---

[1] Kālidāsa devotes nearly the whole of the thirteenth chapter of his Raghu-vanśa to this subject, which he makes a convenient pretext for displaying his geographical and topographical knowledge, as in the Megha-dūta. Bhava-bhūti does the same in the seventh act of his drama, Mahā-vīra-ćaritra; and Murāri, the same in his play on the same subject.

It is clear, too, that a moral lesson is intended to be conveyed by the whole narrative. Under the story of the conflict between the armies of the noble Rāma and the barbarous races of the South, figured by the Rākshasas, there appears to lie a typical representation of the great mystery of the struggle ever going on between the powers of good and evil. With regard, however, to any other allegorical and figurative ideas involved, as, for example, that Rāma is a mere impersonation of the Solar energy[1]; Sīta, of agriculture or of civilization introduced into the South of India by immigrants from the North; the Rākshasas, of night, darkness or winter—whatever ingenuity there may be in any or all of these theories, it seems very questionable whether any such conceptions ever entered into the mind of the author or authors of any part of the poem.

Time would fail, if we were to attempt even the briefest epitome of all the episodes in the Rāmāyaṇa. I note two others in addition to those already given. That of Viśvā-

---

[1] Certainly Rāma belongs to the Solar race of kings, but this points to the connection of the Epic Vishṇu (of whom Rāma came to be regarded as an incarnation) with the Solar Vishṇu of the Veda. Professor Weber remarks that as Rāma is at a later period called Rāma-ćandra, and is even in one place called Ćandra alone, the mildness so conspicuous in his character might be explained by supposing that he was originally a kind of moon-genius, and that the legend in the Taittirīya-brāhmaṇa (see note 1, p. 348) representing the love of Sītā (the field-furrow) for the Moon might be regarded by some zealous mythologists as the first germ of the story of the Rāmāyaṇa; the beautifying ointment (*anga-rāga*) which Anasūyā, wife of Atri, poured over the limbs of Sītā (III. 2), representing the dew spread over the furrow in which the moonlight is reflected. Weber, however, thinks that as the name Rāma-ćandra was not given to the second Rāma till a late date (the first application of it occurring in Bhava-bhūti's Mahā-vīra-ćaritra III. 18), the converse is rather true, viz. that a poetical spirit among the Brāhmans connected Rāma with the Moon merely on account of the mildness of his character.

mitra (I. 51–65), which is one of the most interesting, may be thus abridged[1]:

Viśvāmitra, son of Gādhi, was a prince of the Lunar race, sovereign of Kanoj, and the district of Magadha. He had a tremendous conflict with the Brāhman Vaśishṭha for the possession of the cow of plenty (Kāma-dhenu, also called S'avalā), which no doubt typified the earth (*go*) or India. At the command of Vaśishṭha, the cow created hordes of barbarians, such as Pahlavas (Persians), S'akas (Scythians), Yavanas (Greeks), Kambojas, &c., by whose aid Vaśishṭha conquered Viśvāmitra. Hence the latter, convinced of the superior power inherent in Brāhmanism, determined to raise himself to that dignity, and in order to effect this object, increased the rigour of his austerities for thousands of years. The gods, who always had a hard struggle to hold their own against resolute ascetics, did what they could to interrupt him, and partially succeeded. Viśvāmitra yielded for a time to the seductions of the nymph Menakā, sent by them to entice his thoughts towards sensual objects. A daughter (S'akuntalā) was the result of this temporary backsliding. However, in the end, the obstinate ascetic was too much for the whole troop of deities. He obtained complete power over his passions, and when the gods still refused to brāhmanize him, he began creating new heavens and new gods, and had already manufactured a few stars, when the celestial host thought it prudent to concede the point, and make him a veritable Brāhman.

Another curious episode is the story of the Ganges (I. 36–44)[2]:

Gan·gā, the personified Ganges, was the eldest daughter of Himavat, lord of mountains, her younger sister being Umā. Sagara, a king of Ayodhyā, of the Solar race, had 60,000 sons, who were directed by their father to look for a horse which had been stolen by a Rākshasa at an Aśva-medha or horse-sacrifice. Having first searched the earth unsuccessfully, they proceeded to dig up the ground towards the lower regions. Meeting with the sage Kapila, they accused him of the theft, which enraged him to such a degree, that without more ado he reduced them all to ashes. Sagara's grandson some time afterwards found their remains, and commenced performing the funeral obsequies of his relatives, but was told that it was necessary for Gan·gā to water the ashes with her sacred stream. Neither Sagara, however, nor his grandson could devise any means for

[1] The episode of Viśvāmitra includes under it the story of Ambarīsha given at p. 30 of this volume.

[2] The story is also told in the Mahā-bhārata, Vana-parvan 9920, &c.

effecting the descent of the heavenly river. It was reserved for his great-grandson, Bhagīratha, by his austerities to bring down the sacred stream from heaven. In her descent she fell first with great fury on the head of S'iva, who undertook to break her fall.

Mr. Ralph Griffith has translated the description of this descent with great skill and taste. I subjoin a portion of his version (vol. i. p. 194):

On S'iva's head descending first
  A rest the torrents found,
Then down in all their might they burst
  And roared along the ground.
On countless glittering scales the beam
  Of rosy morning flashed,
Where fish and dolphins through the stream
  Fallen and falling dashed.
Then bards who chant celestial lays,
  And nymphs of heavenly birth,
Flocked round upon that flood to gaze
  That streamed from sky to earth.
The gods themselves from every sphere,
  Incomparably bright,
Borne in their golden cars drew near
  To see the wondrous sight.
The cloudless sky was all aflame
  With the light of a hundred suns,
Where'er the shining chariots came
  That bore those holy ones.
So flashed the air with crested snakes
  And fish of every hue,
As when the lightning's glory breaks
  Through fields of summer blue.
And white foam-clouds and silver spray
  Were wildly tossed on high,
Like swans that urge their homeward way
  Across the autumn sky.

Then, by further austerities, Bhagīratha forced the sacred river to flow over the earth, and to follow him thence to the ocean (therefore called Sāgara), and thence to the lower regions (Pātāla), where she watered the ashes of Sagara's sons, and became the means of conveying their souls to heaven. Hence a common name for the Ganges is Bhāgīrathī.

Another name for the river Ganges is Jāhnavī, because in its course it inundated the sacrificial ground of the sage Jahnu, who thereupon without any ceremony drank up its waters, but consented to discharge them again from his ears.

Notwithstanding the wilderness of exaggeration and hyperbole through which the reader of the Indian Epics has occasionally to wander, there are in the whole range of the world's literature few more charming poems than the Rāmāyaṇa. The classical purity, clearness, and simplicity of its style, the exquisite touches of true poetic feeling with which it abounds, its graphic descriptions of heroic incidents and nature's grandest scenes, the deep acquaintance it displays with the conflicting workings and most refined emotions of the human heart, all entitle it to rank among the most beautiful compositions that have appeared at any period or in any country. It is like a spacious and delightful garden; here and there allowed to run wild, but teeming with fruits and flowers, watered by perennial streams, and even its most tangled thickets intersected with delightful pathways. The character of Rāma is nobly pourtrayed. It is only too consistently unselfish to be human. We must, in fact, bear in mind that the poet is bent on raising his hero to the rank of a god. Yet though occasionally dazzled by flashes from his superhuman nature, we are not often blinded or bewildered by it. At least in the earlier portion of the poem he is not generally represented as more than a heroic, nobleminded, pious, and virtuous man,—a model son, husband, brother,—whose bravery, unselfish generosity, filial obedience, tender attachment to his wife, fraternal affection, and freedom from all resentful feelings, we cannot help admiring. When he falls a victim to the spite of his father's second wife, he cherishes no sense of wrong. When the sentence of banishment is pronounced, not a murmur escapes his lips. In noble language he expresses his resolution to sacrifice himself rather than allow his parent to break his pledged word; and he persists in this determination, notwithstanding the entreaties of his mother Kauśalyā, the taunting remarks of his fiery brother Lakshmaṇa, and his own anxious fear for the safety of his wife Sītā, who resolves to accompany him. Again, after the death of his father, when Bharata urges Rāma to accept the government, and when all the citizens add their entreaties, and the atheistical Jāvāli his sophistical arguments (see p. 354), Rāma replies:

There is nothing greater than truth; and truth should be esteemed the most sacred of all things. The Vedas have their sole foundation in truth. Having promised obedience to my father's commands, I will neither, through covetousness nor forgetfulness nor blind ignorance, break down the barrier of truth (II. cix. 17).

As to Sītā, she is a paragon of wife-like virtues. Her pleadings for permission to accompany her husband into banishment breathe such noble devotion to her lord and master, that I close my examples with a few extracts[1]:

A wife must share her husband's fate. My duty is to follow thee
Where'er thou goest. Apart from thee, I would not dwell in heaven itself.
Deserted by her lord, a wife is like a miserable corpse.
Close as thy shadow would I cleave to thee in this life and hereafter.
Thou art my king, my guide, my only refuge, my divinity.
It is my fixed resolve to follow thee. If thou must wander forth
Through thorny trackless forests, I will go before thee, treading down
The prickly brambles to make smooth thy path. Walking before thee, I
Shall feel no weariness: the forest-thorns will seem like silken robes;
The bed of leaves, a couch of down. To me the shelter of thy presence
Is better far than stately palaces, and paradise itself.
Protected by thy arm, gods, demons, men shall have no power to harm me.
With thee I'll live contentedly on roots and fruits. Sweet or not sweet,

---

[1] I have translated these nearly literally, but not consecutively, in the sixteen-syllable metre of the original. The substance of them will be found in the text of Gorresio's Rāmāyaṇa, vol. ii. p. 74, &c.

If given by thy hand, they will to me be like the food of life.
Roaming with thee in desert wastes, a thousand years will be a day;
Dwelling with thee, e'en hell itself would be to me a heaven of bliss.

As if in support of the prophecy recorded in the beginning of the work (see p. 340) the story of Rāma down to the death of Rāvaṇa and recovery of Sītā, is still regularly recited every year throughout a great part of India, at an annual festival in the beginning of October, called Rāma-līlā [1]. Moreover, Hindū writers never seem tired of working up the oft-repeated tale into various forms. Hence the history of the adventures of Rāma, or at least some reference to them, is found in almost every work of the subsequent literature. I conclude this Lecture with instances:

In the Mahā-bhārata (Vana-parvan 15872–16601) the Rāmopākhyāna is told very nearly as in the Rāmāyaṇa, but there is no mention of Vālmīki as its author, and no allusion to the existence of the great sister Epic. Mārkaṇḍeya is made to recount the narrative to Yudhi-shṭhira, after the recovery of Draupadī (who had been carried off by Jayad-ratha, as Sītā was by Rāvaṇa), in order to show that there were other examples in ancient times of virtuous people suffering violence at the hands of wicked men. It is probable (and even Professor Weber admits it to be

[1] On the day in the month Aśvin or beginning of October, when the Bengālīs consign their images of Durgā to the waters (i. e. at the Durgā-pūjā, of which the 4th day is called Daśahara, and during which for a whole fortnight all business is suspended, and even thieves and rogues allow themselves a vacation), Hindūs of other provinces perform the Rāma-līlā, a dramatic representation of the carrying off of Sīta, concluding with the death of Rāvaṇa, of which that day is the anniversary. Rāma's birth is celebrated on the 9th of the month Ćaitra (April), called Rāma-navamī. The sequel of the story of Rāma, as contained in the Uttara-kāṇḍa and Uttara-rāma-ćarita, is not so popularly known. See an article in the 'Indian Antiquary' for May 1872, by the Rev. K. M. Banerjea. It is noteworthy that the Rāma legends have always retained their purity, and, unlike those of Brahmā, Kṛishṇa, S'iva, and Durgā, have never been mixed up with indecencies and licentiousness. In fact, the worship of Rāma has never degenerated to the same extent as that of some of these other deities.

possible) that the Mahā-bhārata episode was epitomized from the Rāmāyaṇa, and altered here and there to give it an appearance of originality. There are, however, remarkable differences. The story in the Mahā-bhārata, although generally treating Rāma as a great human hero only, begins with the circumstances which led to the incarnation of Vishṇu, and gives a detailed account of what is first mentioned in the Uttara-kāṇḍa of the Rāmāyaṇa—the early history of Rāvaṇa and his brother. The birth of Rāma, his youth, and his father's wish to inaugurate him as heir-apparent are then briefly recounted. Daśaratha's sacrifice, Rāma's education, his winning of Sītā, and other contents of the Bāla-kāṇḍa are omitted. The events of the Ayodhyā-kāṇḍa and much of the Araṇya-kāṇḍa are narrated in about forty verses. A more detailed narrative begins with the appearance before Rāvaṇa of the mutilated S'ūrpa-ṇakhā (see p. 355), but many variations occur; for instance, Kabandha is killed, but not restored to life (see p. 358); the story of S'avarī is omitted, and there is no mention of the dream sent by Brahmā to comfort Sītā (see p. 358)[1].

There are other references to, and brief epitomes of parts of the story of the Rāmāyaṇa in the Mahā-bhārata, e. g. in Vana-parvan 11177–11219; in Droṇa-parvan 2224–2246; in S'ānti-parvan 944–955; in Hari-vaṇśa 2324–2359, 8672–8674, 16232.

The story of Rāma is also (as Professor Weber observes) referred to in the *Mṛiććhakaṭikā* (Act I); and although not mentioned in Kālidāsa's dramas, it is alluded to in his *Megha-dūta* (verses 1, 99); and in his *Raghu-vaṇśa*—which is a kind of abridged Rāmāyaṇa—the poet Vālmīki is named (XV. 63, 64). Moreover, the Rāmāyaṇa forms the basis of a Prākṛit work called the *Setu-bandha* (ascribed to one Kālidāsa, and mentioned in Daṇḍin's *Kāvyādarśa* I. 34), as well as of the *Bhaṭṭi-kāvya*, or grammatical poem of Bhaṭṭi (written, according to Lassen, Ind. Alt. III. 512, in Valabhi-pura under king S'rīdhara-sena, between 530 and 545 of the Christian era), and of the two celebrated dramas of Bhava-bhūti, called *Mahā-vīra-ćaritra* and *Uttara-rāma-ćaritra* (whose date is

---

[1] These and other differences have led Professor Weber to suggest the inquiry whether the Mahā-bhārata version may not be more primitive than that of the Rāmāyaṇa, and possibly even the original version, out of which the other was developed. 'Or ought we,' he asks, 'to assume only that the Mahā-bhārata contains the epitome of an earlier recension of our text of the Rāmāyaṇa; or should both texts, the Rāmopākhyāna and the Rāmāyaṇa, be regarded as resting alike upon a common ground-work, but each occupying an independent stand-point?'

fixed by Lassen between 695 and 733). The last of these dramas quotes verses from the Rāmāyaṇa in three places, one in the second and two in the sixth Act. Indeed, the dramatic literature which makes use of the adventures of Rāma for the subject-matter of the plots of its plays is extensive. Besides the two dramas of Bhava-bhūti, there is the *Hanuman-nāṭaka* or *Mahā-nāṭaka*, 'great drama,' in fourteen acts, fabled to have been composed by the monkey-chief Hanumat himself, who first wrote it on the rocks, and then to please Vālmīki (lest it should throw his Rāmāyaṇa into the shade), cast it into the sea, whence some portions were recovered in Bhoja's time and arranged by Miśra-dāmodara (probably about the tenth century). There is also the *Anargha-rāghava* or *Anarghya-rāghava* in seven acts by Murāri; the *Prasanna-rāghava* by Jaya-deva (probably not the author of the Gīta-govinda); the *Abhirāma-maṇi* in seven acts by Sundara-miśra; the *Ćampū-rāmāyaṇa* by Vidarbha-rāja (or Bhoja) in five acts; the *Rāghavābhyudaya;* the *Bāla-rāmāyaṇa* by Rāja-śekhara; the *Udātta-rāghava;* the *Ćhalita-rāma;* (the last three quoted by the well known work on the *Ars poetica* called *Sāhitya-darpaṇa*); the *Dūtāṅgada*, a short piece by Su-bhaṭa, and others.

Other works mentioned by Weber as noticing the Rāmāyaṇa are that of *Varāha-mihira*—written between 505 and 587 of our era—which takes for granted that Rāma was honoured as a demigod about that time; the *Śatruñjaya-māhātmya* written in Valabhi under king Śīlāditya about A. D. 598; the *Vāsava-dattā* of Subandhu (about the beginning of the seventh century, Weber's Indische Streifen I. 373, 380), in which mention is made of the Sundara-kāṇḍa as a section of the Rāmāyaṇa; the *Kādambarī* of Bāṇa (written a little later, Indische Streifen I. 354), in which repeated reference is made to the great Epic (I. 36, 45, 81); the *Sapta-śataka* of Hāla (35, 316), on which Weber has written a treatise; the *Praćaṇḍa-pāṇḍava* of Rāja-śekhara (about the end of the tenth century); the *Daśa-rūpa* of Dhanañjaya (I. 61, about the same date); the *Sapta-śatī* of Govardhana (32, about the tenth century or later); the *Damayantī-kathā* of Trivikrama-bhaṭṭa (11); the *Rāja-taraṅgiṇī* (I. 166); the *Sārṅgadhara-paddhati* (Böhtlingk, Ind. Spr. 1586), &c.

The eighteen Purāṇas (which are to a great extent drawn from the two great Epics) contain, of course, numerous allusions to the Rāmāyaṇa, and sometimes relate the whole story. The *Agni-purāṇa* has an epitome of the seven Books in seven chapters. The *Padma* and *Skanda* also devote several chapters to the same subject. The *Vishṇu-purāṇa* has also a section (IV. 4) about Rāma, and in III. 3 describes Vālmīki as the Vyāsa of the 24th Dvāpara. The *Brahmāṇḍa-purāṇa*—a confused medley of various subjects—has a *Rāmāyaṇa-māhātmya*, and in this Purāṇa is also contained the well known Adhyātma-rāmāyaṇa, 'Spiritual Rāmāyaṇa,' divided into seven Books, bearing the same titles as those of Vālmīki's Rāmāyaṇa. Its object is to show that Rāma was a manifestation of the Supreme Spirit, and Sītā (identified with Lakshmī), a type of Nature.

This Adhyātma-rāmāyaṇa contains two chapters, held to be especially sacred: 1. The *Rāma-hṛidaya* or first chapter, in which the inner or hidden nature of Rāma is explained and his identification with Vishṇu, as the Supreme Spirit, is asserted; 2. the *Rāma-gītā* or fifth chapter of the seventh Book, in which the author, who is evidently a Vedāntist, sets forth the advantage of giving up all works in order to meditate upon and become united with the Supreme Spirit.

There is also a remarkable work called *Vāsishṭha-rāmāyaṇa* (or *Yoga-vāsishṭha* or *Vāsishṭham Mahā-rāmāyaṇam*) in the form of an exhortation with illustrative narratives addressed by Vasishṭha to his pupil, the youthful Rāma, on the best means of attaining true happiness, and considered to have been composed as an appendage to the Rāmāyaṇa by Vālmīki himself.

We ought also here to mention the celebrated Hindī Rāmāyaṇa by the poet Tulasī-dāsa (Tulsī-dās). This poem is so well known and so greatly esteemed in some parts of India, that it is sometimes affirmed that there are three epic poems called Rāmāyaṇa: 1. that of Vālmīki, 2. that attributed to Vyāsa called Adhyātma-rāmāyaṇa, 3. the Hindī Epic by Tulasī-dāsa.

I conclude the list by noting the following comparatively modern artificial poems on the same subject: 1. the *Rāghavapāṇḍavīya* by Kavi-rāja, a very singular production, much admired and imitated by later Indian writers, being nothing less than a poem worded with such dexterous 'double-entendre,' that it may serve as an epitome of either the Rāmāyaṇa or Mahā-bhārata; 2. the *Rāghava-vilāsa* by Viśva-nātha (author of the Sāhitya-darpaṇa); 3. the *Rāma-vilāsa* by Rāma-ćaraṇa; 4. another *Rāma-vilāsa* by Hari-nātha (in imitation of the Gīta-govinda); 5. the *Rāmaćandra-ćaritra-sāra* by Agni-veśa; 6. the *Raghu-nāthābhyudaya* mentioned by Professor Weber[1].

With regard to the composition called *Ćampū*, this is a kind of highly artificial style in alternations of prose and verse (*gadya* and *padya*).

---

[1] The story of the Rāmāyaṇa and Mahā-bhārata, as given in full by Mr. Talboys Wheeler in his History of India, is most interesting and instructive, although it does not profess to be an analysis made by himself from the original Sanskṛit.

## LECTURE XIII.

*The Itihāsas or Epic Poems—The Mahā-bhārata.*

I PASS on now to the Mahā-bhārata—probably by far the longest epic poem that the world has ever produced. Its main design is to describe the great contest between the descendants of king Bharata[1]. He was the most renowned monarch of the Lunar dynasty, and is alleged to have reigned in the neighbourhood of Hastinā-pur or ancient Delhi, and to have extended his authority over a great part of India, so that India to this day is called by the natives Bhārata-varsha. The great Epic, however, is not so much a poem with a single subject as a vast cyclopædia or thesaurus of Hindū mythology, legendary history, ethics, and philosophy. The work, as we now possess it, cannot possibly be regarded as representing the original form of the poem. Its compilation appears to have proceeded gradually for centuries. At any rate, as we have already indicated (pp. 319, 320), it

[1] The title of the poem is *Mahā-bhāratam*, a compound word in the neuter gender, the first member of which, *mahā* (for *mahat*), means 'great,' and the second, *bhārata*, 'relating to Bharata.' The title of a book is often in the neuter gender, some word like *kāvyam*, 'a poem,' being understood. Here the word with which Mahā-bhāratam agrees may be either *ākhyānam*, 'a historical poem,' or *yuddham*, 'war.' It is curious that in the *San͘graha-parva*, or introductory summary (l. 264), the word Mahā-bhārata is said to be derived from its large size and great weight because the poem is described as outweighing all the four Vedas and mystical writings together. Here is the passage :—*Ekataś ćaturo Vedān Bhāratam̢ ćaitad ekataḥ Purā kila suraiḥ sarvaiḥ sametya tulayā dhṛitam Ćaturbhyaḥ sarahasyebhyo Vedebhyo hy adhikam̢ yadā, Tadā prabhṛiti loke 'smin* [*mahattvād bhāravattvāć-ća*] *Mahā-bhāratam ućyate.*

seems to have passed through several stages of construction and reconstruction, until finally arranged and reduced to orderly written shape by a Brāhman or Brāhmans, whose names have not been preserved [1]. The relationship which the original Brāhman compiler bore to the scattered legends and lays of India, many of them orally transmitted until transferred to the Mahā-bhārata, was similar to that borne by Pisistratus to the Homeric poems. But the Hindūs invest this personage, whoever he was, with a nimbus of mystical sanctity, and assert that he was also the arranger of various other celebrated religious works, such as the Vedas and Purāṇas. He is called Vyāsa, but this is, of course, a mere epithet derived from the Sanskṛit verb *vy-as*, meaning 'to dispose in regular sequence,' and therefore would be equally applicable to any compiler [2].

---

[1] Professor Lassen, in his 'Indische Alterthumskunde' (II. 499, new edition), considers that it may be proved from an examination of the Introduction to the Mahā-bhārata that there were three consecutive workings-up (*bearbeitung*) of that poem by different authors. The first or oldest version, called simply *Bhārata*, which contained only 24,000 verses, began with the history of Manu, the progenitor of the Kshatriya or military class (Ādi-parvan 3126), and a short section—describing the pedigree of Vyāsa, and how he appeared at the Snake-sacrifice, and how, at the request of Janamejaya, he commissioned Vaiśampāyana to relate the story of the strife between the Pāṇḍavas and Kauravas (I. 2208, &c.)—might have formed the introduction (*einleitung*) to this oldest Bhārata. The second reconstruction or recasting of the poem—thought by Professor Lassen to be identical with the Itihāsa mentioned in Āśvalāyana's Gṛihya-sūtras, and recited at S'aunaka's Horse-sacrifice—took place about 400 B.C. It began with the history of king Vasu, whose daughter Satyavatī was mother of Vyāsa; and the section called *Paushya* (I. 661), the antiquity of which is indicated by its being almost entirely in prose, might have served as its introduction. The section called *Pauloma* (I. 851) probably formed the commencement of the third reconstruction of the great Epic, which he considers must have preceded the era of Aśoka.

[2] *Vivyāsa Vedān yasmāt sa tasmād Vyāsa iti smṛitaḥ* (I. 2417). Similarly the name Homerus (Ὅμηρος) is thought by some to come from ὁμοῦ and ἄρω. It may seem strange that the compilation of wholly different works

Many of the legends are Vedic, and of great antiquity; while others, as we have already pointed out, are comparatively modern—probably interpolated during the first centuries of the Christian era. In fact, the entire work, which consists of about 220,000 lines in eighteen Parvans or sections, nearly every one of which would form a large volume, may be compared to a confused congeries of geological strata. The principal story, which occupies little more than a fifth of the whole, forms the lowest layer; but this has been so completely overlaid by successive incrustations, and the mass so compacted together, that the original substratum is not always clearly traceable. If the successive layers can ever be critically analysed and separated, the more ancient from the later

---

composed at very different epochs, such as the Vedas, Mahā-bhārata, and Purāṇas undoubtedly were, should be attributed to the same person; but the close relationship supposed by learned natives to subsist between these productions, will account for a desire to call in the aid of the same great sage in their construction. The following passage from the Vedārtha-prakāśa of Mādhava Āćārya (who lived in the fourteenth century) commenting on the Taittirīya Yajur-veda (p. 1), translated by Dr. Muir in his Sanskṛit Texts, vol. iii. p. 47, attributes the actual composition of the Mahā-bhārata to the sage Vyāsa, and gives a remarkable reason for his having written it:—'It may be said that all persons whatever, including women and S'ūdras, must be competent students of the Veda, since the aspiration after good (*ishṭam me syād iti*) and the deprecation of evil are common to all mankind. But it is not so. For though the expedient exists, and women and S'ūdras are desirous to know it, they are debarred by another cause from being competent students of the Veda. The scripture (*śāstra*) which declares that those persons only who have been invested with the sacrificial cord are competent to read the Veda, intimates thereby that the same study would be a cause of unhappiness to women and S'ūdras (who are not so invested). How then are these two classes of persons to discover the means of future happiness? We answer, from the Purāṇas and other such works. Hence it has been said: Since the triple Veda may not be heard by women, S'ūdras, and degraded twice-born men, the Mahā-bhārata (*Bhāratam ākhyānam*) was, in his benevolence, composed (*kṛitam*) by the Muni.'

additions, and the historical element from the purely fabulous, it may be expected that light will be thrown on the early history of India, religious, social, and political —a subject still veiled in much obscurity, notwithstanding the valuable researches of Professor Lassen and others.

I now give the names of the eighteen sections or Books which constitute the poem, with a brief statement of their contents:

1. *Ādi-parvan,* 'introductory Book,' describes how the two brothers, Dhṛita-rāshṭra and Pāṇḍu, are brought up by their uncle Bhīshma; and how Dhṛita-rāshṭra, who is blind, has one hundred sons—commonly called the Kuru princes—by his wife Gāndhārī; and how the two wives of Pāṇḍu—Pṛithā (Kuntī) and Mādrī—have five sons, called the Pāṇḍavas or Pāṇḍu princes.

2. *Sabhā-parvan* describes the great *Sabhā* or 'assembly of princes' at Hastinā-pura, when Yudhi-shṭhira, the eldest of the five Pāṇḍavas, is persuaded to play at dice with S'akuni and loses his kingdom. The five Pāṇḍavas and Draupadī, their wife, are required to live for twelve years in the woods.

3. *Vana-parvan* narrates the life of the Pāṇḍavas in the Kāmyaka forest. This is one of the longest books, and full of episodes such as the story of Nala and that of the Kirātārjunīya.

4. *Virāṭa-parvan* describes the thirteenth year of exile and the adventures of the Pāṇḍavas while living disguised in the service of king Virāṭa.

5. *Udyoga-parvan.* In this the preparations for war on the side of both Pāṇḍavas and Kauravas are described.

6. *Bhīshma-parvan.* In this both armies join battle on Kuru-kshetra, a plain north-west of Delhi. The Kauravas are commanded by Bhīshma, who falls transfixed with arrows by Arjuna.

7. *Droṇa-parvan.* In this the Kuru forces are commanded by Droṇa, and numerous battles take place. Droṇa falls in a fight with Dhṛishṭa-dyumna (son of Drupada).

8. *Karṇa-parvan.* In this the Kurus are led by Karṇa. Other battles are described. Arjuna kills Karṇa.

9. *Śalya-parvan.* In this S'alya is made general of the Kuru army. The concluding battles take place, and only three of the Kuru warriors, with Duryodhana, are left alive. Bhīma and Duryodhana then fight with clubs. Duryodhana, chief and eldest of the Kurus, is struck down.

10. *Sauptika-parvan.* In this the three surviving Kurus make a night attack on the camp of the Pāṇḍavas and kill all their army, but not the five Pāṇḍavas.

11. *Strī-parvan* describes the lamentations of queen Gāndhārī and the other wives and women over the bodies of the slain heroes.

12. *Śānti-parvan.* In this Yudhi-shṭhira is crowned in Hastinā-pura. To calm his spirit, troubled with the slaughter of his kindred, Bhīshma, still alive, instructs him at great length in the duties of kings (*rāja-dharma* 1995–4778), rules for adversity (*āpad-dharma* 4779–6455), rules for attaining final emancipation (*moksha-dharma* 6456 to end).

13. *Anuśāsana-parvan.* In this the instruction is continued by Bhīshma, who gives precepts and wise axioms on all subjects, such as the duties of kings, liberality, fasting, eating, &c., mixed up with tales, moral and religious discourses, and metaphysical disquisitions. At the conclusion of his long sermon Bhīshma dies.

14. *Āśvamedhika-parvan.* In this Yudhi-shṭhira, having assumed the government, performs an Aśva-medha or 'horse-sacrifice' in token of his supremacy.

15. *Āśramavāsika-parvan* narrates how the old blind king Dhṛita-rāshṭra, with his queen Gāndhārī and with Kuntī, mother of the Pāṇḍavas, retires to a hermitage in the woods. After two years a forest conflagration takes place, and they immolate themselves in the fire to secure heaven and felicity.

16. *Mausala-parvan* narrates the death of Kṛishṇa and Bala-rāma, their return to heaven, the submergence of Kṛishṇa's city Dvārakā by the sea, and the self-slaughter in a fight with clubs (*musala*) of Kṛishṇa's family—the Yādavas—through the curse of some Brāhmans.

17. *Mahāprasthānika-parvan* describes the renunciation of their kingdom by Yudhi-shṭhira and his four brothers, and their departure towards Indra's heaven in Mount Meru.

18. *Svargārohaṇika-parvan* narrates the ascent and admission to heaven of the five Pāṇḍavas, their wife Draupadī, and kindred.

Supplement or *Hari-vanśa-parvan*, a later addition, recounting the genealogy and birth of Kṛishṇa and the details of his early life.

The following is a more complete and continuous account of the story of the poem, which is supposed to be recited by Vaiśampāyana, the pupil of Vyāsa, to Janamejaya, great-grandson of Arjuna.

We have seen that the Rāmāyaṇa commences by recounting the genealogy of the Solar line of kings, of whom Rāmā was one. The heroes of the Mahā-bhārata are of the other great race, called Lunar. Here, however, as in the Solar race, the Brāhman compiler was careful to assign the origin of the second great dynasty of kings to a noted sage and Brāhman. I epitomize the genealogy as essential to the comprehension of the story:

*Soma*, the Moon, the progenitor of the Lunar race, who reigned at Hastinā-pur, was the child of the Ṛishi *Atri*, and had a son named *Budha*, who married Iḷā or Idā, daughter of the Solar prince Ikshvāku, and had by her a son, *Aila* or *Purūravas*. The latter had a son by Urvaśī, named *Āyus*, from whom came *Nahusha*, the father of *Yayāti*. The latter had two sons, *Puru*[1] and *Yadu*, from whom proceeded the two branches of the Lunar line. In the line of *Yadu* we need only mention the last three princes, *Śūra*, *Vasu-deva*[2], and *Kṛishṇa* with his brother *Bala-rāma*. Fifteenth in the other line—that of *Puru*—came *Dushyanta*, father of the great *Bharata*, from whom India is called Bhārata-varsha. Ninth from Bharata came *Kuru*, and fourteenth from him *Śāntanu*. This S'āntanu had by his wife Satyavatī, a son named *Vićitra-vīrya*. *Bhīshma* (also called S'āntanava, Deva-vrata, &c.), who renounced the right of succession and took the vow of a Brahmaćārī[3], was the son of S'āntanu by a former wife, the goddess Gangā, whence one of his names is Gāngeya. *Satyavatī* also had, before her marriage with S'āntanu, borne *Vyāsa* to the sage Parāśara; so that *Vićitra-vīrya*, *Bhīshma*, and *Vyāsa* were half-brothers[4]; and Vyāsa, although he retired into the wilderness, to live a life of contemplation, promised his mother that he would place himself at her disposal whenever she

---

[1] This name *Puru* (nom. case *Purus*) is probably the original of Porus, whose country in the Pañjāb, between the Hydaspes and Acesines, was conquered by Alexander the Great.

[2] Pṛithā or Kuntī, wife of Pāṇḍu, and mother of three of the Pāṇḍu princes, was a sister of Vasu-deva, and therefore aunt of Kṛishṇa.

[3] I. e. perpetual celibacy. *Adya-prabhṛiti me brahmaćaryam bhavishyati; Aputrasyāpi me lokā bhavishyanty akshayā divi* (I. 4060).

[4] Parāśara met with Satyavatī when quite a girl, as he was crossing the river Yamunā (Jumnā) in a boat. The result of their intercourse was a child, Vyāsa, who was called Kṛishṇa, from his swarthy complexion, and Dvaipāyana, because he was brought forth by Satyavatī on an island (*dvīpa*) in the Jumnā. (See Mahā-bhārata I. 2416, 2417, and 4235.)

required his services. Satyavatī had recourse to him when her son Vićitra-vīrya died childless, and requested him to pay his addresses to Vićitra-vīrya's two widows, named Ambikā and Ambālikā. He consented, and had by them respectively two children, *Dhṛita-rāshṭra,* who was born blind, and *Pāṇḍu,* who was born with a pale complexion[1]. When Satyavatī begged Vyāsa to become the father of a third son (who should be without any defect), the elder wife, terrified by Vyāsa's austere appearance, sent him one of her slave-girls, dressed in her own clothes; and this girl became the mother of *Vidura* (whence he is sometimes called Kshattṛi[2]).

*Dhṛita-rāshṭra, Pāṇḍu,* and *Vidura* were thus brothers, sons of Vyāsa, the supposed author or compiler of the Mahā-bhārata. Vyāsa after this retired again to the woods; but, gifted with divine prescience, appeared both to his sons and grandsons whenever they were in difficulties, and needed his advice and assistance.

The two brothers, Dhṛita-rāshṭra and Pāṇḍu, were

---

[1] The mother of Pāṇḍu was also called Kauśalyā; and this name (which was that of the mother of Rāma-ćandra) seems also to be applied to the mother of Dhṛita-rāshṭra. Paleness of complexion, in the eyes of a Hindū, would be regarded as a kind of leprosy, and was therefore almost as great a defect as blindness. The reason given for these defects is very curious. Ambikā was so terrified by the swarthy complexion and shaggy aspect of the sage Vyāsa (not to speak of the *gandha* emitted by his body), that when he visited her she closed her eyes, and did not venture to open them while he was with her. In consequence of this assumed blindness her child was born blind. Ambālikā, on the other hand, though she kept her eyes open, became so colourless with fright, that her son was born with a pale complexion (I. 4275–4290). Pāṇḍu seems to have been in other respects good-looking—*Sā devī kumāram ajījanat pāṇḍu-lakshaṇa-sampannaṃ dīpyamānaṃ vara-śriyā.*

[2] Vyāsa was so much pleased with this slave-girl that he pronounced her free, and declared that her child, Vidura, should be *sarva-buddhimatāṃ varaḥ,* 'the most excellent of all wise men.' Kshattṛi, although described in Manu as the child of a S'ūdra father and Brāhman mother, signifies here the child of a Brāhman father and S'ūdra mother. Vidura is one of the best characters in the Mahā-bhārata, always ready with useful advice (*hitopadeśa*) both for the Pāṇḍavas and for his brother Dhṛita-rāshṭra. His disposition leads him to side with the Pāṇḍu princes and warn them of the evil designs of their cousins.

brought up by their uncle Bhīshma[1], who, until they were of age, conducted the government of Hastinā-pur[2]. Dhṛita-rāshṭra was the first-born, but renounced the throne, in consequence of his blindness. The other brother, Vidura, being the son of a Śūdra woman, could not succeed, and Pāṇḍu therefore, when of age, became king (I. 4361). Meanwhile Dhṛita-rāshṭra married Gāndhārī, also called Saubaleyī or Saubalī, daughter of Subala, king of Gāndhāra. When she first heard that her future husband was blind, she from that moment showed her respect for him, by binding her own eyes with a handkerchief, and always remaining blindfolded in his presence[3]. Soon afterwards a Svayaṃvara was held by king Kuntibhoja, and his adopted daughter, Pṛithā or Kuntī, then chose Pāṇḍu for her husband. She was really the child of a Yādava prince, Śūra, who gave her to his childless cousin Kuntibhoja; under whose care she was brought up:

One day, before her marriage, she paid such respect and attention to a powerful sage named Durvāsas, a guest in her father's house, that he gave her a charm and taught her an incantation, by virtue of which she might have a child by any god she liked to call into her presence. Out of curiosity, she invoked the Sun, by whom she had a child, who was born clothed in armour[4]. But Pṛithā (Kuntī), fearing the censure of her relatives, deserted her offspring, after exposing it in the river. It was found by Adhiratha, a charioteer (*sūta*), and nurtured by his wife Rādhā; whence the child was afterwards called Rādheya, though named

---

[1] They were all three thoroughly educated by Bhīshma. Dhṛita-rāshṭra is described as excelling all others in strength (I. 4356), Pāṇḍu as excelling in the use of the bow, and Vidura as pre-eminent for virtue and wisdom (4358).

[2] Hastinā-pur is also called Gajasāhvaya and Nāgasāhvaya.

[3] *Sā paṭam ādāya kṛitvā bahu-guṇaṃ tadā Babandha netre sve rājan pativrata-parāyaṇā* (I. 4376). She is described as so devoted to her husband that *Vāćā'pi purushān anyān suvratā nānvakīrtayat.*

[4] The Sun afterwards restored her *kanyātva* (I. 4400).

by his foster-parents Vasu-sheṇa. When he was grown up, the god Indra conferred upon him enormous strength, and changed his name to Karṇa[1].

After Pāṇḍu's marriage to Pṛithā, his uncle Bhīshma wishing him to take a second wife, made an expedition to visit Śalya, king of Madra, and prevailed upon him to bestow his sister Mādrī upon Pāṇḍu, in exchange for vast sums of money and jewels. Soon after this second marriage Pāṇḍu undertook a great campaign, in which he subjugated so many countries, that the kingdom of Hastinā-pur became under him as glorious and extensive as formerly under his ancestor Bharata (I. 4461). Having acquired enormous wealth, he distributed it to Bhīshma, Dhṛita-rāshṭra, and Vidura, and then retired to the woods to indulge his passion for hunting, living with his two wives as a forester on the southern slope of the Himālayas. The blind Dhṛita-rāshṭra, who had a very useful charioteer named Sañjaya, was then obliged, with the assistance of Bhīshma as his regent, to assume the reins of government.

We have next an account of the supernatural birth of Dhṛita-rāshṭra's sons :

One day the sage Vyāsa was hospitably entertained by queen Gāndhārī, and in return granted her a boon. She chose to be the mother of a hundred sons. After two years she produced a mass of flesh, which was divided by Vyāsa into a hundred and one pieces, as big as the joint of a thumb. From these in due time the eldest, Dur-yodhana, 'difficult to be subdued' (sometimes called Su-yodhana, see p. 383, note 2), was born. At his birth, however, various evil omens took place; jackals yelled, asses brayed, whirlwinds blew, and the sky seemed on fire. Dhṛita-rāshṭra, alarmed, called his ministers together, who recommended him to abandon the child, but could not persuade him to take their advice. The miracu-

---

[1] He is also called Vaikartana, as son of Vikartana or the Sun, and sometimes Vṛisha. Karṇa is described (4405) as worshipping the Sun till his back became warm (*ā-prishṭha-tāpāt*, i.e. 'till after midday,' when the sun began to shine behind him). Compare Hitop. book II. v. 32.

lous birth of the remaining ninety-nine sons then occurred in due course[1]. There was also one daughter, called Duḥśalā (afterwards married to Jayad-ratha).

Next follows the description of the supernatural birth of the five reputed sons of Pāṇḍu:

One day, on a hunting expedition, Pāṇḍu transfixed with five arrows a male and female deer. These turned out to be a certain sage and his wife, who had assumed the form of these animals. The sage cursed Pāṇḍu, and predicted that he would die in the embraces of one of his wives. In consequence of this curse, Pāṇḍu took the vow of a Brahmaćārī[2], gave all his property to the Brāhmans, and became a hermit.

Thereupon his wife Pṛithā (also called Kuntī), with his approval, made use of the charm and incantation formerly given to her by Durvāsas, and had three sons, Yudhi-shṭhira, Bhīma, and Arjuna, by the three deities, Dharma, Vāyu, and Indra respectively:

Yudhi-shṭhira was born first, and at the moment of his birth a heavenly voice was heard to utter these words, 'This is the most virtuous of men.' Bhīma, the son of Pṛithā and Vāyu, was born on the same day as Duryodhana. Soon after his birth, his mother accidentally let him fall, when a great prodigy—indicative of the vast strength which was to distinguish him—occurred; for the body of the child falling on a rock shivered it to atoms. On the birth of Arjuna auspicious omens were manifested; showers of flowers fell[3], celestial minstrels filled the air with harmony, and a heavenly voice sounded his praises and future glory.

Mādrī, the other wife of Pāṇḍu, was now anxious to have children, and was told by Pṛithā (Kuntī) to think on any god she pleased. She chose the two Aśvins (see p. 14), who appeared to her, and were the fathers of her twin sons Nakula and Sahadeva. While the five princes were still children, Pāṇḍu, forgetting the curse of the sage whom he had killed in the form of a deer, ventured one

---

[1] Their names are all detailed at I. 4540.

[2] The *brahmaćarya-vrata*, or vow of continence.

[3] Showers of flowers are as common in Indian poetry as showers of blood; the one indicating good, the other portending evil.

day to embrace his wife Mādrī, and died in her arms. She and Prithā (Kuntī) then had a dispute for the honour of becoming a Satī (see p. 315), which ended in Mādrī burning herself with her husband's corpse (I. 4896). Prithā and the five Pāṇḍu princes were then taken by certain Rishis, or holy men—companions of Pāṇḍu—to Hastinā-pur, where they were presented to Dhṛita-rāshṭra, and all the circumstances of their birth and of the death of Pāṇḍu narrated. The news of the death of his brother was received by Dhṛita-rāshṭra with much apparent sorrow; he gave orders for the due performance of the funeral rites, and allowed the five young princes and their mother to live with his own family. The cousins were in the habit of playing together:

In their boyish sports the Pāṇḍu princes excelled the sons of Dhṛita-rāshṭra, which excited much ill feeling; and Duryodhana, spiteful even when a boy, tried to destroy Bhīma by mixing poison in his food, and then throwing him into the water when stupified by its effects (I. 5008). Bhīma, however, was not drowned, but descended to the abode of the Nāgas (or serpent-demons), who freed him from the poison (5052), and gave him a liquid to drink which endued him with the strength of ten thousand Nāgas. From that moment he became a kind of Hercules.

Then Duryodhana, Karṇa, and Śakuni[1] devised schemes for destroying the Pāṇḍu princes, but without success.

The characters of the five Pāṇḍavas are drawn with much artistic delicacy of touch, and maintained with general consistency throughout the poem[2]. The eldest, Yudhi-shṭhira, is the Hindū ideal of excellence—a pattern of justice, integrity, calm passionless composure, chivalrous

---

[1] S'akuni was the brother of Gāndhārī, and therefore maternal uncle (*mātula*) of the Kaurava princes. He was the counsellor of Duryodhana. He is often called Saubala, as Gāndhārī is called Saubalī.

[2] Complete consistency must not be expected in such a poem as the Mahā-bhārata, which was the growth of several centuries. The act of the five Pāṇḍavas, described p. 386, cannot be reconciled with their usual probity and generosity, though committed under great provocation. Bhīma appears to have been most in fault, which is so far consistent.

honour, and cold heroism[1]. Bhīma is a type of brute courage and strength: he is of gigantic stature, impetuous, irascible, somewhat vindictive, and cruel even to the verge of ferocity, making him, as his name implies, 'terrible.' It would appear that his great strength had to be maintained by plentiful supplies of food; as his name Vṛikodara, 'wolf-stomached,' indicated a voracious appetite; and we are told that at the daily meals of the five brothers, half of the whole dish had to be given to Bhīma (I. 7161). But he has the capacity for warm unselfish love, and is ardent in his affection for his mother and brothers. Arjuna rises more to the European standard of perfection. He may be regarded as the real hero of the Mahā-bhārata[2], of undaunted bravery, generous[3], with refined and delicate sensibilities, tender-hearted, forgiving, and affectionate as a woman, yet of superhuman strength, and matchless in arms and athletic exercises. Nakula and Sahadeva are both amiable, noble-minded, and spirited[4]. All five are as unlike as possible to the

---

[1] Yudhi-shṭhira, 'firm in battle,' was probably of commanding stature and imposing presence. He is described as *Mahā-siṇha-gati*, 'having a majestic lion-like gait,' with a Wellington-like profile (*Pralambojjvala-ćāru-ghoṇa*) and long lotus-eyes (*kamalāyatāksha*).

[2] Strictly, as in the Iliad, there is no real hero kept always in view.

[3] Perhaps it may be objected that some of Arjuna's acts were inconsistent with this character. Thus he carried off Subhadrā, the sister of Kṛishṇa, by force. It must be borne in mind, however, that Kṛishṇa himself encourages him to this act, and says, *Prasahya haraṇam Kshatriyāṇām praśasyate* (I. 7927). Compare p. 391.

[4] The five Pāṇḍu princes are known by various other names in the Mahā-bhārata, some of which it may be useful here to note. Yudhi-shṭhira is also called Dharma-rāja, Dharma-putra, and sometimes simply Rājan. His charioteer was called Indrasena. Bhīma's other names are Bhīmasena, Vṛikodara, Bāhuśālin. Arjuna is also called Kirīṭin, Phālguna, Jishṇu, Dhanañjaya, Bībhatsu, Savyasāćin, Pākaśāsani, Guḍā-keśa, S'veta-vāhana, Nara, Vijaya, Kṛishṇa, and sometimes *par excellence* Pārtha, though Bhīma and Yudhi-shṭhira, as sons of Pṛithā, had also this

hundred sons of Dhṛita-rāshṭra, commonly called the *Kuru* princes, or *Kauravas*[1], who are represented as mean, spiteful, dishonourable, and vicious.

So bad indeed are these hundred brothers, and so uniformly without redeeming points, that their characters present few distinctive features. The most conspicuous is the eldest, Duryodhana[2], who, as the representative of the others, is painted in the darkest colours, and embodies all their bad qualities. When the Mahā-bhārata (like the Rāmāyaṇa) is regarded as an allegory, then Duryodhana (like Rāvaṇa) is a visible type of the evil principle in human nature[3] for ever doing battle with the good and divine principle, symbolized by the five sons of Pāṇḍu.

The cousins, though so uncongenial in character, were educated together at Hastinā-pur, the city of Dhṛita-rāshṭra, by a Brāhman named Droṇa[4], who found in the Pāṇḍu princes apt pupils. From him the five sons of Pāṇḍu acquired 'intelligence and learning, lofty aims, religious earnestness, and love of truth.' All the cousins were equally instructed in war and arms; but Arjuna, by

title. Nakula and Sahadeva are called Mādreyau (as sons of Mādrī), and sometimes Yamau (the twins).

[1] This name, however, is occasionally applied to the Pāṇḍavas, as they and the sons of Dhṛita-rāshṭra were equally descendants of Kuru.

[2] 'Difficult to conquer,' cf. p. 408. The names of all are given in Ādi-parvan 4541. Duḥśāsana is one of the most conspicuous.

[3] There are certainly many points in his character, as well as in that of Rāvaṇa, which may be compared to Milton's conception of Satan. Perhaps his intimacy with the Asura Ćārvāka may be intended to mark him out as a type of heresy and infidelity, as well as of every other bad quality. In the case of Rāvaṇa it is remarkable that he gained his power by penance, and that he is described as well-read in the Veda (Rām. VI. xciii. 58). Some Rākshasas, such as Vibhīshaṇa, Atikāya, are described as religious (Rām. VI. lxxi. 31). Cf. Manu VII. 38.

[4] Droṇa appears to have kept a kind of school, to which all the young princes of the neighbouring countries resorted (I. 5220). He married Kṛipī, sister of Kṛipa, and had by her a son, Aśvatthāman.

the help of Droṇa, who gave him magical weapons, excelled all, distinguishing himself in every exercise, 'submissive ever to his teacher's will, contented, modest, affable, and mild,' and both Bhīma and Duryodhana learnt the use of the club from their cousin Bala-rāma (I. 5520).

Their education finished, a tournament was held, at which all the youthful cousins displayed their skill in archery, in the management of chariots (*ratha-ćaryā*), horses, and elephants, in sword, spear, and club exercises, and wrestling. The scene is graphically described (I. 5324):

An immense concourse of spectators cheered the combatants. The agitation of the crowd was like the roar of a mighty ocean. Arjuna, after exhibiting prodigies of strength, shot five separate arrows simultaneously into the jaws of a revolving iron boar, and twenty-one arrows into the hollow of a cow's horn suspended by a string. Suddenly there was a pause. The crowd turned as one man towards a point in the arena, where the sound of a warrior striking his arms in defiance[1] rent the sky like a thunder-clap, and announced the entrance of another combatant. This proved to be a warrior named *Karṇa,* who entered the lists in full armour, and after accomplishing the same feats in archery, challenged Arjuna to single combat. But each champion was required to tell his name and pedigree; and Karṇa's parentage being doubtful (see p. 378), he was obliged to retire, 'hanging his head with shame like a drooping lily.'

Karṇa, thus publicly humiliated, became afterwards a conspicuous and valuable ally of the Kurus against his own half-brothers. His character is well imagined. Feeling keenly the stain on his birth, his nature was chastened by the trial. He exhibited in a high degree fortitude, chivalrous honour, self-sacrifice, and devotion. Especially remarkable for a liberal and generous disposition[2], he never stooped to ignoble practices like his friends the Kurus, who were intrinsically bad men.

---

[1] So in Vishṇu-purāṇa, p. 513: 'Kṛishṇa having dived into the pool struck his arms in defiance, and the snake-king, hearing the sound, came quickly forth.'

[2] He is often to this day cited as a model of liberality. Hence his name, Vasu-sheṇa.

The tutor's fee (*Gurv-artha*, see pp. 204, 249, Manu II. 245, Raghu-vanśa V. 17) which Droṇa required of his pupils for their instruction was, that they should capture Drupada, king of Pañćāla, who was his old schoolfellow, but had insulted him by repudiating his friendship (I. 5446):

They therefore invaded Drupada's territory and took him prisoner; but Droṇa generously spared his life, and gave him back half his kingdom. Drupada, however, burning with resentment, endeavoured to procure the birth of a son, to avenge his defeat and bring about the destruction of Droṇa. Two Brāhmans undertook a sacrifice for him, and two children were born from the midst of the altar, out of the sacrificial fire, a son, Dhṛishṭa-dyumna, and a daughter, Kṛishṇā or Draupadī, afterwards the wife of the Pāṇḍavas (see p. 388).

After this, Yudhi-shṭhira was installed by Dhṛita-rāshṭra as Yuva-rāja or heir-apparent, and by his exploits soon eclipsed the glory of his father Pāṇḍu's reign.

The great renown gained by the Pāṇḍu princes excited the jealousy and ill-will of Dhṛita-rāshṭra, but won the affections of the citizens. The latter met together, and after consultation declared that, as Dhṛita-rāshṭra was blind, he ought not to conduct the government, and that as Bhīshma had formerly declined the throne, he ought not to be allowed to act as regent. They therefore proposed to crown Yudhi-shṭhira at once. When Duryodhana heard of this, he consulted with Karṇa, Śakuni, and Duḥśāsana, how he might remove Yudhi-shṭhira out of the way, and secure the throne for himself:

Urged by Duryodhana, Dhṛita-rāshṭra was induced to send the Pāṇḍava princes on an excursion to the city of Vāraṇāvata, pretending that he wished them to see the beauties of that town, and to be present at a festival there. Meanwhile Duryodhana instigated his friend Puroćana to precede them, and to prepare a house for their reception, which he was to fill secretly with hemp, resin, and other combustible substances, plastering the walls with mortar composed of oil, fat, and lac (*lākshā*, *jatu*). When the princes were asleep in this house, and unsuspicious of danger, he was to set it on fire. The five Pāṇḍavas and their mother left Hastinā-pur amid the tears and regrets of the citizens, and in eight days arrived at Vāraṇāvata, where, after great demonstrations of respect from the inhabitants, they were conducted by Purоćana to the house of lac. Having been warned by Vidura, they soon discovered the dangerous character of the structure, and with the assistance of a miner (*khanaka*) sent by Vidura, dug an underground passage, by which to escape from the interior (I. 5813). Then they devised a counterplot, and agreed together that a degraded outcaste woman (*nishādī*) with her five sons should be invited to a feast, and stupefied with wine. Bhīma was then to set fire to the lac-house in which they were all assembled (see note, p. 381). This was done. Puroćana was burnt, as well as the woman with her five sons, but they themselves escaped by the secret passage (*suruṅgā*). The charred bodies of the woman and her sons being afterwards found, it was supposed that the Pāṇḍava princes had perished in the conflagration, and their funeral ceremonies were actually performed by Dhṛita-rāshṭra. Meanwhile they hurried off to the woods; Bhīma, the strong one, carrying his mother and the twins, and leading his other brothers by the hands when through fatigue they could not move on. Whilst his mother and brothers were asleep under a fig-tree, Bhīma had an encounter with a hideous giant named Hiḍimba, whom he slew[1]. Afterwards he married Hiḍimbā, the sister of this monster, and had a son by her named Ghaṭotkaća.

By the advice of their grandfather Vyāsa, the Pāṇḍava princes next took up their abode in the house of a Brāhman at a city called Ekaćakrā. There they lived for a long time in the guise of mendicant Brāhmans, safe from the persecution of Duryodhana. Every day they went out to beg for food as alms (*bhikshā, bhaiksha*), which their mother Kuntī divided at night, giving half of the whole to Bhīma as his share (cf. p. 382). While resident in the house of the Brāhman, Bhīma delivered his family and the city of Ekaćakrā from a fierce giant (or Rākshasa) named Baka (or Vaka), who forced the citizens to send him every day a dish of food by a man, whom he always devoured as his daintiest morsel at the end of the repast[2].

[1] This forms the subject of a celebrated episode, edited by Bopp.

[2] This story forms a touching episode, which has been printed by Bopp, and translated by Milman.

The turn had come to a poor Brāhman to provide the Rākshasa with his meal. He determined to go himself, but lamented bitterly the hardness of his fate. Upon this, his wife and daughter addressed him in language full of the deepest pathos, each in turn insisting on sacrificing herself for the good of the family. Lastly, the little son, too young to speak distinctly, ran with beaming eyes and smiling face to his parents, and in prattling accents said, 'Weep not, father; sigh not, mother.' Then breaking off and brandishing a pointed spike of grass, he exclaimed, 'With this spike will I kill the fierce man-eating giant.' His parents, hearing this innocent prattle of their child, in the midst of their heart-rending anguish felt a thrill of exquisite delight. In the end Bhīma, who overheard the whole conversation, undertook to convey the meal to the monster, and, of course, speedily despatched him (I. 6202).

After this Vyāsa appeared to his grandsons, and informed them that Draupadī, the daughter of Drupada, king of Pañćāla, was destined to be their common wife[1]:

In real fact she had been in a former life the daughter of a sage, and had performed a most severe penance, in order that a husband might fall to her lot. Śiva, pleased with her penance, had appeared to her, and had promised her, instead of one, five husbands. When the maiden replied that she wanted only one husband, the god answered, 'Five times you said to me, Grant me a husband; therefore in another body you will obtain five husbands' (I. 6433, 7322). This Ṛishi's daughter was thereupon born in the family of Drupada as a maiden of the most distinguished beauty, and was destined to be the wife of the Pāṇḍavas[2].

---

[1] Polyandry is still practised among some hill-tribes in the Ḥimālaya range near Simla, and in other barren mountainous regions, such as Bhotan, where a large population could not be supported. It prevails also among the Nair (Nāyar) tribe in Malabar. Our forefathers, or at least the ancient Britons, according to Cæsar, were given to the same practice: 'Uxores habent deni duodenique inter se communes,' &c. De Bello Gallico, V. 14.

[2] Vyāsa, who is the type and representative of strict Brāhmanism, is made to explain at length the necessity for the marriage of Draupadī to five husbands (which is called a *sūkshma-dharma*, I. 7246). He also gifted Drupada with divine intuition (*ćakshur divyam*) to perceive the divinity of the Pāṇḍavas and penetrate the mystic meaning of what otherwise would have been a serious violation of the laws and institutions

In obedience to the directions of their grandfather, the five Pāṇḍavas quitted Ekaćakrā, and betook themselves to the court of king Drupada, where Draupadī was about to hold her Svayaṃvara:

An immense concourse of princely suitors, with their retainers, came to the ceremony; and king Drupada eagerly looked for Arjuna among them, that, strengthened by that hero's alliance, he might defy Droṇa's anger. He therefore prepared an enormous bow, which he was persuaded none but Arjuna could bend, and proposed a trial of strength, promising to give his daughter to any one who could by means of the

---

of the Brāhmans (7313). Hence Drupada became aware of his daughter's former birth, and that Arjuna was really a portion of the essence of Indra (*Śakrasyāṇśa*), and all his brothers portions of the same god. Draupadī herself, although nominally the daughter of Drupada, was really born, like her brother Dhṛishṭa-dyumna, out of the midst of the sacrificial fire (*vedī-madhyāt*, I. 6931; see p. 385), and was a form of Lakshmī. In no other way could her supernatural birth, and the divine perfume which exhaled from her person, and was perceived a league off (*krośa-mātrāt pravāti*), be accounted for. Vyāsa at the same time explained the mysterious birth of Kṛishṇa and Baladeva;—how the god Vishṇu pulled out two of his own hairs, one white and the other black, which entered into two women of the family of the Yādavas (Devakī and Rohiṇī), and became, the white one Baladeva, the black one Kṛishṇa (I. 7307; Vishṇu-purāṇa V. 1). The Mārkaṇḍeya-purāṇa (ch. 5) shows how the five Pāṇḍavas could be all portions of Indra, and yet four of them sons of other gods. When Indra killed the son of Tvashṭṛi (or Viśvakarman as Prajāpati, the Creator), his punishment for this *brahma-hatyā* was that all his *tejas*, 'manly vigour,' deserted him, and entered Dharma, the god of justice. The son of Tvashṭṛi was reproduced as the demon Vṛitra, and again slain by Indra; as a punishment for which his *bala*, 'strength,' left him, and entered *Māruta*, 'the Wind.' Lastly, when Indra violated Ahalyā, the wife of the sage Gautama, his *rūpa*, 'beauty,' abandoned him, and entered the Nāsatyau or Aśvins. When Dharma gave back the *tejas* of Indra, Yudhi-shṭhira was born; when the Wind gave up Indra's *bala*, Bhīma was born; and when the Aśvins restored the *rūpa* of Indra, Nakula and Sahadeva were born. Arjuna was born as half the essence of Indra. Hence, as they were all portions of one deity, there could be no harm in Draupadī becoming the wife of all five.

bow shoot five arrows simultaneously through a revolving ring into a target beyond. An amphitheatre was erected outside the town, surrounded by tiers of lofty seats and raised platforms, with variegated awnings. Magnificent palaces, crowded with eager spectators, overlooked the scene. Actors, conjurors, athletes, and dancers exhibited their skill before the multitude. Strains of exquisite music floated in the air. Drums and trumpets sounded. When expectation was at its height, Draupadī in gorgeous apparel entered the arena, and the bow was brought. The hundred sons of Dhṛita-rāshṭra strained every nerve to bend the ponderous weapon, but without effect. Its recoil dashed them breathless to the ground, and made them the laughing-stock of the crowd.

Arjuna now advanced, disguised as a Brāhman. I here translate a portion metrically (I. 7049, &c.):

A moment motionless he stood and scanned
The bow, collecting all his energy.
Next walking round in homage, breathed a prayer
To the Supreme Bestower of good gifts;
Then fixing all his mind on Draupadī
He grasped the ponderous weapon in his hand,
And with one vigorous effort braced the string.
Quickly the shafts were aimed; they flew;
The mark fell pierced; a shout of victory
Rang through the vast arena; from the sky
Garlands of flowers crowned the hero's head,
Ten thousand fluttering scarfs waved in the air,
And drum and trumpet sounded forth his triumph.

I need not suggest the parallel which will at once be drawn by the classical scholar between this trial of archery and a similar scene in the Odyssey.

When the suitors found themselves outdone by a mere stripling in the coarse dress of a mendicant Brāhman, their rage knew no bounds. A real battle ensued:

The Pāṇḍu princes protected Drupada, and enacted prodigies. Bhīma tore up a tree, and used it as a club. Karṇa at last met Arjuna in single combat, rushing on him like a young elephant. They overwhelmed each other with showers of arrows, which darkened the air. But not even Karṇa could withstand the irresistible onset of the godlike Arjuna, and he and the other suitors retired vanquished from the field, leaving Draupadī as the bride of Arjuna.

Arjuna having been chosen by Draupadī, the five brothers returned with her to their mother, who being inside the house, and fancying that they had brought alms, called out to them, 'Share it between you' (*bhunkteti sametya sarve*, I. 7132). The words of a parent, thus spoken, could not be set aside without evil consequences; and Drupada, at the persuasion of Vyāsa, who acquainted him with the divinely ordained destination of his daughter[1], consented to her becoming the common wife of the five brothers. She was first married by the family-priest Dhaumya to Yudhi-shṭhira (I. 7340), and then, according to priority of birth, to the other four[2].

The Pāṇḍavas, being now strengthened by their alliance with the powerful king of Pańćāla, threw off their disguises; and king Dhṛita-rāshṭra thought it more politic to settle all differences by dividing his kingdom between them and his own sons. He gave up Hastināpur to the latter, presided over by Duryodhana, and permitted the five Pāṇḍavas to occupy a district near the Yamunā (Jumnā), called Khāṇḍava-prastha, where

---

[1] See note 2, p. 387. Drupada at first objected. Yudhi-shṭhira's excuse for himself and his brothers is remarkable; *Pūrveshām ānupūrvyeṇa yātaṃ vartmānuyāmahe* (I. 7246).

[2] She had a son by each of the five brothers—Prativindhya by Yudhishṭhira; Sutasoma by Bhīma; S'rutakarman by Arjuna; S'atānīka by Nakula; S'rutasena by Sahadeva (I. 8039). Arjuna had also another wife, Subhadrā, the sister of Kṛishṇa, with whom he eloped when on a visit to Kṛishṇa at Dvārakā. By her he had a son, Abhimanyu. He had also a son named Irāvat by the serpent-nymph Ulūpī. Bhīma had also a son, Ghaṭotkaća, by the Rākshasī Hiḍimbā (see p. 386); and the others had children by different wives (Vishṇu-purāṇa, p. 459). Arjuna's son Abhimanyu had a son Parīkshit, who was father of Janamejaya. Parīkshit died of the bite of a snake; and the Bhāgavata-purāṇa was narrated to him between the bite and his death.

they built Indra-prastha (the modern Delhi), and, under Yudhi-shṭhira as their leader, subjugated much of the adjacent territory by predatory incursions (I. 6573).

One day, when Arjuna was bathing in the Ganges, he was carried off by the serpent-nymph Ulūpī, daughter of the king of the Nāgas, whom he married (I. 7809). Afterwards he married Ćitrāṅgadā, daughter of the king of Maṇipura, and had a child by her named Babhru-vāhana (I. 7883).

Wandering for twelve years in the forests, to fulfil a vow, Arjuna came to Prabhāsa, a place of pilgrimage in the west of India, where he met Kṛishṇa[1], the details of whose early life have already been given (p. 334), and who here first formed a friendship with Arjuna, and took him to his city Dvārakā, where he received him as a visitor into his own house (I. 7905). Soon afterwards, some of the relatives of Kṛishṇa celebrated a festival in the mountain Raivataka, to which both Arjuna and Kṛishṇa went. There they saw Bala-rāma, elder brother of Kṛishṇa (p. 335), in a state of intoxication (*kshīva*)[2] with his wife Revatī; and there they saw Subhadrā, Kṛishṇa's sister. Her beauty excited the love of Arjuna, who, after obtaining Kṛishṇa's leave, carried her off (see note 2, p. 390) and married her (I. 7937). In the twelfth year of his absence he returned with her to Indra-prastha.

The Pāṇḍavas and all the people of Indra-prastha then lived happily for some time under the rule of Yudhi-shṭhira, who, elated with his conquests, undertook, assisted by Kṛishṇa, to celebrate the Rājasūya, a great sacrifice,

---

[1] See note 2, p. 387. I enumerate some of the other names by which Kṛishṇa is known in the Mahā-bhārata, as follows: Vāsudeva, Keśava, Govinda, Janārdana, Dāmodara, Dāśārha, Nārāyaṇa, Hṛishīkeśa, Puru-shottama, Mādhava, Madhu-sūdana, Aćyuta. (See V. 2560). In the Draupadī-haraṇa (75) Kṛishṇa and Arjuna are called *Kṛishṇau*.

[2] Compare Megha-dūta, verse 51, where Bala-rāma's fondness for wine is alluded to. See also Vishṇu-purāṇa V. 25.

at which his own inauguration as paramount sovereign was to be performed.

A great assembly (*sabhā*) was accordingly held:

Various princes attended, and brought either rich presents or tribute (II. 1264). Among those who came were Bhīshma, Dhṛita-rāshṭra and his hundred sons, Subala (king of Gandhāra), S'akuni, Drupada, S'alya, Droṇa, Kṛipa, Jayad-ratha, Kuntibhoja, S'iśu-pāla, and others from the extreme south and north (Drāviḍa, Ceylon, and Kāśmīr, II. 1271)[1]. On the day of the inauguration (*abhisheka*) Bhīshma, at the suggestion of the sage Nārada, proposed that a respectful oblation (*argha*) should be prepared and offered in token of worship to the best and strongest person present, whom he declared to be Kṛishṇa. To this the Pāṇḍavas readily agreed; and Sahadeva was commissioned to present the offering. S'iśu-pāla (also called Sunītha), however, opposed the worship of Kṛishṇa; and, after denouncing him as a contemptible and ill-instructed person (II. 1340), challenged him to fight[2]; but Kṛishṇa instantly struck off his head with his discus called Su-darśana[3].

After this, Dhṛita-rāshṭra was persuaded to hold another assembly (*sabhā*) at Hastinā-pur; and Vidura was sent to the Pāṇḍavas, to invite them to be present (II. 1993). They consented to attend; and Yudhi-shṭhira was easily prevailed on by Duryodhana to play with Śakuni. By degrees Yudhi-shṭhira staked everything—his territory, his possessions, and last of all Draupadī. All were successively lost; and Draupadī, then regarded as a slave, was treated with great indignity by Duḥśāsana. He dragged her by the hair of the head into the assembly; upon which Bhīma, who witnessed this insult, swore that

[1] The details in this part of the poem are interesting and curious. As shown by Professor H. H. Wilson, they throw light on the geographical divisions and political condition of India at an early epoch.

[2] Duryodhana also, in a subsequent part of the Mahā-bhārata, evinces scepticism in regard to the divine nature of Kṛishṇa (V. 4368).

[3] The story of S'iśu-pāla and his destruction by Kṛishṇa form the subject of the celebrated poem of Māgha. The particulars of the narrative as told in this book of the Mahā-bhārata are given by Dr. Muir in his Sanskrit Texts, vol. iv. The Vishṇu-purāṇa identifies S'iśu-pāla with the demons Hiraṇya-kaśipu and Rāvaṇa (Wilson, p. 437).

he would one day dash Duḥśāsana to pieces and drink his blood[1] (II. 2302). In the end a compromise was agreed upon. The kingdom was given up to Duryodhana for twelve years; and the five Pāṇḍavas, with Draupadī, were required to live for that period in the woods, and to pass the thirteenth concealed under assumed names in various disguises.

They accordingly retired to the Kāmyaka forest, and took up their abode on the banks of the Sarasvatī.

While they were resident in the forest, various episodes occurred, thus:

Arjuna went to the Himālaya mountains to perform severe penance, and thereby obtain celestial arms. After some time S'iva, to reward him and prove his bravery, approached him as a Kirāta or wild mountaineer living by the chase, at the moment that a demon named Mūka, in the form of a boar, was making an attack upon him. S'iva and Arjuna both shot together at the boar, which fell dead, and both claimed to have hit him first. This served as a pretext for S'iva, as the Kirāta, to quarrel with Arjuna, and have a battle with him. Arjuna fought long with the Kirāta[2], but could not conquer him. At last he recognized the god, and threw himself at his feet. S'iva, pleased with his bravery, gave him the celebrated weapon Pāśupata, to enable him to conquer Karṇa and the Kuru princes in war (III. 1650, 1664).

Many legends were also repeated to console and amuse the Pāṇḍu princes in their time of exile. For instance, we have here introduced (III. 12746–12804) the epic version of the tradition of the Deluge (the earliest account

---

[1] This threat he fulfilled. The incident is noticeable as it is the subject of the well-known drama by Bhaṭṭa-nārāyaṇa called Veṇī-saṃhāra, 'braid-binding,' which describes how the braided hair torn by Duḥśāsana was again bound together by Bhīma, who is made to say *Svayam ahaṃ saṃharāmi*, 'I myself will again bind the braid together.' See Sāhitya-darpaṇa, p. 169.

[2] This forms the subject of a celebrated poem by Bhāravi called the Kirātārjunīya. S'iva was regarded as the god of the Kirātas, who were evidently a race of aborigines much respected by the Hindūs for their bravery and skill in archery.

of which occurs in the Śatapatha-brāhmaṇa, see p. 32 of this volume), as follows:

Manu, the Hindū Noah (not the grandson of Brahmā, and reputed author of the Code, but the seventh Manu, or Manu of the present period, called Vaivasvata, and regarded as one of the progenitors of the human race, Manu I. 61, 62), is represented as conciliating the favour of the Supreme Being by his austerities in an age of universal depravity. A fish, which was an incarnation of Brahmā (cf. p. 329), appeared to him whilst engaged in penance on the margin of a river, and accosting him, craved protection from the larger fish. Manu complied, and placed him in a glass vessel. Having outgrown this, he requested to be taken to a more roomy receptacle. Manu then placed him in a lake. Still the fish grew, till the lake, though three leagues long, could not contain him. He next asked to be taken to the Ganges; but even the Ganges was soon too small, and the fish was finally transferred to the ocean. There he continued to expand, till at last, addressing Manu, he warned him of the coming Deluge.

Manu, however, was to be preserved by the help of the fish, who commanded him to build a ship and go on board, not with his own wife and children, but with the seven Ṛishis or patriarchs; and not with pairs of animals, but with the seeds of all existing things. The flood came; Manu went on board, and fastened the ship, as directed, to a horn in the fish's head. He was then drawn along[1]—(I translate nearly literally):

Along the ocean in that stately ship was borne the lord of men, and through
Its dancing, tumbling billows, and its roaring waters; and the bark,
Tossed to and fro by violent winds, reeled on the surface of the deep,
Staggering and trembling like a drunken woman. Land was seen no more,
Nor far horizon, nor the space between; for everywhere around
Spread the wild waste of waters, reeking atmosphere, and boundless sky.
And now when all the world was deluged, nought appeared above the waves
But Manu and the seven sages, and the fish that drew the bark.
Unwearied thus for years on years the fish propelled the ship across
The heaped-up waters, till at length it bore the vessel to the peak
Of Himavān; then, softly smiling, thus the fish addressed the sage:
Haste now to bind thy ship to this high crag. Know me the lord of all,

[1] There is still a later account of the Deluge in the Bhāgavata-purāṇa, where the fish is represented as an incarnation of Vishṇu. The god's object in descending as a fish seems to have been to steer the ship. In the Assyrian account (as interpreted by Mr. G. Smith) sailors and a helmsman are taken on board.

The great creator Brahmā, mightier than all might—omnipotent.
By me in fish-like shape hast thou been saved in dire emergency.
From Manu all creation, gods, Asuras, men, must be produced;
By him the world must be created—that which moves and moveth not.

Another tale told in this section of the poem (III. 16619, &c.) may be cited for its true poetic feeling and pathos—qualities in which it is scarcely excelled by the story of Admetus and Alcestis. I subjoin the briefest epitome:

Sāvitrī, the beautiful daughter of a king Aśvapati, loved Satyavān, the son of an old hermit, but was warned by a seer to overcome her attachment, as Satyavān was a doomed man, having only one year to live. But Sāvitrī replies[1]:

Whether his years be few or many, be he gifted with all grace
Or graceless, him my heart hath chosen, and it chooseth not again.

The king's daughter and the hermit's son were therefore married, and the bride strove to forget the ominous prophecy; but as the last day of the year approached, her anxiety became irrepressible. She exhausted herself in prayers and penances, hoping to stay the hand of the destroyer; yet all the while dared not reveal the fatal secret to her husband. At last the dreaded day arrived, and Satyavān set out to cut wood in the forest. His wife asked leave to accompany him, and walked behind her husband, smiling, but with a heavy heart. Satyavān soon made the wood resound with his hatchet, when suddenly a thrill of agony shot through his temples, and feeling himself falling, he called out to his wife to support him.

Then she received her fainting husband in her arms, and sat herself
On the cold ground, and gently laid his drooping head upon her lap;
Sorrowing, she call'd to mind the sage's prophecy, and reckoned up
The days and hours. All in an instant she beheld an awful shape
Standing before her, dressed in blood-red garments, with a glittering crown
Upon his head: his form, though glowing like the sun, was yet obscure,
And eyes he had like flames, a noose depended from his hand; and he
Was terrible to look upon, as by her husband's side he stood
And gazed upon him with a fiery glance. Shuddering she started up
And laid her dying Satyavān upon the ground, and with her hands
Joined reverently, she thus with beating heart addressed the Shape:

[1] I translate as closely as I can to the original. This and other select specimens of Indian poetry have been more freely and poetically translated by Mr. R. Griffiths.

Surely thou art a god, such form as thine must more than mortal be!
Tell me, thou godlike being, who thou art, and wherefore art thou here?

The figure replied that he was Yama, king of the dead; that her husband's time was come, and that he must bind and take his spirit:

Then from her husband's body forced he out and firmly with his cord
Bound and detained the spirit, clothed in form no larger than a thumb[1].
Forthwith the body, reft of vital being and deprived of breath,
Lost all its grace and beauty, and became ghastly and motionless.

After binding the spirit, Yama proceeds with it towards the quarter of which he is guardian—the south. The faithful wife follows him closely. Yama bids her go home and prepare her husband's funeral rites; but she persists in following, till Yama, pleased with her devotion, grants her any boon she pleases, *except* the life of her husband. She chooses that her husband's father, who is blind, may recover his sight. Yama consents, and bids her now return home. Still she persists in following. Two other boons are granted in the same way, and still Sāvitrī follows closely on the heels of the king of death. At last, overcome by her constancy, Yama grants a boon without exception. The delighted Sāvitrī exclaims—

Nought, mighty king, this time hast thou excepted: let my husband live;
Without him I desire not happiness, nor even heaven itself;
Without him I must die. 'So be it! faithful wife,' replied the king of death;
'Thus I release him;' and with that he loosed the cord that bound his soul.

During the residence of the five brothers in the forest, Jayad-ratha attempted to carry off Draupadī, while they were absent on a shooting excursion. This resembles in some respects the story of Sītā's forcible abduction by Rāvaṇa in the Rāmāyaṇa (III. 15572), which story, therefore, is here told (15945. See p. 368 of this volume).

In the thirteenth year of exile, the Pāṇḍavas journeyed to the court of king Virāṭa, and entered his service in different disguises:

Yudhi-shṭhira called himself a Brāhman and took the name of Kaṅka (23); Arjuna named himself Vṛihan-nalā, and pretending to be a eunuch (*tṛitīyām prakṛitim gataḥ*), adopted a sort of woman's dress, putting bracelets on his arms and ear-rings in his ears, in order, as he said, to

[1] Compare note 3, p. 206 of this volume.

hide the scars caused by his bow-string. He undertook in this capacity to teach dancing, music, and singing to the daughter of Virāṭa and the other women of the palace, and soon gained their good graces (IV. 310).

One day when Virāṭa and four of the Pāṇḍavas were absent, Duryodhana and his brothers made an expedition against Virāṭa's capital, Matsya, and carried off some cattle. Uttara the son of Virāṭa (in the absence of his father) determined to follow and attack the Kuru army, if any one could be found to act as his charioteer. Vṛihan-nalā (Arjuna) undertook this office, and promised to bring back fine clothes and ornaments for Uttarā and the other women of the palace (IV. 1226). When they arrived in sight of the Kuru army, the courage of Uttara, who was a mere youth, failed him. Vṛihan-nalā then made him act as charioteer, while he himself (Arjuna) undertook to fight the Kauravas. Upon that great prodigies occurred. Terror seized Bhīshma, Duryodhana, and their followers, who suspected that Vṛihan-nalā was Arjuna in disguise, and even the horses shed tears[1] (IV. 1290). Duryodhana, however, declared that if he turned out to be Arjuna, he would have to wander in exile for a second period of twelve years. Meanwhile Arjuna revealed himself to Uttara, and explained also the disguises of his brothers and Draupadī. Uttara, to test his veracity, inquired whether he could repeat Arjuna's ten names, and what each meant. Arjuna enumerated them (Arjuna, Phālguna, Jishṇu, Kirīṭin, S'vetavāhana, Bībhatsu, Vijaya, Kṛishṇa, Savyasāćin, Dhanañjaya), and explained their derivation[2] (IV. 1380). Uttara then declared that he was satisfied, and no longer afraid of the Kuru army (IV. 1393).

Arjuna next put off his bracelets and woman's attire, strung his bow Gāṇḍīva, and assumed all his other weapons, which had been concealed in a S'amī tree. They are described as addressing him suppliantly, and saying, 'We are your servants, ready to carry out your commands[3]' (IV. 1421). He also removed Uttara's standard and placed his own ape-emblazoned banner in front of the chariot. Then was fought a great battle between Arjuna and the Kauravas. In the end the whole Kuru army fled before him, and all the property and cattle of Virāṭa was recovered. Arjuna told Uttara to conceal the real circumstances of the battle, but to send messengers to his father's capital announcing his victory, which so delighted Virāṭa that he ordered the whole city to be decorated.

---

[1] Compare Homer, Iliad XVII. 426.

[2] See Arjuna's other names in note 4, p. 382.

[3] Compare note 1, p. 402.

Not long afterwards Virāṭa held a great assembly, at which the five Pāṇḍavas attended, and took their seats with the other princes. Virāṭa, who did not yet know their real rank, was at first angry at this presumption (IV. 2266). Arjuna then revealed who they were. Virāṭa was delighted, embraced the Pāṇḍavas, offered them all his possessions, and to Arjuna his daughter Uttarā in marriage. Arjuna declined, but accepted her for his son Abhimanyu (IV. 2356).

A council of princes was then called by Virāṭa, at which the Pāṇḍavas, Kṛishṇa, and Bala-rāma were present, and a consultation was held as to what course the Pāṇḍavas were to take:

Kṛishṇa, in a speech, advised that they should not go to war with their kinsmen until they had sent an ambassador to Duryodhana, summoning him to restore half the kingdom. Bala-rāma supported Kṛishṇa's opinion, and recommended conciliation (*sāman*), but Sātyaki, in an angry tone, counselled war (V. 40). Drupada supported him, and recommended that they should send messengers to all their allies, and collect forces from all parts. The upshot was that the family-priest of Drupada was despatched by the Pāṇḍavas as an ambassador to king Dhṛita-rāshṭra at Hastinā-pur, to try the effect of negotiation.

Meanwhile Kṛishṇa and Bala-rāma returned to Dvārakā. Soon afterwards Duryodhana visited Kṛishṇa there, hoping to prevail on him to fight on the side of the Kuru army.

On the same day Arjuna arrived there also, and it happened that they both reached the door of Kṛishṇa's apartment, where he was asleep, at the same moment. Duryodhana succeeded in entering first, and took up his station at Kṛishṇa's head. Arjuna followed behind, and stood reverently at Kṛishṇa's feet. On awaking, Kṛishṇa's eyes first fell on Arjuna. He then asked them both the object of their visit. Duryodhana thereupon requested his aid in battle, declaring that although Kṛishṇa was equally related to Arjuna, yet that, as he (Duryodhana) had entered the room first, he was entitled to the priority. Kṛishṇa answered that, as he had seen Arjuna first, he should give Arjuna the first choice of two things. On the one side, he placed himself, stipulating that he was to lay down his weapons and abstain from fighting. On the other, he placed his army of a hundred million (*arbuda*) warriors, named Nārāyaṇas. Arjuna, without hesitation, chose Kṛishṇa; and Duryodhana, with glee, accepted the army, thinking that as Kṛishṇa was pledged not to fight, he would be unable to help the Pāṇḍavas in battle (V. 154).

Duryodhana next went to Bala-rāma and asked his aid; but Bala-rāma declared that both he and Kṛishṇa had determined to take no part in the strife[1]. Kṛishṇa, however, consented to act as Arjuna's charioteer, and soon afterwards joined Yudhi-shṭhira, who with his brothers was still living in the country of Virāṭa. Various attempts at negotiation followed, and before any actual declaration of war the Pāṇḍavas held a final consultation, at which Arjuna begged Kṛishṇa to undertake the office of a mediator. Kṛishṇa consented and departed for Hastinā-pura:

Midway he was met by Paraśu-rāma and various Ṛishis, who informed him of their resolution to be present at the coming congress of Kuru princes. On reaching Hastinā-pura, Kṛishṇa retired to rest in the house of Vidura. In the morning he performed all the appointed religious ceremonies, dressed himself, put on the jewel Kaustubha (V. 3343), and set out for the assembly. Then followed the great congress. The Ṛishis, headed by Nārada, appeared in the sky, and were accommodated with seats. Kṛishṇa opened the proceedings by a speech, which commenced thus: 'Let there be peace (*śama*) between the Kurus and Pāṇḍavas.' Then, looking towards Dhṛita-rāshṭra, he said, 'It rests with you and me to effect a reconciliation.' When he had concluded a long harangue, all remained riveted and thrilled by his eloquence (V. 3448). None ventured for some time to reply, except Paraśu-rāma, the sage Kaṇva, and Nārada, who all advocated harmony and peace between the rival cousins. At length Duryodhana spoke, and flatly refused to give up any territory: 'It was not our fault,' he said, 'if the Pāṇḍavas were conquered at dice.' Upon that Kṛishṇa's wrath rose, and addressing Duryodhana, he said, 'You think that I am alone, but know that the Pāṇḍavas, Andhakas, Vṛishṇis, Ādityas, Rudras, Vasus, and Ṛishis are all present

---

[1] Compare Megha-dūta, verse 51, where Bala-rāma is described as *Bandhu-prītyā samara-vimukhaḥ*.

here in me.' Thereupon flames of fire, of the size of a thumb, settled on him. Brahmā appeared on his forehead, Rudra on his breast, the guardians of the world issued from his arms, Agni from his mouth. The Ādityas, Sādhyas, Vasus, Aśvins, Maruts with Indra, Viśvadevas, Yakshas, Gandharvas, and Rākshasas were also manifested out of his body; Arjuna was produced from his right arm; Bala-rāma from his left arm; Bhīma, Yudhi-shṭhira, and the sons of Mādrī from his back; flames of fire darted from his eyes, nose, and ears; and the sun's rays from the pores of his skin[1] (V. 4419–4430). At this awful sight, the assembled princes were compelled to close their eyes; but Droṇa, Bhīshma, Vidura, Sañjaya, the Ṛishis, and the blind Dhṛita-rāshṭra were gifted by Kṛishṇa with divine vision that they might behold the glorious spectacle of his identification with every form (cf. p. 147 of this volume). Then a great earthquake and other portents occurred, and the congress broke up. Kṛishṇa, having suppressed his divinity, re-assumed his human form and set out on his return. He took Karṇa with him for some distance in his chariot, hoping to persuade him to take part with the Pāṇḍavas as a sixth brother. But, notwithstanding all Kṛishṇa's arguments, Karṇa would not be persuaded; and, leaving the chariot, returned to the sons of Dhṛita-rāshṭra (V. 4883).

Meanwhile Bhīshma consented to accept the generalship of the Kuru army (V. 5719). Though averse from fighting against his kinsmen, he could not as a Kshatriya abstain from joining in the war, when once commenced[2].

Before the armies joined battle, Vyāsa appeared to his son Dhṛita-rāshṭra, who was greatly dejected at the prospect of the war, consoled him, and offered to confer sight upon him, that he might view the combat. Dhṛita-rāshṭra declined witnessing the slaughter of his kindred, and Vyāsa then said that he would endow Sañjaya (Dhṛita-rāshṭra's charioteer) with the faculty of knowing everything that took place, make him invulnerable, and enable him to transport himself by a thought at any time to any part of the field of battle (VI. 43–47).

---

[1] This remarkable passage, identifying Vishṇu with everything in the universe, is probably a later interpolation.

[2] Bhīshma, though really the grand-uncle of the Kuru and Pāṇḍu princes, is often styled their grandfather (*pitāmaha*); and though really the uncle of Dhṛita-rāshṭra and Pāṇḍu, is sometimes styled their father. He is a kind of Priam in caution and sagacity, but like a hardy old veteran, never consents to leave the fighting to others.

The armies now met on Kuru-kshetra, a vast plain north-west of the modern Delhi; the Kuru forces being commanded by Bhīshma, and the Pāṇḍavas by Dhṛishṭa-dyumna, son of Drupada (VI. 832). While the hosts stood drawn up in battle-array, Kṛishṇa, acting as Arjuna's charioteer, addressed him in a long philosophical discourse, which forms the celebrated episode called Bhagavad-gītā (VI. 830–1532), an epitome of which is given at pp. 136–152 of this volume.

And now as the armies advanced a tumult filled the sky; the earth shook; 'Chafed by wild winds, the sands upcurled to heaven, and spread a veil before the sun.' Awful portents occurred; showers of blood fell[1]; asses were born from cows, calves from mares, jackals from dogs. Shrill kites, vultures, and howling jackals hung about the rear of the marching armies. Thunder roared in the cloudless sky. Then darkness supervened, lightnings flashed, and blazing meteors shot across the darkened firmament; yet,

> The mighty chiefs, with martial ardour fired,
> Scorning Heaven's portents, eager for the fray,
> Pressed on to mutual slaughter, and the peal
> Of shouting hosts commingling, shook the world.

There is to a European a ponderous and unwieldy character about Oriental warfare, which he finds it difficult to realize; yet the battle-scenes, though exaggerated, are vividly described, and carry the imagination into the midst of the conflict. Monstrous elephants career over the field, trampling on men and horses, and dealing destruction with their huge tusks; enormous clubs and iron maces clash together with the noise of thunder;

---

[1] So Jupiter rains blood twice in the Iliad, XI. 53 and XVI. 459. We have also the following in Hesiod, Scut. Herc. 384: Κὰδ δ' ἄρ' ἀπ' οὐρανόθεν ψιάδας βάλεν αἱματοέσσας.

rattling chariots dash against each other; thousands of arrows hurtle in the air, darkening the sky; trumpets, kettle-drums, and horns add to the uproar; confusion, carnage, and death are everywhere.

In all this, however, there is nothing absolutely extravagant; but when Arjuna is described as killing five hundred warriors simultaneously, or as covering the whole plain with dead and filling rivers with blood; Yudhishṭhira, as slaughtering a hundred men 'in a mere twinkle' (*nimesha-mātreṇa*); Bhīma, as annihilating a monstrous elephant, including all mounted upon it, and fourteen foot-soldiers besides, with one blow of his club; Nakula and Sahadeva, fighting from their chariots, as cutting off heads by the thousand, and sowing them like seed upon the ground; when, moreover, the principal heroes make use of mystical god-given weapons, possessed of supernatural powers, and supposed to be themselves celestial beings[1];—we at once perceive that the utter unreality of such scenes mars the beauty of the description. Still it must be borne in mind that the poets who brāhmanized the Indian Epics gifted the heroes

[1] About a hundred of these weapons are enumerated in the Rāmāyaṇa (I. xxix), and constant allusion is made to them in battle-scenes, both in the Rāmāyaṇa and Mahā-bhārata. Arjuna underwent a long course of austerities to obtain celestial weapons from S'iva (see p. 393). It was by the terrific *brahmāstra* that Vaśishṭha conquered Viśvāmitra, and Rāma killed Rāvaṇa. Sometimes they appear to be mystical powers exercised by meditation, rather than weapons, and are supposed to assume animate forms, and possess names and faculties like the genii in the Arabian Nights, and to address their owners (see p. 397). Certain distinct spells, charms, or prayers had to be learnt for their due use (*prayoga*) and restraint (*saṃhāra*). See Rām. I. xxix, xxx, where they are personified; also Raghu-vaṇśa V. 57 (*Sammohanaṃ nāma astram ādhatsva prayoga-saṃhāra-vibhakta-mantram*). When once let loose, he only who knew the secret spell for recalling them, could bring them back; but the *brahmāstra* returned to its possessor's quiver of its own accord.

with semi-divine natures, and that what would be incredible in a mere mortal is not only possible but appropriate when enacted by a demigod[1]. The individual deeds of prowess and single combats between the heroes are sometimes graphically narrated. Each chief has a conch-shell (*śankha*) for a trumpet, which, as well as his principal weapon, has a name, as if personified[2]. Thus we read:

Arjuna blew his shell called Deva-datta, 'god-given,' and carried a bow named Gāṇḍīva. Kṛishṇa sounded a shell made of the bones of the demon Pańćajana and hence called Pāńćajanya, Bhīma blew a great trumpet named Pauṇḍra, and Yudhi-shṭhira sounded his, called Ananta-vijaya, 'eternal victory.'

The first great single-combat was between Bhīshma and Arjuna. It ended in Arjuna transfixing Bhīshma with innumerable arrows, so that there was not a space of two fingers' breadth on his whole body unpierced.

Then Bhīshma fell from his chariot; but his body could not touch the ground, surrounded as it was by countless arrows (VI. 5658). There it remained, reclining as it were on an arrowy couch (*śara-talpe śayāna*). In that state consciousness returned, and the old warrior became divinely supported. He had received from his father the power of fixing the time of his own death[3], and now declared that he intended retaining life till the sun entered the summer solstice (*uttarāyaṇa*). All the warriors on both sides ceased fighting that they might view this wonderful sight, and do homage to their dying relative (VI. 5716). As he lay on his arrowy bed, his head hanging down, he begged for a pillow; whereupon

---

[1] Aristotle says that the epic poet should prefer impossibilities which appear probable to such things as though possible appear improbable (Poetics III. 6). But previously, in comparing epic poetry with tragedy, he observes, 'the surprising is necessary in tragedy, but the epic poem goes further, and admits even the improbable and incredible, from which the highest degree of the surprising results' (III. 4).

[2] Trumpets do not appear to have been used by Homer's heroes. Whence the value of a Stentorian voice. But there is express allusion in Il. XVIII. 219 to the use of trumpets at sieges.

[3] Compare Kirātārjunīya III. 19.

the chiefs brought soft supports, which the hardy old soldier sternly rejected. Arjuna then made a rest for his head with three arrows, which Bhīshma quite approved, and soon afterwards asked Arjuna to bring him water. Whereupon Arjuna struck the ground with an arrow, and forthwith a pure spring burst forth, which so refreshed Bhīshma that he called for Duryodhana, and in a long speech begged him, before it was too late, to restore half the kingdom to the Pāṇḍavas (VI. 5813).

After the fall of Bhīshma, Karṇa advised Duryodhana to appoint his old tutor Droṇa—who was chiefly formidable from his stock of fiery arrows and magical weapons[1]—to the command of the army (VII. 150). Several single combats and general engagements (*sankula-yuddham, tumula-yuddham*), in which sometimes one party, sometimes the other had the advantage, took place. Here is an account of a single combat (VII. 544):

High on a stately car
Swift borne by generous coursers to the fight,
The vaunting son of Puru proudly drove,
Secure of conquest o'er Subhadrā's son.
The youthful champion shrank not from the conflict.
Fierce on the boastful chief he sprang, as bounds
The lion's cub upon the ox; and now
The Puru chief had perished, but his dart
Shivered with timely aim the upraised bow
Of Abhimanyu[2]. From his tingling hand
The youthful warrior cast the fragments off,
And drew his sword, and grasped his iron-bound shield;
Upon the car of Paurava he lept
And seized the chief—his charioteer he slew,
And dragged the monarch senseless o'er the plain[3].

Amongst other battles a great fight was fought between Ghaṭotkaća and Karṇa, in which the former as a Rākshasa

[1] These *āgneyāstra* were received by Droṇa from the son of Agni, who obtained them from Droṇa's father, Bharadvāja.

[2] The name of Arjuna's son by Subhadrā.

[3] The translation of this and the short passage at p. 401 is a slightly altered version of some spirited lines by Professor H. H. Wilson, given in vol. iii. of his collected works edited by Dr. R. Rost.

(son of the Rākshasī Hiḍimbā and Bhīma) assumed various forms, but was eventually slain (VII. 8104). This disaster filled the Pāṇḍavas with grief, but the fortunes of the day were retrieved by Dhṛishṭa-dyumna (son of Drupada), who fought with Droṇa, and succeeded in decapitating his lifeless body,—not, however, till Droṇa had laid down his arms and saved Dhṛishṭa-dyumna from the enormous crime of killing a Brāhman and an Āćārya, by transporting himself to heaven in a glittering shape like the sun. His translation to Brahma-loka was only witnessed by five persons, and before leaving the earth he made over his divine weapons to his son Aśvatthāman. The loss of their general Droṇa caused the flight of the whole Kuru army (VII. 8879), but they appointed Karṇa general, in his place, and renewed the combat:

In this engagement so terrible was the slaughter that the rivers flowed with blood, and the field became covered with mutilated corpses (VIII. 2550, 3899). Numbers of warriors bound themselves by oath (*saṃśaptaka*) to slay Arjuna, but were all destroyed, and an army of Mleććhas or barbarians with thirteen hundred elephants, sent by Duryodhana against Arjuna, were all routed by him (4133).

Then Bhīma and Duḥśāsana joined in deadly conflict. The latter was slain, and Bhīma, remembering the insult to Draupadī, and the vow he made in consequence (see p. 393), cut off his head, and drank his blood on the field of battle (4235).

Then occurred the battle between Karṇa and Arjuna:

Arjuna was wounded and stunned by an arrow shot off by Karṇa, and seemed likely to be defeated had not the wheel of Karṇa's chariot come off. This obliged Karṇa to leap down, and his head was then shot off by one of Arjuna's arrows[1] (VIII. 4798). His death struck terror into the Kuru army, which fled in dismay, while Bhīma and the Pāṇḍu party raised a shout of triumph that shook heaven and earth.

---

[1] This arrow is called in the text *Añjalika* (VIII. 4788). The arrows used in the Mahā-bhārata are of various kinds, some having crescent-shaped heads. It may be useful to subjoin a list of words for arrow, which occur constantly in the description of battles: *śara, vāṇa, ishu, śāyaka, patrin, kāṇḍa, viśikha, nārāća, vipāṭha, pṛishatka, bhalla, tomara* (a kind of lance), *śalya* (a dart), *ishīkā, śilīmukha.*

On the death of Karṇa, Śalya, king of Madra, was appointed to the command of the Kuru army, then much reduced in numbers (IX. 327). Another general engagement followed, and a single combat between Śalya and Bhīma with clubs or maces, in which both were equally matched (IX. 594). Here is a version of the encounter:

Soon as he saw his charioteer struck down,
Straightway the Madra monarch grasped his mace,
And like a mountain firm and motionless
Awaited the attack. The warrior's form
Was awful as the world-consuming fire,
Or as the noose-armed god of death, or as
The peaked Kailāsa, or the Thunderer
Himself, or as the trident-bearing god,
Or as a maddened forest elephant.
Him to defy did Bhīma hastily
Advance, wielding aloft his massive club.
A thousand conchs and trumpets and a shout,
Firing each champion's ardour, rent the air.
From either host, spectators of the fight,
Burst forth applauding cheers: 'The Madra king
Alone,' they cried, 'can bear the rush of Bhīma;
None but heroic Bhīma can sustain
The force of S'alya.' Now like two fierce bulls
Sprang they towards each other, mace in hand.
And first as cautiously they circled round,
Whirling their weapons as in sport, the pair
Seemed matched in equal combat. S'alya's club,
Set with red fillets, glittered as with flame,
While that of Bhīma gleamed like flashing lightning.
Anon the clashing iron met, and scattered round
A fiery shower; then fierce as elephants
Or butting bulls they battered each the other.
Thick fell the blows, and soon each stalwart frame,
Spattered with gore, glowed like the Kiṉśuka,
Bedecked with scarlet blossoms; yet beneath
The rain of strokes, unshaken as a rock
Bhīma sustained the mace of S'alya, he
With equal firmness bore the other's blows.
Now like the roar of crashing thunder-clouds

Sounded the clashing iron; then, their clubs
Brandished aloft, eight paces they retired,
And swift again advancing to the fight,
Met in the midst like two huge mountain-crags
Hurled into contact. Nor could either bear
The other's shock; together down they rolled,
Mangled and crushed, like two tall standards fallen.

After this a great battle was fought between Yudhi-shṭhira and Śalya, who was at first aided and rescued by Aśvatthāman, but was eventually killed (IX. 919).

The Kauravas after suffering continual reverses, rallied their scattered forces for a final charge, which led to a complete rout and general slaughter, Duryodhana, Aśvatthāman (son of Droṇa), Kṛita-varman (also called Bhoja), and Kṛipa (see note 4, p. 383) being the only chiefs of the Kuru army left alive[1]. Nothing remained of eleven whole armies (IX. 1581). Duryodhana, wounded, disheartened, and alarmed for his own safety, resolved on flight:

On foot, with nothing but his mace, he took refuge in a lake, hiding himself under the water, and then, by his magical power, supporting it so as to form a chamber around his body[2]. The Pāṇḍavas informed of his hiding-place, came to the lake, and Yudhi-shṭhira commenced taunting Duryodhana, 'Where is your manliness? where is your pride? where your valour? where your skill in arms, that you hide yourself at the bottom of a lake? Rise up and fight; perform your duty as a Kshatriya' (IX. 1774). Duryodhana answered, that it was not from fear, but fatigue, that he was lying under the water, and that he was ready to fight them all. He entreated them, however, to go and take the kingdom, as he had no longer any pleasure in life, his brothers being killed. Yudhi-shṭhira then continued his sarcasms, till at last, thoroughly roused by his goading words (*vāk-pratoda*), Duryodhana rose up out of the lake, his body streaming with blood and water (IX. 1865).

---

[1] Sañjaya was taken by Dhṛishṭa-dyumna, and would have been killed had not Vyāsa suddenly appeared and demanded that he should be dismissed unharmed (compare p. 377).

[2] So I interpret *astambhayat toyam māyayā* (IX. 1621) and *vishṭabhya apaḥ sva-māyayā* (1680, 1739). Duryodhana is described as lying down and sleeping at the bottom of the lake (1705).

It was settled that a single combat with clubs should take place between Duryodhana and Bhīma; and when Bala-rāma heard that his two pupils (see p. 384) were about to engage in conflict, he determined to be present, that he might ensure fair play[1].

Then followed the great club-fight (*gadā-yuddha*):

The two combatants entered the lists and challenged each other, while Kṛishṇa, Bala-rāma, and all the other Pāṇḍavas sat round as spectators. The fight was tedious, the combatants being equally matched. At last Bhīma struck Duryodhana a blow on his thighs, broke them, and felled him to the ground. Then reminding him of the insult received by Draupadī, he kicked him on the head with his left foot (IX. 3313). Upon this Bala-rāma started up in anger, declaring that Bhīma had fought unfairly (it being a rule in club-fights that no blow should be given below the middle of the body), and that he should ever after be called *Jihma-yodhin* (unfair-fighter), while Duryodhana should always be celebrated as *Ṛiju-yodhin* (fair-fighter).

Bala-rāma thereupon returned to Dvārakā, and the five Pāṇḍavas with Krishṇa entered the camp of Duryodhana, and took possession of it and its treasures as victors (IX. 3492).

The three surviving Kuru warriors (Aśvatthāman, Kṛipa, and Kṛita-varman), hearing of the fall of Duryodhana, hastened to the place where he was lying. There they found him weltering in his blood (IX. 3629), but still alive. He spoke to them, told them not to grieve for him, and assured them that he should die happy in having done his duty as a Kshatriya. Then leaving Duryodhana still lingering alive with broken thighs on the battle-field, they took refuge in a forest.

There, at night, they rested near a Nyagrodha-tree, where thousands

[1] An interesting episode about the *māhātmya* of Tīrthas, and especially of those on the sacred Sarasvatī (IX. 2006), is inserted in this part of the poem. The story of the Moon, who was afflicted with consumption, on account of the curse of Daksha, is also told (2030), as well as the celebrated legend of Vaśishṭha and Viśvāmitra (2296, see p. 363).

of crows were roosting. Aśvatthāman, who could not sleep, saw an owl approach stealthily and destroy numbers of the sleeping crows (X. 41). This suggested the idea of entering the camp of the Pāṇḍavas by night and slaughtering them while asleep (*supta*[1]). Accordingly he set out for the Pāṇḍu camp, followed by Kṛipa and Kṛita-varman. At the gate of the camp his progress was arrested by an awful figure, described as gigantic, glowing like the sun, dressed in a tiger's skin, with long arms, and bracelets formed of serpents. This was the deity S'iva[2]; and after a tremendous conflict with him, Aśvatthāman recognized the god, worshipped and propitiated him (X. 251).

Aśvatthāman then directed Kṛipa and Kṛita-varman to stand at the camp-gate and kill any of the Pāṇḍu army that attempted to escape (X. 327). He himself made his way alone and stealthily to the tent of Dhṛishṭa-dyumna, who was lying there fast asleep. Him he killed by stamping on him, declaring that one who had murdered his father (Droṇa, see p. 405)—a Brāhman and an Ācārya—was not worthy to die in any other way (X. 342). After killing every one in the camp and destroying the whole Pāṇḍu army (except the five Pāṇḍavas themselves with Sātyaki and Kṛishṇa who happened to be stationed outside the camp), Aśvatthāman joined his comrades, and they all three proceeded to the spot where Duryodhana was lying. They found him just breathing (*kiñcit-prāṇa*), but weltering in his blood and surrounded by beasts of prey. Aśvatthāman then announced that he was avenged, as only seven of the Pāṇḍu army were now left; all the rest were slaughtered like cattle (X. 531). Duryodhana hearing this, revived a little, and gathering strength to thank them and say farewell, expired; his spirit rising to heaven and his body entering the ground (X. 536).

Thus perished both armies of Kurus and Pāṇḍavas.

Dhṛita-rāshṭra was so overwhelmed with grief for the death of his sons, that his father Vyāsa appeared to him and consoled him by pointing out that their fate was

---

[1] Hence the name *sauptika* applied to this section of the poem. Compare Homer's narrative of the night adventures of Diomed and Ulysses in the camp of the Trojans (Iliad X).

[2] The description of S'iva in this passage is remarkable. Hundreds and thousands of Kṛishṇas are said to be manifested from the light issuing from his person. Many of S'iva's names also are enumerated as follow: Ugra, Sthāṇu, S'iva, Rudra, S'arva, Īśāna, Īśvara, Giriśa, Varada, Deva, Bhava, Bhāvana, S'itikaṇṭha, Aja, S'ukra, Daksha-kratu-hara, Hara, Viśvarūpa, Virūpāksha, Bahurūpa, Umāpati (X. 252).

pre-destined, and that they could not escape death. He also declared that the Pāṇḍavas were not to blame; that Duryodhana, though born from Gāndhārī, was really a partial incarnation of Kali[1] (*Kaler aṉśa*), and Śakuni of Dvāpara (see p. 333, note).

Vidura also comforted the king with his usual sensible advice, and recommended that the funeral ceremonies (*preta-kāryāṇi*) should be performed. Dhṛita-rāshṭra then ordered carriages to be prepared, and with the women proceeded to the field of battle (XI. 269).

There he met and became reconciled to the five Pāṇḍavas, but his wife Gāndhārī would have cursed them had not Vyāsa interfered. The five brothers next embraced and comforted their mother Pṛithā, who with the queen Gāndhārī, and the other wives and women, uttered lamentations over the bodies of the slain heroes, as one by one they came in sight on the field of battle (XI. 427–755).

Finally, the funeral obsequies (*śrāddha*) were performed at the command of Yudhi-shṭhira (XI. 779), after which he, with his brothers, entered Hastinā-pura in triumph.

All the streets were decorated; and Brāhmans offered him congratulations, which he acknowledged by distributing largesses among them (XII. 1410). Only one person stood aloof. This turned out to be an impostor, a friend of Duryodhana—a Rākshasa named Ćārvāka—who in the disguise of a mendicant reviled him and the Brāhmans. He was, however, soon detected; and the real Brāhmans, filled with fury and uttering imprecations, killed him on the spot (see p. 132).

After this incident, Yudhi-shṭhira, seated on a golden throne, was solemnly crowned (XII. 1443).

Nevertheless, restless and uneasy, and his mind filled with anguish at the slaughter of his kindred, he longed for consolation (*śānti*), and Kṛishṇa recommended him to apply to Bhīshma, who still remained alive on the field of battle, reclining on his soldier's bed (*vīra-śayana*), surrounded by Vyāsa, Nārada, and other holy sages. Accordingly, Yudhi-shṭhira and his brothers, accompanied by Kṛishṇa, set out for Kuru-kshetra,

[1] So also S'akuni is said to be an incarnation of Dvāpara (XVIII. 166).

passing mutilated corpses, skulls, broken armour, and other evidences of the fearful nature of the war. This reminded Kṛishṇa of the slaughter caused by Paraśu-rāma, who cleared the earth thrice seven times of the Kshatriya caste (see p. 331). His story was accordingly narrated to Yudhi-shṭhira (XII. 1707–1805). They then approached Bhīshma lying on his couch of arrows (*śara-saṃstara-śāyinam*), and Kṛishṇa entreated him to instruct Yudhi-shṭhira, and calm his spirit.

Upon that Bhīshma, who had been lying for fifty-eight nights on his spiky bed (XIII. 7732), assisted by Kṛishṇa, Nārada, Vyāsa, and other Ṛishis, commenced a series of long and tedious didactic discourses (contained in the S'ānti-parvan and Anuśāsana-parvan[1]).

Then having finished instructing his relatives, he bade them farewell, and asked Kṛishṇa's leave to depart. Suddenly the arrows left his body, his skull divided, and his spirit, bright as a meteor, ascended through the top of his head to the skies (XIII. 7765). They covered him with garlands and perfumes, carried him to the Ganges, and performed his last obsequies.

And here a European poet would have brought the story to an end. The Sanskṛit poet has a deeper knowledge of human nature, or at least of Hindū nature.

In the most popular of Indian dramas (the Śakuntalā) there occurs this sentiment[2]:

> 'Tis a vain thought that to attain the end
> And object of ambition is to rest.
> Success doth only mitigate the fever
> Of anxious expectation: soon the fear
> Of losing what we have, the constant care
> Of guarding it doth weary.

If then the great national Epic was to respond truly to the deeper emotions of the Hindū mind, it could not

[1] In XII. 1241 we have some curious rules for expiation (*prāyaś-ćitta*), and at 1393 rules for what to eat and what to avoid (*bhakshyā-bhakshya*). Some of the precepts are either taken from or founded on Manu. For instance, compare 6071 with Manu II. 238. Many of the moral verses in the Hitopadeśa will be found in the S'ānti-parvan; and the fable of the three fishes is founded on the story at 4889. For the contents of the Āśvamedhika, Āśramavāsika, and Mausala Parvans, see p. 375.

[2] See my translation of this play, 4th edition, p. 124 (recently published by W. H. Allen & Co., 13, Waterloo Place).

leave the Pāṇḍavas in the contented enjoyment of their kingdom. It had to instil a more sublime moral—a lesson which even the disciples of a divine philosophy are slow to learn—that all who desire rest must aim at union with the Infinite. Hence we are brought in the concluding chapters to a sublime description of the renunciation of their kingdom by the five brothers, and their journey towards Indra's heaven in the mountain Meru. Part of this (XVII. 24, &c.) I now translate:

When the four brothers knew the high resolve of king Yudhi-shṭhira,
Forthwith with Draupadī they issued forth, and after them a dog
Followed: the king himself went out the seventh from the royal city,
And all the citizens and women of the palace walked behind;
But none could find it in their heart to say unto the king, 'Return.'
And so at length the train of citizens went back, bidding adieu.
Then the high-minded sons of Pāṇḍu and the noble Draupadī
Roamed onwards, fasting, with their faces towards the east; their hearts
Yearning for union with the Infinite; bent on abandonment
Of worldly things. They wandered on to many countries, many a sea
And river. Yudhi-shṭhira walked in front, and next to him came Bhīma,
And Arjuna came after him, and then, in order, the twin brothers.
And last of all came Draupadī, with her dark skin and lotus-eyes—
The faithful Draupadī, loveliest of women, best of noble wives—
Behind them walked the only living thing that shared their pilgrimage—
The dog—and by degrees they reached the briny sea. There Arjuna
Cast in the waves his bow and quivers[1]. Then with souls well-disciplined
They reached the northern region, and beheld with heaven-aspiring hearts
The mighty mountain Himavat. Beyond its lofty peak they passed
Towards a sea of sand, and saw at last the rocky Meru, king
Of mountains. As with eager steps they hastened on, their souls intent
On union with the Eternal, Draupadī lost hold of her high hope,
And faltering fell upon the earth.

One by one the others also drop, till only Bhīma, Yudhi-shṭhira, and the dog are left. Still Yudhi-shṭhira walks steadily in front, calm and unmoved, looking neither to the right hand nor to the left, and gathering up his

[1] Arjuna had two celebrated quivers, besides the bow named Gāṇḍīva, given to him by the god Agni. See Kirātārjunīya XI. 16.

soul in inflexible resolution. Bhīma, shocked at the fall of his companions, and unable to understand how beings so apparently guileless should be struck down by fate, appeals to his brother, who, without looking back, explains that death is the consequence of sinful thoughts and too great attachment to worldly objects; and that Draupadī's fall was owing to her excessive affection for Arjuna; Sahadeva's (who is supposed to be the most humble-minded of the five brothers) to his pride in his own knowledge; Nakula's (who is very handsome) to feelings of personal vanity; and Arjuna's to a boastful confidence in his power to destroy his foes. Bhīma then feels himself falling, and is told that he suffers death for his selfishness, pride, and too great love of enjoyment. The sole survivor is now Yudhi-shṭhira, who still walks steadily forward, followed only by the dog:

When with a sudden sound that rang through earth and heaven the mighty god
Came towards him in a chariot, and he cried, 'Ascend, O resolute prince.'
Then did the king look back upon his fallen brothers, and address'd
These words unto the Thousand-eyed in anguish—'Let my brothers here
Come with me. Without them, O god of gods, I would not wish to enter
E'en heaven; and yonder tender princess Draupadī, the faithful wife,
Worthy of endless bliss, let her too come. In mercy hear my prayer.'

Upon this, Indra informs him that the spirits of Draupadī and his brothers are already in heaven, and that he alone is permitted to ascend there in bodily form. Yudhi-shṭhira now stipulates that his dog shall be admitted with him. Indra says sternly, 'Heaven has no place for men accompanied by dogs (*śvavatām*);' but Yudhi-shṭhira is unshaken in his resolution, and declines abandoning the faithful animal. Indra remonstrates—'You have abandoned your brothers and Draupadī; why not forsake the dog?' To this Yudhi-shṭhira haughtily replies, 'I had no power to bring them back to life: how can there be abandonment of those who no longer live?'

The dog, it appears, is his own father Dharma in disguise (XVII. 88 [1]). Reassuming now his proper form, he praises Yudhi-shṭhira for his constancy, and they enter heaven together. There, to his surprise, he finds Duryodhana and his cousins, but not his brothers or Draupadī. Hereupon he declines remaining in heaven without them. An angel is then sent to conduct him to the lower regions and across the Indian Styx (*Vaitaraṇī*) to the hell where they are supposed to be. The scene which now follows may be compared to the Nekyomanteia in the eleventh book of the Odyssey, or to parts of Dante.

The particular hell to which Yudhi-shṭhira is taken is a dense wood, whose leaves are sharp swords, and its ground paved with razors (*asi-patra-vana*, see p. 66, note 2). The way to it is strewed with foul and mutilated corpses. Hideous shapes flit across the air and hover over him. Here there is an awful sensation of palpable darkness. There the wicked are burning in flames of blazing fire. Suddenly he hears the voices of his brothers and companions imploring him to assuage their torments, and not desert them. His resolution is taken. Deeply affected, he bids the angel leave him to share their miseries. This is his last trial. The whole scene now vanishes. It was a mere illusion, to test his constancy to the utmost. He is now directed to bathe in the heavenly Ganges; and having plunged into the sacred stream, he enters the real heaven, where at length, in company with Draupadī and his brothers, he finds that rest and happiness which were unattainable on earth.

---

[1] So I infer from the original, which, however, is somewhat obscure. The expression is *dharma-svarūpī bhagavān*. At any rate, the dog was a mere phantom created to try Yudhi-shṭhira, as it is evident that a real dog is not admitted with Yudhi-shṭhira to heaven.

# LECTURE XIV.

## *The Indian Epics compared with each other and with the Homeric Poems.*

I PROCEED to note a few obvious points that force themselves on the attention in comparing the two great Indian Epics with each other, and with the Homeric poems. I have already stated that the episodes of the Mahā-bhārata occupy more than three-fourths of the whole poem[1]. It is, in fact, not one poem, but a combination of many poems: not a *Kāvya*, like the poem of Vālmīki, by one author, but an *Itihāsa* by many authors. This is one great distinctive feature in comparing it with the Rāmāyaṇa. In both Epics there is a leading story, about which are collected a multitude of other stories; but in the Mahā-bhārata the main narrative only acts as a slender thread to connect together a vast mass of independent legends, and religious, moral, and political precepts; while in the Rāmāyaṇa the episodes, though numerous, never break the solid chain of one principal and paramount subject, which is ever kept in view. Moreover, in the Rāmāyaṇa there are few didactic discourses and a remarkable paucity of sententious maxims.

[1] Although the Mahā-bhārata is so much longer than the Rāmāyaṇa as to preclude the idea of its being, like that poem, the work of one or even a few authors, yet it is the number of the episodes which, after all, causes the disparity. Separated from these, the main story of the Mahā-bhārata is not longer than the other Epic.

It should be remembered that the two Epics belong to different periods and different localities. Not only was a large part of the Mahā-bhārata composed later than the Rāmāyaṇa, parts of it being comparatively modern, but the places which gave birth to the two poems are distinct (see p. 320). Moreover, in the Rāmāyaṇa the circle of territory represented as occupied by the Āryans is more restricted than that in the Mahā-bhārata. It reaches to Videha or Mithilā and Anga in the East, to Su-rāshṭra in the South-west, to the Yamunā and great Daṇḍaka forest in the South. Whereas in the Mahā-bhārata (as pointed out by Professor Lassen) the Āryan settlers are described as having extended themselves to the mouths of the Ganges in the East, to the mouth of the Godāvarī on the Koromandel coast, and to the Malabar coast in the West; and even the inhabitants of Ceylon (Sinhala) bring tribute to the Northern kings. It is well known that in India different customs and opinions frequently prevail in districts almost adjacent; and it is certain that Brāhmanism never gained the ascendancy in the more martial north which it acquired in the neighbourhood of Oude [1], so that in the Mahā-bhārata we have far more allusions to Buddhistic scepticism than we have in the sister Epic. In fact, each poem, though often running parallel to the other, has yet a distinct point of departure; and the Mahā-bhārata, as it became current in various localities, diverged more into by-paths and cross-roads than its sister. Hence the Rāmāyaṇa is in some respects a more finished

[1] Professor Weber (Ind. Stud. I. 220) remarks that the north-western tribes retained their ancient customs, which those who migrated to the east had at one time shared. The former (as represented in the Mahā-bhārata) kept themselves free from those influences of hierarchy and caste, which arose among the inhabitants of Ayodhyā (in the Rāmāyaṇa) as a consequence of their intermingling and coming more in contact with the aborigines.

composition than the Mahā-bhārata, and depicts a more polished state of society, and a more advanced civilization. In fact, the Mahā-bhārata presents a complete circle of post-Vedic mythology, including many myths which have their germ in the Veda, and continually enlarging its circumference to embrace the later phases of Hindūism, with its whole train of confused and conflicting legends[1]. From this storehouse are drawn much of the Purāṇas, and many of the more recent heroic poems and dramas. Here we have repeated many of the legends of the Rāmāyaṇa, and even the history of Rāma himself (see p. 368). Here also we have long discourses on religion, politics, morality, and philosophy, introduced without any particular connexion with the plot. Here again are most of the narratives of the incarnation of Vishṇu, numberless stories connected with the worship of Śiva, and various details of the life of Kṛishṇa. Those which especially bear on the modern worship of Kṛishṇa are contained in the supplement called Hari-vaṉśa, which is itself a long poem—consisting of 16,374 stanzas[2]—longer than the Iliad and Odyssey combined[3]. Hence the religious system of the Mahā-bhārata is far more popular, liberal, and comprehensive than that of the Rāmāyaṇa. It is true that the god Vishṇu is connected with Kṛishṇa in the Mahā-bhārata, as he is with Rāma

[1] It should be noted, that the germs of many of the legends of Hindū epic poetry are found in the Ṛig-veda. Also that the same legend is sometimes repeated in different parts of the Mahā-bhārata, with considerable variations; as, for example, the story of the combat of Indra—god of air and thunder—with the demon Vṛitra, who represents enveloping clouds and vapour. See Vana-parvan 8690 &c.; and compare with Śānti-parvan 10124 &c. Compare also the story of the 'Hawk and Pigeon,' Vana-parvan 10558, with Anuśāsana-parvan 2046.

[2] The Hari-vaṉśa bears to the Mahā-bhārata a relation very similar to that which the Uttara-kāṇḍa, or last Book of the Rāmāyaṇa, bears to the preceding Books of that poem.

[3] The Iliad and Odyssey together contain about 30,000 lines.

in the Rāmāyaṇa, but in the latter Rāma is everything; whereas in the Mahā-bhārata, Kṛishṇa is by no means the centre of the system. His divinity is even occasionally disputed[1]. The five Pāṇḍavas have also partially divine natures, and by turns become prominent. Sometimes Arjuna, sometimes Yudhi-shṭhira, at others Bhīma, appears to be the principal orb round which the plot moves[2]. Moreover, in various passages Śiva is described as supreme, and receives worship from Kṛishṇa. In others, Kṛishṇa is exalted above all, and receives honour from Śiva[3]. In fact, while the Rāmāyaṇa generally represents one-sided and exclusive Brāhmanism[4], the Mahā-bhārata reflects the multilateral character of Hindūism; its monotheism and polytheism, its spirituality and materialism, its strictness and laxity, its priestcraft and anti-priestcraft, its hierarchical intolerance and rationalistic philosophy, combined. Not that there was any intentional variety in the original design of the work, but that almost every shade of opinion found expression in a compilation formed by gradual accretion through a long period.

In unison with its more secular, popular, and *human* character, the Mahā-bhārata has, as a rule, less of mere mythical allegory, and more of historical probability in its

---

[1] As by S'iśu-pāla and others. See p. 392, with notes.

[2] In this respect the Mahā-bhārata resembles the Iliad. Achilles is scarcely its hero. Other warriors too much divide the interest with him.

[3] In the Bhagavad-gītā Kṛishṇa is not merely an incarnation of Vishṇu; he is identified with Brahma, the Supreme Spirit, and is so in numerous other places. It is well known that in Homer the supremacy of one god (Jove), and due subordination of the other deities, is maintained.

[4] Some free thought, however, has found its way into the Rāmāyaṇa; see II. cviii (Schl.); VI. lxii. 15 (Gorr., Bomb. lxxxiii. 14); VI. lxxxiii. 14 (Calc.). It is remarkable that in the Rāmāyaṇa the same gods are appealed to by Rāma and Rāvaṇa, just as by Greeks and Trojans in the Iliad; and Hanumat, when in Laṅkā, heard the Brahma-ghosha in the morning. Rāmāy. V. xvi. 41. This has been noticed by Weber.

narratives than the Rāmāyaṇa. The reverse, however, sometimes holds good. For example, in Rāmāyaṇa IV. xl. we have a simple division of the world into four quarters or regions, whereas in Mahā-bhārata VI. 236 &c. we have the fanciful division (afterwards adopted by the Purāṇas) into seven circular Dvīpas or continents, viz. 1. Jambu-dvīpa or the Earth, 2. Plaksha-dvīpa, 3. Śālmali-dvīpa, 4. Kuśa-dvīpa, 5. Krauñća-dvīpa, 6. Śāka-dvīpa, 7. Push-kara-dvīpa; surrounded respectively by seven oceans in concentric belts, viz. 1. the sea of salt-water (*lavaṇa*), 2. of sugar-cane juice (*ikshu*), 3. of wine (*surā*), 4. of clarified butter (*sarpis*), 5. of curdled milk (*dadhi*), 6. of milk (*dugdha*), 7. of fresh water (*jala*); the mountain Meru, or abode of the gods, being in the centre of *Jambu-dvīpa*, which again is divided into nine Varshas or countries separated by eight ranges of mountains, the Varsha called *Bhārata* (India) lying south of the Himavat range[1].

Notwithstanding these wild ideas and absurd figments, the Mahā-bhārata contains many more illustrations of real life and of domestic and social habits and manners than the sister Epic. Its diction again is more varied than that of the Rāmāyaṇa. The bulk of the latter poem (notwithstanding interpolations and additions) being by one author, is written with uniform simplicity of style and metre (see p. 338, note); and the antiquity of the greater part is proved by the absence of any studied

[1] The eight ranges are Nishadha, Hema-kūṭa, Nishadha on the south of Meru; Nīla, S'veta, S'ṛiṅgin on the north; and Mālyavat and Gandha-mādana on the west and east. Beyond the sea of fresh water is a circle called 'the land of gold,' and beyond this the circle of the Lokāloka mountains, which form the limit of the sun's light, all the region on one side being illuminated, and all on the other side of them being in utter darkness. See Raghu-vaṅśa I. 68. Below the seven Dvīpas are the seven Pātālas (see p. 431), and below these are the twenty-one Hells (note 2, p. 66).

elaboration of diction. The Mahā-bhārata, on the other hand, though generally simple and natural in its language, and free from the conceits and artificial constructions of later writers, comprehends a greater diversity of composition, rising sometimes (especially when the Indra-vajrā metre is employed) to the higher style, and using not only loose and irregular, but also studiously complex grammatical forms[1], and from the mixture of ancient legends, occasional archaisms and Vedic formations.

In contrasting the two Indian poems with the Iliad and the Odyssey, we may observe many points of similarity. Some parallel passages have been already pointed out. We must expect to find the distinctive genius of two different people (though both of the Āryan race) in widely distant localities, colouring their epic poetry very differently, notwithstanding general features of resemblance. The Rāmāyaṇa and Mahā-bhārata are no less wonderful than the Homeric poems as monuments of the human mind, and no less interesting as pictures of human life and manners in ancient times, yet they bear in a remarkable degree the peculiar impress ever stamped on the productions of Asiatic nations, and separating them from European. On the side of art and harmony of proportion, they can no more compete with the Iliad and the Odyssey than the unnatural outline of the ten-headed and twenty-armed Rāvaṇa can bear comparison with the symmetry of a Grecian statue. While the simplicity of the one commends itself to the most refined classical taste, the exaggerations of the other only excite the wonder of Asiatic minds, or if attractive to European, can only please imaginations nursed in an Oriental school.

---

[1] Thus, *jīvase* (I. 732), *kurmi* (III. 10943, and Rāmāy. II. xii. 33), *dhita* for *hita* (Hari-vaṉśa 7799), *pariṇayāmāsa* for *pariṇāyayāmāsa*, *mā bhaiḥ* for *mā bhaishīḥ*, *vyavasishyāmi* for *vyavasāsyāmi*. The use of irregular grammatical forms is sometimes due to the exigency of the metre.

Thus, in the Iliad, time, space, and action are all restricted within the narrowest limits. In the Odyssey they are allowed a wider, though not too wide, a cycle; but in the Rāmāyaṇa and Mahā-bhārata their range is almost unbounded. The Rāmāyaṇa, as it traces the life of a single individual with tolerable continuity, is in this respect more like the Odyssey than the Iliad. In other points, especially in its plot, the greater simplicity of its style, and its comparative freedom from irrelevant episodes, it more resembles the Iliad. There are many graphic passages in both the Rāmāyaṇa and Mahā-bhārata which, for beauty of description, cannot be surpassed by anything in Homer. It should be observed, moreover, that the diction of the Indian Epics is more polished, regular, and cultivated, and the language altogether in a more advanced stage of development than that of Homer. This, of course, tells to the disadvantage of the style on the side of nervous force and vigour; and it must be admitted that in the Sanskṛit poems there is a great redundance of epithets, too liberal a use of metaphor, simile, and hyperbole, and far too much repetition, amplification, and prolixity.

In fact, the European who wishes to estimate rightly the Indian Epics must be prepared not to judge them exclusively from his own point of view. He should bear in mind that to satisfy the ordinary Oriental taste, poetry requires to be seasoned with exaggeration.

Again, an Occidental student's appreciation of many passages will depend upon his familiarity with Indian mythology, as well as with Oriental customs, scenery, and even the characteristic idiosyncrasies of the animal creation in the East. Most of the similes in Hindū epic poetry are taken from the habits and motions of Asiatic animals, such as elephants and tigers[1], or from peculiarities

[1] Thus any eminent or courageous person would be spoken of as 'a tiger of a man.' Other favourite animals in similes are the lion

in the aspect of Indian plants and natural objects. Then, as to the description of scenery, in which Hindū poets are certainly more graphic and picturesque than either Greek or Latin [1], the whole appearance of external nature in the East, the exuberance of vegetation, the profusion of trees and fruits and flowers [2], the glare of burning skies, the freshness of the rainy season, the fury of storms, the serenity of Indian moonlight [3], and the gigantic mould in which natural objects are generally cast—these and many other features are difficult to be realized by a European. We must also make allowance for the difference in Eastern manners; though, after conceding a wide margin in this direction, it must be confessed that the disregard of all delicacy in laying bare the most revolting particulars of certain ancient legends which we now and then encounter in the Indian Epics (especially in the Mahā-bhārata) is

---

(*siṉha*), the ruddy goose (*ćakravāka* or *rathāṅga*), the buffalo (*mahisha*), the boar (*varāha*), the koïl or Indian cuckoo (*kokila*), the heron (*krauńća*), the ox (*gavaya*, i. e. *bos gavaeus*), &c. &c. A woman is sometimes said to have a rolling gait like that of an elephant. It should be noted, however, that similes in the Indian Epics, though far too frequent, are generally confined to a few words, and not, as in Homer, drawn out for three or four lines.

[1] The descriptions of scenery and natural objects in Homer are too short and general to be really picturesque. They want more colouring and minuteness of detail. Some account for this by supposing that a Greek poet was not accustomed to look upon nature with a painter's eye.

[2] The immense profusion of flowers of all kinds is indicated by the number of botanical terms in a Sanskṛit dictionary. Some of the most common flowers and trees alluded to in epic poetry are, the *ćūta* or mango; the *aśoka* (described by Sir William Jones); the *kiṉśuka* (butea frondosa, with beautiful red blossoms); the tamarind (*amlikā*); the jasmine (of which there are many varieties, such as *mālatī*, *jātī*, *yūthikā*, &c.); the *kuruvaka* (amaranth); the saudal (*ćandana*); the jujube (*karkandhu*); the pomegranate (*dāḍima*); the kadamba (*nīpa*); the tamarisk (*pićula*); the *vakula*, *karṇikāra*, *śṛingāṭa*, &c.

[3] See the beautiful description of night in Rāmāyaṇa (Gorr.) I. xxxvi. 15.

a serious blot, and one which never disfigures the pages of Homer, notwithstanding his occasional freedom of expression. Yet there are not wanting indications in the Indian Epics of a higher degree of civilization than that represented in the Homeric poems. The battle-fields of the Rāmāyaṇa and Mahā-bhārata, though spoiled by childish exaggerations and the use of supernatural weapons, are not made barbarous by wanton cruelties[1]; and the descriptions of Ayodhyā and Lan̄kā imply far greater luxury and refinement than those of Sparta and Troy.

The constant interruption of the principal story (as before described) by tedious episodes, in both Rāmāyaṇa and Mahā-bhārata, added to the rambling prolixity of the story itself, will always be regarded as the chief drawback in Hindū epic poetry, and constitutes one of its most marked features of distinction. Even in this respect, however, the Iliad has not escaped the censure of critics. Many believe that this poem is the result of the fusion of different songs on one subject, long current in various localities, intermixed with later interpolations, something after the manner of the Mahā-bhārata. But the artistic instincts of the Greeks required that all the parts and appendages and more recent additions should be blended into one compact, homogeneous, and symmetrical whole. Although we have certainly in Homer occasional digressions or parentheses, such as the description of the 'shield of Achilles,' the 'story of Venus and Mars,' these are not like the Indian episodes. If not absolutely essential to the completeness of the epic conception, they appear to arise naturally out of the business of the plot, and cause

[1] There is something savage in Achilles' treatment of Hector; and the cruelties permitted by Ulysses, in the 22nd Book of the Odyssey, are almost revolting. Compare with these Rāma's treatment of his fallen foe Rāvaṇa, in the Yuddha-kāṇḍa.

no violent disruption of its unity. On the contrary, with Eastern writers and narrators of stories, continuity is often designedly interrupted. They delight in stringing together a number of distinct stories,—detached from each other, yet connected like the figures on a frieze. They even purposely break the sequence of each; so that before one is ended another is commenced, and ere this is completed, others are interwoven; the result being a curious intertwining of stories within stories, the slender thread of an original narrative running through them all. A familiar instance of this is afforded by the well-known collection of tales called 'Hitopadeśa,' and by the 'Arabian Nights.' The same tendency is observable in the composition of the epic poems—far more, however, in the Mahā-bhārata than in the Rāmāyaṇa.

Passing on to a comparison of the plot and the personages of the Rāmāyaṇa with those of the Iliad, without supposing, as some have done, that either poem has been imitated from the other, it is certainly true, and so far remarkable, that the subject of both is a war undertaken to recover the wife of one of the warriors, carried off by a hero on the other side; and that Rāma, in this respect, corresponds to Menelaus, while in others he may be compared to Achilles, Sītā answering to Helen, Sparta to Ayodhyā, Lankā to Troy. It may even be true that some sort of analogy may be traced between the parts played by Agamemnon and Sugrīva, Patroclus and Lakshmaṇa, Nestor and Jāmbavat[1]. Again, Ulysses[2], in one respect, may be compared to Hanumat; and Hector, as the bravest warrior on the Trojan side, may in some points be likened to Indrajit, in others to the indignant Vibhī-

[1] Jāmbavat was the chief of the bears, who was always giving sage advice.

[2] When any work had to be done which required peculiar skill or stratagem, it was entrusted to πολύμητις Ὀδυσσεύς.

shaṇa[1], or again in the Mahā-bhārata to Duryodhana, while Achilles has qualities in common with Arjuna. Other resemblances might be indicated; but these comparisons cannot be carried out to any extent without encountering difficulties at every step, so that any theory of an interchange of ideas between Hindū and Greek epic poets becomes untenable. Rāma's character has really nothing in common with that of Menelaus, and very little with that of Achilles; although, as the bravest and most powerful of the warriors, he is rather to be compared with the latter than the former hero. If in his anger he is occasionally Achillean, his whole nature is cast in a less human mould than that of the Grecian hero. He is the type of a perfect husband, son, and brother. Sītā also rises in character far above Helen, and even above Penelope[2], both in her sublime devotion and loyalty to her husband, and her indomitable patience and endurance under suffering and temptation. As for Bharata and Lakshmaṇa, they are models of fraternal duty; Kauśalyā of maternal tenderness; Daśaratha of paternal love: and it may be affirmed generally that the whole moral tone of the Rāmāyaṇa is certainly above that of the Iliad. Again, in the Iliad the subject is really the anger of Achilles; and when that is satisfied the drama closes. The fall of Troy is not considered necessary to the completion of the plot. Whereas in the Rāmāyaṇa the whole action points to the capture of Lan-kā and destruction of the ravisher. No one too can read either the Rāmāyaṇa or Mahā-bhārata without feeling that they rise above the Homeric poems in this—that a deep religious meaning appears to underlie

---

[1] Hector, like Vibhīshaṇa, was indignant with the ravisher, but he does not refuse to fight on his brother's side.

[2] One cannot help suspecting Penelope of giving way to a little womanly vanity in allowing herself to be surrounded by so many suitors, though she repudiated their advances.

all the narrative, and that the wildest allegory may be intended to conceal a sublime moral, symbolizing the conflict between good and evil, and teaching the hopelessness of victory in so terrible a contest without purity of soul, self-abnegation, and subjugation of the passions.

In reality it is the religious element of the Indian Epics that constitutes one of the principal features of contrast in comparing them with the Homeric. We cannot of course do more than indicate here the bare outlines of so interesting a subject as a comparison between the gods of India, Rome, and Greece. Thus:

Indra[1] and S'iva certainly offer points of analogy to Jupiter and Zeus; Durgā or Pārvatī to Juno; Kṛishṇa to Apollo; S'rī to Ceres; Pṛithivī to Cybele; Varuṇa to Neptune, and, in his earlier character, to Uranus; Sarasvatī, goddess of speech and the arts, to Minerva; Kārttikeya or Skanda, god of war, to Mars[2]; Yama to Pluto or Minos; Kuvera to Plutus; Viśvakarman to Vulcan; Kāma, god of love, to Cupid; Rati, his wife, to Venus[3]; Nārada to Mercury[4]; Hanumat to Pan; Ushas, and in the later mythology Aruṇa, to Eos (Ἠώς) and Aurora; Vāyu to Aeolus; Gaṇeśa, as presiding over the opening and beginning of all undertakings, to Janus; the Aśvinī-kumāras[5] to the Dioscuri (Διόσκουροι), Castor and Pollux.

---

[1] Indra is, as we have already seen (p. 13), the Jupiter Pluvius who sends rain and wields the thunderbolt, and in the earlier mythology is the chief of the gods, like Zeus. Subsequently his worship was superseded by that of Kṛishṇa and S'iva.

[2] It is curious that Kārttikeya, the war-god, is represented in Hindū mythology as the god of thieves—I suppose from their habit of sapping and mining under houses. (See Mṛić-ćhakaṭikā, Act III.) Indian thieves, however, display such skill and ingenuity, that a god like Mercury would appear to be a more appropriate patron. Kārttikeya was the son of S'iva, just as Mars was the offspring of Jupiter.

[3] In one or two points Lakshmī may be compared to Venus.

[4] As Mercury was the inventor of the lyre, so Nārada was the inventor of the Vīṇā or lute.

[5] These ever-youthful twin sons of the Sun, by his wife Sañjñā, transformed into a mare (*aśvinī*), resemble the classical Dioscuri, both by their exploits and the aid they render to their worshippers (see p. 14).

But in Greece, mythology, which was in many respects fully systematized when the Homeric poems were composed[1], never passed certain limits, or outgrew a certain symmetry of outline. In the Iliad and the Odyssey, a god is little more than idealized humanity. His form and his actions are seldom out of keeping with this character. Hindū mythology, on the other hand, springing from the same source as that of Europe, but, spreading and ramifying with the rank luxuriance of an Indian forest, speedily outgrew all harmony of proportions, and surrounded itself with an intricate undergrowth of monstrous and confused allegory. Doubtless the gods of the Indian and Grecian Epics preserve some traces of their common origin, resembling each other in various ways; interfering in human concerns, exhibiting human infirmities, taking part in the battles of their favourite heroes, furnishing them with celestial arms, or interposing directly to protect them.

But in the Rāmāyaṇa and Mahā-bhārata, and in the Purāṇas to which they led, the shape and operations of divine and semi-divine beings are generally suggestive of the monstrous, the frightful, and the incredible. The human form, however idealized, is seldom thought adequate to the expression of divine attributes. Brahmā is four-faced; Śiva, three-eyed and sometimes five-headed; Indra has a thousand eyes; Kārttikeya, six faces; Rāvaṇa, ten heads; Gaṇeśa has the head of an elephant. Nearly every god and goddess has at least four arms, with symbols of obscure import exhibited in every hand[2]. The deeds of

---

[1] Herodotus says (Euterpe, 53) that 'Homer and Hesiod *framed* the Greek Theogony, gave distinctive names to the gods, distributed honours and functions to them, and described their forms.' I conclude that by the verb ποιεῖν, Herodotus did not mean to imply that Homer *invented* the myths, but that he gave system to a mythology already current; see, however, Grote's History of Greece, I. 482 &c.

[2] The Roman god Janus (supposed to be for Dianus and connected with *dies*) was represented by two and sometimes four heads.

heroes, who are themselves half gods, transport the imagination into the region of the wildest chimera; and a whole pantheon presents itself, teeming with grotesque fancies, with horrible creations, half animals half gods, with man-eating ogres, many-headed giants and disgusting demons, to an extent which the refined and delicate sensibilities of the Greeks and Romans could not have tolerated[1].

Moreover, in the Indian Epics the boundaries between the natural and supernatural, between earth and heaven, between the divine, human, and even animal creations, are singularly vague and undefined; troops of deities and semi-divine personages appear on the stage on every occasion. Gods, men, and animals are ever changing places. A constant communication is kept up between the two worlds, and such is their mutual interdependence that each seems to need the other's help. If distressed mortals are assisted out of their difficulties by divine interposition, the tables are often turned, and perturbed gods, themselves reduced to pitiful straits, are forced to implore the aid of mortal warriors in their conflicts with the demons[2]. They even look to mortals for their daily sustenance, and are represented as actually *living on the sacrifices* offered to them by human beings, and at every sacrificial ceremony assemble in troops, eager to feed upon their shares. In fact, sacrifice with the Hindūs is not merely expiatory or placatory; it is necessary for the *food* and *support* of the gods. If there were no sacrifices the gods would starve to death (see Introduction, p. xxxvii, note 1). This alone will account for the interest they take

---

[1] It is true that Homer now and then indulges in monstrous creations; but even the description of Polyphemus does not outrage all probability, like the exaggerated horrors of the demon Kabandha, in the 3rd Book of the Rāmāyaṇa (see p. 358).

[2] Indra does so in the S'akuntalā and Vikramorvaśī.

in the destruction of demons, whose great aim was to obstruct these sources of their sustenance. Much in the same way the spirits of dead men are supposed to depend for existence and happiness on the living, and to be fed with cakes of rice and libations of water at the Śrāddha ceremonies.

Again, not only are men aided by animals which usurp human functions, but the gods also are dependent on and associated with birds and beasts of all kinds, and even with plants. Most of the principal deities are described as using animals for their Vāhanas or vehicles. Brahmā is carried on a swan, and sometimes seated on a lotus; Vishṇu is borne on or attended by a being, half eagle, half man (called Garuḍa); Lakshmī is seated on a lotus or carries one in her hand; Śiva has a bull for his vehicle or companion; Kārttikeya, god of war, has a peacock[1]; Indra has an elephant; Yama, god of death, has a buffalo (*mahisha*[2]); Kāma-deva, a parrot and fish[3]; Gaṇeśa, a rat[4]; Agni, a ram; Varuṇa, a fish; Durgā, a tiger. The latter is sometimes represented with her husband on a bull, Śiva himself being also associated with a tiger and antelope as well as with countless serpents. Vishṇu (Hari, Nārāyaṇa) is also represented as the Supreme Being sleeping on a thousand-headed serpent called Śesha (or Ananta, 'the Infinite').

This Śesha is moreover held to be the chief of a race of Nāgas or semi-divine beings, sometimes stated to be one thousand in number, half serpents half men, their heads being human and their bodies snake-like. They inhabit

---

[1] *Kārttikeya* is represented as a handsome young man (though with six faces). This may account for his being associated with a peacock.

[2] Perhaps from its great power.

[3] A parrot often figures in Indian love-stories. He is also associated with a kind of crocodile as his symbol (whence his name *Makara-dhvaja*). Such an animal is kept in tanks near his temples.

[4] Supposed to possess great sagacity.

the seven Pātālas[1] or regions under the earth, which, with the seven superincumbent worlds, are supposed to rest on the thousand heads of the serpent Śesha, who typifies infinity—inasmuch as, according to a common myth, he supports the Supreme Being between the intervals of creation, as well as the worlds created at the commencement of each Kalpa (note, p. 333). Again, the earth is sometimes fabled to be supported by the vast heads and backs of eight male and eight female mythical elephants, who all have names[2], and are the elephants of the eight

---

[1] Pātāla, though often used as a general term for all the seven regions under the earth, is properly only one of the seven, called in order, *Atala*, *Vitala*, *Sutala*, *Rasātala*, *Talātala*, *Mahātala*, and *Pātāla;* above which are the seven worlds (Lokas), called *Bhū* (the earth), *Bhuvar*, *Svar*, *Mahar*, *Janar*, *Tapaḥ*, and *Brahma* or *Satya* (see note 2, p. 66); all fourteen resting on the heads of the great serpent. The serpent-race who inhabit these lower regions (which are not to be confounded with the Narakas or hells, note 2, p. 26) are sometimes regarded as belonging to only one of the seven, viz. Pātāla, or to a portion of it called Nāga-loka, of which the capital is Bhogavatī. They are fabled to have sprung from Kadrū, wife of Kaśyapa, and some of the females among them (Nāga-kanyās) are said to have married human heroes. In this way Ulūpī became the wife of Arjuna (p. 390, note 2), and, curiously enough, a tribe of the Rājputs claims descent from the Nāgas even in the present day. A particular day is held sacred to the Nāgas, and a festival called Nāga-pañćamī is kept in their honour about the end of July (Śrāvaṇa). Vāsuki and Takshaka are other leading Nāgas, to whom a separate dominion over part of the serpent-race in different parts of the lower regions is sometimes assigned. All the Nāgas are described as having jewels in their heads. Their chiefs, Śesha, Vāsuki, and Takshaka, are said to rule over snakes generally, while Garuḍa is called the enemy of Nāgas (*Nāgāri*); so that the term Nāga sometimes stands for an ordinary serpent. The habit which snakes have of hiding in holes may have given rise to the notion of peopling the lower regions with Nāgas. The Rev. K. M. Banerjea has a curious theory about them (see p. xxxvi. of this volume).

[2] The eight names of the male elephants are given in the Amara-kosha, thus: Airāvata, Puṇḍarīka, Vāmana, Kumuda, Añjana, Pushpa-danta, Sārva-bhauma, Supratīka. Four are named in Rāmāyaṇa (I. xli), Virū-

quarters. When any one of these shakes his body the whole earth quakes (see Rāmāyaṇa I. xli).

In fact, it is not merely in a confused, exaggerated, and overgrown mythology that the difference between the Indian and Grecian Epics lies. It is in the injudicious and excessive use of it. In the Rāmāyaṇa and Mahā-bhārata, the spiritual and the supernatural are everywhere so dominant and overpowering, that anything merely human seems altogether out of place.

In the Iliad and Odyssey, the religious and supernatural are perhaps scarcely less prevalent. The gods are continually interposing and superintending; but they do so as if they were themselves little removed from men, or at least without destroying the dramatic probability of the poem, or neutralizing its general air of plain matter-of-fact humanity. Again, granted that in Homer there is frequent mention of the future existence of the soul, and its condition of happiness or misery hereafter, and that the Homeric descriptions of disembodied spirits correspond in many points with the Hindū notions on the same subject[1]—yet even these doctrines do not stand out with such exaggerated reality in Homer as to make human concerns appear unreal. Nor is there in his poems the slightest allusion to the soul's pre-existence in a former

---

pāksha, Mahā-padma, Saumanas, and Bhadra. Sometimes these elephants appear to have locomotive habits, and roam about the sky in the neighbourhood of their respective quarters (see Megha-dūta 14).

[1] See the following passages, which bear on the existence of the ψυχή after death as an εἴδωλον in Hades: Il. XXIII. 72, 104: Od. XI. 213, 476; XX. 355; XXIV. 14. It is curious that the Hindū notion of the restless state of the soul until the S'rāddha is performed (see p. 255) agrees with the ancient classical superstition that the ghosts of the dead wandered about as long as their bodies remained unburied, and were not suffered to mingle with those of the other dead. See Odyss. XI. 54: Il. XXIII. 72; and cf. Aen. VI. 325: Lucan I. II: Eur. Hec. 30.

body, and its liability to pass into other bodies hereafter—a theory which in Hindū poetry invests present actions with a mysterious meaning, and gives a deep distinctive colouring to Indian theology.

Above all, although priests are occasionally mentioned in the Iliad and the Odyssey, there is wholly wanting in the Homeric poems any recognition of a regular hierarchy, or the necessity for a mediatorial caste of sacrificers [1]. This, which may be called the sacerdotal element of the Indian Epics, is more or less woven into their very tissue. Brāhmanism has been at work in these productions almost as much as the imagination of the poet; and boldly claiming a monopoly of all knowledge, human and divine, has appropriated this, as it has every other department of literature, and warped it to its own purposes. Its policy having been to check the development of intellect, and keep the inferior castes in perpetual childhood, it encouraged an appetite for exaggeration more insatiable than would be tolerated in the most extravagant European fairy-tale. This has been done more in the Rāmāyaṇa than in the Mahā-bhārata; but even in the later Epic, full as it is of geographical, chronological, and historical details, few assertions can be trusted. Time is measured by millions of years, space by millions of miles; and if a battle has to be described, nothing is thought of it unless millions of soldiers, elephants, and horses are brought into the field [2].

This difference in the religious systems of Europe and India becomes still more noteworthy, when it is borne in mind that the wildest fictions of the Rāmāyaṇa and Mahā-

---

[1] A king, or any other individual, is allowed in Homer to perform a sacrifice without the help of priests. See Il. II. 411; III. 392. Nevertheless we read occasionally of a θυοσκόος, or 'sacrifice-viewer,' who prophesied from the appearance of the flame and the smoke at the sacrifice. See Il. XXIV. 221: Odyss. XXI. 144; XXII. 319.

[2] Cf. extract from Aristotle's Poetics, p. 434, note 1, of this volume.

bhārata are *to this very day* intimately bound up with the religious creed of the Hindūs. It is certain that the more intelligent among them, like the more educated Greeks and Romans, regarded and still regard the fictions of mythology as allegorical. But both in Europe and Asia the mass of the people, not troubling themselves about the mystical significance of symbols, took emblem and allegory for reality. And this, doubtless, they are apt to do still, as much in the West as in the East. Among European nations, however, even the ductile faith of the masses is sufficiently controlled by common sense to prevent the fervour of religious men from imposing any great extravagance on their credulity; and much as the Homeric poems are still admired, no one in any part of the world now dreams of placing the slightest faith in their legends, so as to connect them with religious opinions and practices. In India a complete contrast in this respect may be observed. The myths of the Indian Epics are still closely interwoven with *present* faith. In fact, the capacity of an uneducated Hindū for accepting and admiring the most monstrous fictions is apparently unlimited. Hence the absence of all history in the literature of India. A plain relation of facts has little charm for the ordinary Hindū mind.

Even in the delineation of heroic character, where Indian poets exhibit much skill, they cannot avoid ministering to the craving for the marvellous which appears to be almost inseparable from the mental constitution of Eastern peoples.

Homer's characters are like Shakespeare's. They are *true* heroes, if you will, but they are always *men;* never perfect, never free from human weaknesses, inconsistencies, and caprices of temper. If their deeds are sometimes praeterhuman, they do not commit improbabilities which are absolutely absurd. Moreover, he does not seem to delineate his characters; he allows them to delineate themselves. They stand out like photographs, in all the reality of nature. We are not so much told what they do or say[1]. They appear rather to speak and act for themselves. In the Hindū Epics the poet gives us too long and too tedious descriptions in his own person; and, as a rule, his characters are either too good or too bad. How far more natural is Achilles, with all his faults, than Rāma, with his almost painful correctness of conduct! Even the cruel vengeance that Achilles perpetrates on the dead Hector strikes us as more likely to be true than Rāma's magnanimous treatment of the fallen Rāvaṇa. True, even the heroes sometimes commit what a European would call crimes; and the Pāṇḍavas were certainly guilty of one inhuman act of treachery. In their anxiety to provide for their own escape from a horrible death, they enticed an outcaste woman and her five sons into their inflammable lac-house, and then burnt her alive (see p. 386). But the guilt of this transaction is neutralized to a Hindū by the woman being an outcaste; and besides, it is the savage Bhīma who sets fire to the house. Rāma and Lakshmaṇa again were betrayed into a deed of cruelty in mutilating Śūrpa-ṇakhā. For this, however, the fiery Lakshmaṇa was responsible. If the better heroes sin, they do not sin like men. We see in them no portraits of ourselves. The pictures are too much one colour. There are few gradations of light and shadow, and little artistic blending of opposite hues. On the one side we have all gods or demigods; on the other, all demons or fiends. We miss real human

[1] Aristotle says that 'among the many just claims of Homer to our praise, this is one—that he is the only poet who seems to have understood what part in his poem it was proper for him to take himself. The poet, in his own person, should speak as little as possible. . . . . Homer, after a few preparatory lines, immediately introduces a man, a woman, or some other character; for all have their character.' (Poetics III. 3.)

beings with mixed characters. There is no mirror held up to inconsistent humanity. Duryodhana and his ninety-nine brothers are too uniformly vicious to be types of real men. Lakshmaṇa has perhaps the most natural character among the heroes of the Rāmāyaṇa, and Bhīma among those of the Mahā-bhārata. In many respects the character of the latter is not unlike that of Achilles; but in drawing his most human heroes the Indian poet still displays a perpetual tendency to run into extravagance.

It must be admitted, however, that in exhibiting pictures of domestic life and manners the Sanskrit Epics are even more true and real than the Greek and Roman. In the delineation of women the Hindū poet throws aside all exaggerated colouring, and draws from nature. Kaikeyī, Kauśalyā, Mandodarī (the favourite wife of Rāvaṇa[1]), and even the hump-backed Mantharā (Rāmāyaṇa II. viii), are all drawn to the very life. Sītā, Draupadī, and Damayantī engage our affections and our interest far more than Helen, or even than Penelope. Indeed, Hindū wives are generally perfect patterns of conjugal fidelity; nor can it be doubted that in these delightful portraits of the Pativratā or 'devoted wife' we have true representations of the purity and simplicity of Hindū domestic manners in early times[2]. We may also gather from the epic poems

[1] What can be more natural than Mandodarī's lamentations over the dead body of Rāvaṇa, and her allusions to his fatal passion for Sītā in Rāmāyaṇa VI. 95 (Gorresio's ed.)?

[2] No doubt the devotion of a Hindū wife implied greater inferiority than is compatible with modern European ideas of independence. The extent to which this devotion was carried, even in little matters, is curiously exemplified by the story of Gāndhārī, who out of sympathy for her blind husband never appeared in public without a veil over her face (see p. 378). Hence, during the grand sham-fight between the Kuru and Pāṇḍu princes, Vidura stood by Dhṛita-rāshṭra, and Kuntī by Gāndhārī, to describe the scene to them (see p. 384).

many interesting hints as to the social position occupied by Hindū women before the Muhammadan conquest. No one can read the Rāmāyaṇa and Mahā-bhārata without coming to the conclusion that the habit of secluding women, and of treating them as inferiors, is, to a certain extent, natural to all Eastern nations, and prevailed in the earliest times[1]. Yet various passages in both Epics clearly establish the fact, that women in India were subjected to

[1] It was equally natural to the Greeks and Romans. Chivalry and reverence for the fair sex belonged only to European nations of northern origin, who were the first to hold 'inesse foeminis sanctum aliquid' (Tac. Germ. 8). That Hindū women in ancient times secluded themselves, except on certain occasions, may be inferred from the word *asūryam-paśyā*, given by Pāṇini as an epithet of a king's wife ('one who never sees the sun')—a very strong expression, stronger even than the *parda-nishīn* of the Muhammadans. It is to be observed also that in the Rāmāyaṇa (VI. xcix. 33) there is clear allusion to some sort of seclusion being practised; and the term *avarodha*, 'fenced or guarded place,' is used long before the time of the Muhammadans for the women's apartments. In the Ratnāvalī, however, the minister of king Vatsa, and his chamberlain and the envoy from Ceylon, are admitted to an audience in the presence of the queen and her damsels; and although Rāma in Rāmāyaṇa VI. 99 thinks it necessary to excuse himself for permitting his wife to expose herself to the gaze of the crowd, yet he expressly (99, 34) enumerates various occasions on which it was allowable for a woman to show herself unveiled. I here translate the passage, as it bears very remarkably on this interesting subject. Rāma says to Vibhīshaṇa—

'Neither houses, nor vestments, nor enclosing walls, nor ceremony, nor regal insignia (*rāja-satkāra*), are the screen (*āvaraṇa*) of a woman. Her own virtue alone (protects her). In great calamities (*vyasaneshu*), at marriages, at the public choice of a husband by maidens (of the Kshatriya caste), at a sacrifice, at assemblies (*saṃsatsu*), it is allowable for all the world to look upon women (*strīṇāṃ darśanaṃ sārvalaukikam*).'

Hence S'akuntalā appears in the public court of king Dushyanta; Damayantī travels about by herself; and in the Uttara-rāma-ćarita, the mother of Rāma goes to the hermitage of Vālmīki. Again, women were present at dramatic representations, visited the temples of the gods, and performed their ablutions with little privacy; which last custom they still practise, though Muhammadan women do not.

less social restraint in former days than they are at present, and even enjoyed considerable liberty [1]. True, the ancient lawgiver, Manu, speaks of women as having no will of their own, and unfit for independence (see p. 259 of this volume); but he probably described a state of society which it was the aim of the priesthood to establish, rather than that which really existed in his own time. At a later period the pride of Brāhmanism, and still more recently the influence of Muhammadanism, deprived women of even such freedom as they once enjoyed; so that at the present day no Hindū woman has, *in theory*, any independence. It is not merely that she is not her own mistress: she is not her own property, and never, under any circumstances, can be. She belongs to her father first, who gives her away to her husband, to whom she belongs *for ever* [2]. She is not considered capable of so high a form of religion as man [3], and she does not mix

---

[1] In Mahā-bh. I. 4719 we read: *An-āvṛitāḥ kila purā striya āsan kāma-ćāra-vihāriṇyaḥ svatantrāḥ*, &c.

[2] Hence when her husband dies she cannot be remarried, as there is no one to give her away. In fact, the remarriage of Hindū widows, which is now permitted by law, is utterly opposed to all modern Hindū ideas about women; and many persons think that the passing of this law was one cause of the mutiny of 1857. It is clear from the story of Damayantī, who appoints a second Svayaṃvara, that in early times remarriage was not necessarily improper; though, from her wonder that the new suitor should have failed to see through her artifice, and from her vexation at being supposed capable of a second marriage, it may be inferred that such a marriage was even then not reputable.

[3] See, however, the stories of Gārgī and Maitreyī (Bṛihad-āraṇyaka Upanishad, Röer's transl. pp. 198, 203, 242). No doubt the inferior capacity of a woman as regards religion was implied in the epic poems, as well as in later works. A husband was the wife's divinity, as well as her lord, and her best religion was to please him. See Sītā's speech, p. 366 of this volume; and the quotation from Mādhava Āćārya (who flourished in the fourteenth century), p. 373, note. Such verses as the following are common in Hindū literature: *Bhartā hi paramaṃ nāryā*

freely in society. But in ancient times, when the epic songs were current in India, women were not confined to intercourse with their own families; they did very much as they pleased, travelled about, and showed themselves unreservedly in public[1], and, if of the Kshatriya caste, were occasionally allowed to choose their own husbands from a number of assembled suitors[2]. It is clear, moreover, that, in many instances, there was considerable dignity and elevation about the female character, and that much mutual affection prevailed in families. Nothing can be more beautiful and touching than the pictures of domestic and social happiness in the Rāmāyaṇa and Mahā-bhārata. Children are dutiful to their parents[3] and submissive to their superiors; younger brothers are respectful to elder brothers; parents are fondly attached to their children, watchful over their interests and ready to sacrifice themselves for their welfare; wives are loyal, devoted,

---

*bhūshaṇam bhūshaṇair vinā*, 'a husband is a wife's chief ornament even without (other) ornaments.' Manu says (V. 151), *Yasmai dadyāt pitā tv enām bhrātā vānumate pituḥ, Taṃ śuśrūsheta jīvantaṃ saṃsthitaṃ ća na laṅghayet.* See p. 287 of this volume. In IV. 198, Manu classes women with S'ūdras.

[1] Especially married women. A wife was required to obey her husband implicitly, but in other respects she was to be independent (*svātantryam arhati*, Mahā-bhār. I. 4741).

[2] The Svayaṃvara, however, appears to have been something exceptional, and only to have been allowed in the case of the daughters of kings or Kshatriyas. See Draupadī-svayaṃvara 127; Mahā-bhār. I. 7926.

[3] Contrast with the respectful tone of Hindū children towards their parents, the harsh manner in which Telemachus generally speaks to his mother. Filial respect and affection is quite as noteworthy a feature in the Hindū character now as in ancient times. It is common for unmarried soldiers to stint themselves almost to starvation-point, that they may send home money to their aged parents. In fact, in proportion to the weakness or rather total absence of the *national* is the strength of the *family* bond. In England and America, where national life is strongest, children are less respectful to their parents.

and obedient to their husbands, yet show much independence of character, and do not hesitate to express their own opinions; husbands are tenderly affectionate towards their wives, and treat them with respect and courtesy; daughters and women generally are virtuous and modest, yet spirited and, when occasion requires, firm and courageous; love and harmony reign throughout the family circle. Indeed, in depicting scenes of domestic affection, and expressing those universal feelings and emotions which belong to human nature in all time and in all places, Sanskṛit epic poetry is unrivalled even by Greek Epos. It is not often that Homer takes us out of the battle-field; and if we except the lamentations over the bodies of Patroclus and Hector, the visit of Priam to the tent of Achilles, and the parting of Hector and Andromache, there are no such pathetic passages in the Iliad as the death of the hermit-boy (p. 350), the pleadings of Sītā for permission to accompany her husband into exile (p. 366), and the whole ordeal-scene at the end of the Rāmāyaṇa. In the Indian Epics such passages abound, and, besides giving a very high idea of the purity and happiness of domestic life in ancient India, indicate a capacity in Hindū women for the discharge of the most sacred and important social duties.

We must guard against the supposition that the women of India at the present day have altogether fallen from their ancient character. Notwithstanding the corrupting example of Islāmism, and the degrading tendency of modern Hindūism, some remarkable instances may still be found of moral and even intellectual excellence[1]. These, however, are exceptions, and we may rest assured, that until Asiatic women, whether Hindū or Muslim, are elevated and educated, our efforts to raise Asiatic nations

---

[1] In some parts of India, especially in the Marāṭhī districts, there is still considerable freedom of thought and action allowed to women.

to the level of European will be fruitless[1]. Let us hope that when the Rāmāyaṇa and Mahā-bhārata shall no longer be held sacred as repositories of faith and storehouses of trustworthy tradition, the enlightened Hindū may still learn from these poems to honour the weaker sex; and that Indian women, restored to their ancient liberty and raised to a still higher position by becoming partakers of the 'fulness of the blessing' of Christianity, may do for our Eastern empire what they have done for Europe—soften, invigorate, and dignify the character of its people.

I close my present subject with examples of the religious and moral teaching of the two Indian Epics. A few sentiments and maxims, extracted from both poems, here follow:

A heavy blow, inflicted by a foe[2],
Is often easier to bear, than griefs,
However slight, that happen casually.
Rāmāyaṇa (ed. Bombay) II. lxii. 16.

To carry out an enterprise in words
Is easy, to accomplish it by acts
Is the sole test of man's capacity.
Rāmāyaṇa (ed. Gorresio) VI. lxvii. 10.

Truth, justice, and nobility of rank
Are centred in the King; he is a mother,
Father, and benefactor of his subjects.
Rāmāyaṇa (ed. Bombay) II. lxvii. 35.

In countries without monarchs, none can call
His property or family his own;
No one is master even of himself.
Rāmāyaṇa (ed. Gorresio) II. lxix. 11.

---

[1] Manu gives expression to a great truth when he says (III. 145), *Sahasraṃ tu pitṛīn mātā gauraveṇātirićyate*, 'a mother exceeds in value a thousand fathers.'

[2] Though some of these translations were made years ago from Böhtlingk's admirable collection of Indische Sprüche, I have since been assisted in my renderings of many examples by Dr. Muir's 'Religious and Moral Sentiments freely translated from Indian writers,' lately printed at Edinburgh, with an appendix and notes. I may not have succeeded so well as Dr. Muir, but rhymeless metre may have enabled me to keep somewhat closer to the original.

Where'er we walk, Death marches at our side;
Where'er we sit, Death seats himself beside us;
However far we journey, Death continues
Our fellow-traveller and goes with us home.
Men take delight in each returning dawn,
And with admiring gaze, behold the glow
Of sunset. Every season, as it comes,
Fills them with gladness, yet they never reck
That each recurring season, every day
Fragment by fragment bears their life away.
As drifting logs of wood may haply meet
On Ocean's waters, surging to and fro,
And having met, drift once again apart;
So fleeting is a man's association
With wife and children, relatives and wealth,
So surely must a time of parting come.

Rāmāyaṇa (ed. Bombay) II. cv. 24–27.

Whate'er the work a man performs,
The most effective aid to its completion—
The most prolific source of true success—
Is energy without despondency.

Rāmāyaṇa (ed. Bombay) V. xii. 11.

Fate binds a man with adamantine cords,
And drags him upwards to the highest rank
Or downward to the depths of misery.

Rāmāyaṇa (ed. Bombay) V. xxxvii. 3.

He who has wealth has strength of intellect;
He who has wealth has depth of erudition;
He who has wealth has nobleness of birth;
He who has wealth has relatives and friends;
He who has wealth is thought a very hero;
He who has wealth is rich in every virtue.

Rāmāyaṇa (ed. Bombay) VI. lxxxiii. 35, 36.

Time is awake while mortals are asleep,
None can elude his grasp or curb his course,
He passes unrestrained o'er all alike.

Mahā-bh. I. 243.

Thou thinkest: I am single and alone—
Perceiving not the great eternal Sage
Who dwells within thy breast. Whatever wrong
Is done by thee, he sees and notes it all.

Mahā-bh. I. 3015.

Heaven, Earth, and Sea, Sun, Moon, and Wind, and Fire,
Day, Night, the Twilights, and the Judge of souls,
The god of justice and the Heart itself,
All see and note the conduct of a man[1].

Mahā-bh. I. 3017.

A wife is half the man, his truest friend,
Source of his virtue, pleasure, wealth—the root
Whence springs the line of his posterity.

Mahā-bh. I. 3028.

An evil-minded man is quick to see
His neighbour's faults, though small as mustard-seed;
But when he turns his eyes towards his own,
Though large as Bilva[2] fruit, he none descries.

Mahā-bh. I. 3069.

If Truth and thousands of Horse-sacrifices
Were weighed together, Truth would weigh the most[3].

Mahā-bh. I. 3095.

Death follows life by an unerring law;
Why grieve for that which is inevitable?

Mahā-bh. I. 6144.

Conquer a man who never gives by gifts;
Subdue untruthful men by truthfulness;
Vanquish an angry man by gentleness;
And overcome the evil man by goodness[4].

Mahā-bh. III. 13253.

Triple restraint of thought and word and deed,
Strict vow of silence, coil of matted hair,
Close shaven head, garments of skin or bark,
Keeping of fasts, ablutions, maintenance
Of sacrificial fires, a hermit's life,
Emaciation—these are all in vain,
Unless the inward soul be free from stain.

Mahā-bh. III. 13445.

To injure none by thought or word or deed,
To give to others, and be kind to all—

---

[1] Compare Manu VIII. 86, p. 284 of this volume.

[2] This is the Aegle Marmelos (*Bel*) or Bengal Quince, bearing a large fruit. It is esteemed sacred to Mahā-deva. Compare St. Matthew vii. 3, 4.

[3] Hitopadeśa IV. 135.

[4] See Rom. xii. 21. Compare the Pāli Rājovāda Jātaka (Fausböll's Ten Jātakas, p. 5), *Akkodhena jine kodham, Asādhum sādhunā jine, Jine kadariyam dānena, Saććena alika-vādinam.* See also Dhamma-pada 223.

This is the constant duty of the good.
High-minded men delight in doing good,
Without a thought of their own interest;
When they confer a benefit on others,
They reckon not on favours in return [1].

Mahā-bh. III. 16782, 16796.

An archer shoots an arrow which may kill
One man, or none; but clever men discharge
The shaft of intellect, whose stroke has power
To overwhelm a king and all his kingdom.

Mahā-bh. V. 1013.

Two persons will hereafter be exalted
Above the heavens—the man with boundless power
Who yet forbears to use it indiscreetly,
And he who is not rich and yet can give [2].

Mahā-bh. V. 1028.

Sufficient wealth, unbroken health, a friend,
A wife of gentle speech, a docile son,
And learning that subserves some useful end—
These are a living man's six greatest blessings.

Mahā-bh. V. 1057.

Good words, good deeds, and beautiful expressions
A wise man ever culls from every quarter,
E'en as a gleaner gathers ears of corn.

Mahā-bh. V. 1126.

The gods defend not with a club or shield
The man they wish to favour—but endow him
With wisdom; and the man whom they intend
To ruin, they deprive of understanding [3];
So that to him all things appear distorted.
Then, when his mind is dulled and he is ripe
To meet his doom, evil appears to him
Like good, and even fortunate events
Turn to his harm and tend to his destruction.

Mahā-bh. V. 1122, 2679.

To curb the tongue and moderate the speech,
Is held to be the hardest of all tasks [4].
The words of him who talks too volubly
Have neither substance nor variety.

Mahā-bh. V. 1170.

---

[1] Compare St. Luke vi. 35. [2] Compare St. Mark xii. 41–44.
[3] *Quos Deus vult perdere prius dementat.* [4] St. James iii. 8.

Darts, barbëd arrows, iron-headed spears,
However deep they penetrate the flesh,
May be extracted; but a cutting speech,
That pierces, like a javelin, to the heart,
None can remove; it lies and rankles there.

Mahā-bh. V. 1173.

Repeated sin destroys the understanding,
And he whose reason is impaired, repeats
His sins. The constant practising of virtue
Strengthens the mental faculties, and he
Whose judgment stronger grows, acts always right.

Mahā-bh. V. 1242.

Bear railing words with patience, never meet
An angry man with anger, nor return
Reviling for reviling, smite not him
Who smites thee; let thy speech and acts be gentle.

Mahā-bh. V. 1270, 9972.

If thou art wise, seek ease and happiness
In deeds of virtue and of usefulness;
And ever act in such a way by day
That in the night thy sleep may tranquil be;
And so comport thyself when thou art young,
That when thou art grown old, thine age may pass
In calm serenity. So ply thy task
Throughout thy life, that when thy days are ended,
Thou may'st enjoy eternal bliss hereafter.

Mahā-bh. V. 1248.

Esteem that gain a loss which ends in harm;
Account that loss a gain which brings advantage.

Mahā-bh. V. 1451.

Reflect that health is transient, death impends,
Ne'er in thy day of youthful strength do aught
To grieve thy conscience, lest when weakness comes,
And thou art on a bed of sickness laid,
Fear and remorse augment thy sufferings.

Mahā-bh. V. 1474.

Do naught to others which if done to thee
Would cause thee pain; this is the sum of duty.

Mahā-bh. V. 1517.

How can a man love knowledge yet repose?
Would'st thou be learned, then abandon ease.
Either give up thy knowledge or thy rest.

Mahā-bh. V. 1537.

No sacred lore can save the hypocrite,
Though he employ it craftily, from hell;
When his end comes, his pious texts take wing,
Like fledglings eager to forsake their nest.

Mahā-bh. V. 1623.

When men are ripe for ruin, e'en a straw
Has power to crush them, like a thunderbolt.

Mahā-bh. VII. 429.

By anger, fear, and avarice deluded,
Men do not strive to understand themselves,
Nor ever gain self-knowledge. One is proud
Of rank, and plumes himself upon his birth,
Contemning those of low degree; another
Boasts of his riches, and disdains the poor;
Another vaunts his learning, and despising
Men of less wisdom, calls them fools; a fourth
Piquing himself upon his rectitude,
Is quick to censure other peoples' faults.
But when the high and low, the rich and poor,
The wise and foolish, worthy and unworthy,
Are borne to their last resting-place—the grave—
When all their troubles end in that last sleep,
And of their earthly bodies naught remains
But fleshless skeletons—can living men
Mark differences between them, or perceive
Distinctions in the dust of birth or form?
Since all are, therefore, levelled by the grave,
And all must sleep together in the earth—
Why, foolish mortals, do ye wrong each other?

Mahā-bh. XI. 116.

Some who are wealthy perish in their youth,
While others who are fortuneless and needy,
Attain a hundred years; the prosperous man
Who lives, oft lacks the power to enjoy his wealth.

Mahā-bh. XII. 859.

A king must first subdue himself, and then
Vanquish his enemies. How can a prince
Who cannot rule himself, enthral his foes?
To curb the senses, is to conquer self.

Mahā-bh. XII. 2599.

Who in this world is able to distinguish
The virtuous from the wicked, both alike

The fruitful earth supports, on both alike
The sun pours down his beams, on both alike
Refreshing breezes blow, and both alike
The waters purify? Not so hereafter—
Then shall the good be severed from the bad;
Then in a region bright with golden lustre—
Centre of light and immortality—
The righteous after death shall dwell in bliss[1].
Then a terrific hell awaits the wicked—
Profound abyss of utter misery—
Into the depths of which bad men shall fall
Headlong, and mourn their doom for countless years.

Mahā-bh. XII. 2798.

He who lets slip his opportunity,
And turns not the occasion to account,
Though he may strive to execute his work,
Finds not again the fitting time for action.

Mahā-bh. XII. 3814.

Enjoy thou the prosperity of others,
Although thyself unprosperous; noble men
Take pleasure in their neighbour's happiness.

Mahā-bh. XII. 3880.

Even to foes who visit us as guests
Due hospitality should be displayed;
The tree screens with its leaves, the man who fells it[2].

Mahā-bh. XII. 5528.

What need has he who subjugates himself
To live secluded in a hermit's cell?
Where'er resides the self-subduing sage,
That place to him is like a hermitage.

Mahā-bh. XII. 5961.

Do good to-day, time passes, Death is near.
Death falls upon a man all unawares,
Like a ferocious wolf upon a sheep.
Death comes when his approach is least expected.
Death sometimes seizes ere the work of life
Is finished, or its purposes accomplished.

---

[1] Compare St. Matthew xiii. 43, xxv. 46.

[2] This verse occurs in Hitopadeśa I. 60. Cf. Rom. xii. 20. Professor H. H. Wilson was induced to commence the study of Sanskṛit by reading somewhere that this sentiment was to be met with in Sanskṛit literature.

Death carries off the weak and strong alike,
The brave and timorous, the wise and foolish,
And those whose objects are not yet achieved.
Therefore delay not ; Death may come to-day.
Death will not wait to know if thou art ready,
Or if thy work be done. Be active now,
While thou art young, and time is still thy own.
This very day perform to-morrow's work,
This very morning do thy evening's task.
When duty is discharged, then if thou live,
Honour and happiness will be thy lot,
And if thou die, supreme beatitude [1].

Mahā-bh. XII. 6534.

The building of a house is fraught with troubles,
And ne'er brings comfort; therefore, cunning serpents
Seek for a habitation made by others,
And creeping in, abide there at their ease.

Mahā-bh. XII. 6619.

Just as the track of birds that cleave the air
Is not discerned, nor yet the path of fish
That skim the water, so the course of those
Who do good actions, is not always seen.

Mahā-bh. XII. 6763, 12156.

Let none reject the meanest suppliant
Or send him empty-handed from his door.
A gift bestowed on outcasts or on dogs
Is never thrown away or unrequited.

Mahā-bh. XIII. 3212.

Time passes, and the man who older grows
Finds hair and teeth and eyes grow ever older.
One thing alone within him ne'er grows old—
The thirst for riches and the love of gold.

Mahā-bh. XIII. 3676, 368a.

This is the sum of all true righteousness—
Treat others, as thou would'st thyself be treated.
Do nothing to thy neighbour, which hereafter
Thou would'st not have thy neighbour do to thee.
In causing pleasure, or in giving pain,
In doing good, or injury to others,

[1] The order of the text has been slightly changed in this translation, and a few liberties taken in the wording of it.

In granting, or refusing a request,
A man obtains a proper rule of action
By looking on his neighbour as himself[1].

Mahā-bh. XIII. 5571.

No being perishes before his time,
Though by a hundred arrows pierced; but when
His destined moment comes, though barely pricked
By a sharp point of grass, he surely dies[2].

Mahā-bh. XIII. 7607.

Before infirmities creep o'er thy flesh;
Before decay impairs thy strength and mars
The beauty of thy limbs; before the Ender,
Whose charioteer is sickness, hastes towards thee,
Breaks up thy fragile frame and ends thy life[3],
Lay up the only treasure: do good deeds;
Practise sobriety and self-control;
Amass that wealth which thieves cannot abstract,
Nor tyrants seize, which follows thee at death,
Which never wastes away, nor is corrupted[4].

Mahā-bh. XIII. 12084.

Heaven's gate is very narrow and minute[5],
It cannot be perceived by foolish men,
Blinded by vain illusions of the world.
E'en the clear-sighted who discern the way,
And seek to enter, find the portal barred
And hard to be unlocked. Its massive bolts
Are pride and passion, avarice and lust.

Mahā-bh. XIV. 2784.

Just heaven is not so pleased with costly gifts,
Offered in hope of future recompense,
As with the merest trifle set apart
From honest gains, and sanctified by faith[6].

Mahā-bh. XIV. 2788.

---

[1] Compare St. Matthew xxii. 39, St. Luke vi. 31.

[2] This occurs also in Hitopadeśa II. 15.

[3] Compare Eccles. xii. 1. [4] Compare St. Matthew vi. 19, Job xxi. 23.

[5] Compare St. Matthew vii. 14.

[6] Compare St. Matthew vi. 1–4, St. Mark xii. 43, 44.

# LECTURE XV.

*The Artificial Poems. Dramas. Purāṇas. Tantras. Nīti-śāstras.*

I CAN only notice very briefly the remaining classes of Indian writings which follow on the Rāmāyaṇa and Mahā-bhārata. In their religious bearing, as constituting part of Smṛiti, and as chiefly drawn from the two great Epics, the eighteen Purāṇas possess the next claim on our attention. It will be convenient, however, to introduce here an enumeration of some of the more celebrated artificial poems and dramas, which are connected with the Epics, adding a few explanations and examples, but reserving the fuller consideration of these and other departments of Sanskṛit literature to a future opportunity.

## *The Artificial Poems.*

Some of the best known of the artificial poems are:

1. The *Raghu-vanśa* or 'history of Raghu's race,' in nineteen chapters, by Kālidāsa, on the same subject as the Rāmāyaṇa, viz. the history of Rāma-ćandra, but beginning with a longer account of his ancestors; 2. the *Kumāra-sambhava*, by Kālidāsa, on the 'birth of Kumāra' or Kārttikeya, god of war, son of S'iva and Pārvatī,—originally in sixteen cantos, of which only seven are usually edited, though nine more have been printed in the *Pandit* at Benares; 3. the *Megha-dūta*, 'cloud-messenger,' also by Kālidāsa—a poem of 116 verses, in the Mandākrāntā metre (well edited by Professor Johnson), describing a message sent by a banished Yaksha to his wife in the Himālayas; a cloud being personified and converted into the messenger; 4. the *Kirātārjunīya*, 'battle of the Kirāta and Arjuna,' by Bhāravi, in eighteen cantos, on a subject taken from the fourth chapter of Mahā-bhārata III, viz. the penance performed by Arjuna, one of the Pāṇḍava princes, and his combat with S'iva disguised as a Kirāta or wild mountaineer (see p. 393); 5. the *Śiśupāla-badha* or 'destruction of S'iśu-pāla,'

a poem in twenty cantos, by Māgha, on a subject taken from the seventh chapter of the Sabhā-parvan of the Mahā-bhārata, viz. the slaying of the impious S'iśu-pāla by Kṛishṇa at a Rājasūya sacrifice performed by Yudhishṭhira (see p. 392); 6. the *Naishadha* or *Naishadhīya*, by S'rī-harsha [1], on a subject drawn from an episode in the sixth chapter of the Vana-parvan of the Mahā-bhārata, viz. the history and adventures of Nala, king of Nishadha.

The above six are sometimes called Mahā-kāvyas, 'great poems,' not with reference to their length (for they are generally short), but with reference to the subjects of which they treat. To these may be added:

7. The *Ṛitu-saṃhāra* or 'collection of the seasons,' a short but celebrated poem by Kālidāsa, on the six seasons of the year (viz. *Grīshma*, the hot season; *Varshā*, the rains; *Śarad*, autumn; *Hemanta*, the cold season; *Śiśira*, the dewy season; *Vasanta*, the spring); 8. the *Nalodaya* or 'rise of Nala,' an artificial poem, also ascribed to one Kālidāsa, but probably not the composition of the celebrated poet of that name, on much the same subject as the Naishadha, and describing especially the restoration of the fallen Nala to prosperity and power; 9. the *Bhaṭṭi-kāvya*, 'poem of Bhaṭṭi,' according to some the work of Bhartṛi-hari or his son, on the same subject as the Rāmāyaṇa, written at Valabhī (Ballabhi) in the reign of S'rīdhara-sena (probably the king who reigned in Gujarāt from about A.D. 530–544); its aim being to illustrate the rules of Sanskṛit grammar, as well as the figures of poetry and rhetoric, by introducing examples of all possible forms and constructions, as well as of the Alan-kāras (see p. 454); it is divided into two great divisions, viz. *Śabda-lakshaṇa*, 'illustration of grammar,' and *Kāvya-lakshaṇa*, 'illustration of poetry,' together comprising twenty-two chapters; 10. the *Rāghava-pāṇḍavīya*, an artificial poem by Kavi-rāja, giving a narrative of the acts of both the descendants of Raghu and Pāṇḍu, in such language that it may be interpreted as a history of either one or the other family; 11. the *Amaru-śataka* or *Amarū-śataka*, 'hundred verses of Amaru,' on erotic subjects, to which a mystical interpretation is given, especially as they

---

[1] He is supposed to have lived about the year 1000 (cf. note, p. 486). This S'rī-harsha was the greatest of all sceptical philosophers, and wrote a book called *Khaṇḍana-khaṇḍa-khādya* for the refutation of all other systems. It is alluded to in Naishadha VI. 113 (Premaćandra's commentary). The commentator Nārāyana does not seem to have understood this. There are some philosophical chapters in the Naishadha.

are supposed to have been composed by the great philosopher S'ankarāćārya, when, according to a popular legend, he animated the dead body of king Amaru, his object being to become the husband of his widow, that he might argue on amatory subjects with the wife of a Brāhman, named Mandana; 12. the *Gīta-govinda* or 'Kṛishṇa in his character of Govinda (the Cow-finder or Herdsman) celebrated in song,' by Jaya-deva, a lyrical or erotic poem, thought to have been composed about the twelfth or thirteenth century of our era; it was written nominally to celebrate the loves of Kṛishṇa and the Gopīs, especially of Kṛishṇa and Rādhā; but as the latter is supposed to typify the human soul, the whole poem is regarded as susceptible of a mystical interpretation.

Some of these poems, especially the Raghu-vanśa, Kumāra-sambhava, Megha-dūta, and Ṛitu-saṃhāra of Kālidāsa (who, according to native authorities, lived a little before the commencement of the Christian era, but is now placed in the third century[1]), abound in truly poetical ideas, and display great fertility of imagination and power of description; but it cannot be denied that even in these works of the greatest of Indian poets there are occasional fanciful conceits, combined with a too studied and artificial elaboration of diction, and a constant tendency to what a European would consider an almost puerile love for alliteration and playing upon words (*wort-spiel*). Some of the other poems, such as the Kirātārjunīya, Śiśupāla-badha, Nalodaya, Naishadha, and Bhaṭṭi-kāvya, are not wanting in occasional passages containing poetical feeling, striking imagery, and noble sentiment; but they are artificial to a degree quite opposed to European canons of taste; the chief aim of the composers being to exhibit their artistic skill in bringing out the capabilities of the Sanskṛit language, its ductility, its adaptation to every kind of style from the most diffuse to the most concise, its power of compounding words, its intricate grammatical structure, its complex system of metres, and the fertility of its resources in the employment of rhyme, rhythm, and alliteration.

[1] Professor Weber places him either in the third or sixth century.

In fact, there is nothing in the whole range of Greek or Latin or any other literature that can be compared with these poems. Nearly every verse in them presents a separate puzzle—so that when one riddle is solved, little is gained towards the solution of the next—or exhibits rare words, unusual grammatical forms, and intricate compounds, as it were twisted together into complicated verbal knots, the unravelment of which can only be effected by the aid of a native commentary.

Of course, in such cases the sense, and even the strict grammatical construction are sometimes sacrificed to the display of ingenuity in the bending and straining of words to suit a difficult metre or rhyme; and this art is studied as an end in itself, the ideas to be conveyed by the language employed being quite a secondary matter. To such an extreme is this carried, that whole verses are sometimes composed with the repetition of a single consonant [1], while in other cases a string of epithets is employed, each of which will apply to two quite distinct words in a sentence, and thus be capable of yielding different senses, suited to either word, according to the will of the solver of the verbal puzzle.

Again, stanzas are sometimes composed so as to form fanciful shapes or figures, such as that of a lotus (*padma-*

---

[1] English, I fear, would be quite unequal to such a task as the production of a verse like the following from the Kirātārjunīya (XV. 14)—

*Na nonanunno nunnono nānā nānānanā nanu* |
*Nunno nunnonanunneno nānena nunnanunnanut* ||

Or the following from Māgha (XIX. 114)—

*Dādadoduddaduddādī dādādodūdadīdadoḥ* |
*Duddādaṃ dadade dudde dadādadadadodadaḥ* ||

Though in Latin we have something similar in Ennius, *O Tite tute Tati tibi tanta tyranne tulisti.* It must be admitted, however, that the celebrated nursery stanza beginning *Peter Piper picked a peck of pepper* is an effort in the same direction.

*bandha*); or so that the lines or parts of the lines composing the verses, whether read horizontally, diagonally, or perpendicularly, or in opposite directions, will yield significant and grammatical sentences of some kind, the sense being a matter of subordinate consideration. This is called the Fanciful-shape (*ćitra*) ornament.

The formation of the octopetalous *Lotus-stanza* is described in Sāhitya-darpaṇa X. p. 268. One of the commonest of these artificial stanzas, called *Sarvato-bhadra*, is a verse so contrived that the same syllables occur in each Pāda of the verse, whether read backwards or forwards, or from the centre to each extremity, while all the Pādas together read the same either downwards or upwards, whether the reader commence at the centre or each extremity. An example of this verse occurs in Kirātārjunīya XV. 25.

Still more complicated forms are occasionally found, as described by Dr. Yates in his edition of the Nalodaya.

Thus we have the *muraja-bandha*, a stanza shaped like a *drum;* the *khaḍga-bandha*, like a *sword;* the *dhanu-bandha*, like a *bow;* the *srag-bandha*, like a *garland;* the *vṛiksha-bandha*, like a *tree;* and the *go-mūtrikā*, like a *stream of cow's urine*, in uneven or undulating lines.

The art, too, of inventing and employing an almost endless variety of rhetorical figures called Alan̄kāras, 'ornaments of speech,' for the sake of illustrating the various sentiments, feelings, and emotions depicted in dramatic and erotic poetry, is studied to a degree quite unknown in other languages, the most refined subtlety being shown in marking off minute gradations of simile, comparison, metaphor, &c. There are numerous works on this subject—which may be called a kind of *Ars poetica* or *rhetorica*—some of the best known of which are:

1. The *Sāhitya-darpaṇa*, 'mirror of composition,' by Viśvanātha-kavi-rāja (said to have lived in Dacca about the fifteenth century), giving rules and canons for literary composition from simple sentences to epic poems and dramas, illustrated by examples from standard authors, especially dramatic (see p. 466, note). 2. The *Kāvyādarśa*, 'mirror of poetry,' by Daṇḍin. 3. The *Kāvya-prakāśa*, 'illumination of poetry,' by Mammaṭa (the commentary to which, by Govinda, is called Kāvya-pradīpa). 4. The *Daśa-rūpaka*, 'description of the ten kinds of dramatic composition called

Rūpakas,' by Dhanañjaya (p. 465, note). 5. The *Kāvyālankāra-vṛitti*, 'explanation of the ornaments of poetry,' by Vāmana. 6. The *Sarasvatī-kaṇṭhābharaṇa*, 'necklace of the goddess of speech,' by Bhoja-deva. 7. The *Śṛingāra-tilaka*, 'mark of love,' a work by Rudra-bhaṭṭa, describing and illustrating by examples the various emotions, feelings, and affections of lovers, male and female (*nāyaka* and *nāyikā*), as exhibited in dramas, &c. 8. The *Rasa-mañjarī*, 'cluster of affections,' a work on the Rasas[1], by Bhānu-datta, of much the same character as the last.

I add here a brief description of some of the commonest Alankāras. They are divided into two classes: A. *Śabdālankāra*, those produced by the mere sound of words; B. *Arthālankāra*, those arising from the meaning. The tenth Books of the Sāhitya-darpaṇa and Bhaṭṭi-kāvya are devoted to the illustration of this subject.

Examples of A. are, 1. *Anuprāsa*, a kind of alliteration or repetition of the same consonants, although the vowels may be dissimilar, e.g. *Samālingan angan*. 2. *Yamaka*, more perfect alliteration or repetition of vowels and consonants, e.g. *Sakalaiḥ sakalaiḥ*. Various kinds of Yamaka will be found in Bhaṭṭi-kāvya X. 2–21; and in Kirātārjunīya XV. 52 there is a *Mahā-yamaka*.

Examples of B. are, 1. *Upamā*, comparison or simile (the subject of comparison is called *upameyam*, sometimes *prastuta, prakṛita, prakrānta, vastu, vishaya;* while the object to which it is compared is called *upamānam*, sometimes *a-prastuta, a-prakṛita*, &c.). It is essential to an *Upamā* that the *upameya*, the *upamāna*, and common attribute (*sāmānya-dharma*) should be all expressed, and the complete subordination of the *upamāna* to the *upameya* preserved; thus 'her face is like the moon in charmingness,' where 'her face' is the *upameya;* 'moon,' the *upamāna;* and 'charmingness,' the common quality. If the latter is omitted it is a *luptopamā* (see Bhaṭṭi-kāvya X. 30–35). 2. *Utprekshā*, a comparison in which the *upamāna* is beginning to encroach on the *upameya* and to assume equal prominence. It is thirty-two-fold, under two classes, one called *vāćya* when a word like *iva* is expressed, as 'her face shines as if it were a moon;' the other *pratīyamāna* when *iva* is understood (cf.

[1] There are ten Rasas or 'feelings,' enumerated as exemplified in dramatic composition: 1. *Śṛingāra*, love; 2. *Vīra*, heroism; 3. *Bībhatsa*, disgust; 4. *Raudra*, anger; 5. *Hāsya*, mirth; 6. *Bhayānaka*, terror; 7. *Karuṇa*, pity; 8. *Adbhuta*, wonder; 9. *Śānta*, calmness; 10. *Vātsalya*, parental fondness. Some authors only allow 1–8.

Bhaṭṭi-k. X. 44). 3. *Rūpaka*, 'superimposition,' consisting in the superimposition (*āropa*) of a fancied form over the original subject, the *upameya* and *upamāna* being connected as if possessing equal prominence, and their resemblance implied rather than expressed; thus 'moon-face,' 'her face is the moon' (Bhaṭṭi-k. X. 28). 4. *Atiśayokti*, hyperbole, exaggeration, pleonasm (Bhaṭṭi-k. X. 42), in which the *upameya* is swallowed up in the *upamāna*, as when 'her moon' is used for 'her face,' or 'her slender stem' for 'her figure.' 5. *Tulya-yogitā*, in which the *upamāna* or *upameya* is connected with the common quality, as 'a snow-white flower' (Bhaṭṭi-k. X. 61; Kumāra-s. I. 2). 6. *Dṛishṭānta*, exemplification by comparing or contrasting similar attributes (Māgha II. 23). 7. *Dīpaka*, 'illuminator,' i. e. using an illustrative expression, placed either in the beginning (*ādi*), middle (*madhya*), or end (*anta*) of a verse to throw light on a description (Bhaṭṭi-k. X. 22–24; Kumāra-s. II. 60). 8. *Vyāja-stuti*, artful or indirect eulogy in which praise is rather implied than directly expressed (Bhaṭṭi-k. X. 59). 9. *Ślesha* (*lit.* coalescence), paronomasia, using distinct words which have identity of sound, the meaning being different; thus *vidhau* may mean 'in fate' if it comes from *vidhi*, or 'in the moon' if from *vidhu*. 10. *Vibhāvanā*, description of an effect produced without a cause (Kumāra-sambhava I. 10). 11. *Viśeshokti*, description of a cause without its natural effect. 12. *Arthāntara-nyāsa*, transition to another matter, i. e. the turning aside to state a general truth as an illustration of a particular case (Bhaṭṭi-k. X. 36; Kirātārjunīya VII. 15). 13. *Arthāpatti*, inference of one fact from another. 14. *Sāra*, climax. 15. *Kāraṇa-mālā*, series of causes. 16. *Vyatireka*, contrast or dissimilitude. 17. *Ākshepa*, hint. 18. *Sahokti*, a hyperbolical description of simultaneous action connected by the word *saha*. 19. *Parikara*, employment of a number of significant epithets. 20. *Saṃsṛishṭi*, conjunction, i. e. the employment of more than one figure in the same verse independently of each other (Bhaṭṭi-k. X. 70). When there is a commixture or combination of more than one figure, it is called *Sankara;* especially when they are combined as principal and subordinates (*aṅgāṅgi-bhāva*).

To give examples from all the artificial poems enumerated (pp. 449, 450) would be wearisome. It will be sufficient to select a passage from Kālidāsa's Raghu-vanśa, and a few of the moral sentiments scattered through the Kirātārjunīya and the Śiśupāla-badha. I first translate Raghu-vanśa X. 16–33. The inferior gods are supposed to be addressing Vishṇu as the Supreme Being (cf. a similar address in Kumāra-sambhava II):

Hail to thee, mighty lord, the world's creator,
Supporter and destroyer, three in one—
One in thy essence, tripartite in action[1]!
E'en as heaven's water—one in savour—gains
From different receptacles on earth
Diversity of flavours, so dost thou,
Unchangeable in essence, manifest
Changes of state in diverse qualities[2].
Unmeasured and immeasurable, yet
Thou measurest the world; desireless, yet
Fulfilling all desire; unconquered and
A conqueror; unmanifested, yet
A manifester; uniformly one,
Yet ever multiform from various motives.
Thy manifold conditions are compared
To those of clearest crystal, which reflects
Varieties of hue from diverse objects.
Though ever present in the heart, thou art
Held to be infinitely distant; free
From passion, yet austere in self-restraint;
Full of all pity, yet thyself untouched
By misery; the ever ancient one,
Yet never growing ancient; knowing all,
Yet never known; unborn, yet giving birth
To all; all-ruling, yet thyself unruled;
One in thyself, yet many in thy aspects.
Men hymn thy praises in seven songs; and say
Thou liest sleeping on the earth's seven seas[3];
Thy face is seven-flamed fire, and thou thyself
The sole asylum of the world's seven spheres[4].
From the four mouths of thee, pourtrayed as four-faced,
Proceeds the knowledge of life's fourfold objects,
Time's quadruple divisions through four ages[5],
Man's fourfold distribution into castes.
On thee abiding in man's heart, the source
Of light, with minds and senses all subdued,
The pious meditate in hope of bliss.
Of thee the mystic nature who can fathom?
Unborn, yet taking birth; from action free,

[1] See p. 324. [2] See p. 324, note 1. [3] See p. 419.
[4] See p. 430. [5] See p. 333, note 1.

Yet active to destroy thy demon-foes;
Seeming asleep, yet ever vigilant;
Possessing senses fitted for enjoyment,
Yet in all points restrained; protecting all
Thy creatures, yet apparently indifferent.
The ways which lead to everlasting bliss,
Though variously distinguished in the Veda,
Converge to thee alone; e'en as the streams
Of Gangā's waters to their ocean home.
Thou art the only way, the only refuge
Of all whose hearts are fixed on thee, whose acts
Are centred in thee, and whose worldly longings,
Checked and suppressed, have passed away for ever.
Thy greatness is displayed before our eyes
In this thy world and these thy mighty works;
Yet through the Veda and by inference
Alone can thy existence be established[1].
How then can we, the finite, tell thy essence?
Since merely by the thought of thee thy creatures
Are purified, much more have other acts
Which have thee for their object, full reward.
As jewels lying deep in ocean's bed,
And fires deep hidden in the solar orb
Are far beyond the reach of mortals, so thy deeds
Exceed our praises. Naught is unattained
By thee, and naught is unattainable;
Yet love, and love alone, for these thy worlds
Moves thee to act, leads to thy incarnations[2].
That in the celebration of thy praises
Our voices are restrained, deign to ascribe
This to our limited capacities,
Not to the limitation of thy glory.

I next translate some moral sentiments and wise sayings from the Kirātārjunīya of Bhāravi:

Those who wish well towards their friends disdain
To please them by fair words which are not true (I. 2).

---

[1] This is an allusion to the three Pramāṇas of the Sāṅkhya, viz. Pratyaksha, Anumāna, and Āpta-vaćana or S'abda; see p. 92.

[2] See p. 323.

Better to have a great man for one's foe
Than court association with the low (I. 8).

As drops of bitter medicine, though minute,
May have a salutary force, so words
Though few and painful, uttered seasonably,
May rouse the prostrate energies of those
Who meet misfortune with despondency (II. 4).

Do nothing rashly, want of circumspection
Is the chief cause of failure and disaster.
Fortune, wise lover of the wise, selects
Him for her lord who ere he acts, reflects (II. 30).

He who with patience and deliberation
Prepares the ground whence issue all his actions,
Obtains, like those who water seeds and roots,
An ample harvest of autumnal fruits (II. 31).

The body's truest ornament consists
In knowledge of the truth; of sacred knowledge
The best embellishment is self-control;
Of self-control the garniture is courage,
Courage is best embellished by success (II. 32).

In matters difficult and dark, concealed
By doubt and disagreement of opinion,
The Veda, handed down by holy men,
Explained with clearness, and well put in practice,
Like a bright lamp throws light upon the way,
Guiding the prudent lest they go astray (II. 33).

To those who travel on the rugged road
Trodden by virtuous and high-minded men,
A fall, if pre-ordained by destiny,
Becomes equivalent to exaltation;
Such falls cause neither evil nor distress,
The wise make failures equal to success (II. 34).

Would'st thou be eminent, all passion shun,
Drive wrath away by wisdom; e'en the sun
Ascends not to display his fullest light
Till he has chased away the mists of night (II. 36).

That lord of earth, who equable in mind,
Is on occasion lenient and kind,
Then acts in season with severity,
Rules like the sun by his own majesty (II. 38).

The man who every sacred science knows,
Yet has not strength to keep in check the foes
That rise within him, mars his Fortune's fame
And brings her by his feebleness to shame (II. 41).

Be patient if thou would'st thy ends accomplish,
For like to patience is there no appliance
Effective of success, producing surely
Abundant fruit of actions, never damped
By failure, conquering impediments (II. 43).

If the constituent members of a state
Be in disorder, then a trifling war
May cause a ruler's ruin, just as fire
Caused by the friction of the dried-up branches
Of one small tree, may devastate a mountain (II. 51).

Success is like a lovely woman, wooed
By many men, but folded in the arms
Of him alone who free from over-zeal
Firmly persists and calmly perseveres (III. 40).

The drops upon a lovely woman's face
Appear like pearls; no marks avail to mar,
But rather to her beauty add a grace (VII. 5).

The noble-minded dedicate themselves
To the promotion of the happiness
Of others—e'en of those who injure them.
True happiness consists in making happy (VII. 13, 28).

Let not a little fault in him who does
An act of kindness, minish aught its value (VII. 15).

If intercourse with noble-minded men,
Though short and accidental, leads to profit,
How great the benefit of constant friendship! (VII. 27.)

As persons though fatigued forbear to seek
The shelter of the fragrant sandal-trees,
If deadly serpents lurk beneath their roots,
So must the intercourse of e'en the virtuous,
If vicious men surround them, be avoided (VII. 29).

A woman will not throw away a garland,
Though soiled and dirty, which her lover gave;
Not in the object lies a present's worth,
But in the love which it was meant to mark (VIII. 37).

To one who pines in solitude apart
From those he loves, even the moon's cool rays
Appear unbearable; for in affliction
Even a pleasant object heightens grief (IX. 30).

Wine is averse from secresy; it has
A power to bring to light what is concealed—
The hidden qualities both good and bad (IX. 68).

True love is ever on the watch, and sees
Risks even in its loved one's happiness (IX. 70).

Youth's glories are as transient as the shadow
Of an autumnal cloud; and sensual joys,
Though pleasant at the moment, end in pain (XI. 12).

Soon as a man is born, an adversary
Confronts him, Death the Ender; ceaseless troubles
Begin; his place of birth—the world—
Must one day be abandoned; hence the wise
Seek the full bliss of freedom from existence (XI. 13).

Riches and pleasure are the root of evil;
Hold them not dear, encourage not their growth;
They are aggressors hard to be subdued,
Destroyers of all knowledge and of truth (XI. 20).

To one united with a much-loved object
The empty turns to fulness; evil fortune
Brings festive joys; and disappointment, gain;
But not to him who lives in separation—
He in the midst of friends feels solitary;
The pleasant causes grief; and life itself,
Before so dear, pains like a piercing shaft (XI. 27, 28).

The enemies which rise within the body,
Hard to be overcome—thy evil passions—
Should manfully be fought; who conquers these
Is equal to the conqueror of worlds (XI. 32).

Why give thyself to pleasure? this day's joys
Are thought upon to-morrow, then like dreams
They pass away and are for ever lost (XI. 34).

Who trusts the passions finds them base deceivers:
Acting like friends, they are his bitterest foes;
Causing delight, they do him great unkindness;
Hard to be shaken off, they yet desert him (XI. 35).

The clear and quiet minds of prudent men,
Though ruffled on the surface and disturbed
Like the deep waters of the ocean, fear
To pass the limits of self-mastery (XI. 54).

The friendship of the bad is like the shade
Of some precipitous bank with crumbling sides,
Which falling buries him who sits beneath (XI. 55).

The natural hostility of beasts
Is laid aside when flying from pursuers;
So also when calamities impend
The enmity of rivals has an end (XII. 46).

The following are from Book II. of the Śiśupāla-badha of Māgha (I translate nearly literally):

Alliance should be formed with friendly foes,
Not with unfriendly friends; of friend and foe
The test is benefit and injury (37)[1].

He who excites the wrath of foes and then
Sits down inactively, is like a man
Who kindles withered grass and then lies near
While a strong wind is blowing from beyond (42).

He who by virtue of his rank, his actions,
And qualities, effects no useful purpose,
Is like a chance-invented word; his birth
Is useless, for he merely bears a name (47).

A man of feeble character resembles
A reed that bends with every gust of wind (50).

Soft words, intended to alleviate,
Often foment the wrath of one enraged,
Like drops of water poured on burning butter (55).

A rambling speech whose meaning is confused,
Though long, is spoken easily; not so
A clear, connected, logical discourse (73).

Two only sources of success are known—
Wisdom and effort; make them both thine own
If thou would'st rise and haply gain a throne (76).

Science is like a couch to sapient men;
Reclining there, they never feel fatigue (77).

---

[1] This verse occurs also in Hitopadeśa IV. 16.

A subtle-witted man is like an arrow,
Which rending little surface, enters deeply;
But they whose minds are dull, resemble stones,
Dashing with clumsy force, but never piercing (78).
The foolish undertake a trifling act
And soon desist, discouraged; wiser men
Engage in mighty works and persevere (79).
The undertaking of a careless man
Succeeds not, though he use the right expedients;
A clever hunter, though well placed in ambush,
Kills not his quarry if he fall asleep (80).
A monarch's weapon is his intellect;
His minister and servants are his limbs;
Close secresy of counsel is his armour;
Spies are his eyes; ambassadors, his mouth (82).
That energy which veils itself in mildness
Is most effective of its object; so
The lamp that burns most brightly owes its force
To oil drawn upwards by a hidden wick (85).
Wise men rest not on destiny alone,
Nor yet on manly effort, but on both (86).
Weak persons gain their object when allied
With strong associates; the rivulet
Reaches the ocean by the river's aid (100).
A good man's intellect is piercing, yet
Inflicts no wound; his actions are deliberate,
Yet bold; his heart is warm, but never burns;
His speech is eloquent, yet ever true (109).

## *The Dramas.*

If we bear in mind that the nations of modern Europe can scarcely be said to have possessed a dramatic literature before the fifteenth century of the present era, the antiquity of the extant Hindū plays, some of which may be traced back to about the first or second century of our era, will of itself appear a remarkable circumstance. But to the age of these dramas must be added their undoubted literary value as repositories of much true poetry, though of an Oriental type. They are also valuable as representing the early condition of Hindū society, and as serving to illustrate some of its present peculiarities; for notwithstanding the increasing intercourse with Europe, India, like other Eastern countries, is slow in delivering itself from subjection to the stereotyped laws of tradition which appear to be stamped on its manners and social practices.

In all likelihood the germ of the dramatic representations of the Hindūs, as of the Greeks, is to be sought for in public exhibitions of dancing, which consisted at first of simple movements of the body, executed in harmony with singing and music. Indeed, the root *naṭ* and the nouns *nāṭya* and *nāṭaka*, which are now applied to dramatic acting, are probably mere corruptions of *nṛit*, 'to dance,' *nṛitya*, 'dancing,' and *nartaka*, 'a dancer.' Of this dancing various styles were gradually invented, such as the *Lāsya* and *Tāṇḍava*[1], to express different actions or various sentiments and emotions.

Very soon dancing was extended to include pantomimic gesticulations accompanied with more elaborate musical performances, and these gesticulations were aided by occasional exclamations between the intervals of singing. Finally, natural language took the place of music and singing, while gesticulation became merely subservient to emphasis in dramatic dialogue.

When we come to actual dramatic writing we are obliged to confess that its origin, like that of epic poetry, and of nearly every department of Sanskrit composition, is lost in remote antiquity. There is evidence that plays were acted in India as early as the reign of Aśoka, in the third century B.C. At that period intercourse between

---

[1] The *Tāṇḍava* is a boisterous dance regarded as the peculiar invention of S'iva; the *Lāsya* is said to have been invented by Pārvatī; the *Rāsa-maṇḍala* is the circular dance of Kṛishṇa.

India and Greece had certainly commenced, but it does not appear that the Hindūs borrowed either the matter or form of any of their dramas from the Greeks. (See Lassen's Ind. Alt. II. 507.)

Semitic nations have never inclined towards theatrical representations. The book of Job is a kind of dramatic dialogue. The same may be said of parts of the Song of Solomon, and there is occasional dialogue in the Makāmāt of *al Harīrī* and Thousand and One Nights; but neither the Hebrews nor Arabs seem to have carried dramatic ideas beyond this point. Among the Āryans, on the other hand, as well as among the Chinese, the drama appears to have arisen naturally. At least, its independent origin in Greece and India—both which countries also gave birth independently to epic poetry, grammar, philosophy, and logic—can scarcely be called in question, however probable it may be that an interchange of ideas took place in later times. In fact, the Hindū drama, while it has certainly much in common with the representations of other nations, has quite a distinctive character of its own which invests it with great interest.

At the same time the English reader, when told that the author of the earliest Hindū drama which has come down to us—the *Mṛić-ćhakaṭikā* or 'Clay-cart'—probably lived in the first or second century of the Christian era, will be inclined to wonder at the analogies it offers to our own dramatic compositions of about fifteen centuries later. The dexterity with which the plot is arranged, the ingenuity with which the incidents are connected, the skill with which the characters are delineated and contrasted, the boldness and felicity of the diction are scarcely unworthy of our own great dramatists. Nor does the parallel fail in the management of the stage-business, in minute directions to the actors and various scenic artifices. The asides and aparts, the exits and the entrances, the manner, attitude, and gait of the speakers, their tones of voice, tears, smiles, and laughter are as regularly indicated as in a modern drama.

A great number of other ancient plays besides 'the Clay-cart' are extant, and many of the most celebrated have been printed. To classify these Hindū dramas according to European ideas, or even to arrange them under the general heads of tragedy and comedy, is impossible. Indeed, if a calamitous conclusion be necessary to constitute a tragedy, Hindū plays are never tragedies[1]. They are rather mixed representations, in which happiness and misery, good and evil, right and wrong, justice and injustice are allowed to blend in confusion until the end of the drama. In the last act harmony is restored, tranquillity succeeds to agitation, and the minds of the spectators, no longer perplexed by the ascendency of evil, are soothed and purified by the moral lesson deducible from the plot, or led to acquiesce in the inevitable results of Adṛishṭa (see p. 69). Such dramatic conceptions are, in truth, exactly what might be expected to prevail among a people who look upon no occurrence in human life as really tragic, but regard evil and suffering of all kinds as simply the unavoidable consequences of acts done by each soul, of its own free will, in former bodies.

Nevertheless, to invest the subject of dramatic composition with dignity, a great sage is, as usual (compare p. 372), supposed to be its inventor. He is called Bharata, and is regarded as the author of a system of music, as well as of an Alaṅkāra-śāstra containing Sūtras or rules. His work is constantly quoted as the original authority for dramatic composition[2]. On Bharata's Sūtras followed

---

[1] A rule states that the killing of a hero is not to be hinted at. This does not always hold good. No one, however, is killed on the stage.

[2] Dr. Fitz-Edward Hall has a MS. of the work in 36 Books, of which 18, 19, 20, and 34 were printed at the end of his Daśa-rūpa. Dr. Heymann is now editing the whole work.

various treatises which laid down minute precepts and regulations for the construction and conduct of plays, and subjected dramatic writing to the most refined and artificial rules of poetical and rhetorical style.

Besides the *Daśa-rūpaka*, *Kāvya-prakāśa*, *Kāvyādarśa*, and *Sāhitya-darpaṇa*, &c., mentioned at pp. 453, 454, others are named which treat of dramatic composition as well as of ornaments (*alan̄kāra*) and figures of rhetoric. For example: the *Kāvyālan̄kāra-vṛitti*, by Vāmana; the *Alan̄kāra-sarvasva*, by Bhāma; the *Alan̄kāra-kaustubha*, by Kavi Karṇa-pūraka; the *Kuvalayānanda*, by Apyaya [or Apya]-dīkshita; the *Ćandrāloka*, by Jaya-deva; and a work on music, singing, and dancing, called the *San̄gīta-ratnākara*, by S'ārn̄gadeva, thought by Wilson to have been written between the twelfth and thirteenth centuries.

These treatises classify Sanskṛit plays very elaborately under various subdivisions; and the Sāhitya-darpaṇa—a favourite authority[1]—divides them into two great classes, viz. 1. *Rūpaka*, 'principal dramas,' of which there are ten species; 2. *Upa-rūpaka*, 'minor or inferior dramas,' of which eighteen are enumerated. The trouble taken to invent titles for every variety of Hindū play, according to far more subtle shades of distinction than those denoted by our drama, melodrama, comedy, farce, and ballet, proves that dramatic composition has been more elaborately cultivated in India than in European countries. The ten species of *Rūpaka* are as follow:

1. The *Nāṭaka*, or 'principal play,' should consist of from five to ten acts (*an̄ka*), and should have a celebrated story (such as the history of Rāma) for its plot (*vastu*). It should represent heroic or godlike characters, and good deeds; should be written in an elaborate style, and be full of noble sentiments. Moreover, it should contain all the five 'joints' or 'junctures' (*sandhi*)[2] of the plot; the four kinds of action

[1] The Sāhitya-darpaṇa is in ten sections, treating of the nature and divisions of poetry, the various powers of a word, varieties of style, ornaments of style and blemishes (*dosha*). I have here consulted the late Dr. Ballantyne's translation of part of it, published at Benares.

[2] These five junctures are, 1. the *mukha* or 'opening;' 2. the *prati-mukha* or 'first development of the germ (*vīja*) of the plot;' 3. the

(*vṛitti*); the sixty-four members (*anga*) or peculiar properties; and the thirty-six distinctive marks (*lakshaṇa*). The hero or leading character (*nāyaka*) should be of the kind described as high-spirited but firm[1], being either a royal sage of high family (as Dushyanta in the S'akuntalā), or a god (as Kṛishṇa), or a demigod (*divyādivya*), who, though a god (like Rāma-ćandra), thinks himself a man (*narābhimānī*, see note 3, p. 360). The principal sentiment or flavour (*rasa*, see p. 454, note) should be either the erotic (*śṛingāra*) or heroic (*vīra*), and in the conclusion (*nirvahaṇa*) the marvellous (*adbhuta*). It should be composed like the end of a cow's tail (*go-puććhāgra*), i.e. so that each of the acts is gradually made shorter. If it also contain the four *Patākā-sthānaka* or 'striking points,' and the number of its acts (*anka*) be ten, it is entitled to be called a *Mahā-nāṭaka*. An example of the *Nāṭaka* is the S'akuntalā, and of the *Mahā-nāṭaka* is the Bāla-rāmāyaṇa (see p. 488). 2. The *Prakaraṇa* should resemble the Nāṭaka in the number of its acts as well as in other respects; but the plot must be founded on some mundane or human story, invented by the poet, and have love for its principal sentiment, the hero or leading character being either a Brāhman (as in the Mṛić-ćhakaṭikā), or a minister (as in the Mālatī-mādhava), or a merchant (as in the Pushpa-bhūshita), of the description called firm and mild (*dhīra-praśānta*), while the heroine (*nāyikā*) is sometimes a woman of good family, sometimes a courtesan, or both. 3. The *Bhāṇa*, in one act, should consist of a variety of incidents, not progressively developed, the plot being invented by the poet. It should only have the opening and concluding juncture (see note, p. 466). An example is the *Līlā-madhukara*. 4. The *Vyāyoga*, in one act, should have a well-known story for its plot, and few females in its *dramatis personae*. Its hero should be some celebrated personage of the class called firm and haughty (*vīroddhata*). Its principal sentiments or flavours (*rasa*, see p. 454, note) should be the comic (*hāsya*), the erotic (*śṛingāra*), and the unimpassioned (*śānta*). 5. The *Samavakāra*, in four acts, in which a great variety of subjects are mixed together (*samavakīryante*); it dramatizes a well-known story, relating to gods and demons. An example is the *Samudra-mathana*, 'churning of the ocean' (described in Bharata's S'āstra IV). 6. The

---

*garbha* or 'actual development and growth of the germ;' 4. the *vimarsha* or 'some hindrance to its progress;' 5. the *nirvahaṇa* or *upa-saṃhṛiti*, 'conclusion.'

[1] There are four kinds of heroes: 1. high-spirited but firm (*dhīrodātta*); 2. firm and haughty (*dhīroddhata*); 3. gay and firm (*dhīralalita*); 4. firm and mild (*dhīra-praśānta*).

*Ḍima*, in four acts, founded on some celebrated story; its principal sentiment should be the terrible (*raudra*); it should have sixteen heroes (a god, a Yaksha, a Rākshasa, a serpent, goblin, &c.). An example is the *Tripura-dāha*, 'conflagration of Tripura' (described in Bharata's S'āstra IV). 7. The *Īhā-mṛiga*, in four acts, founded on a mixed story (*miśra-vṛitta*), partly popular, and partly invented; the hero and rival hero (*prati-nāyaka*) should be either a mortal or a god. According to some it should have six heroes. It derives its name from this, that the hero seeks (*īhate*) a divine female, who is as unattainable as a deer (*mṛiga*). 8. The *Anka* or *Utsṛishṭikānka*, in one act, should have ordinary men (*prākṛita-narāḥ*) for its heroes; its principal sentiment should be the pathetic (*karuṇa*), and its form (*sṛishṭi*) should transgress (*utkrānta*) the usual rules. An example is the *Śarmishṭhā-yayāti*. 9. The *Vīthī*, in one act, is so called because it forms a kind of garland (*vīthī*) of various sentiments, and is supposed to contain thirteen members (*anga*) or peculiar properties. An example is the *Mālavikā*. 10. The *Prahasana*, properly in one act, is a sort of farce representing reprobate characters (*nindya*), and the story is invented by the poet, the principal sentiment being the comic (*hāsya*); it may be either pure (*śuddha*), of which the Kandarpa-keli, 'love-sports,' is an example; or mixed (*sankīrṇa*), like the Dhūrta-ćarita, 'adventures of a rogue;' or it may represent characters transformed (*vikṛita*) by various disguises.

The eighteen Upa-rūpakas need not be so fully described. Their names are as follow:

1. The *Nāṭikā*, which is of two kinds—*Nāṭikā* pure, and *Prakaraṇikā* differing little from the Nāṭaka and Prakaraṇa. The Ratnāvalī is an example of the Nāṭikā. 2. The *Troṭaka*, in five, seven, eight, or nine acts; the plot should be founded on the story of a demigod, and the Vidūshaka or 'jesting Brāhman' should be introduced into every act. An example is the Vikramorvaśī. 3. The *Goshṭhī*. 4. The *Saṭṭaka*. 5. The *Nāṭya-rāsaka*. 6. The *Prasthāna*. 7. The *Ullāpya*. 8. The *Kāvya*. 9. The *Prenkhana*. 10. The *Rāsaka*. 11. The *Saṃlāpaka*. 12. The *Śrī-gadita*, in one act, dedicated chiefly to the goddess S'rī. 13. The *Śilpaka*. 14. The *Vilāsikā*. 15. The *Durmallikā*. 16. The *Prakaraṇī*. 17. The *Hallīśa*, chiefly consisting in music and singing. 18. The *Bhāṇikā*.

As I have elsewhere stated (see Introduction to translation of the Śakuntalā), it is probable that in India, as in Greece, scenic entertainments took place at religious festivals, and especially at the Spring festival (*Vasantotsava*, corresponding to the present Holī) in the month Phālguna. Kālidāsa's Śakuntalā seems to have been acted at the commencement of the summer season—a period sacred to Kāma-deva, the Indian god of love. We are told that it was enacted before an audience 'consisting chiefly of men of education and discernment.' As the greater part of every play was written in Sanskṛit, which was certainly not the vernacular of the country at the time when the dramas were performed, few spectators could have been present who were not of the learned classes (see Introduction to this volume, p. xxix). This circumstance is in accordance with the constitution of Hindū society, whereby the productions of literature, as well as the offices of state, were reserved for the privileged castes. The following is a brief account of the construction of an ordinary Hindū Nāṭaka:

Every play opens with a prologue (*prastāvanā*), or, to speak more correctly, an introduction, designed to prepare the way for the entrance of the *dramatis personae.* The prologue commences with a benediction (*nāndī*) or prayer[1] (pronounced by a Brāhman, or if the stage-manager happens to be a Brāhman, by the manager himself), in which the poet invokes the favour of his favourite deity in behalf of the audience. The blessing is generally followed by a dialogue between the manager and one or two of the actors, in which an account is given of the author of the drama, a complimentary tribute is paid to the critical acumen of the spectators, and such a reference is made to past occurrences or present circumstances as may be necessary for the elucidation of the plot. At the conclusion of the prologue, the manager, by some abrupt exclamation, adroitly introduces one of the dramatic personages, and the real performance commences. The play being thus opened, is carried forward in scenes and acts; each scene being marked by the entrance of one character and the exit of another. The *dramatis personae* are divided into three classes—the inferior characters (*nīća*), who are said to speak Prākṛit in a monotonous unaccented tone (*anudāttoktyā*); the middling (*madhyama*); and the superior (*pradhāna*). These latter are to speak Sanskṛit with

[1] The fact that scarcely a single work in Sanskṛit literature is commenced without a prayer to some god, is, as Professor Banerjea has remarked, a testimony to the universal sentiment of piety animating the Hindū race.

accent and expression (*udāttoktyā*). The commencement of a new act, like that of the whole piece, is often marked by an introductory monologue or dialogue spoken by one or more of the *dramatis personae*, and called *Vishkambha* or *Praveśaka*. In this scene allusion is made to events supposed to have occurred in the interval of the acts, and the audience is prepared to take up the thread of the story, which is then skilfully carried on to the concluding scene. The piece closes, as it began, with a prayer for national prosperity, addressed to the favourite deity, and spoken by one of the principal personages of the drama.

Although, in the conduct of the plot, and the delineation of character, Hindū dramatists show considerable skill, yet in the plot itself, or, in the story on which it is founded, they rarely evince much fertility of invention. The narrative of Rāma's adventures and other well-known fictions of Hindū mythology are constantly repeated. Love, too, according to Hindū notions, is the subject of most of their dramas. The hero and heroine are generally smitten with attachment for each other at first sight, and that, too, in no very interesting manner. By way of relief, however, an element of life is introduced in the character of the *Vidūshaka* or 'jester,' who is the constant companion of the hero; and in the young maidens, who are the confidential friends of the heroine, and soon become possessed of her secret. By a curious regulation, the jester is always a Brāhman; yet his business is to excite mirth by being ridiculous in person, age, and attire. Strictly he should be represented as grey-haired, hump-backed, lame, and ugly. He is a species of buffoon, who is allowed full liberty of speech, being himself a universal butt. His attempts at wit, which are rarely very successful, and his allusions to the pleasures of the table, of which he is a confessed votary, are absurdly contrasted with the sententious solemnity of the despairing hero, crossed in the prosecution of his love-suit. On the other hand, the shrewdness of the heroine's confidantes never seem to fail them under the most trying circumstances; while their sly jokes and innuendos, their love of fun, their girlish sympathy with the progress of the love-affair, their warm affection for their friend, heighten the interest of the plot, and contribute to vary its monotony.

Let me now introduce a few remarks on certain well-known plays, some of which have been already mentioned. And first with regard to the earliest extant Sanskṛit drama—the *Mṛić-ćhakaṭikā* or 'Clay-cart.'

This was attributed (probably out of mere flattery) to a royal author, king S'ūdraka, who is said to have reigned in the first or second century B.C. Its real author is unknown, and its exact date is, of course, uncertain. According to Professor Weber, so much at least may be affirmed, 'that it was composed at a time in which Buddhism was flourishing in full vigour.' Some, indeed, may be inclined to infer from the fact of its describing a *Śramaṇa* or Buddhist ascetic as appointed to the head of the Vihāras or monasteries, that one hundred years after Christ is too early an epoch to allow for the possibility of representing Buddhism as occupying such a position in India. At any rate, the date of this drama ought not to be placed before the first century of our era[1]. The play is in ten acts, and though too long and tedious to suit European theatrical ideas, has nevertheless considerable dramatic merit, the plot being ingeniously developed, and the interest well sustained by a rapid succession of stirring incidents and picturesquely diversified scenes of every-day life. In fact, its pictures of domestic manners, and descriptions of the natural intercourse of ordinary men and women, followed by the usual train of social evils, make it more interesting than other Sanskṛit dramas, which, as a rule, introduce too much of the supernatural, and abound in overwrought poetical fancies unsuited to occidental minds.

The hero or leading character (*nāyaka*) of the 'Clay-cart' is Ćāru-datta, a virtuous Brāhman, who by his extreme generosity has reduced himself to poverty. The heroine (*nāyikā*) is Vasanta-senā, a beautiful and wealthy lady, who although, according to the strictest standard of morality, not irreproachable in character, might still be described as conforming to the Hindū conception of a high-minded liberal woman. Moreover, her naturally virtuous disposition becomes strictly so from the moment of her first acquaintance with Ćāru-datta. Her affections are

[1] Professor Lassen assigns it to about 150 after Christ.

then concentrated upon him, and she spurns the king's brother-in-law, named Saṃsthānaka, a vicious, dissipated man, whose character is well depicted in striking contrast to that of Ćāru-datta. As the one is a pattern of generosity, so the other stands out in bold relief as a typical embodiment of the lowest forms of depravity. They are both probably drawn to the life, but the latter delineation is the most remarkable as an evidence of the corruption of Oriental courts in ancient times, when it was often possible for a man, more degraded than a brute, to prosecute with impunity the selfish gratification of the worst passions under the shelter of high rank [1].

At the commencement of the second act, a gambler is introduced running away from the keeper of a gaming-house, named Māthura, and from another gambler. I here translate the scene [2]:

*1st Gambler.* The master of the tables and the gamester are at my heels, how can I escape them? Here is an empty temple, I will enter it walking backwards, and pretend to be its idol.

*Māthura.* Ho! there! stop thief! a gambler has lost ten Suvarṇas, and is running off without paying—Stop him! stop him!

*2nd Gambler.* He has run as far as this point; but here the track is lost.

*Māth.* Ah! I see, the footsteps are reversed; the rogue has walked backwards into this temple which has no image in it.

(They enter, and make signs to each other on discovering the object of their search, standing motionless on a pedestal.)

*2nd Gambler.* Is this a wooden image, I wonder?

*Māth.* No, no, it must be made of stone, I think. (So saying, they shake and pinch him.) Never mind, sit we down here and play out our game. (They commence playing.)

*1st Gambler.* (Still acting the image, but looking on, and with difficulty restraining his wish to join in the game—Aside.) The rattling of

---

[1] That this sort of personage was commonly found at the courts of Eastern kings is evident from the fact of his forming, under the name of the 'S'akāra,' one of the stock characters in the *dramatis personae* of Indian plays. He is a king's brother-in-law through one of his inferior wives, and is required by theatrical rules to be represented as foolish, frivolous, vicious, selfish, proud, and cruel.

[2] I have made use of Stenzler's excellent edition, and also consulted Professor H. H. Wilson's free translation. I hope to give an epitome of the whole play in a Second Series of Lectures.

dice is as tantalizing to a penniless man as the sound of drums to a dethroned monarch; verily it is sweet as the note of a nightingale.

*2nd Gambler.* The throw is mine! the throw is mine!

*Māth.* No, no, it is mine, I say.

*1st Gambler.* (Forgetting himself and jumping off the pedestal.) No, I tell you, it is mine.

*2nd Gambler.* We've caught him.

*Māth.* Yes, rascal! you're caught at last. Hand over the Suvarṇas.

*1st Gambler.* Worthy sir, I'll pay them in good time.

*Māth.* Hand them over this very minute, I say. (They beat him.)

*1st Gambler.* (Aside to 2nd Gambler.) I'll pay you half, if you will forgive me the rest.

*2nd Gambler.* Agreed.

*1st Gambler.* (Aside to Māthura.) I'll give you security for half if you will let me off the other half.

*Māth.* Agreed.

*1st Gambler.* Then, good morning to you, sirs, I'm off.

*Māth.* Hallo! stop there, where are you going so fast? Hand over the money.

*1st Gambler.* See here, my good sirs; one has taken security for half, and the other has let me off the other half. Isn't it clear I have nothing to pay?

*Māth.* No, no, my fine fellow; my name is Māthura, and I'm not such a fool as you take me for. Don't suppose I'm going to be cheated out of my ten Suvarṇas in this way; hand them over, you scoundrel.

Upon that they set to work beating the unfortunate gambler, whose cries for help bring another gamester, who happens to be passing, to his rescue. A general scuffle now takes place, and in the midst of the confusion the first gambler escapes. In his flight he comes to the house of Vasanta-senā, and, finding the door open, rushes in. Vasanta-senā inquires who he is, and what he wants. He then recites his story, and makes known to her that he was once in the service of Ćāru-datta, who discharged him on account of reduced circumstances. Hence he had been driven to seek a livelihood by gambling. The mention of Ćāru-datta at once secures Vasanta-senā's aid, and the pursuers having now tracked their fugitive to the door of her house, she sends them out a jewelled bracelet, which satisfies their demands, and they retire. The gambler expresses the deepest gratitude, hopes in return to be of use to Vasanta-senā, and announces his intention of abandoning his disreputable habits, and becoming a Buddhist mendicant.

The following is a soliloquy of which he delivers himself

after he has settled down into an ascetical life (Act VIII). I translate somewhat freely:

Hear me, ye foolish, I implore.
Make sanctity your only store;
Be satisfied with meagre fare;
Of greed and gluttony beware;
Shun slumber, practise lucubration,
Sound the deep gong of meditation.
Restrain your appetites with zeal,
Let not these thieves your merit steal;
Be ever storing it anew,
And keep eternity in view.
Live ever thus like me austerely,
And be the home of Virtue merely.
Kill your five senses, murder then
Women and all immoral men.
Whoe'er has slain these evils seven
Has saved himself, and goes to heaven.
Nor think by shaven face and head
To prove your appetites are dead;
Who shears his head and not his heart
Is an ascetic but in part;
But he whose heart is closely lopped,
Has also head and visage cropped.

In the end, Ćāru-datta and Vasanta-senā are happily married, but not till the Buddhist mendicant has saved the life of both.

I pass on to the greatest of all Indian dramatists, *Kālidāsa.* He is represented by some native authorities (though on insufficient grounds) to have lived in the time of a celebrated king, Vikramāditya, whose reign forms the starting-point of the Hindū era called *Saṃvat*, beginning fifty-seven years B.C. This king had his capital in Ujjayinī (Oujein); he was a great patron of literature, and Kālidāsa is described as one of the nine illustrious men called the nine jewels of his court. It is, however, more probable that Kālidāsa lived and composed his works about the commencement of the third century[1]. His well-known poems have already been noticed at pp. 449–451[2]. He only wrote three plays—the *Śakuntalā*, the *Vikramorvaśī*, and the *Mālavikāgnimitra*. Of these, the Śakuntalā, in seven acts, is by far the most celebrated and popular. I have endeavoured in my translation of this beautiful drama (fourth edition, published by W. H. Allen & Co.)[3] to give some idea of the merits of a work which drew unqualified praise from such a poet as

---

[1] Professor Lassen places Kālidāsa about the year 250 after Christ. Dr. Bhāu Dājī assigns him to the reign of a Vikramāditya in the sixth century. Kālidāsa probably lived at Ujjayinī, as he describes it with much feeling in the Megha-dūta, and to this circumstance may probably be traced his supposed connection with the great Vikramāditya.

[2] Besides these, he is said to have written a poem called the *Setu-kāvya* or *Setu-bandha*, describing the building of Rāma's bridge, and written for Pravara-sena, king of Kaśmīr. A work on metres, called the S'ruta-bodha, is also attributed to him. This last may be by another Kālidāsa. No doubt many works were ascribed to the greatest Indian poet, as to the greatest Indian philosopher, S'an-karāćārya, which they neither of them wrote.

[3] As every Orientalist knows, Sir W. Jones was the first to translate the S'akuntalā, but he had only access to the Bengāl (Bengālī) recension. Two other recensions exist, one in the North-west (commonly called the Devanāgarī) and one in the South of India. The last is the shortest, and the Bengāl version is the longest. The Devanāgarī recension, translated by me into English, is generally considered the purest. Nevertheless Dr. R. Pischel in a learned dissertation maintains that the palm belongs to the Bengālī, and it must be admitted that in some cases the Bengāl version contains readings which appear more likely to represent the original. Professor Böhtlingk's edition of the Devanāgarī recension is well known. My edition of the same recension, with literal translations of the difficult passages and critical notes (published by Stephen Austin of Hertford), is now out of print. Dr. C. Burkhard has lately published a new edition of this recension with a useful vocabulary. A good edition of the Bengāl recension was prepared in Calcutta by Pandit Prem Chunder Tarkabāgish, and brought out in 1860 under the superintendence of Professor E. B. Cowell.

Goethe in the following words (Mr. E. B. Eastwick's translation):

Wouldst thou the young year's blossoms and the fruits of its decline,
And all by which the soul is charmed, enraptured, feasted, fed?
Wouldst thou the earth and heaven itself in one sole name combine?
I name thee, O S'akoontalā! and all at once is said.

I merely extract from my own translation of the *Śakuntalā* two passages. The following is the hero Dushyanta's description of a peculiar sensation to which he confesses himself subject, and to which perhaps the minds of sensitive persons, even in Western countries, are not altogether strangers (Act V. Translation, p. 121):

Not seldom in our happy hours of ease,
When thought is still, the sight of some fair form,
Or mournful fall of music breathing low,
Will stir strange fancies, thrilling all the soul
With a mysterious sadness, and a sense
Of vague, yet earnest longing. Can it be
That the dim memory of events long past,
Or friendships formed in other states of being,
Flits like a passing shadow o'er the spirit?

Here is a specimen of the poetical similes which occur constantly throughout the drama (Act V. Translation, p. 129)[1]:

The loftiest trees bend humbly to the ground
Beneath the teeming burden of their fruit;
High in the vernal sky the pregnant clouds
Suspend their stately course, and, hanging low,
Scatter their sparkling treasures o'er the earth:
And such is true benevolence; the good
Are never rendered arrogant by riches.

The two other dramas composed by Kālidāsa are the *Vikramorvaśī*, 'Urvaśī won by valour,' and the *Māla-*

[1] This verse occurs also in Bhartṛi-hari II. 62. He was the author of 300 moral, political, and erotic verses called *Śṛingāra-śataka*, *Nīti-ś°*, and *Vairāgya-ś°*.

*vikāgnimitra,* 'story of Mālavikā and Agnimitra,' the first of which is unequalled in poetical beauty by any other Indian drama except the Śakuntalā. The *Vikramorvaśī* is in only five acts, and its subject is easily told[1]:

Urvaśī, a nymph of heaven—the heroine of the piece—is carried off by a demon, and is rescued by the hero, king Purūravas, who, of course, falls in love with her. The usual impediments arise, caused by the inconvenient fact that the king has a wife already; but in the end the nymph is permitted by the god Indra to marry the mortal hero. Subsequently, in consequence of a curse, Urvaśī becomes metamorphosed into a plant, and Purūravas goes mad. She is afterwards restored to her proper form through the efficacy of a magical gem, and her husband recovers his reason. They are happily reunited, but it is decreed that when Urvaśī's son is seen by his father Purūravas she is to be recalled to heaven. This induces her to conceal the birth of her son Āyus, and to intrust him for some years to the care of a female ascetic. Accidentally father and son meet, and Urvaśī prepares to leave her husband; but Indra compassionately revokes the decree, and the nymph is permitted to remain on earth as the hero's second wife.

As to the *Mālavikāgnimitra,* which is also rather a short play in five acts, the excellent German translation of it by Professor Weber of Berlin, published in 1856, and the scholarlike edition published in 1869 by Shankar P. Pandit of the Dekhan College[2], have set at rest the vexed question of its authenticity, by enabling the student to compare it with Kālidāsa's acknowledged writings. So many analogies of thought, style, and diction in the Mālavikāgnimitra have been thus brought to light, that few can now have any doubt about the authorship of the extant drama. According to the statement in its own

---

[1] Various editions of this play have been published; one by Lenz, another by myself. By far the best edition is by Dr. Bollensen. Professor H. H. Wilson's spirited verse translation is well known. A prose translation was made by Professor E. B. Cowell and published in 1851.

[2] A previous edition was published at Bonn in 1840 by Dr. Tullberg.

prologue, it is evidently the veritable production of the author of the Śakuntalā and Vikramorvaśī. Nevertheless, its inferiority to the two masterpieces of Kālidāsa—notwithstanding considerable poetical and dramatic merit, and great beauty and simplicity of style—must be admitted on all hands. Perhaps this may be accounted for by supposing the Mālavikāgnimitra to have been Kālidāsa's first theatrical composition. Or possibly the scenes in which the dramatic action is laid, afforded the poet no opportunity (as in the other two plays) of displaying his marvellous powers of describing the beauties of nature and the habits of animals in rural and sylvan retreats. Its hero, king Agnimitra, is certainly a more ordinary and strictly human character than the semi-mythical Dushyanta and Purūravas, and the same may be said of its heroine Mālavikā, as compared with Śakuntalā and Urvaśī; but the plots of the three plays resemble each other in depending for their interest on the successful prosecution of love-intrigues under very similar difficulties and impediments.

In the Mālavikāgnimitra[1], king Agnimitra (son of Pushpamitra, founder of the S'un-ga dynasty of Magadha kings) falls in love with a girl named Mālavikā—belonging to the train of his queen Dhāriṇī's attendants—from accidentally seeing her portrait. As usual, the Vidūshaka is employed as a go-between, and undertakes to procure the king a sight of the original. It happens that the principal queen, Dhāriṇī, has caused Mālavikā to be instructed in music, singing, and dancing. Hence in the second act a sort of concert (*Sangīta*), or trial of skill, is arranged, at which Mālavikā executes a very difficult part in a particular musical time—called the *Madhya-laya*—with wonderful brilliancy. This, of course, captivates the king, and destroys his peace of mind. In spite of the opposition of his two queens, Dhāriṇī and Irāvatī, and notwithstanding other hindrances, he contrives to carry on an intrigue with Mālavikā. Not that he attempts to marry her by unlawful means, nor

[1] I have consulted Professor H. H. Wilson's epitome of the play in the appendix to his Hindū Theatre.

even against the wishes of his other wives. Polygamy is, of course, held to be legitimate in the household of Oriental Rājas. The difficulty consists in conciliating his two queens. This, however, he contrives in the end to accomplish, and their assent to his union with Mālavikā is at last obtained. In the course of the plot a *Parivrājikā* or Buddhist female mendicant is introduced, which is regarded by Professor Weber as an argument for the antiquity of the drama. In the prologue Bhāsa and Saumilla are mentioned as two poets, predecessors of Kālidāsa.

I here give an example of a wise sentiment from the prelude. The stage-manager, addressing the audience, says:

All that is old is not on that account
Worthy of praise, nor is a novelty
By reason of its newness to be censured.
The wise decide not what is good or bad,
Till they have tested merit for themselves.
A foolish man trusts to another's judgment.

I come now to a more modern Indian dramatist named *Bhavabhūti* and surnamed *Śrī-kaṇṭha*, 'whose voice is eloquence.' His reputation is only second to that of Kālidāsa. In the prelude to two of his plays he is described as the son of a Brāhman named Nīlakaṇṭha (his mother being Jatūkarṇī), who was one of the descendants of Kaśyapa, living in a city called Padma-pura, and a follower of the Black Yajur-veda. He is said to have been born somewhere in the district Berar, and to have flourished at the court of Yaśovarman, who reigned at Kanouj (Kanyā-kubja) about A.D. 720[1]. Like Kālidāsa, he only wrote three plays. These are called the *Mālatī-mādhava*, *Mahā-vīra-ćarita*, and *Uttara-rāma-ćarita*[2]. Of these three the Mālatī-mādhava, in ten acts, is perhaps the best known to English Sanskṛit scholars. The style

[1] According to Professor Lassen he lived about the year 710. Kanouj, now in ruins, ranks in antiquity next to Ayodhyā. It is situated in the North-west, on the Kālīnadī, a branch of the Ganges, in the district of Furruckabad.

[2] *Ćarita* is sometimes written *ćaritra*.

is more laboured and artificial than that of Kālidāsa's plays, and some of the metres adopted in the versification are of that complex kind which later Hindū poets delight to employ for the exhibition of their skill[1]. In the prelude the poet is guilty of the bad taste of praising his own composition. Its plot, however, is more interesting than that of Kālidāsa's plays; its action is dramatic, and its pictures of domestic life and manners are most valuable, notwithstanding too free an introduction of the preternatural element, from which, as we have seen, the Mṛić-ćhakaṭikā is exceptionally free. The story of the *Mālatī-Mādhava* has been well epitomized by Colebrooke[2]. I give here but a bare outline:

Two ministers of two neighbouring kings have agreed together privately that their children, Mādhava and Mālatī, shall in due time marry each other. Unhappily for the accomplishment of their project, one of the kings requires the father of Mālatī to make a match between his daughter and an ugly old court-favourite named Nandana. The minister, fearing to offend the monarch, consents to sacrifice his daughter. Meanwhile Mādhava is sent to finish his studies under an old Buddhist priestess named Kāmandakī, who had been Mālatī's nurse, and who contrives that she and Mādhava shall meet and fall in love, though they do not at that time make known their mutual attachment. Soon afterwards the king prepares to enforce the marriage of Mālatī with his favourite Nandana. The news, when brought to Mālatī, makes her desperate. Another meeting takes place in Kāmandakī's garden between her and her lover Mādhava, who is followed to the garden by a friend, Makaranda. During their interview a great tumult and terrific screams are heard. A tiger has escaped from an iron cage and spreads destruction everywhere. Madayantikā, sister of Nandana, happens to be passing and is attacked by the tiger. Mādhava and Makaranda both rush to the rescue. The latter kills the animal and thus saves Madayantikā, who is then brought in a half-fainting state into the garden. On recovering she naturally falls in love with her preserver Makaranda.

---

[1] Colebrooke especially mentions the Daṇḍaka metre, for an account of which see page 166 of this volume.

[2] See Professor E. B. Cowell's edition of his Essays, vol. ii. p. 123.

The two couples are thus brought together, and Mālatī affiances herself there and then to Mādhava. At this very moment a messenger arrives to summon Madayantikā, Nandana's sister, to be present at Nandana's marriage with Mālatī, and another messenger summons Mālatī herself to the king's palace. Mādhava is mad with grief, and in despair makes the extraordinary resolution of purchasing the aid of evil demons by going to the cemetery and offering them living flesh, cut off from his own body, as food. The cemetery happens to be near the temple of the awful goddess Ćāmuṇḍā (a form of Durgā), presided over by a sorceress named Kapāla-kuṇḍalā and her preceptor, a terrible necromancer, Aghora-ghaṇṭa. They have determined on offering some beautiful maiden as a human victim to the goddess. With this object they carry off Mālatī, before her departure, while asleep on a terrace, and bringing her to the temple are about to kill her at Ćāmuṇḍā's shrine, when her cries attract the attention of Mādhava, who is at that moment in the cemetery, offering his flesh to the demons. He rushes forward, encounters the sorcerer Aghora-ghaṇṭa, and after a terrific hand-to-hand fight kills him and rescues Mālatī, who is thus restored to her family. The remainder of the story, occupying the five concluding acts, is tediously protracted and scarcely worth following out. The preparations for Mālatī's marriage to Nandana go on, and the old priestess Kāmandakī, who favours the union of Mālatī with her lover Mādhava, contrives that, by the king's order, the bridal dress shall be put on at the very temple where her own ministrations are conducted. There she persuades Makaranda to substitute himself for the bride. He puts on the bridal dress, is taken in procession to the house of Nandana, and goes through the form of being married to him. Nandana, disgusted with the masculine appearance of his supposed bride, leaves Makaranda in the inner apartments, thus enabling him to effect an interview with Nandana's sister Madayantikā—the object of his own affections. Makaranda then makes himself known, and persuades her to run away with him to the place where Mālatī and Mādhava have concealed themselves. Their flight is discovered; the king's guards are sent in pursuit, a great fight follows, but Makaranda assisted by Mādhava defeats his opponents. The bravery and handsome appearance of the two youths avert the king's anger, and they are allowed to join their friends unpunished. In the midst of the confusion, however, Mālatī has been carried off by the sorceress Kapāla-kuṇḍalā in revenge for the death of her preceptor Aghora-ghaṇṭa. Mādhava is again in despair at this second obstacle to his union, but an old pupil of the priestess Kāmandakī, named Saudāminī, who has acquired extraordinary magical powers by her penances, opportunely appears on the scene, delivers Mālatī from the sorceress, and brings about the happy marriage of Mālatī with Mādhava and of Madayantikā with Makaranda.

The following description of Mādhava's first interview with Mālatī is from the first act[1]:

One day by curiosity impelled
I sought the temple of the god of love.
There I roved to and fro, glancing around,
Till weary with my wandering I stood
Close to a pool that laved a Vakul tree
In the court-yard and precints of the temple.
The tree's sweet blossoms wooed a swarm of bees
To cull their nectar; and in idleness,
To while away the time, I laid me down
And gathered round me all the fallen flowers
To weave a garland, when there issued forth
From the interior fane a lovely maid.
Stately her gait, yet graceful as the banner
Waved by victorious Love o'er prostrate men;
Her garb with fitting ornaments embellished
Bespoke a youthful princess, her attendants
Moved proudly as became their noble rank;
She seemed a treasury of all the graces,
Or Beauty's store-house, where collected shone
A bright assemblage of all fairest things
To frame a perfect form; or rather was she
The very guardian goddess of love's shrine;
Or did the great Creator mould her charms
From some of Nature's loveliest materials—
The moon, the lotus-stalk, and sweetest nectar?
I looked and in an instant both my eyes
Seemed bathed with rapture and my inmost soul
Was drawn towards her unresistingly,
Like iron by the iron-loving magnet.

The other two plays of Bhava-bhūti, called *Mahā-vīra-ćarita* and *Uttara-rāma-ćarita*, form together a dramatic

[1] Some expressions in my version have been suggested by Professor H. H. Wilson's, but I have endeavoured to make my own closer to the original.

version of the story of the second Rāma or Rāma-ćandra, as narrated in Vālmīki's Rāmāyaṇa and Kālidāsa's Raghu-vanśa.

The *Mahā-vīra-ćarita*[1], in seven acts (often quoted in the Sāhitya-darpaṇa under the title *Vīra-ćarita*), dramatizes the history of Rāma, the great hero (*mahā-vīra*), as told in the first six Books of the Rāmāyaṇa, but with some variations.

The author informs us in the prologue that his object in composing the play was 'to delineate the sentiment (*rasa*) of heroism (*vīra*, see note, p. 454) as exhibited in noble characters.' The marvellous (*adbhuta*) sentiment is also said to be depicted, and the style of the action is called *Bhāratī*[2]. The first five acts carry the story to the commencement of the conflict between Rāma and Rāvaṇa and between his army and the Rākshasas; but no fighting is allowed to take place on the stage, and no one is killed before the spectators. Indra and his attendant spirits are supposed to view the scene from the air, and they describe its progress to the audience; as, for example, the cutting off of Rāvaṇa's heads, the slaughter of the demons, the victory of Rāma and recovery of Sītā. The seventh and last act represents the aërial voyage of Rāma, Lakshmaṇa, Sītā, Vibhīshaṇa, and their companions in the celestial car Pushpaka (once the property of Rāvaṇa) from Lan-kā back to Ayodhyā. As they move through the air, they descry some of the scenes of their previous adventures, and many poetical descriptions are here introduced. The car at one time passes over the Daṇḍaka forest, and even approaches the sun. At length it descends at Ayodhyā. Rāma and Lakshmaṇa are re-united to Bharata and S'atrughna, and the four brothers once more embrace each other. Rāma is then consecrated king by Vasishṭha and Viśvāmitra.

---

[1] Mr. John Pickford, one of my former Boden Scholars, some time Professor at Madras, has made a translation of this play from the Calcutta edition of 1857, and Professor H. H. Wilson has given an epitome of it in the appendix to his Hindū Theatre.

[2] The word Bhāratī may perhaps mean simply 'language.' But we may note here that the Sāhitya-darpaṇa enumerates four kinds of style or dramatic action (*vṛitti*), viz. 1. the *Kaiśikī*, vivacious and graceful; 2. the *Sātvatī* or *Sāttvatī*, abounding in descriptions of brave deeds and characterized by the marvellous; 3. the *Ārabhaṭī*, supernatural and terrible; 4. the *Bhāratī*, in which the vocal action is mostly in Sanskṛit.

The *Uttara-rāma-ćarita*[1], in seven acts, continues the narrative and dramatizes the events described in the seventh Book or Uttara-kāṇḍa of the Rāmāyaṇa (see pp. 339–341). I give a brief epitome[2]:

Rāma, when duly crowned at Ayodhyā, seemed likely to enter upon a life of quiet enjoyment with his wife. But this would not have satisfied the Hindū conception of the impossibility of finding rest in this world (compare p. 411), nor harmonized with the idea of the pattern man Rāma, born to suffering and self-denial. We are first informed that the family-priest Vasishṭha, having to leave the capital for a time to assist at a sacrifice, utters a few words of parting advice to Rāma, thus: 'Remember that a king's real glory consists in his people's welfare.' Rāma replies: 'I am ready to give up everything, happiness, love, pity—even Sītā herself—if needful for my subjects' good.' In accordance with this promise he employs an emissary (named Durmukha) to ascertain the popular opinion as to his own treatment of his subjects, and is astonished to hear from Durmukha that they approve all his conduct but one thing. They find fault with him for having taken back his wife after her long residence in a stranger's house (*para-gṛiha-vāsa*). In short, he is told that they still gossip and talk scandal about her and Rāvaṇa. The scrupulously correct and over-sensitive Rāma, though convinced of his wife's fidelity after her submission to the fiery ordeal (p. 360), and though she is now likely to become a mother, feels himself quite unable to allow the slightest cause of offence to continue among the citizens. Torn by contending feelings, he steals away from his wife, while asleep, and directs Lakshmaṇa to seclude her somewhere in the woods. This is the first act. An interval of twelve years elapses before the second act, during which time Sītā is protected by divine agencies. In this interval, too, her twin sons, Kuśa and Lava, are born and entrusted to the care of Vālmīki, the author of the Rāmāyaṇa, who educates them in his hermitage. This leads to the introduction at the beginning of the second act of Vālmīki's stanza (drawn from him by his *śoka* or sorrow on beholding a bird, one of a pair, killed by a hunter), quoted from the Rāmāyaṇa (I. ii. 18), where it is said to be the first S'loka ever invented. An incident now occurs which leads

[1] The whole of this play is translated in Professor H. H. Wilson's Hindū Theatre.

[2] I have consulted the Rev. K. M. Banerjea's article in the 'Indian Antiquary' for May 1872.

Rāma to revisit the Daṇḍaka forest, the scene of his former exile. The child of a Brāhman dies suddenly and unaccountably. His body is laid at Rāma's door. Evidently some national sin is the cause of such a calamity, and an aërial voice informs him that an awful crime is being perpetrated; for a S'ūdra, named S'ambūka, is practising religious austerities instead of confining himself to his proper province of waiting on the twice-born (Manu I. 91). Rāma instantly starts for the forest, discovers S'ambūka in the sacrilegious act, and strikes off his head. But death by Rāma's hand confers immortality on the S'ūdra, who appears as a celestial spirit, and thanks Rāma for the glory and felicity thus obtained. Before returning to Ayodhyā, Rāma is induced to visit the hermitage of Agastya in the woods. Sītā now reappears on the scene. She is herself invisible to Rāma, but able to thrill him with emotions by her touch. Rāma's distraction is described with great feeling. 'What does this mean?' he says, 'heavenly balm seems poured into my heart; a well-known touch changes my insensibility to life. Is it Sītā, or am I dreaming?' This leads on to the last act of the drama. In the end, husband and wife are re-united, but not without supernatural agencies being again employed, and not until Pṛithivī, the Earth, who, it appears, had taken charge of Sītā, restores her to the world. Vālmīki then introduces Kuśa and Lava to Rāma, who recognizes in them his two sons. Happiness is once more restored to the whole family, and the play closes.

We may note as remarkable that at the beginning of the fourth act a dialogue takes place between two young pupils of Vālmīki, who are delighted because some guests, having visited the hermitage, afford hopes of a feast at which flesh meat is to constitute one of the dishes. Manu's rule (V. 41; see p. 256 of this volume) is cited, whereby a *Madhu-parka* or offering of honey to a guest is directed to be accompanied with a dish of beef or veal; for on these occasions householders may kill calves, bulls, and goats (*vatsatarīm mahoksham vā mahājam vā nirvapanti gṛiha-medhinaḥ*).

As a specimen of the poetry of the play, I here give Rāma's description of his love for his wife (translated by Professor H. H. Wilson):

Her presence is ambrosia to my sight;
Her contact fragrant sandal; her fond arms,
Twined round my neck, are a far richer clasp
Than costliest gems, and in my house she reigns
The guardian goddess of my fame and fortune.
Oh! I could never bear again to lose her.

Two other well-known plays, the *Ratnāvalī* and the *Mudrā-rākshasa* (both translated by Professor H. H. Wilson), ought to be mentioned.

The *Ratnāvalī*, or 'jewel-necklace,' is a short play in four acts, attributed (like the Mṛić-ćhakaṭikā, see p. 471) to a royal author, king *Śrī Harsha-deva*[1].

There is nothing of the supernatural about this drama. It may be called a comedy in which the characters are all mortal men and women, and the incidents quite domestic. The play is connected with what appears to have been a familiar story, viz. the loves and intrigues of a certain king *Udayana*, and *Vāsava-dattā*, a princess of Ujjayinī. This tale is told in the Kathā-sarit-sāgara. The king is there called Udayana (see the account in Wilson's Essays, Dr. Rost's edition, I. 191), and is said to have carried off Vāsava-dattā, who is there the daughter of Ćaṇḍa-mahāsena, while in the Ratnāvalī she is daughter of Pradyota, and is not said to be a princess of Ujjayinī. The same story (along with the stories of S'akuntalā and Urvaśī) is alluded to towards the end of the second act of the Mālatī-mādhava, and according to Professor Wilson is referred to by Kālidāsa in the Megha-dūta when he speaks of the *Udayana-kathā* as frequently recited in Ujjayinī (verse 32). Dr. Fitz-Edward Hall has shown in his Preface to Subandhu's *Vāsava-dattā* that this romance has scarcely any feature in common with the Ratnāvalī story except the name of its heroine. The plot of the Ratnāvalī resembles in its love-intrigues that of the Vikramorvaśī, Mālavikāgnimitra, &c., and in like manner presents us with a valuable picture of Hindū manners in medieval times. The poet seems to have had no scruple in borrowing ideas and expressions from Kālidāsa. The hero of the piece is generally spoken of as 'the King,' or else as *Vatsa-rājaḥ*, king of Vatsa—a country

---

[1] This is probably a different S'rī Harsha from the author of the *Naishadha* or *Naishadhīya* (at p. 450). The *Nāgānanda* (see p. 488), a Hindū-Buddhist drama, is attributed to the same author. Hindū poets appear to have been in the habit of flattering kings and great men in this way. Professor E. B. Cowell is inclined to assign the Nāgānanda to a poet named *Dhāvaka*, mentioned in the Kāvya-prakāśa, while he conjectures that *Bāṇa*, the author of the Kādambarī, may have written the *Ratnāvalī*, which would place the date of this play (as shown by Dr. Fitz-Edward Hall) in the seventh century of our era. One native commentator on the Kāvya-prakāśa asserts that *Dhāvaka* wrote the *Ratnāvalī*.

or people whose capital was *Kauśāmbhī*. He is, however, called *Udayana* at the end of the first act, and before the play commences he is supposed to be already married to *Vāsava-dattā*. His minister's name is *Yaugandharāyaṇa* or *Yogandharāyaṇa*, his Vidūshaka or jovial companion is called *Vasantaka*, and his general *Rumaṇvat*.

The first scene introduces a curious description of the sports and practical jokes practised at the Spring festival (now called Holī), when plays were generally acted, and still continue to be performed in some parts of India. *Sāgarikā* (otherwise called *Ratnāvalī*, from her jewel-necklace), a princess of Laṅkā (Ceylon), is accidentally brought to the king's court, falls in love with him, and paints his picture. The king is, of course, equally struck with her. His queen's jealousy is excited by the discovery of the picture. She even succeeds in imprisoning *Sāgarikā* and putting fetters on her feet, and more than the ordinary impediments threaten to stop the progress of the love-affair. All difficulties, however, are eventually removed, and the play ends, as usual, by the king's conciliating his first wife and gaining a second.

I give one specimen of a sentiment uttered by the hero on hearing of the death of a brave enemy. He says: *Mṛityur api tasya ślāghyo yasya ripavaḥ purusha-kāraṃ varṇayanti*; that is,

> How glorious is the death of that brave man
> Whose very enemies applaud his prowess!

The *Mudrā-rākshasa*, or 'signet-ring Rākshasa[1],' is by *Viśākha-datta*, and is a political drama in seven acts, attributed to the twelfth century.

This play is noteworthy as introducing the well-known Ćandra-gupta, king of Pāṭaliputra, who was happily conjectured by Sir W. Jones to be identical with the Sandrakottus described by Megasthenes in Strabo as the most powerful Rāja immediately succeeding Alexander's death, and whose date (about 315 B.C.) serves as the only definite starting-point in Hindū chronology. Another celebrated character is his crafty minister Ćāṇakya, the Indian *Macchiavelli*, and writer on Nīti or 'rules of

---

[1] If this title *Mudrā-rākshasa* is a compound similar to *Vikramorvaśī* and *Abhijñāna-śakuntalam*, where there is *madhyama-pada-lopa*, it might be translated, 'Rākshasa known by the signet-ring;' but it may possibly be one in which the terms are inverted. Some translate it as a *Dvandva*, 'Rākshasa and the signet-ring.' In the fifth act, Ćāṇakya's emissary Siddhārtha enters, bearing a letter marked with the signet-ring of the minister Rākshasa (*amātya-rākshasasya mudrā-lāñćhito lekhaḥ*).

government and polity,' and the reputed author of numerous moral and political precepts commonly current in India. He is represented as having slain king Nanda and assisted Ćandra-gupta to the throne. The principal design of the play is to describe how this wily Brāhman Ćāṇakya (also called Vishṇu-gupta) effects a reconciliation between a person named Rākshasa, the minister of the murdered Nanda, and the persons on whose behalf he was killed. At the beginning of act VII. there is a curious scene in which a Ćaṇḍāla or executioner leads a criminal to the place of execution (*badhya-sthāna*). The latter bears a stake (*śūla*) on his shoulder, and is followed by his wife and child. The executioner calls out,

'Make way, make way, good people! let every one who wishes to preserve his life, his property, or his family, avoid transgressing against the king as he would poison.' (Cf. Mṛić-ćhakaṭikā, act X.)

With regard to the interesting Hindū-Buddhist drama called *Nāgānanda* or 'joy of the snake-world,' I must refer those who wish for an account of its contents to Professor Cowell's Preface prefixed to Mr. Boyd's recent translation (see note, p. 486).

Some other well-known plays have been before noticed:

Thus, for example, the student will find mentioned at p. 369 the *Hanuman-nāṭaka*, a *Mahā-nāṭaka* in fourteen acts[1]; the *Bāla-rāmāyaṇa*, a *Mahā-nāṭaka* in ten acts, by *Rāja-śekhara* (edited by Paṇḍit Govinda Deva S'āstrī of Benares in 1869); the *Prasanna-rāghava* in seven acts (edited by the same in 1868); the *Anargha-rāghava;* and the *Veṇī-saṃhāra* at p. 393, note 1. The *Hāsyārṇava*, a comic and satirical piece in two acts, is described in the appendix to Professor Wilson's Hindū Theatre.

Before, however, taking leave of the Hindū Theatre I ought to note a curious allegorical and philosophical play by Kṛishṇa-miśra, who is supposed to have lived in the twelfth century of our era. The play is called *Prabodha-ćandrodaya*, i. e. 'rise of the moon of (true) intelligence or knowledge,' and its *dramatis personae*

[1] I possess an old and valuable MS. of this play, which I hope may one day be used in editing it. The edition published in Calcutta by Mahārāja Kālī-kṛishṇa Bahādur, in 1840, was not from the purest recension. It was lithographed at Bombay about ten years ago.

remind one of some of our old Moralities—acted in England about the time of Henry VIII—in which the Virtues and Vices were introduced as persons for the purpose of inculcating moral and religious truth.

Thus in an old English Morality called *Every-man* some of the personifications are—God, Death, Every-man, Fellowship, Kindred, Good-deeds, Knowledge, Confession, Beauty, Strength, Discretion. In *Hycke-scorner*—Contemplation, Pity, Imagination, Free-will. In *Lusty Juventus*—Good Counsel, Knowledge, Satan, Hypocrisy, Fellowship, Abominable Living, God's Merciful Promises. Similarly in the Hindū Morality *Prabodha-ćandrodaya* we have Faith, Volition, Opinion, Imagination, Contemplation, Devotion, Quietude, Friendship, &c. &c., on one side; Error, Self-conceit, Hypocrisy, Love, Passion, Anger, Avarice, on the other. The two sets of characters are, of course, opposed to each other, the object of the play being to show how the former become victorious over the latter, the Buddhists and other heretical sects being represented as adherents of the losing side.

## V. *The Purāṇas.*

I must now advert briefly to the eighteen Purāṇas. They constitute an important department of Sanskṛit literature in their connection with the later phases of Brāhmanism, as exhibited in the doctrines of emanation, incarnation, and triple manifestation (*tri-mūrti*, see pp. 324–327), and are, in real fact, the proper Veda of popular Hindūism, having been designed to convey the exoteric doctrines of the Veda to the lower castes and to women. On this account, indeed, they are sometimes called a fifth Veda (see note 2, p. 372). Their name *Purāṇa* signifies 'old traditional story,' and the eighteen ancient narratives to which this name is applied are said to have been compiled by the ancient sage *Vyāsa* (also called Kṛishṇa-dvaipāyana and Bādarāyaṇa), the arranger of the Vedas and Mahā-bhārata (p. 372, with note 2), and the supposed founder of the Vedānta philosophy (p. 111, note 2). They are composed chiefly in the simple Śloka metre (with occasional passages in prose), and are, like the Mahā-bhārata, very encyclopedical in their range of subjects. They must not, however, be confounded with the Itihāsas, which are properly the histories of heroic *men*, not *gods*, though these men were afterwards deified. The Purāṇas are properly the history of the gods themselves, interwoven with every variety of legendary tradition on other subjects. Viewing them as a whole, the theology they teach is anything but simple, consistent, or uniform. While nominally tritheistic—to suit the three developments of Hindūism explained at p. 327—the religion of the Purāṇas is practically polytheistic and yet essentially pantheistic. Underlying their whole teaching may be discerned the one grand doctrine which is generally found at the root of Hindū theology, whether Vedic or Purānic—pure uncompromising pantheism. But interwoven with the radically pantheistic and Vedāntic texture of these compositions, tinged as it is with other philosophical ideas (especially the Sān-khyan doctrine of Prakṛiti), and diversified as it is with endless fanciful mythologies, theogonies, cosmogonies, and mythical genealogies, we have a whole body of teaching on nearly every subject of knowledge. The Purāṇas pretend to give the history of the whole universe from the most remote ages, and claim to be the inspired revealers of scientific as well as theological truth. They dogmatize on physical science, geography, the form of the earth (see p. 419), astronomy, chronology; and even in the case of one or two Purāṇas, anatomy, medicine, grammar, and the use of military weapons. All this cycle of very questionable omniscience is conveyed in the form of leading dialogues (connecting numerous subordinate dialogues), in some of which a well-known and supposed divinely inspired sage, like Parāśara, is the principal speaker, and answers the enquiries put to him by his disciples; while in others, Loma-harshaṇa (or

Roma-harshaṇa), the pupil of Vyāsa, is the narrator, being called Sūta, that is, 'Bard' or 'Encomiast,' as one of an order of men to whom the reciting of the Itihāsas and Purāṇas was especially intrusted[1].

Strictly, however, every Purāṇa is supposed to treat of only five topics: 1. The creation of the universe (*sarga*); 2. Its destruction and re-creation (*prati-sarga*); 3. The genealogy of gods and patriarchs (*vaṉśa*); 4. The reigns and periods of the Manus (*manv-antara*); 5. The history of the solar and lunar races of kings (*vaṉśānućarita*[2]).

---

[1] A Sūta was properly the charioteer of a king, and was the son of a Kshatriya by a Brāhmaṇī. His business was to proclaim the heroic actions of the king and his ancestors, as he drove his chariot to battle, or on state occasions. He had therefore to know by heart the epic poems and ancient ballads, in which the deeds of heroes were celebrated, and he had more to do with reciting portions of the Mahā-bhārata and Itihāsas than with the Purāṇas. In Mahā-bh. I. 1026 it is said that Sauti or Ugra-śravas (son of the Sūta Loma-harshaṇa) had learnt to recite a portion of the Mahā-bhārata from his father. Generally it is declared that Loma-harshaṇa learnt to recite it from Vaiśampāyana, a pupil of Vyāsa.

[2] Certainly the recounting of royal genealogies is an important part of the Purāṇas. It consists, however, of a dry chronicle of names. Similar chronicles were probably written by the early Greek historians, called λογογράφοι (Thuc. I. 21); but these developed into real histories, which the Indian never did. It was the duty of bards to commit their masters' genealogies to memory, and recite them at weddings or great festivals, and this is done by Bhāṭs in India to this day. In Rāmāyaṇa I. lxx. 19, however, it is the family-priest Vasishṭha who, before the marriage of the sons of Daśaratha with the daughters of Janaka, recites the genealogy of the solar line of kings reigning at Ayodhyā. This dry genealogy of a race of kings is sometimes called *Anuvaṉśa*. Several similar catalogues of the lunar race (Soma-vaṉśa or Aila-vaṉśa), who first reigned at Pratishṭhāna, and afterwards at Hastinā-pura, are found in the Mahā-bhārata (see especially one in prose, with occasional Ślokas called *Anu-vaṉśa-śloka* interspersed, Mahā-bh. I. 3759 &c.). Professor Lassen gives valuable lists at the end of vol. i. of his Ind. Alt. It must be noted that both the *solar* and *lunar* races have collateral lines or branches. A principal branch of the *solar* consisted of the kings of *Mithilā* or *Videha*,

On this account the oldest native lexicographer Amarasiṉha (see p. 171), whose date was placed by Professor H. H. Wilson at the end of the first century B.C., gives the word *Pañća-lakshaṇa*, 'characterized by five subjects,' as a synonym of Purāṇa. No doubt some kind of Purāṇas must have existed before his time, as we find the word mentioned in the Gṛihya-sūtras of Āśvalāyana (see p. 203 of this volume), and in Manu (see p. 215, note 1, and p. 256 of this volume). The fact that very few of the Purāṇas now extant, answer to the title Pañća-lakshaṇa, and that the abstract given in the Matsya-purāṇa of the contents of all the others, does not always agree with the extant works, either in the subjects described, or number of verses enumerated[1], proves that, like the Rāmāyaṇa and Mahā-bhārata, they were preceded by more ancient works. In all probability there were *Mūla* or original Purāṇas, as there once existed also a *Mūla* Rāmāyaṇa and *Mūla* Mahā-bhārata. Indeed, in the Bhāgavata-purāṇa XII. vii. 7, six *Mūla-saṃhitāḥ* or original collections are specially declared to have been taught by Vyāsa to six sages, his pupils; and these six collections may have formed the

---

commencing with the bad king *Nimi*, who perished for his wickedness (Manu VII. 41). His son was *Mithi* (who gave his name to the city), and his son was *Janaka* (so called as the real 'father of the race'); the great and good Janaka, learned in Brahmanical lore, being, it appears, a descendant of this first Janaka. The *lunar* race, to which the Pāṇḍavas belonged, had two principal branches, that of the *Yādavas* (commencing with *Yadu*, and comprising under it *Arjuna Kārtavīrya* and *Kṛishṇa*), and that of the kings of *Magadha*. The Yādavas had also a collateral line of kings of *Kāśī* or *Vārāṇasī*. For the solar and lunar genealogies see pp. 346 and 376 of this volume.

[1] Thus the *Bhavishya-purāṇa* ought to consist of a revelation of future events by Brahmā, but contains scarcely any prophecies. This work is rather a manual of religious observances; and the commencement, which treats of creation, is little else than a transcript of Manu. We may note, however, that S'an̄kara Āćārya often quotes the extant Vishṇu-purāṇa.

bases of the present works, which, as we shall presently see, are arranged in three groups of six. At any rate, it appears certain that the Purāṇas had an ancient groundwork, which may have been in some cases reduced by omissions or curtailments, before serving as a basis for the later superstructures. This groundwork became more or less overlaid from time to time by accretions and incrustations; the epic poems, and especially the Mahā-bhārata, constituting the principal sources drawn upon for each successive augmentation of the original work. Nevertheless, it must always be borne in mind that the mythology of the Purāṇas is more developed than that of the Mahā-bhārata, in which (as properly an Itihāsa, and therefore only concerned with kings and heroic men) Vishṇu and Śiva are often little more than great heroes, and are not yet regarded as rival gods. In medieval times, when the present Purāṇas were compiled, the rivalry between the worshippers of Vishṇu and Śiva was in full force—the fervour of their worship having been stimulated by the Brāhmans as an aid to the expulsion of Buddhism—and the Purāṇas themselves were the expression and exponent of this phase of Hindūism. Hence the great antiquity ascribed to the present works by the Hindūs, although it may have had the effect of investing them with a more sacred character than they could otherwise have acquired, is not supported by either internal or external evidence. The oldest we possess can scarcely date from a period more remote than the sixth or seventh century of our era.

Of course the main object of most of the Purāṇas is, as I have already hinted, a sectarian one. They aim at exalting one of the three members of the Tri-mūrti, Brahmā, Vishṇu, or Śiva; those which relate to *Brahmā* being sometimes called *Rājasa* Purāṇas (from his own peculiar Guṇa *rajas*); those which exalt *Vishṇu* being designated *Śattvika* (from his Guṇa *sattva*); and those which prefer

*Śiva* being styled *Tāmasa* (from his Guṇa *tamas*). The reason for connecting them with the three Guṇas will be understood by referring to p. 324.

I now give the names of the eighteen Purāṇas according to the above three divisions:

*A.* The Rājasa Purāṇas, or those which relate to Brahmā, are, 1. *Brahma*, 2. *Brahmāṇḍa*, 3. *Brahma-vaivarta*, 4. *Mārkaṇḍeya*, 5. *Bhavishya*, 6. *Vāmana*.

*B.* The S'attvika Purāṇas, or those which exalt Vishṇu, are, 1. *Vishṇu*, 2. *Bhāgavata*, 3. *Nāradīya*, 4. *Garuḍa*, 5. *Padma*, 6. *Vārāha*. These six are usually called Vaishṇava Purāṇas.

*C.* The Tāmasa, or those which glorify S'iva, are, 1. *Śiva*, 2. *Linga*, 3. *Skanda*, 4. *Agni*, 5. *Matsya*, 6. *Kūrma*. These six are usually styled S'aiva Purāṇas. For the 'Agni,' an ancient Purāṇa called '*Vāyu*,' which is probably one of the oldest of the eighteen, is often substituted.

Although it is certainly convenient to group the eighteen Purāṇas in these three divisions in accordance with the theory of the Tri-mūrti or triple manifestation, it must not be supposed that the six Purāṇas in the first, or *Rājasa* group, are devoted to the exclusive exaltation of *Brahmā*, whose worship has never been either general or popular (see note 2, p. 327).

Though these six Purāṇas abound in legends connected with the first member of the Triad, they resemble the other two groups in encouraging the worship of either Vishṇu or S'iva, and especially of Vishṇu as the lover Kṛishṇa. According to Professor H. H. Wilson some of them are even favourites with the S'āktas (see p. 502 of this volume), as promoting the adoration of the goddess Durgā or Kālī, the personified energy of S'iva.

One of their number, the *Mārkaṇḍeya*, is (as Professor Banerjea has shown in the Preface to his excellent edition of this work) quite unsectarian in character.

This *Mārkaṇḍeya-purāṇa* is, therefore, probably one of the oldest—perhaps as old as the eighth century of our era. Part of it seems to be devoted to Brahmā, part to Vishṇu, and part consists of a *Devī-māhātmya* or exaltation of the female goddess. At the commencement *Jaimini*, the pupil of Vyāsa, addresses himself to certain sapient birds (who had been Brāhmans in a previous birth) and requests the solution of four theological and moral difficulties, viz. 1. Why did Vishṇu, himself being *nirguṇa* (see p. 95), take human form? 2. How could Draupadī become the common wife of the five Pāṇḍavas (see p. 387, with notes)? 3. Why had Bala-rāma to expiate the crime of Brahmanicide committed by him while intoxicated (see p. 391)? 4. Why did the five sons of Draupadī meet with untimely deaths, when Kṛishṇa and Arjuna were their protectors (see p. 390, note 2, and p. 409)?

Another of this group of Purāṇas, the *Brahma-vaivarta*, inculcates the worship of the young Kṛishṇa (*Bāla-kṛishṇa*) and his favourite Rādhā, now so popular in India; from which circumstance this work is justly regarded as the most modern of all the Purāṇas.

Of course it will be inferred from the statement at p. 329 that the second group of Purāṇas—the *Sāttvika* or *Vaishṇava*—is the most popular. Of these the *Bhāgavata* and *Vishṇu*, which are sometimes called *Mahā-purāṇas*, 'great Purāṇas,' are by far the best known and most generally esteemed.

The *Bhāgavata-purāṇa*[1], in twelve Books, is perhaps the most popular of all the eighteen Purāṇas, since it is devoted to the exaltation of the favourite god Vishṇu or Kṛishṇa, one of whose names is Bhagavat.

It is related to the Ṛishis at Naimishāraṇya by the Sūta (see p. 491), but he only recites what was really narrated by the sage S'uka, son of Vyāsa, to Parīkshit, king of Hastinā-pura, and grandson of Arjuna, who in consequence of a curse was condemned to die by the bite of a snake in seven days, and who therefore goes to the banks of the Ganges to prepare for death. There he is visited by certain sages, among whom is S'uka, who answers his inquiry (how can a man best prepare to die?) by relating the Bhāgavata-purāṇa as he received it from Vyāsa.

Colebrooke believed it to be the work of the grammarian Vopadeva (p. 178 of this volume).

This Purāṇa has been well edited at Bombay with the commentary of Śrīdhara-svāmin.

---

[1] A magnificent edition was commenced by Eugène Burnouf at Paris in the 'Collection Orientale,' but its completion was prevented by that great scholar's death.

Its most important Book is the tenth, which gives the early life of Kṛishṇa. This Book has its Hindī counterpart in the Prem Sāgar, and has been translated into nearly all the languages of India.

An epitome of this part of the work has already been given at p. 334. As an example of the style of the Purāṇas I here give the text of the story related at p. 337 of this volume. It is condensed in *Bhāgavata-purāṇa* X. lxxxix. 1, thus:

*Srī-Śuka uvāća | Sarasvatyās taṭe rājann Ṛishayaḥ satram āsata | Vitarkaḥ samabhūt teshāṃ trishv adhīśeshu ko mahān || Tasya jijñāsayā te vai Bhṛigum Brahma-sutaṃ nṛipa | Taj jñaptyai preshayām-āsuḥ so 'bhyagād Brahmanaḥ sabhām || Na tasmai prahvaṇaṃ stotram ćakre sattva-parīkshayā | Tasmai ćukrodha Bhagavān prajvalan svena tejasā || Sa ātmany utthitam manyum ātma-jāyātmanā prabhuḥ | Aśīśamad yathā vahniṃ sva-yonyā vāriṇātmanaḥ || Tataḥ Kailāsam agamat sa taṃ devo maheśvaraḥ | Parirabdhuṃ samārebha utthāya bhrātaram mudā || Naiććhat tvam asy utpathaga iti devaś ćukopa ha | Śūlam udyamya taṃ hantum ārebhe tigma-loćanaḥ || Patitvā pādayor Devī sāntvayāmāsa taṃ girā | Atho jagāma Vaikuṇṭhaṃ yatra devo Janārdanaḥ || Śayānaṃ Śriya utsaṅge padā vakshasy atāḍayat | Tata utthāya Bhagavān saha Lakshmyā satāṃ gatiḥ || Sva-talpād avaruhyātha nanāma śirasā munim | Āhate svāgatam Brahman nishīdātrāsane kshaṇam | Ajānatām āgatān vaḥ kshantum arhatha naḥ prabho || Atīva komalau tāta ćaraṇau te mahā-mune | Ity uktvā vipra-ćaraṇau mardayan svena pāṇinā || Punīhi sahalokam māṃ loka-pālāṅś-ća mad-gatān | Pādodakena bhavatas tīrthānāṃ tīrtha-kāriṇā || Adyāham Bhagaval lakshmyā āsam ekānta-bhājanam | Vatsyaty urasi me bhūtir bhavat-pāda-hatāṅhasaḥ ||*

The above story affords a good example of the view taken by the Bhāgavata of the comparative excellence of the three members of the Tri-mūrti.

In VIII. vii. 44, the following sentiment occurs:

When other men are pained the good man grieves—
Such care for others is the highest worship
Of the Supreme Creator of mankind.

Perhaps the *Vishṇu-purāṇa* as conforming most nearly to the epithet *Pañća-lakshaṇa* (see p. 492), will give the best idea of this department of Sanskrit literature.

It is in six Books, and is, of course, dedicated to the exaltation of Vishṇu, whom it identifies with the Supreme Being. Book I. treats of the creation of the universe; the peopling of the world and the descent of mankind from seven or nine patriarchs[1], sons of Brahmā; the destruction of the universe at the end of a Kalpa (see p. 333, note) and its re-creation (*prati-sarga*); and the reigns of kings during the first Manvantara. Book II. describes the various worlds, heavens, hells, and planetary spheres; and gives the formation of the seven circular continents and concentric oceans as described at p. 419 of this volume. Book III. describes the arrangement of the Vedas, Itihāsas, and Purāṇas by Vyāsa, and the institution and rules of caste, in which it follows and resembles Manu. Book IV. gives lists of kings and dynasties. Book V. corresponds to Book X. of the Bhāgavata-purāṇa and is devoted to the life of Kṛishṇa. Book VI. describes the deterioration of mankind during the four ages, the destruction of the world by fire and water, and its dissolution at the end of a Kalpa.

The above is a bare outline of the contents of this Purāṇa. It is encyclopedical, like the others, and is rich in philosophical speculations and curious legends. A passage illustrating the Sāṅkhyan tone of its philosophy will be found quoted at p. 101 of this volume. The great sage Parāśara, father of Vyāsa (p. 376, note 4), is supposed to relate the whole Purāṇa to his disciple Maitreya. The narrative begins thus[2]:

Having adored Vishṇu, the lord of all, and revered Brahmā and the rest, and done homage to the Guru, I will relate a Purāṇa, equal to the Vedas [*Praṇamya Vishṇum viśveśam Brahmādīn praṇipatya ća* | *Gurum praṇamya vakshyāmi Purāṇam Veda-sammitam*, I. 3].

The metre is generally the simple Śloka, with occasional stanzas in the Indra-vajrā, Vaṉśa-sthavila, &c.

---

[1] The seven patriarchs or sages (*saptarshayaḥ*, sometimes identified with the seven stars of the Great Bear) were created by Brahmā as progenitors of the human race, and are called his mind-born sons; they are, *Marīći*, *Atri*, *Aṅgiras*, *Pulastya*, *Pulaha*, *Kratu*, and *Vasishṭha*. To these two others are added in Vishṇu-purāṇa I. vii, viz. *Daksha* and *Bhṛigu*. In Manu I. 35, *Nārada* is also added, making ten.

[2] In my translations I have consulted Professor H. H. Wilson's great work, but I have had the text of the Bodleian MS. before me.

The following is a metrical version of the prayer of Parāśara, addressed to Vishṇu, at the beginning of Book I. 2, (with which compare similar descriptions of the Supreme Being in the Upanishads and Bhagavad-gītā, pp. 45, 143–146 of this volume):

Hail to thee, mighty Lord, all-potent Vishṇu !
Soul of the Universe, unchangeable,
Holy, eternal, always one in nature,
Whether revealed as Brahmā, Hari, S'iva—
Creator or Preserver or Destroyer—
Thou art the cause of final liberation;
Whose form is one, yet manifold; whose essence
Is one, yet diverse; tenuous, yet vast;
Discernible, yet undiscernible;
Root of the world, yet of the world composed;
Prop of the universe[1], yet more minute
Than earth's minutest particles; abiding
In every creature, yet without defilement;
Imperishable, one with perfect wisdom.

There is a curious story of the churning of the ocean for the production of the *Amṛita*, 'ambrosial food of immortality,' in Book I. 9, (compare p. 330 of this volume.) It is noteworthy as differing considerably from that in Rāmāyaṇa I. xlv. The passage represents Indra and the gods as having lost all their strength—in consequence of a curse pronounced on them by the choleric sage Durvāsas—and so becoming subject to the demons. The gods apply to Vishṇu in their distress, and even Brahmā adores him in a long hymn. I give a portion of the story metrically, changing the order of the text in one or two places:

The gods addressed the mighty Vishṇu thus—
'Conquered in battle by the evil demons
We fly to thee for succour, Soul of all,
Pity and by thy might deliver us.'

---

[1] In the original these three attributes are, *Mūla-bhūto jagataḥ*, *jaganmayaḥ*, and *ādhāra-bhūto viśvasya*.

Hari the lord, creator of the world,
Thus by the gods implored, all graciously
Replied—'Your strength shall be restored, ye gods;
Only accomplish what I now command;
Unite yourselves in peaceful combination
With these your foes; collect all plants and herbs
Of diverse kinds from every quarter; cast them
Into the sea of milk; take Mandara,
The mountain, for a churning-stick, and Vāsuki,
The serpent, for a rope; together churn
The ocean to produce the beverage—
Source of all strength and immortality—
Then reckon on my aid, I will take care
Your foes shall share your toil, but not partake
In its reward or drink th' immortal draught.'
Thus by the god of gods advised, the host
United in alliance with the demons.
Straightway they gathered various herbs and cast them
Into the waters, then they took the mountain
To serve as churning-staff, and next the snake
To serve as cord, and in the ocean's midst
Hari himself, present in tortoise-form,
Became a pivot for the churning-staff.
Then did they churn the sea of milk; and first
Out of the waters rose the sacred Cow,
God-worshipped Surabhi—eternal fountain
Of milk and offerings of butter; next,
While holy Siddhas wondered at the sight,
With eyes all rolling, Vāruṇī uprose—
Goddess of wine. Then from the whirlpool sprang
Fair Pārijāta, tree of Paradise, delight
Of heavenly maidens, with its fragrant blossoms
Perfuming the whole world. Th' Apsarasas
Troop of celestial nymphs, matchless in grace,
Perfect in loveliness, were next produced.
Then from the sea uprose the cool-rayed moon,
Which Mahā-deva seized; terrific poison
Next issued from the waters; this the snake-gods
Claimed as their own. Then seated on a lotus
Beauty's bright goddess, peerless S'rī, arose
Out of the waves; and, with her, robed in white
Came forth Dhanvantari, the gods' physician.

High in his hand he bore the cup of nectar—
Life-giving draught—longed for by gods and demons.
Then had the demons forcibly borne off
The cup, and drained the precious beverage,
Had not the mighty Vishṇu interposed.
Bewildering them, he gave it to the gods;
Whereat incensed the demon troops assailed
The host of heaven, but they with strength renewed
Quaffing the draught, struck down their foes, who fell
Headlong through space to lowest depths of hell.

The following is part of the prayer of Mućukunda, Book V. 23:

Lord of the Universe, the only refuge
Of living beings, the alleviator
Of pain, the benefactor of mankind,
Show me thy favour and deliver me
From evil; O creator of the world,
Maker of all that has been and will be,
Of all that moves and is immoveable,
Thyself composed of what possesses form,
And what is formless; limitless in bulk,
Yet infinitely subtle; lord of all,
Worthy of praise, I come to thee my refuge,
Renouncing all attachment to the world,
Longing for fulness of felicity—
Extinction of myself, absorption into thee.

The following account of the Kali or fourth age of the world—the age of universal degeneracy—is from Book VI. 1, (compare p. 333, note 1, of this volume):

Hear what will happen in the Kali age.
The usages and institutes of caste,
Of order and of rank, will not prevail,
Nor yet the precepts of the triple Veda.
Religion will consist in wasting wealth,
In fasting and performing penances
At will; the man who owns most property
And lavishly distributes it, will gain
Dominion over others; noble rank
Will give no claim to lordship; self-willed women
Will seek their pleasure, and ambitious men

Fix all their hopes on riches gained by fraud.
Then women will be fickle and desert
Their beggared husbands, loving them alone
Who give them money. Kings instead of guarding
Will rob their subjects, and abstract the wealth
Of merchants, under plea of raising taxes.
Then in the world's last age the rights of men
Will be confused, no property be safe,
No joy and no prosperity be lasting.

There are eighteen *Upa-purāṇas* or 'secondary Purāṇas,' subordinate to the eighteen *Mahā* or principal Purāṇas, but as they are of less importance I shall do little more than simply give their names as follow:

1. *Sanatkumāra;* 2. *Nara-siṉha* or Nṛi-siṉha; 3. *Nāradīya* or Vṛihan-nāradīya[1]; 4. *Śiva;* 5. *Durvāsasa;* 6. *Kāpila;* 7. *Mānava;* 8. *Auśanasa;* 9. *Vāruṇa;* 10. *Kālikā;* 11. *Śāmba;* 12. *Nandi;* 13. *Saura;* 14. *Pārāśara;* 15. *Āditya;* 16. *Māheśvara;* 17. *Bhāgavata* (thought to be a misreading for Bhārgava); 18. *Vāśishṭha.* Another list given by Professor H. H. Wilson varies a little, thus: 1. *Sanatkumāra;* 2. *Nara-siṉha;* 3. *Nandā;* 4. *Śiva-dharma;* 5. *Durvāsasa;* 6. *Bhavishya;* 7. *Kāpila;* 8. *Mānava;* 9. *Auśanasa;* 10. *Brahmāṇḍa;* 11. *Vāruṇa;* 12. *Kālikā;* 13. *Māheśvara;* 14. *Śāmba;* 15. *Saura;* 16. *Pārāśara;* 17. *Bhāgavata;* 18. *Kaurma.*

With regard to the second or *Nara-siṉha Upa-purāṇa* we have an abstract of its contents by Rājendralāla Mitra in his Notices of MSS. (No. 1020), whence it appears that the general character of these works is very similar to that of the principal Purāṇas. For example, Chapters 1–5 give the origin of creation; 6. the story of Vaśishṭha; 18. the praises of Vishṇu; 22. the solar race; 23. the lunar race; 30. the terrestial sphere. That this work was well known at least five hundred years ago is proved by the fact that Mādhavāćārya quotes from it.

## *The Tantras.*

I have already alluded to the Tantras, which represent a phase of Hindūism generally later than that of the

[1] According to Rājendralāla Mitra this is called *Vṛihat* to distinguish it from the Nāradīya, one of the Mahā-purāṇas. He gives an abstract of it in No. 1021 of his valuable Notices of MSS.

Purāṇas, although some of the Purāṇas and Upa-purāṇas, such as the Skanda, Brahma-vaivarta, and Kālikā, are said to teach Tāntrika doctrines, by promoting the worship of Prakṛiti and Durgā.

The Tantras are very numerous, but none have as yet been printed or translated in Europe. Practically they constitute a fifth Veda (in place of the Purāṇas) for the Śāktas or worshippers of the active energizing will (*śakti*) of a god—personified as his wife, or sometimes as the female half of his essence[1].

It must here be remarked that the principal Hindū deities are sometimes supposed to possess a double nature, or, in other words, two characters, one quiescent, the other active. The active is called his *Śakti*.

Sometimes only eight S'aktis are enumerated and sometimes nine, viz. *Vaishṇavī, Brahmāṇī, Raudrī, Māheśvarī, Nārasiṉhī, Vārāhī, Indrāṇī, Kārttikī*, and *Pradhānā*. Others reckon fifty forms of the S'akti of Vishṇu, besides *Lakshmī;* and fifty of S'iva or Rudra, besides *Durgā* or *Gaurī*. *Sarasvatī* is named as a S'akti of Vishṇu and Rudra, as well as of Brahmā. According to the Vāyu-purāṇa, the female nature of Rudra (S'iva) became two-fold, one half *Asita* or white, and the other half *Sita* or black, each of these again becoming manifold. The white or mild nature includes the S'aktis *Umā, Gaurī, Lakshmī, Sarasvatī*, &c.; the black or fierce nature includes *Durgā, Kālī, Ćaṇḍī, Ćāmuṇḍā*, &c.

This idea of personifying the will of a deity may have been originally suggested by the celebrated hymn (129) in the tenth Maṇḍala of the Ṛig-veda, which, describing the creation, says that Will or Desire (*Kāma*), the first germ (*prathamaṃ retas*) of Mind, brought the universe into existence (see p. 22 of this volume).

But in all probability, the Tāntrika doctrine owes its development to the popularizing of the Sāṅkhya theory

---

[1] It is remarkable, as noticed by Professor H. H. Wilson, that Kullūka-bhaṭṭa, in commenting on Manu II. 1, says, *Śrutiś-ća dvi-vidhā vaidikī tāntrikī ća*, 'revelation is two-fold, Vedic and Tāntric.'

of *Purusha* and *Prakṛiti* (as described at p. 96 and p. 101 of this volume). The active producing principle, whether displayed in creation, maintenance, or destruction—each of which necessarily implies the other—became in the later stages of Hindūism a living visible personification. Moreover, as destruction was more dreaded than creation or preservation, so the wife of the god Śiva, presiding over dissolution, and called *Kālī, Durgā, Pārvatī, Umā, Devī, Bhairavī*, &c., became the most important personage in the whole Pantheon to that great majority of worshippers whose religion was actuated by superstitious fears. Sometimes the god himself was regarded as consisting of two halves, representing the male principle on his right side, and the female on his left[1]—both intimately united, and both necessary to re-creation as following on dissolution. It may be easily imagined that a creed like this, which regarded the blending of the male and female principles, not only as the necessary cause of production and reproduction, but also as the source of strength, vigour, and successful enterprise, soon degenerated into corrupt and superstitious practices. And, as a matter of fact, the Tāntrika doctrines have in some cases lapsed into a degrading system of impurity and licentiousness.

Nevertheless the original Tantra books, which simply inculcate the worship of the active energizing principle of

---

[1] This is the *Ardha-nārī* or half male half female form of S'iva. There are two divisions of the S'āktas: 1. the *Dakshiṇāćārins*, 'right-doers,' 'right-hand worshippers,' or *Bhaktas*, 'devoted ones,' who worship the goddess Pārvatī or Durgā openly, and without impure practices; 2. the *Vāmāćārins*, 'left-doers,' 'left-hand worshippers,' or *Kaulas*, 'ancestral ones,' who are said to perform all their rites in secret, a naked woman representing the goddess. The sacred books appealed to by 1. are called the *Nigamas;* by 2. the *Āgamas.* The forms of worship are said to require the use of some one of the five *Ma-kāras*, 'words beginning with the letter *m*,' viz. 1. *madya*, wine; 2. *māṉsa*, flesh; 3. *matsya*, fish; 4. *mudrā*, mystical gestures; 5. *maithuna*, intercourse of sexes.

the deity—full as they are of doubtful symbolism, strange mysticism, and even directions for witchcraft and every kind of superstitious rite—are not necessarily in themselves impure. On the contrary, the best of them are believed to be free from gross allusions, however questionable may be the tendency of their teaching. The truth, I believe, is that they have never yet been thoroughly investigated by European scholars. When they become more so, their connection with a popular and distorted view of the Sāṅkhyan theory of creation, and perhaps with some corrupt forms of Buddhism, will probably be made clear. It is certain that among the Northern Buddhists, especially in Nepāl, a kind of worship of the terrific forms of Śiva and Durgā appears to have become interwoven with the Buddhistic system.

In all probability, too, the mystical texts (*Mantras*) and magical formularies contained in the Tantras will be found to bring them into a closer relationship with the Atharva-veda than has been hitherto suspected.

As so little is known of these mystical writings, it is not possible to decide at present as to which are the most ancient, and still less as to the date to be assigned to any of them. It may, however, be taken for granted that the extant treatises are, like the extant Purāṇas, founded on older works; and if the oldest known Purāṇa is not older than the sixth or seventh century (see p. 493), an earlier date can scarcely be attributed to the oldest known Tantra[1]. Perhaps the *Rudra-yāmala* is one of the most esteemed. Others are the *Kālikā*, *Mahā-nirvāṇa* (attributed to Śiva), *Kulārṇava* (or text-book of the Kaulas, see note, p. 503), *Śyāmā-rahasya*, *Śaradā-tilaka*, *Mantra-mahodadhi*, *Uḍḍīśa*, *Kāmada*, *Kāmākhyā*.

---

[1] It has been noted that the oldest native lexicographer, Amara Siṉha, does not give the meaning 'sacred treatise' to the word *tantra*, as later writers do.

I now note some of the subjects of which they treat, merely premising that the Tantras are generally in the form of a dialogue between Śiva and his wife Durgā or Pārvatī, the latter inquiring as to the correct mode of performing certain secret ceremonies, or as to the mystical efficacy of various Mantras used as spells, charms, and magical formularies; and the former instructing her.

Properly a *Tantra*, like a Purāṇa, ought to treat of five subjects, viz. 1. the creation; 2. the destruction of the world; 3. the worship of the gods; 4. the attainment of all objects, especially of six superhuman faculties; 5. the four modes of union with the Supreme Spirit. A great variety of other subjects, however, are introduced, and practically a great number of Tantras are merely handbooks or manuals of magic and witchcraft, and collections of Mantras for producing and averting evils. Such, at least, must be the conclusion arrived at, if we are to judge of them by the bare statement of their contents in the Catalogues published by Rājendralāla Mitra and others. I select the following as specimens of what they contain:

Praise of the female energy; spells for bringing people into subjection; for making them enamoured; for unsettling their minds; for fattening; for destroying sight; for producing dumbness, deafness, fevers, &c.; for bringing on miscarriage; for destroying crops; for preventing various kinds of evil; modes of worshipping Kālī; methods of breathing in certain rites; language of birds, beasts, &c.; worship of the female emblem, with the adjuncts of wine, flesh-meat, women, &c.

This last is said to be the subject of the Kāmākhyā-tantra.

## VI. *The Nīti-śāstras.*

This department of Sanskrit literature may be regarded as including, in the first place, Nīti-śāstras proper, or works whose direct object is moral teaching; and, in the second, all the didactic portion of the epic poems and other works.

The aim of the *Nīti-śāstras proper* is to serve as guides to correct conduct (*nīti*) in all the relations of domestic, social, and political life. They are either, *A*. collections of choice maxims, striking thoughts, and wise sentiments, in the form of metrical stanzas; or, *B.* books of fables in prose, which string together stories about animals and amusing apologues for the sake of the moral they contain, or to serve as frameworks for the introduction of metrical precepts. These latter often represent wise sayings orally current, or are cited from the regular collections and from other sources.

But besides the Nīti-śāstras proper, almost every department of Sanskṛit literature contributes its share to moral teaching.

Any one who studies the best Hindū writings cannot but be struck by the moral tone which everywhere pervades them. Indian writers, although they do not trouble themselves much about the history of past generations, constantly represent the present condition of human life as the result of actions in previous existences. Hence a right course of present conduct becomes an all-important consideration as bearing on future happiness; and we need not be surprised if, to satisfy a constant longing for *Nīti* or guidance and instruction in practical wisdom, nearly all departments of Sanskṛit literature—Brāhmaṇas, Upanishads, Law-books, Epic poems, and Purāṇas—are more or less didactic, nearly all delight in moralizing and philosophizing, nearly all abound in wise sayings and prudential rules. Scarcely a book or writing of any kind begins without an invocation to the Supreme Being or to some god supposed to represent his overruling functions, and as each work proceeds the writers constantly suspend the main topic, or turn aside from their regular subject for the purpose of interposing moral and religious reflections, and even long discourses, on the duties of life. This is especially the case in the Mahā-bhārata.

Examples of the religious precepts, sentiments, and aphothegms, scattered everywhere throughout Sanskṛit literature, have already been given in this volume (see, for instance, pp. 282–294, 440, 457)[1].

We now, therefore, turn, in conclusion, to the *two divisions of Nīti-śāstras proper.*

*A.* With regard to the regular collections of moral maxims, sentiments, &c., these are generally in metrical stanzas, and sometimes contain charming allusions to natural objects and domestic life, with occasional striking thoughts on the nature of God and the immortality of the soul, as well as sound ethical teaching in regard to the various relations and conditions of society. They are really mines of practical good sense. The knowledge of human nature displayed by the authors, the shrewd advice they give, and the censure they pass on human frailties—often in pointed, vigorous, and epigrammatic language—attest an amount of wisdom which, if it had been exhibited in practice, must have raised the Hindūs to a high position among the nations of the earth. Whether, however, any entire collection of such stanzas can be attributed to any one particular author is doubtful. The Hindūs, for the reasons we have already stated, have always delighted in aphothegms. Numbers of wise sayings have, from time immemorial, been constantly quoted in conversation. Many thus orally current were of such antiquity that to settle their authorship was impossible. But occasional attempts were made to give permanence to the floating wisdom of the day, by stringing together in stanzas the most celebrated maxims and sayings like beads on a necklace; each necklace representing a separate topic, and the authorship of a

[1] I need scarcely mention here so well-known and valuable a work as Dr. Böhtlingk's *Indische Sprüche,* which contains a complete collection of maxims, &c., in three volumes, and gives the text of each aphothegm critically, with a German translation.

whole series being naturally ascribed to men of known wisdom, like Bhartṛi-hari and Ćāṇakya (see p. 487), much in the same way as the authorship of the Purāṇas and Mahā-bhārata was referred to the sage Vyāsa (see p. 372). Among these collections it will be sufficient to note:

1. The three hundred aphothegms, ascribed to *Bhartṛi-hari*[1] (see p. 512), of which the 1st S'ataka, or collection of a hundred verses, is on love (*śriṅgāra*), and therefore more lyrical than didactic, the 2nd is on good conduct (*nīti*), and the 3rd on the renunciation of worldly desires (*vairāgya*). 2. The *Vṛiddha-ćāṇakya* or *Rājanīti-śāstra*. 3. The *Ćāṇakya-śataka* or hundred verses (109 in one collection translated by Weber) of *Ćāṇakya*, minister of Ćandra-gupta (see under Mudrā-rākshasa, p. 487). 4. The *Amaru-śataka* or one hundred erotic stanzas of Amaru (already described at p. 450). 5. The *Śārṅgadhara-paddhati*, 'Śārṅgadhara's collection,' an anthology professing to collect sententious verses from various sources and to give the names of most of the authors, to the number of about 247[2]. Some verses, however, are anonymous.

There are numerous other collections of didactic and erotic stanzas, some of which are quite modern, e.g. the *Subhāshitārṇava*, *Śānti-śataka*, *Nīti-saṅkalana*, *Kavitāmṛita-kūpa*, *Kavitārṇava*, *Jñāna-sudhākara*, *Śloka-mālā*, the *Bhāminī-vilāsa* by Jagan-nātha, the *Ćaura-pañćāśika* by Vihlaṇa (edited with Bhartṛi-hari by Von Bohlen).

*B.* As to the collections of fables and apologues, these form a class of composition in which the natives of India are wholly unsurpassed.

Sir W. Jones affirmed that the Hindūs claimed for themselves three inventions: 1. the game of chess (*ćatur-aṅga*, see p. 264 of this volume); 2. the decimal figures (see p. 193); 3. the method of teaching by fables. To these might be added: 4. grammar (p. 173); 5. logic (p. 73).

It is thought that both the Greek fabulist Aesop and the Arabian Lokmān[3] (*Lukmān*) owed much to the Hindūs.

---

[1] Edited by Von Bohlen, with a Latin translation, in 1833.

[2] See Professor Aufrecht's article on this anthology in vol. xxvii of the Zeitschrift der Deutschen Morgenländischen Gesellschaft.

[3] According to Herodotus and Plutarch, Aesop lived in the latter part of the sixth century B.C., and was once a slave at Samos. On being

Indeed, in all likelihood, some ancient book of Sanskṛit apologues, of which the present representative is the *Pañća-tantra*, and which has been translated or paraphrased into most of the dialects of India, as well as into Hebrew, Arabic, Syriac, Pahlavī, Persian, Turkish, Italian, French, German, English, and almost every known language of the literary world, is the original source of all the well-known fables current in Europe and Asia for more than two thousand years since the days of Herodotus (II. 134)[1].

This *Pañća-tantra*[2]—which is itself the original source

---

freed, he travelled about and visited Croesus, &c. As to Lokmān, probably such a person once lived, though thought by some to be an imaginary character. He is certainly more likely to have borrowed ideas from Indian fabulists than from Job, or Abraham, whose nephew he is said by some Arabic writers to have been. The 31st chap. of the Kurān is called after him, God being made to say, 'We have given him wisdom.'

[1] A Pahlavī version of the Pañća-tantra was the first real translation. It was made in the time of Nūshīrvān, about A. D. 570, and perished with much of the Pahlavī literature when the Arabs invaded Persia. Before its destruction it had been translated into Arabic, about A. D. 760, and was called *Kalīla wa Damna* (=Sanskṛit *Karataka* and *Damanaka*, the names of two jackals) or fables of the Brāhman Bīdpāi. The well-known Persian *Anvār-i-Suhaili*, 'lights of Canopus,' of Husain Vā'iz, written about the beginning of the fifteenth century, was also an amplification of the Pañća-tantra. Abū-l Fazl, Akbar's celebrated minister, also translated it into simpler Persian and called it *'Iyār-i-Dānish*, 'criterion of knowledge.' An Urdū version, called *Ḳhirad Afroz*, 'illuminator of the understanding,' was made in 1803 by Hāfizu'd dīn Ahmad. The Hebrew version is attributed to one Rabbi Joël. This was translated into Latin by John of Capua at the end of the fifteenth century; and from this various Italian, Spanish, and German translations were made. The English Pilpay's fables is said to have been taken from a French translation. The best of the Turkish versions, called *Humāyūn Nāmah*, was made, according to Mr. E. B. Eastwick, in the reign of the Emperor Sulaimān I, by 'Alī Chalabī bin Sālih.

[2] Edited by Kosegarten in 1848, and lately in India by Professors Bühler and Kielhorn. Translated into German, with an elaborate Introduction, by Professor Benfey in 1859.

of a still later work, the well-known class-book *Hitopadeśa*, 'friendly instruction'—derives its name from being divided into five chapters (*Tantras*); but it is also commonly called the *Pañćopākhyāna*, 'five collections of stories.' The date of the extant Pañća-tantra is usually placed about the end of the fifth century. But the fables of which it consists are many of them referable to a period long preceding the Christian era.

It has even been conjectured that the notion of instructing in domestic, social, and political duties by means of stories in which animals figure as the speakers, first suggested itself to Hindū moralists when the doctrine of metempsychosis had taken root in India. We have seen that a most elaborate theory of transmigration of souls through plants, animals, men, and gods was propounded by Manu at least 500 years B.C., to which date we have conjecturally assigned the existing Code of the Mānavas (see p. 67, note 1, and p. 280). Accordingly there is evidence that contemporaneously with the rise of Brāhmanism in Manu's time, and the consequent growth of antagonistic systems like Buddhism and the Sān·khya philosophy, fables were commonly used to illustrate the teaching of these systems. Thus:

In the whole fourth Book of the *Sān·khya-pravaćana* (see p. 89, note 1) there are constant exemplifications of philosophical truth by allusions to the habits of animals, as recorded in popular stories and proverbs. (For example, *sarpa-vat*, 'like the serpent,' IV. 12; *bhekī-vat*, 'like the female frog,' IV. 16; *śuka-vat*, 'like the parrot,' IV. 25, &c.) Again, one of Kātyāyana's Vārttikas or supplements to a rule of the grammarian Pāṇini (IV. 2, 104; cf. IV. 3, 125) gives a name for the popular fable of the crows and owls (*Kākolūkikā*), the actual title of the fourth Tantra of the Pañća-tantra, *Kākolūkīya*, being formed according to another rule of Pāṇini (IV. 3, 88). This fable is also alluded to in the Sauptika-parvan of the Mahā-bhārata (see p. 409 of this volume). In that Epic, too, other well-known fables are related. For example, the story of the three fishes occurring in Hitopadeśa, Book IV, is found in Śānti-parvan 4889 &c., and that of Sunda and Upasunda in Ādi-parvan 7619.

The fables of the Pańća-tantra and Hitopadeśa are supposed to be narrated by a learned Brāhman named Vishṇu-śarman for the improvement of some young princes, whose royal father had expressed himself grieved by their idle, dissolute habits. Of course, the fables are merely a vehicle for the instruction conveyed. They are strung together one within another, so that before one is finished another is commenced, and moral verses from all sources are interwoven with the narratives.

A still larger collection of tales exists in Sanskṛit literature. It is called the *Kathā-sarit-sāgara*, 'ocean of rivers of stories,' and was compiled by *Soma-deva Bhaṭṭa* of Kaśmīr, towards the end of the eleventh or beginning of the twelfth century, from a still larger work named *Vṛihat-kathā* (ascribed to *Guṇāḍhya*):

The *Kathā-sarit-sāgara*[1] consists of eighteen Books (*Lambakas*), containing in all 124 chapters (*Taraṅgas*). The second and third Books contain the celebrated story of Udayana (see p. 487). A contemporary of Soma-deva was *Kalhaṇa*, who is said to have written the *Rāja-taraṅgiṇī*, 'stream of kings'—a chronicle of the kings of Kaśmīr—about A.D. 1148. This is almost the only work in the whole range of Sanskṛit literature which has any historical value. It is mostly composed in the common Śloka metre, and consists of eight chapters (*Taraṅgas*)[2].

Other collections of tales and works of fiction—which are not, however, properly Nīti-śāstras—are the following:

1. The *Daśa-kumāra-ćarita*, 'adventures of ten princes,' a series of tales in prose (but called by native authorities a *Kāvya* or poem) by *Daṇḍin*, who lived in the eleventh century. The style is studiously

---

[1] The whole work has been excellently edited by Dr. Hermann Brockhaus, all but the first five Lambakas being in the Roman character.

[2] The first six Books were edited and the whole work translated into French by M. Troyer in 1840, and analysed by Professor H. H. Wilson. See Dr. Rost's edition of his works.

difficult, long compounds and rare grammatical forms being used. It was edited, with a long Introduction, by Professor H. H. Wilson in 1846. 2. The *Vetāla-pańća-vinśati*, 'twenty-five tales of a demon,' ascribed to an author named *Jambhala-datta.* It is the original of the well-known Hindī collection of stories called *Baitāl-paćīsī.* The stories are told by a Vetāla, or spirit, to king Vikramāditya, who tries to carry off a dead body occupied by the Vetāla. 3. The *Sinhāsana-dvātrinśat* (sometimes called *Vikrama-ćarita* or 'adventures of Vikramāditya'), stories related by the thirty-two images on king Vikramāditya's throne which was dug up near Dhārā, the capital of king *Bhoja,* to whom the tales are told, and who is supposed to have flourished in the tenth or eleventh century. It is the original of the Bengālī *Batriś Sinhāsan.* 4. The *Śuka-saptati* or 'seventy tales of a parrot,' translated into many modern dialects of India (e. g. into Hindūstānī under the title *Totā-kahānī;* several Persian versions called *Tūtī-nāma* being also extant). 5. The *Kathārṇava,* 'ocean of stories,' a collection of about thirty-five comparatively modern stories, attributed to S'iva-dāsa. 6. The *Bhoja-prabandha*, a work by *Ballāla,* celebrating the deeds of king Bhoja. 7. The *Kādambarī,* a kind of novel by *Vāṇa* or *Bāṇa,* who flourished in the seventh century at the court of Harsha-vardhana or S'īlāditya, king of Kanauj. An analysis of this work is given by Professor Weber (vol. i. p. 352 of his Indische Streifen). Good editions have been printed at Calcutta. 8. The *Vāsava-dattā,* a romance by *Subandhu,* written, according to Dr. Fitz-Edward Hall, not later than the early part of the seventh century (see the elaborate Preface to his excellent edition of the work in 1859). This and the previous story, although written in prose, are regarded (like 1) as Kāvyas or poems, and are supposed, like the Rāghava-pāṇḍavīya (p. 450), to contain numerous words and phrases which convey a double sense.

I conclude with examples from Bhartṛi-hari's aphothegms, from the Pańća-tantra, and from the Hitopadeśa.

The following are specimens from *Bhartṛi-hari:*

Here in this world love's only fruit is won,
When two true hearts are blended into one;
But when by disagreement love is blighted,
'Twere better that two corpses were united (I. 29).

Blinded by self-conceit and knowing nothing,
Like elephant infatuate with passion,
I thought within myself, I all things knew;
But when by slow degrees I somewhat learnt,

By aid of wise preceptors, my conceit,
Like some disease, passed off; and now I live
In the plain sense of what a fool I am (II. 8).

The attribute most noble of the hand
Is readiness in giving; of the head,
Bending before a teacher; of the mouth,
Veracious speaking; of a victor's arms,
Undaunted valour; of the inner heart,
Pureness the most unsullied; of the ears,
Delight in hearing and receiving truth—
These are adornments of high-minded men
Better than all the majesty of Empire (II. 55).

Better be thrown from some high peak,
Or dashed to pieces, falling upon rocks;
Better insert the hand between the fangs
Of an envenomed serpent; better fall
Into a fiery furnace, than destroy
The character by stains of infamy (II. 77).

Now for a little while a child, and now
An amorous youth; then for a season turned
Into the wealthy householder; then stripped
Of all his riches, with decrepit limbs
And wrinkled frame, man creeps towards the end
Of life's erratic course; and, like an actor,
Passes behind Death's curtain out of view[1] (III. 51).

I now give, as an example of an Indian apologue, a nearly literal translation of a fable in the Pańća-tantra (Book V. 8th story):

## *The Two-headed Weaver*[2].

Once upon a time there lived in a certain place a weaver (*kaulika*) named Manthara, all the wood-work of whose loom one day fell to pieces while he was weaving. Taking his axe (*kuṭhāra*), he set off to cut fresh timber to make a new loom, and finding a large Siṇśapā tree by the sea-side, and thinking to himself, 'This will furnish plenty of wood for

---

[1] The parallel in Shakespeare need scarcely be suggested.

[2] I have omitted some verses in this story, and taken a few liberties. In my translations I have consulted Professor H. H. Wilson, and Professor Benfey's German translation.

my purpose,' began to fell it. In the tree resided a spirit (*vyantara*), who exclaimed on the first stroke of the axe, 'Hallo, there! what are you about? this tree is my dwelling, and I can't allow you to destroy it; for here I live very happily, inhaling the fresh breezes cooled by the ocean's spray.' The weaver replied, 'What am I to do? unless I get wood, my family must starve. Be quick, then, and look out for another house; for cut your present one down I must, and that too instantly.' The spirit replied, 'I am really quite pleased with your candour, and you shall have any boon you like to ask for; but you shall not injure this tree.' The weaver said he would go home and consult a friend and his wife; and would then come back and let the spirit know what gift he would be willing to take in compensation for the loss of the tree. To this the spirit assented. When the weaver returned home, he found there a particular friend of his—the village barber (*nāpita*). To him he confided all that had occurred, telling him that he had forced the spirit to grant him a boon, and consulting his friend as to what he should demand. The barber said, 'My good fellow, ask to be made a king; then I'll be your prime minister, and we'll enjoy ourselves gloriously in this world and gain felicity in the next. Don't you know the saying?—

A king by gifts on earth achieves renown
And, when he dies, in heaven obtains a crown.'

The weaver approved his friend's suggestion, but said he must first consult his wife. To this the barber strenuously objected, and reminded him of the proverb,

'Give women food, dress, gems, and all that's nice,
But tell them not your plans, if you are wise.

Besides, the sagacious son of Bhṛigu has said as follows:

If you have ought to do and want to do it,
Don't ask a woman's counsel, or you'll rue it.'

The weaver admitted the justice of his friend the barber's observations, but insisted that *his* wife was quite a model woman and wholly devoted to her husband's welfare, and that he felt compelled to ask her opinion. Accordingly he went to her, and told her of the promise he had extorted from the spirit of the tree, and how the barber had recommended his asking to be made a king. He then requested her advice as to what boon he should solicit. She replied, 'You should never listen, husband, to barbers. What can they possibly know about anything? Surely you have heard the saying,

No man of sense should take as his adviser
A barber, dancer, mendicant, or miser.

Besides, all the world knows that royalty leads to a perpetual round of troubles. The cares of peace and war, marching and encamping, making allies and quarrelling with them afterwards, never allow a monarch a moment's enjoyment. Let me tell you then,

> If you are longing to be made a king,
> You've set your heart upon a foolish thing;
> The vase of unction at your coronation
> Will sprinkle you with water and vexation.' (Cf. p. xxxvii, 3.)

The weaver replied, 'What you say, wife, is very just, but pray tell me what I am to ask for.' His wife rejoined, 'I recommend you to seek the means of doing more work. Formed as you now are, you can never weave more than one piece of cloth at a time. Ask for an additional pair of hands and another head, with which you may keep a loom going both before and behind you. The profits of the first loom will be enough for all household expenses, and with the proceeds of the second you'll be able to gain consequence and credit with your tribe, and a respectable position in this world and the next.'

'Capital! capital!' exclaimed the husband, mightily pleased with his excellent wife's advice. Forthwith he repaired to the tree, and addressing the spirit, said, 'As you have promised to grant me anything I ask for, give me another pair of arms, and an additional head.' No sooner said than done. In an instant he became equipped with a couple of heads and four arms, and returned home, highly delighted with his new acquisitions. No sooner, however, did the villagers see him, than, greatly alarmed, they exclaimed, 'A goblin! a goblin!' and between striking him with sticks and pelting him with stones, speedily put an end to his existence.

The following sentiments are also from the Panćatantra:

> Praise not the goodness of the grateful man
> Who acts with kindness to his benefactors.
> He who does good to those who do him wrong
> Alone deserves the epithet of good (I. 277).

> The misery a foolish man endures
> In seeking riches, is a hundred-fold
> More grievous than the sufferings of him
> Who strives to gain eternal blessedness (II. 127).

> Hear thou a summary of righteousness,
> And ponder well the maxim: Never do
> To other persons what would pain thyself (III. 104).

The little minded ask: Belongs this man
To our own family? The noble-hearted
Regard the human race as all akin (V. 38).

As a conclusion, I subjoin some sentiments from the *Hitopadeśa* or book of 'friendly advice.' My translations are from Professor Johnson's excellent edition:

Fortune attends the lion-hearted man
Who acts with energy; weak-minded persons
Sit idly waiting for some gift of fate.
Banish all thought of destiny, and act
With manly vigour, straining all thy nerve;
When thou has put forth all thy energy
The blame of failure will not rest with thee (Introd. 31).

Even a blockhead may respect inspire,
So long as he is suitably attired;
A fool may gain esteem among the wise,
So long as he has sense to hold his tongue (Introd. 40).

A piece of glass may like a jewel glow,
If but a lump of gold be placed below;
So even fools to eminence may rise
By close association with the wise (Introd. 41).

Never expect a prosperous result
In seeking profit from an evil quarter—
When there is taint of poison in the cup,
E'en th' ambrosial draught, which to the gods
Is source of life immortal, tends to death (I. 5).

Subjection to the senses has been called
The road to ruin, and their subjugation
The path to fortune; go by which you please (I. 29).

A combination of e'en feeble things
Is often potent to effect a purpose;
E'en fragile straws, when twisted into ropes,
May serve to bind a furious elephant (I. 35).

A man of truest wisdom will resign
His wealth, and e'en his life, for good of others;
Better abandon life in a good cause,
When death in any case is sure to happen (I. 45).

He has all wealth who has a mind contented.
To one whose foot is covered with a shoe
The earth appears all carpeted with leather (I. 152).

'Tis right to sacrifice an individual
For a whole household, and a family
For a whole village, and a village even
For a whole country's good; but for one's self
And one's own soul, one should give up the world (I. 159).

Make the best use of thy prosperity,
And then of thy reverses when they happen.
For good and evil fortune come and go,
Revolving like a wheel in sure rotation (I. 184).

Strive not too anxiously for a subsistence,
Thy Maker will provide thee sustenance;
No sooner is a human being born
Than milk for his support streams from the breast (I. 190).

He by whose hand the swans were painted white,
And parrots green, and peacocks many-hued,
Will make provision for thy maintenance[1] (I. 191).

How can true happiness proceed from wealth,
Which in its acquisition causes pain;
In loss, affliction; in abundance, folly (I. 192)?

A friend, the sight of whom is to the eyes
A balm—who is the heart's delight—who shares
Our joys and sorrows—is a treasure rare.
But other friendly persons who are ready
To share in our prosperity, abound.
Friendship's true touchstone is adversity (I. 226).

Whoever, quitting certainties, pursues
Uncertain things, may lose his certainties (I. 227).

By drops of water falling one by one,
Little by little, may a jar be filled;
Such is the law of all accumulations
Of money, knowledge, and religious merit (II. 10).

That man is sapient who knows how to suit
His words to each occasion, his kind acts
To each man's worth, his anger to his power (II. 48).

Is anything by nature beautiful
Or the reverse? Whatever pleases each,
That only is by each thought beautiful (II. 50).

---

[1] Compare St. Matthew vi. 26.

Disinclination to begin a work
Through fear of failure, is a mark of weakness;
Is food renounced through fear of indigestion (II. 54)?

If glass be used to decorate a crown,
While gems are taken to bedeck a foot,
'Tis not that any fault lies in the gem,
But in the want of knowledge of the setter[1] (II. 72).

A man may on affliction's touchstone learn
The worth of his own kindred, wife, and servants;
Also of his own mind and character (II. 79).

A feverish display of over-zeal
At the first outset, is an obstacle
To all success; water, however cold,
Will penetrate the ground by slow degrees (III. 48).

Even a foe, if he perform a kindness,
Should be esteemed a kinsman; e'en a kinsman,
If he do harm, should be esteemed a foe.
A malady, though bred within the body
Does mischief, while a foreign drug that comes
From some far forest does a friendly work (III. 101).

Whither have gone the rulers of the earth,
With all their armies, all their regal pomp,
And all their stately equipages? Earth,
That witnessed their departure, still abides (IV. 68).

E'en as a traveller, meeting with the shade
Of some o'erhanging tree, awhile reposes,
Then leaves its shelter to pursue his way,
So men meet friends, then part with them for ever[2] (IV. 73).

Thou art thyself a stream whose sacred ford
Is self-restraint, whose water is veracity,
Whose bank is virtue, and whose waves are love;
Here practise thy ablutions; by mere water
The inner man can ne'er be purified (IV. 90).

---

[1] 'Is such a thing as an emerald made worse than it was, if it is not praised?' Marcus Aurelius. Farrar's 'Seekers after God,' p. 306.

[2] Compare p. 441, l. 11, of this volume.

Many parallels in European writers will naturally suggest themselves to the educated reader while perusing the foregoing pages. I have purposely avoided cumbering my notes with obvious comparisons.

# INDEX.

Observe—In the following Index the numbers indicate the pages. When more than one page is given the numbers are separated by semicolons. A unit separated from a preceding number by a comma indicates the number of a foot-note. The Roman numerals denote the pages of the Introduction.

---

*Addition to note* 1, *page* 232.

Since this note was printed off, I have received a letter from Mr. Sinclair, in which he informs me that the name *Chitpāvan* is supposed to mean 'the race of the corpse' or 'race of the burning-ground,' and refers me to the 'Journal of the Royal Asiatic Society,' Bombay Branch, January 1850, p. 47. He also requests me to correct *Pataṇe*, which is a misprint for Pathare, and to explain that *Marwāḍī* merely means 'a merchant from Marwāḍ' (i. e. Marwar).

# THE INDO-ROMANIC ALPHABET

WITH THE

## EQUIVALENT SANSKṚIT LETTERS AND RULES FOR PRONUNCIATION.

### VOWELS.

*A, a,* for अ, pronounced as in rur*a*l; *Ā, ā,* for आ, ा, as in t*a*r, f*a*ther; *I, i,* for इ, ि, as in f*i*ll; *Ī, ī,* for ई, ी, as in pol*i*ce; *U, u,* for उ, ु, as in f*u*ll; *Ū, ū,* for ऊ, ू, as in r*u*de; *Ṛi, ṛi,* for ऋ, ृ, as in mer*ri*ly; *Ṝi, ṝi,* for ॠ, ॄ, as in mar*i*ne; *E, e,* for ए, े, as in pr*ey*; *Ai, ai,* for ऐ, ै, as in *ai*sle; *O, o,* for ओ, ो, as in g*o*; *Au, au,* for औ, ौ, as in H*au*s (German); *ṅ* or *ṃ,* for ं, i.e. the Anusvāra, sounded like *n* in French mo*n*, or like any nasal; *ḥ,* for ः, i. e. the Visarga or a distinctly audible aspirate.

### CONSONANTS.

*K, k,* for क्, pronounced as in *k*ill, see*k*; *Kh, kh,* for ख्, as in in*kh*orn; *G, g,* for ग्, as in *g*un, do*g*; *Gh, gh,* for घ्, as in lo*gh*ut; *Ṅ, ṅ,* for ङ्, as in si*n*g (si*ṅ*).

*Ć, ć,* for च्, as in dol*c*e (in music),=English *ch* in *ch*ur*ch*, lur*ch* (lur*ć*); *Ćh, ćh,* for छ्, as in chur*chh*ill (ćur*ćh*ill); *J, j,* for ज्, as in *j*et; *Jh, jh,* for झ्, as in he*dge-h*og (he*jh*og); *Ñ, ñ,* for ञ्, as in si*n*ge (si*ñj*).

*Ṭ, ṭ,* for ट्, as in *t*rue (*ṭ*ru); *Ṭh, ṭh,* for ठ्, as in an*th*ill (an*ṭh*ill); *Ḍ, ḍ,* for ड्, as in *d*rum (*ḍ*rum); *Ḍh, ḍh,* for ढ्, as in re*dh*aired (re*ḍh*aired); *Ṇ, ṇ,* for ण्, as in *n*o*n*e (*ṇ*u*ṇ*).

*T, t,* for त्, as in wa*t*er (as pronounced in Ireland); *Th, th,* for थ्, as in nu*t-h*ook (but more dental); *D, d,* for द्, as in *d*ice (more like *th* in *th*is); *Dh, dh,* for ध्, as in a*dh*ere (more dental); *N, n,* for न्, as in *n*ot, i*n*.

*P, p,* for प्, as in *p*ut, si*p*; *Ph, ph,* for फ्, as in u*ph*ill; *B, b,* for ब्, as in *b*ear, ru*b*; *Bh, bh,* for भ्, as in a*bh*or; *M, m,* for म्, as in *m*ap, ja*m*.

*Y, y,* for य्, as in *y*et; *R, r,* for र्, as in *r*ed, yea*r*; *L, l,* for ल्, as in *l*ie; *V, v,* for व्, as in *v*ie (but like *w* after consonants, as in t*w*ice).

*Ś, ś,* for श्, as in *s*ure, se*ss*ion; *Sh, sh,* for ष्, as in *sh*un, hu*sh*; *S, s,* for स्, as in *s*ir, hi*ss*. *H, h,* for ह्, as in *h*it.

Fuller directions for pronunciation will be found in a 'Practical Grammar of the Sanskṛit Language,' by Monier Williams, third edition, published by the Delegates of the Clarendon Press, Oxford, and sold by Macmillan & Co., and by W. H. Allen & Co., 13, Waterloo Place. Also in a Sanskṛit-English Dictionary, published by the same.

# ORIENTAL WORKS

BY

## MONIER WILLIAMS, M.A.,

BODEN PROFESSOR OF SANSKṚIT IN THE UNIVERSITY OF OXFORD.

---

1. AN ENGLISH-SANSKṚIT DICTIONARY, in one vol. 4to. Published under the patronage of the Court of Directors of the East India Company. W. H. Allen & Co., Waterloo Place, London. 1851. Price £3 3*s*.

2. A SANSKṚIT-ENGLISH DICTIONARY, in one vol. 4to. Published for the University of Oxford by Macmillan & Co., Bedford Street, Covent Garden, London; also W. H. Allen & Co., London. 1872. Price £4 14*s*. 6*d*.

   'This is a most laboriously and carefully constructed and excellent work, which no student of Sanskṛit can do without.'—W. D. Whitney, Professor of Sanskṛit and Comparative Philology in Yale College (from the *Harvard College Courant*).

3. A PRACTICAL GRAMMAR OF THE SANSKṚIT LANGUAGE, arranged with reference to the Classical Languages of Europe, for the use of English Students. Third Edition. Published for the University of Oxford by Macmillan & Co.; also W. H. Allen & Co., London. 1864. Price 15*s*.

   'I am accustomed to recommend Williams's Grammar to any one who takes up the study (of Sanskṛit) by himself, without a teacher, because it is more intelligible and easily managed.'—W. D. Whitney (from the *Harvard College Courant*).

4. A SANSKṚIT MANUAL, containing the Accidence of Grammar, and Progressive Exercises for Composition, and a Vocabulary by A. E. Gough. Second Edition. W. H. Allen & Co., London. 1868. Price 7*s*. 6*d*.

5. ŚAKUNTALĀ; a Sanskṛit Drama. The Devanāgarī Recension of the Text, with Critical Notes and Literal Translations. W. H. Allen & Co., London. 1853. Price 21*s*.

6. A FREE TRANSLATION IN ENGLISH PROSE AND VERSE OF THE SANSKṚIT DRAMA ŚAKUNTALĀ. Fourth Edition. W. H. Allen & Co., London. 1872. Price 8*s*.

7. ANOTHER EDITION OF THE ABOVE, illuminated and illustrated. Stephen Austin, Hertford. 1855.

8. VIKRAMORVAŚĪ; a Sanskṛit Drama, published as a Class-Book for the East India College. W. H. Allen & Co., London. 1849. Price 5*s*.

9. STORY OF NALA; a Sanskṛit Poem, with full Vocabulary, and Dean Milman's Translation. Published at the Oxford University Press. 1860. Price 15*s*.

10. THE STUDY OF SANSKṚIT IN RELATION TO MISSIONARY WORK IN INDIA; a Lecture delivered before the University of Oxford on April 19, 1861, with Notes and Additions. Williams & Norgate, London; J. H. & James Parker, Oxford. Price 2*s*.

11. INDIAN EPIC POETRY; being the Substance of Lectures delivered in Oxford. Williams & Norgate, London and Edinburgh. 1863. Price 5*s*.

12. A PRACTICAL HINDŪSTĀNĪ GRAMMAR. Second Edition. Longmans & Co., London. 1865. Price 5*s*.

13. AN EASY INTRODUCTION TO THE STUDY OF HINDŪSTĀNĪ. Longmans & Co., London. 1859. Price 2*s*. 6*d*.

14. HINDŪSTĀNĪ PRIMER. Longmans & Co., London. 1859. Price 1*s*. 8*d*.

15. BĀGH O BAHĀR; the Hindūstānī Text, with Notes and Introductory Essay on the Application of the Roman Alphabet to the Languages of India. Longmans & Co., London. 1859. Price 6*s*. 6*d*.

16. ORIGINAL PAPERS illustrating the History of the Application of the Roman Alphabet to the Languages of India. Longmans & Co., London. 1859. Price 12*s*.

**Adam W. (late of Calcutta) Theories of History.**
8vo. 15s. (See page 26).

**Advice to Officers in India.**
By JOHN McCOSH, M.D. Post 8vo. 8s.

**Allen's Series.** 2s. each.
1.—World We Live In. (See page 29).
2.—Earth's History. (See page 6).
3.—Geography of India. (See page 8).
4.—2000 Examination Questions in Physical Geography.
5.—Hall's Trigonometry.

**Analytical History of India.**
From the earliest times to the Abolition of the East India Company in 1858. By ROBERT SEWELL, Madras Civil Service. Post 8vo. pp. 28 & 334. 8s.
*** The object of this work is to supply the want which has been felt by students for a condensed outline of Indian History which would serve at once to recall the memory and guide the eye, while at the same time it has been attempted to render it interesting to the general reader by preserving a medium between a bare analysis and a complete history.

**Ancient and Mediæval India.**
2 vols. 8vo. 30s. (See page 16).

**Anderson's (P.) English in Western India.**
8vo. 14s.

**Ansted's (D. T.) Physical Geography.**
5th Edition. With Maps. Crown 8vo. 7s. (See page 22).

**Ansted's (D. T.) We Live In.**
Fcap. 2s. 25th Thousand, with Illustrations. (See page 29).

**Ansted's (D. T.) Earth's History.**
Fcap. 2s. (See page 6).

**Ansted's (D. T.)**
Two Thousand Examination Questions in Physical Geography. pp. 180. Price 2s.

**Ansted's (D. T.) Ionian Islands.**
8vo. 8s. (See page 14.)

**Ansted's (D T.) and R. G. Latham's Channel Islands.**
8vo. 16s (See page 14).

**At Home in Paris.**
By BLANCHARD JERROLD. 2 Vols. Post 8vo. 16s.

**Atterbury Memoirs, &c.**
The Memoir and Correspondence of Francis Atterbury, Bishop of Rochester, with his distinguished contemporaries. Compiled chiefly from the Atterbury and Stuart Papers. By FOLKESTONE WILLIAMS, Author of "Lives of the English Cardinals," &c., 2 vols. 8vo. 14s.

**Authors at Work.**
By CHARLES PEBODY. Post 8vo. 10s. 6d.

**Bengal Artillery.**
A Memoir of the Services of the Bengal Artillery from the formation of the Corps. By the late CAPT. E. BUCKLE, Assist.-Adjut.Gen.Ben.Art. Edit. by J. W. KAYE. 8vo. Lond. 1852. 10s.

**Bernays, (Dr. A. J.) Students' Chemistry.**
Crown 8vo. 5s. 6d. (See page 25).

**Binning's (R. M.) Travels in Persia, &c.**
2 vols. 8vo. 16s.

**Birth of the War God.**
A Poem. By KALIDASA. Translated from the Sanscrit into English Verse. By RALPH T. H. GRIFFITH, ESQ. 5s.

**Blanchard's (S.) Yesterday and To-day in India.**
Post 8vo. 6s. (See page 29).

**Blenkinsopp's (Rev. E. L.) Doctrine of Development**
In the Bible and in the Church. 2nd edit. 12mo. 6s. (See page 5).

**Boileau (Major-General J. T.)**
A New and Complete Set of Traverse Tables, showing the Differences of Latitude and the Departures to every Minute of the Quadrant and to Five Places of Decimals. Together with a Table of the lengths of each Degree of Latitude and corresponding Degree of Longitude from the Equator to the Poles; with other Tables useful to the Surveyor and Engineer. Royal 8vo. 12s.

**Botany of the Himalaya Mountains.**
And other Branches of Natural History of the Himalaya Mountains, and of the Flora of Cashmere. By J. FORBES ROYLE, M.D., V.P.R.S. 2 vols. folio. London, 1839. £7 7s.

*** *This Book is now very scarce.*

**Bowring's Flowery Scroll.**
A Chinese Novel. Translated and Illustrated with Notes by SIR J. BOWRING, late H.B.M. Plenipo. China. Post 8vo. 10s. 6d.

**Briggs' (Gen. J.) India and Europe Compared.**
Post 8vo. 7s. (See page 12).

**Burgess' Report of the First Season's Operations in the** Belgâm and Kaladgi Districts, January to May, 1874. Archæological Survey of Western India. Prepared at the India Museum. 4to. £2 2s.

**Catholic Doctrine of the Atonement.**
An Historical Inquiry into its Development in the Church, with an Introduction on the Principle of Theological Development. By H. NUTCOMBE OXENHAM, M.A. Sec. Edit. 8vo. 10s. 6d.

"It is one of the ablest and probably one of the most charmingly written treatises on the subject which exists in our language."—*Times.*

**Celebrated Naval and Military Trials.**
By PETER BURKE, Serjeant-at-Law. Author of "Celebrated Trials connected with the Aristocracy." Post 8vo. 10s. 6d.

**Central Asia (Sketches of).**
By A. VAMBERY. 8vo. 16s. (See page 28).

**Cochrane, (John) Hindu Law.**
20s. (See page 13).

**Cruise of H.M.S. "Galatea,"**
Captain H.R.H. the Duke of Edinburgh, K.G., in 1867–1868. By the REV. JOHN MILNER, B.A., Chaplain; and OSWALD W. BRIERLY. Illustrated by a Photograph of H.R.H. the Duke of Edinburgh; and by Chromo-Lithographs and Graphotypes from Sketches taken on the spot by O. W. BRIERLY. 8vo. 16s.

"It is written in a lively and spirited style, and, putting aside the interest it gains as the history of the hearty and loyal reception which the Prince everywhere received, it is a very readable volume of travel. . . . It is throughout interestingly written, and will well repay perusal."—*Standard.*

"The book is full of adventures, and will be read with interest by all."—*Observer.*

**Cunningham's (Alex.) Ladakh.**
Royal 8vo. £1 1s. Without Plates. (See page 15).

**Danvers (Fred. Chas.) On Coal.**
With Reference to Screening, Transport, &c. 8vo. 10s. 6d.

**Doctrine of Development in the Bible and in the Church.**
By REV. E. L. BLENKINSOPP, M.A., Rector of Springthorp. 2nd edit. 12mo. 6s.

"This is a thoroughly well written and carefully digested treatise. The thoughtful theologian will be charmed with its clear and convincing line of argument."—*Church Review.*

**Dollinger's First Age of Christianity.**
From the German. By REV. H. NUTCOMBE OXENHAM. 8vo. 12s. 6d. (See page 13.)

**Doran (Dr. J.) Annals of the English Stage.**
2 Vols. 8vo. 18s. *Also Cheap Edition*, post 8vo. 6s. (See p.25.)

**Drain of Silver to the East,**
And the Currency of India. By W. NASSAU LEES. Post 8vo. 8s.

**Drury.—The Useful Plants of India,**
With Notices of their chief value in Commerce, Medicine, and the Arts. By COLONEL HEBER DRURY. Second Edition, with Additions and Corrections. Royal 8vo. 16s.

**Earth's History,**
Or, First Lessons in Geology. For the use of Schools and Students. By D. T. ANSTED. Third Thousand. Fcap. 8vo. 2s.

**East India Calculator,**
By T. THORNTON. 8vo. London, 1823. Reduced to 10s.

**Edgar's (J. G.) Modern History.**
12mo. 6s. 6d.

**Edinburgh (The Duke of) Cruise of the "Galatea."**
With Illustrations. 8vo. 16s. (See page 5).

**Edwards' (H. S.) Russians at Home.**
With Illustrations. Post 8vo. 6s. (See page 24).

**Edwards' (H. S.) History of the Opera.**
2 Vols., 8vo. 10s. 6d. (See page 10).

**Elementary Mathematics.**
A Course of Elementary Mathematics for the use of candidates for admission into either of the Military Colleges; of applicants for appointments in the Home or Indian Civil Services; and of mathematical students generally. By Professor J. R. YOUNG. In one closely-printed volume. 8vo., pp. 648. 12s.

"In the work before us he has digested a complete Elementary Course, by aid of his long experience as a teacher and writer; and he has produced a very useful book. Mr. Young has not allowed his own taste to rule the distribution, but has adjusted his parts with the skill of a veteran."—*Athenæum.*

**English Cardinals.**
The Lives of the English Cardinals, from Nicholas Breakspeare (Pope Adrien IV.) to Thomas Wolsey, Cardinal Legate. With Historical Notices of the Papal Court. By FOLKESTONE WILLIAMS. In 2 vols. 14s.

"It is not only a meritorious addition to our biographical literature, but a useful work in aid of the later history of the Mother Church of England. It is a Work evincing much erudition, and the Author has spared no pains in the researches necessary to authenticate and illustrate his materials."—*Morning Post.*

**English Homes in India.**

By Mrs. Keatinge. Part I.—The Three Loves. Part II.—The Wrong Turning. Two vols., Post 8vo. 16s.

These volumes were written by a lady well known in Indian Society, and form a truthful picture of Indian life as it now is.

"Two most charming volumes, containing stories of no common attractiveness."—*Homeward Mail.*

"The stories are written with much spirit and force, and abundance of incident sustains the interest throughout."—*Examiner.*

**Essays Military and Political,**

Written in India by the late Sir Henry Montgomery Lawrence, K.C.B., Chief Commissioner of Oude and Provisional Governor-General in India. 8vo. 14s.

Contents —Military Defence of our Indian Empire. Written in 1844.—The Kingdom of Oude. Written in 1845.—Mahrattah History and Empire. Written in 1845.—Lord Hardinge's Indian Administration. Written in 1847.—The Indian Army. Written in 1855-6.—Army Reform. Written in 1856.

**First Age of Christianity and the Church.**

By John Ignatius Döllinger, D.D., Professor of Ecclesiastical History in the University of Munich, &c., &c. Translated from the German by Henry Nutcombe Oxenham, M.A., late Scholar of Baliol College, Oxford. Second edition. 8vo. pp. 440. 12s. 6d.

Contents.—Book I.—Christ and the Apostles.—Ministry and Teaching of Christ.—St. Peter and St. Paul, St. James, St. Jude, St. John, and the remaining Apostles.

Book II.—Doctrine of the Apostles.—Scripture and Tradition. The Trinity, Incarnation, and Redemption.—The Church and the Sacraments.—The last things, and the future, of the Church and the World.

Book III.—Constitution, Worship, and Life of the Apostolic Church.—Orders and Offices of Ministry and Spiritual Gifts.—Ordinances of Discipline and Worship, and Religious Ideas.—Ecclesiastical Institutions and Customs.—Social and Political Relations.

"We are very glad to see the Work of so temperate and large-minded, and patient a theologian in an English dress. Mr. Oxenham has performed his part as translator with much skill.—*Guardian.*

**Forbes (Dr. Duncan) History of Chess.**

8vo. 7s, 6d. (See page 10).

**Franz Schubert.**
A Musical Biography, from the German of Dr. Heinrich Kreisle von Hellborn. By Edward Wilberforce, Esq., Author of "Social Life in Munich." Post 8vo. 6s.

**Gazetteers of India.**
Thornton, 4 vols., 8vo. £2 16s.
" 8vo. 21s.
" (N.W.P., &c.) 2 vols., 8vo. 25s.
Pharaoh's S. India. 8vo. With 4to. Atlas. £3 3s.

**Gazetteer of Southern India.**
With the Tenasserim Provinces and Singapore. Compiled from original and authentic sources. Accompanied by an Atlas, including plans of all the principal towns and cantonments. Royal 8vo. with 4to. Atlas. £3 3s.

**Gazetteer of the Punjaub, Affghanistan, &c.**
Gazetteer of the Countries adjacent to India, on the north-west, including Scinde, Affghanistan, Beloochistan, the Punjaub, and the neighbouring States. By Edward Thornton, Esq. 2 vols. 8vo. £1 5s.

**Geography of India.**
Comprising an account of British India, and the various states enclosed and adjoining. Fcap. pp. 250. 2s.

**Geological Papers on Western India.**
Including Cutch, Scinde, and the south-east coast of Arabia. To which is added a Summary of the Geology of India generally. Edited for the Government by Henry J. Carter, Assistant Surgeon, Bombay Army. Royal 8vo. with folio Atlas of maps and plates; half-bound. £2 2s.

**German Life and Manners**
As seen in Saxony. With an account of Town Life—Village Life—Fashionable Life—Married Life—School and University Life, &c. Illustrated with Songs and Pictures of the Student Customs at the University of Jena. By Henry Mayhew, 2 vols. 8vo., with numerous illustrations. 18s.

*A Popular Edition of the above.* With illustrations. Cr. 8vo. 7s.
"Full of original thought and observation, and may be studied with profit by both German and English—especially by the German." *Athenæum.*

**Glyn's (A. C.) Civilization in the 5th Century.**
2 vols. post 8vo. £1 1s. (See page 19).

**Grady's (S. G.) Mohamedan Law of Inheritance & Contract.**
8vo. 14s.

**Grady's (S. G.) Institutes of Menu.**
8vo 12s. (See page 12).

**Griffith's Ralph (T. H.) Birth of the War God.**
8vo. 5s. (See page 4).

**Hall's Trigonometry.**
The Elements of Plane and Spherical Trigonometry. With an Appendix, containing the solution of the Problems in Nautical Astronomy. For the use of Schools. By the REV. T. G. HALL, M.A., Professor of Mathematics in King's College, London. 12mo. 2s.

**Hamilton's Hedaya.**
A new edition, with the obsolete passages omitted, and a copious Index added by S. G. Grady. 8vo. £1 15s.

**Handbook of Reference to the Maps of India.**
Giving the Lat. and Long. of places of note. 18mo. 3s. 6d.
*** *This will be found a valuable Companion to Messrs. Allen & Co.'s Maps of India.*

**Harcourt's (Capt. A. F. P.) Himalayan Districts.**
Kooloo, Lahoul, and Spiti. Post 8vo. 10s. 6d.

**Hedaya.**
Translated from the Arabic by WALTER HAMILTON.
*A New Edition,* with Index by S. G. GRADY 8vo. £1 15s.

**Henry VIII.**
An Historical Sketch as affecting the Reformation in England. By CHARLES HASTINGS COLLETTE. Post 8vo. 6s.

**Hindu Law.**
By Sir Thomas Strange. 2 vols. Royal 8vo., 1830. 15s.

**Historical Results**
Deducible from Recent Discoveries in Affghanistan. By H. T. PRINSEP. 8vo. Lond. 1844. 15s.

**Histories of India.**
Thornton, 6 vols., 8vo. £2 8s. (See page 26).
Thornton, 1 vol., 8vo. 12s.
Trotter, 2 vols., 8vo. 32s. (See page 27).
Sewell (Analytical). Crown 8vo. 8s. (See page 3).
Owen, India on the Eve of the British Conquest. 8s.

**History of Civilization in the Fifth Century.**
Translated by permission from the French of A. Frederic Ozanam, late Professor of Foreign Literature to the Faculty of Letters at Paris. By ASHBY C. GLYN, B.A., of the Inner Temple, Barrister-at-Law. 2 vols., post 8vo. £1 1s.

**History of Chess,**

From the time of the Early Invention of the Game in India, till the period of its establishment in Western and Central Europe. By DUNCAN FORBES, LL.D. 8vo. 7s. 6d.

**History of China,**

From the Earliest Records to A.D. 420. By THOMAS THORNTON, Esq., Member of the Royal Asiatic Society. 8vo., cloth. 8s.

**History of the Opera,**

From Monteverde to Donizetti. By H. SUTHERLAND EDWARDS Second edition. 2 vols., Post 8vo. 10s. 6d.

**History of the Punjaub,**

And of the Rise, Progress, and Present Condition of the Sikhs. By T. THORNTON. 2 Vols. Post 8vo. 8s.

**Horses of the Sahara, and the Manners of the Desert.**

By E. DAUMAS, General of the Division Commanding at Bordeaux, Senator, &c., &c. With Commentaries by the Emir Abd-el-Kadir (Authorized Edition). 8vo. 6s.

"We have rarely read a work giving a more picturesque and, at the same time, practical account of the manners and customs of a people, than this book on the Arabs and their horses."—*Edinburgh Courant.*

**Hough (Lieut.-Col. W.) Precedents in Military Law.**

8vo. cloth. 25s.

**Illustrated Horse Doctor.**

Being an Accurate and Detailed Account, accompanied by more than 400 Pictorial Representations, characteristic of the various Diseases to which the Equine Race are subjected; together with the latest Mode of Treatment, and all the requisite Prescriptions written in Plain English. By EDWARD MAYHEW, M.R.C.V.S. Author of "The Illustrated Horse Management." 8vo. 18s. 6d.

CONTENTS.—The Brain and Nervous System.—The Eyes.—The Mouth.—The Nostrils.—The Throat.—The Chest and its contents.—The Stomach, Liver, &c.—The Abdomen.—The Urinary Organs.—The Skin.—Specific Diseases.—Limbs —The Feet.—Injuries.—Operations.

"The book contains nearly 600 pages of valuable matter, which reflects great credit on its author, and, owing to its practical details, the result of deep scientific research, deserves a place in the library of medical, veterinary, and non-professional readers."—*Field.*

"The book furnishes at once the bane and the antidote, as the drawings show the horse not only suffering from every kind of disease, but in the different stages of it, while the alphabetical summary at the end gives the cause, symptoms and treatment of each."—*Illustrated London News.*

## Illustrated Horse Management.

Containing descriptive remarks upon Anatomy, Medicine, Shoeing, Teeth, Food, Vices, Stables; likewise a plain account of the situation, nature, and value of the various points; together with comments on grooms, dealers, breeders, breakers and trainers; also on carriages and harness. Embellished with more than 400 engravings from original designs made expressly for this work. By E. MAYHEW. 8vo 18s 6d.

CONTENTS.—The body of the horse anatomically considered PHYSIC.—The mode of administering it, and minor operations. SHOEING.—Its origin, its uses, and its varieties. THE TEETH. —Their natural growth, and the abuses to which they are liable.

FOOD.—The fittest time for feeding, and the kind of food which the horse naturally consumes. The evils which are occasioned by modern stables. The faults inseparable from most present erections which are used as stables. The so-called "incapacitating vices," which are the results of injury or of disease. Stables as they should be. GROOMS.—Their prejudices, their injuries, and their duties. HORSE DEALERS.—Who they are: their mode of dealing: their profits: their morality, and their secrets. POINTS.—Their relative importance, and where to look for their development. BREEDING.—Its inconsistencies and its disappointments. BREAKING AND TRAINING.—Their errors and their results. CARRIAGES.—Their cost: their make: their excellences and their management. SADDLERY, HARNESS, AND STABLE SUNDRIES.—Of what these consist; their application and their preservation.

"Mr. Mayhew thoroughly comprehends the matter, and all the masters of studs—we may say every owner of a single pony or ass—will derive much profit and an equal amount of pleasure by perusing this volume, for the book is not only distinguished by common sense but by its power of amusing."—*Athenæum.*

"No horseman who can afford to buy it will regret the purchase of Mr. Mayhew's Horse Management."—*Spectator.*

## India Directory (The).

For the Guidance of Commanders of Steamers and Sailing Vessels. Founded upon the Work of the late CAPTAIN JAMES HORSBURGH, F.R.S.

PART I.—The East Indies, and Interjacent Ports of Africa and South America. Revised, Extended, and Illustrated with Charts of Winds, Currents, Passages, Variation, and Tides. By COMMANDER ALFRED DUNDAS TAYLOR, F.R.G.S. £1 18s.

**Indian Administration.**
By H. G. KEENE. Post 8vo. 5s.

**Indian Army and Civil Service List.**
Issued in January and July of each year, by permission of the Secretary of State for India in Council. 12mo. 6s. bd. 7s. 6d.

**Indian Code of Civil Procedure.**
In the Form of Questions and Answers. With Explanatory and Illustrative Notes. By ANGELO J. LEWIS. 12. 6d.

**Indian Criminal Law and Procedure,**
By M. H. STARLING, ESQ., LL.B. 1870. £1 10s. (See page 13).

**Indian Penal Code.**
In the Form of Questions and Answers. With Explanatory and Illustrative Notes By ANGELO J. LEWIS. 7s. 6d.

**Indian and Military Law.**
Mahommedan Law of Inheritance, &c. A Manual of the Mahommedan Law of Inheritance and Contract; comprising the Doctrine of the Soonee and Sheca Schools, and based upon the text of Sir H. W. MACNAGHTEN'S Principles and Precedents, together with the Decisions of the Privy Council and High Courts of the Presidencies in India. For the use of Schools and Students. By STANDISH GROVE GRADY, Barrister-at-Law, Reader of Hindoo, Mahommedan, and Indian Law to the Inns of Court. 8vo. 14s.

Hedaya, or Guide, a Commentary on the Mussulman Laws, translated by order of the Governor-General and Council of Bengal. By CHARLES HAMILTON. Second Edition, with Preface and Index by STANDISH GROVE GRADY. 8vo. £1 15s.

Institutes of Menu in English. The Institutes of Hindu Law or the Ordinances of Menu, according to Gloss of Collucca. Comprising the Indian System of Duties, Religious and Civil, verbally translated from the Original, with a Preface by SIR WILLIAM JONES, and collated with the Sanscrit Text by GRAVES CHAMNEY HAUGHTON, M.A., F.R.S., Professor of Hindu Literature in the East India College. New edition, with Preface and Index by STANDISH G. GRADY, Barrister-at-Law, and Reader of Hindu, Mahommedan, and Indian Law to the Inns of Court. 8vo., cloth. 12s.

Indian Criminal Law and Procedure (including the Procedure in the High Courts, and that in the Courts not established by Royal Charter); with Forms of Charges, and notes on Evidence, illustrated by a large number of English cases and cases decided by the High Courts in India: and an Appendix of selected Acts passed by the Legislative Council relating to Criminal Matters. By M. H. STARLING, ESQ., LL.B., of the Inner Temple, Barrister-at-Law. Second edition, comprising the Criminal Procedure Amendment Act of 1869. Royal 8vo. 1870. £1 10s.

*In this work the sections of the Penal Code have been arranged in groups, and to each group has been appended a short paragraph containing information collected from the schedule to the Criminal Procedure Code, as amended by the subsequent Acts, respecting the Courts competent to try offenders, the mode of arrest, and the power to take bail. Forms of charges, and the evidence necessary to support them, will also be found in the proper places. The sections of both Codes, relating to punishments, have been collected together, so that the whole law on that subject will be found arranged consecutively in one chapter. The book on Procedure contains the Criminal Procedure Code and the High Court Procedure Acts, as well as portions of English statutes in force in India, illustrated and elucidated by notes containing the decisions of the High Courts on those sections which have been the subject of judicial notice. This work is thus a complete handbook of law and procedure, which is not the case with any of the works published in either of the Presidencies.*

Indian Code of Criminal Procedure. Being Act X. of 1872, Passed by the Governor-General of India in Council on the 25th of April, 1872. 8vo. Price 12s.

Indian Code of Civil Procedure. In the form of Questions and Answers, with Explanatory and Illustrative Notes. By ANGELO J. LEWIS, Barrister-at-law. 12mo. 12s. 6d.

Indian Penal Code. In the Form of Questions and Answers. With Explanatory and Illustrative Notes. BY ANGELO J. LEWIS, Barrister-at-Law. Post 8vo. 7s. 6d.

Hindu Law. Principally with reference to such portions of it as concern the Administration of Justice in the Courts in India. By SIR THOMAS STRANGE, late Chief Justice of Madras. 2 vols. Royal 8vo., 1830. 15s.

Hindu Law. Defence of the Daya Bhaga. Notice of the Case on Prosoono Coomar Tajore's Will. Judgment of the Judicial Committee of the Privy Council. Examination of such Judgment. By JOHN COCHRANE, Barrister-at-Law. Royal 8vo. 20s.

Law and Customs of Hindu Castes, within the Dekhan Provinces subject to the Presidency of Bombay, chiefly affecting Civil Suits. By ARTHUR STEELE. Royal 8vo. £1 1s.

Law relating to India, and the East India Company, with Notes and Appendix. Fifth Edition. 4to. London, 1855. £3 3s.

Manual of Military Law. For all ranks of the Army, Militia and Volunteer Services. By Colonel J. K. PIPON, Assist. Adjutant General at Head Quarters, & J. F. COLLIER, Esq., of the Inner Temple, Barrister-at-Law. Third and Revised Edition. Pocket size. 5s.

Precedents in Military Law; including the Practice of Courts-Martial; the Mode of Conducting Trials; the Duties of Officers at Military Courts of Inquests, Courts of Inquiry, Courts of Requests, &c., &c. The following are a portion of the Contents:—

1. Military Law. 2. Martial Law. 3. Courts-Martial. 4. Courts of Inquiry. 5. Courts of Inquest. 6. Courts of Request. 7. Forms of Courts-Martial. 8. Precedents of Military Law. 9. Trials of Arson to Rape (Alphabetically arranged.) 10. Rebellions. 11. Riots. 12. Miscellaneous. By Lieut.-Col. W. HOUGH, late Deputy Judge-Advocate-General, Bengal Army, and Author of several Works on Courts-Martial. One thick 8vo. vol. 25s.

The Practice of Courts Martial. By HOUGH & LONG. Thick 8vo. London, 1825. 26s.

**Indian Infanticide.**

Its Origin, Progress, and Suppression. By JOHN CAVE-BROWN, M.A. 8vo. 5s.

**Ionian Islands in 1863.**

By PROFESSOR D. T. ANSTED, M.A., F.R.S., &c. 8vo., with Maps and Cuts. 8s.

"What Mr. Ansted saw in the Ionian Islands he saw well and under good auspices, and has noted down carefully."—*Saturday Review.*

**Japan, the Amoor and the Pacific.**

With notices of other Places, comprised in a Voyage of Circumnavigation in the Imperial Russian Corvette *Rynda*, in 1858—1860. By HENRY A. TILLEY. Eight Illustrations. 8vo. 16s.

**Jersey, Guernsey, Alderney, Sark, &c.**

THE CHANNEL ISLANDS. Containing: PART I.—Physical Geography. PART II.—Natural History. PART III.—Civil History. PART IV.—Economics and Trade. By DAVID THOMAS ANSTED, M.A., F.R.S., and ROBERT GORDON LATHAM, M.A., M.D., F.R.S. New and Cheaper Edition in one handsome 8vo. Volume, with 72 Illustrations on Wood by Vizetelly, Loudon, Nicholls, and Hart; with Map. 16s.

"This is a really valuable work. A book which will long remain the standard authority on the subject. No one who has been to the Channel Islands, or who purposes going there will be insensible of its value."—*Saturday Review.*

"It is the produce of many hands and every hand a good one."

**Jerrold's (Blanchard) at Home in Paris.**
2 Vols. Post 8vo. 16s.

**Kaye (Sir J. W.) The Sepoy War in India.**
Vol. 1. 18s. (See page 24).
Vol. 2. £1.
Vol. 3. (In Preparation.)

**Kaye (Sir J. W.) History of the War in Affghanistan.**
3 Vols. Crown 8vo. £1 5s.

**Kaye (Sir J. W.) Christianity in India.**
8vo. 16s.

**Kaye (Sir J. W.) H. St. G. Tucker's Life and Correspondence.**
8vo. 10s.

**Kaye's (Sir J. W.) Memorials of Indian Governments.**
By H. St. George Tucker. 8vo. 10s.

**Keene's (H. G.) Mogul Empire.**
8vo. 9s.

**Keene's (H. G.) Administration in India.**
Post 8vo. 9s.

**Ladakh.**
Physical, Statistical and Historical, with Notices of the surrounding Countries by Alexander Cunningham, Bengal Engineers. 8vo.; without the plates, £1 1s.

**Lady Morgan's Memoirs.**
Autobiography, Diaries and Correspondence. 2 Vols. 8vo., with Portraits. 18s.

**Latham's (Dr. R. G.) Nationalities of Europe.**
2 Vols. 8vo. 12s. (See page 21).

**Law and Customs of Hindu Castes,**
By Arthur Steele. Royal 8vo. £1 1s.

**Law Relating to India,**
Fifth Edition. 4to. London, 1855. £3 3s. (See page 16).

**Lawrence's (Sir Henry) Essays on Indian Subjects.**
8vo. 14s. (See page 7).

**Lees' (Dr. W. N.) Drain of Silver to the East.**
Post 8vo. 8s.

**Lewin's Wild Races of the South Eastern Frontier of India.**
Including an Account of the Loshai Country. Post 8vo. 10s. 6d.

**Lewis's (A. J.) Indian Penal Code.**
Post 8vo. 7s. 6d. (See page 12).

**Lewis's Indian Code of Civil Procedure.**
Post 8vo. 12s. 6d. (See page 12).

**Leyden and Erskine's Baber.**
MEMOIRS OF ZEHIR-ED-DIN MUHAMMED BABER, EMPEROR OF HINDUSTAN, written by himself in the Jaghatai Turki, and translated partly by the late JOHN LEYDEN, Esq., M.D., and partly by WILLIAM ERSKINE, Esq., with Notes and a Geographical and Historical Introduction, together with a Map of the Countries between the Oxus and Jaxartes, and a Memoir regarding its construction. By CHARLES WADDINGTON, of the East India Company's Engineers. 4to. Lond. 1826. £1 5s.

**Liancourt's and Pincott's Primitive and Universal Laws of** the Formation and development of language; a Rational and Inductive System founded on the Natural Basis of Onomatops. 8vo. 12*s.* 6*d.*

**Mahommedan Law of Inheritance and Contract.**
By STANDISH GROVE GRADY, Barrister-at-Law. 8vo. 14s.

**Manning (Mrs.) Ancient and Mediæval India.**
Being the History, Religion, Laws, Caste, Manners and Customs, Language, Literature, Poetry, Philosophy, Astronomy, Algebra, Medicine, Architecture, Manufactures, Commerce, &c., of the Hindus, taken from their writings. Amongst the works consulted and gleaned from may be named the Rig Veda, Sama Veda, Vajur Veda, Sathapatha Brahmana, Baghavat Gita, The Puranas, Code of Menu, Code of Yajna-valkva, Mitakshara, Daya Bagha, Mahabharata, Atriya, Charaka, Susruta, Ramayana, Raghu Vansa, Bhattikavia, Sakuntala Vikramorvasi, Malali and Madhava, Mudra Rakshasa, Retnavali, Kumara Sambhava, Prabodah, Chandrodaya, Megha Duta, Gita Govinda, Panchatantra, Hitopadesa, Katha Sarit, Sagara, Ketala, Panchavinsati, Dasa Kumara Charita, &c. By Mrs. MANNING, with Illustrations. 2 vols., 8vo. 30s.

"Mrs. Manning's book will probably long and deservedly remain a standard handbook on the Literature, Arts, and Sciences of Ancient India."—*Saturday Review.*

**Manual of Military Law.**
By Colonel J. K. PIPON, and J. F. COLLIER, Esq., of the Inner Temple, Barrister-at-Law. 5s.

**Mayhew's (Edward) Illustrated Horse Doctor.**
8vo. 18s. 6d. (See page 10).

**Mayhew's (Edward) Illustrated Horse Management.**
8vo. 18s. 6d. (See page 11)

**Mayhew's (Henry) German Life and Manners.**
2 vols., 8vo. 18s.
Also a cheaper edition, Post 8vo. 7s. (See page 8).

**Max Muller's Rig-Veda-Sanhita.**
The Sacred Hymns of the Brahmins; together with the Commentary of Sayanacharya. Published under the Patronage of the Secretary of State for India in Council. 6 vols., 4to. £13 10s.

**Meadow's (T.) Notes on China.**
8vo. 9s.

**Memorable Events of Modern History.**
By J. G. Edgar, Author of the Boyhood of Great Men, &c. Post 8vo. With Illustrations. 6s. 6d.

**Mexico.**
Travels in Mexico, South America, &c , &c. By G. T. Vigne, Esq., Author of Travels in Cashmere, &c., &c. 2 vols., Post 8vo. With Illustrations. 21s.

---

**Military Works—chiefly issued by the Government.**

Field Exercises and Evolutions of Infantry.
Pocket edition, 1s.

Queen's Regulations and Orders for the Army. 8vo. 3s. 6d.; Pocket Edition, 1s. New Edition, corrected to 1874.

Rifle Exercise and Musketry Instruction. 1s.

Musketry Regulations, as used at Hythe. 1s.

Dress Regulations for the Army. 1*s*. 6*d*.

Infantry Sword Exercise. 6d.

Infantry Bugle Sounds. 6d.

Handbook of Battalion Drill. By Lieut. H. C. Slack. 2s; or with Company Drill, 2s. 6d.

Handbook of Brigade Drill. By Lieut. H. C. Slack. 3s.

Elementary and Battalion Drill. Condensed and Illustrated, together with duties of Company Officers, Markers, &c., in Battalion. By Captain Malton. 2s. 6d.

Handbook of Company Drill; also of Skirmishing, Battalion, and Shelter Trench Drill. By Lieut. Charles Slack. 1s.

Regulations for the Movements and Formation of a Division of Cavalry. 12mo. 3s.

Cavalry Sword, Carbine, Pistol and Lance Exercises, together with Field Gun Drill. Pocket Edition. 1s.

Cavalry Regulations. For the Instruction, Formations, and Movements of Cavalry. 12mo., cloth. 3s.

Trumpet and Bugle Sounds for Mounted Service and Artillery. 1s. 6d.

The Training of Cavalry Remount Horses. By the late Capt. L. E. NOLAN, of the 15th Hussars. A new edition. 8vo. 10s.

Manual of Artillery Exercises, 1873. 8vo. 5s.

Manual of Field Artillery Exercises. 1875. 4*s*.

Standing Orders and Dress Regulations for Royal Artillery. 8vo. 5s.

Principles and Practice of Modern Artillery. By Lt.-Col. C. H. OWEN, R.A. 8vo. Illustrated. 15s.

Artillerist's Manual and British Soldiers' Compendium. By Major F. A. GRIFFITHS. 11th Edition. 5s.

Compendium of Artillery Exercises—Smooth Bore, Field, and Garrison Artillery for Reserve Forces. By Captain J. M. McKenzie. 3s. 6d.

Principles of Gunnery. By JOHN T. HYDE, M.A., late Professor of Fortification and Artillery, Royal Indian Military College, Addiscombe. Second edition, revised and enlarged. With many Plates and Cuts, and Photograph of Armstrong Gun. Royal 8vo. 14s.

Notes on Gunnery. By Captain Goodeve. Revised Edition. 1s.

Text Book of the Construction and Manufacture of Rifled Ordnance in the British Service. By STONEY & JONES. Second Edition. Paper, 3s. 6d., Cloth, 4s. 6d.

Handbooks of the 9, 16, and 64-Pounder R. M. L. Converted Guns. 6d. each.

Handbook of 40-Pounder B. L. Gun. 6*d*.

Treatise on Fortification and Artillery. By Major HECTOR STRAITH. Revised and re-arranged by THOMAS COOK, R.N., and JOHN T. HYDE, M.A. 7th Edition. Royal 8vo. Illustrated by Four Hundred Plans, Cuts, &c. £2 2s.

Military Surveying and Field Sketching. The Various Methods of Contouring, Levelling, Sketching without Instruments, Scale of Shade, Examples in Military Drawing, &c., &c., &c. As at present taught in the Military Colleges. By Major W. H. RICHARDS, 55th Regiment. Late Instructor in Military Surveying, Royal Military College, Sandhurst. New Edition. 12s.

Treatise on Military Surveying; including Sketching in the Field, Plan-Drawing, Levelling, Military Reconnaissance, &c. By Lieut.-Col. BASIL JACKSON, late of the Royal Staff Corps. The Fifth Edition. 8vo. Illustrated by Plans, &c. 14s.

Elementary Principles of Fortification. A Text-Book for Military Examinations. By J. T. Hyde, M.A. Royal 8vo. With numerous Plans and Illustrations. 10s. 6d.

Military Train Manual. 1s.

The Sappers' Manual. Compiled for the use of Engineer Volunteer Corps. By Col. W. A. Frankland, R.E. With numerous Illustrations. 2s.

Ammunition. A descriptive treatise on the different Projectiles Charges, Fuzes, Rockets, &c., at present in use for Land and Sea Service, and on other war stores manufactured in the Royal Laboratory. 6s.

Hand-book on the Manufacture and Proof of Gunpowder, as carried on at the Royal Gunpowder Factory, Waltham Abbey. 5s.

Regulations for the Training of Troops for service in the Field and for the conduct of Peace Manœuvres. 2s.

Hand-book Dictionary for the Militia and Volunteer Services, Containing a variety of useful information, Alphabetically arranged. Pocket size, 3s. 6d.; by post, 3s. 8d.

Royal Warrant regulating First Appointments, Regimental Promotion, &c., in the Army, with Appendices. 2s.

A Military System of Gymnastic Exercises, for the use of Instructors. By Archibald Maclaren. Crown 8vo. 1s. 6d.

A System of Fencing, for the use of Instructors. By A. Maclaren. 1s.

Gymnastic Exercises, System of Fencing, and Exercises for the Regulation Clubs. In one volume. Crown 8vo. 2s.

Army Equipment. Prepared at the Topographical and Statistical Department, War Office. By Col. Sir Henry James, R.E., F.R.S., &c., Director.

Part. 1.—*Cavalry*. Compiled by Lieut. H. M, Hozier, 2nd Life Guards. Royal 8vo. 4s.

Part 4.—*Military Train*. Compiled by Lieut. H. M. Hozier, 2nd Life Guards. Royal 8vo. 2s. 6d.

Part 5.—*Infantry*. Compiled by Capt. F. Martin Petrie. Royal 8vo. With Plates. 5s.

Part 6.—*Commissariat*. Compiled by Lieut. H. M. Hozier, 2nd Life Guards. Royal 8vo. 1s. 6d.

Part 7.—*Hospital Service*. Compiled by Capt. Martin Petrie. Royal 8vo. With Plates. 5s.

Text-Book on the Theory and Motion of Projectiles; the History, Manufacture, and Explosive Force of Gunpowder; the History of Small Arms. For the use of Officers sent to the School of Musketry. 2s.

Revised Army Regulations. Vol. 1. Royal Warrant for the Pay, Promotion, Non-effective Pay and Allowances of Her Majesty's British Forces serving elsewhere than in India. Parts 1 and 2. Pay and Non-effective Pay. 4s.

Notes on Ammunition. 2nd Edition. Corrected up to September 1874, Paper, 2s., Cloth, 3s.

Regulations and Instructions for Encampments, 1872. Price 6d.

Rules for the Conduct of the War Game. 2s.

Medical Regulations for the Army, Instructions for the Army, Comprising duties of Officers, Attendants, and Nurses, &c. 1s. 8d.

Purveyors' Regulations and Instructions, for Guidance of Officers of Purveyors' Department of the Army. 3s.

Priced Vocabulary of Stores used in Her Majesty's Service. 1875. 4s.

Transport of Sick and Wounded Troops. By DR. LONGMORE. 5s.

Precedents in Military Law. By LT-COL. W. HOUGH. 8vo. 25s.

The Practice of Courts-Martial, by HOUGH & LONG. Thick 8vo. 26s.

Manual of Military Law. For all ranks of the Army, Militia, and Volunteer Services. By Colonel J. K. PIPON, and J. F. COLLIER, Esq. Third and Revised Edition. Pocket size. 5s.

Regulations applicable to the European Officer in India. Containing Staff Corps Rules, Staff Salaries, Commands, Furlough and Retirement Regulations, &c. By GEORGE E. COCHRANE, late Assistant Military Secretary, India Office. 1 vol., post 8vo. 7s. 6d.

Reserve Force; Guide to Examinations, for the use of Captains and Subalterns of Infantry, Militia, and Rifle Volunteers, and for Serjeants of Volunteers. By Captain G. H. GREAVES. 2nd edition. 8vo. 2s.

The Military Encyclopædia; referring exclusively to the Military Sciences, Memoirs of distinguished Soldiers, and the Narratives of Remarkable Battles. By J. H. STOCQUELER. 1853. 8vo. 12s.

The Operations of War Explained and Illustrated. By Col. HAMLEY. New Edition Revised, with Plates. Royal 8vo. 30s.

Lessons of War. As taught by the Great Masters and Others; Selected and Arranged from the various operations in War. By FRANCE JAMES SOADY, Lieut.-Col., R.A. Royal 8vo. 21s.

The Soldiers' Pocket Book for Field Service. By Col. SIR GARNET J. WOLSELEY. 2nd Edition. Revised and Enlarged. 4s. 6d.

A Precis of Modern Tactics, compiled from the Works of recent Continental Writers. By CAPTAIN HOME. 8vo. 8s. 6d.

Armed Strength of Austria. By Captain COOKE. Part II. £1 2s.

Armed Strength of Denmark. 3s.

Armed Strength of Russia. Translated from the German. 7s.

Armed Strength of Sweden and Norway. 3s. 6d.

The Franco-German War of 1871. By CAPT. C. H. CLARKE. Vol. I. £1 6s.

The Campaign of 1866 in Germany. 1 Vol. Royal 8vo. With Atlas, folio. 21s.

Celebrated Naval and Military Trials. By PETER BURKE. Post 8vo., cloth. 10s. 6d.

Military Sketches. By SIR LASCELLES WRAXALL, Bart. Post 8vo., cloth. 6s.

Military Life of the Duke of Wellington. By JACKSON and SCOTT. 2 Vols. 8vo. Maps, Plans, &c. 12s.

Single Stick Exercise of the Aldershot Gymnasium. 4*d.*

Treatise on Military Carriages, and other Manufactures of the Royal Carriage Department. 5s.

---

**Mogul Empire.**

From the death of Aurungzeb to the overthrow of the Mahratta Power, by HENRY GEORGE KEENE, B.C.S. 8vo. 9s.

*This Work fills up a blank between the ending of Elphinstone's and the commencement of Thornton's Histories.*

**Mysteries of the Vatican;**

Or Crimes of the Papacy. From the German of DR. THEODORE GREISENGER. 2 Vols. post 8vo. 21s.

**Nationalities of Europe.**

By ROBERT GORDON LATHAM, M.D. 2 Vols. 8vo. 12s.

"The mass of facts gathered from all quarters, and crowded together into the pages of these volumes is something wonderful."

**Nirgis and Bismillah.**

NIRGIS; a Tale of the Indian Mutiny, from the Diary of a Slave Girl: and BISMILLAH; or, Happy Days in Cashmere. By HAFIZ ALLARD. Post 8vo. 10s. 6d.

**Notes on China.**

Desultory Notes on the Government and People of China and on the Chinese Language. By T. T. MEADOWS, 8vo. Lond., 1847. 9s.

**Notes on the North Western Provinces of India.**

By a District Officer. 2nd Edition. Post 8vo., cloth. 5s.

CONTENTS.—Area and Population.—Soils.—Crops.—Irrigation.—Rent.—Rates.—Land Tenures.

"We have never read a book on India that has interested us more, or which to our thinking contains compressed into so small a space more valuable information or so many suggestive remarks. We recommend the book most strongly to all thoughtful readers."—*Athenæum.*

**Owen (Sidney) India on the Eve of the British Conquest.**

A Historical Sketch. By SIDNEY OWEN, M.A. Reader in Indian Law and History in the University of Oxford. Formerly Professor of History in the Elphinstone College, Bombay. Post 8vo. 8s.

**Oxenham's (Rev. H. N.) Atonement.**

8vo. 10s. 6d. (See page 5).

**Oxenham's (Rev. H. N.) First Age of Christianity, &c.**

8vo. 12s. 6d. (See page 7).

**Ozanam's (A. F.) Civilisation in the Fifth Century.**

From the French. By The Hon. A. C. GLYN. 2 Vols. post 8vo. 21s.

**Pathologia Indica,**

Based upon Morbid Specimens from all parts of the Indian Empire. By ALLAN WEBB, B.M.S. Second Edition. Royal 8vo. 14s.

**Pharmacopœia of India.**

By EDWARD JOHN WARING, M.D , &c. 8vo. 6s. (See page 2).

**Physical Geography.**

By PROFESSOR D. T. ANSTED, M.A., F.R.S., &c. Fifth Edition. Post 8vo., with Illustrative Maps. 7s.

CONTENTS:—PART I.—INTRODUCTION.—The Earth as a Planet.—Physical Forces.—The Succession of Rocks. PART II.—EARTH —Land.—Mountains.—Hills and Valleys.—Plateaux and Low Plains. PART III.—WATER.—The Ocean.—Rivers.—Lakes and Waterfalls.—The Phenomena of Ice.—Springs. PART IV.—AIR.—The Atmosphere. Winds and Storms.—Dew, Clouds, and Rain.—Climate and Weather. PART V.—FIRE.—Volcanoes and Volcanic Phenomena.—Earthquakes. PART VI.—LIFE —The Distribution of Plants in the different Countries of the Earth.—The Distribution of Animals on the Earth.—The Distribution of Plants and Animals in Time.—Effects of Human Agency on Inanimate Nature.

"The Book is both valuable and comprehensive, and deserves a wide circulation."—*Observer.*

**Pilgrimage to Mecca (A.)**
By the Nawab Sikandar Begum of Bhopal. Translated from the Original Urdu. By MRS. WILLOUGHBY OSBORNE. Followed by a Sketch of the History of Bhopal. By COL. WILLOUGHBY-OSBORNE, C.B. With Photographs, and dedicated, by permission, to HER MAJESTY, QUEEN VICTORIA. Post 8vo. £1 1s.

This is a highly important book, not only for its literary merit, and the information it contains, but also from the fact of its being the first work written by an Indian lady, and that lady a Queen.

**Pebody (Charles) Authors at Work.**
Francis Jeffrey—Sir Walter Scott—Robert Burns—Charles Lamb—R. B. Sheridan—Sydney Smith—Macaulay—Byron Wordsworth—Tom Moore—Sir James Mackintosh. Post 8vo. 10s. 6d.

**Pollock (Field Marshal Sir George) Life & Correspondence.**
By C. R. Low. 8vo. Pp. 34 and 560, with portrait. 18s.

**Primitive and Universal Laws of the Formation and** Development of Language. 8vo. 12s. (See page 16.).

**Prinsep's Political and Military Transactions in India.**
2 Vols. 8vo. London, 1825. 18s.

**Practice of Courts Martial.**
By HOUGH & LONG. In one thick 8vo. Volume. London, 1825. 26s.

**Precedents in Military Law;**
By LIEUT.-COL. W. HOUGH. One thick 8vo. Vol. 25s.

**Prichard's Chronicles of Budgepore, &c.**
Or Sketches of Life in Upper India. 2 Vols., Foolscap 8vo. 12s.

**Prinsep's (H. T.) Historical Results.**
8vo. 15s.

**Prinsep's (H. T.) Thibet.**
Post 8vo. 5s.

**Races and Tribes of Hindostan.**
The People of India. A series of Photographic Illustrations of the Races and Tribes of Hindustan. Prepared under the Authority of the Government of India, by J. FORBES WATSON, and JOHN WILLIAM KAYE. The Work will contain about 450 Photographs on mounts, in Eight Volumes, super royal 4to. £2 5s. per volume.

*Volumes* 1 *to* 6 *are now ready.* £13 10*s.*

**Republic of Fools (The).**
Being the History of the People of Abdera in Thrace, from the German of C. M. Von Wieland. By Rev. HENRY CHRISTMAS, M.A. 2 Vols. crown 8vo. 12s.

**Richards (Major W. H.) Military Surveying, &c.**
14s. (See page 18).

**Royle's (Dr. J. F.) Botany of the Himalaya Mountains.**
2 Vols. royal 4to. £7 7s. (See page 4).

**Russians at Home.**
Unpolitical Sketches, showing what Newspapers they read, what Theatres they frequent; and how they eat, drink and enjoy themselves; with other matter relating chiefly to Literature, Music, and Places of Historical and Religious Interest in and about Moscow. By H. SUTHERLAND EDWARDS. Second Edition, post 8vo., with Illustrations. 6s.

"This is not only one of the most amusing books that we have read for a long time, but also the best and most reliable account of Russian Life and Manners which has hitherto been given to the public."—*Spectator.*

**Sepoy War in India.**
A History of the Sepoy War in India, 1857—1858. By Sir JOHN WILLIAM KAYE, Author of "The History of the War in Affghanistan." Vol. I, 8vo. 18s. Vol. II. £1. Vol. III. in preparation.

CONTENTS OF VOL. I.:—BOOK I.—INTRODUCTORY.—The Conquest of the Punjab and Pegu.—The "Right of Lapse."—The Annexation of Oude.—Progress of Englishism. BOOK II.—THE SEPOY ARMY: ITS RISE, PROGRESS, AND DECLINE.—Early History of the Native Army.—Deteriorating Influences.—The Sindh Mutinies.—The Punjaub Mutinies. Discipline of the Bengal Army. BOOK III.—THE OUTBREAK OF THE MUTINY.—Lord Canning and his Council.—The Oude Administration and the Persian War.—The Rising of the Storm.—The First Mutiny.—Progress of Mutiny.—Excitement in Upper India—Bursting of the Storm.—APPENDIX.

CONTENTS OF VOL II.:—BOOK IV.—THE RISING IN THE NORTH-WEST.—The Delhi History.—The Outbreak at Meerut.—The Seizure of Delhi.—Calcutta in May.—Last Days of General Anson.—The March upon Delhi, BOOK V.—PROGRESS OF REBELLION IN UPPER INDIA.—Benares and Alla-

**Sepoy War in India—continued.**

habad.—Cawnpore.—The March to Cawnpore.—Re-occupation of Cawnpore. BOOK VI.—THE PUNJAB AND DELHI.—First Conflicts in the Punjab.—Peshawur and Rawul Pinder.—Progress of Events in the Punjab.—Delhi.—First Weeks of the Siege.—Progress of the Siege.—The Last Succours from the Punjab.

**Sewell's (Robert) Analytical History of India.**

Crown 8vo. 8s. (See page 3).

**Social Life in Munich.**

By EDWARD WILBERFORCE, ESQ., Second Edition. Dedicated, by permission, to the Bishop of Oxford. Post 8vo. 6s.

"A very able volume. Mr. Wilberforce is a very pleasant and agreeable writer whose opinion is worth hearing on the subject of modern art which enters largely into the matter of his discourse."—*Saturday Review.*

**Sin: Its Causes and Consequences.**

An attempt to Investigate the Origin, Nature, Extent and Results of Moral Evil. A Series of Lent Lectures. By the REV. HENRY CHRISTMAS, M.A., F.R.S. Post 8vo. 5s.

**Starling (M. H.) Indian Criminal Law and Procedure.**

Second Edition. Royal 8vo. 1870. 30s. (See page 13).

**Strange's (Sir T.) Hindu Law.**

2 Vols. Royal 8vo. 1830. 15s. (See page 13).

**Student's Chemistry.**

Being the Seventh Edition of Household Chemistry, or the Science of Home Life. By ALBERT J. BERNAYS, PH. DR. F.C.S., Professor of Chemistry and Practical Chemistry at St. Thomas' Hospital, Medical, and Surgical College. Post 8vo. 5s. 6d.

**"Their Majesties Servants":**

Annals of the English Stage. Actors, Authors, and Audiences. From Thomas Betterton to Edmund Kean. By Dr. DORAN, F.S.A., Author of "Table Traits," "Lives of the Queens of England of the House of Hanover." &c. Post 8vo. 6s.

"Every page of the work is barbed with wit, and will make its way point foremost. . . . . . provides entertainment for the most diverse tastes."—*Daily News.*

**Textile Manufactures and Costumes of the People of India,**

As originally prepared under the Authority of the Secretary of State for India in Council. By J. Forbes Watson, M.A., M.D., F R.A.S., Reporter on the Products of India. Folio, half-morocco. With numerous Coloured Photographs. £3 5s.

*This work—by affording a key to the Fashions of the People, and to the Cotton, Silk, and Wool Textiles in actual use in India—is of special interest to Manufacturers, Merchants, and Agents; as also to the Student and lover of ornamental art.*

"We congratulate Dr. Forbes Watson on having produced so useful and so practical a work, and on having diffused knowledge upon all material points connected with the clothing of the people of India, which heretofore had been unattainable. His book is written in a clear and thoroughly intelligible style throughout; it is handsomely got up, and embellished by numerous coloured photographs, from which the various styles of costume and portion of clothing, male and female, will be more readily understood than from mere description. The colours, too, of the various fabrics are given from the articles themselves, and we would in particular invite attention to the plates at page 118, all or most being figures of respectable Mohammedans in Upper India in rich dresses, as conveying excellent impressions of colour and effect in native Indian costume."—*Times.*

**Theories of History.**

An Inquiry into the Theories of History,—Chance,—Law,—Will. With Special Reference to the Principle of Positive Philosophy. By William Adam 8vo. 15s.

"The whole book bears the evident mark of maturity of thought. The third chapter is full of thoughtful and able argument, in which the positions of Comté, and even of Mill, are powerfully and successfully assailed."—*Spectator.*

"It is well thought and weightily written. We have not come across a book of the present day for a considerable while so far removed from the common run of writing and of thinking as this one is."—*Athenæum.*

**Thomson's Lunar and Horary Tables.**

For New and Concise Methods of Performing the Calculations necessary for ascertaining the Longitude by Lunar Observations, or Chronometers; with directions for acquiring a knowledge of the Principal Fixed Stars and finding the Latitude of them. By David Thomson. Sixty-first edit. Royal 8vo. 10s.

**Thornton's History of India.**

The History of the British Empire in India, by Edward Thornton, Esq. Containing a Copious Glossary of Indian Terms, and a Complete Chronological Index of Events, to aid the Aspirant for Public Examinations. Third edition. 1 vol. 8vo. With Map. 12s.

*** *The Library Edition of the above in 6 volumes, 8vo., may be had, price £2 8s.*

**Thornton's Gazetteer of India.**

Compiled chiefly from the records at the India Office. By EDWARD THORNTON. 1 vol., 8vo., pp. 1015. With Map. 21s.

*** *The chief objects in view in compiling this Gazetteer are:—*

*1st. To fix the relative position of the various cities, towns, and villages, with as much precision as possible, and to exhibit with the greatest practicable brevity all that is known respecting them; and*

*2ndly. To note the various countries, provinces, or territorial divisions, and to describe the physical characteristics of each, together with their statistical, social, and political circumstances.*

*To these are added minute descriptions of the principal rivers and chains of mountains; thus presenting to the reader, within a brief compass, a mass of information which cannot otherwise be obtained, except from a multiplicity of volumes and manuscript records.*

*The Library Edition.*

4 vols., 8vo. Notes, Marginal References, and Map. £2 16s.

**Thugs and Dacoits of India.**

A Popular Account of the Thugs and Dacoits, the Hereditary Garotters and Gang Robbers of India. By JAMES HUTTON. Post 8vo. 5s.

**Tibet, Tartary, and Mongolia.**

By HENRY T. PRINSEP, Esq. Second edition. Post 8vo. 5s.

**Tilley's (H. A.) Japan, &c.**

8vo. 16s. (See page 14).

**Tod's (Col. Jas.) Travels in Western India.**

Embracing a visit to the Sacred Mounts of the Jains, and the most Celebrated Shrines of Hindu Faith between Rajpootana and the Indus, with an account of the Ancient City of Nehrwalla. By the late Lieut.-Col. JAMES TOD, Illustrations. Royal 4to. £2 2s.

*** *This is a companion volume to Colonel Tod's Rajasthan.*

**Trotter's History of India.**

The History of the British Empire in India, from the Appointment of Lord Hardinge to the Death of Lord Canning (1844 to 1862). By LIONEL JAMES TROTTER, late Bengal Fusiliers. 2 vols. 8vo. 16s. each.

"The work is full of interesting matter, comprising every event of importance during the exciting period of the Rebellion, told in a concise, straightforward, and impartial manner."—*Observer.*

"The arrangement of the matter, the style, and, above all, the spirit which pervades Captain Trotter's pages, are worthy of great commendation."—*Calcutta Englishman.*

"It appears to us that Mr. Trotter has been eminently successful in his treatment of a very exciting and interesting period of recent history."—*London Review.*

**Turkish Cookery Book (The).**
A Collection of Receipts from the best Turkish Authorities. Containing—Soups, Krbabs or Roast Meats, Boiled Meats, &c., Fricasseed or Stewed Meats, Balls of Minced Meats, &c., Fried Dishes, Pastry with Meat, &c., Meat, Vegetables, &c., Stuffed Dishes, Rice cooked with Meat, &c., Hot Sweet Pastry, Cold Sweet Dishes, Omelets, Salads, Pickles, Stewed Fruits, Various Kinds of Sherbets with Fruit in them, Syrups, Jams, or Preserves. Done into English by FARABI EFENDI. 12mo. Cloth. 3s. 6d.

**Vambery's Sketches of Central Asia.**
Additional Chapters on My Travels and Adventures, and of the Ethnology of Central Asia. By Armenius Vambery. 8vo. 16s.

"A valuable guide on almost untrodden ground."—*Athenæum.*

**View of China,**
For Philological Purposes. Containing a Sketch of Chinese Chronology, Geography, Government, Religion, and Customs. Designed for the use of Persons who study the Chinese Language. By the Rev. ROBERT MORRISON. 4to. Macao, 1817. 6s.

**Waring's Pharmacopœia of India.**
8vo. 6s. (See page 22).

**Watson's (Dr. J. Forbes) Textile Manufactures of India.**
Folio. £3 5s. (See page 26).

**Watson's (Dr. J. F.) and J. W. Kaye, The People of India.**
A Series of Photographs. Vols. 1 to 6, £13 10. (See page 3).

**Webb's (Dr. A.) Pathologia Indica.**
8vo. 14s. (See page 22).

**Wellesley's Despatches.**
The Despatches, Minutes, and Correspondence of the Marquis Wellesley, K.G., during his Administration in India. 5 vols. 8vo. With Portrait, Map, &c. £6 10s.

*This work should be perused by all who proceed to India in the Civil Services.*

**Wellington in India.**
The Military History of the Duke of Wellington in India. 12mo. 1s.

**Wilberforce's (Edward) Social Life in Munich.**
Post 8vo. 6s. (See page 25).

**Wilberforce's (E.) Life of Schubert.**
Post 8vo. 6s.

**Wilk's South of India.**
3 vols. 4to. £5 5s.

**Williams' (F.) Lives of the English Cardinals.**
2 vols., 8vo. 14s. (See page 6).

**Williams' (F.) Life, &c., of Bishop Atterbury.**
2 vols., 8vo. 14s. (See page 4).

**Woolrych's (Serjeant W. H.)**
Lives of Eminent Serjeants-at-Law of the English Bar.

By Humphry William Woolrych, Serjeant-at-Law.

2 vols. 8vo. 30s.

**World we Live In.**
Or First Lessons in Physical Geography. For the use of Schools and Students. By D. T. Ansted, M.A., F.R.S., &c. 25th Thousand. Fcap. 8vo. 2s.

**Wraxall's Caroline Matilda.**
Queen of Denmark, Sister of George 3rd. From Family and State Papers in the possession of Sir Lascelles Wraxall, Bart. 3 vols., 8vo. 18s.

**Wraxall's Military Sketches.**
By Sir Lascelles Wraxall, Bart. Post 8vo. 6s. (See p. 21).

"The book is clever and entertaining from first to last."—*Athenæum.*

**Wraxall's Scraps and Sketches.**
By Sir Lascelles Wraxall, Bart. 2 vols., Post 8vo. 12s.

**Yesterday and To-Day in India.**
By Sidney Laman Blanchard. Post 8vo. 6s.

Contents.—Outward Bound.—The Old Times and the New.—Domestic Life.—Houses and Bungalows.—Indian Servants.—The Great Shoe Question.—The Garrison Hack.—The Long Bow in India.—Mrs. Dulcimer's Shipwreck.—A Traveller's Tale, told in a Dark Bungalow.—Punch in India.—Anglo-Indian Literature.—Christmas in India.—The Seasons in Calcutta.—Farmers in Muslin.—Homeward Bound.—India as it Is.

**Young's (J. R.) Course of Mathematics.**
8vo. 12s. (See page 6).

A SELECTION FROM

# MESSRS. ALLEN'S CATALOGUE

## OF BOOKS IN THE EASTERN LANGUAGES, &c.

### HINDUSTANI, HINDI, &c.

[*Dr. Forbes's Works are used as Class Books in the Colleges and Schools in India.*]

Forbes's Hindustani-English Dictionary in the Persian Character, with the Hindi words in Nagari also; and an English Hindustani Dictionary in the English Character; both in one volume. By DUNCAN FORBES, LL.D. Royal 8vo. 42s.

Forbes's Hindustani Grammar, with Specimens of Writing in the Persian and Nagari Characters, Reading Lessons, and Vocabulary. 8vo. 10s. 6d.

Forbes's Hindustani Manual, containing a Compendious Grammar, Exercises for Translation, Dialogues, and Vocabulary, in the Roman Character. New Edition, entirely revised. By J. T. PLATTS. 18mo. 3s. 6d.

Forbes's Bagh o Bahar, in the Persian Character, with a complete Vocabulary. Royal 8vo. 12s. 6d.

Forbes's Bagh o Bahar in English, with Explanatory Notes, illustrative of Eastern Character. 8vo. 8s.

Forbes's Tota Kahani; or, "Tales of a Parrot," in the Persian Character, with a complete Vocabulary. Royal 8vo. 8s.

Small's (Rev. G.) Tota Kahani; or, "Tales of a Parrot." Translated into English. 8vo. 8s.

Forbes's Baital Pachisi; or, "Twenty-five Tales of a Demon," in the Nagari Character, with a complete Vocabulary. Royal 8vo. 9s.

Platt's J. T., Baital Pachisi; translated into English. 8vo. 8s.

Forbes's Ikhwanu s Safa; or, "Brothers of Purity," in the Persian Character. Royal 8vo. 12s. 6d.

[*For the higher standard for military officers' examinations.*]

Ikhwanu S Safa; or, "Brothers of Purity," Translated from the Hindustani of Maulavi Ikram Ali. By JOHN PLATTS, Esq., Inspector of Public Instruction in the North Circle, Central Provinces. Carried through the Press by E. B. EASTWICK, Esq., C.B., M.P., F.R.S., &c., 8vo. 10s. 6d.

Platts' Grammar of the Urdu or Hindustani Language. 8vo. 12s.

Forbes's Oriental Penmanship; a Guide to Writing Hindustani in the Persian Character. 4to. 8s.

Forbes's Hindustani Dictionary, the Two Volumes in One, in the English Character. Royal 8vo. 36s.

Forbes's Smaller Dictionary, Hindustani and English, in the English Character. 12s.

Forbes's Bagh o Bahar, with Vocaby., English Character. 5s.

Singhasan Battisi. Translated into Hindi from the Sanscrit. A New Edition. Revised, Corrected, and Accompanied with Copious Notes. By SYED ABDOOLAH. Royal 8vo. 12s. 6d.

Robertson's Hindustani Vocabulary. 3s. 6d.

Eastwick's (E. B.) Prem Sagur. 4to. 30s.

Eastwick's (E. B.) English Version of the Prem. Sagur. 4to. 12s.

Akhlaki Hindi, translated into Urdu, with an Introduction and Notes. By SYED ABDOOLAH. Royal 8vo. 12s. 6d.

## SANSCRIT.

Haughton's Sanscrit and Bengali Dictionary, in the Bengali Character, with Index, serving as a reversed dictionary. 4to. 30s.

Williams's English and Sanscrit Dictionary. 4to., cloth. £3 3s.

Williams's (Monier) Sanscrit Grammar. 8vo. 15s.

Williams's (Monier) Sanscrit Manual; to which is added, a Vocabulary, by A. E. GOUGH. 18mo. 7s. 6d.

Gough's (A. E.) Key to the Exercises in Williams's Sanscrit Manual. 18mo. 4s.

Wilkin's (Sir Charles) Sanscrit Grammar. 4to. 15s.

Haughton's Menu, with English Translation. 2 vols. 4to. 24s.

Johnson's Hitopadesa, with Vocabulary. 15s.

Hitopadesa, Sanscrit, with Bengali and English Trans. 10s. 6d.

Johnson's Hitopadesa, English Translation of the. 4to. 5s.

Wilson's Megha Duta, with Translation into English Verse, Notes, Illustrations, and a Vocabulary. Royal 8vo. 6s.

Williams's (Monier) Sakuntala, with Literal English Translation of all the Metrical Passages, Schemes of the Metres, and copious Critical and Explanatory Notes. Royal 8vo. 21s.

Williams's (Monier) Sakuntala. Translated into English Prose and Verse. Fourth Edition. 8s.

Williams's (Monier) Vikramorvasi. The Text. 8vo. 5s.

Cowell's (E B.) Translation of the Vikramorvasi. 8vo. 3s. 6d.

Thompson's (J. C.) Bhagavat Gita. Sanscrit Text. 5s.

## PERSIAN.

Richardson's Persian, Arabic, and English Dictionary. Edition of 1852. By F. JOHNSON. 4to. £4.

Forbes's Persian Grammar, Reading Lessons, and Vocabulary. Royal 8vo. 12s. 6d.

Ibraheem's Persian Grammar, Dialogues, &c. Royal 8vo. 12s. 6d.

Gulistan (The). Carefully collated with the original MS., with a full Vocabulary. By JOHN PLATTS, late Inspector of Schools, Central Provinces, India. Royal 8vo. 12s. 6d.

Gulistan. Translated from a revised Text, with Copious Notes. By JOHN PLATTS. 8vo. 12s. 6d.

Ouseley's Anwari Soheili. 4to. 30s.

Eastwick's Translation of the Anwari Soheili. Royal 8vo. 21s.

Keene's (Rev. H. G.) First Book of The Anwari Soheili. Persian Text. 8vo. 5s.

Ouseley's (Col.) Akhlaki Mushini. Persian Text. 8vo. 5s.

Keene's (Rev. H. G.) Akhlaki Mushini. Translated into English. 8vo. 3s. 6d.

## BENGALI.

Haughton's Bengali, Sanscrit, and English Dictionary, adapted for Students in either language; to which is added an Index, serving as a reversed dictionary. 4to. 30s.

Forbes's Bengali Grammar, with Phrases and Dialogues. Royal 8vo. 12s. 6d.

Forbes's Bengali Reader, with a Translation and Vocabulary. Royal 8vo. 12s. 6d.

Batris Singhasan. 8vo. 5s.

Tota Itihas. 8vo. 5s.

Nabo Nari. 12mo. 7s.

Sykes's English Bengali Dictionary. 6s.

Bakyabali, or Idiomatical Sentences. English and Bengali. 6s. 6d.

## ARABIC.

Richardson's Arabic, Persian and English Dictionary. Edition of 1852. By F. JOHNSON. 4to., cloth. £4.

Forbes's Arabic Grammar, intended more especially for the use of young men preparing for the East India Civil Service, and also for the use of self instructing students in general. Royal 8vo. 18s.

Palmer's Arabic Grammar. 8vo. 18s.

Forbes's Arabic Reading Lessons, consisting of Easy Extracts from the best Authors, with Vocabulary. Royal 8vo., cloth. 15s.

Beresford's Arabic Syntax. Royal 8vo. 6s.

## TELOOGOO.

Brown's Dictionary, Reversed; with a Dictionary of the Mixed Dialects used in Teloogoo. 3 vols. in 2, royal 8vo. £5.

Campbell's Dictionary. Royal 8vo. 30s.

Brown's Grammar. 8vo. 16s.

Brown's Reader. 8vo. 3 vols. 27s.

Brown's Dialogues, Teloogoo and English. 8vo. 5s. 6d.

Selections, or Test Book. 8vo. 18s.

Pancha Tantra. 8s.

Percival's English-Teloogoo Dictionary. 10s. 6d.

## TAMIL.

Rottler's Dictionary, Tamil and English. 4to. 42s.

Babington's Grammar (High Dialect). 4to. 12s.

Beschi's Grammar (Common Dialect.) 8vo. 7s.

Rhenius's Grammar. 8vo. 14s.

Pope's Tamil Handbook. 8vo. 18s. 6d.

Pope's Tamil Prose Reading Book. Part I. 8vo. 10s.

Pope's First Lessons in Tamil. 12mo. 12s.

Babington's Gooroo Paramartan, with Translation and Vocabulary. 8s.

Pancha Tantra Katha. 2s. 6d.

Katha Manjiri. 8vo. 6s.

Percival's Tamil Dictionary. 2 vols. 10s. 6d.

## GUZRATTEE.

Mavor's Spelling, Guzrattee and English. 7s. 6d.

Bal Mitra. Vol. 1. 8vo. 6s. 6d.

Shapurji Edalji's Dictionary, Guzrattee and English. 21s.

## MAHRATTA.

Molesworth's Dictionary, Mahratta and English. 4to. 42s.

Molesworth's Dictionary, English and Mahratta. 4to. 42s.

Stevenson's Grammar. 8vo., cloth. 17s. 6d.

Esop's Fables. 12mo. 2s. 6d.

Fifth Reading Book. 7s.

## MALAY.

Marsden's Dictionary. 4to. 25s.

Marsden's Grammar. 4to. 12s. 6d.

## CHINESE.

Morrison's Dictionary. 6 vols. royal 4to. £10.

Marshman's—Clavis Sinica, a Chinese Grammar. 4to. £2 2s.

Summer's Grammar. Royal 8vo. 28s.

Morrison's View of China, for Philological purposes; containing a Sketch of Chinese Chronology, Geography, Government, Religion and Customs, designed for those who study the Chinese language. 4to. 6s.

## MISCELLANEOUS.

Reeve's English-Carnatica and Carnatica-English Dictionary. 2 vols. (Very slightly damaged). £8.

Collett's Malayalam Reader. 8vo. 12s. 6d.

Esop's Fables in Carnatica. 8vo. bound. 12s. 6d.

David's Turkish Grammar. 15s.

Wilson's Glossary of Judicial and Revenue Terms, and of useful Words occurring in Official Documents relating to the Administration of the Government of British India. From the Arabic, Persian, Hindustani, Sanskrit, Hindi, Bengali, Uriya, Marathi, Guzarathi, Telugu, Karnaṭa, Tamil, Malayalam, and other Languages. Compiled and published under the authority of the Hon. the Court of Directors of the E. I. Company. 4to., cloth. £1 10s.

*Messrs. Wm. H. Allen & Co.'s Catalogues of Printed and Lithographed Books in the Eastern Languages, to which is added a list of Oriental Manuscripts, may be had gratis on application.*